Current and Prospective Applications of Virtual Reality in Higher Education

Dong Hwa Choi
Park University, USA

Amber Dailey-Hebert
Park University, USA

Judi Simmons Estes
Park University, USA

IGI Global
PUBLISHER of TIMELY KNOWLEDGE

A volume in the Advances in Higher Education and Professional Development (AHEPD) Book Series

Published in the United States of America by
IGI Global
Information Science Reference (an imprint of IGI Global)
701 E. Chocolate Avenue
Hershey PA, USA 17033
Tel: 717-533-8845
Fax: 717-533-8661
E-mail: cust@igi-global.com
Web site: http://www.igi-global.com

Library of Congress Cataloging-in-Publication Data

Names: Choi, Dong Hwa, 1964- editor. | Dailey-Hebert, Amber, 1977- editor. | Estes, Judi Simmons, 1947- editor.
Title: Current and prospective applications of virtual reality in higher education / Dong Hwa Choi, Amber Dailey-Hebert, Judi Simmons Estes, editors.
Description: Hershey, PA : Information Science Reference, 2020. | Includes bibliographical references and index. | Summary: "This book provides research on the integration of virtual reality in education programs and establishes foundations for course design, program development, and institutional strategic planning. The book covers an overall understanding and approach to virtual reality in education, specific applications of using virtual reality in higher education, and prospects and issues of virtual reality in the future"-- Provided by publisher.
Identifiers: LCCN 2020002714 (print) | LCCN 2020002715 (ebook) | ISBN 9781799849605 (hardcover) | ISBN 9781799853336 (paperback) | ISBN 9781799849612 (ebook)
Subjects: LCSH: Virtual reality in higher education. | Education, Higher--Effect of technological innovations on.
Classification: LCC LB2395.7 .C87 2020 (print) | LCC LB2395.7 (ebook) | DDC 378.1/73468--dc23
LC record available at https://lccn.loc.gov/2020002714
LC ebook record available at https://lccn.loc.gov/2020002715

This book is published in the IGI Global book series Advances in Higher Education and Professional Development (AHEPD) (ISSN: 2327-6983; eISSN: 2327-6991)

British Cataloguing in Publication Data
A Cataloguing in Publication record for this book is available from the British Library.

For electronic access to this publication, please contact: eresources@igi-global.com.

Advances in Higher Education and Professional Development (AHEPD) Book Series

Jared Keengwe
University of North Dakota, USA

ISSN:2327-6983
EISSN:2327-6991

Mission

As world economies continue to shift and change in response to global financial situations, job markets have begun to demand a more highly-skilled workforce. In many industries a college degree is the minimum requirement and further educational development is expected to advance. With these current trends in mind, the **Advances in Higher Education & Professional Development (AHEPD) Book Series** provides an outlet for researchers and academics to publish their research in these areas and to distribute these works to practitioners and other researchers.

AHEPD encompasses all research dealing with higher education pedagogy, development, and curriculum design, as well as all areas of professional development, regardless of focus.

Coverage

- Adult Education
- Assessment in Higher Education
- Career Training
- Coaching and Mentoring
- Continuing Professional Development
- Governance in Higher Education
- Higher Education Policy
- Pedagogy of Teaching Higher Education
- Vocational Education

IGI Global is currently accepting manuscripts for publication within this series. To submit a proposal for a volume in this series, please contact our Acquisition Editors at Acquisitions@igi-global.com or visit: http://www.igi-global.com/publish/.

The Advances in Higher Education and Professional Development (AHEPD) Book Series (ISSN 2327-6983) is published by IGI Global, 701 E. Chocolate Avenue, Hershey, PA 17033-1240, USA, www.igi-global.com. This series is composed of titles available for purchase individually; each title is edited to be contextually exclusive from any other title within the series. For pricing and ordering information please visit http://www.igi-global.com/book-series/advances-higher-education-professional-development/73681. Postmaster: Send all address changes to above address.

Titles in this Series

For a list of additional titles in this series, please visit:
http://www.igi-global.com/book-series/advances-higher-education-professional-development/73681

Higher Education Response to Exponential Societal Shifts
Jerrid P. Freeman (Northeastern State University, USA) Cari Keller (Northeastern State University, USA) and Renee Cambiano (Northeastern State University, USA)
Information Science Reference • © 2020 • 290pp • H/C (ISBN: 9781799824107) • US $195.00

New Models for Technical and Vocational Education and Training
Moses Makgato (Tshwane University of Technology, South Africa) and Antje Barabasch (Swiss Federal Institute for Vocational Education and Training, Switzerland)
Information Science Reference • © 2020 • 400pp • H/C (ISBN: 9781799826071) • US $175.00

Optimizing Higher Education Learning Through Activities and Assessments
Yukiko Inoue-Smith (University of Guam, Guam) and Troy McVey (University of Guam, Guam)
Information Science Reference • © 2020 • 300pp • H/C (ISBN: 9781799840367) • US $195.00

Integrating Social Justice Education in Teacher Preparation Programs
Courtney K. Clausen (Utah State University, USA) and Stephanie R. Logan (Springfield College, USA)
Information Science Reference • © 2020 • 340pp • H/C (ISBN: 9781799850984) • US $185.00

Antiracist Professional Development for In-Service Teachers Emerging Research and Opportunities
Jenice L. View (George Mason University, USA) Elizabeth K. DeMulder (George Mason University, USA) Stacia M. Stribling (George Mason University, USA) and Laura L. Dallman (George Mason University, USA)
Information Science Reference • © 2020 • 275pp • H/C (ISBN: 9781799856498) • US $165.00

Handbook of Research on Diversity and Social Justice in Higher Education
Jared Keengwe (University of North Dakota, USA)
Information Science Reference • © 2020 • 380pp • H/C (ISBN: 9781799852681) • US $255.00

Accessibility and Diversity in the 21st Century University
Gary A. Berg (California State University Channel Islands (Retired), USA) and Linda Venis (UCLA (Retired), USA)
Information Science Reference • © 2020 • 331pp • H/C (ISBN: 9781799827832) • US $195.00

Higher Education Accessibility Behind and Beyond Prison Walls
Dani V. McMay (State University of New York at Fredonia, USA) and Rebekah D. Kimble (Via Evaluation, USA)
Information Science Reference • © 2020 • 335pp • H/C (ISBN: 9781799830566) • US $255.00

IGI Global
PUBLISHER of TIMELY KNOWLEDGE

701 East Chocolate Avenue, Hershey, PA 17033, USA
Tel: 717-533-8845 x100 • Fax: 717-533-8661
E-Mail: cust@igi-global.com • www.igi-global.com

This volume is dedicated to all of those individuals who think outside the box, embrace the unknown, and pioneer technological developments. These innovators spur on the rest of us who ride on their coat tails. Technology is leading the possibility of transforming the teaching-learning process in an engaging student-centered manner that reinvents the concept of school and classroom.

In memory of my son, Jeremy Blake Estes, who was a self-taught computer whiz from the moment he set hands on his Apple IIe in 1983; watching him taught me to embrace the unknown with zeal. JSE

Table of Contents

Preface xiii

Acknowledgment xviii

Chapter 1
This History and Evolution of Virtual Reality 1
Amber Dailey-Hebert, Park University, USA
Judi Simmons Estes, Park University, USA
Dong Hwa Choi, Park University, USA

Chapter 2
A Literature Review on the Use of Three-Dimensional Virtual Worlds in Higher Education 21
Reza Ghanbarzadeh, School of Business and Tourism, Southern Cross University, Australia
Amir Hossein Ghapanchi, College of Engineering and Science, Victoria University, Australia

Chapter 3
Virtual Reality, Augmented Reality, and Mixed Reality in Education: A Brief Overview 48
Nicoletta Sala, Institute for Complexity Studies, Italy & Institute for Scientific and Interdisciplinary Studies (ISSI), Switzerland

Chapter 4
Technical Details and Educational Applications for Virtual Reality Technologies 74
Yongzhi Wang, Park University, USA

Chapter 5
Facilitation Strategies to Moderate Synchronous Virtual Discussion Groups in Teacher Training 96
Kevin Oh, University of San Francisco, USA
Natalie Nussli, University of Applied Sciences and Arts Northwestern Switzerland, Switzerland
Melisa Kaye, San Jose State University, USA
Nicole Michele Cuadro, University of San Francisco, USA

Chapter 6
Developing an Immersive Virtual Classroom: TeachLivE – A Case Study 118
Kathleen M. Ingraham, University of Central Florida, USA
Annette Romualdo, University of Central Florida, USA
Angelica Fulchini Scruggs, University of Central Florida, USA
Eric Imperiale, University of Central Florida, USA
Lisa Dieker, University of Central Florida, USA
Charles E. Hughes, University of Central Florida, USA

Chapter 7
Creating a Virtual Reality Lab: Using a Student-Centered Approach.. 145
Benjamin Zibers, Park University, USA
Judi Simmons Estes, Park University, USA

Chapter 8
Engaging Students in a Computer Diversity Course Through Virtual Worlds 170
Yvonne Pigatt, Community College of Baltimore County, USA
James Braman, Community College of Baltimore County, USA

Chapter 9
Board Games, Zombies, and Minecraft: Gamification in Higher Education.................................... 194
Susan Keim, Park University, USA
Zac Jarrard, Park University, USA

Chapter 10
AI and AR: A Copacetic Approach in the New Educational Environment 216
Anita M. Cassard, H. W. Taft University, USA
Brian W. Sloboda, University of Phoenix, USA

Chapter 11
Virtual Reality in Social Work Education: Models, Meaning, and Purpose for Enhanced Learning. 232
Debra L. Olson-Morrison, Park University, USA

Chapter 12
Using Virtual Reality in College Student Mental Health Treatment 257
Nidhi Sinha, Indian Institute of Technology, Hyderabad, India

Compilation of References 274

About the Contributors 319

Index... 325

Detailed Table of Contents

Preface xiii

Acknowledgment xviii

Chapter 1
This History and Evolution of Virtual Reality 1
Amber Dailey-Hebert, Park University, USA
Judi Simmons Estes, Park University, USA
Dong Hwa Choi, Park University, USA

Virtual reality (VR) is a continuously evolving technology that is gradually being integrated into the teaching-learning process, within institutions of higher education. VR has the potential to transform the instructional process, enhance student learning, and engage students in a more interactive manner than has occurred historically. While technology integration within the instructional process has been initiated within institutions of higher education, mass adoption among faculty has not yet occurred. This chapter provides an introduction to VR, discusses the evolution of VR, applications in higher education and other fields, and a progression of features, tools, and functionality that can be used to innovate learning in higher education.

Chapter 2
A Literature Review on the Use of Three-Dimensional Virtual Worlds in Higher Education 21
Reza Ghanbarzadeh, School of Business and Tourism, Southern Cross University, Australia
Amir Hossein Ghapanchi, College of Engineering and Science, Victoria University, Australia

Three-dimensional virtual worlds (3DVW) have been substantially adopted in teaching and learning worldwide. The current study conducted a literature review of the published research relevant to the application of 3DVWs in higher education. A literature search was performed on nine scientific databases, and following scrutiny according to inclusion criteria, 176 papers were selected for review. The literature review process was summarized, reviews undertaken by the authors, and results about the applicability of 3DVWs in higher education were extracted. A wide variety of application areas for 3DVWs in higher education were found and classified into five main categories. Various 3DVW platforms and virtual environments used for educational goals were also identified. This study found that a wide range of virtual environments and tools have been implemented by 3DVW technology and applied for teaching and learning in higher education.

Chapter 3
Virtual Reality, Augmented Reality, and Mixed Reality in Education: A Brief Overview 48
Nicoletta Sala, Institute for Complexity Studies, Italy & Institute for Scientific and Interdisciplinary Studies (ISSI), Switzerland

Virtual reality (VR), augmented reality (AR), and mixed reality (MR) are three different technologies developed in the last decades of the 20th century. They combine hardware and software solutions. They permit the creation of three-dimensional (3D) virtual worlds and virtual objects. This chapter describes how VR, MR, and AR technologies find positive application fields in educational environments. They support different learning styles, offering potential help in teaching and in learning paths.

Chapter 4
Technical Details and Educational Applications for Virtual Reality Technologies............................. 74
Yongzhi Wang, Park University, USA

The application of virtual reality (VR) in higher education has drawn attention. Understanding the state of the art for VR technologies helps educators identify appropriate applications and develop a high-quality engaging teaching-learning process. This chapter provides a comprehensive survey of current hardware and software supports on VR. Secondly, important technical metrics in VR technology are considered with comparisons of different VR devices using identified metrics. Third, there is a focus on software tools and an explore of various development frameworks, which facilitate the implementation of VR applications. With this information as a foundation, there is a VR use in higher education. Finally, there is a discussion of VR applications that can be potentially used in education.

Chapter 5
Facilitation Strategies to Moderate Synchronous Virtual Discussion Groups in Teacher Training 96
Kevin Oh, University of San Francisco, USA
Natalie Nussli, University of Applied Sciences and Arts Northwestern Switzerland, Switzerland
Melisa Kaye, San Jose State University, USA
Nicole Michele Cuadro, University of San Francisco, USA

This chapter reports on an exploratory case study investigating strategies to facilitate group discussions in Second Life, a three-dimensional virtual world. The purpose was to identify best practices for discussion facilitation in-world from the perspective of a virtual host and a discussion facilitator. A host and a facilitator moderated four virtual group discussions with 16 in-service teachers enrolled in a graduate technology class. The chapter discusses several themes that emerged from the host's and the facilitator's debriefings. Key themes include the need for a careful selection of the communication modality (text or voice or a combination), strategies to promote interactivity among the participants, the critical need for at least one facilitator in addition to the host, the need for clear ground rules for the participants, and clear guidelines for the host and the facilitator. Several challenges experienced during the process of facilitating these virtual events are discussed and recommendations are made to address these difficulties. This chapter is of interest to educators who are planning to substitute in-class group discussions with synchronous group discussions in-world.

Chapter 6
Developing an Immersive Virtual Classroom: TeachLivE – A Case Study 118
Kathleen M. Ingraham, University of Central Florida, USA
Annette Romualdo, University of Central Florida, USA
Angelica Fulchini Scruggs, University of Central Florida, USA
Eric Imperiale, University of Central Florida, USA
Lisa Dieker, University of Central Florida, USA
Charles E. Hughes, University of Central Florida, USA

As virtual reality (VR) technologies continue to improve and become more accessible, educators are increasingly incorporating VR learning experiences in teacher education contexts. This chapter is a case study of TeachLivE™, a virtual classroom platform designed for practicing teaching in a safe virtual space. This chapter describes the system, development, and challenges faced when incorporating immersive VR technologies. Recommendations are provided for future research, development, use, and facilitation of immersive VR learning experiences.

Chapter 7
Creating a Virtual Reality Lab: Using a Student-Centered Approach 145
Benjamin Zibers, Park University, USA
Judi Simmons Estes, Park University, USA

Use of virtual reality (VR) has increased in higher education in recent years and is projected to continue to increase. At the same time, there is a growing emphasis for institutions of higher education to re-envision learning spaces and teaching strategies that are student-centered rather than faculty centered. Use of VR, by faculty, requires a new pedagogy of teaching as well as a willingness to explore the use of an unknown technology in delivering curriculum. Having access to a technology lab that uses VR can be a welcomed support for faculty. VR can be expensive and creating a VR lab may not seem doable in settings other than large, well-funded universities. This chapter describes a technology lab that was established at a small Midwest liberal arts university, funded by a student technology fee and created by a student-led technology committee.

Chapter 8
Engaging Students in a Computer Diversity Course Through Virtual Worlds 170
Yvonne Pigatt, Community College of Baltimore County, USA
James Braman, Community College of Baltimore County, USA

Virtual world technology allows for an immersive 3D experience with rich content and interactive potential for students. Through this richness and interactivity, educators have abundant creative power to design and facilitate meaningful learning experiences and collaboration opportunities. In this chapter, the authors discuss one such initiative using Second Life as an educational space for a community college course activity to enhance student engagement. A brief literature review of the educational use of virtual worlds will be presented, which underpin our pedagogical methodology for the project framework. Focusing on a specific community college course titled "Diversity in a Technological Society," the course goals and project requirements will be discussed. The chapter concludes with a detailed description of the proposed methodology for the next phase, recommendations, and future work.

Chapter 9
Board Games, Zombies, and Minecraft: Gamification in Higher Education 194
Susan Keim, Park University, USA
Zac Jarrard, Park University, USA

Games have been played throughout human history and in all cultures, exposing almost everyone to gameplay in some form. Higher education is exploring ways faculty can leverage games to enhance course development and the student learning experience. The primary pedagogical use of games is gamification, in which gaming is used to transform learning activities. This chapter will 1) provide an overview of gamification theory and practice in higher education, 2) share ideas for faculty to consider when using gamification as a teaching tool, and 3) explore how the game Minecraft was used through educational and practical applications to teach a local government course.

Chapter 10
AI and AR: A Copacetic Approach in the New Educational Environment 216
Anita M. Cassard, H. W. Taft University, USA
Brian W. Sloboda, University of Phoenix, USA

This chapter presents some of the possibilities and approaches that are used in the application of AI (artificial intelligence) and AR (augmented reality) in the new learning environments. AI will add another dimension to distance learning or eLearning that in some cases already includes AR (augmented reality) virtual learning environments. Because of this advent in available technology and the impact it will have on learning, assessment of newly structured parameters and their impact on student outcomes is crucial when measuring student learning. For some of us there might be a concern about the domination of AI as seen in the movie The Terminator, but we can take ease in the notion that it is not only AI versus humans. A new version of human augmented intelligence (HI) is being developed as we speak.

Chapter 11
Virtual Reality in Social Work Education: Models, Meaning, and Purpose for Enhanced Learning. 232
Debra L. Olson-Morrison, Park University, USA

The use of virtual reality (VR) as a learning tool occupies a whole new and exciting domain for social work education. Engaging in virtual worlds expands the potential for students to connect with the learning experience on multiple levels, pedagogically aligns with stimulating affective processes to enhance cognitive engagement, and aligns with the domains of knowledge acquisition in competency-based social work education. In this chapter the author outlines the affordances necessary for student engagement in a virtual learning experience (VLE). The author explores applications for virtual reality in social work education and outlines several distinct opportunities for virtually-enhanced classroom learning. Practical guidelines to assist instructors in facilitating a VR learning experience are proposed, and the chapter concludes with commentary on the future of VR in social work education.

Chapter 12
Using Virtual Reality in College Student Mental Health Treatment 257
Nidhi Sinha, Indian Institute of Technology, Hyderabad, India

When students leave home to attend college, they encounter many adjustments and new experiences. Some students have difficulty coping with the challenges they experience and over time may develop mild to severe mental health issues. Mental health illness among college students is associated with long-term adverse academic outcomes, including dropout. With an exponential rise in mental health issues among university students, there is a dire need to reach out to newer technologies to help students effectively cope with academic and social challenges. Given the increased accessibility and practicality of virtual reality (VR) use in mental health, it becomes paramount to extend the utility of VR to university counselling settings including the preliminary assessment, diagnosis, and treatment strategies to guide students to effectively address any mental health challenges. There are potential implications and challenges associated with the use of VR within universities' counselling settings as well.

Compilation of References 274

About the Contributors 319

Index 325

Preface

The hardest part of learning something new is not embracing new ideas, but letting go of old ones. Todd Rose (Harvard Faculty, Graduate School of Education)

Since 2016, when the first edition of this collection was published, we've seen many advancements and improvements in the emergent technologies that support teaching and learning – few more dramatic than the evolution of virtual reality (VR). In 2017, Campus Technology shared an article on the *'5 VR Trends to Watch in Education'* that outlined the following trends: 1) more affordable headsets, 2) hand controllers that will bring increased interactivity, 3) easy-to-use content creation platforms, 4) 360-degree cameras, and 5) social VR spaces (Ravipati, 2017). Only a few years later, these trends have indeed helped shape the VR we know today and the evolution of the technology itself. In fact, it is rather interesting to review the projected (and actual) growth of VR that has occurred in the past 4 years. According to Statistica Research (2020), in 2016 approximately 1.8 billion dollars accounted for the consumer virtual reality software and hardware market size; this has grown to over 9.6 billion in 2020 (more than six times the amount in only four years) and is projected to reach over 16.3 billion by 2022.

In the past 4 years an emergence and growth in e-sports, mobile applications, and low (or no) cost solutions have grown exponentially. Likewise, the use of VR has also aligned with easy-to-use content creation platforms and VR use in social contexts, particularly in the wake of the COVID-19 global pandemic - as users sought more realistic ways to connect during extended periods of isolation. For example, as the pandemic led to the closure of gyms, VR served as a useful tool for indoor training, with VR health exercise tracker apps, and via new innovations such as the YUR virtual reality smartwatch. Co-founder of YUR reported over 5 million workouts logged by over 600,000 users, who had more time to spend at home to join and participate (Rogers, 2020). Likewise, other industries benefitted from the use of VR during this time to offer lifesaving benefits. For example, the VR medical training system built by Oxford Medical Simulation was offered at no cost during the pandemic to help overtaxed hospitals and medical facilities quickly train over 17,000 medical staff on patient care (Weiss, 2020). Similarly, as schools around the world closed their doors amidst the pandemic, classwork and learning continued in online and virtual environments (Allen, 2020). For example, a professor at the University of North Carolina used AltspaceVR to build a virtual 3D version of his classroom, which allowed students to 'walk around' in the classroom and break out into groups during 'class' (Brka, 2020).

With the progress that has occurred during the past 4 years, and the anticipated projections for the years ahead, the current state of the world is shaping our reality and the rapid adoption of VR technologies unlike any time in history. Revisiting the quote from Thomas Friedman, "People don't change when you tell them they should, they change when they tell themselves they must." (Friedman, 2005, p. 462). As people around the world are finding that they 'must' learn to think/communicate/work/evolve in new and unfamiliar ways, VR is primed for expansion. Unlike any other time in history, individuals are motivated to engage with VR unlike and our current global reality is creating a catalyst for the use of virtual reality. This holds unprecedented opportunity to establish a higher baseline for digital literacy among all learners today – particularly those who have been most resistant to the benefits and potential VR holds.

This collection, our second edition, was created to share advances that have occurred during the past four years since our first edition and to help create a framework for the applications of VR in learning and education in particular. In this collection, the reader will find a plethora of topics highlighting and related to VR. For example, a comprehensive literature review from experts in the field with empirical data and evidence to support VR work is presented. An exploration of new and innovative uses for VR in the classroom will be discussed, along with many ways to integrate cost-free solutions to promote connection in new ways. As a final example, unorthodox strategies to promote student engagement through owning and empowering the learner role in the knowledge creation process itself will be presented, as well as the building of knowledge creating cultures within learning. Let the exploration of VR begin!

SECTION 1: THE EVOLUTION OF VIRTUAL REALITY IN HIGHER EDUCATION

This collection appropriately begins with four chapters, collectively setting a foundational understanding of VR as a technology that has evolved with advances in applications and uses that have included a broadening of definition, as well as higher education practices unimaginable in 1989 when the term "virtual reality" was coined.

First, in Chapter 1, Amber Dailey-Hebert, Judi Simmons Estes and Dong Hwa Choi (USA) provide a discussion of the history of virtual reality (VR) use in higher education and its significant evolution in more recent years. In order to understand the latest updates and progression of features, tools, and functionality that can be used to innovate learning in higher education today, this chapter shares an introduction to virtual reality, explores the history and evolution of VR, and discusses the use of VR in learning today.

Reza Ghanbarzadeh and Amir Hossein Ghapanchi (Australia) provide a robust review of the literature on three dimensional virtual words (3DVW) in higher education in Chapter 2. This literature review analyzes 176 articles from nine major databases, including both empirical and technical studies on the topic of VR in higher education. The authors identified a wide variety of application areas for 3DVW's in higher education and classified them into five main categories. This study found that a wide range of virtual environments and tools have been implemented by 3DVW technology and applied for teaching and learning in higher education.

Next, in Chapter 3, a brief overview of virtual reality (VR), augmented reality (AR), and mixed reality (MR), used in education, is presented by Nicoletta Melida Sala (Italy). Specifically, a description is provided for how VR, AR, and MR are applied in a variety of diverse educational environments in the United States, Italy, Morocco, Romania, and Switzerland, providing a global perspective. Conclusively, the author establishes an expectation for potential use of VR as an evolutionary teaching and learning tool.

In Chapter 4, Yongzhi Wang (USA) posits that understanding the state of the art for VR technologies helps educators identify appropriate applications and develop high-quality engaging teaching-learning environments. Additionally, a comprehensive survey of current hardware and software supports on VR are explored, important technical metrics in VR technology are considered, and there is a focus on software tools and an explore of various development frameworks, which facilitate the implementation of VR applications.

SECTION 2: STUDENT-CENTERED USE OF VIRTUAL REALITY IN HIGHER EDUCATION

Several chapters on virtual reality in higher education are provided in Section 2 of the collection. Here, across a broad range of course context and disciplines, we see a focus on how VR is being used to directly support and integrate a more student-centered approach to learning.

In Chapter 5, an investigation of strategies to facilitate best practices in online synchronous graduate student discussions in Second Life® are discussed. Kevin Oh, Natalie Nussli (Switzerland), Melisa Kaye, and Nicole Michele Cuadro (USA) examine discussion facilitation from the perspective of a host and a facilitator who moderated four virtual group discussions with in-service teachers. The chapter discusses several themes that emerged from the debriefings, including practices that engage students. The authors explore selected areas that are critical for educators to consider when planning to transfer group discussions, or any type of communicative interaction for learning purposes, to a 3D environment.

Developing an Immersive Virtual Classroom:TeachLivE™ a Case Study, in Chapter 6, examines the development cycle and challenges of incorporating newer immersive VR technologies into existing VR platforms using the TeachLivE™ simulation platform as a case example. TeachLivE™ is a platform used in teacher education to provide opportunities for teacher candidates to practice instructional strategies and behavior management techniques. The authors of the chapter, Kathleen M. Ingraham, Annette Romualdo, Angelica Fulchini Scruggs, Eric Imperiale, Lisa Dieker, and Charles Hughes (USA), provide recommendations for future research, development, use, and facilitation of immersive VR learning experiences.

To continue the exploration into student-centered VR use, Chapter 7 by Ben Zibers and Judi Simmons Estes (USA), share a new approach to VR use from a small liberal arts Midwest college, that empowers and places students at the center of decision-making and leadership. This chapter describes how a student-led technology committee created a relatively low-cost technology lab funded through an annual student technology fee. Planning and implementation of the lab experiences were determined primarily by students with guidance from student services staff. The guiding principles of the lab were to offer virtual reality experiences for individual student exploration and faculty course topic specific explorations.

In Chapter 8, Yvonne Pigatt and James Braman (USA) share their experience using Second Life® (SL) to pilot a study on the diversity of in-world users, the capabilities of the platform, and the potential for dynamic interactivity through built-in scripting language. The purpose of using SL in the diversity course, discussed in this chapter, was twofold: 1) To increase student engagement in the context of the course by increasing participation, student enthusiasm and assignment quality and 2) To teach a new emerging technology. This chapter begins with background discussion of virtual worlds and creating and using a virtual educational space. Secondly, the chapter shares the pilot study completed at a community college, including the difficulties inside and outside the classroom. A third section discusses the pilot study and recommendations. Lastly, future research directions and conclusions are provided.

SECTION 3: APPLICATIONS AND CONSIDERATIONS FOR VIRTUAL REALITY

In the last section of the collection, readers are challenged to explore innovative uses, practical applications, and considerations for virtual reality use in higher education today.

In Chapter 9, Susan Keim and Zac Jarrad's (USA) integration of using gamification to improve and engage learners. This chapter offers an overview of academic literature on gamification and, more specifically, shares experiences of using Minecraft to teach a Local Government course. Additional tips and strategies are provided to assist those who would like to integrate VR into their own course development process, and the authors provide steps and ideas to consider for doing so.

In Chapter 10, Anita Cassard and Brian W. Sloboda (USA) present a discussion of artificial intelligence (AI) and augmented reality (AR) used in education – specifically, focused in translation tasks, such as conversing across a language barrier. Tools include Google Translate, AI-powered AR glasses, AR contact lenses, and heads-up display capabilities without glasses. The authors share their perspectives and forward-thinking vision for the future of AI and how it will impact learning.

Debra L. Olson-Morrison (USA) explores the use of VR in the context of Social Work Education to create meaning, purpose, and enhanced learning in Chapter 11. The author shows how engaging in virtual worlds expands the potential for students to connect with the learning experience on multiple levels, pedagogically aligns with stimulating affective processes to enhance cognitive engagement and aligns with the domains of knowledge acquisition in competency-based social work education. Olson-Morrison outlines the affordances necessary for student engagement in a virtual learning experience and outlines several distinct opportunities for virtually- enhanced classroom learning. Practical guidelines to assist instructors in facilitating a VR learning experience are proposed, and the chapter concludes with commentary on the future of VR in social work education.

Finally, in Chapter 12, Nidhi Sinha (India) expands on how VR can be used to support student mental health at the collegiate level. As students may have difficulty coping with new adjustments and experiences living on their own, mental illness can develop and lead to dropout or poor academic performance. In this chapter, the author explores the utility of VR to university counselling settings; including the preliminary assessment, diagnosis, and treatment strategies to guide students to effectively address any mental health challenges. This chapter also shares the challenges and considerations for using VR within universities' counselling settings.

REFERENCES

Allen, J. (2020, March 13). *How technological innovation in education is taking on COVID-19*. Forbes. https://www.forbes.com/sites/jeanneallen/2020/03/13/how-technological-innovation-in-education-is-taking-on-covid-19/#cb540977bc72

Brka, L. (2020, April 6). An 'immersive experience': Professor uses virtual reality to replicate the classroom. *The Daily Tar Heel*. https://www.dailytarheel.com/article/2020/04/virtual-reality-classroom-0407

Friedman, T. L. (2005). *The world is flat: A brief history of the twenty-first century*. Macmillan.

Ravipati, S. (2017, May 16). 5 VR Trends to watch in education. *Campus Technology*. https://campustechnology.com/articles/2017/05/16/5-vr-trends-to-watch-in-education.aspx

Rogers, S. (2020, April 7). Virtual reality games to keep you fit during COVID-19 lockdown, *Forbes*. Retrieved from: https://www.forbes.com/sites/solrogers/2020/04/07/virtual-reality-games-to-keep-you-fit-during-covid-19-lockdown/#66e3e0ae4c16

Statistica Research. (2020, March 3). *Virtual Reailty (VR) Statistics and Fact*. https://www.statista.com/topics/2532/virtual-reality-vr/

Weiss, T. R. (2020, April 2). 17,000 doctors and nurses training for COVID-19 pandemic using VR technology. *Tech Republic*. https://www.techrepublic.com/article/free-medical-vr-training-system-being-offered-to-help-combat-the-covid-19-pandemic/

Acknowledgment

We would like to thank our generous colleagues for their helpful and insightful ideas, reviews, and feedback of chapter manuscripts: James Braman, Anita M. Cassard, Nicole Michele Cuadro, Lisa Dieker, Reza Ghanbarzadeh, Amir Hossein Ghapanchi, Charles Hughes, Eric Imperiale, Kathleen M. Ingraham, Zac Jarrard, Melisa Kaye, Susan Keim, Natalie Nussli, Kevin Oh, Debra L. Olson-Morrison, Yvonne Pigatt, Annette Romualdo, Nicoletta Sala, Angelica Fulchini Scruggs, Nidhi Sinha, Brian W. Sloboda, Yongzhi Wang, Ben Zibers. These individuals not only offered critiques and valuable suggestions, but also recommended additional resources to help inform this project and expand our knowledge base on the topic of virtual reality. Finally, the editors would like to extend thanks to the staff at IGI Global who guided the development process and successful completion of this project.

Chapter 1
This History and Evolution of Virtual Reality

Amber Dailey-Hebert
Park University, USA

Judi Simmons Estes
Park University, USA

Dong Hwa Choi
Park University, USA

ABSTRACT

Virtual reality (VR) is a continuously evolving technology that is gradually being integrated into the teaching-learning process, within institutions of higher education. VR has the potential to transform the instructional process, enhance student learning, and engage students in a more interactive manner than has occurred historically. While technology integration within the instructional process has been initiated within institutions of higher education, mass adoption among faculty has not yet occurred. This chapter provides an introduction to VR, discusses the evolution of VR, applications in higher education and other fields, and a progression of features, tools, and functionality that can be used to innovate learning in higher education.

AN INTRODUCTION TO VIRTUAL REALITY

Virtual Reality (VR) is a computer-generated environment designed to simulate three-dimensional (3D) physical environments that provide user interaction. Three-dimensional immersive virtual worlds are one of the most exciting emerging technologies being used today and have been shown to improve learning satisfaction while providing opportunities to practice and apply professional skills (Hodgson et al., 2019). While these emergent technologies offer a unique venue to enact learning and practice skills, they also require training, support, and opportunities for experimentation. Therefore, it is important to understand the broad scope through defining VR, identifying characteristics of VR, and describing VR in practice.

DOI: 10.4018/978-1-7998-4960-5.ch001

Defining Virtual Reality

While there are countless uses for VR in education and industry, there are equally as many definitions; definitions of VR have shifted as the related hardware and software applications have evolved, moving from a single user interface to massively multiplayer online worlds (MMOW). For example, in 1996 Schroeder first posited that computer-generated display allows or compels users to have a sense of being present in an environment, other than the one they are actually in, and to interact with that environment (Schroeder, 2008). By 2003, Sherman and Craig expanded the definition of VR when they defined it as "a medium composed of interactive computer simulation that senses the participant's position and actions and replaces or augments the feedback to one or more senses, giving the feeling of being mentally immersed or present in the simulation (a virtual world)" (p. 13). In 2010, Kapp and O'Driscoll defined a virtual world as an "immersed 3D virtual environment in which a learner acts through an avatar to engage with the other avatars for the explicit purpose of learning" (p. 55). As time and technology progressed, the concept of immersive learning in VR expanded significantly to represent the user being physically present in a non-physical world (Freina & Ott, 2015).

More recently, Sherman and Craig (2018) defined VR as having elements that include: "the virtual world, immersion, interactivity, as well as people on the creating and receiving sides of the medium" (p.6). Immervisive Virtual Reality (IVR) often uses head mounted displays and integrates motion sensors to bridge the gap between the simulation environment and real-world conditions (Frederiksen et al., 2019). Hence, as the capabilities and applications of the VR and IVR functions have expanded, definitions and instructional uses for VR have changed. Often, visual, auditory, manipulation and other perceptual stimuli are incorporated within software and hardware applications of technology in a sequence of programmed events to which a person is expected to react and with which to engage directly through a complete sensory experience.

A Broad Overview of Virtual Reality

VR can be overwhelming to understand, particularly given the nuanced uses of evolving technology, terms, applications, and more. Therefore, this section will provide a broad overview of VR and pertinent language. Given the expansive growth of VR in recent years, (and with the inclusion of immervise virtual reality (IVR), mixed reality (MR), augmented reality (AR), and new functionalities within all), a new term, "Extended Reality" (XR) is used to encompass all of the terms used for co-existing realities. The Horizon Report Panel "expanded the definition of redesigning learning spaces from a trend accommodating more active learning in the physical classroom to one that includes attention to the learner experience in emerging learning spaces programmed into extended reality (XR)" (Alexander et al., 2019, p. 6). Figure 1 below, adapted from Vera (2019), offers a helpful figure to demonstrate the progression of realities and the differences between each.

Figure 1. Extended Reality
Adapted from Vera, L. (2019, Apr 10). What does extended reality mean? Premo.
Retreived from: https://3dcoil.grupopremo.com/blog/what-does-extended-reality-mean/

Extended Reality (XR)

Augmented Reality (AR) uses a digital overlay of objects in the user's physical environment and requires the use of a camera, screen and processor. AR might be the best technology "to train people in specific tasks, to provide helpful information in order to develop certain complex activities for education, to enable damaged or incomplete art objects to be displayed in museums and also to set certain rooms before buying furniture, by means of a smartphone or tablet – as in the IKEA Place App." (Vera, 2019, para.11).

Mixed Reality (MR) is "also known as hybrid reality because it is based on the combination of real and virtual objects which coexist and interact in real time. This technology creates mixed environments where virtual objects can react to real objects in the physical surrounding world. It represents one step beyond AR in the way toward the VR scenario, but still including the physical world and real objects as a basis. Applications are similar for MR and AR, including the possible interaction between real and virtual elements." (Vera, 2019, para. 13).

VR is an environment that allows the user to "be immersed in a completely new experience, a virtual environment were you can move, feel, and interact through specific devices. The user is completely isolated from the real world and immersed in a synthetic one where a person can feel as being there." (Vera, 2019, para. 14). One type of highly interactive, fully immersive, multisensory VR is commonly referred to as Immersive Virtual Reality (IVR). Unlike VR, IVR can induce a psychological state in which the individual perceives him or herself as existing within, being immersed in, or having presence in the VRE (Blascovich & Bailenson, 2005, p. 230). The users'sensation of presence caused by immersion in IVR helps distinguish it from more familiar types of VR like 3D movies, desktop 3D simulations, or 3D video games. Additionally, IVR is typically more interactive than other types of multimedia as users can manipulate representations of real-world objects using a handheld device (Lee &Wong, 2014).

Characteristics of Virtual Reality

As VWE's have evolved, so too have the characteristics and terminology used in VR. VR can create entrance into a world far from reality and/or allow users to participate in activities that would otherwise be impossible in the realworld (Lau & Lee 2015). Designs of VWs are quite diverse, ranging from the replication of real classrooms to imaginary worlds (Prasolova-Førland, 2008). Dickey (2005a) posited that 3D virtual worlds typically share three features: 1) the illusion of 3D space, 2) avatars that serve as visual representations of users and 3) an interactive chat tool for users to communicate with one another. Five years later, Hew and Cheung (2010) added a fourth feature; 4) the ability for a user to 'act' on the virtual world; this added feature provides the user with more opportunity for active engagement within the virtual world environment. For example, objects have properties that allow them to be taken or dropped, which makes it possible for students to learn by doing rather than simply learning by listening to the instructor or reading assigned content in a text.

The environment created through VR is referred to as a virtual world (VW), virtual world environment (VWE), and/or a virtual world learning environment (VWLE). Simply, a VWE is an artificial physical environment created using digital technology viewed two-dimensionally (2D); a complex three-dimensional (3D) environment contains digital objects and human avatars in real-time, and the complete sensory experience through immersive virtual reality (IVR). VWLE's can accommodate a wider range of learning styles and goals, encourage collaborative and resource-based learning and allow greater sharing and re-use of resources (Britain, 1999). These VR environments are used to support multiple learning styles and encourage such collaborative exchange through social learning as well. This social focus evolved when innovators of VR noticed that users were responsive to the collaborative community and in 2003, the immersive virtual world of Second Life® (SL) was launched (Linden Lab, 2013), allowing users opportunities for interaction, exploration, and collaboration. In SL, the user typically has some digital representation of self, known as an avatar. Users create their own identity and embody themselves through their avatars and by representing self as avatars, users report feeling socially and psychologically connected (Biocca et al., 2003). Additionally, users can interact and communicate with each other in real time by using voice and text chat and/or gestures.

Providing the opportunity to manipulate and interact with objects in the VWs expanded the scope and application for learning. Bojonova (2011) suggested that through avatars, users can navigate, explore, create, and communicate in a virtual space as if it were an extension of the real world, but without the physical limitations and risk of the real world. One of the most attractive features of VWs, and their use in learning environments, is the ability to extend beyond mere text and lecture to promote active learning, the application of knowledge and skills, and the ability to put learning into practice.

Technological advances and their affordances in the classroom have allowed educators to deliver information more accurately and easily to their students (Keengwe & Onchwari 2011). Specifically, VWs serve as optimal learning environments to promote the application of both content knowledge and procedural knowledge in a safe space (Noteborn et al., 2013). Furthermore, VR promotes the 'knowledge creating cultures' (Scardamalia & Bereiter, 2006), which allow learners to not only collaborate virtually, but to create and produce new knowledge and experiences together. Regardless of specific hardware, software, or uses for VR, Smart, Cascio and Paffendof (2007) posited that while VWs may appear in different forms, they possess a number of recurrent features:

- Persistence of an in-world environment
- Hared space allowing multiple users to participate simultaneously
- Virtual embodiment in the form of an avatar (a 3D representation of the self)
- Interactions that occur between users and objects in a 3D environment
- Immediacy of action such that interactions occur in real time
- Similarities to the real world (topography, movement, physics); a sense of being in the environment

More recently, Sherman and Craig (2018, p.6) found VR to include the following features that are defined more broadly, but expand to include individuals who are creating and using the medium:

- The virtual world
- Immersion
- Interactivity
- People on the creating and receiving sides of the medium

It's also important to note, the cost and price for such technologies has become more affordable and, consequently, currently reach wider markets; making VR more accessible, with more users exploring ways to create, build, and integrate it in their learning activities. Recent developments have also allowed more accessibility via mobile devices which support easier integration for VR to be a valuable tool in education, mentoring, and training (Limet al., 2019).

VR: AN EVOLUTION OF TECHNOLOGY-ENABLED LEARNING

Within educational institutions, effectively integrating technology into instruction has been ever evolving. There have always been 'early adopters' of innovation (initiated by a few), and gradual adaptations of innovation by many. Technology integration into instruction is actually a developmental process with more than a 70-year history, receiving policy and fiduciary support from governmental agencies in some instances. In this section, a brief history of emergent technology use in education will be presented, followed by some of today's most innovative projects, and developments that we can anticipate in the future.

Emergent Technology in Education: A Brief History (1944-2020)

Today, Silicon Valley is viewed as the U.S. birthplace of technological innovations. However, institutions of higher education have been the historical venues of new technological knowledge. In fact, the first operational computer was introduced in 1944 at Harvard with early educational uses primarily occurring within departments of mathematics, science and engineering for the purposes of critical thinking and problem-solving (Levien, 1972). As early as 1954, B. F. Skinner combined his theories related to direct instruction and programmed learning to provide students with individualized instruction; the skill base of each student was targeted and sequentially higher level skills were provided based on successful responses. Skinner (1954) referred to the technology that he developed as *teaching machines* (https://www.youtube.com/watch?v=jTH3ob1IRFo).

In 1959, at the University of Illinois, Donald Bitier began the first, large-scale project for the use of computers in education, serving elementary school reading programs, a community college, and undergraduate programs (Office of Technology Assessment, 1982). In 1963, only 1% of U.S. secondary schools used computers for instructional purposes, by 1974, 55% of the schools had access to computers, over two million students used computers in their classes and 23% of these classrooms were using computers primarily for instruction (Molner, 1975).

The Office of Technology Assessment, established in 1972, was intended to provide Congress with objective and authoritative analysis of the complex scientific and technical issues of the late 20th century. A report, *Teachers and Technology: Making the Connection* (Office of Technology Assessment, 1995), included one chapter focused specifically on *Helping Teachers Learn About and Use Technology Resources* (https://www.princeton.edu/~ota/ns20/year_f.html), recognizing the importance of training teachers (as the person responsible) for integrating technology into instruction.

In 1981, IBM became the first mainframe manufacturer to develop a personal computer used primarily for drill & practice, and by 1986, 25% of high schools used PCs for college and career guidance, while K-8 schools were primarily buying Apple II and Macintosh computers (http://web.csulb.edu/~murdock/histofcs.html). In 1992, the Office of Science and Technology Policy (OSTP), a department of the Executive Office of the President, initiated a government-wide effort to dramatically expand the U.S. portion of the Internet; the purpose was interconnecting the nation's educational infrastructure to its knowledge and information centers so that all may could share access to digital libraries, databases and diverse scientific instruments (OSTP, 1992).

As early as 1994, digital video, VR, and 3D systems captured the attention of many business professionals. Digital video systems were the forerunners of VR emerging as a new paradigm in computer technology. Object-oriented authoring systems such as HyperCard, Hyperstudio, and Authorware were growing in popularity and use, particularly as a resource for instructional delivery by teachers, however in many K-12 schools there was a lack of availability to students (http://web.csulb.edu/~murdock/histofcs.html). The original educational intent of VR was for the learner to interact with electronically generated artificial environments as if they were real and to develop procedural knowledge in the process. In early 1990, Howard Rheingold expanded the concept and use of VR to the gaming industry (Mazuryk & Gervautz,1996; Rheingold, 1991) but the cost and clunky nature of VR goggles and data gloves inhibited mass adoption during the 90's (Virtual Reality, n.d.).

The Internet did not became commercialized and decommissioned until 1995 (Harris & Gerich, 1996) and as the internet grew in access, capability, and use, so did the VR movement. Such developments and applications highlighted the need to consider the future of VR from both the technical and social aspects (Mazuryk & Gervautz, 1996). By 2000 innovators of VR noticed that users were responsive to the collaborative community and in 2003, the less immersive VW of Second Life® was launched (Linden Lab, 2013), where users could create their own avatars and socialize in a virtual space together.

By 2012 the USC Institute for Creative Technologies released a viewer that used a smartphone display for VR. This discovery moved Oculus Rift from protype to production between 2013-2016 and changed the face of VR by providing a path to low-cost HMDs (Sherman & Craig, 2018). By 2016, industry stakeholders launched hand-held controllers, gaming head displays, and development kits for users, finally making VR more affordable, accessible, and adoptable by industry, personal use, gaming, and educational sectors. Today, universities have varsity e-sports teams that continue to grow in popularity and profitability, with only seven colleges and universities hosting esports in 2016 to 63 institutions by 2018, and projections of esports to be a $2.3 billion market in 2022 with significant investments from sponsors and advertisers (Brightman, 2017; eSports, 2019). VR continues to evolve and expand in unforeseen areas; such technology will progress and evolve at exponential rates in the years to come.

VR Adoption and Integration Into Practice

In 2007, the EDUCAUSE Horizon Report predicted a two to three year time frame for the adoption of VWs in education (The New Media Consortium, 2007). In the 2019 EDUCAUSE Horizon Report (Alexander, et al., 2019), an adoption of mixed reality and artificial intelligence is listed as an important development in technology in higher education,. projected to occur in two to three years. One of the factors in this seemingly slow adoption of technology use in higher education may be reluctance of faculty. In the same report, the evolved roles of faculty with educational technology strategies is listed as a significant challenge that is "difficult," with difficult defined as those that we understand but for which solutions are illusive.

There is growing interest in using many types of VR for educational purposes as educators recognize that teaching with technology is able to create more effective learning environments (Keengwe & Onchwari, 2011; Merchant et al., 2014). However, simply using new technology because it is available can often be ineffective (Sweller, 2008). Successful instruction using IVR requires technology to be incorporated in well-designed contexts that apply theoretical approaches to accomplishing objectives (Mikropoulos & Natsis, 2011). Every faculty member should learn how to select and use the most appropriate technological tools so they can become proficient in teaching with technology. The challenge confronting faculty is that they not only have to gain technological knowledge and skills but also need to adopt what might be a new pedagogy involving active learning. Using technology for the sake of using technology accomplishes little. The power of technology, and the power of VR user, is the potential to transform the teaching-learning process. This concept is presented in the SAMR model that provides a framework of four levels of technology integration (Puentedura, 2006).

1. **Substitution:** Tech acts as a direct substitute, no functional change.
2. **Augmentation:** Tech acts as a direct substitute, with functional improvement.
3. **Modification:** Tech allows for significant task redesign.
4. **Redefinition:** Tech allows for the creation of new tasks, previously inconceivable.

When a teacher does not understand the pedagogy of technology integration, then using technology to transform learning is unlikely to happen. One of the functions of using VR is that it provides students with experiences previously inconceivable. Another function is the use of VR inherently provides the student with an active learning experience within an active learning classroom. "The transition to active learning classrooms and spaces in higher education has gained considerable momentum in recent years" (Alexander et al., 2019, p. 11). Dawley (2009) posited an emerging pedagogical framework that includes active learning and "social network knowledge construction." Such a pedagogy addresses the need for new strategies in teaching and learning in both face to face and within distance learning courses, particularly when VR is used to transform the learning experience. An example of a VW being used in education is Second Life® (SL). This framework incorporates user-centered content, social networking, and VWs in the teaching-learning process.The social construction of knowledge in the VW provides students with the opportunity to provide physical representations of newly acquired knowledge in a variety of formats that can synthesized and shared with other users.

Use of VR as a tool to deepen knowledge and demonstration of student outcomes, is an example of how "Learning solutions are designed and deployed using increasingly sophisticated technology, creating a need for learners to gain new skills to meaningfully engage with those tools" (Alexander et al., 2019, p. 14). Even though educational institutions are increasingly including SL as a technology based tool in teaching and learning, there is a lack of research in guiding educators in course design and pedagogy within the SL environment (Mutekwe et al., 2013). In fact, there is a paucity of research on how faculty are using a pedagogy to guide their integration of technology into instruction while demonstrating effectiveness in obtaining student outcomes. Affordances of VR that could be useful to educators include the ability to assume multiple perspectives, contextual learning, and transfer of knowledge and skills to real-world situations (Mikropoulos & Natsis 2011). VR provides opportunities to navigate 3D models and environments, in a way that allows students to view learning experiences from an entirely new perspective (Moro et al., 2017).

Fortunately, it appears VR use in educational practice is showing growth, emerging as gaming, esports, and shared open-access content. For example, in addition to use of SL, educators are using Minecraft to teach about local government, civic planning, and geographic skills (Scarlett, 2015), using VR for students to experience past historical events and locations or to explore the solar system (Detlefsen, 2014; Roussou, 2004), and in training medical students to make decisions and perform surgical procedures in a safe VR space (Harrington et al., 2018; Liu, 2014). Social work education is using a VW format as a resource for achieving competence in the field, as students study human behavior in the social environment as well as assessment of clients using a biopsychsocial and spiritual format (Holloway et al., 2009) .

While there is no question that challenges exist for the adoption of educational innovations for VR use, the opportunities that exist in the realm of VR and learning are exponential. There is significant growth in the use of VR within academic organizations offering virtual campus tours, the expansion of digital libraries, institutional museums and much more. Some leaders in innovation who seek to provide a more rich understanding of VR include Stanford's *Virtual Human Interaction Lab*. With numerous projects and dozens of publications, the researchers investigate topics related to social issues, interactions, and applications for VR (Ahn et al., 2015; Cummings & Bailenson, 2015). Standford is not alone in dedicated work to better understand and explore the VR space for learning. The University of Minnesota's *Virtual Realty Design Lab* represents an interdisciplinary partnership between the College of Design and Computer Science & Engineering for a six-year project focused on a more immersive experience using perception headsets to investigate the learning effects of "Social VR". (http://vr.design.umn.edu).

Other academic institutions are also leading the way to explore this unknown frontier, such as the University of Southern California's *Institute for Creative Technologies* Medical Virtual Reality Group, that specializes in mental health therapy, motor and cognitive skills rehabilitation, assessment, and clinical skills training (http://medvr.ict.usc.edu). Today, these immersive learning-scapes have become quite popular, particularly in medical and engineering programs that require the practical application of skills or the building and modeling of a design. The medical profession has typically served as an early adopter of emergent technologies and has been proactive in their uses for VR as well. One example includes the work of PULSE a simulation game for health care professionals which has been in development since 2005 by an international team of academicians, as well as subject-matter experts in medicine and human-factors research. that "allows them to train and practice on avatars without the risk of harming patients. "Three-dimensional virtual reality is capable of encompassing most medical issues and can be used for clinical learning by all health care disciplines" (Dunne & McDonald, 2010). Many universities and learning institutions are not only using VR in practice, but are dedicating research centers and funding collaborative efforts to support the expansion of such work on their campuses.

In regard to strategies that support educators, the concept of a virtual technology coach and its potential to support NETS*C Standards still needs to be considered in future studies (Sugar & Slagter van Tryon, 2014). Virtual communities of practices for teachers (Lewis et al., 2011) have been offered in an online setting. A key facet of school technology integration needs point to the alignment between the NETS*C, International Society for Technology in Education's (2012) education coach standards for skills necessary in promoting teachers' classroom integration of technology, and the apparent value teachers place on their ability to learn more deeply about technology integration within a collaborative community. To better support and offer additional training and guidance, there is evidence of potential for avatar-based, avatar-led instruction and training on demand through e-coaching (Warner, 2012). Such options could utilize VR to train educators, offering hands-on experience using the VWfrom a learner perspective. In the past, faculty resistance to using technology in general, and VR specifically included lack of understanding and skill in how the tools can taransform learning and cost. With recent advancements in technology these limitations are becoming resolved, creating new educational opportunities (Trelease, 2016).

Research suggests that students like using VWs for the following reasons: 1) the ability to fly and move around freely in a 3D space, 2) to socialize and meet new people and 2) to experience virtual field trips and simulated experiences (Dickey, 2005b). In short, students liked being embodied in the learning content and context, as opposed to the traditional flat, one-dimensional, text-driven digital displays. In addition to the content and procedural knowledge students can develop, VR helps to better prepare learners for the unscripted future they face, a future that is dynamic and constantly changing as a result of emergent technologies that shape it (Dailey-Hebert et al., 2008). Providing a state-of-the- art learning experience for students will not only benefit colleges and universities in their competitive environment, but also aid in preparing students for their entry into the workforce (Miller, 2014). This opportunity provides one key to moving forward with a vision for the future of VR in education.

Not only is VR expanding in educational practice, but the potential and promise for innovative uses of such technologies is evident in other fields which may directly inform and improve upon VR uses as a model in the future. Today, outside of education, VR is being used in the treatment of chronic pain in both pediatric and adult patients (Gupta et al., 2018), to help rehabilitate stroke victims (Saposnik & Levin, 2011), to enhance the design and manufacturing process in industry (Ong & Nee, 2013), to train medical staff in a virtual clinical learning lab (Pulse Simulation Technology, 2008), to take a jury through a crime scene (Hullinger, 2015), and to customize a virtual shopping experience and explore merchandise from the comfort of one's own home (Chang, 2015). The possibilities, applications, and uses for VR continue to be explored and continue to enhance these domains as a result.

Moving Forward: VR in Education Today

In this section, VR use in education will be highlighted through a few examples of curricular innovations that are and will continue to, shape the future of VR as currently known and beyond. It has been hypothesised that VLEs will increase student practice time, leading to better understanding and improved learning outcomes (Moro et al., 2017). VR is in its infancy; a field that is rapidly evolving. There is a paucity of research related to student outcomes when using VR as a learning tool as compared to other tools, but there is promising evidence that when use of VR is planned strategically that the interactive and engaging nature can transform the teaching learning process as the following examples demonstrate.

Innovative Education

The Innovation Education, a constructivist learning pedagogy developed within the Icelandic education system in 1991, is aimed at searching for needs and problems in the student's environment and involving students in finding appropriate solutions or applying and developing known solutions, a process of ideation (Thorsteinsson, 2013). Building on the original IE work, computer-based technologies were introduced in order to develop new ways of supporting students work in IE classes. For example, Thorsteinsson, Page, and Niculescu (2010) explored the possibilities of using virtual reality for cooperative idea generation and then attempted to assess the relationship between a student's cooperation and the design process, learning experiences and the pedagogy employed by the teacher. One output was the development of a VRLE in which children could interact collaboratively, communicate, and host their innovation education work within a social learning process. This is a prime example of how VR, as a technology tool, can be used to transform the teaching-learning process when integrated into a pedagogy of education aligned with curriculum and desired student outcomes.

VR Games as Learning Tools

VR expansion into the gaming world grew significantly and continues to be the most popular application of VR reality today (Chouhan & Sharma, 2015). For example, KZero's radar charts indicate that the number of virtual worlds and Massively Multiplayer On-line Role Playing Games (MMORPGs) totaled 900 as of 2013; KZero's universe chart revealed 1,899 million registered users in VWs and massively multiplayer online games (MMOs) as of 2013 (KZero, 2013). Given the popularity and engagement of such VR games, serious games as a learning tool have emerged and been effective in increasing underegraduate academic performance (Malaquias et al., 2018) and having positive affects in the workplace (Heili & Michel, 2011; Michel, 2013).

In Grenoble France, professors developed a curriculum they call *GemInGame*, in which students create, develop, and co-brand serious games as part of their curriculum. Students are able to partner with external organizations to create and co-brand serious games for employee training, giving students the opportunity to not only engage in a gaming system for the sake of learning, but to create and produce new serious games for market in the VR environment (Lépinard & Vandangeon-Derumez, 2019).

Oculus Rift

Oculus Rift is an evolving technology that was created in 2012, as a high-quality, head-mounted display device that is worn like goggles to experience an immersive VW experiences mimicking real-life (Anthes et al., 2016). In 2016, after the release of two developer kits Oculus Rift DK1 and DK2, the first consumer-grade Oculus Rift CV1 became available for the general public (Robinson, 2016). Examples of applications of Oculus Rift in education, have included providing a virtual tour of a college campus (http://www.youvisit.com/tour/yale); a virtual lecture presented in a virtual classroom (Tsaramirsis et al., 2016); and a lesson on spine anatomy (Moro et al., 2017). Already a leader in virtual reality technology, the Occulus company was purchased by the social media leader Facebook in 2014; CEO Mark Zuckerberg blogged, "We're going to make Oculus a platform for many other experiences. Imagine enjoying a courtside seat at a game, studying in a classroom of students and teachers all over the world, or consulting with a doctor face-to-face" (The Associated Press, 2014, para.1).

CAVE Automatic Virtual Environment

The IVR system known as the Cave Automatic Virtual Environment (CAVE) is typically an open three-walled room measuring 10 feet wide, 10 feet tall, and 10 feet deep (Mechdyne Corporation, 2012), with the floor and each wall illuminated with computer-generated objects. Special head-tracking glasses are worn by users to facilitate interacting with projected simulations and overlap with a three-dimensional aspect giving the perception of being inside a physical room. CAVEs use information from infrared detectors on the location of the glasses to redraw the scene in real time to the user's perspective (Mechdyne Corporation, 2012). A handheld controller can also be used to move objects and change perspectives. Unlike most other VR systems, a user has the full ability to physically walk around and interact with virtual objects in the CAVE. Multiple users can be in the CAVE at the same time to observe and engage in discussions about the simulation. Behavior in the CAVE thus closely mimics experiences in the real-world (Blascovich & Bailenson, 2011, 2005; Dunleavy et al., 2009). A potential problems with CAVEs and other IVR's (Immersive Virtual Reality) is a risk of overwhelming users with unnecessary information and distract from overall learning. A way to lessen the risks of this potential problem if to establish instructional strategy guidelines and strategies that are applied to a framework of best practice, with effective incorporation of technology (Ritz & Buss, 2016).

Scalable Game Design

Alexander Repenning, Director of Scalable Game Design (SGD), housed at the University of Colorado, Boulder, began an effort in 1995 to reinvent computer science education in public schools through game design starting at the middle school level. SGD merged with the Computational Thinking Foundation, a 501(c)3 non-profit in 2019; their work providing workshops and trainings to students and teachers will continue. (http://sgd.cs.colorado.edu/wiki/Scalable_Game_Design_wiki). SGD is mentioned because of the pioneering work in development of computational thinking tools that evolved as game and simulation authoring systems including programming VR game skills taught to students K-16 and their teachers. The simulation authoring systems include AgentSheets™ for two-dimensional games and AgentCubes™ for three-dimensional games (Repenning et al., 2012). Brand and Repenning (2017) have examined the challenges and advantages of 3D programming in the AgentCubes Online programming environment. 3D imagery and its associated programming provide a means for personalizing projects and may increase a learner's motivation to learn about technology. Results indicate that students, across genders and ethnicities, are not only highly motivated to learn computer science through game design but they also learn essential computational thinking skills. (Webb et al., 2012). A discussion of SGD is included in this discussion of VR and higher education because it is important for schools of education to be including similar opportunities in their curriculum in order to prepare teacher candidates to integrate into their own classrooms. Repenning et al. (2019) have discussed the viability of mandatory pre-service teacher coursework in computer science education, not just knowledge and skills but as importantly pedagogy of technology use in the classroom.

Mobile Devices and VR

The 2019 Horizon Report listed as one of the important development in technology for higher education, an adoption of mobile learning within one year or less (Alexander et al., 2019). McCormack et al. (2020) listed mobile devices in teaching and learning as one of the 2020 top 10 strategic techniques in higher education. Moro et al. (2017) posit that consumer-grade VR has recently become available for both desktop and mobile platforms and may redefine the way that faculty teach. It is likely that personal phones will be increasingly be used within the college classroom as a learning tool.

Currently, VR is more robust for an Android phone, but there are a number of ways to use VR with an iPhone, offering affordability and accessibility (Pierce, 2015). The following are needed to gain access to VR on an iPhone or any smartphone: 1) a viewing device, such as Google Cardboard of the Gear VR, that provide two lenses and an immersive viewing environment, and 2) VR content apps (Costello, 2020). As of now, VR on the iPhone is often a passive experience in which the user views content, though some viewers include buttons to interact with apps and some apps support basic interactions. For example, the Samsung Gear VR headset includes a feature that lets the user move through menus and select content in VR by tapping the side of the headset (Costello, 2020).

Newer mobile devices, such as Google Cardboard ($20 USD) or the Gear VR ($99 USD), also now have the capacity to depict VR with attachments. These devices provide a reduction in the cost of setup for educational institutions as compared to desk-top devices, and could potentially utilze the students own mobile phones in the future as more and more devices become VR-compatible (Moro et al., 2017).

CONCLUSION

The purpose of education is not simply for students to acquire knowledge and skills, but to be interested and engaged in the learning process, to successfully collaborate with peers, to develop critical thinking and problem-solving skills to tackle unforeseen challenges, and to view themselves as life-long learners who are capable of applying knowledge, skills, and digital literacy to real-life situations. The utilization of VR to promote such development has been evident in the past and holds great promise for the future, as the evolution of technology tools, features, and functionalities continue to evolve. In reviewing the evolution and rapid progress of VR today, it's important to take stock of where it began, the advancements which make it more accessible to a wider audience, and the opportunities that exist in education for integration and adoption.

REFERENCES

Ahn, S. J., Bostick, J., Ogle, E., & Bailenson, J. N. (2015). *Embodying nature's experiences: Taking the perspective of nature with immersive virtual environments to promote connectedness with nature.* Paper to be presented at the Annual Association for Education in Journalism and Mass Communication (AEJMC) Conference, San Francisco, CA. Retrieved May 2020 from https://vhil.stanford.edu/pubs/

Alexander, B., Ashford-Rowe, K., Barajas-Murphy, N., Dobbin, G., Knott, J. McCormack, M., Pomerantz, J., Seilhamer, R., & Weber, N. (2019). Educause Horizon Report: 2019 Higher Education Edition. Louisville, CO: Educause.

Anthes, C., García-Hernandez, R. J., Wiedemann, M., & Kranzlmüller, D. (2016, March). *State of the art of virtual reality technology.* Paper presented at the 2016 IEEE Aerospace Conference, Yellowstone, MT. 10.1109/AERO.2016.7500674

Biocca, F., Harms, C., & Burgoon, J. K. (2003). Toward a more robust theory and measure of social presence: Review and suggested criteria. *Presence (Cambridge, Mass.), 12*(5), 456–480. doi:10.1162/105474603322761270

Blascovich, J., & Bailenson, J. (2005). Immersive virtual environments and education simulations. In S. Cohen, K. E. Portney, D. Rehberger, & C. Thorsen (Eds.), *Virtual decisions: Digital simulations for teaching reasoning in social science and humanities immersive virtual environments* (pp. 229–253). Lawrence Erlbaum Associates.

Blascovich, J., & Bailenson, J. (2011). *Infinite reality: Avatars, eternl life, new worlds, and the dawn of the virtual evolution.* William Morrow & Company.

Bojanova, I. (2011). Physical presence through virtual worlds. *IT Professional, 13*(4), 4–5. doi:10.1109/MITP.2011.66

Brand, C., & Repenning, A. (2017). Helping teacher and students learn to use 3D in agent cubes online. 2017 IEE Blocks and beyond workshop (B & B), 103-104.

Brightman, J. (2017). Global esports revenue to hit $2.3 billion in 2022. *Gamesindustry.biz*. Retreived from: https://www.gamesindustry.biz/articles/2017-12-11-global-esports-revenue-to-hit-usd2-3-billion-in-2020-superdata

Britain, S. (1999). A framework for pedagogical evaluation of virtual world learning environments. JISC Technology Applications Programme, Report 41: Joint Information Systems Committee of the Higher Educational Funding Council, Manchester, UK.

Chang, L. (2015). Go shopping from the comfort of your own home with your virtual reality headset. *Digital Trends*. Retrieved July 1, 2015 from http://www.digitaltrends.com/cool/retail/

Chouhan, R., & Sharma, G. K. (2015). Virtual Reality: In gaming. *International Journal of Multidisciplinary Consortium*, *2*(2), 36.

Costello, S. (2020). Everything you need to know about virtual reality on i-phone. *Lifewire*. Retrieved May 3, 2020 from https://www.lifewire.com/virtual-reality-on-iphone-4125903

Cummings, J. J., & Bailenson, J. N. (2015). How immersive is enough? A meta-analysis of the effect of immersive technology on user presence. *Media Psychology*, 1–38.

Dailey-Hebert, A., Donnelli-Sallee, E., & DiPadova-Stocks, L. (2008). Service-eLearning as integrated pedagogy: An introduction. In A. Dailey-Hebert, E. Donnelli-Sallee, & L. DiPadova-Stocks (Eds.), *Service-eLearning: Educating for citizenship* (pp. 1–5). Information Age Publishing.

Dawley, L. (2009). Social network knowledge construction: Emerging virtual world pedagogy. *On The Horizon, 17*(2), 109-121. doi:10.1108/10748120910910965494

Detlefsen, J. (2014). *The Cosmic Perspective: Teaching Middle-School Children Astronomy Using Ego-Centric Virtual Reality* (Unpublished master's thesis). Alborg University, Alborg, Denmark. Retrieved June 2, 2020 from https://projekter.aau.dk/projekter/files/198097322/Portfolio_JanDetlefsen.pdf

Dickey, M. D. (2005a). Brave new (interactive) worlds: A review of the design affordances and constraints of two 3D virtual worlds as interactive learning environments. *Interactive Learning Environments*, *13*(1-2), 121–137. doi:10.1080/10494820500173714

Dickey, M. D. (2005b). Three-dimensional virtual worlds and distance learning: Two case studies of Active Worlds as a medium for distance learning. *British Journal of Educational Technology*, *36*(3), 439–451. doi:10.1111/j.1467-8535.2005.00477.x

Dunleavy, M., Dede, C., & Mitchell, R. (2009). Affordances and Limitations of Immersive Participatory Augmented Reality Simulations for Teaching and Learning. *Journal of Science Education and Technology*, *18*(1), 7–22. doi:10.100710956-008-9119-1

Dunne, J. R., & McDonald, C. L. (2010). Pulse!!: A model for research and development of virtual-reality learning in military medical education and training. *Military Medicine*, *175*(7S), 25–27. doi:10.7205/MILMED-D-10-00158 PMID:23634475

eSports. (2019). Collegiate varsity esports programs. *Game Designing*. Retrieved from https://www.gamedesigning.org/schools/varsity-esports/

Frederiksen, J. G., Sørensen, S. M. D., Konge, L., Svendsen, M. B. S., Nobel-Jørgensen, M., Bjerrum, F., & Andersen, S. A. W. (2020). Cognitive load and performance in immersive virtual reality versus conventional virtual reality simulation training of laparoscopic surgery: A randomized trial. *Surgical Endoscopy*, *34*(3), 1244–1252. doi:10.100700464-019-06887-8 PMID:31172325

Freina, L., & Ott, M. (2015, April). A literature review on immersive virtual reality in education: state of the art and perspectives. In *The International Scientific Conference eLearning and Software for Education* (*Vol. 1*, p. 133). "Carol I" National Defence University.

Gupta, A., Scott, K., & Dukewich, M. (2018). Innovative technology using virtual reality in the treatment of pain: Does it reduce pain via distraction, or is there more to it? *Pain Medicine*, *19*(1), 151–159. doi:10.1093/pm/pnx109 PMID:29025113

Harrington, C. M., Kavanagh, D. O., Quinlan, J. F., Ryan, D., Dicker, P., O'Keeffe, D., Traynor, O., & Tierney, S. (2018). Development and evaluation of a trauma decision-making simulator in Oculus virtual reality. *American Journal of Surgery*, *215*(1), 42–47. doi:10.1016/j.amjsurg.2017.02.011 PMID:28262203

Harris, S. R., & Gerich, E. (1996). Retiring the NSFNET backbone service: Chronicling the end of an era. *ConneXiona, 10*(4). Retrieved June 2, 2020 from https://www.merit.edu/wp-content/uploads/2019/06/Retiring-the-NSFNET-Backbone-Service_-Chronicling-the-End-of-an-Era-1.pdf

Heili, J., & Michel, H. (2011, October). Do students Trained using serious games become better sales representatives? An experiment to study the performance of academic serious games. In *European Conference on Games-Based Learning* (p. 230). Redding, UK: Academic Conferences International Limited. Retrieved June 2, 2020 from http://ja.games.free.fr/ludoscience/EVirtuoses/AppelAComEVirtuo2012/Articles/01_ImpactSG.pdf

Hew, K. F., & Cheung, W. S. (2010). Use of three-dimensional (3-D) immersive virtual worlds in K-12 and higher education settings: A review of the research. *British Journal of Educational Technology*, *4*(1), 33–55. doi:10.1111/j.1467-8535.2008.00900.x

Hodgson, P., Lee, V. W. Y., Chan, J. C. S., Fong, A., Tang, C. S. Y., Chang, L., & Wong, C. (2019). Immersive virtual reality (VR) in higher education: development and implementation. In M. C. Dieck & T. Jung (Eds.), *Augmented reality and virtual reality: The power of AR and VR in business* (pp. 161–173). Springer. doi:10.1007/978-3-030-06246-0_12

Holloway, S., Black, P., Hoffman, K., & Pierce, D. (2009). Some considerations of the import of the 2008 EPAS for curriculum design. *Council on Social Work Education.* Retrieved May 4, 2020 from https://www.bu.edu/ssw/files/pdf/2008EPASCurriculumDesign1.pdf

Hullinger, J. (2015). *Six innovative uses for virtual reality. The Idea Factory.* Retrieved July 1, 2015 from http://theweek.com/articles/562851/6

International Society for Technology in Education. (2012). *Digital age coaching*. Retrieved July 7, 2015 from http://www.iste.org/standards/nets-for-coaches

Kapp, K., & O'Driscoll, T. (2010). *Learning in 3D*. Pfeiffer.

Keengwe, J., & Onchwari, G. (2011). Fostering meaningful student learning through constructivist pedagogy and technology integration. In L. A. Tomei (Ed.), *Learning tools and teaching approaches through ICT advancements* (pp. 239–249). IGI Global.

KZero. (2013). *Kzero Worldswide*. Retrieved May 15, 2013 from http://www.kzero.co.uk/blog/category/education-and-academia

Lai, K.-W. (2008). ICT supporting the learning process: The premise, reality, and promise. In J. Voogt & G. Knezek (Eds.), *International Handbook of Information Technology in Primary and Secondary Education* (pp. 215–230). Springer. doi:10.1007/978-0-387-73315-9_13

Lau, K. W., & Lee, P. Y. (2015). The use of virtual reality for creating unusual environmental stimulation to motivate students to explore creative ideas. *Interactive Learning Environments, 23*, 3-18. doi:10.1080/10494820.2012.745426

Lee, E. A., & Wong, K. W. (2014). Learning with desktop virtual reality:low spatial ability learners are more positively affected. *Computers & Education, 79*, 49–58. doi:10.1016/j.compedu.2014.07.010

Lépinard, P., & Vandangeon-Derumez, I. (2019). Apprendre le management autrement: la ludopédagogie au service du développement des soft skills des étudiant·e·s. *XXVIIIe Conférence Internationale de Management Stratégique.*

Levien, R. E. (1972). *The Emerging Technology: Instructional Uses of the Computer in Higher Education*. McGraw-Hill Book Company.

Lewis, L. A., Koston, Z., Quartley, M., & Adsit, J. (2011). Virtual communities of practice: Bridging research and practice using Web 2.0. *Journal of Educational Technology Systems, 39*(2), 155–161. doi:10.2190/ET.39.2.e

Lim, D. H., Han, S. J., Oh, J., & Jang, C. S. (2019). Application of Virtual and Augmented Reality for Training and Mentoring of Higher Education Instructors. In *Handbook of Research on Virtual Training and Mentoring of Online Instructors* (pp. 325–344). IGI Global. doi:10.4018/978-1-5225-6322-8.ch015

Linden Lab. (2013). *Infographic: 10 years of second life*. Retrieved July 1, 2015 from http://www.lindenlab.com/releases/infographic

Liu, Y. (2014, July). Virtual neurosurgical education for image-guided deep brain stimulation neurosurgery. In *Audio, Language and Image Processing (ICALIP), 2014 International Conference on* (pp. 623-626). IEEE. 10.1109/ICALIP.2014.7009869

Malaquias, R., DeOliveira Malzquias, F., Borges, D., Junior., & Zambra, P. (2018). The use of a serious game and academic performance of undergraduate accounting students: an empirical analysis. *Turkish Online Journal of Distance Education, 19*(2), 117-127. Retrieved May 25, 2020 from http://static.dergipark.org.tr/article-download/7b29/972a/43f3/5ad4fcaca63ef.pdf?

Mazuryk, T., & Gervautz, M. (1996). *Virtual reality, history, applications, technology and future, 1-72. Institute of Computer Graphics*. Vienna University of Technology, Austria. Retrieved August 29, 2015 from https://www.cg.tuwien.ac.at/research/publications/1996/mazuryk-1996-VRH/TR-186-2-96-06Paper.pdf

McCormack, M., Brooks, D. C., & Shulman, B. (2020). *The Top 10 Strategic Technologies for 2020.* EDUCAUSE Center for Analysis and Research (ECAR).

Mechdyne Corporation. (2012). *CAVE 2: The hybrid work environment.* Retrieved May 24, 2020 from https://www.mechdyne.com/hardware.aspx?name=CAVE2

Michel, H. (2013, January). From «Haute-Couture» to «Ready-to-Wear»: Typology of Serious Games Implementation Strategies in Higher Education. In *European Conference on Games Based Learning* (p. 386). Academic Conferences International Limited.

Mikropoulos, T. A., & Natsis, A. (2011). Educational virtual environments: A ten-year review of empirical research (1999–2009). *Computers & Education, 56*(3), 769–780. doi:10.1016/j.compedu.2010.10.020

Miller, R. (2014). The application of virtual reality in higher education distance learning. *Journal of Applied Learning Technology, 4*(4), 15–18.

Molnar, A. R. (1975). Viable Goals for New Educational Technology Efforts: Science Education and the New Technological Revolution. *Educational Technology, 15*(9), 16–22.

Moro, C., Stromberga, Z., Raikos, A., & Stirling, A. (2017). The effectiveness of virtual and augmented reality in health sciences and medical anatomy. *Anatomical Sciences Education, 10*(6), 549–559. doi:10.1002/ase.1696 PMID:28419750

Moro, C., Stromberga, Z., & Stirling, A. (2017). Virtualisation devices for student learning: Comparison between desktop-based (Oculus Rift) and mobile-based (Gear VR) virtual reality in medical and health science education. *Australasian Journal of Educational Technology, 33*(6), 1–10. doi:10.14742/ajet.3840

Mueller, J., Wood, E., Willoughby, T., Ross, C., & Specht, J. (2008). Identifying discriminating variables between teachers who fully integrate computers and teachers with limited integration. *Computers & Education, 51*(4), 1523–1537. doi:10.1016/j.compedu.2008.02.003

Mutekwe, E., Ndofirepi, A., Maphosa, C., Wadesango, N., & Machingambi, S. (2013). A swot analysis of the rise and pedagogical implications of the social constructivist epistemology in educational practice. *Anthrpologist, 15*(1), 53–65. doi:10.1080/09720073.2013.11891292

Noteborn, G., Dailey-Hebert, A., Bohle-Carbonell, K., & Gijselears, W. (2013). Essential knowledge for academic performance: Educating in the virtual world to promote active learning. In *Teacher and Teacher Education.* Elsvier. http://authors.elsevier.com/sd/article/S0742051X1300156X

Office of Science and Technology Policy (OSTP). (1992). *Grand Challenges: High Performance Computing and Communications.* Retrieved July 25, 2015 from http://www.hpcc.gov

Office of Social and Economic Data Analysis (OSEDA). (2001). *Final results from the e-MINTS teacher survey.* Author.

Office of Technology Assessment. (1982). Informational technology and its impact on American education. U.S. Congress.

Office of Technology Assessment (OTA). (1995). *Teachers and technology: Making the connection.* U.S. Government Printing Office.

Ong, S. K., & Nee, A. Y. C. (2013). *Virtual and augmented reality applications in manufacturing*. Springer Science & Business Media.

Pierce, D. (2015, March 6). The Future of Virtual Reality is inside your smartphone. *Wired*. Retrieved from http://www.wired.com/2015/03/future-virtual-reality-inside-smartphone/

Prasolova-Førland, E. (2008). Analyzing place metaphors in 3D educational collaborative virtual environments. *Computers in Human Behavior*, *24*(2), 185–204. doi:10.1016/j.chb.2007.01.009

Puentedura, R. (2006). Transformation, technology, and education [Blog post]. Retreived May 3, 2020 from http://hippasus.com/resources/tte/

Pulse Simulation Technology. (2008). Retrieved July 1, 2015 from https://www.youtube.com/watch?v=Q11aWO6dg2Q

Repenning, A., Lamprou, A., Petralito, S., & Basawapatna, A. (2019). *Mandatory pre-service teacher Computer Science Education: Exploring a demographic shift in Switzerland*. Paper presented at the Innovation and Technology in computer Science Education, (ITiCSE'19), Aberdeen, UK.

Repenning, A., Webb, D., & Ioannidou, A. (2010). *Scalable game design and the development of a checklist for getting computational thinking into public schools*. Association for Computer Machinery (ACM).

Rheingold, H. (1991). *Virtual reality: The revolutionary technology of computer generated artificial worlds*. Simon & Schuster Publishing.

Ritz, L. T., & Buss, A. R. (2016). A framework for aligning instructional design strategies with affordances of CAVE immerisive virtualy reality systesm. *Techn Trends: Linking Research in Practice to Improve Learning*, *60*(6), 549–556. doi:10.100711528-016-0085-9

Robinson, A. (2016). Oculus Rift Review: Virtual reality is always almost here. *The Verge*. Retrieved May 24, 2020 from https://www.theverge.com/2016/3/28/11284590/oculus-rift-vr-review

Roussou, M. (2004, June). Examining young learners' activity within interactive virtual environments. In *Proceedings of the 2004 conference on Interaction design and children: building a community* (pp. 167-168). ACM. 10.1145/1017833.1017872

Saposnik, G., & Levin, M. (2011). Virtual reality in stroke rehabilitation a meta-analysis and implications for clinicians. *Stroke*, *42*(5), 1380–1386. doi:10.1161/STROKEAHA.110.605451 PMID:21474804

Scardamalia, M., & Bereiter, C. (2006). Knowledge building: Theory, pedagogy, and technology. In K. Sawyer (Ed.), *Cambridge Handbook of the Learning Sciences* (pp. 97–118). Cambridge University Press.

Scarlett, M. (2015). Gaming Geography: Using Minecraft to Teach Essential Geographic Skills. In D. Rutledge & D. Slykhuis (Eds.), *Proceedings of SITE 2015--Society for Information Technology & Teacher Education International Conference* (pp. 838-840). Las Vegas, NV: Association for the Advancement of Computing in Education (AACE). Retrieved November 5, 2019 from https://www.learntechlib.org/primary/p/150098/

Schroeder, R. (2008). Defining VirtualWorlds and Virtual Environments. *Journal of Virtual Worlds Research*, *1*(1). Advance online publication. doi:10.4101/jvwr.v1i1.294

Sherman, W. R., & Craig, A. B. (2003). *Understanding virtual reality. Interface, application and design.* Morgan-Kaufmann Publishers. doi:10.1162/105474603322391668

Sherman, W. R., & Craig, A. B. (2018). *Understanding virtual reality: Interface, application, and design.* Morgan Kaufmann.

Skinner. (1954). *The science of learning and art of teaching*. Cambrige, MA: Harvard Education Review.

Smart, J., Cascio, J., & Paffendof, J. (2007). *Metaverse roadmap: pathways to the 3D web*. Retrieved July 5. 2015, from http://www.metaverseroadmap.org/overview

Sugar, W., & Slagter van Tryon, P. J. (2014). Development of a virtual technology coach to support technology integration for K-12 educators. *TechTrends*, *58*(3), 54–62. doi:10.100711528-014-0752-7

Sweller, J. (2008). Cognitive load theory and the use of educational technology. *Educational Technology*, *48*, 32–35. doi:10.100711423-019-09701-3

The Associated Press. (2014). *Facebook to buy Oculus virtual reality firm for $2B*. Retrieved July 1, 2015 from http://www.cbc.ca/news/technology/facebook-to-buy-oculus-virtual-reality-firm-for-zb-1,2586318

The New Media Consortium. (2007). *The Horizon Report*. New Media Consortium.

Thorsteinson, G. (2002). Innovation and practical use of knowledge. *DATA International Research Conference 2002. The Design and Technology Association*, 177–183.

Thorsteinsson, G. (2013). Developing an understanding of the pedagogy of using a virtual reality learning environment (VRLE) to support innovation education. In L. Shavinina (Ed.), The Routledge International handbook of innovation education (pp. 454-470). London: Routledge.

Thorsteinsson, G., & Page, T. (2008). Innovative technology education using a virtual reality learning environment. Pedagogy Studies/Pedigogika: Vilnius Pedagogical University.

Thorsteinsson, G., Page, T., & Niculescu, A. (2010). Using virtual relity for developing design communication. *Studies in Informatics and Control*, *19*(1), 93–106. doi:10.24846/v19i1y201010

Trelease, R. B. (2016). From chalkboard, slides, and paper to e-learning: How computing technologies have transformed anatomical sciences education. *Anatomical Sciences Education*, *9*(6), 583–602. doi:10.1002/ase.1620 PMID:27163170

Tsaramirsis, G., Buhari, S. M., Al-Shammari, K. O., Ghazi, S., Nazmudeen, M. S., & Tsaramirsis, K. (2016). Towards simulation of the classroom learning experience: Virtual reality approach. *3rd International Conference on Computing for Sustainable Global Development (INDIACom)*, 1343-1346.

Vera, L. (2019, Apr 10). What does extended reality mean? *Premo*. Retreived from: https://3dcoil.grupopremo.com/blog/what-does-extended-reality-mean/

Virtual Reality. (n.d.a). Retrieved June 24, 2015, from http://www.merriamwebster.com/dictionary/virtualreality

Virtual Reality. (n.d.b). Retrieved June 24, 2015, from https://en.wikipedia.org/wiki/Virtual_reality

Warner, T. (2012). E-coaching systems: Convenient, anytime, anywhere, and nonhuman. *Performance Improvement*, *51*(9), 22–28. doi:10.1002/pfi.21305

Webb, D., Repenninga, A., & Koh, K. (2012). Toward an emergent theory of broadening participation in computer science education. In *Proceeding of the Association for Computer Machinery (ACM) Special Interest Group on Computer Science Conference (SIGCSE).* Raleigh, NC: ACM. 10.1145/2157136.2157191

ADDITIONAL READING

Blascovich, J., & Bailenson, J. (2011). *Infinite Reality: Avatars, eternal life, new worlds and the dawn of the virtual revolution*. Harper Collins Publishing.

Blascovich, J., & Bailenson, J. (2012). *Infinite Reality: The hidden blueprint of our virtual lives*. Harper Collins Publishing.

Gill, L., & Dalgarno, B. (2010). How does pre-service teacher preparedness to use ICTs for learning and teaching develop during the first two years of teacher training? In C. Steel, M. J. Keppell, P. Gerbic, & S. Housego (Eds.), *ascilite2010 Sydney* (pp. 371–381)., Retrieved from http://www.ascilite.org.au/conferences/sydney10/Ascilite%20conference%20proceedings%202010/Gillfull.pdf

Kay, J., & FitzGerald, S. (2008). *Educational uses of Second Life*. Retrieved July 7, 2015 from http://sleducation.wikispaces.com/educationaluses

Kock, N. (2008). E-collaboration and e-commerce in virtual worlds: The potential of Second Life and World of Warcraft. *International Journal of e-Collaboration*, *4*(3), 1–13. doi:10.4018/jec.2008070101

Mayo, M. J. (2009). Video games: A route to large scale STEM education? *Science*, *323*(5910), 79–82. doi:10.1126cience.1166900 PMID:19119223

Monahan, T., McArdle, G., & Bertolotto, M. (2008). Virtual reality for collaborative e-learning. *Computers & Education*, *50*(4), 1339–1353. doi:10.1016/j.compedu.2006.12.008

Peterson, M. (2006). Learner interaction management in an avatar and chat-based virtual world. *Computer Assisted Language Learning*, *19*(1), 79–103. doi:10.1080/09588220600804087

Repenning, A., Webb, D. C., Koh, K. H., Nickerson, H., Miller, S. B., Brand, K., Many Horses, I. H., Basawapatna, A., Gluck, F., Grover, R., Gutierrez, K., & Repenning, N. (2015, April). Scalable game design: A strategy to bring systemic computer science education to schools through game design and simulation creation. *ACM Transactions on Computing Education,15*(2), 31 pages. DOI: . doi:10.1145/2700517

Rienties, B. C., Reeb-Gruber, S., Daly, P., & Van den Bossche, P. (2011). Proceedings of the 18th ED-INEB Conference: *From Innovation to Crème de la Crème Education.*

Tapscott, D. (2009). *Grown Up Digital. How The Net Generation Is Changing Your World.* McGraw Hill.

Warburton, S. (2009). Second Life in higher education: Assessing the potential for and the barriers to deploying virtual worlds in learning and teaching. *British Journal of Educational Technology*, *40*(3), 414–426. doi:10.1111/j.1467-8535.2009.00952.x

KEY TERMS AND DEFINITIONS

Artificial Intelligence (AI): Intelligence demonstrated by machines. The theory and development of computer systems able to perform tasks that normally require human intelligence, such as visual perception, speech recognition, decision-making, and translation between languages.

Augmented Reality (AR): An enhanced version of reality created by the use of technology to overlay digital information on an image of something being viewed through a device. It is an interactive experience of a real-world environment where the objects that reside in the real world are enhanced by computer-generated perceptual information.

eSports: A form of competition sports using video games. Esports often take the form of organized, multiplayer video game competitions, particularly between professional players, individually or as teams.

Extended Reality (XR): Refers to all real-and-virtual combined environments and human machine interactions generated by computer technology and wearables. It includes representative forms such as augmented reality, mixed reality, and virtual reality and the areas interpolated among them (https://g.co/kgs/r1facN).

Head-Mounted Display (HMD): A display device, worn on the head or as part of a helmet, that has a small display optic in front of one or each eye. HMD has many uses including gaming, aviation, engineering and medicine. HMD's are the primary components are virtual reality headsets.

Immersive Virtual World: Immersion into a virtual reality is a perception of being physically present in a non-physical world. The perception is created by surrounding the user of the VR system in images, sound or other stimuli that provide an engrossing total environment.

Mixed Reality (MR): The merging of real and virtual worlds to produce new environments and visualizations, where physical and digital objects co-exist and interact in real time.

Three Dimensional (3D): A solid figure or an object or shape that has three dimensions – length, width, and height. They have thickness and depth.

Two-Dimensional (2D): A flat, plane figured or shape that has two dimensions – length and width. They do not have any thickness and can be measured in only two faces.

Virtual Learning Environment (VLE): The environment created through virtual reality. Any networked application that permits both interaction with the computing environment and the work of other users. (email, chat, web-based document sharing applications are all examples of virtual environments. It is a networked common operating system.

Virtual Reality (VR): An artificial environment which is experienced through sensory stimuli (such as sights and sounds) provided by a computer and in which one's actions partially determine what happens in the environment.

Virtual Reality Simulators: The equipment used for human immersion in virtual reality with the purpose of entertainment, education or training of the public. (examples include a virtual amusement ride, virtual gaming simulator, virtual motion simulator).

Virtal World (VW): Computer-based simulated environment which may be populated by many users who can create a personal avatar and simultaneously and independently explore the virtual world, participat in activities and communicate with others.

Wearables: Electronic devices that can be incorporated into clothing or worn on the body as implants or accessories. (These might include smartwatches, fitness trackers, google glasses, and VR.)

Chapter 2
A Literature Review on the Use of Three-Dimensional Virtual Worlds in Higher Education

Reza Ghanbarzadeh
https://orcid.org/0000-0001-9073-1576
School of Business and Tourism, Southern Cross University, Australia

Amir Hossein Ghapanchi
College of Engineering and Science, Victoria University, Australia

ABSTRACT

Three-dimensional virtual worlds (3DVW) have been substantially adopted in teaching and learning worldwide. The current study conducted a literature review of the published research relevant to the application of 3DVWs in higher education. A literature search was performed on nine scientific databases, and following scrutiny according to inclusion criteria, 176 papers were selected for review. The literature review process was summarized, reviews undertaken by the authors, and results about the applicability of 3DVWs in higher education were extracted. A wide variety of application areas for 3DVWs in higher education were found and classified into five main categories. Various 3DVW platforms and virtual environments used for educational goals were also identified. This study found that a wide range of virtual environments and tools have been implemented by 3DVW technology and applied for teaching and learning in higher education.

INTRODUCTION

A Three-Dimensional Virtual World (3DVW) is a computer-based, simulated and graphical environment, usually accessible on the World Wide Web, that is intended for users to inhabit and interact using personalized graphical and animated self-representations, known as avatars (Boulos et al., 2007). Virtual worlds are online spaces where individuals can interact with three-dimensional representations of physical locations or phenomena. The simulated environment could appear similar to the real world

DOI: 10.4018/978-1-7998-4960-5.ch002

(with real rules, real-time actions, interactions and communications) or depict a fantasy virtual world. Recently, Internet-based 3DVW have thrived and hold promise to significantly impact the way people communicate and interact with each other.

Inside 3DVWs, people can manipulate elements and experience telepresence. Increasingly, researchers, organizations and educational communities are recognizing these environments as legitimate communication media which can be used as an effective media in teaching and learning. Users of these environments not only have the opportunity to interact with each other in a sociocultural and delightful activities but also can follow virtual wealth through activities such as selling and buying lands as well as creating and trading virtual goods using virtual currencies (Ba et al., 2010).

The purpose of this chapter is to 1) identify the main activities in the application of 3DVWs in higher education, 2) highlight various 3D virtual world platforms that researchers have used in learning and teaching, 3) categorize various virtual environments designed for educational purposes. Therefore, the current chapter attempts to answer the following three research questions:

1. For what purposes have 3DVWs been used in higher education?
2. What types of 3DVW platforms have been used by researchers in higher education?
3. What kinds of virtual environments have been created for educational activities using 3DVWs?

BACKGROUND

3DVWs have been broadly adopted to favor socialization and education. These virtual worlds offer the possibility of simulating the real world or designing unique fantasy worlds. By interacting with these platforms, people can actively experience simulated realities, which can aid in understanding various concepts and in supporting independent viewpoints for users as they accomplish specific tasks. Users can easily share the virtual environment for performing highly synchronous collaborative tasks, manipulating the same virtual objects (De Lucia et al., 2009).

Numerous advances in information technology are transfiguring teaching and learning styles, especially in higher education. During the past decade, educators from a variety of backgrounds have started using the online virtual environments to support their teaching and learning activities. 3DVWs support a higher level of interactivity and richness for interaction, collaboration and communication than traditional media. They also have the potential to create engaging and meaningful experiences for students and learners. In recent years, there has been remarkable growth in the application of these environments for distance education and e-learning. These immersive platforms offer various tools to create sophisticated and highly interactive simulations using in-world programming, modeling and scripting tools. 3DVWs support teaching and learning in an educational context and they offer the functionality and capability to manage the various aspects of education such as lecturing, presentation, administration and assessment of coursework.

A wide variety of organizations, educational groups, and government agencies currently provide regular events, seminars, and workshops in virtual worlds. Furthermore, many educational institutions and organizations are creating virtual learning environments to deliver courses (face-to-face and online) and events that include 3DVW presentations, discussions, simulations and role-playing. Not only do 3DVWs amplify learning beyond the capabilities afforded by teleconferencing and online web presentation tools, they also create opportunities for field trips that go far beyond the traditional learning spaces (Linden Research, 2011).

Many studies have been conducted on the application of 3DVWs in learning and teaching. For example, Hew and Cheung (2013) discussed evidence-based educational approaches related to the application of Web 2.0 technologies in both K-12 and higher education settings. In their study, Saleeb and Dafoulas (2010b) analytically derived advantageous and disadvantageous categories and sub-categories of applying 3DVWs for conducting e-learning. Hew and Cheung (2010) reviewed past empirical research studies on the application of 3DVWs in educational settings such as K-12 and higher education and found that virtual worlds may be applied for the communication spaces, simulation of space, and experiential spaces.

RESEARCH METHOD

A literature review was conducted on the application of 3DVWs in higher education. The current literature review follows the steps used in a variety of previous studies e.g. the reviews conducted by Ghanbarzadeh et al., (2015) and Ghanbarzadeh et al., (2014). In this section, the steps in the literature review process will be described, including the procedure for deciding upon the inclusion and exclusion of pertinent literature, and data extraction and analysis during the search process will be discussed in detail.

Search Criteria, Databases, and Keywords

To start the literature review process, inclusion and exclusion criteria were established:

- Both empirical and technical studies were included.
- Studies related to education settings other than higher education were excluded.
- Studies in languages other than English were excluded.

Nine relevant scientific databases were used in the search of the keywords: ScienceDirect, ProQuest Computing, Scopus, IEEE Xplore, Association for Information Systems Electronic Library (AISel), Web of Science (via Thomson Reuters), Inspec (via Thomson Reuters), ERIC (Via ProQuest) and PsycARTICLES (via Ovid). The databases were selected based on their comprehensiveness in locating pertinent articles, chapters, presentations, papers; these nine databases cover thousands of sources.

Based on various search patterns proposed by each search engine, the advanced search option provided by each database was used for the search operations. 48 search keywords were selected and categorized into three main categories: three-dimensional, virtual world, and higher education. By using the selected search terms, title, abstract and keywords of the articles were searched in accordance with the various search patterns offered by each search engine. The key words that were used in the search are shown in Table 1.

The process of searching for and selecting relevant literature for the current study was completed in six different stages. Figure 1 shows this process.

In the first stage, nine scientific databases were selected. In Stage 2, by using the keywords demonstrated in Table 1, search on the databases were carried out. In Stages 3, 4 and 5, papers were excluded based on their titles, abstracts, and full text, respectively. Finally, after exclusions, at the end of the

Table 1. Key words used in the search

("3D" OR "3 D" OR "3-D" OR "3_D" OR "three-dimensional" OR "three dimensional" OR "3 dimensional" OR "three D" OR "three-D") *AND* *("virtual world" OR "virtual life" OR "virtual space" OR "virtual environment" OR "virtual reality" OR "virtual community" OR "virtual inhabited world" OR "inhabited space" OR "second life" OR "active world" OR "avatar" OR "virtual immersive world" OR "Multi user virtual environment" OR "MUVE")* *AND* *("educate" OR "education" OR "educational" OR "educating" OR "distance education" OR "distance learning" OR "train" OR "training" OR "lecture" OR "lecturing" OR "pedagogy" OR "pedagogical" OR "learn" OR "learning" OR "teach" OR "teaching" OR "instruct" OR "instruction" OR "instructing" OR "edutainment" OR "university" OR "universities" OR "higher education" OR "tertiary sector" OR "tertiary education")*

Figure 1. Stages in the procedure of searching for and selecting studies

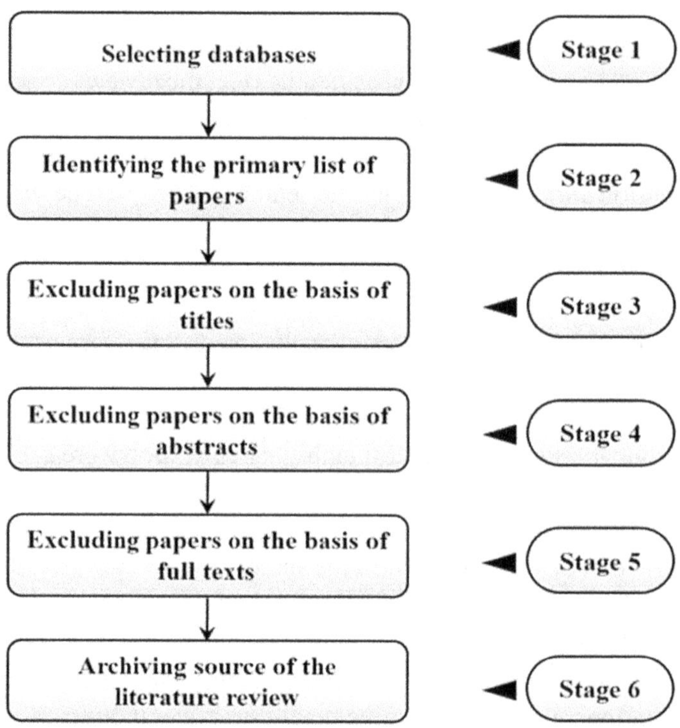

procedure, the total number of relevant papers was 176, which was a reasonable number for generating an appropriate conclusion. Therefore, the search process stopped at the end of Stage 6.

To select papers for the literature review, we considered the following inclusion and exclusion criteria:

1. As we investigated various perspectives of utilization of 3DVWs in higher education, we reviewed both the empirical evidence and design guidelines. Therefore, we targeted both the empirical and technical studies in the current literature review.
2. We examined only peer-reviewed publications (e.g. journals, conference papers, book chapters) that were found in electronic databases. All non-peer-reviewed publications were excluded.

3. Studies focusing on applications of 3DVWs in K–12 education or in non-academic organizations were excluded.
4. Studies in languages other than English were excluded.

Table 2. Number of related papers selected from each scientific database

Scientific Data Bases	Related Studies
IEEE Xplore	62
ERIC (Via ProQuest)	38
ScienceDirect	28
Inspec (via Thomson Reuters)	19
AISeL	12
Scopus	11
ProQuest	5
Web of Science (via Thomson Reuters)	1
PsycARTICLES (via Ovid)	0
Total number of related papers	176

Table 2 indicates the number of related papers which were selected from each scientific database.

Data Extraction and Analysis

The data extracted from each of the selected 176 papers includes:

- Performed activities by using 3DVWs for learning and teaching in higher education
- Utilized 3DVW platform
- Created 3D virtual educational environments for the study

To perform a data analysis, full text of all extracted papers were read in their entirety in order to identify all information related to each of the mentioned research questions; then each paper was classified and labeled according to its main area of research and application area of 3DVWs. To make a better classification, the categorizing operation was performed two times. First, each paper was reviewed by one of the authors and an appropriate category code allocated, therefore, all papers were classified in various categories. To clarify the classification, the process was repeated for the second time by the other author. The results were discussed in a meeting with professionals in the same research field. During the meeting, all categories were discussed and revised, and some of them were merged. Finally, all papers were classified into five major research categories based on the main activity and application areas of 3DWVs: virtual lecturing, discussion, field trip, simulation, and gaming. After this, some demographic information extracted from each paper, then investigated and finalized. Figure 2 shows the procedure undertaken in the data analysis process.

Figure 2. The procedure of data analysis

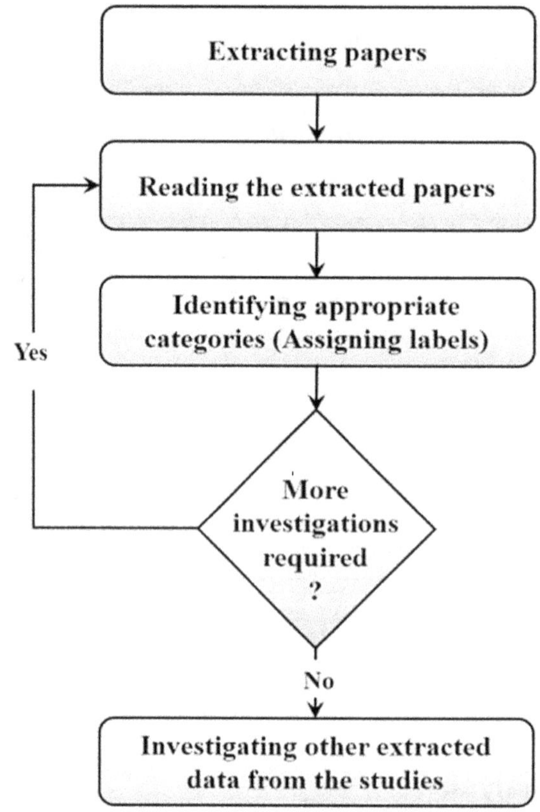

RESULTS

The purpose of this study, as stated in the introduction section, was to conduct a literature review on the application areas of 3DVWs in learning and teaching in higher education, in order to answer three research questions in relation to the technology and higher education. In this section a discussion of findings will be presented for each of the research questions.

Applications for 3DVWs in Higher Education

The results of the current literature review revealed that 3DVWs have been adopted and applied in a wide range of areas in higher education for teaching and learning. According to the nature of educational activities performed, articles were sorted into five main categories: virtual lecturing, discussion, field trip, simulation, and gaming. Some of the studies implemented two or more activities simultaneously. Figure 3 depicts the major categories of application areas of 3DVWs in the higher education settings.

Figure 3. The major categories of application areas of 3DVWs in the higher education setting

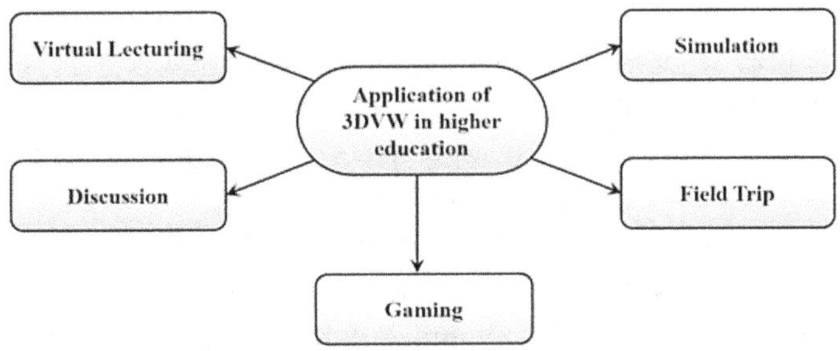

Virtual Lecturing

In this application, by using 3DVWs, a virtual replica of a classroom setting, or a laboratory as commonly used for presentations and lectures, is designed. The instructor could use two or more screens for presenting slides, videos, pictures, web resources, and even an online-desktop when a part of the desktop needs to be shared with the students. Students usually attend the virtual classroom using their own avatars and there are possibilities to make contact between the instructor and the students using two mechanisms, text chat and online voice. For voice chat, instructor and students need to have microphones and headsets hooked up to their computers. 49% of the investigated studies in the literature have content relevant to virtual lecturing, and they have mainly established a virtual lecturing activity to deliver a course to the students.

For instance, in order to understand the reaction and perception of students when using Second Life in a blended learning session with the involvement of the instructors, Zulkanain, Rahim, and Azizan (2016) conducted an exploratory study. Kawulich and D'Alba (2019) used Second Life for teaching research methods to a doctoral-level qualitative research class. In a quantitative research, Al-Hatem et al. (2018) examined impacts of second life on student nurses' confidence and motivation in developing their self-regulated learning performance. In the study of Lorenzo-Alvarez et al. (2019), attitudes and perceptions of 3rd-year medical students, as well as family physicians, toward a radiographic interpretation course in Second Life was evaluated. In another study, second life was used to enhance Mandarin essay writing by learners of Chinese as a second language in Singapore (Lan et al., 2019). Gazave and Hatcher (2017) used a 3D virtual world to implement Team-based learning (TBL) in an online undergraduate anatomy course. In a qualitative study, Linganisa et al. (2018) investigated the perception of fourth-year information systems and technology (IST) students on the usefulness of Second Life as a learning platform. Chen et al. (2010) assessed the relative effectiveness of a 3DVW-based learning environment and traditional face-to-face learning environment, and by performing a quantitative research, they found that when an interactive instructional strategy is applied in education, there is no remarkable difference for perceived learning and satisfaction between the two environments. Pereira et al. (2019) used Second Life to teach the first semester veterinary students the clinical reasoning process, and compared the results with the traditional classroom setting. Barry et al. (2013), Callaghan et al. (2009), Dafoulas et al. (2012), Dreher et al. (2009), Mendonça et al. (2011), Sharma et al. (2013), and Yalcinalp et al. (2012) carried out studies related to this category.

Discussion

Discussion boards and online meetings are other application in the 3DVW-related virtual learning programs. During the distance discussions or meetings, students engage in several social activities, such as discussing a subject matter, sharing their perspective(s), presenting students' projects, consultation, asking questions, etc. Voice, video and text-based communication are used for discussions. For example, by using text chat, students or educators could send private and public messages or post text messages in discussion forums inside the 3DVWs. For voice and live video chat, users need to have microphones, cameras and headsets hooked up to their computers. Additionally, there is the possibility of automatic recording of entire sessions as reviewable logs.

Approximately, 32% of studies have used virtual worlds as a tool for discussions and meetings in higher education. For instance, Lorenzo et al. (2012) found that 3DWV platforms can provide better capabilities for removing barriers between students and between instructors and students. The problematic issue in this application was technical difficulties in establishing video, voice and/or text communications. For example, there could be glitches in sending and receiving video, voice and text, especially when the number of simultaneous participants was high. Balcikanli (2012) used Second Life® to create an interactive discussion environment for two groups of language learners and found that it played a crucial role in encouraging them to apply the authentic language. Studies of Nikolaou and Tsolakidis (2012), Loureiro and Bettencourt (2011), Di Blas and Poggi (2007), Prasolova-Forland (2004), and Zhao et al. (2010) are classified into this category as they involve virtual meeting or discussion room for various educational purposes.

Field Trip

Field trips are mainly used as an application for self-learning. A virtual representation of a specific place such as a museum, a gallery, a hotel, a hospital, and a scientific site is designed to create visitor awareness about the place and provide information that students need. Students are able to navigate their avatars into the designed environment to visit the virtual site. Students usually perform a virtual trip to a virtual place, visit the site, read the provided information, and observe some activities inside the site.

Almost 14% of studies in the literature used 3DVWs for conducting field trip programs. For example, Aydogan et al. (2010) have built a hydroelectric power plant in Second Life® with all its important parts to teach how to produce electricity. Using avatars, students walked around and flew towards the power plant to figure out how it worked. In another study, access to a number of digital 3D models of European theatre designs was provided and participants visited the Theatre of Epidaurus during a virtual field trip; participants also explored Shakespeare's Globe Theatre (Nicholls & Philip, 2012). Huang et al. (2013) used 3DVW for tourism education, and the majority of the hypotheses in their research model identify the factors impacting student learning experience within a 3DVW. For example, they examined the association between students' perceptions of autonomy and positive emotions, which was supported ($\beta = 0.487$, $p < 0.05$) suggesting that the perceptions of autonomy in a 3DVW predicts students' feelings of positive emotion.

Simulation

Other studies in the current review applied 3DVWs for simulation purposes in higher education. Simulation is the act of imitation of a real-world system's or process's operation over time. By definition, it is the emulation of a real-world system, an activity or a process operation over a time period. It is a powerful action that is used for teaching and learning processes that generally are impossible or very hard to practice in the real world. It is a powerful tool that is commonly used to teach processes that are generally difficult to practice in the real world (Wang & Zhu, 2009). By using virtual worlds' designing and programming tools, as well as simulation techniques, the virtual clones of a specific place or an environment is modelled and designed for training purposes. By working with simulated environments, students get familiar with various concepts which are usually inaccessible in the real world.

Twenty-eight percent of studies used 3DVWs for simulation-related teaching and learning. For example, Aydogan and Aras (2019) designed, simulated and virtually implemented a new basic programmable logic controllers (PLC) laboratory on Second Life for the purpose of online PLC training. In a study conducted by Grenfell (2013), students were working to simulate the development of a virtual art exhibition space. In another study, researchers simulated an on-line garment store in Second Life with static objects, such as buildings, sofas, costumes, advertising boards, direction boards, etc. (Dong et al., 2010). They found that to provide a successful educational service in 3DVWs, more attention should be paid to the ease of use during the whole service lifetime. Molka-Danielsen and Chabada (2010) simulated an emergency evacuation within Second Life®. Irwin et al. (2019) utilized a created nursing environment in Second Life® for three nursing courses in order to develop nursing skills among undergraduate students. In another study, a collaborative simulation was applied to educate students on construction safety (Le & Park, 2012). Brown et al. (2012) presented a simulation of handing over the 24-hour care requirements of patients in intensive care during the first hour of a shift. According to (Cheng & Wang, 2011), the simulation experience with a 3DVW for marketing was very important and irreplaceable in comparison with other ICT-based pedagogy. To achieve a higher level of simulation potential, improvements in visual effects and realism of the virtual platforms are required. Winkelmann et al. (2019) used Second Life to implement a virtual laboratory experiment for students enrolled in a General Chemistry 2 course.

Gaming

One of the significant effects of IT-based technologies on students is that they are interested in playing computer games. Computer games are useful and educationally effective approaches to teach various educational concepts. For many years, electronic games have supported entertainment-based learning. Computer games are effective approaches to teach various educational concepts. Students who play computer games tend to learn the intended concepts, and in most of the cases, they find it a relatively enjoyable experience of learning (Wang & Zhu, 2009).

About 11% of the studies in the review have used virtual worlds for gaming and machinima to improve teaching and learning in the higher education setting. For example, to determine whether and how a 3DVW enhanced software engineering education, researchers designed a Second Life-based game for computer science students (Ye et al., 2007). Arango-López et al. (2019) created a platform, CREANDO, that allows the creation and edition of pervasive gaming experiences in closed spaces on university campuses, in order to increase the motivation of higher education students in educational processes. In another study, authors designed a 3D virtual quest game to enhance English vocabulary acquisition through interaction, negotiation of meaning and observation (Kastoudi, 2011). Wang and Zhu (2009) developed a game within Second Life® for software engineering education. Students, by playing the game, were able to realize the process of developing a software. Merchant et al. (2012), in their quantitative study, designed a game in Second Life® to enable students to see molecules from multiple perspectives. They found 3D virtual reality-based instruction effective in enhancing students' chemistry achievement.

3DVWs Platforms Used in Teaching and Learning

Since the advent of the first generation of 3DVWs, various companies have developed their own virtual world platform, and currently, there are a wide variety of 3DVW platforms. Individuals and numerous companies and organizations around the world are using various samples of these platforms for their own purposes. There are a wide variety of active 3DVW platforms at the moment, however, this literature review sought to identify the platforms most widely used by researchers in their educational programs.

Figure 4 presents percentages of various 3DWV platforms found in the review of 176 studies. Second Life was the most frequently discussed 3DVW platform used for learning and teaching purposes in higher education; Second Life was discussed in 61% of studies. Fourteen percent of the studies used their own, self-developed 3DVW platform mainly using a designed single-purpose virtual world for extending educational activities. Open Simulator was discussed in 7% of the studies, as a platform utilized for learning and teaching in higher education. Five percent of the papers discussed using other platforms such as Vacademia, Zora 3-D, Croquet and AliveX3D. Active World and AET Zone are the other platforms which were discussed respectively in 3% and 2% of studies. In 8% of the studies, authors

Table 3. Number of studies for each 3DVW platform

3D Virtual World Platform	Number of Studies
Second Life ®	107
Self-Developed	24
Open Simulator	12
Active World	5
AET Zone	3
Unknown	14
Vacademia	2
Barnsborough(AWEDU)	1
Croquet	1
GEARS	1
QA (Quest Atlantis)	1
Virtools Dev	1
Virtual Incubator World (VIW)	1
WonderLands/TEAL	1
Zora 3-D	1
AliveX3D	1

did not specify the type of 3DVW that they have applied, therefore, the used platforms considered as unknown. Table 3 indicates all 3DWV platforms used in the literature, and the exact number of studies which used each one.

Gamage, Tretiakov, and Crump (2011) investigated educators' perceptions of Second Life® affordances for learning by conducting in-depth semi-structured interviews with 22 educators. Chen et al. (2009) assessed the efficacy of two instruction strategies in Second Life®, and their effects on interactivity, social presence, and perceived learning. Garcia-Zubia et al. (2010) described the implementation of a new remote lab that allowed students to control a micro robot from Second Life®. Stiubiener et al. (2011) in their study presented two tools developed to facilitate the use and to automate the process of using Open Simulator for educational purposes. Dickey (2005) presented two exploratory case studies of different, but exemplary educational activities using Active Worlds for formal and informal education. In another study, Bronack et al. (2008) used the AET Zone platform for their teaching and learning purposes.

Figure 4. Percentage of applied 3DVW platforms in higher education

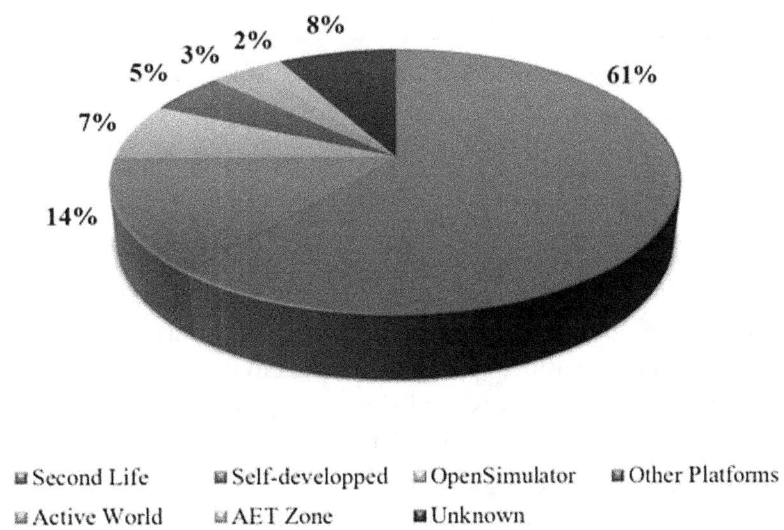

Categorization of Learning Environments for Educational Purposes

3DVW technology provides the ability for users to design and create different kinds of virtual and 3D environments for various purposes. In all of the studies in the current literature review, researchers designed and developed specific spaces inside the virtual worlds in relation to their educational activities. The created virtual environments were categorized and 17 categories were identified. The majority of the studies created two or more categories of environments simultaneously. Table 4 shows the list of all virtual environments in higher education as well as the number of papers in each category in the literature.

As it can be noted in Table 4, in 69 studies, researchers designed virtual classroom environments for their programs. These environments resemble actual classrooms or lecture theaters (having a number of seats, a lectern for instructor, a presentation display and video display), where students' and instructors' avatars can attend and communicate with each other using voice or text chat tools. Students can see the

Table 4. Virtual environments used in higher education and the number of related studies

Virtual Environments	Number of Studies
Virtual classroom	69
Simulated place	34
Meeting area	22
Other environments	21
Virtual campus	15
Virtual laboratory	15
Gaming environment	11
Virtual library	9
Replica of known place	9
Virtual messaging environment	8
Board room	4
Sandbox area	4
Video room	3
Quiz environment	3
Poster room	1
Outdoor environment	1
Staff room	1

presentation slides and educational videos and they can even see the instructor's face in an online and real-time video. For Example, Gao et al. (2009), Loureiro and Bettencourt (2011), Marcelino et al. (2012), and Yalcinalp et al. (2012) designed various virtual classroom environments inside the 3DVW platforms.

In 34 of the reviewed studies, researchers used simulated places for teaching and learning. In most cases, a specific place has been modeled, simulated and created; therefore, students can learn different things by visiting, interacting with and going around these places. For example, Cheng and Wang (2011) designed a 3D virtual supermarket to help business students transform abstract class theory into the concrete application ability in the real world. Brown et al. (2012) developed a simulated 3D ICU (Intensive Care Unit) for students to practice key steps in handing over the 24/7 care requirements of intensive care patients during the first hour of a shift. In another study, authors designed a virtual hydroelectric power plant in Second Life to teach students how to produce electricity (Aydogan et al., 2010). Students can also observe the detail of the power plant's structure, which cannot be shown even in a technical trip due to the plant being in-service.

Virtual meeting areas have been designed and used in 22 studies. These areas are mainly furnished by seats and chairs, and they contain presentations and video displays. The avatars can get together in the place and they can use microphones/speakers (voice chat) or text chat tools for sending public or private messages to each other. The main purpose of these places is to hold across-distance meetings with students, instructors or staff. For example, Bronack et al. (2008), Nikolaou and Tsolakidis (2012), and Andreas and Tsiatsos (2008) developed a virtual meeting area to hold educational meetings.

Fifteen studies discussed the development of a university campus for their activities. They designed various parts of a real campus and students could enter the campus using their avatars and visit different sections inside. In some cases, a replica of a real-world university campus is designed so the virtual campus exactly resembles the real one. In other cases, researchers designed different buildings and views for the campus and they only inserted the parts, buildings or rooms that students needed to attend or visit. For example, Bers and Chau (2010), Nishide (2011), and Nishide and Ueshima (2004) developed a campus using 3DVWs for their teaching and learning programs in higher education.

Virtual laboratories are the other virtual environments which have been created and developed by researchers for higher education in 15 studies. These laboratories are simulated environments that present the ability to perform most of the activities of the real laboratories in a virtual manner. For instance, Winkelmann et al. (2019) implemented a virtual laboratory for General Chemistry 2 course within Second Life®. Muller et al. (2012) designed a virtual mechatronics lab in Open Simulator, developed for mechatronics training, which combines immersive 3D worlds and real lab equipment. Zhong and Liu (2012) created a virtual chemistry laboratory to discuss the technical difficulties that users face when developing 3D virtual worlds. A physics laboratory was designed by dos Santos, Guetl et al. (2010) in order to support students understanding of physics concepts.

Eleven studies implemented gaming environments and activities within 3DVW. For example, in the study of Arango-López et al. (2019) a platform was created that allows students to create and edit pervasive gaming experiences.

In nine papers, virtual libraries were implemented, and in nine other studies, researchers developed a replica of a known place or a popular attraction in the world to help students get familiar with the place and atmosphere. These virtual clones are mainly used for field trips and similar activities. For example, Hsu (2012) created a virtual island of France for tourism education. In two other studies, researchers used Second Life to simulate a Saami tent and a Kalasha valley and dwellings for archaeology students (Edirisingha et al., 2009; Salmon et al., 2010).

Virtual messaging environments have also been created and used in educational settings for communication purposes. In these environments, users of virtual worlds can interact with each other using voice or text chat tools. For example, Traphagan et al. (2010) used a text chat tool for students to complete all course activities collaboratively with group members. Wigham and Chanier (2013) offer a classification of verbal and nonverbal communication acts in Second Life and outline relationships between the different types of acts by using a voice forum.

In addition to the environments mentioned, other virtual spaces have been designed for different educational purposes. Some of the other virtual environments are video rooms, virtual libraries, board rooms, poster rooms, outdoor environments, staff rooms, sandbox areas, and other miscellaneous environments.

DISCUSSION AND FUTURE DIRECTION FOR RESEACH AND PRACTICE

The principal objective of the present review was to characterize the various application areas of 3DVWs in conjunction with higher education. Following, we will take a deeper look at the aims of this study and discuss the lessons we have learned. The 176 articles retained for review demonstrate the breadth of research foci in this topic. To gain a general understanding of virtual world research in higher education, according to the application areas of this technology, we classified these research studies into 5 main categories. Figure 5 illustrates the frequency of studies included in each of these categories of activities and shows that most of the papers contained more than one activity in the context and were included in more than one category.

Figure 5. Percentage of studies included in each category of activities

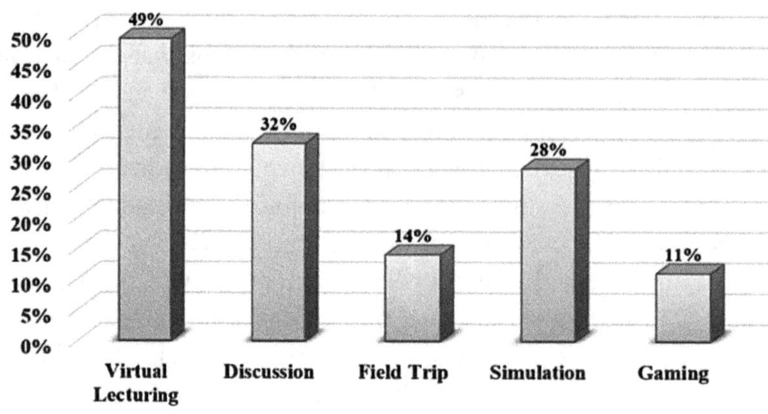

The virtual lecturing category contains the largest percentage of papers (49%). This indicates the capability of 3DVW technologies to facilitate online lectures and distance learning. The possibility of presenting lectures and classroom activities through voice, video, slide, animation and other online facilities provided by 3DVWs as well as the feeling of presence in a real classroom by students and instructors has made this technology as a mature tool to be used in higher education. Discussion and meeting (32%) and simulation (28%) are the next most common applications of 3DVWs in higher education. The great potential of this technology enabled educational systems to hold online and real-time meetings and seminars. Most 3DVW platforms provide the feasibility of simulating and modelling real-world activities through in-world programming and building tools. As shown in Figure 5, these technologies have been utilized for field trips activities in 14% of the reviewed studies. Despite the great potential of 3DVWs in gaming, studies paid less attention to this category with total of 11% of all studies.

A total of 7% of all studies, 13 out of 176, only conducted reviews, surveys and investigation of the impact of using these technologies on education. For example, Fırat (2010) evaluated the pedagogical capabilities of 3DVWs and determined the educational application of these technologies in Turkey. Hew and Cheung (2013) presented a literature review to investigate the impact of applying technologies based on Web 2.0 on K–12 and higher education students' learning performance. Boulos et al. (2007) presented the educational potential of 3DVWs for educators as well as medical and health librarians. Wang and Lockee (2010) provided a content analysis for investigating studies on the application of 3DVWs in distance education. Hew and Cheung (2010) reviewed previous empirical studies on the application of 3DVWs in education settings. Another study explored Second Life's potential and the problems 3D virtual environments present to instructors and educators (Warburton, 2009). Pricer (2011) presented a 'Webliography' which provides resources discussing the application of various forms of computer simulations such as 3DVWs for immersive education. To assess the impact of 3DVWs on education, Eschenbrenner et al. (2008) conducted a literature review to identify applications, benefits, opportunities and issues. Saleeb and Dafoulas (2010b) analytically derived the advantageous and disadvantageous themes and sub-concepts of using 3DVWs for e-learning. They also investigated the impact of architectural features of educational virtual buildings and classrooms within 3DVWs on the comfort of higher education students and staff, and they presented design preferences and propositions to enhance virtual campus learning spaces, internally and externally (Saleeb & Dafoulas, 2010a).

One of the principle goals of this research was to classify various application areas of 3DVWs in the field of education. Therefore, based on the literature, the authors provide five meaningful categories of applications in higher education (virtual lecturing, discussion, field trip, simulation, and gaming). Hence, future research can explore additional applications of these environments in the education sector. They can identify various criteria to evaluate value-added activities and strategies for effective integration of this technology into a curriculum. Future research also needs to be more creative to figure out new effective ways of teaching and learning rather than to replicate the traditional methods of education. In spite of the considerable level of academic research related to the educational application of 3DVWs, research pertaining to the practical applications of such tools are seemingly inadequate, particularly as opportunities continue to arise and continue to evolve in utilizing this technology in the field of education.

The investigated studies tended to pay more attention to qualitative data collection and analysis approaches than quantitative ones. Among the studies, approximately 11% employed a quantitative approach, and most studies used only qualitative research methods to collect educators' and students' feedback. Although some studies used multiple methods, the emphasis of the data collection was on qualitative data. The data resources mainly included interviews, participatory observation, platform log files, screen captured images, environment videos, notes, class logs and chat logs. Future research may employ quantitative data methods as well as mixed method approaches to get results that can be better generalized.

The current literature review and the results provide various implications for a wide range of organizations, universities, educational communities, schools, academic staff, educators, instructors and individuals which are able to use this study to consider all the capabilities and derived experiences that are associated with the application of 3DVWs in the professional and pedagogical objectives they want to achieve. This study also identifies any gaps that were apparent in the published research. Despite the fact that researchers paid more attention to educational benefits of 3DVWs, some gaps still exist in the literature and future research should be conducted to explore improvements to previous studies. The mentioned implications as well as existing gaps in conjunction with the topic will be discussed as following:

Collaborative Learning

According to the findings, the focus of previous studies was mainly on the possibilities of using 3DVWs for delivering distance courses, and the students' learning outcomes in the investigated studies were mostly positive for distance education. Nevertheless, as these technologies provide effective opportunities for students in respect to collaborative learning, teamwork and self-directed learning, future studies may best contribute by investigating the impacts of such technologies on individual and group student outcomes and experiences. By using various communication tools provided by 3DVWs (e.g. text chat, voice chat, online video conferencing), students can interact with each other and their educators at the same time. Moreover, 3DVWs provide synchronous communication regardless of the students' location. These environments can be designed to be a social hub, places for people to meet and a place for various events. Educators and instructors can take advantage of this technology for collaboration purposes among students. On the other hand, students with social disorders, especially those who have difficulty communicating with others for various reasons, could benefit from this technology and improve their learning and social interactive behavior. Learning as construction or co-construction can be performed easily within these environments which provide facilities for creating, mixing, and mashing up objects and content. Therefore, 3DVWs can be seen as a great collaborative tool with which multiple users can experiment with each other. Edirisingha et al. (2009) found that in spite of the fact that the creation of participants' real identity through an avatar is complex in virtual words, their experience of socialization gave them positive feelings. Ellison and Matthews (2010) found that using 3DVWs for a 3D construction-based project had various positive effects on learners.

Gaming and Machinima

Gaming and machinima aspect of 3DVWs has also received little attention in the higher education field. Machinima, in definition, is the "art of making animated movies in a 3D virtual environment in real time" (Marino, 2004). Entertainment environments and leisure activities, as well as using computers and video games, have been identified as significant educational resources. Games help impart knowledge, develop course-related skills and reinforce positive habits in students of all ages, in the form of play. Future studies are expected to put more attention to this capability of 3DVWs in teaching and learning programs. For example, the findings of Terzidou, Tsiatsos, Dae, Samaras, & Chasanidou, (2012) revealed that there is a positive attitude toward adoption of 3DVWs used from game-based learning techniques. The main problems in the 3DVW gaming applications in education are a lack of appropriate hardware performance; having low visual, acoustic and graphics specifications in comparison with different gaming consoles (which reduces the attractiveness of the environment); and the need for greater Internet speed. Another consideration of 3DVW-based games is that there is no winner and loser, which reduces some students' interest in playing.

Geographical Context

According to findings of the current study, the majority of studies in the literature in this field were conducted in North America and Europe, and there are only a limited number of studies from other countries of the world. A comparative research within various cultural and social environments is recommended in order to more effectively comprehend the influence of geographical contexts on the use of 3DVWs in higher education.

3DVW-based vs. Traditional Classroom

One of the significant questions about the applicability of 3DVWs in higher education is whether these technologies can provide comparable learning outcomes for trainees attending real-world classrooms. In the current literature review, the researchers found a wide range of studies that covered this research topic and, according to students' and educators' feedback, they demonstrate that 3DVWs have the ability to enhance teaching and learning outcomes significantly, having a general positive impact on students' achievement and providing more options for delivering education in comparison with real-world and in-person classes. Based on the reported results, the majority of studies in the literature have come up with the same results and even better results of real-world lectures. For instance, Okutsu et al. (2013) investigated the learning outcomes of a 3DVW-based course on students. They did not find a significant difference between the exam scores of the 3DVW group and the real-world group. According to Zhao et al. (2011), 3DVWs can create a more colourful learning environment than traditional teaching, and students can recognise the experience of immersion, flexibility and interactivity.

Distance Learning Opportunities

The findings show that the focus of previous studies was mainly on the possibilities of using 3DVWs to deliver distance courses, and the students' learning outcomes based on those studies were mostly positive. Due to Internet-based characteristics, 3DVWs, provide effective opportunities to conduct distance learning and e-learning programs for students using this technology. Lectures, seminars, laboratories and workshops can be held easily using this technology, and students and educators can attend courses in the virtual venue using their own avatar from various locations all around the world.

Simulation and Modeling

Modeling is "the act of representing a system or subsystem formally" (Davis II et al., 1999). According to the promising potential of 3DVWs for modeling and simulation purposes, research or practice that may not have been practical or feasible in real life can be created through simulations in 3D virtual environments (Eschenbrenner et al., 2008), and virtual simulations using these kinds of technologies are an acceptable strategy to deliver scenarios that focus on practical skills. By using the simulation techniques, instructors, educators and trainers are able to collaborate with learners and solve problem-based scenarios in a team. Simulation also allows them to construct technical skills actively through interaction in a 3D virtual environment without having the hazard of risks or danger of making mistakes in a specific activity. Organizations such as universities, manufacturers and educational communities can model and simulate various systems, laboratories, product lines and activities, with virtual instruments and equipment that simulate real-world operations at a very low cost for education. Particularly, utilizing 3DVWs seems to be a proper method to learn design-based and visually-intensive courses like object modelling and computer graphics. Using 3DVWs seems to be particularly appropriate for learning design-based and visually intensive courses like object modelling and computer graphics. For example, Molka-Danielsen and Chabada, (2010) used Second Life® to simulate evacuation and training exercises, and they found that, despite the differences of human behaviors within virtual worlds, using a simulated environment for education has real value and experiential learning takes place.

Virtual Field Trips

By using 3DVWs, there is a possibility of holding virtual field trips inside virtual environments for educational purposes. It is a guided and narrated tour of a virtual simulation of a real place or an imaginary location inside a 3DVW that can be selected by educators and arranged so that students can visit, follow the instructions and perform an exploration with just moving around the virtual space. By traveling to virtual locations, students can get familiar with various spectacular, historical and travel points all around the world. To illustrate, by developing a virtual field trip for university students in a virtual world, Mathews et al. (2012) found that this kind of learning method is an innovative learning opportunity.

Hardware and Software Integration

A 3DVW gives developers the ability to connect and control other hardware and software to add more facilities to virtual learning and teaching environments. For example, developers can control various types of hardware from their virtual land, by adding programs and scripts to their objects within the virtual environment. Developers are also able to connect other educational applications such as Blackboard to some of the virtual worlds like Second Life to take more advantages of those applications inside the virtual learning environment. For instance, Second Life supports a programming language, Linden Scripting Language (LSL), which is a capable tool allowing control of in-world objects as well as integration and connection with other applications and hardware. Since virtual worlds support 3D shape functions, inside these environments students are able to create and sculpt shapes and showcase their individual works to others for peer review; the application of this technology is related to learning as construction or co-construction (Hew & Cheung, 2013). These environments provide facilities for reusing, remixing, and mashing up user-created objects and content; therefore, they can be seen as an effective collaborative tool with which multiple users can experiment with each other.

Virtual Campus

By creating a virtual campus, universities and colleges can provide attractive virtual environments to extend their educational programs. A virtual campus provides a specific place as a framework for learning activities as well as a set of virtual tools to benefit educational process (Clark & Maher, 2001). Various activities can be done inside the virtual lands of 3DVWs beside the educational programs such as open day programs, orientation programs, public ceremonies or any other extracurricular activities. A virtual campus can also be accessed from any Internet-connected personal computer from remote locations providing a more effective learning environment for all its students giving them the opportunity to access the learning materials and resources from own place.

Development

The current review revealed a lack of attention to the development aspect of 3DVWs. Most of the virtual worlds provide building tools and programming languages to fill in the gaps left by the platform engine. Programmers and developers can add new functionalities to objects, design new objects with new actions and even integrate other applications or hardware with their virtual environment. According to the findings of this study, few studies covered this functionality of 3DVWs; therefore, the powerful ability of 3DVWs in integrating these tools with other e-learning applications to improve their functionality could be investigated in depth. The most significant difficulty regarding development within these worlds is that students need to learn the fundamental concepts of computer graphics design as well as programming languages.

Teaching Material

Studies in the literature paid less attention to a potential of 3DVW technology in providing facilities for teaching material and resources. The technology can help educators and educational organizations to develop a rich resource of course materials through the ability of 3DVWs to store, present, play, upload and download various file formats (e.g. images, videos, voices, animations, textures, slides, other documents), as well as to connect the virtual environments to the Internet to open dynamic and static web pages. It is also possible to add visual and animated effects in order to ease access to the material and make the materials more appealing. The technology is very mature and rich for this purpose, which can make self-training and distance learning applicable. The main concern is the need for higher Internet speed and higher performance hardware to access the resources easily. Another issue can be the cost of uploading documents, videos, sounds and other files to the virtual environment, as most of the virtual world platforms charge for each file upload.

Massive Open Online Courses

Massive Open Online Courses (MOOCs) as a new method in education can also benefit from 3DVWs. MOOCs are free online courses aimed at large-scale participation and open access on the web. Many academics across the world recently have become interested in using MOOCs for delivering education around the globe on an unprecedented scale. In accordance with their basic specifications, 3DVWs can add more value to MOOCs in the educational system. 3DVWs as online infrastructures are open on a global scale; they support a massive number of residents and users, and various kinds of courses can take place within these platforms either synchronously or asynchronously. More research and practice is needed to understand the implications of this technology on MOOCs and to assess opportunities and challenges for incorporating 3DVWs into MOOCs units at the higher education and university level.

Sense of Presence

One of the main reasons for the success of 3DVW in the education field, specifically in lecturing and presenting courses, is its tremendous ability to provide users with a virtual presence within an immersive virtual environment. By using an avatar, everyone can experience a virtual presence in the virtual classroom or a laboratory area. Students can touch everything and see everything by using the visual effects.

Barriers and Issues

In the current study, some challenges related to the use of 3DWVs in higher education were identified. There is also a need for more research into the issues and barriers of using this technology, as the current studies tend to deal with only the advantages and positive aspects of the use of 3DVWs in higher education. The problems and barriers of these environments, such as complexity, speed, compatibility, behaviour, health, safety, security, cost, user adoption, and so on need to be considered, as well as factors associated with adoption and students' intention to use 3DVWs in educational activities. In order to make this technology more accessible and user-friendly, and to reduce the complexity for educators and trainees, especially those who are unfamiliar with designing and programming techniques, further studies and research are required.

The most important issues which could affect the efficiency of 3DVWs in this application area were lower hardware performance, limited Internet speed and technical problems. Furthermore, in most experiences, there is no possibility to limit students' behaviours within the virtual classroom and the type and appearance of their avatar. The lack of a personal computer or smart device as well as limited access to the Internet also could be a significant problem for a student.

Limitations

Our attempts to perform the present literature review have highlighted a number of limitations, most of which can influence future research. We believe that the research methods in the current study were thorough and exhaustive, and we aimed for a comprehensive coverage of the literature in this field, but there is a possibility of omitted relevant research during the filtering process. Therefore, we do not guarantee that we have taken all of the application areas of this technology in higher education into account as a massive number of studies relevant to this topic have been published, and some studies might have been missed. As the quality of results of a literature review study is extremely dependent on the quality of the identified papers in that study, an evaluation of the quality of the results in this study is not possible. Generally, any literature review is limited to its search terms, and the current review is not an exception in this regard. As there are only a limited percentage of the studies in the literature from countries other than the United States and in Europe, we cannot present a global conclusion regarding to the application areas of 3DVWs in the higher education sector. A further limitation of the present study is that it included only published research.

CONCLUSION

To provide a big picture of application areas of 3DVWs in the higher education sector, a literature review was conducted on the available body of knowledge. Consequently, five main categories of curricular activities were developed for which 3DVWs have been used to date: virtual lecturing, discussion, field trip, simulation and gaming. The authors also identified the most applied 3DVWs platforms in higher education. Additionally, the 3D virtual environments created for educational purposes have been identified and classified into seventeen main categories. Virtual classroom, virtual laboratory, virtual meeting area, simulated places and replicas of popular places are the most common 3D virtual environments in the literature that are used for educational pedagogical activities in higher education. The findings offer researchers, educators and educational institutions some informed directions for utilizing these technologies to achieve specific learning outcomes. They can use this technology as a creative, powerful and efficient tool to develop new and effective ways of teaching and learning. In order to close the gap between academic research and practical applications some suggestions can be made: First, educational applications should be widespread, in accordance with the proposals obtained from the researchers conducting studies in this field. Second, universities and other educational communities and organizations should lead the use of 3DVWs for their educational purposes in the future.

REFERENCES

Al-Hatem, A. I., Masood, M., & Al-Samarraie, H. (2018). Fostering student nurses' self-regulated learning with the Second Life environment: An empirical study. *Journal of Information Technology Education, 17*, 285–307. doi:10.28945/4110

Andreas, K., & Tsiatsos, T. (2008, March). Selecting a networked virtual environment platform and the design of a collaborative e-learning environment. In *22nd International Conference on Advanced Information Networking and Applications-Workshops (aina workshops 2008)* (pp. 44-49). IEEE.

Arango-López, J., Valdivieso, C. C. C., Collazos, C. A., Vela, F. L. G., & Moreira, F. (2019). CREANDO: Tool for creating pervasive games to increase the learning motivation in higher education students. *Telematics and Informatics, 38*, 62–73. doi:10.1016/j.tele.2018.08.005

Aydogan, H., & Aras, F. (2019). Design, simulation and virtual implementation of a novel fundamental programmable logic controllers laboratory in a 3D virtual world. *International Journal of Electrical Engineering Education*. Advance online publication. doi:10.1177/0020720919856249

Aydoğan, H., Aras, F., & Karakas, E. (2010, June). An assessment on distance education in a 3D virtual environment: How to produce electricity in a hydroelectric power plant. In *2010 2nd International Conference on Education Technology and Computer* (Vol. 1, pp. V1-346). IEEE.

Ba, S., Ke, D., Stallaert, J., & Zhang, Z. (2010). Why give away something for nothing? Investigating virtual goods pricing and permission strategies. *ACM Transactions on Management Information Systems*, *1*(1), 1–22. doi:10.1145/1877725.1877729

Balcikanli, C. (2012). Language learning in Second Life: American and Turkish Students' Experiences. *Turkish Online Journal of Distance Education*, *13*(2), 131–146.

Barry, D. M., Kanematsu, H., Fukumura, Y., Kobayashi, T., Ogawa, N., & Nagai, H. (2013). US Students Carry out Nuclear Safety Project in a Virtual Environment. *Procedia Computer Science*, *22*, 1354–1360. doi:10.1016/j.procs.2013.09.224

Bers, M., & Chau, C. (2010). The virtual campus of the future: Stimulating and simulating civic actions in a virtual world. *Journal of Computing in Higher Education*, *22*(1), 1–23. doi:10.100712528-009-9026-3

Boulos, M. N. K., Hetherington, L., & Wheeler, S. (2007). Second Life: An overview of the potential of 3-D virtual worlds in medical and health education. *Health Information and Libraries Journal*, *24*(4), 233–245. doi:10.1111/j.1471-1842.2007.00733.x PMID:18005298

Bronack, S., Sanders, R., Cheney, A., Riedl, R., Tashner, J., & Matzen, N. (2008). Presence Pedagogy: Teaching and Learning in a 3D Virtual Immersive World. *International Journal on Teaching and Learning in Higher Education*, *20*(1), 59–69.

Brown, R., Rasmussen, R., Baldwin, I., & Wyeth, P. (2012). Design and implementation of a virtual world training simulation of ICU first hour handover processes. *Australian Critical Care*, *25*(3), 178–187. doi:10.1016/j.aucc.2012.02.005 PMID:22436543

Callaghan, M. J., McCusker, K., Losada, J. L., Harkin, J. G., & Wilson, S. (2009, August). *Integrating virtual worlds & virtual learning environments for online education. In 2009 International IEEE Consumer Electronics Society's Games Innovations Conference*. IEEE.

Chen, X., Siau, K., & Nah, F. F.-H. (2009). 3-D virtual worlds: Education and learning. *Proceedings of the Eighth Annual Workshop on HCI Research in MIS (SIGHCI 2009).*

Chen, X., Siau, K., & Nah, F. F.-H. (2010). 3-D Virtual World Education: An Empirical Comparison With Face-To-Face Classroom. *Thirty First International Conference on Information Systems (ICIS)*, 260.

Cheng, Y., & Wang, S.-H. (2011). Applying a 3D virtual learning environment to facilitate student's application ability–The case of marketing. *Computers in Human Behavior*, *27*(1), 576–584. doi:10.1016/j.chb.2010.10.008

Clark, S., & Maher, M. L. (2001). The role of place in designing a learner centred virtual learning environment. In *Computer Aided Architectural Design Futures 2001* (pp. 187–200). Springer. doi:10.1007/978-94-010-0868-6_15

Dafoulas, G., Saleeb, N., & Loomes, M. (2012, June). The impact of 3D virtual environments on communication patterns. In *2012 International Conference on Information Technology Based Higher Education and Training (ITHET)* (pp. 1-5). IEEE. 10.1109/ITHET.2012.6246065

Davis, I. I. J., Goel, M., Hylands, C., Kienhuis, B., Lee, E. A., Liu, J., Liu, X., Muliadi, L., Neuendorffer, S., Reekie, J., Smyth, N., Tsay, J., & Xiong, Y. (1999). *Overview of the Ptolemy project* (Vol. 99). ERL Technical Report UCB/ERL No. M99/37, Dept. EECS, University of California, Berkeley, CA.

De Lucia, A., Francese, R., Passero, I., & Tortora, G. (2009). Development and evaluation of a virtual campus on Second Life: The case of SecondDMI. *Computers & Education, 52*(1), 220–233. doi:10.1016/j.compedu.2008.08.001

Di Blas, N., & Poggi, C. (2007). European virtual classrooms: Building effective "virtual" educational experiences. *Virtual Reality (Waltham Cross), 11*(2-3), 129–143. doi:10.100710055-006-0060-4

Dickey, M. D. (2005). Three-dimensional virtual worlds and distance learning: Two case studies of Active Worlds as a medium for distance education. *British Journal of Educational Technology, 36*(3), 439–451. doi:10.1111/j.1467-8535.2005.00477.x

Dong, P., Ma, B., & Wang, F. (2010, May). Development and evaluation of an experiential learning service in 3D virtual world. In *2010 International Conference on Service Sciences* (pp. 374-378). IEEE. 10.1109/ICSS.2010.37

dos Santos, F. R., Guetl, C., Bailey, P. H., & Harward, V. J. (2010, April). Dynamic virtual environment for multiple physics experiments in higher education. In *IEEE EDUCON 2010 Conference* (pp. 731-736). IEEE. 10.1109/EDUCON.2010.5492507

Dreher, C., Reiners, T., Dreher, N., & Dreher, H. (2009, June). 3D virtual worlds as collaborative communities enriching human endeavours: Innovative applications in e-Learning. In *2009 3rd IEEE International Conference on Digital Ecosystems and Technologies* (pp. 151-156). IEEE.

Edirisingha, P., Nie, M., Pluciennik, M., & Young, R. (2009). Socialisation for learning at a distance in a 3-D multi-user virtual environment. *British Journal of Educational Technology, 40*(3), 458–479. doi:10.1111/j.1467-8535.2009.00962.x

Ellison, K., & Matthews, C. (2010). Virtual history: A socially networked pedagogy of Enlightenment. *Educational Research, 52*(3), 297–307. doi:10.1080/00131881.2010.504065

Eschenbrenner, B., Nah, F. F.-H., & Siau, K. (2008). 3-D virtual worlds in education: Applications, benefits, issues, and opportunities. *Journal of Database Management, 19*(4), 91–110. doi:10.4018/jdm.2008100106

Fırat, M. (2010). Learning in 3D virtual worlds and current situation in Turkey. *Procedia: Social and Behavioral Sciences, 9*, 249–254. doi:10.1016/j.sbspro.2010.12.145

Gamage, V., Tretiakov, A., & Crump, B. (2011). Teacher perceptions of learning affordances of multi-user virtual environments. *Computers & Education*, *57*(4), 2406–2413. doi:10.1016/j.compedu.2011.06.015

Gao, F., Noh, J. J., & Koehler, M. J. (2009). Comparing role-playing activities in Second Life and face-to-face environments. *Journal of Interactive Learning Research*, *20*(4), 423–443.

Garcia-Zubia, J., Irurzun, J., Angulo, I., Hernandez, U., Castro, M., Sancristobal, E., Orduna, P., & Ruiz-de Garibay, J. (2010, April). SecondLab: A remote laboratory under Second Life. In *IEEE EDUCON 2010 Conference* (pp. 351-356). IEEE.

Gazave, C. M., & Hatcher, A. R. (2017). Evaluating the use of Second Life™ for virtual team-based learning in an online undergraduate anatomy course. *Medical Science Educator*, *27*(2), 217–227. doi:10.100740670-017-0374-8

Ghanbarzadeh, R., Ghapanchi, A. H., & Blumenstein, M. (2015, May). Characteristics of research on the application of three-dimensional immersive virtual worlds in health. In *International Conference on Health Information Science* (pp. 213-224). Springer. 10.1007/978-3-319-19156-0_22

Ghanbarzadeh, R., Ghapanchi, A. H., Blumenstein, M., & Talaei-Khoei, A. (2014). A Decade of Research on the Use of Three-Dimensional Virtual Worlds in Health Care: A Systematic Literature Review. *Journal of Medical Internet Research*, *16*(2), e47. doi:10.2196/jmir.3097 PMID:24550130

Grenfell, J. (2013). Immersive interfaces for art education teaching and learning in virtual and real world learning environments. *Procedia: Social and Behavioral Sciences*, *93*, 1198–1211. doi:10.1016/j.sbspro.2013.10.016

Hew, K. F., & Cheung, W. S. (2010). Use of three-dimensional (3-D) immersive virtual worlds in K-12 and higher education settings: A review of the research. *British Journal of Educational Technology*, *41*(1), 33–55. doi:10.1111/j.1467-8535.2008.00900.x

Hew, K. F., & Cheung, W. S. (2013). Use of Web 2.0 technologies in K-12 and higher education: The search for evidence-based practice. *Educational Research Review*, *9*, 47–64. doi:10.1016/j.edurev.2012.08.001

Hsu, L. (2012). Web 3D simulation-based application in tourism education: A case study with Second Life. *Journal of Hospitality, Leisure, Sport and Tourism Education*, *11*(2), 113–124. doi:10.1016/j.jhlste.2012.02.013

Huang, Y.-C., Backman, S. J., Chang, L.-L., Backman, K. F., & McGuire, F. A. (2013). Experiencing student learning and tourism training in a 3D virtual world: An exploratory study. *Journal of Hospitality, Leisure, Sport and Tourism Education*, *13*, 190–201. doi:10.1016/j.jhlste.2013.09.007

Irwin, P., Coutts, R., & Graham, I. (2019, September). Looking Good Sister! The Use of a Virtual World to Develop Nursing Skills. In *Australasian Simulation Congress* (pp. 33-45). Springer. 10.1007/978-981-32-9582-7_3

Kastoudi, D. (2011). *Using a Quest in a 3D Virtual Environment for Student Interaction and Vocabulary Acquisition in Foreign Language Learning. In European Association for Computer-Assisted Language Learning*. EUROCALL.

Kawulich, B. B., & D'Alba, A. (2019). Teaching qualitative research methods with Second Life, a 3-dimensional online virtual environment. *Virtual Reality (Waltham Cross), 23*(4), 375–384. doi:10.100710055-018-0353-4

Lan, Y. J., Lyu, B. N., & Chin, C. K. (2019). Does 3D immersive experience enhance Mandarin writing by CSL students? *Language Learning & Technology, 23*(2), 125–144.

Le, Q. T., & Park, C. S. (2012, August). Construction safety education model based on second life. In *Proceedings of IEEE International Conference on Teaching, Assessment, and Learning for Engineering (TALE) 2012* (pp. H2C-1). IEEE. 10.1109/TALE.2012.6360336

Linden Research. (2011). *Second Life education: The virtual learning advantage.* Retrieved from http://lecs-static-secondlife-com.s3.amazonaws.com/work/SL-Edu-Brochure-010411.pdf

Linganisa, A., Ako-Nai, A., & Ajayi, N. (2018, December). The Potential of Second Life as a Platform for Learning: Student's Perspective. In *2018 International Conference on Intelligent and Innovative Computing Applications (ICONIC)* (pp. 1-5). IEEE. 10.1109/ICONIC.2018.8601201

Lorenzo, C.-M., Ángel Sicilia, M., & Sánchez, S. (2012). Studying the effectiveness of multi-user immersive environments for collaborative evaluation tasks. *Computers & Education, 59*(4), 1361–1376. doi:10.1016/j.compedu.2012.06.002

Lorenzo-Alvarez, R., Ruiz-Gomez, M. J., & Sendra-Portero, F. (2019). Medical students' and family physicians' attitudes and perceptions toward radiology learning in the Second Life virtual world. *AJR. American Journal of Roentgenology, 212*(6), 1295–1302. doi:10.2214/AJR.18.20381 PMID:30860900

Loureiro, A., & Bettencourt, T. (2011). The Extended Classroom: Meeting students' needs using a virtual environment. *Procedia: Social and Behavioral Sciences, 15*, 2667–2672. doi:10.1016/j.sbspro.2011.04.167

Marcelino, R., Silva, J. B., Gruber, V., & Bilessimo, M. S. (2012, July). 3D virtual worlds using open source platform and integrated remote experimentation. In *2012 9th International Conference on Remote Engineering and Virtual Instrumentation (REV)* (pp. 1-2). IEEE.

Marino, P. (2004). *The art of machinima: 3D game-based filmmaking.* ParaglyphPress.

Mathews, S., Andrews, L., & Luck, E. (2012). Developing a Second Life virtual field trip for university students: An action research approach. *Educational Research, 54*(1), 17–38. doi:10.1080/00131881.2012.658197

Mendonça, R. F., Carreira, S. M., & Sampaio, P. N. (2011, April). VirtualLabs@ UMa: A customizable 3D learning platform for experimental activities. In *2011 International Conference on Multimedia Computing and Systems* (pp. 1-6). IEEE. 10.1109/ICMCS.2011.5945594

Merchant, Z., Goetz, E. T., Keeney-Kennicutt, W., Kwok, O. M., Cifuentes, L., & Davis, T. J. (2012). The learner characteristics, features of desktop 3D virtual reality environments, and college chemistry instruction: A structural equation modeling analysis. *Computers & Education, 59*(2), 551–568. doi:10.1016/j.compedu.2012.02.004

Molka-Danielsen, J., & Chabada, M. (2010, January). Application of the 3D multi user virtual environment of second life to emergency evacuation simulation. In *2010 43rd Hawaii international conference on system sciences* (pp. 1-9). IEEE.

Müller, D., Chilliischi, A., & Langer, S. (2012, July). Integrating immersive 3D worlds and real lab equipment for teaching mechatronics. In *2012 9th International Conference on Remote Engineering and Virtual Instrumentation (REV)* (pp. 1-6). IEEE.

Nicholls, J., & Philip, R. (2012). Solo life to Second Life: The design of physical and virtual learning spaces inspired by the drama classroom. *Research in Drama Education, 17*(4), 583–602. doi:10.1080/13569783.2012.727628

Nikolaou, A., & Tsolakidis, C. (2012, September). The role of three dimensional virtual environments in the development of Personal Learning Networks. In *2012 15th International Conference on Interactive Collaborative Learning (ICL)* (pp. 1-7). IEEE. 10.1109/ICL.2012.6402114

Nishide, R. (2011). Prospects for digital campus with extensive applications of virtual collaborative space. *Journal of Interactive Learning Research, 22*(3), 421–443.

Nishide, R., & Ueshima, S. (2004, January). Digital campus project: A" dream university" over the Internet Web. *Proceedings. Second International Conference on Creating, Connecting and Collaborating through Computing, 2004*, 122–129.

Okutsu, M., DeLaurentis, D., Brophy, S., & Lambert, J. (2013). Teaching an aerospace engineering design course via virtual worlds: A comparative assessment of learning outcomes. *Computers & Education, 60*(1), 288–298. doi:10.1016/j.compedu.2012.07.012

Pereira, M. M., Artemiou, E., McGonigle, D., Köster, L., Conan, A., & Sithole, F. (2019). Second Life and Classroom Environments: Comparing Small Group Teaching and Learning in Developing Clinical Reasoning Process Skills. *Medical Science Educator, 29*(2), 431–437. doi:10.100740670-019-00706-4

Prasolova-Forland, E. (2004, November). Supporting social awareness among university students in 3D CVEs: Benefits and limitations. In *2004 International Conference on Cyberworlds* (pp. 127-134). IEEE. 10.1109/CW.2004.59

Pricer, W. F. (2011). At issue: Immersive Education, an Annotated Webliography. *Community College Enterprise, 17*(1), 41–50.

Saleeb, N., & Dafoulas, G. (2010a, June). Architectural propositions for enhancement of learning spaces within 3D virtual learning environments. In *2010 International Conference on Information Society* (pp. 410-415). IEEE. 10.1109/i-Society16502.2010.6018738

Saleeb, N., & Dafoulas, G. (2010b, June). Pedagogical immigration to 3D virtual worlds: A critical review of underlying themes and their concepts. In *2010 International Conference on Information Society* (pp. 401-409). IEEE. 10.1109/i-Society16502.2010.6018737

Salmon, G., Nie, M., & Edirisingha, P. (2010). Developing a five-stage model of learning in Second Life. *Educational Research, 52*(2), 169–182. doi:10.1080/00131881.2010.482744

Sharma, S., Agada, R., & Ruffin, J. (2013, April). *Virtual reality classroom as an constructivist approach. In 2013 Proceedings of IEEE Southeastcon*. IEEE.

Stiubiener, I., Barbosa, W., Kamienski, C. A., & Schweitzer, C. M. (2011, October). Using Virtual Worlds in distance learning environments. In 2011 Frontiers in Education Conference (FIE) (pp. F3C-1). IEEE. doi:10.1109/FIE.2011.6142822

Terzidou, T., Tsiatsos, T., Dae, A., Samaras, O., & Chasanidou, A. (2012, July). Utilizing virtual worlds for game based learning: Grafica, a 3D educational game in second life. In *2012 IEEE 12th International Conference on Advanced Learning Technologies* (pp. 624-628). IEEE.

Traphagan, T. W., Chiang, Y.-V., Chang, H. M., Wattanawaha, B., Lee, H., Mayrath, M. C., Woo, J., Yoon, H.-J., Jee, M. J., & Resta, P. E. (2010). Cognitive, social and teaching presence in a virtual world and a text chat. *Computers & Education, 55*(3), 923–936. doi:10.1016/j.compedu.2010.04.003

Wang, F., & Lockee, B. B. (2010). Virtual Worlds in Distance Education: A Content Analysis Study. *Quarterly Review of Distance Education, 11*(3), 183–186.

Wang, T., & Zhu, Q. (2009, March). A software engineering education game in a 3-D online virtual environment. In *2009 First International Workshop on Education Technology and Computer Science* (Vol. 2, pp. 708-710). IEEE. 10.1109/ETCS.2009.418

Warburton, S. (2009). Second Life in higher education: Assessing the potential for and the barriers to deploying virtual worlds in learning and teaching. *British Journal of Educational Technology, 40*(3), 414–426. doi:10.1111/j.1467-8535.2009.00952.x

Wigham, C. R., & Chanier, T. (2013). A study of verbal and nonverbal communication in Second Life–the ARCHI21 experience. *ReCALL, 25*(01), 63–84. doi:10.1017/S0958344012000250

Winkelmann, K., Keeney-Kennicutt, W., Fowler, D., Lazo Macik, M., Perez Guarda, P., & Ahlborn, C. J. (2019). Learning gains and attitudes of students performing chemistry experiments in an immersive virtual world. *Interactive Learning Environments*, 1–15.

Yalcinalp, S., Sen, N., Kocer, G., & Koroglu, F. (2012). Higher education student's behaviors as avatars in a web based course in Second Life. *Procedia: Social and Behavioral Sciences, 46*, 4534–4538. doi:10.1016/j.sbspro.2012.06.291

Ye, E., Liu, C., & Polack-Wahl, J. A. (2007). *Enhancing software engineering education using teaching aids in 3-D online virtual worlds. Frontiers in Education.*

Zhao, H., Sun, B., Wu, H., & Hu, X. (2010, November). Study on building a 3D interactive virtual learning environment based on OpenSim platform. In *2010 International Conference on Audio, Language and Image Processing* (pp. 1407-1411). IEEE. 10.1109/ICALIP.2010.5684986

Zhao, W., Sun, K., & Li, X. J. (2011, May). Investigation on Situational Networked Learning Environment in Virtual Campus. In *2011 3rd International Workshop on Intelligent Systems and Applications* (pp. 1-5). IEEE. 10.1109/ISA.2011.5873408

Zhong, Y., & Liu, C. (2012, June). User evaluation of a domain-oriented end-user design environment for building 3D virtual chemistry experiments. In *2012 First International Workshop on User Evaluation for Software Engineering Researchers (USER)* (pp. 5-8). IEEE. 10.1109/USER.2012.6226585

Zulkanain, N. A., Rahim, E. E. A., & Azizan, F. F. (2016, August). Exploratory study on the relationship of students' perceptions towards the instructors' involvement in Second Life. In *2016 4th International Conference on User Science and Engineering (i-USEr)* (pp. 100-104). IEEE.

KEY TERMS AND DEFINITIONS

Avatar: A computer user's digital, graphical, and animated self-representation which is completely manipulated by its owner.

Blackboard: A virtual learning environment and course management system developed by Blackboard Inc.

E-Learning: A kind of learning which is conducted by using information and communication technologies and electronic media.

Higher Education: Education provided by colleges, universities, or similar educational establishments.

Linden Scripting Language: A scripting programming language that gives behavior to Second Life's primitives, objects, and avatars.

Machinima: Use of video game and computer graphics to create animated cinematic production.

Open Simulator: An open source multi-platform and multi-user 3D application server.

Second Life: A 3D virtual world platform developed by Linden Lab Inc. in 2003.

Simulation: The act of imitation of a real-world system's or process's operation over time.

Three-Dimensional Virtual World (3DVW): A computer-based 3D graphical and simulated environment in which users can interact via their own avatars.

Virtual Lecturing: The act of delivering of lectures by utilizing the Internet, Web, and virtual world technologies.

Chapter 3
Virtual Reality, Augmented Reality, and Mixed Reality in Education: A Brief Overview

Nicoletta Sala
Institute for Complexity Studies, Italy & Institute for Scientific and Interdisciplinary Studies (ISSI), Switzerland

ABSTRACT

Virtual reality (VR), augmented reality (AR), and mixed reality (MR) are three different technologies developed in the last decades of the 20th century. They combine hardware and software solutions. They permit the creation of three-dimensional (3D) virtual worlds and virtual objects. This chapter describes how VR, MR, and AR technologies find positive application fields in educational environments. They support different learning styles, offering potential help in teaching and in learning paths.

INTRODUCTION

Virtual Reality

In the 19th century, formal education was based on lectures and recitations. The Swiss pedagogues Johann Heinrich Pestalozzi (1746-1827) was one of the first that studied what is commonly known as "hands-on learning". He observed that students learn best through physical activity and if they use their senses (Pestalozzi, 1803). Nowadays, modern educational environments find in the new technologies a way to improve the learning paths. For example, VR, AR, and MR can stimulate the senses of the students, involving them in learning activities.

In 1987, Yaakov Garb used the term "virtual reality" as title of a paper. VR is the capability to represent the world with visual symbols (Garb, 1987). Garb's point of view is far from computer technology. While Garb used the term 'virtual reality' as the title of a paper on 1987, the term was used to represent

DOI: 10.4018/978-1-7998-4960-5.ch003

the world with visual symbols. It was two years later when Lanier used the term specific to the world of computer technology (Lanier, 1989). He referred the term to the world of computers: VR exists only as an electronic image, without any connection with the real world. As Krueger (1991) stated, "The term therefore typically refers to three-dimensional (3D) realities implemented with stereo viewing goggles and reality gloves" (p. xiii). VR is a technology which involves information technology, computer graphics and electronics, and it gives its users the illusion of being immersed in a computer-generated virtual world with the ability to interact with it. VR has also been defined as an experience in which the users are immersed in a responsive virtual world. This implies users' dynamic control of viewpoints. (Brooks, 1999).

Burdea and Coiffet (2003) describe VR as a simulation in which computer graphics are used to create a realistic-looking world. The synthetic world is dynamic, responding to the user's input (gesture, verbal command, etc.). This introduces the real-time interactivity, which is a key feature of this technology, but computer science evolution requires a new definition of VR. More recently, the Encyclopædia Britannica (2019) describes VR as a technology that permits the use of modeling and computer simulation, where a person can interact with a sensory environment or with an artificial three-dimensional visual environment.

In 1997, Rosenblum & Cross define the three primary requirements of a VR system. They are:

- Immersion refers to a realistic feeling that allows users to have exposure to a virtual environment. The perception is created surrounding the user by the VR technologies and by its devices (e.g., data gloves, head mounted display, sound or other sensorial stimuli), that provide an engrossing total environment (Wu et al., 2015). Immersion requires physically involving the user, both by capturing exclusive visual attention and by transparently responding to 3D input, through use of devices such as a head-tracker, 3D mouse, wand, data glove, or fully instrumented body suit;
- Interaction is a kind of action that occurs as two or more objects have an effect upon one another. In VR what is realized through the 3D control devices to investigate and control the virtual environment; and
- Visual realism provides an accurate representation of the virtual world using computer graphics tools.

Immersion is a feature of VR and MR. characterized by different degrees of user involvement.

It is a unique experience that is connected with the real world and the virtuality. Astheimer et al. (1994) define immersion as the feeling of a user, that his virtual environment is real. In a 2004 paper titled *Postmodernism and the Three Types of Immersion*, Adams presented three main categories of immersion: tactical, strategic, and narrative. Tactical immersion gives the users the experience that they are accurately performing actions in the virtual world with convincing feedback. Strategic immersion is associated with mental challenge. Narrative immersion occurs when users become invested in a story, and is similar to what is experienced while reading a book or watching a movie. Björk and Holopainen (2004), divide immersion into three similar categories, but they call them: sensory-motoric immersion, cognitive immersion, and emotional immersion, respectively. In addition, they also add a new category named spatial immersion that occurs when a user feels the simulated world is perceptually convincing (Björk & Holopainen, 2004).

Interaction refers to the natural interaction between the users and the virtual scenes. VR, AR, and MR systems involve interface hardware components. For VR they consist of:

- The input devices which report, in real time, the position and the movements of the users in the virtual worlds. Input devices permit users to give electrical signals to the computer that can be transformed as specific commands. Input devices can include gloves, trackers, keyboards, and mouse (2D or 3D);
- The output devices (visual, aural, and haptic) give the users the illusion to be immersed in the virtual environments. For example, the visual display, which is an output tool, is a kind of helmet that places a television-like screen over each eye, blocking one's view of the physical world. Instead, of the physical world, one sees a 3D rendition of a place created by computer graphics workstation.
- The graphic rendering system generates the virtual scenarios and the virtual environments; and
- The database construction and virtual object modelling software realize virtual scenarios and detailed and realistic models of the virtual world. In particular, the software handles the geometry, texture, intelligent behavior, and physical modelling of any object included in the virtual world.

Visual realism refers on the ability of VR to create an immersive 3D spatial experience when the user perceives that is to a virtual world (for example, being a player in a videogame). This is affected by the perceived feeling of artificiality and transportation (Benford et al., 1998). To be credible, this perception requires different interactions which should be in real-time (Riva, 2006). For example, the user requires instant feedback of his movements, position, and sensations (Martín-Gutiérrez et al., 2017).

More recently, visual realism was defined as the extent to which an image appears to people as a photo rather than generated by computer (Fan et al., 2017).

Augmented Reality

Augmented reality is a technology which overlays computer generated information into a virtual world.

In this way, the environment is "augmented" by more information.

In 1990, the researcher Thomas Caudell coined the term "Augmented Reality" with his colleague David Mizell and applied this technology to support an industrial process at Boeing (Höllerer & Feiner, 2004).

As Caudell and Mizell stated (1992, p.660): "This technology is used to "augment" the visual field of the user with information necessary in the performance of the current task, and therefore we refer to the technology as "augmented reality." In 2002, Feiner defined AR as a technology which refers to computer displays that add virtual information to a user's sensory perceptions (Feiner, 2002, p.36).

AR is a direct or indirect view of a real-world environment with elements augmented by computer-generated sensory input such as graphics, sound, and video. For example, the user's view of the world is enriched by virtual objects. They usually provide information about the real environment. Some researchers described the implementation of AR using three characteristics: (1) the combination of real-world and virtual elements, (2) which are interactive in real-time, and which (3) are registered in 3D. For example, the display of virtual objects or information is connected to the real-world (Azuma, 1997; Kaufmann & Schmalstieg, 2003; Kim et al., 2018). In 1994, Paul Milgram and Fumio Kishino introduced Mixed Reality (MR), sometimes referred to as hybrid reality. They also introduced the "virtuality continuum" which extends itself from the completely real to the completely virtual environment passing through AR and augmented virtuality ranges.

Hardware components for AR include the following: a processor, a display, sensors, and input devices. (Bauer et al., 2001; Feiner, 2002; Harrison et al., 2019; Laughlin et al., 2018; Mount et al., 2016),

Modern mobile computing devices, such as tablet computers and smartphones, contain these four elements. Devices often include a camera and other components (GPS, Microelectromechanical systems (MEMS) sensors such as an accelerometer, etc.) making them suitable AR platforms.

Mixed Reality

MR is seen as the merging of real and virtual worlds to produce new scenarios and new environments, where physical and digital objects co-exist and interact together in real time (Croatti & Ricci, 2018).

The hardware components for MR have been described by Milgram and Kishimo (1994):

- Monitor based (non-immersive) video displays, for example "window-on-the-world"(WoW) displays;
- Video displays that uses immersive head-mounted displays (HMD's), rather than WoW monitors;
- HMD's equipped with a see-through capability, with which computer generated graphics can be optically superimposed, using half-silvered mirrors, onto directly viewed real-world scenes;
- Same as the previous point, but using video, rather than optical, viewing of the "outside" world;
- Completely graphic display environments, either completely immersive, partially immersive or otherwise, to which video "reality" is added; and
- Completely graphic but partially immersive environments (e.g. large screen displays) in which real physical objects in the user's environment play a role in the computer generated scene, such as in reaching in and "grabbing" something with one's own hand.

Figure 1. Reality-virtuality continuum
(Milgram & Kishino, 1994)

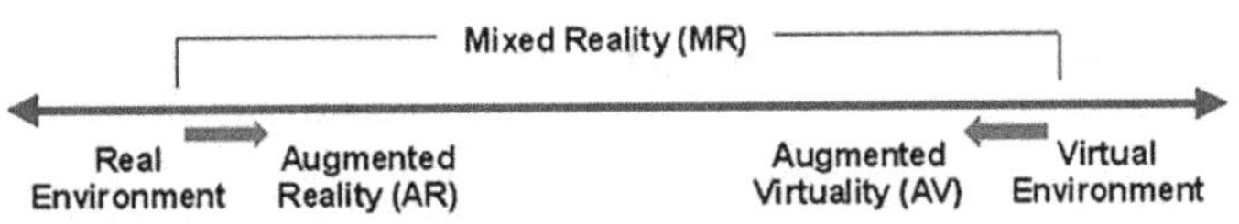

Figure 1 shows the reality-virtuality continuum by Milgram and Kishino (1994), where is one part of the general area of mixed reality (van Krevelen & Poelman, 2010). In particular, they affirm that in virtual environments, VR can replace the surrounding environment by a virtual one. Milgram et al. (1994) introduced a three-dimensional taxonomic framework for classifying MR displays, comprising: Extent of World Knowledge (EWK), Reproduction Fidelity (RF) and Extext of Presence Metaphor (EPM) (see Figure 2). AR is different from VR and MR. In fact, VR immerses users in a fully artificial digital environment. AR overlays virtual objects on the real-world environment with spatial registration that enables geometric persistence concerning placement and orientation within the real world. Prior technologies that overlaid data or images not spatially registered to real-world geometries are referred to as heads-up display technologies. MR not only overlays, but also anchors virtual objects to real-world objects, allowing the user to interact with combined virtual–real objects. Figure 3 shows the difference between these three technologies.

Figure 2. Three dimensional taxonomic framework for classifying MR displays
(Milgram, Takemura, Utsumi, & Kishino, 1994, p. 291)

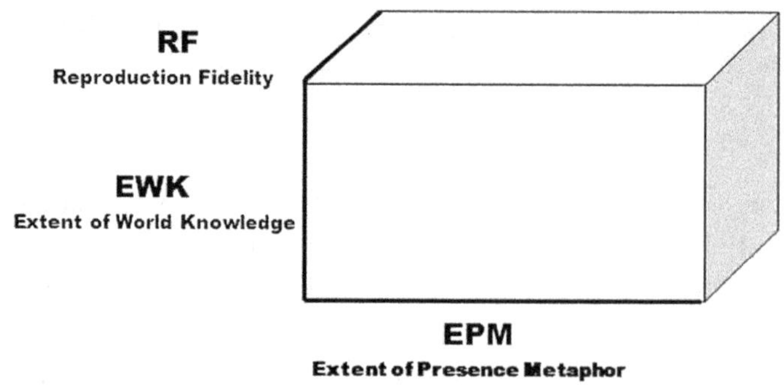

Figure 3. Differences between VR, AR, and MR.

VIRTUAL REALITY	AUGMENTED REALITY	MIXED REALITY
The user is immersed in a digital experience, creating a digital simulation of a real environment. The real world is hidden.	AR overlays digital information onto a real world. Interactive objects are layered on top of a physical environment without the ability to manipulate the augmented objects.	The capabilities of VR and AR are blended producing an environment where physical and digital objects coexist and interact in real time.

This chapter presents an overview of the use of VR, AR, and MR technologies in educational fields, and intends to answer the following question: "Are these technologies good educational tools for learning environments?" To answer to this question, the chapter presents a set of applications of these technologies in different schools settings. Such settings may include use in primary schools to create collaborative environments to facilitate the learning, in universities (for example, to create virtual objects and virtual prototypes for training students of industrial design to new digital prototyping systems) and in different countries.

A paragraph is dedicated to the Virtual Worlds and their use in education (Childs, 2010; Duncan et al., 2012, Gregory et al., 2015; Harrys & Rea, 2019; Stefan, 2016). All these experiences emphasize that VR, MR, and AR have positive impacts in the educational environments. VR, AR, and MR present multiple entry points for personal learning strategies and offers didactic paths that privilege an intuitive approach (Chiang et al., 2014; Freina & Ott, 2015; Jee et al., 2014; Johnston et al., 2018; Maas et al., 2020; Sala, 2016; Tilhou et al., 2020).

HISTORY OF VR, AR AND MR USE IN EDUCATION

The Decade 1989-1999

This decade was characterized by the first attempts to use VR and AR technologies in didactic and educational paths with different ages of students. Several studies confirmed and recognized the potential of VR in education. Its potential was demonstrated by measured results. For example, Winn affirmed the reasons for using VR in education. In particular, immersive VR furnishes a non-symbolic experience which helps students in their learning path (Winn, 1993).

In 1995, a set of studies describe the applications of VR in surgical education and in medicine. For example, Ota et al. (1995) presented VR as an emerging technology that can teach surgeons new procedures and can determine their level of competence before they operate on real patients. They affirmed that VR in medical training could reduce expensive animal training model enhancing the operative field.

In 1996, Christine Byrne explored VR as an educational tool, testing students' assembling of a virtual molecule of water, using an immersive virtual environment with haptic input. The immersive virtual world was created by high school students. Instead of sitting in a classroom and passively viewing images of atomic orbital, students placed electrons into an atom see the atomic orbital appear as the electron buzzes. Byrne posited that interactivity was found to be significant, but immersion was found to be insignificant. She also affirmed that the results of her study have not shown VR to be superior to other methods of instruction; but interactivity, a VR's feature, could be important (Byrne, 1996). This study emphasized that VR does not furnish only passive interactions, but it reconstruction of reality is a model where users can act. Users react and behave as in real environment. This important feature overcomes the inherent limitations of perception, which should be applicable only to objects physically perceptible.

In Youngblut's 1998 survey of research, she concluded that VR can be used with different ages of students (from elementary schools to colleges). VR introduces important aspects of constructivist learning. The role of the teacher changed to facilitator that helped students in their learning paths, building ideas. Students enjoy using pre-developed applications and developing their own virtual worlds (Youngblut, 1998).

In the same decade, single user interfaces for AR have been developed for different application fields. For example, in medical visualization (Bajura et al., 1992), in manufacturing (Caudell & Mizell, 1992), and in computer-aided instruction (Feiner et al., 1993).

These applications have shown that AR technologies can allow a person to interact with the real world in ways never seen before.

In 1996, Schmalsteig et al. presented the StudierStube project, an example of collaborative learning with AR. In this educational approach, they used as devices the head mounted displays to permit to the users the collaboratively view 3D models of scientific data superimposed on the real world.

The Decade: 2000-2010

This decade was characterized by the rapid development of electronic components which allowed to decrease the costs of VR and AR technologies. This permitted applications in different educational areas, unthinkable a few years ago. In this period, MR began to spread. It is certainly the last born of the three technologies and the least known. Unlike VR, AR systems permit users to see the real world and, at the same time, virtual imagery objects attached to real locations, this represents an improvement in the teaching and learning paths (Billinghurst, 2002). AR can be applied to enhance collaborative learning experiences (Billinghurst et al., 2001). In 2002, Sala et al. described the connections between VR, fractal geometry, and computer graphics to realize some virtual worlds, where the students also generated trees, mountains, lakes, and special effects using fractal algorithms (Sala et al., 2002). In 2004, Woods et al. described some examples of AR applications in educational field. In particular, they showed the educational benefits of virtual and augmented reality technologies. In 2005, Sala and Sala analyzed the contribution of multimedia technologies and VR in university courses of mathematics and information technology to a faculty of architecture in Switzerland. In this educational project, the term "virtual reality" has been used to cover both immersive and non-immersive VR. The technology was used first to help architecture students to visualize in 3D, since this is arguably the most difficult part of understanding architecture. The topic dedicated to the polyhedra and their interconnections between nature and architecture is an excellent example of an abstract topic that is difficult to learn.

The undergraduate students used the VR technologies in different ways (Sala & Sala, 2005).

For example,

- to observe and to rotate the platonic solids and the polyhedra from the different points of view (outside and inside the virtual objects),
- to create some virtual objects using VRML (Virtual Reality Modeling Language),
- to observe and to interact the molecules of carbon (C60 and C70),
- to observe and to manipulate the geodesic domes,
- to study and to observe the symmetry present in the crystals, and
- to create virtual trees using fractal algorithms.

VR can be a medium to create virtual towns and virtual worlds, where the students design virtual territories using fractal algorithms (Guérin et al., 2002; Sala, 2009).

In 2005, Huges et al. describe MR technology into diverse applications, for example for military training, situational awareness, and community learning. MR applied in edutainment, promises the potential to revolutionize learning and teaching, making learners' experience more "engaging" (Liu et al., 2007).

Mixed reality deals with combining the best aspects of Virtual Reality and Augmented Reality, in order to be as marketable as possible. This emerging technology has a high potential for teacher educators, classroom teachers, and students with disabilities (Dieker et al., 2008).

More Recent Years: 2011-2020

These years are characterized by further evolution of VR, AR and MR. There is also an expansion of the application fields of these technologies, introducing more interactivity and participation in the teaching and in the learning. For example, AR can help to realize interactive learning environments (Wu et al., 2018). AR systems can be used to enhance collaborative learning experiences (Billinghurst et al., 2001), enabling innovative and interactive teaching methods in which information in 3D format facilitates knowledge acquisition and student discussion (Wu et al., 2013). AR can also realize interactive environments for learning (Chen & Wang, 2015), enabling innovative and interactive teaching methods in which information in 3D format facilitates knowledge acquisition and student discussion (Wu et al., 2013). AR can support the teaching of natural science, as described by Shen et al. (2019). This technology assists learners in understanding the composition and characteristics of matter.

Dieker et al. (2016) describe the TeachLive™ Lab at the University of Central Florida (UCF) which is one of the first laboratories which uses a mixed reality simulation environment to prepare pre-service teachers or retrain in-service teachers. Tang et al. (2018) describe a MR application for teaching product design to university students. They affirm that for students or individuals with learning difficulties, mixed reality (MR) allows interaction and feedback from the users. This aspect is particularly important for enhancing experience in teaching and learning. Moreover, the benefits to insert mixed reality into educational paths include better engagement, giving to the students the opportunities to experience and better remember what they have learned (Hughes et al., 2005; Tanget al., 2018).

Generally, VR, AR and MR technologies are used separately in the educational field. Only recently, there are some researches which present their contemporary application in the same educational fields. An example is described in the work by Hamacher et al. (2016) which present an interesting application in urology.

MR technology works by anchoring virtual objects to fixed points of real space, so that with each movement of the user, the digital object moves appropriately (Johnson, 2016). The virtual objects can be manipulated by the users. They can move or modify them at will, as it was previously not possible with Augmented Reality. Mixed reality support the creation of environments which contain a combination of real and virtual world information (Hoffmann et al., 2016; Quint et al., 2015; Sargent, 2020). This technology can introduce new accessible learning methods delivered through mobile. This approach is important in medical and health education, where the required knowledge acquisition is typically much more self-directed, experiential, and hands-on than in many other disciplines (Birt et al., 2018). The future is the integration of these three technologies. For example, how these technologies improve the interpretation of spatial, temporal, and contextual contents (Pérez-López & Contero, 2013).

VR, AR AND MR ACROSS DISCIPLINES

An interesting application field of VR is in medicine, and in particular in surgical education (Ammanuel et al., 2019; Gallagher et al., 2005; Kononowicz et al., 2016; Uppot et al., 2019). Kononowicz et al. (2016) describe the use of virtual patient simulation on the health professional education. They wrote:

Virtual patients may be ineffective when technology per se drives the learning instead of addressing actual learning needs. Virtual patient activities should be aligned with overall learning objectives and should be well integrated with existing educational activities; otherwise the new possibilities might be ignored or rejected or might create a learning overload.

Ammanuel et al. (2019) show applications of transforming 2D radiologic images into 3D model by using thresholding and segmentation and import into VR interface at an affordable cost. For example, visualization of 3D anatomic structures in a virtual environment gives another tool for teaching students and patients about anatomy of the body. Other studies introduce telepresence surgery, 3D visualization of anatomy for medical education, complex medical database visualization, VR surgical simulators, and virtual prototyping of surgical equipment and operating rooms, and rehabilitation (Ghezzi & Corleta, 2016, Latifi & Latifi, 2018, Bhattarai et al., 2019, Shakya et al., 2019).

In another field, Computer Numerical Control (CNC) courses teach students how to set-up, maintain, operate and dismantle machining tools that are controlled by computers. Tsai, Kao, & Lee (2012) investigated the effect of VR on students' intention to learn the designed VR machine tool in a CNC practice course based on affordance theory. The proposed theoretical model was empirically evaluated by using survey data collected from 170 students. The research result might provide a reference for academy and industry to design an improved VR system to satisfy student's expectation. This approach has influenced other researches in these field (Jose et al, 2016; Niu et al., 2014; Postlethwaite et al., 2017). A series of experimental tests have been carried out to assess the educational validity of the instructional tool, which has been devised. These studies demonstrated VR can help in the comprehension of some core machining concepts. In particular, novice students benefit from free navigation in the virtual environment, training themselves in the use of a real lathe. VR allows the training in safety.

The abstractness of scientific topics creates difficulties in their understanding, but VR can reduce this problem creating virtual environments "ad hoc" dedicated to the explanation of complex scientific topics, where the immersion and the interaction play central role. In fact, through the presence as avatars in the immersive spaces, the students can feel a sense of control within the virtual environments and more easily engage with the scientific experiences emulated by computers (Byrne, 1996; Millar, 1991; Sala, 2016; Youngblut, 1998; Zoller, 1990). VR has been integrated in a training path to visualize the projects connected to the territory or to realize some "virtual buildings" which students can visit (Sala, 2016).

In order to effectively apply VR as an educational tool in architecture and other technical areas it has been observed a set of problems connected to the technology. For example,

- low resolution of inexpensive viewing devices which made unrealistic objects,
- difficulties to maintain high frame rates on personal computers, and
- high costs of hardware and software devices to realize immersive VR.

About the augmented reality, it can find application in the teaching of scientific disciplines. For example, physics, mathematics, and chemistry, can greatly benefit students by helping them acquire more manual skills with the techniques explained during the lessons or to involve them in more in the study of the discipline (Auliya & Munasiah, 2019; Buesing & Cook, 2013; Crăciun & Bunoiu, 2016; Crăciun, Bunoiu, 2017; Kapp et al., 2019; Strzys et al., 2017).

These educational experiences emphasize that one current problem with using VR is the cost to realize immersive VR environments. The price may drop if the market grows, but in terms of products for education, currently there is high cost for modest quality hardware and software (Sala, 2016). Recently, thanks to the rapid development of mobile processors and optics fabrication capabilities, virtual reality (VR) near-eye display devices have been developed (Zhan et al., 2020). This could open new scenarios in the application of VR, AR, and MR technologies in teaching, training and learning.

VIRTUAL WORLDS

In 2008, the term 'virtual worlds' had a coherent definition in the works written by Bell and Schroeder (Girvan, 2018). A Virtual World is a computer simulated environment that enables users to interact with each other without geographical confines. Virtual reality is connected to computer graphics to render Virtual Worlds (VW) and virtual scenes. Computer graphics, connected to the development of new programming languages and to the advanced computer technologies, have high potentiality, especially in the field of 3D animations for creating online virtual reality environments and virtual worlds. Virtual worlds are computer-based simulated environments where the users can interact via an alter ego in the computer representation in real time with different devices, for example head mounted displays, and data gloves (Damer, 1997).

This "alter ego" is named avatar. The avatar is: an online manifestation of human's desire to try out alternative identities (Hemp, 2006). The word derives by the Sanskrit "avatāra", an incarnation of the Hindu god Vishnu. Through their presence as an avatar in the immersive space, the user can easily feel a sense of control within the environments and more easily engage with the experiences as they unfold (de Freitas, 2008). Avatars can move themselves through virtual territories quickly generating with fractal algorithms, which can be codified in different computer languages (Java, C++, VRML) (Sala, 2016).

The technological evolutions of WWW and of computer graphics techniques have generated online virtual worlds, which can be considered virtual communities or scenarios for 3D virtual games. IMVU, Planet Calypso, Planet Arkadia, Woozworld are examples in this field. Other online virtual worlds can offer positive applications in educational fields. Duncan, Miller, and Jiangin (2012) present a taxonomy for using virtual worlds in education. They classify six categories, according to the content or influence in online education. These categories are the following (see Figure 4).

Figure 4. Hierarchy relationships between categories within the Duncan, Miller and Jiang taxonomy (Duncan, Miller, & Jiangin, 2012, p. 956)

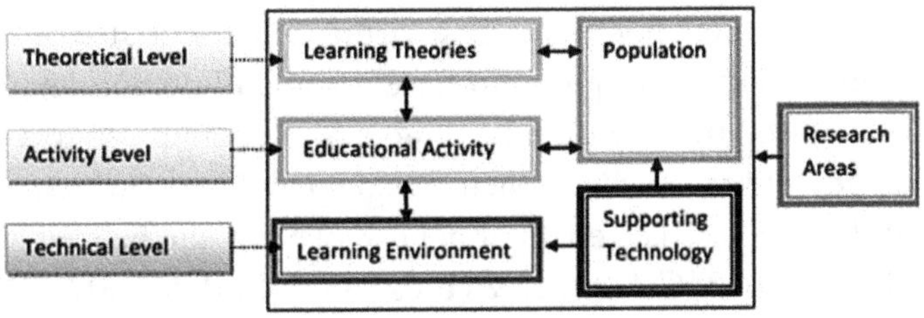

- Population (users aged 18+),
- Educational Activities (for example, visit 3D representation of a cathedral to understand construction techniques),
- Learning Theories (e.g., constructivist or collaborative learning),
- Learning Environment (where the users are working, e.g. inside a simulation of museum),
- Supporting Technologies (e.g. audio, display or tactile equipment), and
- Research Areas (e.g., case studies on interface).

To analyze the application of the virtual world and VR in the healthcare education, Pensieri and La Marca (2019) analyze 2,252 articles published between 2012 and 2019 on PubMed and they organized them in sections. For example, simulation for students; simulation for residents/novice; advanced simulation for professionals; application in the medical/dental/nursing field; review and metaanalysis on simulations or VR and planning of presurgical/surgical or diagnostic cases. Pensieri and La Marca found that the greater use of VR is about: students/residents training and professionals skills improvement. Their analysis demonstrates the versatility of these instruments in this educational field.

Harris and Rea (2019) describe the use of Web 2.0 and virtual world technologies in information systems classes. They discuss the different types of Web 2.0 technologies, looking at how they are used in information systems education. They also analyze some of the advantages and disadvantages of using them in the classroom. In agreement with the Dickey's classifications (Dickey, 2003) for using Virtual Worlds, they present the following advantages (Dickey, 2003):

- Ability to collaborate within the virtual world,
- Accessible 24/7,
- Demonstrate simulations not available in a regular classroom,
- Allow students to apply skills and knowledge to model solutions, and
- Provide a larger community within which students can learn from others.

Harrys and Rea (2019) observe that there are challenges to effectively using virtual worlds in education. In particular, the high technical requirements for computer systems, the steep learning curve to control avatars in virtual worlds, and the lack of environmental control unless situated in a private area (2019, p. 141).

Second Life®

Second Life ®(SL) is one of the most popular online virtual worlds. It also defined as a Social Virtual World (SVW). It was developed by San Francisco-based Linden Lab and launched on June 23, 2003. This virtual world can be accessed freely via Linden Lab's own client programs, or via alternative Third Party Viewers. The Second Life users are also called "residents". They can create their avatars, which are virtual representations of themselves. The educational use of SL is the base of a set of research projects and technical papers (Bal et al., 2015; Calongne, & Hiles, 2007; Childs, 2007, 2010; Duncan et al., 2012; Falloon, 2010; Hew, & Cheung, 2010; Inman et al., 2010; Jestice & Kahai, 2010; Kamel Boulos et al., 2007; Kopp & Burkle, 2010; McKeown, 2007; Mladenovic et al., 2012; Oliver & Carr, 2009; Petrakou, 2010; Salmon, 2009; Trahan et al., 2012; Wang & Braman, 2019). Kamel Boulos et al . (2007) introduce three-dimensional (3D) virtual worlds and their educational potential to medical/health librarians and educators. They affirm that the virtual world named Second Life® could be ideal for those studying at a distance from their parent institution, becoming an equitable method of interaction.

In a 2009 paper titled *Using Virtual Worlds in Education: Second Life as an Educational Tool*, Baker, Wentz, and Woods claim that Second Life has a high potential for its use in education, but they also suggest that the teachers have to prepare the students for this social experience. They affirm:

SL is similar to a public square, where we can meet people from other cultures or countries. All students have to remember that behind every avatar there is a real person. Consider SL to be one tool in your toolbox. (2009, p. 62)

Grimes and Bartolacci (2012) introduce some of the possibilities for using Second Life® as a platform for network and information security training with a focus on the profiling of online behavior. In particular, they refer the initial attempts of its use at one of the Pennsylvania State University's campuses. About SL the authors affirm that SL presents an environment where the cyber eavesdropping, and even would-be criminal acts such as fraud, can be demonstrated with little or no real world harm or consequences. This could create a rift between the virtual world, where anything goes, and the real one, with its rules.

In 2016, Gallego, Bueno, and Noyes analyze the motivation of Second Life users with regard to e-learning. They propose a model based on Uses and Gratification Theory (UGT) that comprises the following seven constructs:

- Convenience,
- Entertainment,
- Socializing,
- Status seeking,
- Information seeking,
- Sharing experience, and
- Continuance intention.

This study confirms the positive influence of convenience, sharing experiences, and entertainment on the intention to continue to use Second Life e-learning. It also emphasizes the positive impact of status, and information seeking on sharing experiences. Implications of this study are considered in agreement to the three following categories: academic, managerial, and technology.

Other Virtual Worlds

Virtual worlds have opened up the potential for learners, teachers and trainers to collaborate easily in immersive 3D environments. The use of virtual worlds was facilitated by the web-based applications that allowed a range of options including sharing files and documents (in different formats), holding conferences and events, and the hosting of virtual lectures. Some virtual worlds are oriented to social networking, for example, Kaneva that is a 3D Virtual World that supported 2D web browsing, and shared media. Where it is possible to build virtual worlds with 3D graphics, interact with the environment and meet new people. Others have a variety of environments to choose. For example, IMVU, an avatar based social experience provides goth, rock, emo, sci-fi, and fashion.

In Active Worlds, the users can chat together or build buildings or areas thanks to a list of available objects. It allows users to have their own worlds, making 3D graphics tools available. The ability to build allows users to create their own environment. For example, a user can request a vacant lot of land and build a house from it using walls of various sizes, deciding to add windows, doors, furniture, embellishments, etc. Another virtual world is The Sims. It is a strategic life-simulation video game developed by Maxis and published by Electronic Arts in 2000. It is a simulation of the daily activities of one or more virtual people ("Sims") in a suburban household near a fictional city.

OpenSim (OpenSimulator) allows to the users to create a virtual world and run it on their own computer. It is an open source multi-platform, multi-user 3D application server. Fernández-Avilés et al. (2016) have developed several 3D laboratories in virtual environment. They realized the chemical, physical, electronics, and topography laboratories based on open source platform OpenSim. They summarize the main advantages of using virtual labs in five point (Fernández-Avilés et al., 2016, p. 271):

- To facilitate the realization of teaching practices via the Internet;
- To encourage autonomous student work, as well as customizing the learning process;
- To enable the access to the equipment full-time;
- To offer practices that in real life would not be possible to perform due to safety reasons such as handling of dangerous materials (radioactive, nuclear, electrical or biological); and
- To provide access to external groups: high school students, students from other universities, people with disabilities.

Virtual worlds are also connected to the gamification, and they have a high potential in the teaching and learning (Fonseca et al., 2017; Grivokostopoulou et al., 2016; Zhang et al., 2017).

An example is GUINEVERE (Games Used IN Engaging Virtual Environments for Real-time Language Education), which is a European project on the potential of the *game-based learning* in 3D immersive environment for the language learning (Cinganotto, 2019; Thomas et al., 2018). In 3D virtual worlds through a virtual presence, students are able to visualize, to experience, in space and time, different environments. They can also touch and examine virtual objects. Tilhou et al. (2020) claim that 3D VR is applied in science classrooms in middle and high schools. It facilitates a branch of constructivism: the pedagogical approach of inquiry-based learning (IBL) (Tilhou et al., 2020).

FUTURE RESEARCH DIRECTIONS

For a long time, VR was considered to be useful only for the learning of simple manual and operative skills (e.g., hazardous conditions in laboratory activities). Technology evolution will open new scenarios and applications of VR, now. VR will become a medium to introduce cyber ethics education, too. An example in this field is proposed by Matsuda, Nakayama, and Tamada (2015). They introduce the e-learning material that they developed using three-dimensional Virtual Reality (3D-VR) technology in cyber ethics education. They introduce a new method that teaches students to use three types of knowledge in their analyses of moral judgment problems: knowledge of ethical codes, ICT, and rational judgment. The authors verified that this method is more effective than the conventional method.

VR and AR are technologies which help the distance learning and the e-learning (Hamada et al., 2016; Penland et al., 2019; Tretsiakova-McNally et al., 2017; Violante & Vezzetti, 2015).

Holley and Hobbs (2020) suggests that AR is not only bridges virtual and real worlds but also creates an enhanced reality through a creative process. They argue that the educational values of AR are not solely based on the use of technologies but are closely related to how AR is designed, implemented and integrated into formal and informal learning settings. The transfers of technology for educational use, re-use and re-purpose are key emergent themes in research as employers demand ever more technology enabled graduates, with high-level cognitive skills.

Technological evolution of computer graphics and of WWW will increase online virtual worlds for collaborative learning with social sharing. For example, Wang and Braman (2019) present a case study of the integration of Second Life® (SL) into an introductory computer course. The authors describe that the integration of SL activities improved students' learning experience. The students involved in the SL activities show better performance and higher learning motivation. Wagner and Ip (2019) test the usefulness of SL as an action learning environment in a senior course for management information systems students. They describe that the learning in the SL environment helps the students' perceived value of learning through the Action Learning steps. In constructivist activities, the virtual worlds have the potential to provide a new environment in which to engage learners (Girvan & Savage, 2019).

Gregory and Wood state critically (Gregory & Wood, 2018, p.199):

Far from languishing in the "trough of disillusionment", as the authors of this collection show, virtual worlds have now come of age as educators continue to explore the pedagogical affordances of these technologies for engaging students in authentic activities designed to improve their technical and employability skills.

Recent studies in VR and AR describe how they can support science, technology, engineering and mathematics (STEM) learning (Ibáñez & Delgado-Kloos, 2018; Westlake, 2019). Holley and Hobbs (2020) suggest that AR is not only bridges virtual and real worlds but also creates an enhanced reality through a creative process. They argue that the educational values of AR are not solely based on the use of technologies but are closely related to how AR is designed, implemented and integrated into formal and informal learning settings. The transfers of technology for educational use, re-use and re-purpose are key emergent themes in research as employers demand ever more technology enabled graduates, with high-level cognitive skills.

In recent years, VR, AR, and MR have begun to take advantage of the wireless networks, but the problems connected to the bandwidth and the latency have limited the telepresence and collaborative virtual and augmented reality applications (Orlosky et al., 2017). New 5G technology can solve these problems. 5G is the 5th generation mobile network. This technology is opening new scenarios in VR, AR and MR. 5G will reinvent digital media, by enabling us to step into a high-resolution 3D world, where the user will experience a new sense of immersion. With the implementation of 5G technology and advances in haptics technology, there will be a future where a surgeon, through a robotic interface, can reliably operate on patients in isolated parts of the world (Kim et al., 2018).

CONCLUSION

This chapter presents an overview of the application VR, AR, and MR technologies in a variety of teaching and in learning environments, from primary schools to graduate courses.

The application of these technologies in education can be seen as a set which influence, support and improve teaching methods, strengthening the educational process and helping to develop new ways of learning. Using these technologies the students can design their virtual world learning environments (Jacka & Booth, 2019).

Figure 5. The features and applications of VR, AR, and MR

Features and Applications of VR, AR, and MR			
	Virtual Reality	**Augmented Reality**	**Mixed Reality**
What is it?	Digital environment that shut out the real world.	Virtual objects overlaid on a real world environment.	Virtual environment combined with the real world.
Features	Closed and fully immersive. Complete immersion in the virtual environment. Freedom of movement in the digital atmosphere with sound effects.	Open and partial immersive. Real world enhanced with digital objects. Digital contents on top of the real world.	Interaction with both virtual and real environment. Digital contents interact with the real world.
Applications	Video games, training, collaboration, simulation, virtual worlds, education, edutainment.	Video games, training, commerce, education, park themes, edutainment.	Engineering, healthcare, education, edutainment.
Devices	Data gloves, headset, special hand controllers.	Special AR handset (used wherein the digital content on a small screen).	Microsoft HoloLens, Mixed Reality headset.
Applications in educational fields	Virtual reality can be used to enhance student learning and engagement.	Augmented reality can help make classes more interactive and allow learners to focus more on practice instead of just theory.	In mixed reality, students can touch and manipulate objects generating a greater understanding of them, interacting with data sets, complex formulae and abstract concepts, which could be more difficult to understand through a traditional lesson.

Recently, these technologies find application in robotics. In particular, Virtual, Augmented, and Mixed (VAM) Reality can be used for Human-Robot Interaction (VAM-HRI). In this technology, the robots can interact with humans in mixed reality. Virtual reality is a tool for developing interactive robots, the design of new augmented reality interfaces and mediate communication between humans and robots, comparisons of the capabilities and perceptions of robots and virtual agents, and best design practices (Williams et al., 2018, 2019).

The initial question was: Are virtual reality, augmented reality and mixed reality good educational tools for learning environments? The answer can be positive, but it is important to consider that VAM realities are not "panacea" for all educational environments. There are some teaching scenarios where these technologies can be used for improving teaching, learning, and collaboration. In contrast, there are other educational environments where these technologies should not be used.

Figure 5 summarizes the features and applications of VR, AR, and MR.

In conclusion, the use of these technologies opens up new potentialities for engrossing learning experiences. The traditional lectures will soon be objects from the past. Digital reality could be the natural evolution from virtual worlds, virtual reality, augmented reality, and mixed reality. It will allow students to participate in accurate workplace scenarios far earlier than now possible (Gregory et al., 2019).

REFERENCES

Adams, E. W. (2004). Postmodernism and the three types of immersion. *Gamasutra*. Retrieved from http://designersnotebook.com/Columns/063_Postmodernism/063_postmodernism.htm

Ammanuel, S., Brown, I., Uribe, J., & Rehani, B. (2019). Creating 3D models from radiologic images for virtual reality medical education modules. *Journal of Medical Systems*, *43*(6), 166. doi:10.100710916-019-1308-3 PMID:31053902

Astheimer, P., Dai, F., Göbel, M., Kruse, R., Müller, S., & Zachmann, G. (1994). Realism in virtual reality. In *Artificial life and virtual reality* (pp. 189–209). John Wiley.

Auliya, R. N., & Munasiah, M. (2019, October). Mathematics learning instrument using augmented reality for learning 3D geometry. *Journal of Physics: Conference Series*, *1318*(1), 012069. doi:10.1088/1742-6596/1318/1/012069

Azuma, R. (1997). A Survey of Augmented Reality. *Presence (Cambridge, Mass.)*, *6*(4), 355–385. doi:10.1162/pres.1997.6.4.355

Bajura, M., Fuchs, H., & Ohbuchi, R. (1992). Merging virtual objects with the real world: Seeing ultrasound imagery within the patient. *Computer Graphics*, *26*(2), 203–210. doi:10.1145/142920.134061

Baker, S. C., Wentz, R. K., & Woods, M. M. (2009). Using virtual worlds in education: Second Life® as an educational tool. *Teaching of Psychology*, *36*(1), 59–64. doi:10.1080/00986280802529079

Bal, A., Crittenden, V., Halvorson, W., Pitt, L., & Parent, M. (2015, January). Second best in Second Life: Teaching marketing cases in a virtual world environment. In *Proceedings of the 2010 Academy of Marketing Science (AMS) Annual Conference* (pp. 211-211). Springer International Publishing. 10.1007/978-3-319-11797-3_119

Bauer, M., Bruegge, B., Klinker, G., MacWilliams, A., Reicher, T., Riss, S., & Wagner, M. (2001, October). Design of a component-based augmented reality framework. In *Proceedings IEEE and ACM International Symposium on Augmented Reality* (pp. 45-54). IEEE. 10.1109/ISAR.2001.970514

Benford, S., Greenhalgh, C., Reynard, G., Brown, C., & Koleva, B. (1998). Understanding and constructing shared spaces with mixed-reality boundaries. *ACM Transactions on Computer-Human Interaction*, *5*(3), 185–223. doi:10.1145/292834.292836

Bhattarai, A., Alsadoon, A., Prasad, P. W. C., Pham, L., Haddad, S., Hsu, J., & Deva, A. (2019). A novel multiple communication paths for surgical telepresence videos delivery of the maxilla area in oral and maxillofacial surgery. *International Journal of Computer Assisted Radiology and Surgery*, *14*(5), 873–883. doi:10.100711548-018-01904-y PMID:30649669

Billinghurst, M. (2002). *Augmented Reality in Education.* Retrieved from http://solomonalexis.com/downloads/ar_edu.pdf

Billinghurst, M., Kato, H., & Poupyrev, I. (2001). The MagicBook: A transitional AR interface. *Computers & Graphics*, *25*(5), 745–753. doi:10.1016/S0097-8493(01)00117-0

Birt, J., Stromberga, Z., Cowling, M., & Moro, C. (2018). Mobile mixed reality for experiential learning and simulation in medical and health sciences education. *Information*, *9*(2), 31. doi:10.3390/info9020031

Björk, S., & Holopainen, J. (2004). *Patterns in Game Design.* Charles River Media.

Brooks, F. P. (1999). What's real about virtual reality? *IEEE Computer Graphics and Applications*, *19*(6), 16–27. doi:10.1109/38.799723

Buesing, M., & Cook, M. (2013). Augmented reality comes to physics. *The Physics Teacher*, *51*(4), 226–228. doi:10.1119/1.4795365

Burdea, G. C., & Coiffet, P. (2003). *Virtual reality technology* (2nd ed.). Wiley-IEEE Press. doi:10.1162/105474603322955950

Byrne, C. M. (1996). *Water on tap: The use of virtual reality as an educational tool* (Doctoral dissertation). University of Washington.

Calongne, C., & Hiles, J. (2007). Blended Realities: A Virtual Tour of Education in Second Life. *Proceedings of TCC Worldwide Online Conference 2007*, 70-90. Retrieved from http://etec.hawaii.edu/proceedings/2007/calongne.pdf

Caudell, T. P., & Mizell, D. W. (1992, January). Augmented reality: An application of heads-up display technology to manual manufacturing processes. In *Proceedings of the twenty-fifth Hawaii international conference on system sciences* (Vol. 2, pp. 659-669). IEEE. 10.1109/HICSS.1992.183317

Chen, C. P., & Wang, C. H. (2015, December). The effects of learning style on mobile augmented-reality-facilitated English vocabulary learning. In *2015 2nd International Conference on Information Science and Security (ICISS)* (pp. 1-4). IEEE. 10.1109/ICISSEC.2015.7371036

Chiang, T. H. C., Yang, S. J., & Hwang, G. J. (2014). An augmented reality-based mobile learning system to improve students' learning achievements and motivations in natural science inquiry activities. *Journal of Educational Technology & Society*, *17*(4), 352–365.

Childs, M. (2007). Real Learning in Virtual Worlds. *Warwick International Journal, 30*(2).

Childs, M. (2010). *Learners' experience of presence in Virtual Worlds* (Doctoral dissertation). Institute of Education. Retrieved from https://files.warwick.ac.uk/mchilds1/files/childs+thesis+final.pdf

Cinganotto, L. (2019). Gamification and virtual worlds for language learning. *Form@ re-Open Journal per la formazione in rete, 19*(1), 133-148.

Crăciun, D., & Bunoiu, M. (2016, July). Augmented reality in Romanian science education Pros and cons. In *The International Scientific Conference eLearning and Software for Education* (*Vol. 3*, pp. 193-199). "Carol I" National Defence University.

Crăciun, D., & Bunoiu, M. (2017, December). Boosting physics education through mobile augmented reality. In. AIP Conference Proceedings: Vol. 1916. *No. 1* (p. 050003). AIP Publishing. doi:10.1063/1.5017456

Croatti, A., & Ricci, A. (2018, June). A model and platform for building agent-based pervasive mixed reality systems. In *International Conference on Practical Applications of Agents and Multi-Agent Systems* (pp. 127-139). Springer. 10.1007/978-3-319-94580-4_10

Damer, B. (1997). *Avatars! Exploring and building virtual worlds on the Internet*. Retrieved from http://www.digitalspace.com/avatars/book/chtu/chtu1.htm

De Freitas, S. (2008). *Serious virtual worlds: A scoping study.* Retrieved from http://citeseerx.ist.psu.edu/viewdoc/download?doi=10.1.1.176.1630&rep=rep1&type=pdf

Dickey, M. D. (2003). Teaching in 3D: Pedagogical Affordances and Constraints of 3D Virtual Worlds for Synchronous Distance Education. *Distance Education*, *24*(1), 105–121. doi:10.1080/01587910303047

Dieker, L., Hynes, M., Hughes, C., & Smith, E. (2008). Implications of mixed reality and simulation technologies on special education and teacher preparation. *Focus on Exceptional Children*, *40*(6), 1. doi:10.17161/foec.v40i6.6877

Dieker, L. A., Lignugaris-Kraft, B., Hynes, M., & Hughes, C. E. (2016). Mixed reality environments in teacher education: Development and future applications. *Online in Real Time: Using WEB 2.0 for Distance Education in Rural Special Education*, 122-131.

Duncan, I., Miller, A., & Jiang, S. (2012). A taxonomy of virtual worlds usage in education. *British Journal of Educational Technology*, *43*(6), 949–964. doi:10.1111/j.1467-8535.2011.01263.x

Encyclopædia Britannica. (2019). Virtual Reality (VR). *Encyclopædia Britannica Online*. Retrieved from: https://www.britannica.com/technology/virtual-reality#ref884313

Falloon, G. (2010). Using avatars and virtual environments in learning: What do they have to offer? *British Journal of Educational Technology*, *41*(1), 108–122. doi:10.1111/j.1467-8535.2009.00991.x

Fan, S., Ng, T. T., Koenig, B. L., Herberg, J. S., Jiang, M., Shen, Z., & Zhao, Q. (2017). Image visual realism: From human perception to machine computation. *IEEE Transactions on Pattern Analysis and Machine Intelligence*, *40*(9), 2180–2193. doi:10.1109/TPAMI.2017.2747150 PMID:28866484

Feiner, S. (2002, April). Augmented Reality: A New Way of Seeing. *Scientific American*, *286*(4), 36–41. doi:10.1038cientificamerican0402-48 PMID:11905108

Feiner, S., Macintyre, B., & Seligmann, D. (1993). Knowledge-based augmented reality. *Communications of the ACM*, *36*(7), 53–62. doi:10.1145/159544.159587

Fernández-Avilés, D., Dotor, D., Contreras, D., & Salazar, J. C. (2016, February). Virtual labs: A new tool in the education: Experience of Technical University of Madrid. In *2016 13th International Conference on Remote Engineering and Virtual Instrumentation (REV)* (pp. 271-272). IEEE.

Fonseca, D., Villagrasa, S., Navarro, I., Redondo, E., Valls, F., & Sánchez, A. (2017, April). Urban gamification in architecture education. In *World Conference on Information Systems and Technologies* (pp. 335-341). Springer.

Freina, L., & Ott, M. (2015, April). A literature review on immersive virtual reality in education: state of the art and perspectives. In *The International Scientific Conference eLearning and Software for Education* (*Vol. 1*, p. 133). "Carol I" National Defence University.

Gallagher, A. G., Ritter, E. M., Champion, H., Higgins, G., Fried, M. P., Moses, G., Smith, C. D., & Satava, R. M. (2005). Virtual reality simulation for the operating room: Proficiency-based training as a paradigm shift in surgical skills training. *Annals of Surgery*, *241*(2), 364–372. doi:10.1097/01.sla.0000151982.85062.80 PMID:15650649

Gallego, M. D., Bueno, S., & Noyes, J. (2016). Second Life adoption in education: A motivational model based on Uses and Gratifications theory. *Computers & Education*, *100*, 81–93. doi:10.1016/j.compedu.2016.05.001

Garb, Y. (Winter 1987). Virtual Reality, *Whole Earth Review,* (57).

Ghezzi, T. L., & Corleta, O. C. (2016). 30 years of robotic surgery. *World Journal of Surgery*, *40*(10), 2550–2557. doi:10.100700268-016-3543-9 PMID:27177648

Girvan, C. (2018). What is a virtual world? Definition and classification. *Educational Technology Research and Development*, *66*(5), 1087–1100. doi:10.100711423-018-9577-y

Girvan, C., & Savage, T. (2019). Virtual worlds: A new environment for constructionist learning. *Computers in Human Behavior*, *99*, 396–414. doi:10.1016/j.chb.2019.03.017

Gregory, S., O'Connell, J., Butler, D., McDonald, M., Kerr, T., Schutt, S., . . . Gregory, B. (2019). *New applications, new global audiences: Educators repurposing and reusing 3D virtual and immersive learning resources*. Retrieved from https://ro.uow.edu.au/cgi/viewcontent.cgi?article=4204&context=eispapers1

Gregory, S., Scutter, S., Jacka, L., McDonald, M., Farley, H., & Newman, C. (2015). Barriers and enablers to the use of virtual worlds in higher education: An exploration of educator perceptions, attitudes and experiences. *Journal of Educational Technology & Society*, *18*(1), 3–12.

Gregory, S., & Wood, D. (2018). Conclusion. In S. Gregory & D. Wood (Eds.), *Authentic Virtual World Education*. Springer. doi:10.1007/978-981-10-6382-4_12

Grimes, G., & Bartolacci, M. (2012). Second Life: a virtual world platform for profiling online behavior for network and information security education? An initial investigation. In M. Bartolacci & S. Powell (Eds.), *Research, practice, and educational advancements in telecommunications and networking* (pp. 285–289). Information Science Reference., doi:10.4018/978-1-4666-0050-8.ch017

Grivokostopoulou, F., Perikos, I., & Hatzilygeroudis, I. (2016, December). An innovative educational environment based on virtual reality and gamification for learning search algorithms. In *2016 IEEE Eighth International Conference on Technology for Education (T4E)* (pp. 110-115). IEEE. 10.1109/T4E.2016.029

Guérin, E., Tosan, E., & Baskurt, A. (2002). *Modeling and approximation of fractal surfaces with projected IFS attractors. In Emergent Nature: Patterns, Growth and Scaling in the Science*. World Scientific.

Hamacher, A., Kim, S. J., Cho, S. T., Pardeshi, S., Lee, S. H., Eun, S. J., & Whangbo, T. K. (2016). Application of virtual, augmented, and mixed reality to urology. *International Neurourology Journal, 20*(3), 172–181. doi:10.5213/inj.1632714.357 PMID:27706017

Hamada, E. K., Mohamed, E. A., Mohamed, S., & Youssef, M. (2016). An augmented reality approach to integrate practical activities in e-learning systems. *International Journal of Advanced Computer Science & Applications, 1*(7), 107–117.

Harris, A. L., & Rea, A. (2019). Web 2.0 and virtual world technologies: A growing impact on IS education. *Journal of Information Systems Education, 20*(2), 3.

Harrison, G. A., Smith, D. A., Black, J. M., & Ghaneie, E. (2019). *U.S. Patent No. 10,215,989*. Washington, DC: U.S. Patent and Trademark Office.

Hemp, P. (2006). Avatar-based marketing. *Harvard Business Review, 84*(6), 48–57.

Hew, K. F., & Cheung, W. S. (2010). Use of three-dimensional (3-D) immersive virtual worlds in K-12 and higher education settings: A review of the research. *British Journal of Educational Technology, 41*(1), 33–55. doi:10.1111/j.1467-8535.2008.00900.x

Hoffmann, M., Meisen, T., & Jeschke, S. (2016). Shifting virtual reality education to the next level–Experiencing remote laboratories through mixed reality. In *Engineering Education 4.0* (pp. 235–249). Springer. doi:10.1007/978-3-319-46916-4_19

Höllerer, T. H., & Feiner, S. K. (2004). Mobile Augmented Reality. In H. A. Karimi & A. Hammad (Eds.), *Telegeoinformatics: Location-Based Computing and Services* (pp. 392–421). CRC Press.

Holley, D., & Hobbs, M. (2020). Augmented Reality For Education. In: Peters, M.A and Heraud, R., eds. Encyclopedia of Educational Innovation. Delhi, India: Springer Nature.

Holley, D., & Hobbs, M. (2020). Augmented Reality For Education. In Encyclopedia of Educational Innovation. Delhi, India: Springer Nature.

Hughes, C. E., Stapleton, C. B., Hughes, D. E., & Smith, E. M. (2005). Mixed reality in education, entertainment, and training. *IEEE Computer Graph, 25*(6), 24–30. doi:10.1109/MCG.2005.139 PMID:16315474

Ibáñez, M. B., & Delgado-Kloos, C. (2018). Augmented reality for STEM learning: A systematic review. *Computers & Education, 123*, 109–123. doi:10.1016/j.compedu.2018.05.002

Inman, C., Wright, V. H., & Hartman, J. A. (2010). Use of Second Life in K-12 and higher education: A review of research. *Journal of Interactive Online Learning, 9*(1), 44–63.

Jacka, L., & Booth, K. (2019). Students as designers of virtual world learning environments. In Pre-Service and In-Service Teacher Education: Concepts, Methodologies, Tools, and Applications (pp. 1697-1712). IGI Global. doi:10.4018/978-1-5225-7305-0.ch079

Jee, H. K., Lim, S., Youn, J., & Lee, J. (2014). An augmented reality-based authoring tool for E-learning applications. *Multimedia Tools and Applications, 68*(2), 225–235. doi:10.100711042-011-0880-4

Jestice, R. J., & Kahai, S. (2010). *The effectiveness of virtual worlds for education: an empirical study.* Paper presented at the Sixteenth Americas Conference on Information Systems (AMCIS), Lima, Peru.

Johnson, E. (2016). *What are the differences among virtual, augmented and mixed reality?* Retrieved from https://www.vox.com/2015/7/27/11615046/whats-the-difference-between-virtual-augmented-and-mixed-reality

Johnston, A. P., Rae, J., Ariotti, N., Bailey, B., Lilja, A., Webb, R., ... McGhee, J. (2018). Journey to the centre of the cell: Virtual reality immersion into scientific data. *Traffic (Copenhagen, Denmark), 19*(2), 105–110. doi:10.1111/tra.12538 PMID:29159991

Jose, J., Unnikrishnan, R., Marshall, D., & Bhavani, R. R. (2016, December). Haptics enhanced multi-tool virtual interfaces for training carpentry skills. In *2016 International Conference on Robotics and Automation for Humanitarian Applications (RAHA)* (pp. 1-6). IEEE. 10.1109/RAHA.2016.7931900

Kamel Boulos, M. N., Hetherington, L., & Wheeler, S. (2007). Second Life: An overview of the potential of 3-D virtual worlds in medical and health education. *Health Information and Libraries Journal, 24*(4), 233–245. doi:10.1111/j.1471-1842.2007.00733.x PMID:18005298

Kapp, S., Thees, M., Strzys, M. P., Beil, F., Kuhn, J., Amiraslanov, O., Javaheri, H., Lukowicz, P., Lauer, F., Rheinländer, C., & Wehn, N. (2019). Augmenting Kirchhoff's laws: Using augmented reality and smartglasses to enhance conceptual electrical experiments for high school students. *The Physics Teacher, 57*(1), 52–53. doi:10.1119/1.5084931

Kaufmann, H., & Schmalstieg D. (2003). Mathematics and geometry education with collaborative augmented reality. *Computers and Graphics, 27*(3), 7. doi:10.1016/S0097- 8493(03)00028-1358

Kim, S. J., Bae, Y. M., & Choi, Y. J. (2018). Design and Implementation of Real-time Augmented Reality Building Information System Combined with 3D Map. *Journal of The Korea Computer Graphics Society, 24*(4), 39–54. doi:10.15701/kcgs.2018.24.4.39

Kim, S. S., Dohler, M., & Dasgupta, P. (2018). The Internet of Skills: Use of fifth-generation telecommunications, haptics and artificial intelligence in robotic surgery. *BJU International, 122*(3), 356–358. doi:10.1111/bju.14388 PMID:29750403

Kononowicz, A. A., Woodham, L., Georg, C., Edelbring, S., Stathakarou, N., Davies, D., Masiello, I., Saxena, N., Tudor Car, L., Car, J., & Zary, N. (2016). Virtual patient simulations for health professional education. *Cochrane Database of Systematic Reviews*, 5. doi:10.1002/14651858.CD012194

Kopp, G., & Burkle, M. (2010). Using Second Life for just-in-time training: Building teaching frameworks in virtual worlds. *International Journal of Advanced Corporate Learning*, *3*(3), 19–25. doi:10.3991/ijac.v3i3.1373

Krueger, M. W. (1991). *Artificial reality* (2nd ed.). Addison-Wesley.

Lanier, J. (1989). Interview with Jaron Lanier. *Whole Earth Review*, *64*, 108–119.

Latifi, K., & Latifi, R. (2018). Telemedicine and Telepresence for Surgery and Trauma. *Surgical Critical Care and Emergency Surgery: Clinical Questions and Answers*, 477-481.

Laughlin, B. D., Murrish, R. E., & Vandenbrande, J. H. (2018). *U.S. Patent No. 10,026,227*. Washington, DC: U.S. Patent and Trademark Office.

Liu, W., Cheok, A. D., Mei-Ling, C. L., & Theng, Y. L. (2007, September). Mixed reality classroom: learning from entertainment. In *Proceedings of the 2nd international conference on Digital interactive media in entertainment and arts* (pp. 65-72). ACM.

Maas, M. J., & Hughes, J. M. (2020). Virtual, augmented and mixed reality in K–12 education: A review of the literature. *Technology, Pedagogy and Education*, *29*(2), 231–249. doi:10.1080/1475939X.2020.1737210

Martín-Gutiérrez, J., Mora, C. E., Añorbe-Díaz, B., & González-Marrero, A. (2017). Virtual technologies trends in education. *Eurasia Journal of Mathematics, Science and Technology Education*, *13*(2), 469–486.

Matsuda, T., Nakayama, H., & Tamada, K. (2015). Using 3D virtual reality technology in cyber ethics education: How can we really evaluate and change students' attitudes? In Human rights and ethics: concepts, methodologies, tools, and applications (pp. 1621-1636). Hershey, PA: Information Science Reference. doi:10.4018/978-1-4666-6433-3.ch089

McKeown, L. (2007). Taking action learning online in the 3D virtual worlds of Second Life. *International Review of Research in Open and Distance Learning*, *8*(3). Advance online publication. doi:10.19173/irrodl.v8i3.507

Milgram, P., & Kishino, F. (1994). A taxonomy of mixed reality visual displays. *IEICE Trans. Information and Systems. E (Norwalk, Conn.)*, *77-D*(12), 1321–1329. http://etclab.mie.utoronto.ca/people/paul_dir/IEICE94/ieice.html

Milgram, P., Takemura, H., Utsumi, A., & Kishino, F. (1994). Augmented reality: A class of displays on the reality-virtuality continuum, *SPIE. Telemanipulator and Telepresence Technologies*, *2351*, 282–291. doi:10.1117/12.197321

Millar, R. (1991). Why is science hard to learn? *Journal of Computer Assisted Learning*, *7*(7), 66–74. doi:10.1111/j.1365-2729.1991.tb00229.x

Mladenovic, S., Kuvac, H., & Štula, M. (2012). Virtual learning environment. In *Virtual learning environments: concepts, methodologies, tools and applications* (pp. 1–16). Information Science Reference., doi:10.4018/978-1-4666-0011-9.ch101

Mount, B., Latta, S., Poulos, A., McCulloch, D., Bennett, D., Hastings, R., & Scott, J. (2016). *U.S. Patent No. 9,497,501*. Washington, DC: U.S. Patent and Trademark Office.

Niu, Z., Wang, A., Xu, H., Li, L., & Li, Z. (2014). Teaching reform of the Introduction to Metal Cutting Machine Tools course for the Excellent Engineers Training Plan. *World Transactions on Engineering and Technology Education, 12*(2), 294–297.

Oliver, M., & Carr, D. (2009). Learning in virtual worlds: Using communities of practice to explain how people learn from play. *British Journal of Educational Technology, 40*(3), 14. doi:10.1111/j.1467-8535.2009.00948.x

Orlosky, J., Kiyokawa, K., & Takemura, H. (2017). Virtual and augmented reality on the 5G highway. *Journal of Information Processing, 25*(0), 133–141. doi:10.2197/ipsjjip.25.133

Ota, D., Loftin, B., Saito, T., Lea, R., & Keller, J. (1995). Virtual reality in surgical education. *Computers in Biology and Medicine, 25*(2), 127–137. doi:10.1016/0010-4825(94)00009-F PMID:7554831

Penland, J. L., Laviers, K., Bassham, E., & Nnochiri, V. (2019). Virtual Learning: A Study of Virtual Reality for Distance Education. In Handbook of Research on Blended Learning Pedagogies and Professional Development in Higher Education. IGI Global. doi:10.4018/978-1-5225-5557-5.ch009

Pensieri, C., & La Marca, A. (2019). Virtual worlds and virtual reality. An analysis in the healthcare education. *Form@ re, 19*(1), 256.

Pérez-López, D., & Contero, M. (2013). Delivering educational multimedia contents through an augmented reality application: A case study on its impact on knowledge acquisition and retention. *Turkish Online Journal of Educational Technology-TOJET, 12*(4), 19–28.

Pestalozzi, H. (1803). *ABC der Anschauung, oder Anschauungs-Lehre der Massverhaltnisse*. Gessner.

Petrakou, A. (2010). Interacting through avatars: Virtual worlds as a context for online education. *Computers & Education, 54*(4), 1020–1027. doi:10.1016/j.compedu.2009.10.007

Postlethwaite, D., Zboray, D., Gandee, C., Aditjandra, A., Wallace, M., & Lenker, Z. (2017). *U.S. Patent No. 9,836,987*. Washington, DC: U.S. Patent and Trademark Office.

Quint, F., Sebastian, K., & Gorecky, D. (2015). A mixed-reality learning environment. *Procedia Computer Science, 75*, 43–48. doi:10.1016/j.procs.2015.12.199

Riva, G. (2006). *Virtual reality. In Encyclopaedia of Biomedical Engineering*. John Wiley & Sons.

Rosenblum, L. J., & Cross, R. A. (1997). The challenge of virtual reality. In W. R. Earnshaw, J. Vince, & H. Jones (Eds.), *Visualization & Modeling* (pp. 325–399). Academic Press.

Sala, N. (2009). Fractal Geometry in Artificial Worlds and in Second Life. *Chaos and Complexity Letters, 4*(1), 23–34.

Sala, N. (2016). Virtual Reality and Education: Overview Across Different Disciplines. In Emerging Tools and Applications of Virtual Reality in Education (pp. 1-25). IGI Global.

Sala, N., Metzeltin, S., & Sala, M. (2002). Applications of mathematics in the real world: territory and landscape. *Proceedings International Conference The Humanistic Renaissance in Mathematics Education*, 326-333.

Sala, N., & Sala, M. (2005). Virtual reality in education. In D. Carbonara (Ed.), *Technology literacy applications in learning environments* (pp. 358–367). Idea Group Inc. doi:10.4018/978-1-59140-479-8.ch025

Salmon, G. (2009). The future for (second) life and learning. *British Journal of Educational Technology, 40*(3), 13. doi:10.1111/j.1467-8535.2009.00967.x

Sargent, D. L. (2020). The Evolution of Teacher Education Through Emerging Technologies of Mixed Reality Simulation. In *Next Generation Digital Tools and Applications for Teaching and Learning Enhancement* (pp. 16–30). IGI Global. doi:10.4018/978-1-7998-1770-3.ch002

Schmalsteig, D., Fuhrmann, A., Szalavari, Z., & Gervautz, M. (1996). Studierstube – An Environment for Collaboration in Augmented Reality. *CAVE '96 Workshop Proceedings.*

Shakya, K., Khanal, S., Alsadoon, A., Prasad, P. W. C., Hsu, J., Deva, A., ... Elchouemic, A. (2019). Remote surgeon hand motion and occlusion removal in mixed reality in breast surgical telepresence: Rural and remote care. *American Journal of Applied Sciences, 15*(11), 497–509. doi:10.3844/ajassp.2018.497.509

Shen, L. C., Wu, T. T., & Hsu, W. C. (2019, December). The Application of Augmented Reality to the Education of Chemistry–Take the Course of Nature Science in Junior High School as an Example. In *International Conference on Innovative Technologies and Learning* (pp. 41-48). Springer. 10.1007/978-3-030-35343-8_5

Stefan, L. (2016). Virtual worlds in online Education and Training–an evaluation report. In *Conference proceedings of "eLearning and Software for Education"* (No. 2, pp. 453-459). "Carol I" National Defence University Publishing House.

Strzys, M. P., Kapp, S., Thees, M., Kuhn, J., Lukowicz, P., Knierim, P., & Schmidt, A. (2017). Augmenting the thermal flux experiment: A mixed reality approach with the HoloLens. *The Physics Teacher, 55*(6), 376–377. doi:10.1119/1.4999739

Tang, Y. M., Au, K. M., & Leung, Y. (2018). Comprehending products with mixed reality: Geometric relationships and creativity. *International Journal of Engineering Business Management, 10.* Advance online publication. doi:10.1177/1847979018809599

Thomas, M., Benini, S., Schneider, C., Rainbow, C. A., Can, T., Simsek, T., ... Cinganotto, L. (2018). Digital Game-Based Language Learning in 3D Immersive Environments: The Guinevere Project. *Conference Proceedings: Innovation in Language Learning.*

Tilhou, R., Taylor, V., & Crompton, H. (2020). 3D Virtual Reality in K-12 Education: A Thematic Systematic Review. In *Emerging Technologies and Pedagogies in the Curriculum* (pp. 169–184). Springer. doi:10.1007/978-981-15-0618-5_10

Trahan, M. P., Adams, N. B., & Dupre, S. (2012). Virtual learning environments: Second Life MUVEs to leverage student ownership. In Virtual Learning Environments: Concepts, Methodologies, Tools and Applications (pp. 200-213). Hershey, PA: Information Science Reference. doi:10.4018/978-1-4666-0011-9.ch113

Tretsiakova-McNally, S., Maranne, E., Verbecke, F., & Molkov, V. (2017). Mixed e-learning and virtual reality pedagogical approach for innovative hydrogen safety training of first responders. *International Journal of Hydrogen Energy*, *42*(11), 7504–7512. doi:10.1016/j.ijhydene.2016.03.175

Tsai, J. P., Kao, Y. C., & Lee, R. S. (2012, July). Investigating the effect of virtual reality application on teaching assistance for machine tools operation education. In *2012 IEEE/ASME International Conference on Advanced Intelligent Mechatronics (AIM)* (pp. 626-631). IEEE. 10.1109/AIM.2012.6265919

Uppot, R. N., Laguna, B., McCarthy, C. J., De Novi, G., Phelps, A., Siegel, E., & Courtier, J. (2019). Implementing virtual and augmented reality tools for radiology education and training, communication, and clinical care. *Radiology*, *291*(3), 570–580. doi:10.1148/radiol.2019182210 PMID:30990383

van Krevelen, D. W. F., & Poelman, R. (2010). A survey of augmented reality technologies, applications and limitations. *The International Journal of Virtual Reality: a Multimedia Publication for Professionals*, *9*(2), 1–20. doi:10.20870/IJVR.2010.9.2.2767

Violante, M. G., & Vezzetti, E. (2015). Virtual interactive e-learning application: An evaluation of the student satisfaction. *Computer Applications in Engineering Education*, *23*(1), 72–91. doi:10.1002/cae.21580

Wagner, C., & Ip, R. K. (2019). Action learning with Second Life-A pilot study. *Journal of Information Systems Education*, *20*(2), 13.

Wang, Y., & Braman, J. (2019). Extending the classroom through Second Life. *Journal of Information Systems Education*, *20*(2), 12.

Westlake, J. (2019). Exploring the Potential of Using Augmented Reality and Virtual Reality for STEM Education. In *Learning Technology for Education Challenges: 8th International Workshop, LTEC 2019, Proceedings* (36-44). Springer.

Williams, T., Szafir, D., Chakraborti, T., & Ben Amor, H. (2018, March). Virtual, augmented, and mixed reality for human-robot interaction. In *Companion of the 2018 ACM/IEEE International Conference on Human-Robot Interaction* (pp. 403-404). ACM. 10.1145/3173386.3173561

Williams, T., Szafir, D., Chakraborti, T., & Phillips, E. (2019, March). Virtual, Augmented, and Mixed Reality for Human-Robot Interaction (VAM-HRI). In *2019 14th ACM/IEEE International Conference on Human-Robot Interaction (HRI)* (pp. 671-672). IEEE.

Winn, W. (1993). *A conceptual basis for educational applications of virtual reality (Technical Report TR-93-9)*. Human Interface Technology Laboratory, University of Washington. Retrieved from http://www.hitl.washington.edu/publications/r-93-9/

Woods, E., Billinghurst, M., Looser, J., Aldridge, G., Brown, D., Garrie, B., & Nelles, C. (2004). Augmenting the science centre and museum experience. *Proceedings of the 2nd International Conference on Computer Graphics and Interactive Techniques in Australasia and South East Asia (GRAPHITE '04)*, 230–236. 10.1145/988834.988873

Wu, F., Liu, Z., Wang, J., & Zhao, Y. (2015, March). Establishment virtual maintenance environment based on VIRTOOLS to effectively enhance the sense of immersion of teaching equipment. In *2015 International Conference on Education Technology, Management and Humanities Science (ETMHS 2015)*. Atlantis Press. 10.2991/etmhs-15.2015.93

Wu, H. K., Lee, S. W. Y., Chang, H. Y., & Liang, J. C. (2013). Current status, opportunities and challenges of augmented reality in education. *Computers & Education*, *62*, 41–49. doi:10.1016/j.compedu.2012.10.024

Wu, P. H., Hwang, G. J., Yang, M. L., & Chen, C. H. (2018). Impacts of integrating the repertory grid into an augmented reality-based learning design on students' learning achievements, cognitive load and degree of satisfaction. *Interactive Learning Environments*, *26*(2), 221–234. doi:10.1080/10494820.2017.1294608

Youngblut, C. (1998). *Educational uses of virtual reality technology* (IDA Document D-2128). Retrieved from Institute for Defense Analyses website: https://www.sustainable-design.ie/sustain/VE_Education-D2128.pdf

Zhan, T., Zou, J., Xiong, J., Liu, X., Chen, H., Yang, J., Liu, S., Dong, Y., & Wu, S. T. (2020). Practical Chromatic Aberration Correction in Virtual Reality Displays Enabled by Cost-Effective Ultra-Broadband Liquid Crystal Polymer Lenses. *Advanced Optical Materials*, *8*(2), 1901360. doi:10.1002/adom.201901360

Zhang, B., Robb, N., Eyerman, J., & Goodman, L. (2017). Virtual worlds and gamification to increase integration of international students in higher education: An inclusive design approach. *International Journal of E-Learning & Distance Education/Revue internationale du e-learning et la formation à distance, 32*(2).

Zoller, U. (1990). Students' misunderstandings and misconceptions in college freshman chemistry (general and organic). *Journal of Research in Science Teaching*, *27*(10), 1053–1065. doi:10.1002/tea.3660271011

KEY TERMS AND DEFINITIONS

Augmented Reality: It is a direct or indirect view of a real-world environment whose elements are augmented (or supplemented) by computer-generated sensory input such as graphics, sound, and video. For example, the user's view of the world is supplemented with virtual objects, usually to provide information about the real environment. Augmentation is in real-time.

Avatar: It is the graphical representation of the user or the user's alter ego in a virtual world. The word derives from Hindu mythology, and it represents the descent of a deity to the earth in an incarnate form or some manifest shape.

Edutainment: Educational entertainment is medium which educates through entertainment. The term was coined by Walt Disney, in 1954.

Fractal Geometry: It is geometry used to describe the irregular pattern and irregular shapes present in nature. Fractals display the characteristic of self-similarity, an unending series of motifs within motifs repeated at all length scales. The term "fractal" was coined, in 1975, by Polish-born, French and American mathematician, Benoit Mandelbrot (1924-2010).

Gamification: It is the application of game principles and game-design elements in non-game contexts. For example, in the educational environment.

Immersion: In virtual reality, immersion is a perception of being physically present in a non-physical world. The perception is created surrounding the user by the virtual reality technologies and by its devices, for example data gloves, head mounted display, sound, or other sensorial stimuli, that provide an engrossing total environment.

Inquiry-Based Learning (IBL): It is a form of active learning where students are given a carefully scaffolded sequence of tasks and are asked to solve and make sense of them, working individually or in groups.

Interaction: Into virtual reality, interaction is often described as the ability of the user to move within the virtual world and to interact with the objects of the virtual world. If the user can explore the virtual world and move objects within the interactive environment.

Mixed Reality: Is the merging of virtual and real worlds to produce new environments and new kinds of visualizations, where digital and physical objects co-exist and interact together in real time. The two worlds are "mixed" together to create a realistic environment. A user can navigate this environment and interact with both real and virtual objects.

Robotics: Is a branch of technology that deals with the design, construction, operation, and application of robots.

Second Life®: Is one of the most popular online virtual worlds. It was developed by San Francisco-based Linden Lab and launched on June 23, 2003. The Second Life users are also called "residents".

Uses and Gratification Theory (UGT): Is an approach to understand why and how people actively seek out specific media to satisfy specific needs.

Virtual Prototyping (VP): The construction and testing of a virtual prototype is called virtual prototyping. It is a computer simulation of a physical product.

Virtual Reality (VR): The term was coined in 1989, by American writer and computer scientist Jaron Zepel Lanier. It is modern technology which gives its users the illusion of being immersed in a computer generated virtual world with the ability to interact with it.

Virtual Reality Systems: Set of hardware and software components which permit to realize a virtual reality environment.

Virtual World: It is a computer-based simulated environment where the users can interact via alter ego in the computer representation in real time with different devices, for example head mounted displays, and data gloves.

Chapter 4
Technical Details and Educational Applications for Virtual Reality Technologies

Yongzhi Wang
https://orcid.org/0000-0002-7117-4097
Park University, USA

ABSTRACT

The application of virtual reality (VR) in higher education has drawn attention. Understanding the state of the art for VR technologies helps educators identify appropriate applications and develop a high-quality engaging teaching-learning process. This chapter provides a comprehensive survey of current hardware and software supports on VR. Secondly, important technical metrics in VR technology are considered with comparisons of different VR devices using identified metrics. Third, there is a focus on software tools and an explore of various development frameworks, which facilitate the implementation of VR applications. With this information as a foundation, there is a VR use in higher education. Finally, there is a discussion of VR applications that can be potentially used in education.

INTRODUCTION

Virtual Reality (VR) uses computer technology to create a simulated environment with the user inside an experience. Instead of viewing a screen, users are immersed within and able to interact with virtual worlds (VWs). VR technologies have been developing at unparalleled speed and drawn wide attention. Successful uses flourish in various entertainment areas, including gaming, image processing, computer graphics, online shopping, etc. Lately, VR has been expanding as an advanced technology in areas such as conferencing, tourism, and education. There are three main types of VR used today: non-immersive, semi-immersive, and fully-immersive simulations.

Non-immersive is the lowest immersive and least expensive type of VR. It demands the lowest developed components, which permits users to react with a 3D environment via a stereo display monitor

DOI: 10.4018/978-1-7998-4960-5.ch004

or glasses. Typical applications of this type of VR system include three-dimensional (3D) modeling and computer-aided design (CAD) systems (Burdea & Coiffet, 2003).

The semi-immersive VR system is all referred to as a hybrid system (Gadh, 1998) or augmented reality(AR) system. The goal of the semi-immersive VR system is to make the user unaware of their surroundings to the extent that they assume a new identity or interact in new and exciting ways. Some applications of semi-immersive VR are being used in aviation, health care, construction, and education. Oftentimes, experiences include a large concave monitor and a display system; for example, it resembles the big screen experience that can be seen in IMAX theaters and using high-end computer graphics. Another example of a semi-immersive VR experience is the Cave Automatic Virtual Environment (CAVE), where the driving simulator is one of its applications (Barrett, 2012).

The fully immersive VR system provides a maximum level of immersion. This system is a digital technology that enables users to experience real-world artificial environments. It usually includes tracking devices, head-mounted display (HMD), and data gloves. Examples include Oculus Quest, Oculus Rift S, PlayStation VR, Oculus Go, HTC Vive, Valve Index, and Pansonite 3D VR Glasses, etc., which present the users with 3D animations generated by the computer that gives the users the sensation of being part of the virtual environment. Typical user experience includes a virtual walk in a building.

Various terminologies, such as artificial reality (AR), virtual world (VW), virtual learning environment (VLE) and cyberspace, are used in discussions of VR. Overall, interaction is a way to communicate with the system, but unlike the traditional interaction between a human and a computer using a keyboard or mouse, the interaction in VR is performed in a simulated 3-dimensional space. Real time feedback and human engagement are a standard of proficiency in VR systems. The experience of user engagement will be constantly improved, as display and tracking devices become cheaper, more robust and better-designed.

In this chapter, technical metrics in VR technology and metrics of different types of VR devices will be discussed. Secondly, software and various development frameworks, which facilitate the implementation of VR applications, are examined. Third, will be a discussion of the application of VR on education. Lastly, a list of VR applications that can be potentially used for education will be discussed.

BACKGROUND

In 1957, Morton Heilig, a cinematographer, invented the Sensorama (U.S. Patent No. 3,050,870, 1962), a theatre cabinet multimedia device that offered viewers an interactive experience as shown in Figure 1. In 1961, Comeau and Bryan, two Philco Corporation engineers, created the first head-mounted display (HMD) called the Headsight. The display had two video screens, one for each eye, as well as a magnetic tracking device. It was the first motion-tracking device ever created. Headsight was primarily used to move a remote camera allowing a user to look around an environment without physically being there. In 1966, Thomas Furness, a military engineer, developed the first flight simulator for the Air Force. This sparked a lot of interest in VR technology and how it could be used for training purposes (Furness, n.d.). In 1968, Ivan Sutherland, a Harvard professor and computer scientist invented the first VR/AR head-mounted display called 'The Sword of Damocles' (Sutherland, 1965).

As VR has evolved, it has been used in different fields, including: education (Englund et al., 2017), learning and social skills training (Schmidt et al., 2017), military training (Alexander et al., 2017), gaming (Meldrum et al., 2012; Zyda, 2005), architectural design (Song et al., 2017), simulations of surgical

Figure 1. The Sensorama VR systems
(U.S. Patent No. 3,050,870, 1962)

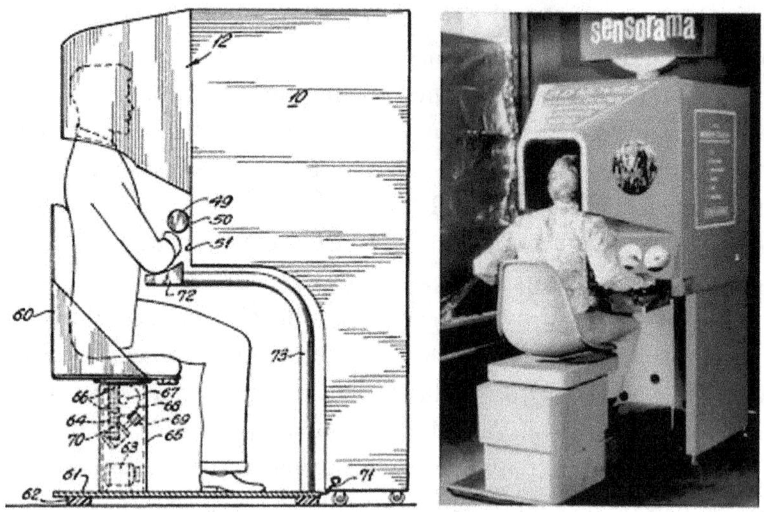

procedures (Gallagher et al., 2005); assistance to the elderly and psychological treatments are other fields in which VR is emerging (Freeman et al., 2017; Neri et al., 2017).

In 1982, the movie Tron brought the concept of VR to the masses. Geared at gamers, the characters were immersed in a fully virtual environment that simulated a video game. In 1991, The Virtuality Group released a series of games and arcade machines, this brought VR to the general public (Virtuality, n.d.). Players would wear a pair of VR goggles and play immersive games in real-time as shown in Figure 3. Note that the term 'virtual reality' was actually coined in 1987 by John Lanier, a computer scientist, researcher, and artist. Lanier and founded the Visual Programming Lab (VPL) and developed a range of VR gear, including the Dataglove (alongside Tom Zimmerman) and the EyePhone HMD, making VPL the first company to sell VR goggles.

A few of these devices were connected by the network for multi-player virtual gaming experiences. In 1991, Sega attempted to bring similar gaming experience to homes with its console. The company never released the Sega VR headset accessory because developers were worried it was too realistic and users would get hurt. In 1995, Nintendo launched its first portable console called "Virtual Boy" that could display 3D graphics. It was a flop due to some reasons such as, the expensive price that tagged $180, lack of colored graphics, and poor software support (Virtual Boy, 2020).

In 2001, SAS cube was introduced as the first PC based cubic room. The SAS library eventually led to the Virtools VR Pack (SAS Cube, n.d.). In 2007, Google with Immersive Media announced Street View. The technology launched with imagery for five mapped cities. In 2013, 25 years after the first wave of virtual reality, there was a project called Oculus Rift, the aim of this project was to provide an affordable high-quality Head-Mounted Display (HMD) (Oculus Rift S, n.d.).

Over the last 10 years, the world of VR has rapidly evolved as a result of competition between Amazon, Apple, Facebook, Google, Microsoft, Sony, and Samsung; each has VR and AR divisions. However, consumers outside of the field of consumer science, remain slow to adopt VR technology because of the cost (Sherman & Craig, 2019). In the last five years, new technologies and components have been

Figure 2. A pair of virtual reality goggles worn by players
("Virtual Reality Goggles," n.d.)

designed and developed in order to offer products at an affordable price. As a result, prototypes are more affordable (Anthes et al., 2016).

In summary, decades have passed since the onset of devices that were the foundation of what we know today as VR. While wide spread adoption has been slow, the depth and breadth of the VR experience far exceeds anything Sutherland (1965) or Helig (1962) imagined. The details of technology have become varied and plenty.

TECHNOLOGY DETAILS

In general, the VR system consists of two main subsystems, hardware and software. The hardware can be divided into a computer, which serves as the VR engine, and input and output (I/O) devices, while the software can be divided into applications and databases as shown in Figure 3.

Figure 3. The main components of a virtual reality system

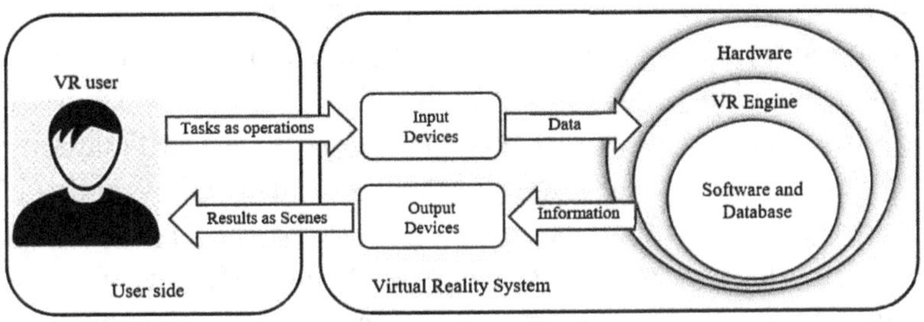

Computers

To power the content creation and production, significant computing power is required, thereby making PC/consoles/smartphones important aspects of VR systems. The process of selecting a computer for a VR experience, there are several factors to consider; graphic display and image generation are some of the most important factors and resource-consuming tasks in a VR system. The choice of computer depends on the application field, the user, the I/O devices, the level of immersion, and the graphic output required. These are important factors to consider in making a choice of a computer given the need for calculating and generating graphical models, object rendering, lighting, mapping, texturing, simulation and display in real-time. The computer also handles the interaction with users through the I/O devices.

A major factor to consider when selecting the VR engine is processing power. The computer processing power is the number of senses (graphical, sound, or haptic, etc.) that can be rendered in a particular time frame as pointed. The VR engine could be a standard PC with processors and powerful graphics accelerator, or a distributed computer system interconnected through a high-speed network. Computers are used to process inputs and outputs sequentially.

Input Devices

Input devices provide users a sense of immersion and determine the way a user communicates with the computer. Input devices help users to navigate and interact within a VR environment, making the experience intuitive and natural as possible. A user's sense of immersion increases when the devices that are used for navigation are efficient and smooth and simulate real life experience of the user. Depending on the desired level of immersion, different systems for user navigation can be used. The most commonly used input devices include the following: joysticks, force balls/tracking balls, controller wands, data gloves, trackpads, on-device control buttons, motion trackers, bodysuits, treadmills and motion platforms.

These input devices are the interface users use to interacts with the VW. Input devices send signals to the VR system about the user's actions, therefore, provide appropriate reactions back to the user through the output devices in real-time. They can be classified into a tracking device, point input device, bio-controllers, and voice device.

Output Devices

Output devices are used for presenting the VR content or environment to the users and it is utmost devices to generate an immersive feeling. Based on the senses, the possible classifications of output devices are graphics (visual), audio (aural), haptic (contact or force), smell or taste. The first three classifications are commonly used in virtual reality systems, while the other two are still uncommon.

Like input devices, current state-of-art VR does not allow a perfect simulation of human senses. Most systems support visual feedback; only some of them are enhanced by audio or haptic information.

Two possible common graphics output options are the stereo display monitor and the Head-Mounted Display (HMD), which provide a higher level of immersion. In the HMD, two independent lenses produce slightly different images, interpreted by the brain, and generate a 3D view of the virtual world for the user. Audio or sound is an important output channel. 3D sound produces different sounds from different directions to make the VR effect more real. Haptic allows the user to feel about virtual objects. Users can achieve haptic sensory experiences through mechanical devices or electronic signals.

Virtual Reality Software and Tools

Planning to design for virtual reality (VR) requires the right software and tools. VR technology can be widely used only if it has a rich ecosystem. Software tools are essential to developing high-quality VR applications; such software can be classified into VR modeling tools and VR development tools.

VR Modeling Tools

Whether you choose traditional design tools or ready-made models when designing for VR, the user must be kept in mind. There are many modeling tools available for designing VR applications. 3D Max, Cinema 4D, Maya, and Modo are all examples of full-featured, diverse 3D graphic applications used to create 3D graphics and models. These models can be export to a format that the development environment can understand as part of 3D workflow. Depending on the need, importing single models for environments may be needed or importing entire scenes created in these 3D packages. Developing specific VR objects might use different software such as CATIA, Pro/E, Solidworks, UG, etc.

VR Development Tools

VR is a complicated and integrated technology that depends on many other technologies, such as real-time 3D computer graphics, tracking technology, sound processing, and haptic technology. Furthermore, software development flexibility and real-time interaction are needed. Developing a VR system from basic languages and library, such as C/C++, Java, and OpenGL requires a large amount of work and also make the system reliability very low. Therefore, development tools usually are used for VR application development. The VR development tools used for VR content creation include VW authoring tools and VR toolkits/software development kits (SDK). However, it is not uncommon to use application program interfaces (APIs) of libraries, such as OpenGL optimizer and Java 3D library. Careful consideration is needed in choosing VR development tools due to the differences provided by different software packages. Differences are related to model input availability, interface compatibility, file format, animation ease, collision detection, supported I/O devices and supported community to the users.

Technical Metrics

The following metrics are identified to evaluate the hardware configuration of VR devices.

- Screen Size. Screen size is the physical size of the screen that uses to show the content of VR.
- Screen Material. Screen material refers to the material the VR screen is using, i.e., LCD and LED.
- Resolution. Resolution (Image resolution, n.d.) is used to evaluate the precision of the screen image, which refers to how many pixels the monitor can display. It determines the quality of the image details (i.e., a higher resolution gives a clearer picture).
- Refresh Rate. Refresh Rate in Hz means the number of times the electron beam repeatedly scans the image on the screen. The higher the refresh rate, the better the stability of the displayed image.
- FOV (Field of view) (Angle of view, n.d.). FOV is the angle range of the image a VR product can receive. The size of the FOV determines the field of view. A larger angle field gives a greater field

of view and thus a smaller optical zoom. In general, the target object beyond this angle will not be collected in the lens.

- Audio Input / Output. Audio Input / Output refers to the equipment that can be used to process audio. Input is any pathway through which an audio signal can go into the component. The output is any pathway through which an audio signal can be sent out.
- Connector. Connector refers to the interface type of VR products, such as USB, DP, Bluetooth and so on.
- Sensor / Tracking Technology. Sensor / Tracking Technology refers to VR products used to detect human activities and reactions.
- Response Time. Response Time is the response speed of each pixel of the display to the input signal. The shorter the response time, the less the user feels to pull back shadow when viewing the dynamic image.
- Development Framework. Development Framework refers to the software tools and technologies that are used to develop the VR system.

Hardware Products and Configurations

The Head-Mounted Display (HMD) is the most popular VR component, which can be worn on the head or as part of a helmet. It has a small display optic in front of each eye. HMDs are considered as the main component of the headsets for virtual reality. They contain magnetometers, accelerometers, and gyroscopes; then they use sensor fusion to combine this information with the optical tracking (Anthes et al., 2016; Chang et al., 2016). HMD provides a large number of uses, including engineering, aviation, gaming, and medicine. It is the mainstream form of VR solution, which achieves the best immersive effect and is affordable. In this section, the configurations of popular HMDs are explained. The metrics of different VR hardware devices are reviewed in Table 1.

Stationary Head-Mounted Displays

Stationary head-mounted displays often need to be connected to a computer, which performs the major image processing and rendering jobs. The image rendering results are transmitted to the display headset through a high-speed data wire. The mobility of users is restricted due to such a data wire. The mainstream devices in this category include:

- HTC VIVE Pro Eye (VIVE Pro Eye, n.d.). It has the latest eye movement tracking. Through tracking and analyzing eye movement, attention and focus, it creates a more immersive virtual scene. HTC VIVE Pro Eye uses eye-tracking results as input, thus no longer relies on the joystick. Users only need to face and look at the menu to operate. HTC VIVE Pro Eye allows users to operate the page with their eyes movements and blinks. In a virtual meeting, chat and remote collaboration, it boosts expressive and non-verbal interaction.
- 3 Glasses D3 (3Glasses, n.d.). It has a low delay and high refresh rate. It uses a new generation of fast LCD and the screen black insertion technology to completely clear the afterglow of the previous frame. 3 Glasses D3 adopts a 2.5k high color game screen, thus, it provides a more realistic immersion effect. The response time of the 3 Glasses D3 is less than 5ms, which makes the picture

Table 1. The detailed metrics of virtual reality hardware.

Metrics	HTC VIVE Pro Eye	VIVE Focus	Oculus Rift S	Oculus Quest	3 Glasses D3	Gear VR
Screen Size	3.5 inches	3.5 inches	5.5 inches	N/A	5.5 inches	Due to phone
Screen Material	AMOLED	AMOLED	LCD	OLED	Fast LCD	OLED
Resolution (per eye)	1440 x 1600	1440 x 1600	1280 x 1440	1440 x 1600	1280 x 1440	1280 x 1440
Refresh Rate	90Hz	75 Hz	80Hz	72Hz	70Hz	60Hz
FOV	110°	110°	90°	100°	100°	101°
Audio Input/ Output	Built-in dual microphone/ Improved ergonomic earphone	Built-in microphon, Built-in speaker	Built-in audio	Built-in audio	Built-in audio	Built-in audio
Connector	USB-C 3.0, DP 1.2, Bluetooth	USB Type-C	DP1.2, USB3.0	USB Type-C	HDMI 1.4B, USB2.0	USB Type-C
Sensor / Tracking Technology	SteamVR tracking, Eye Tracking, Gyroscope, Gravity Sensor	World scale 6-DOF large space tracking technology	Oculus Insight	*Oculus Insight*	*3DOF, 9-axis Gyroscope*	Acceleration Sensor, Gyro Sensor, Proximity Sensor
Response Time	N/A	<=20ms	2ms	N/A	<=5ms	<=20ms
Development Framework	Vive Pro Eye Dev Kit	Wave SDK based on Unity	Oculus based on Unity	Oculus SDK based on Unity	PC SDK based on Unity	Oculus mobile SDK, android studio, jdk1.7 and above

smoother and reduces the sense of vertigo. In addition, D3 also improves its buckle structure to make it more comfortable to wear.

- Oculus Rift S (Oculus Rift S, n.d.). It has the richest VR game resource base. The Oculus store has hundreds of high-quality VR games and exclusive content. The new generation of Oculus Rift S's lenses has a clearer picture quality, moreover, it can bring a bright and vivid picture experience. Also, it reduces the screen effect which can achieve a smooth game experience on a variety of computers. Oculus Rift S has an oculus insight tracking system. No matter where it is heading, oculus insight can transform the player's actions into VR scenes, and supports the game area mobile tracking function without using external sensors.

Figure 4. Three products for Stationary HMDs, the HTC VIVE pro eye (left), the 3 glasses D3 (center) and the oculus rift S (right)

Mobile Head-Mounted Displays

Mobile head-mounted displays often need a common smartphone or embedded device for displaying and processing data. They provide a simple case in use by holding the phone or display lenses at a specified distance (Anthes, García-Hernández, Wiedemann, & Kranzlmüller, 2016). The popular devices in this context include:

- VIVE Focus. (VIVE Focus, n.d.). It uses inside-out tracking technology and six degrees of freedom to realize world-scale large space positioning. With ultra-high-definition 3K AMOLED screen, it gives users an immersive VR interaction mode. VIVE Focus doesn't need to connect to a mobile phone or computer, just wear it and experience the VR world anytime and anywhere.
- Oculus Quest (Oculus Quest, n.d.). It only needs a VR headset and controller to play games anytime and anywhere. Quest has an oculus insight tracking system. Regardless of where it is heading, oculus insight can convert the player's actions into VR scenes and supports the game area mobile tracking function without using external sensors. Oculus Quest is easy to set up whether at home or in another place.
- Samsung Gear VR (Samsung Gear VR, n.d.). It allows users to explore new horizons and enjoy magical landscapes through a 101° super wide vision. Through the built-in gyroscope sensor and acceleration sensor, Samsung gear VR realizes stable and accurate head tracking, thus ensuring a smooth visual experience.

Figure 5. Three products for Mobile HMDs, the Oculus Quest (left), the VIVE Focus (center), and the Gear VR (right)

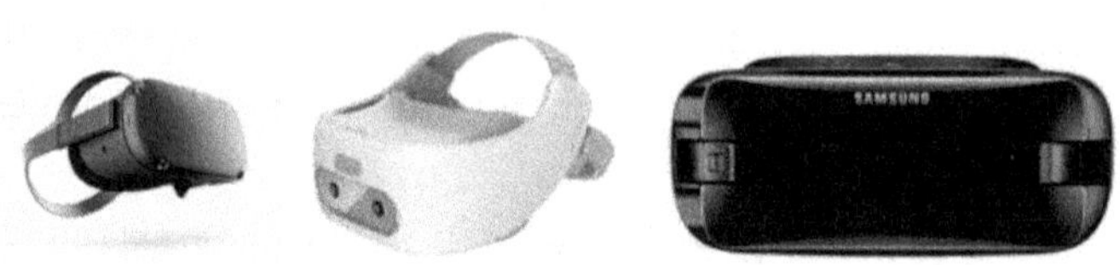

In the last few years, the utilization of VR technology in education was significantly fulfilled. In the early 1960s, the first VR device appeared to be able to create a full virtual reality experience. However, the high price of this technology has significantly reduced its use. Virtual reality systems can be widely used with the advent of virtual reality helmets designed for educational purposes and the modern gaming industry. In this section, I will first introduce several successful stories of using VR in education. After that, I will discuss the benefits of using VR in education, and various APPs that can be used in education.

USING VR IN EDUCATION

There are several examples of VR use in education (Ali, Ullah, Alam, & Rafique, 2014; Civelek, Ucar, Ustunnel, Aydin, 2014; Silva, Freitas, Neto, Lins, Teichrieb, & Teixeira, 2014). Colleges and universities are launching new labs and academic centers dedicated to research on the topics of AR, VR, and

360-degree imaging. An academic conference was offered completely via VR by Lethbridge College in Alberta and Centennial College in Toronto (Merging Realities, n.d.). Major courses of study in VR and AR have increased in higher education across the United States, including programs at the Savannah School of Design (GA), Shenandoah University (VA) and Drexel University (PA) (B.F.A. in Immersive Reality, n.d.; Virtual Reality & Immersive Media Program, n.d.; Virtual Reality Design, n.d.). Some education experts have expected the timing for the broad adoption of these technologies in education at the two-year to three-year horizon. For example, Gartner has predicted (Virtual Reality (VR) in Higher Ed, 2017) that by the year 2021, 60 percent of higher education institutions in the United States will "intentionally" be using VR to create simulations and put students into immersive environments. Following are six current examples.

1. Recreating Past Experiences for New Learners. Some true stories and media manipulation gathered students from different departments such as Culture & Media, Journalism & Design, and Theatre together at The New School (NY) (XReality Center, n.d.) in a class co-taught by two instructors. The students' task was to study and recreate the original news from "fake news," broadcasted by world radios during wars.
2. Grasping Concepts. San Diego State University's Instructional Technology Services unit launched a Virtual Immersive Teaching and Learning (VITaL) initiative in 2017 (Virtual Immersive Teaching and Learning, n.d.). As a result, some of the faculty members have tested the use of AR, VR, mixed reality and 360-degree-video tools for use in numerous disciplines. Instructors can check out gear to immerse their students in new learning environments in their chosen spaces. Another way is to use the VITaL Studio to accommodate up to 40 students at four different stations. Among many types of experimentation, an instructor in the astronomy department has found that VR is a perfect fit for teaching students about astronomy. The instructor explained in a university essay that concepts that are difficult to understand with verbal explanations became easy when students test them visually using VR technology.
3. Stagecraft for Theater Students. Maine's Husson University project helps theater guests visualize the stage design for their performances (Husson University to Demonstrate New Augmented Reality App for Theatrical Set De-signers, 2019). Husson University's integrated technology department has begun the development of an app for iPhones and iPads called *AR Stagecraft*, which leverages Apple's ARKit to give users an immersive AR experience on an empty stage. Students in Husson's entertainment production program are currently designing theater sets in computer-aided drafting (CAD) class, which will be imported into the AR Stagecraft app and provide users the experience of walking through a set on stage before construction ever begins.
4. Virtual Reconstruction of History. Since 2005, students and faculty members from the University of Denver, Colorado, Anthropology Department have worked with members of the public to research, interpret and preserve Amache (DU Amache Research Project, n.d.). Amache is a Japanese-American internment camp in World War II. Although the project consists of digital objects linked to the site that has been created for those who are physically unable to visit, now a team is using drone image capture to produce a 3D reconstruction of the camp. Eventually, a composite of those photos will be used to feed a VR app, thus, that will allow viewers to move through the site via a headset and an AR app. Also. it will permit users to hold up their devices and see what was there during the camp's operation.

5. Going on Space Walks. NASA is taking advantage of ideas from higher education to develop innovative helmet-based displays that use Microsoft HoloLens technology (May, 2015). These devices provide instructions to astronauts on how to interact with inside and outside the spacecraft using the augmented reality display environment. The latest NASA Spacesuit User for Student User Interface Technologies (NASA, 2019) is a good opportunity for students from all over the world to learn more about space.
6. Practicing Clinical Care. Students in Western Carolina University's (NC) School of Nursing have tested the use of VR for experiential learning in emergencies (Western Carolina University, 2019). The idea is to help nurses' community gain exposure to clinical situations that might not occur often in real life. It also helps them feel comfortable with their responses. For initial testing of the setup, participants donned VR headsets to enter a scene in which a patient has come into a clinic experiencing an allergic reaction to the medication and difficulty with breathing. The students had to make quick decisions about the patient's care and prioritize their responses at numerous points during the simulation. Therefore, using virtual reality in clinical education allows learners to participate in real-life experiences without real-life consequences.

BENEFITS OF USING VR IN EDUCATION

Based on some research students spend about 25% of their time on their mobile devices in unrelated topics to their studies in the classrooms. Technologies in virtual reality help to improve the learning environment, thus students do not waste their time looking at their smartphones. Instead, they are fully involved with VR tools, as they provide a desirable environment for learning and change the entire traditional learning process to an exciting experience. It is gradually transforming existing traditional education into new technological heights that impact learners positively (McCoy, 2016; Tindell & Bohlander, 2012).

General Educational Benefits

VR has a several educational benefits:

1. VR enhances visualization. VR is by far the most advanced technology that heightens visualization by alternating different experiences and realities. It is an intuitive way of exploring diverse subject areas and places that people can never visit with unreachable objects such as the Moon or Jupiter. VR makes the impossible happen by making it seem real.
2. VR improves education quality. Pictures make learning easier; thus, VR offers students an in-depth understanding of different subject areas. The immersive learning experience facilitates better retention of the educational material due to the VR simulations. Eventually, it significantly impacts the quality of education across the board.
3. VR boosts collaborative learning. Today, learners find the traditional classroom setting quite dull. VR integration is an effective method to arouse learners' interest and enhance their learning experience. It will also reduce smartphone addiction among the millennial generation and help them focus on studying.

4. VR improves global outreach. VR is an international platform with no language barriers. The developers incorporate multi-language support into the software; thus, any international students can have an equal opportunity to learn via VR apps.
5. VR supports better student appraisal. A successful education thrives on timely and constructive feedback. VR rewards performance and trials no matter how small. For instance, it adopts the gaming reward system to motivate good performance.
6. VR stimulates academic interest. Students of all ages prefer video content for reading. Therefore, VR motivates curiosity and enthusiasm by delivering relevant video content in the student-friendly form.
7. VR introduces edutainment. VR technology incorporates fun in the classroom. It is not hard to sit and learn new knowledge from exciting videos and incredible 3D visuals. Entertainment in learning is an advantage because students will be more motivated to learn and participate in all the lessons interactively. It will boost their overall performance since they enjoy what they are doing.
8. VR improves research. Virtual Reality is a powerful technology in improving research in diverse fields such as medicine. Due to the advances in medical science and education, VR plays a vital role in coming up with improved solutions for disease management and health interventions.

Student Engagement Benefits

From the student's perspective, participation is one of the most important factors of education and training. Using VR can improve participation due to the following points:

1. It provides outstanding visualizations that are not possible in the traditional classroom. Virtual reality is useful because it provides us a way to explore different realities and alternate our experiences. By wearing a VR headset, learners are encountering high-quality visualizations that can mark them in a positive way. The traditional teaching methods can never reach such an effective way of emphasizing things through visualizations.
2. It creates interest. No matter what age students have, they will always love to sit and watch something instead of reading it. VR technology is quite interesting, as it can create amazing experiences that could never be "experienced" in real life. Students will definitely feel more motivated to learn with the use of this technology.
3. It increases students engagement. In the present, teachers find it very difficult to make a positive engagement in the classroom. With VR technology in education, this aspect will disappear, as most students will be tempted to talk about their experiences within their virtual reality.
4. It improves the quality of education in different fields. By taking medicine as the first example. In 2016, innovative doctors are taking advantage of VR technology in order to explore new aspects of medicine and teach others better (Virtual Reality in the Healthcare Industry, n.d.). The second example would be the content writing and editing field. Virtual reality often helps to find mistakes in content and provides good editing features (Case Study: How VR Assists in Writing Skills Training, 2019).
5. It eliminates the language barrier. The language barrier is often a big issue when it comes to education. If students plan to study in a different country, they must understand and speak the language. VR permits integrated translations. With virtual reality, every possible language can be implemented

within the software. Therefore, the language will no longer represent a barrier to student's education plans.

VR Applications in Education

There already exist a number of VR applications that can be used for education. In the following paragraph, I will discuss those applications.

- Discovery VR. (Discovery VR, 2016). This application uses virtual reality to deliver a new immersive communication channel for its audience. Discovery channel audiences enjoy exclusive 360-degree videos via a special VR app. They watch contents related to wild nature, environmental problems, space adventures, culture and history, and more.
- Star Chart. (Star Chart, 2019). With this app, students can learn about constellations by aiming their phones at the night sky. There are additional features that allow students to interact with facts about planets and space discovery.
- Nanome. (Nanome, 2019). This is a Minecraft-like app designed to redefining nano-world studies. Users of Nanome manipulate atoms that design macromolecules in real-time then study and modify the result. The app is aimed at boosting scientific research by freeing the human brain from imagining and describing complex concepts. Instead, users can focus on collaboration and creativity. Nanome suits both learning and research. It helps understand and interact with visualized molecules. Possible fields of application include the pharmaceutical industry, medicine, organic chemistry, biology and more particularly everything related to molecular studies.
- Google Translate. (Google Translate, 2019). While conventional Google Translate may not sound like a VR app, its new camera feature allows students to translate 30 languages by aiming their camera at the text to be translated. Students can watch in real-time as the text is translated. It is great for language students.
- Anatomy 4D. (Anatomy 4D, 2017). This VR app allows us to study the human body with simple, live images. It is ideal for students of biology or anyone interested in the inner workings of the body.
- Kolb Antarctica Experience. (Kolb Antarctica Experience, 2018). This VR app was initially designed to help students gain more awareness of the Antarctic world. The app implements Kolb experiential learning methods to encourage students to achieve a deeper knowledge of the topic. By using the app, students will get an overview of the day of an Antarctic scientist.
- Virtual Speech VR. (Virtual Speech VR, 2016). In realistic scenarios, this VR app provides a good chance for speech education. This app can be used as part of an online course designed by Virtual Speech startup. It also can be used for in-person training as a stand-alone app.
- 3D Organon VR Anatomy. (3D Organon VR Anatomy, 2016). This VR app provides a comprehensive atlas of the human body. When users launch the app, they can see a human model in front of them, a menu with anatomical systems to choose from (skeleton, muscles, nervous system, etc.) and descriptions of the chosen parts. Users can play around with parts of the body, extracting them from the model and putting them aside to get a closer look inside the body. Moreover, they can bring them into their hands to grasp important anatomical concepts from all angles.

VR USE IN OTHER FIELDS

The high precision virtual model opens the doors to the use of virtual reality in training and in various fields such as medicine, engineering, aviation, technical maintenance, and so on. As a result, students can take advantage of virtual reality to accomplish many risky or difficult tasks in the real world such as:

- Learn the skills required to manage and communicate with tricky objects.
- Take journeys to the ancient worlds and discover them.
- Give an ideal opportunity to study the structure of the human body by diving inside it.
- Offer theoretical and practical classes in and around the virtual world with educational programs focused on technology for virtual reality.
- Build extreme environments and situations that help users to test and learn without severe consequences.

Let alone the field of medical and nursing training, virtual reality has been widely used at different levels, including nurse education in a collaborative immersive system (Green et al., 2014), medical training in a virtual hospital (Kleven, 2014), medical professional training (Ma et al., 2014), a simulated caries removal exercise for dental students (Eve et al., 2014), and the surgical education system (Yoshida et al., 2014), which uses an HMD and finger tracking to show the practitioners the exact movements of the expert's fingers during surgery.

There are few cases of technical reports or surveys that attempt to cover the entire virtual reality range. One of them is by Muhanna (2015) which also provides a taxonomy covering different kinds of virtual reality. In his study, he emphasizes the theoretical and manufacturing field rather than the current advancement in consumer virtual reality and sets a robust emphasis on CAVE-like systems. Bowman has shown a diversity of classifications for interaction (Bowman & Hodges, 1999) and for navigation techniques (Bowman et al., 1998). Initial research by Mine (1995) classified the key interaction and navigation in virtual environments. (Zhou & Deng, 2009) afford a concise overview of developments in research but primarily focus on the latest technologies used for image processing to create virtual environments. Gabbard (1997) provided guidelines for user evaluation including best practices for application design. Welch and Foxlin, (2002) delivered a summary of exists tracking techniques that explore and compare their advantages and disadvantages. Howard (2019) investigated the impact of input/output hardware, and game elements on virtual reality interventions for cognitive, emotional, and physical outcome development. I denote that there are multiple methods to measure the metrics of VR products. For example, (Chang, Hsu, Hsu, & Chen, 2016) measure the performance of VR products from four aspects: initial delay, setting a delay, precision, and sensitivity. However, I believe my measurement is more comprehensive.

FUTURE TRENDS

Despite the rapid developments of VR technology, there is a variety of issues that are already considered by developers and researchers that are difficult to consistently address. The problems are primarily concentrated at frame rate and resolution. Most VR can achieve no more than 4K of resolution. However, the very short distance between the eye device and optics of magnifying still makes the pixels visible, which compromises the immersive experience, and, to some extends, undermine the education effect. Although there exist high-resolution VR devices, such as Pimax Vision 8K X, which can provide 3840 x 2160 (8K) pixels resolution, the price is much higher than most 4K VR's (currently more than $1,800). (Pimax Vision 8K X, n.d.) On the other hand, a higher resolution and framerate requests a much higher video rendering capacity and network bandwidth, which might become another bottleneck. For example, when an 8K-pixel VR device plays a video with 30 fps (frames per second), it needs to consume and process 8K x 2 x 30 x 3=1.44 GBytes of data each second, assuming each color pixel can be represented with 3 bytes. As technologies (processing, network, display) evolve, VR with higher resolution will undoubtedly become more practical and affordable.

CONCLUSION

The second wave of VR has brought a plethora of new developments. The HMD display technology is now affordable and dramatically improved. Moreover, the tools appear promising in the fields of I/O devices. Mobile screens may reach high resolution by 2021, bringing many new benefits to the VR industry. Many efforts are being made to continue the development of VR technology (Andersen & Thorpe, 2009; Slater, 2009; Sundar, Xu, & Bellur, 2010), including the following:

- Hardware improvement, such as increasing resolution, improving optics and adding per-user lens positioning capabilities;
- Mobility improvement, which will remove the mobility restrictions from large computers and connected cables;
- Processing improvement, which will improve the computation capacity and further enhance the immersive experience.

One of the key benefits of VR is to enable students to learn from experience. VR helps in constructing 3D objects and enhancing the visualization effect. Furthermore, VR allows students to learn in an intuitive way. The practical implications of VR are enormous because VR provides a new way of learning skills that were difficult to teach in traditional environments. The use of technology for developing student skills is one of the essential uses of VR in education.

When using VR, students can learn and practice communication skills and quickly assess their progress through speech analytics. VR is a perfect tool to learn communication skills because many people have anxiety about speech. Therefore, practicing speech in VR provides a secure atmosphere that results in less student anxiety.

Immersive VR can provide some advantages in learning, such as:

- It offers a clear perception of physically inaccessible items and activities,
- It facilitates training in a secure environment,
- It prevents potential true risks, and
- It improves the participation of learners and encourages them by expanding and developing learning methods.

VR is continuing to grow in both popularity and accessibility. More and more higher education institutions are embracing VR technology. According to Internet2 (n.d.), the VR/AR in Research and Education Study found that 28% of higher education institutions are integrating VR into their campuses. With easy mobile access and affordable VR viewing hardware, more and more universities and colleges will find utility in offering immersive experiences for students. In general, VR has many diverse applications that could be used in higher education. The key is to being using VR in one department and as success is experienced, continue use in other departments.

REFERENCES

Alexander, T., Westhoven, M., & Conradi, J. (2017). Virtual environments for competency-oriented education and training. In J. I. Kantola, T. Barath, S. Nazir, & T. Andre (Eds.), *Advances in Human Factors, Business Management, Training and Education* (pp. 23–29). Springer. doi:10.1007/978-3-319-42070-7_3

Ali, N., Ullah, S., Alam, A., & Rafique, J. (2014). 3D interactive virtual chemistry laboratory for simulation of high school experiments. *Conference: International Conference on Computer Graphics, Animation and Gaming Technologies (EURASIA Turkey 2014)*, 1-6.

Anatomy 4D. (2017). [Mobile application software]. Retrieved May 20, 2020 from https://www.google.com/search?source=univ&tbm=isch&q=Anatomy+4D+(2017).&sa=X&ved=2ahUKEwjTq4Ca4MPpAhVRb60KHcYNDj0QsAR6BAgGEAE&biw=1370&bih=604

Andersen, S. M., & Thorpe, J. S. (2009). An IF–THEN theory of personality: Significant others and the relational self. *Journal of Research in Personality*, *43*(2), 163–170. doi:10.1016/j.jrp.2008.12.040

Angle of View. (n.d.). In *Wikipedia*. Retrieved December 15, 2019, from https://en.wikipedia.org/wiki/Angle_of_view#Measuring_a_camera's_field_of_view

Anthes, C., García-Hernández, R. J., Wiedemann, M., & Kranzlmüller, D. (2016). State of the art of virtual reality technology. In *2016 IEEE Aerospace Conference*, (pp. 1-19). IEEE. 10.1109/AERO.2016.7500674

Barrett, M. (2012). *Using virtual reality modelling to enhance electrical safety and design in the built environment* (Unpublished doctoral dissertation). Technological University Dublin, Republic of Ireland. doi:10.21427/D7W31P

B.F.A. in Immersive Reality. (n.d.). Retrieved May 20, 2020, from https://www.scad.edu/academics/programs/immersive-reality/degrees/bfa

Bowman, D. A., & Hodges, L. F. (1999). Formalizing the design, evaluation, and application of interaction techniques for immersive virtual environments. *Journal of Visual Languages and Computing*, *10*(1), 37–53. doi:10.1006/jvlc.1998.0111

Bowman, D. A., Koller, D., & Hodges, L. F. (1998). A methodology for the evaluation of travel techniques for immersive virtual environments. *Virtual Reality (Waltham Cross)*, *3*(2), 120–131. doi:10.1007/BF01417673

BoyV. (2020, April 1). Retrieved 2020, from https://en.wikipedia.org/wiki/Virtual_Boy

Burdea, G. C., & Coiffet, P. (2003). *Virtual reality technology*. John Wiley & Sons. doi:10.1162/105474603322955950

Case Study: How VR Assists in Writing Skills Training. (2019). Retrieved May 20, 2020, from https://en-vr.101.com/news/06182019/053429513.shtml

Chang, C.-M., Hsu, C.-H., Hsu, C.-F., & Chen, K.-T. (2016). Performance measurements of virtual reality systems: Quantifying the timing and positioning accuracy. In *Proceedings of the 24th ACM International Conference on Multimedia* (pp. 655-659). ACM. 10.1145/2964284.2967303

Chart, S. (2019). [Mobile application software]. Retrieved May 20, 2020 from https://play.google.com/store/apps/details?id=com.escapistgames.starchart&hl=en_US

Civelek, T., Ucar, E., Ustunel, H., & Aydın, M. K. (2014). Effects of a Haptic Augmented Simulation on K-12 Students' Achievement and their Attitudes towards Physics. *Eurasia Journal of Mathematics. Science and Technology Education*, *10*(6), 565–574. doi:10.12973/eurasia.2014.1122a

CubeS. A. S. (n.d.). Retrieved 2020, from https://benayoun.com/z_a/sascube/index.en.html

Desktop, V. (2019). [Windows application software]. Retrieved December 7th, 2019 from https://www.vrdesktop.net/

DU Amache Research Project. (n.d.). Retrieved May 20, 2020, from http://portfolio.du.edu/amache

Earth, V. R. (2017). [Mobile application software]. Retrieved May 20, 2020 from https://play.google.com/store/apps/details?id=uk.hls.earth&hl=en

Englund, C., Olofsson, A. D., & Price, L. (2017). Teaching with technology in higher education: Understanding conceptual change and development in practice. *Higher Education Research & Development*, *36*(1), 73–87. doi:10.1080/07294360.2016.1171300

Eve, E. J., Koo, S., Alshihri, A. A., Cormier, J., Kozhenikov, M., Donoff, R. B., & Karimbux, N. (2014). Performance of dental students versus prosthodontics residents on a 3D immersive haptic simulator. *Journal of Dental Education*, *78*(4), 630–637. PMID:24706694

Freeman, D., Reeve, S., Robinson, A., Ehlers, A., Clark, D., Spanlang, B., & Slater, M. (2017). Virtual reality in the assessment, understanding, and treatment of mental health disorders. *Psychological Medicine*, *47*(14), 2393–2400. doi:10.1017/S003329171700040X PMID:28325167

Furness, T. (n.d.). *Thomas Furness: American Electrical Engineer*. Retrieved May 20, 2020 from https://www.britannica.com/biography/Thomas-Furness

Gabbard, J. L. (1997). *A taxonomy of usability characteristics in virtual environments* (Unpublished doctoral dissertation). Virginia Tech.

Gadh, R. (1998). *Virtual reality—a new technology for the mechanical engineer*. John Wiley & Sons, Inc.

Gallagher, A. G., Ritter, E. M., Champion, H., Higgins, G., Fried, M. P., Moses, G., Smith, C. D., & Satava, R. M. (2005). Virtual reality simulation for the operating room: Proficiency-based training as a paradigm shift in surgical skills training. *Annals of Surgery*, *241*(2), 364–372. doi:10.1097/01.sla.0000151982.85062.80 PMID:15650649

3. Glasses. (n.d.). Retrieved December 19, 2019 from https://www.3glasses.com/en

Green, J., Wyllie, A., & Jackson, D. (2014). Virtual worlds: A new frontier for nurse education? *Collegian (Royal College of Nursing, Australia), 21*(2), 135–141. doi:10.1016/j.colegn.2013.11.004 PMID:25109212

Heilig, M. L. (1962). *U.S. Patent No. 3,050,870.* Washington, DC: U.S. Patent and Trademark Office.

History, N. (n.d.). Retrieved May 20, 2020 from https://www.nintendo.co.uk/Corporate/Nintendo-History/Nintendo-History-625945.html

History of Sega. (n.d.). Retrieved May 20, 2020 from https://segaretro.org/History_of_Sega

Howard, M. (2019). Virtual reality interventions for personal development: A meta-analysis of hardware and software. *Human-Computer Interaction, 34*(3), 205–239. doi:10.1080/07370024.2018.1469408

Husson University to Demonstrate New Augmented Reality App for Theatrical Set Designers. (2019). Retrieved December 19, 2020, from https://www.husson.edu/news/2019/04/husson-university-to-demonstrate-new-augmented-reality-app-for-theatrical-set-designers

Image resolution. (n.d.). In *Wikipedia.* Retrieved May 20, 2020, from https://en.wikipedia.org/wiki/Image_resolution

Internet2. (n.d.). Retrieved 2020, from https://www.internet2.edu/

Kleven, N. F. (2014). *Virtual University hospital as an arena for medical training and health education.* Institutt for datateknikk og informasjonsvitenskap. Retrieved May 20, 2020 from https://ntnuopen.ntnu.no/ntnu-xmlui/handle/11250/253752

Kolb Antarctica Experience. (2018). Kolb (1.0.077) [Windows application software]. Retrieved May 20, 2020 from https://store.steampowered.com/app/831450/Kolb_Antarctica_Experience/

Ma, M., Jain, L. C., & Anderson, P. (2014). *Virtual, augmented reality and serious games for healthcare 1* (Vol. 1). Springer. doi:10.1007/978-3-642-54816-1

May, S. (2015, December 12). *STEM Engagement at Johnson.* Retrieved 2020, from https://www.nasa.gov/centers/johnson/stem/home/index.html

McCoy, B. (2016). Digital distractions in the classroom: Student classroom use of digital devices for non-class related purposes. *Journal of Medical Education, 7*(1), 5–32.

Meldrum, D., Glennon, A., Herdman, S., Murray, D., & McConn-Walsh, R. (2012). Virtual reality rehabilitation of balance: Assessment of the usability of the Nintendo Wii® Fit Plus. *Disability and Rehabilitation. Assistive Technology, 7*(3), 205–210. doi:10.3109/17483107.2011.616922 PMID:22117107

Mine, M. R. (1995). *Virtual environment interaction techniques.* UNC Chapel Hill CS Dept.

Muhanna, M. A. (2015). Virtual reality and the CAVE: Taxonomy, interaction challenges and research directions. *Journal of King Saud University-Computer and Information Sciences, 27*(3), 344–361. doi:10.1016/j.jksuci.2014.03.023

Nanome (2019). Nanome (1.15) [Windows application software]. Retrieved from https://nanome.ai/

NASA Spacesuit User Interface Technologies for Students (SUITS). (2019). Retrieved 2020, from https://www.nasa.gov/stem-ed-resources/nasa-spacesuit-user-interface-technologies-for-students-suits-design-challenge.html

Neri, S. G., Cardoso, J. R., Cruz, L., Lima, R. M., De Oliveira, R. J., Iversen, M. D., & Carregaro, R. L. (2017). Do virtual reality games improve mobility skills and balance measurements in community-dwelling older adults? Systematic review and meta-analysis. *Clinical Rehabilitation*, *31*(10), 1292–1304. doi:10.1177/0269215517694677 PMID:28933612

Oculus Rift, S. (n.d.). Retrieved May 20, 2020 from https://www.oculus.com/rift-s/features/

3D . Organon V. R. Anatomy. (2016). [Windows application software]. Retrieved December 19, 2019 from https://store.steampowered.com/app/548010/3D_Organon_VR_Anatomy/

PC SDK. (n.d.). In *Oculus Developer Center, Overview*. Retrieved May 20, 2020 from https://developer.oculus.com/rift/

Pimax Vision 8K X. (n.d.). Retrieved May 20, 2020, from https://www.tomshardware.com/news/pimax-vision-8k-x-vr-headset

Quest, O. (n.d.). In *Oculus*. Retrieved May 20, 2020, from https://www.oculus.com/quest/?locale=en_US

Realities, M. (2020, March). Retrieved May 20, 2020, from https://lethbridgecollege.ca/mergingrealities

Samsung Gear, V. R. (n.d.). Retrieved May 20, 2020 from https://www.samsung.com/global/galaxy/gear-vr/

Schmidt, M., Beck, D., Glaser, N., & Schmidt, C. (2017) A Prototype Immersive, Multi-user 3D Virtual Learning Environment for Individuals with Autism to Learn Social and Life Skills: A Virtuoso DBR Update. Communications in Computer and Information Science, 725, 185-188.

Sherman, W. R., & Craig, A. B. (2019). *Understanding virtual reality: interface, application, and design*. Elsevier.

Silva, M., Freitas, D., Neto, E., Lins, C., Teichrieb, V., & Teixeira, J. M. (2014). Glassist: using augmented reality on Google Glass as an aid to classroom management. *2014 XVI Symposium on Virtual and Augmented Reality*, 37-44. 10.1109/SVR.2014.41

Slater, M. (2009). Place illusion and plausibility can lead to realistic behaviour in immersive virtual environments. *Philosophical Transactions of the Royal Society of London. Series B, Biological Sciences*, *364*(1535), 3549–3557. doi:10.1098/rstb.2009.0138 PMID:19884149

Song, H., Chen, F., Peng, Q., Zhang, J., & Gu, P. (2018). Improvement of user experience using virtual reality in open-architecture product design. *Proceedings of the Institution of Mechanical Engineers. Part B, Journal of Engineering Manufacture*, *232*(13), 2264–2275. doi:10.1177/0954405417711736

Sutherland, I. E. (1965). The ultimate display. Multimedia: From Wagner to virtual reality. In *Proceedings of the IFIP Congress*. INFERENCE.

Sutori. (n.d.). Retrieved May 20, 2020 from https://www.sutori.com/item/1961-headsight-developed-by-comeau-and-bryan-the-headsight-projected-screen-f

Tindell, D. R., & Bohlander, R. W. (2012). The use and abuse of cell phones and text messaging in the classroom: A survey of college students. *College Teaching*, *60*(1), 1–9. doi:10.1080/87567555.2011.604802

Translate, G. (2019). [Mobile application software]. Retrieved from https://apps.apple.com/us/app/google-translate/id414706506

Virtual Immersive Teaching and Learning (VITaL). (n.d.). Retrieved May 20, 2020, from https://its.sdsu.edu/vital/

Virtual Reality & Immersive Media Program. (n.d.). Retrieved May 20, 2020 from https://drexel.edu/westphal/academics/undergraduate/virtual-reality/

Virtual Reality Design. (n.d.). Retrieved May 20, 2020, from https://www.su.edu/applied-technology/virtual-reality-design/

Virtual Reality in the Healthcare Industry. (n.d.). Retrieved 2May 20, 2020, from https://visualise.com/virtual-reality/virtual-reality-healthcare

Virtual Reality (VR) in Higher Ed. (2017, August 3). Retrieved May 20, 2020, from https://blogs.gartner.com/marty-resnick/virtual-reality-vr-in-higher-ed/

Virtual Speech, V. R. (2016). VirtualSpeech (2.28) [Mobile application software]. Retrieved from https://virtualspeech.com/

Virtuality. (n.d.). Retrieved May 20, 2020, from https://virtuality.com/ /

VIVE Focus. (n.d.). In *VIVE Enterprise*. Retrieved May 20, 2020, from https://enterprise.vive.com/us/product/vive-focus/

VIVE Pro Eye. (n.d.). In *VIVE Enterprise*. Retrieved May 20, 2020 from https://enterprise.vive.com/us/product/vive-pro-eye-office/

Wave, S. D. K. (n.d.). In *VIVE Developer Resources*. Retrieved May 20, 2020 from https://developer.vive.com/resources/mobile-vr/

Welch, G., & Foxlin, E. (2002). Motion tracking survey. *IEEE Computer Graphics and Applications*, *22*(6), 24–38. doi:10.1109/MCG.2002.1046626

Western Carolina University. (2019, April 11). *Nursing students test virtual reality simulation technology at MAHEC*. Retrieved May 20, 2020 from https://news-prod.wcu.edu/2019/04/wcu-school-of-nursing-students-test-virtual-reality-simulation-technology-at-mahec/

XReality Center. (n.d.). Retrieved May 20, 2020, from https://xrcenter.newschool.edu/

Yoshida, S., Kihara, K., Takeshita, H., & Fujii, Y. (2014). Instructive head-mounted display system: Pointing device using a vision-based finger tracking technique applied to surgical education. *Videosurgery, & Techniques Other Miniinvasive, PMC*, *9*(3), 449. doi:10.5114/wiitm.2014.44132 PMID:25337172

YouTube VR. (2020). [Mobile application software]. Retrieved December 17, 2019 from https://play.google.com/store/apps/details?id=com.google.android.apps.youtube.vr&hl=en_IN

Zhou, N. N., & Deng, Y. L. (2009). Virtual reality: A state-of-the-art survey. *International Journal of Automation and Computing*, *6*(4), 319–325. doi:10.100711633-009-0319-9

Zyda, M. (2005). From visual simulation to virtual reality to games. *Computer*, *38*(9), 25–32. doi:10.1109/MC.2005.297

ADDITIONAL READING

Immersive Web Developer Home. (n.d.). Retrieved 2020, from https://immersiveweb.dev/

Livatino, S., & Koffel, C. (2007, June). Handbook for evaluation studies in virtual reality. In *2007 IEEE Symposium on Virtual Environments, Human-Computer Interfaces and Measurement Systems* (pp. 1-6). IEEE. 10.1109/VECIMS.2007.4373918

Netflix, V. R. (2018). [Mobile application software]. Retrieved May 20, 2020 from https://play.google.com/store/apps/details?id=com.netflix.android_vr&hl=en

Poetker, B. (2019). The very real history of BR (+A look ahead). Retrieved May 20, 2020 from https://learn.g2.com/history-of-virtual-reality

Rift, O. (2017). [Mobile application software]. Retrieved from https://play.google.com/store/apps/details?id=com.picselica.OceanRiftDaydream&hl=en

Skalski, P., & Tamborini, R. (2007). The role of social presence in interactive agent-based persuasion. *Media Psychology*, *10*(3), 385–413. doi:10.1080/15213260701533102

SRanipal SDK. (n.d.). *In VIVE Developer Resources*. Retrieved May 20, 2020 from https://developer.vive.com/resources/knowledgebase/vive-sranipal-sdk/

Sundar, S. S., Xu, Q., & Bellur, S. (2010, April). Designing interactivity in media interfaces: A communications perspective. *In Proceedings of the SIGCHI Conference on Human Factors in Computing Systems* (pp. 2247-2256). ACM. 10.1145/1753326.1753666

Unity, V. R. (n.d.). *Getting started with VR development in Unity*. Retrieved May 20, 2020 from https://docs.unity3d.com/Manual/VROverview.html

UNREAL ENGINE 4 (UE4) (n.d.). *Unreal engine for AR, VR, and MR*. Retrieved May 20, 2020 from https://www.unrealengine.com/en-US/vr?lang=en-US

KEY TERMS AND DEFINITIONS

Augmented Reality: Augmented reality is a technology that superimposes a computer-generated image on a user's view of the real world, thus providing a composite view.

Collaborative Virtual Environments: Collaborative virtual environments, or CVEs, are used to collaborate and interact with many participants who may be in different locations and at different distances.

Education: Education is the process of facilitating learning, or the acquisition of knowledge, skills, values, beliefs, and habits.

Hardware: Hardware is the collection of physical parts of a device. Generally, hardware is the parts of a device that you can physically touch.

Interactive: Being interactive is acting one upon or with the other.

Learning Environment: A learning environment is the diverse physical locations, contexts, and cultures in which students learn.

Mixed Reality: Mixed reality is the incorporation of real and virtual worlds to produce new environments and visualizations, where physical and digital objects coexist and interact in real-time.

Software: Software is the programs and other operating information used by a computer or any other device.

Virtual Reality: Virtual reality (VR) is an artificial environment that is created based on two main subsystems, namely hardware and software, and presented to the user in such a way that the user suspends belief and accepts it as a real environment.

Chapter 5
Facilitation Strategies to Moderate Synchronous Virtual Discussion Groups in Teacher Training

Kevin Oh
https://orcid.org/0000-0002-7764-5347
University of San Francisco, USA

Natalie Nussli
https://orcid.org/0000-0002-2411-0023
University of Applied Sciences and Arts Northwestern Switzerland, Switzerland

Melisa Kaye
https://orcid.org/0000-0002-3443-9551
San Jose State University, USA

Nicole Michele Cuadro
https://orcid.org/0000-0002-9677-681X
University of San Francisco, USA

ABSTRACT

This chapter reports on an exploratory case study investigating strategies to facilitate group discussions in Second Life, a three-dimensional virtual world. The purpose was to identify best practices for discussion facilitation in-world from the perspective of a virtual host and a discussion facilitator. A host and a facilitator moderated four virtual group discussions with 16 in-service teachers enrolled in a graduate technology class. The chapter discusses several themes that emerged from the host's and the facilitator's debriefings. Key themes include the need for a careful selection of the communication modality (text or voice or a combination), strategies to promote interactivity among the participants, the critical need for

DOI: 10.4018/978-1-7998-4960-5.ch005

at least one facilitator in addition to the host, the need for clear ground rules for the participants, and clear guidelines for the host and the facilitator. Several challenges experienced during the process of facilitating these virtual events are discussed and recommendations are made to address these difficulties. This chapter is of interest to educators who are planning to substitute in-class group discussions with synchronous group discussions in-world.

INTRODUCTION

Holding a social meeting in a three-dimensional (3D) virtual world rather than in a physical space can be a challenge (Konstantinidis, 2017). Numerous considerations are involved when planning a gathering in a synthetic world, including clarifying the purpose (e.g., social, educational, or business), choosing a location (public or private access), and considering a suitable format (e.g., lectures, discussions, exploratory fieldtrips, or task-based activities).

The notion of multimodal communication is another critical aspect of virtual worlds. It not only consists of verbal-mode voice and text chat but also of non-verbal mode aspects, such as avatar movement, kinesics, proxemics, and appearance (Peterson, 2006; Wigham & Chanier, 2013). Compared to two-dimensional (2D) online environments, the multimodal nature of virtual worlds has been associated with richer and more effective collaborative learning (Dalgarno & Lee, 2009), offers an authentic environment for communication (Liou, 2012), increased student engagement, and better learning outcomes (Claman, 2015).

Due to the complexity of the communication modalities, the expert facilitation of a virtual group discussion deserves special attention. This chapter revolves around the facilitation of virtual group discussion events for educational purposes. Girvan and Savage (2013), for example, provide excellent prior, during, and post guidelines with regard to individual and group interviews conducted in Second Life®, which is a three-dimensional semi-immersive virtual world where users can interact, collaboratively work on projects, explore regions, navigate in different ways (walk, run, fly, dive, etc.), and communicate with each other in real time using voice or text. Girvan and Savage (2013) highlight a facilitator's skills set, such as the ability to manage multiple threads simultaneously.

Similarly, Schmeil et al. (2013) have formulated guidelines based on their experience in organizing and conducting social conferences in virtual worlds. One of their suggestions is to create break-out rooms, or so-called "satellites", instead of having everyone gather in the same virtual room. The satellite approach might increase the participants' willingness to engage and interact with each other more informally. Although a satellite offers more privacy than a whole-group discussion, each satellite might still need its own private facilitator, depending on the purpose or task.

Wang et al. (2014) highlight the complexity of group discussions in virtual worlds. The authors note potentially challenging factors, such as the combined use of text, voice, and avatar gestures, and offer pragmatic advice with an emphasis on advance preparation, skillful multitasking, and co-facilitation to ensure smooth communication within a group. Their participants expressed great appreciation for the co-facilitation because it helped them manage the overwhelming amount of information coming in from multiple communication channels.

This study is situated in an educational online learning context at graduate level. Similar to many virtual worlds studies, the case study described in this chapter takes a pragmatic rather than a theoretical approach (Wang & Burton, 2013). The chapter examines effective facilitation of avatar-based group discussions in a 3D virtual world through examining a graduate technology course case study. This examination includes an exploration of selected areas that are critical for educators to be aware of when planning to transfer group discussions, or any type of communicative interaction for learning purposes, to a 3D environment.

BACKGROUND

This section offers an introduction to (1) the facilitator's role and skills required to moderate a group discussion, (2) communication modalities (text vs. voice), (3) the challenges of promoting participation and interactivity, and (4) a sense of social and physical presence.

The Facilitator's Role and Skills

A high degree of mental multitasking is involved in a synchronous group discussion in a virtual world (Prude, 2013), especially if a combination of communication modalities is used. Wang et al. (2014) highlight the need for this dexterity and emphasize that a facilitator needs to "balance technical, communication, administrative, and logistical elements proficiently and simultaneously" (p. 144). A skilled facilitator of a virtual group discussion is able to help promote a sense of presence by ensuring that the conversation flows naturally and at an authentic pace. One key way to provide for this is immediate feedback. Providing immediate responses in a synchronous discussion has the potential to increase a sense of presence, cohesion, and engagement (Mount et al., 2009). In addition, the concepts of synchronicity and immediacy (i.e., direct interaction with others) in virtual conversations may also enhance one's sense of flow (Prude, 2013).

Wang et al. (2014) highlight the importance of extensive facilitator preparation. Compared to face-to-face discussions, the preparations for virtual discussions appear to be much more time-consuming (Wang et al., 2014). The facilitator guides the participants to the virtual group locations, assists with technical difficulties, and helps with the communication settings.

The amount of preparation and training provided to the participants depends on whether text or voice or a combination of both is used, which is discussed next.

Communication Modalities

When conducting interactive learning events in-world, the mode of communication must be chosen carefully. Text or voice chat, each offers a variety of unique advantages and drawbacks, which are outlined below.

Advantages of Text Chat

Even beginning users of virtual worlds can easily use text chat. Before posting, one can edit and proofread one's contributions (Girvan & Savage, 2013). Text chat is generally free of technical problems.

One can scroll up and down to read or revisit others' contributions. Text chat allows for an immediate download of the group chat logs (i.e., ready-made transcripts), which facilitates later analysis (Girvan & Savage, 2013). If the discussion involves break-out groups, such as satellites (Schmeil et al., 2013), the participants can be asked to download a chat log of their private chat.

Drawbacks of Text Chat

There is an extensive list of potential drawbacks. One of the key challenges is that text chat may slow down the conversation (Girvan & Savage, 2019). There may be awkward moments of silence while everyone is typing. If these silences are too long, they may result in the participants feeling disengaged. Girvan and Savage (2013) recommend that the facilitator type up the questions in advance so that they can easily and quickly be copied and pasted into the text chat box. It is also suggested that the setting called "typing animation while chatting" be turned on in order to visualize which avatar is typing and for how long.

Another potential caveat is the text chat format. With a mid-sized group, the text chat might "fill up" quickly with multiple responses, thereby affecting the reading ease. Having to scroll up and down constantly might frustrate participants, especially slow readers or slow typists. They might not only miss potentially important content but also disengage from the discussion due to an inability to process the incoming information efficiently. Contributions to the text chat may be less elaborate and potentially less substantial, depending on the typing speed and the effects of time-consuming self-editing (Girvan & Savage, 2013).

Advantages of Voice Chat

Producing verbal language compared to text chat is much faster. Depending on their personal preferences, participants using voice might feel more encouraged to elaborate. Some participants might prefer using voice because they know there will be no written record of what they say (Nussli et al., 2019). Although there might be a risk of "chatting over each other", the flow of conversation tends to be much more natural, authentic, and faster than text chat. Girvan and Savage (2013) recommend a turn-taking policy for beginning users, although such an approach might slow down the pace, depending on the participants' expertise in virtual communication.

Drawbacks of Voice Chat

Using voice chat requires specific settings, which, technically, might be overwhelming for inexperienced users of virtual worlds. An additional disadvantage of voice chat is that no ready-made transcripts are available for analysis. Even though voice chat has the potential of humanizing a conversation, there is no guarantee for increased interaction. A discussion still requires facilitation to promote interaction and engagement, even if it is just a non-verbal sign of encouragement, such as "[Avatar name] nods" (Girvan & Savage, 2013, p. 31).

Challenges of Promoting Participation and Interactivity

Participation

Encouraging participants' active engagement in a virtual discussion event may be more challenging in virtual worlds than in other environments, which is why a different set of strategies is required to monitor the participants' attention (Wigert et al., 2012; Jiang, 2017). Keeping virtual participants engaged is critical to a state that Girvan and Savage (2013, 2019) call 'invisible while present'. They refer to the participants' avatar being visible, although it is unclear whether the participant 'behind' the avatar is there or not. For example, if a participant seems to be absent, this could be due to technical issues, disengagement, or engagement in back-channeling (i.e., using private chat). Girvan and Savage (2013) recommend that the participants be asked to notify the host or facilitator of any absence that may be required and to announce once they are back. Another option is to move from one location to the next so that participants need to pay attention.

Interactivity

Promoting interactivity during a learning activity in a 3D virtual world may be more challenging than in a traditional face-to-face environment. In an exploratory case study situated in Second Life® by Nussli et al. (2019), the discussion group co-host frequently asked follow-up questions after the host had asked a set of introductory questions. The goal was to prompt deeper reflection and to promote interactivity. Whereas some participants perceived these follow-up questions as an effective mechanism to make the conversation more interactive, other participants felt even more overwhelmed than they already were due to the unfamiliar discussion format in a 3D virtual world.

Verbal and non-verbal interaction is critical to establishing a sense of personal relationship. Whereas exploratory learning activities set in virtual worlds may naturally promote collaboration and interaction, the group discussion format requires the facilitator to use specific strategies to help participants communicate with each other, taking into account generational preferences for the communication mode.

Sense of Social and Physical Presence

Social presence has been defined as identifying with a community, experiencing and conveying a sense of intimacy, and communicating purposefully in a trusting environment through instant and synchronous interaction with others (Garrison, 2009; Gunawardena, 1995; Gunawardena & Zittle, 1997; Lambert & Fisher, 2013; Lowenthal & Dunlap, 2018; Wei et al., 2012).

Similarly, higher levels of social presence have been associated with enriched communication, higher engagement, significantly higher learning achievements, and higher satisfaction with both the social aspects of a virtual experience and the quality of communication (Hostetter & Busch, 2013; Lambert & Fisher, 2013; Siriaraya & Ang, 2012; Tu, 2001).

In particular, avatars (Fig. 1) have great potential to support a sense of physical presence because they provide a means to communicate non-verbally by using a range of gestures and facial expressions (Konstantinidis, 2017; Murgado-Armenteros et al., 2012).

Relatedly, Wei et al. (2012) emphasize the impact of immediacy on the perception of one's social presence. Other indicators of social presence in virtual worlds include virtual sharing acts (e.g., offering

Figure 1. Avatars in a group discussion and lecture event

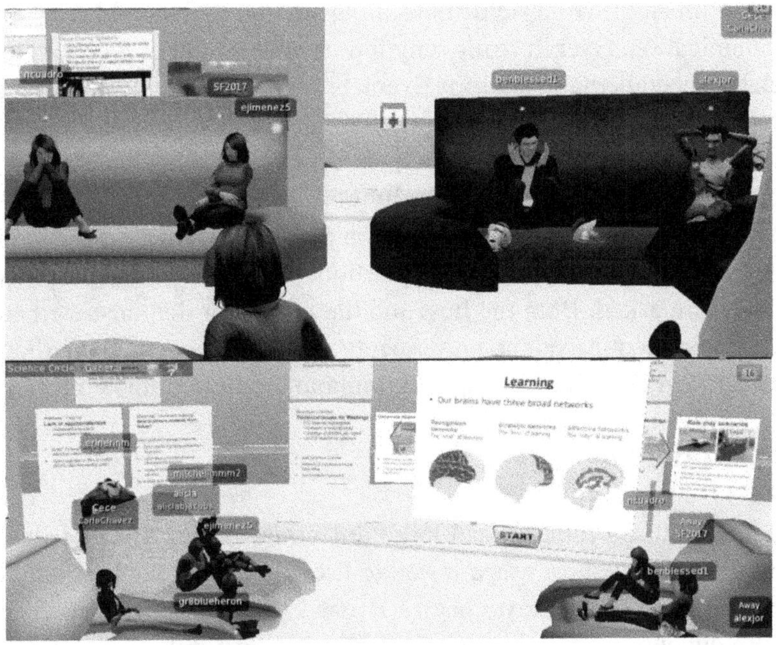

a cup of coffee), observing real-life social norms; showing politeness (e.g., apologizing for being late); using humor; using voice to humanize the conversation; expressing intonation in writing; and showing social emotionality (Gilbert et al., 2011). The connection between the use of voice and a sense of presence is not fully established though. In a study by Wilkes (2016), for example, voice used in virtual environments failed to be a significant contributor to the participants' sense of presence. Colleges and universities who use virtual worlds for teaching purposes, usually own their virtual space (i.e., a virtual region), thus ensuring that only enrolled students can access their virtual space.

Public or private issues may heavily impact participants' sense of social presence. Tu (2001) explored Chinese students' sense of social presence in 3D virtual environments. Although the students felt comfortable expressing their thoughts online, they feared that public accessibility to their posts might violate their privacy and cause them to lose face. Thus, it is recommended that educators consider students' communicative preferences before launching online discussions about potentially sensitive topics (Tu, 2001).

The case study described in this chapter was guided by three research questions, namely: (a) What are the best practices in terms of facilitating a group discussion in a virtual world?, (b) What are the potential challenges that hosts and facilitators might experience while moderating a group discussion in a virtual world?, and (c) Which strategies might help to create a sense of presence when facilitating a group discussion in a virtual world?

SETTING A CONTEXT FOR THE CASE STUDY

The insights described in this chapter emerged from an exploratory case study conducted with sixteen adult participants who were recruited from a technology class for educational specialists studying at a university in the U.S. Of the sixteen participants, 13 (81%) were female and three (19%) were male. The case study began with an in-world fieldtrip/training session in Second Life® to learn the basics of navigation and communication. Over the following four weeks, a total of four sessions were held online as part of the regularly scheduled curriculum (Event 1: two sessions with different participants each, Event 2: two sessions with different participants each). Groups included eight participants each, plus the host and the facilitator as well as a non-participant observer. Each event started with a microphone check. All participants were welcomed individually both by the host and the facilitator. The session design included the following: lecture, first discussion question, lecture continued, second discussion question, lecture continued, and third discussion question. To increase engagement with the topic, only open-ended questions were asked. Both the host and the facilitator demonstrated an ongoing presence by acknowledging and commenting on the participants' contributions, praising them, asking questions to deepen the discourse, and providing prompts to promote the flow of the conversation.

Communication Modality

The communication modalities (Table 1) had to be renegotiated after Event 1 due to a major lack of participant interactivity. Only the host was allowed to use voice in Event 1, whereas the facilitator and the participants were limited to using text chat. In Event 2, the facilitator also used voice extensively. The participants were encouraged to use voice as well. The host only used voice and refrained from using text chat. This change was implemented in the hope that using voice would promote participant engagement and provide a more natural and authentic pace.

Table 1. Overview of the communication modalities in the two events

Role	Event 1		Event 2	
	Voice Chat	Text Chat	Voice Chat	Text Chat
Host	☑	-	☑	-
Facilitator	-	☑	☑	☑
Participants	-	☑	☑	☑

Ground Rules

Starting a synchronous group discussion by communicating a set of clear ground rules has the potential to alleviate initial anxiety and to prepare participants for the discussion (Jiang, 2017). Three sets of ground rules, one each for the participants, the host, and the facilitator, were adapted and synthesized from previous research (Girvan & Savage, 2013, 2019; McVey, 2008; Nussli & Oh, 2017; Nussli et al., 2019). Whereas the host's function was to provide a lecture and to ask questions for reflection and answer participants' questions, the facilitator's role was to personalize the communication by commenting on each individual's contributions, to help build a sense of presence, to promote engagement, to validate and acknowledge contributions, to ask follow-up questions, and to troubleshoot, if necessary. Tables 2 to 4 display the ground rules.

Table 2. Ground rules for the participants

Theme	Ground Rules for Participants
Mode of communication	Participants use text chat only (host uses voice).
Timing	Don't start typing until the host has finished talking so that everyone can pay attention to the host's message.
Message length	Break down long or complex messages into several short posts.
Clear references	Even if you can't type as fast as your colleagues, it's still important that you post your contribution. Just make sure to state explicitly who or what you're responding to.
Personalizing communication	If you type up a response to someone else's comment, always start with a clear and personal reference, such as, *"Mike,..."*.
Asking questions	If you didn't understand the host's question (e.g., due to the sound quality), ask that the question be typed up.
Intonation	Use intonation if you like, such as, *"Goooood question, Jenny."*
Acknowledge and praise	Praise someone if you like what you've heard or read, such as in *"Nice intro to this, P., very provocative."*
Social Politeness	If you're late, ask for permission to join the conversation in progress (as you might in real life).
Internet abbreviations	Feel free to use text message shorthand, such as "afk" (away from keyboard) or "brb" (be right back).
Proofread	Proofread your spelling before posting in order to avoid severe typos, which may impair your discussion partners' understanding or result in embarrassing surprises.
Troubleshooting	If you experience technical issues, ask the facilitator for help. Use the private rather than the group chat to request assistance so that you do not distract the other discussion participants.

DEBRIEFINGS BETWEEN HOST AND FACILITATOR

Insights from the Host and Facilitator First Debriefing

After completion of Event 1, the instructor and the facilitator conducted an online debrief using Zoom video conferencing. They discussed the extent to which they had adhered to the ground rules, the challenges they had experienced, and how to address those challenges in the next event. Strategies supportive of creating a sense of presence were also reviewed.

- Which of the strategies (see ground rules in Tables 3 and 4) did you actually use? In your opinion, which of the strategies you used promoted the discussion most effectively? Provide an example.
- Describe any additional strategies that you could have used to promote the discussion flow.
- Which strategies turned out to be ineffective with regard to moving the discussion along? How might these strategies be improved?
- In your opinion, which strategies effectively promoted a sense of presence among the participants? Provide an example.
- How well did the division of roles (host using voice / vs. facilitator using text) work out?
- With regard to Event 2: What changes are you planning, if any?

- Consider the strategies you have used to facilitate the discussion and/or create a sense of community: Which ones only work in a 3D platform (as opposed to an online discussion in a 2D

Table 3. Ground rules for the host

Theme	Ground Rules for the Host
Mode of communication	Use voice only.
Timing	Start on time.
Reminder	Communicate ground rules before starting the lecture, for example, *"Please refrain from comments until after the topic introduction"* or *"Please refrain from posting your comments as long as the host is speaking."*
Types of questions	Ask open-ended questions. Provide time for participants to ask questions.
Share	Share your own opinion.
Keep conversation going.	Clarify when necessary. For example, if there's no response from anyone, you may have to rephrase or give an example.
Personalize	Address everyone by name.
Social politeness	Show politeness, such as welcoming someone (back).
Providing summaries	Be prepared to provide a short summary of the main points contributed by the discussants.
Troubleshooting	Leave the troubleshooting to the facilitator so that you can focus on the lecture and discussion.

Table 4. Ground rules for the facilitator

Theme	Ground Rules for the Facilitator
Mode of communication	Use text only. (For Event 2, this ground rule was modified to "use text and voice".)
Personalizing communication	Greet everyone individually, as in, *"Welcome, O"*. Address everyone by name, as in, "*Jennifer, thank you for sharing your experience.*" You may also use the initial of their first name, e.g., *"Interesting, B."* or nicknames, e.g., *"Paulie, can you elaborate?"*.
Latecomers	Welcomes latecomers.
Supporting host	When the host asks key questions, type them in the text chat.
Enforce ground rules	If participants start posting text messages to the text chat BEFORE the host has finished talking, remind them of the ground rules.
Promote flow	Keeping the conversation going. If the discussion ebbs, ask probing questions.
Interact	Offer praise for stimulating thoughts, as in, "*Good one, O*". Acknowledge comments *(Yep, P., I hear that. - Oh really, N.?)* Use humor as appropriate.
Troubleshooting	Troubleshoot, if necessary (for example, if a participant can't hear the host, type up what the host said). Use private chat for troubleshooting. The group chat should only be used for the discussion.
Managing text chat	Repost a question: – if the question is no longer visible in the chat channel due to multiple responses or – if it has been a while since the host asked the question (through voice) or – if the discussion is going off track.
Equal contributions	Keep track of the frequency of participant contributions. If there are participants who have failed to contribute anything, address them directly and ask for their opinion.
Neutral	Stay neutral. Do not share your own opinion. Do not show favoritism.

environment)?

Adherence to Ground Rules

The host and facilitator observed all but two ground rules. They did not post the questions to the text chat because these were already included in the slides, which had been shared with all participants prior to the virtual event. No internet abbreviations were used, such as "OT" (off topic) or "POV" (in my point of view) because it was unclear to which extent the participants were familiar with these abbreviations.

Limited Interactivity

The lack of interactivity during Event 1 prompted the host and the facilitator to discuss the possibility of allowing the facilitator and the participants to use voice in Event 2.

[Host]: Like you said last night, it would be interesting to see how they did if we changed it to a verbal chat rather than just a text chat.
[Facilitator]: I think it's going to take longer.
[Host]: I think so too. They are not going to be as succinct.
[Facilitator]: There are pros and cons.
[Host]: We don't have eye contact or some sort of method. Once you bring in the verbal communication, they will stop using the text and like you said we don't know who's going to take turns. You're going to run into issues there.

Despite a number of concerns, it was decided that the facilitator should be allowed to use both voice and text. Thus, the facilitator's role was redefined and extended. Similarly, it was also agreed that the participants would be encouraged but not forced to use voice. For Event 2, all participants would be directed to post their initial contributions to the text chat, whereas follow-up thoughts could be delivered through text chat or voice, depending on the participant's preference.

In addition to the modifications above, it was agreed that the seating arrangement for Event 2 would be renegotiated. For example, the seats in the sandbox could be rearranged in U-shape style with an opening facing the PowerPoint slides so that the participants could 'look' at each other while still having a good view of the slides. Being able to see each other and share a couch might also increase the participants' willingness to interact.

Pace

The facilitator tried to promote the flow of the conversation and posted comments such as "good answer" to acknowledge the participants' contributions, but because there were eight participants in each group it was challenging to comment on every single post. One facilitator commented,

"Everything comes up at once because they were all done at the same time. I had a hard time reading everything." The issue of facilitator feedback was aggravated by a lack of reader-friendliness of the text chat, "... the text chat was small. It was challenging for me to read everything even when I made it the largest it could be."

There are various options how to address this issue of responding to all participant contributions: smaller discussion groups (fewer than eight), turn-taking policy (i.e., have certain people answer first), more practice opportunities (i.e., repeated discussion group participation over a longer period of time), and more time to read and react to peers' contributions although excessively long periods of silence would have to be avoided. The same strategy might be transferable to the facilitation of group discussions. If participants use voice, one way to avoid that they are "chatting over each other" would be to suggest going around clock-wise or counter clock-wise and ensure that the seating arrangement supports this directive (e.g., semi-circular sofa).

Troubleshooting in Private Chat

In both events, the group chat was initially used for troubleshooting. The following excerpt from Event 1 shows that troubleshooting in the group chat heavily interfered with the ongoing conversation. The facilitator and participant A were trying to fix a sound issue while participants B and C were answering the facilitator's question about project-based learning (PBL). Even the host left comments in the text chat to try to help with the troubleshooting.

[Facilitator]: Does PBL have to be a long project?

[Participant A]: btw, i still can't hear the professor. i am using headphones and i hear typing and bird noises

[Host]: [name], you may need to move closer to the front.

[Participant A]: Professor, ok i will

[Participant B]: No I have done both long and small PBL projects.

[Host]: [name] in the upper right corner, please select the audio settings. and Check them.

[Participant C]: The recent unit we are working on is about how to find triangles mathematically. On the first day of the unit we used the layout of a baseball field. This allowed students to discover multiple right triangles which they then graphed into their notebooks and found the different lengths of each side. After finding the lengths for multiple triangles, students were able to discover the relationship between all three side of a triangle and with different triangle types.

[Participant A]: Professor, I did. All possible boxes are checked and the volumes are up

[Facilitator]: in a real world, we face short and long projects to solves, so I concur

[Host]: [name], Perhaps try to log out and log back in again.

[Participant A]: Professor, okay. brb

[Participant A]: I can hear. Thank you.

The above excerpt suggests not only that troubleshooting should be moved to the private chat, but also that the division of roles between the host and the facilitator needs to be clearer and that whoever is in charge of troubleshooting must be very skilled in multi-tasking. The facilitator must not only be skilled in troubleshooting and simultaneous involvement in the ongoing discussion. The facilitator must also be able to handle multiple devices (computer, tablet, smartphone) and platforms (virtual world, email, WhatsApp, instant messaging, Skype, phone, etc.) simultaneously in order to be accessible for those participants who are logged out of the virtual world and have trouble logging back in.

Miscellaneous Challenges

Due to some of the participants' avatar names, the host and facilitator had problems identifying who was behind an avatar, resulting in the recommendation that the participants include their first name when they come up with their avatar names. The participants occasionally included questions in their posts, but some of these questions went unanswered, leading to the recommendation that the host should try to address as many of the participants' questions as possible. Because the event duration was limited to approximately one hour each, there was insufficient time to develop an authentic discussion. For Event 2, it was decided to reduce the number of lecture slides to free up more time for discussion. This adjustment would provide the participants with more time to reflect and comment on their peers' contributions.

Sense of Presence

The host and the facilitator discussed which strategies might have the potential to create a sense of presence in a synchronous 3D platform, especially in comparison to a 2D environment, such as a discussion board.

Key factors emerging from this debrief included (a) being able to chat in real time; (b) seeing visual representations of each other; (c) getting immediate, real-time feedback; (d) doing one-on-one verbal check-ins with each individual participant before the discussion starts; and (e) feeling comfortable in the setting.

[Host]: Just allowing them to chat. Maybe just the chat alone gave them a sense of presence.

[Facilitator]: Without the chat, we could have gone 40 minutes and we wouldn't even know if they were engaged or not. They could have something else open up, we wouldn't know. And also seeing each other as avatars… It makes them feel as if they were in a classroom. The virtual area, it had a screen, it had seats, and when people were typing you saw the avatars moving. It gives them more of a classroom feel than just 2D.

[Host]: If we had another lecture area set up where they had to stand.

[Facilitator]: That would be uncomfortable. I like the sitting part. And I think it's synchronous because a lot of times, online lectures could happen asynchronously and they don't feel part of a group, there's no community, they're learning on their own. But this, they're able to comment right away and get feedback immediately.

Insights from Host and Facilitator Second Debriefing

After completion of Event 2, the host and the facilitator again conducted an online debrief via Zoom video conferencing.

Adherence to Ground Rules

Similar to Event 1, both the host and the facilitator followed the ground rules. The facilitator acknowledged and commented on the participants' contributions, again with the objective of promoting interactivity and helping to create a sense of presence, although the latter was challenging due to the rather rigid and controlled structure of the event.

[Facilitator]: During both sessions, I did my best to praise somebody for sharing. I would also thank them for sharing every time they contributed something. That seemed to work out pretty well. [...] I feel like we have both acknowledged comments, offered praise for stimulating thoughts, I kept asking questions and I think I elicited a response from two people right at the beginning who didn't contribute anything.

Improving Lecture and Discussion Format

The host and facilitator then discussed the strategies that had been ineffective with regard to moving the discussion along and considered ways to improve them.

[Host]: So I think in looking at the first event versus the second event, in the first event, we simply praised and agreed with the things students were sharing, whereas this time we were probing and it worked out really well.

[Facilitator]: I think the strategy the most ineffective was in my mind the way we structured lecture, question, lecture, question, lecture, question, because there was really not a lot of time to get into the questions and make them come alive. [...] I was wondering about, like I was just saying, about students' interactions with each other and I think that part of that would be (a) the teacher stepping back and (b) having a lot more time because the discussion questions made it so short and so possibly an entire discussion with no lecture. So it might just be the question and a couple of talking points or something.

Instead of having a lecture, the focus should be moved onto the discussion portion of future events. To prioritize the discussion and stimulate engagement, the facilitator frequently asked provocative questions.

[Facilitator]: I also think that in the second discussion, this week's discussion about Universal Design Learning, we asked more provocative questions. So we moved away from simply agreeing with students or praising students for participation and tried to probe more, what do you mean by this or could you give me an example for that. I think that really promoted the flow of the discussion as well.

[Host]: I agree.

Troubleshooting in Private Chat

In Event 2, the facilitator initially started troubleshooting in the private chat, but once it became clear that the issue could not be resolved quickly, the facilitator switched to private chat to avoid interference with the ongoing event.

[Facilitator]: And also, I think that when I first was responding to R., I was trying to help her problem-solve. I was doing this in the general chat, and then other people chimed in. And to my mind there's nothing worse than being singled out as having tech problems and no one else does and then you know you're like you're trying to fix it and trying to be innocuous. And I think the instant messaging hopefully helped and I was able to carry on a conversation with her and I did screen-capture the conversation with her. She was pretty grateful for that. I just added, you know, when you said something that wasn't on your slide or when someone spoke out loud, I would just type in a little bit.

[Host]: That's great because I could see her dropping out of the conversation altogether and I'm honestly surprised that she didn't.

Division of Roles

The host and the facilitator next discussed their division of roles and responsibilities. The facilitator, in particular, was mindful of the host's role as the participants' instructor and of her own role as a "guest". Yet, the facilitator was also intent on promoting interaction and often took the initiative of asking follow-up questions. The addition of voice was perceived as a clear benefit to moving the discussion forward and making it more personal.

[Host]: I mentioned earlier it [comment: the division of roles] was different for this session. You were able to use your voice, actually the speech tool, to share out verbally rather than just in the text chat and you also did include your comments in the chat as well. And I think that worked out better, honestly.

[Facilitator]: I think so too. I think it's a little bit of an artificial situation to say, "OK the text chat person is never going to speak." But at the same time, I tried to defer to you always. So if you were talking I was not and I tried to keep in mind the support role rather than the co-facilitator role.

[Host]: And last night, you brought up a lot of good points. For me, it was really hard to go from my lecture and thinking about what I was going to say next and reading through the chat discussion. So having you as that facilitator and really boosting the chat facilitation was really beneficial to me.

[Facilitator]: Oh good, I'm glad. Because it was a little hard for me to tell whether I was sticking my nose in too much or whether that was helpful. But I kind of got the sense that managing the slides and your lecture and you said you couldn't access your notes for everything, that you had your hands full and also just being in charge of the students' administrative issues and making sure that everybody was there and did what they needed to do, that I could jump in the conversation and take up the slack.

[Host]: It worked out really well.

Critical Need for a Host and a Facilitator

One major difference between a face-to-face discussion and a synchronous discussion in a virtual 3D platform is the need for a facilitator, as well as a host, because there are many more tasks to attend to, as outlined in the excerpt below. During Event 2 the host was unable to get into Second Life and missed the first ten minutes of the event. The facilitator stepped into the role of host and started moderating the event right away.

[Host]: There must have been an update or something changed since our last session. For me that was less than 24 hours ago. I think I was coming into that level of frustration, it was hard to transition straight into a lecture. Luckily tonight I had all my notes lined up so that was ready to go but having the technical issues, that really threw me off.

[Facilitator]: I am always extremely thrown off when I have technical issues, but you recovered really nicely and between the two of us, it went well. I am not sure how with just one instructor how well things would go if there were any technical difficulties because you immediately get distracted whether it's your difficulties or your students' difficulties. And I think it's also worth noting you and I we were speaking, we were text-chatting in the main chat, we were instant-messaging in SL, and we were texting each other on our phones. The amount of technology to fix the technology was huge and also necessary.

During these ten minutes, the facilitator was unavailable for troubleshooting. Also, it was impossible for her to simultaneously display PowerPoint slides, provide input, ask guiding questions, and read and react to the participants' responses. Educators wishing to use virtual worlds in their teaching should be digitally fluent and able to multitask on various technical tools and devices. They should be prepared to assume the role of the host to moderate the teaching event and, if necessary, to switch to the role of the facilitator to keep the discussion on track. Both roles are critical to the success of a group discussion in a virtual world.

Using Voice to Increase Participants' Engagement

While the use of text chat may have been a more traditional approach to the synchronous discussion, encouraging voice responses from the participants did, indeed, increase engagement.

[Host]: I think the facilitator in this one we didn't have to push very much to keep the conversation going, I think it was pretty natural to them.

[Facilitator]: It went way better than the first ones.

[Host]: I agree. I think having them be aware that they might be chosen to speak held them more accountable for their responses.

Giving the facilitator a 'voice' also made it easier to create and maintain a conversation with the participants.

[Host]: During the second event, the lectures about UDL [Universal Design for Learning], we included the addition of the facilitator verbally reaching out to students and also having at least one student contribute to the discussion verbally for each question, which I thought was a pretty useful tool.

Finding more effective ways to increase the participants' engagement still remains one of the main challenges. One strategy could be to provide more opportunities for the participants to engage with each other more informally.

[Facilitator]: And I have to say before you were able to log on because there was some down time the students were actually talking to teach other via chat, which was the first time I'd seen them really actively engage with each other. In future studies, it would be super important to figure out how to get them to talk to each other and not just us.

Chat Logs

The chat logs substantiate the host's and the facilitator's accounts. An analysis of the chat logs showed that the host and the facilitator used various facilitation strategies, namely, they (a) greeted students both individually and as a group, (b) praised all contributions to the discussion, (c) elicited examples from the participants, (d) frequently used humor to help compensate for a lack of real-life social cues, (e) occasionally encouraged elaboration, (f) consistently used names to personalize replies, (g) elicited input by reaching out to participants by name, especially to the quiet ones, (h) provided specific feedback by indicating a participant's name, and (i) empathized with participants. Most of these strategies correspond with the guidelines recommended by Girvan and Savage (2013, 2019), for example, that the facilitator should be able to manage multiple threads simultaneously.

Limitations clearly include the small sample size. However, this study did not analyze the participants' reactions but focused on the host's and the facilitator's perspectives. Another limitation is that no group discussions were held in other semi-immersive virtual worlds, such as Active World, Open Sim, or ReactionGrid. Experiences with the communication modalities and group set-up could be very different in these virtual worlds. The ground rules were only tested in this specific setting with graduate students in a teacher education program. The ground rules need to be (re-)formulated and modified with a specific target group in mind. They need to take into account the participants' learning needs, technology background, and willingness to communicate in online spaces.

SOLUTIONS AND RECOMMENDATIONS

The host and the facilitator frequently had to demonstrate their multitasking skills, similar to the facilitators described by Wang et al. (2014) who "often found themselves communicating with the co-facilitators through text messaging and private backchannel audio communications" (p. 145). In the same vein, they had to help troubleshoot technical difficulties that some group members were experiencing while, at the same time, commenting on other group members' experiences shared in the discussion (Wang et al., 2014). The critical need for at least one facilitator was clearly demonstrated in multiple situations.

The host and the facilitators experienced a variety of challenges. First, the changes with regard to the communication modalities in Event 2 were not enough to boost the degree of interactivity among the participants, although communication in virtual worlds has been associated with higher levels of focused interaction (Gilbert et al., 2011) and student engagement (Claman, 2015).

Dividing the participants into smaller groups and having them discuss in break-out rooms would have been more effective than a whole-group discussion in the same virtual space for the entire event duration. Creating "satellites", as suggested by Schmeil et al. (2013), could have offered a way to increase interaction and participation and might also have motivated the quieter students to participate more.

In addition to the ground rules shown in Tables 2 to 4, the recommendations shown in Table 5 are based both on previous research and the host's and the facilitator's experiences described in this chapter. Educators may find these helpful in planning a virtual group discussion.

Table 5. Recommendations for group discussion facilitation

Themes	Recommendations
Critical need for facilitator(s)	At least one facilitator, in addition to the host, skilled in multitasking and trouble-shooting should moderate the group discussion.
Division of roles	To ensure smooth communication and avoid confusion among participants, the roles of the host and the facilitator should be distinct and clearly communicated at the beginning of a virtual event. Participants should know whom to contact and how if they need assistance with technical issues (private chat) or if they have a question about the content (group chat).
Adherence to ground rules	The ground rules should be communicated prior to the virtual group discussion. Should the participants fail to observe them, the facilitator should remind them of the ground rules, as needed.
Strategies to foster a sense of presence	Creating a seating arrangement that supports interaction (e.g., semi-circle couch), using voice to humanize the conversation, and choosing an event format that capitalizes the discussion aspect (rather than incorporating lecture components).
Communication modalities	The potential advantages and drawbacks of each communication modality (text vs. voice) and the impact on participation and interactivity should be carefully considered when planning a virtual group discussion. If participants use voice, a turn-taking policy will help to avoid "chatting over" each other.

FUTURE RESEARCH DIRECTIONS

More insights into the highly multimodal communication modalities of virtual worlds should be gained by researching a variety of virtual worlds offering different text, audio, and video modalities. In Active Worlds, for instance, text chat is not only posted to the chat window, as is the case in Second Life®, but it also appears above avatars' heads in the form of speech bubbles (Wigham & Chanier, 2015). To what extent different communication modalities impact the facilitator's role offers another avenue for investigation. Role rotation and role assignment (Jiang, 2017) may offer a way to increase participation and personal investment during synchronous group discussions.

The effectiveness of the facilitation of group discussions in virtual environments also depends on a facilitator's degree of cultural responsiveness. Online facilitators need to be familiar with the tenets of culturally responsive teaching (CRT). Further research is needed to explore how CRT skills interplay with online facilitation skills and what it takes to moderate multicultural online groups effectively. Synchronous group events in virtual worlds offer potential to establish inclusion in culturally diverse learning environments.

Colleges and universities increasingly work with fully immersive virtual reality. Over the past fifteen years, extensive educational research has been conducted in semi-immersive virtual environments, such as virtual worlds. Unique affordances and challenges have been discussed from multiple perspectives, resulting in multiple taxonomies. As a next step, research needs to continue investigating the potential of fully immersive virtual reality and its applicability for education at all levels.

CONCLUSION

This chapter has presented findings from group discussions and lectures set in Second Life® with participants enrolled in a graduate level technology class. The purpose is to replicate a lecture and discussion format in a virtual world in order to identify (in)effective facilitation strategies and potential challenges. The authors have described the lessons learned in the process of facilitating these virtual events and offer recommendations for the incorporation of virtual discussions for educational purposes.

The best practices that are discussed include a careful selection and orchestration of the communication modalities, a purposeful planning regarding the role of the host and the facilitator(s), strategies to promote participation and interactivity, and clear ground rules for all parties involved. A lack of interactivity emerged as the biggest challenge and prompted the authors to experiment with varied combinations of communication modalities, the increased use of voice chat, higher involvement of the facilitator, and a modified set-up of the activity. Finally, the chapter also discusses which strategies might help to create a sense of presence when facilitating a group discussion in a virtual world. Creating a sense of immediacy, for example by chatting in real time and getting instant feedback; seeing each others' avatars and movements; and creating a relaxing, low-stress environment emerged as the key factors.

Given the increasing use of 3D online platforms for educational purposes, educators should continue to experiment using virtual group discussions to identify the factors that make such events successful and meaningful. Education needs to have virtual environments as an option to provide a different mode of educational platforms. Virtual environments not only eliminate physical boundaries, but they also provide students with opportunities to feel more present during class time as they move around as avatars and interact with each other and with the virtual environment. Especially in times when humans are not allowed to interact freely, such as we are experiencing now due to a global pandemic, and in times of school lockdowns, educators still need to make sure to provide opportunities for collaborative learning, communities of inquiry, experiential and exploratory learning, and interaction.

ACKNOWLEDGMENT

The authors are grateful to Prof. Hajime Nishimura for his kind permission to let the project team use *Science Circle* for the virtual group discussions and lectures.

REFERENCES

Claman, F. L. (2015). The impact of multiuser virtual environments on student engagement. *Nurse Education in Practice*, *15*(1), 13–16. doi:10.1016/j.nepr.2014.11.006 PMID:25532889

Dalgarno, B., & Lee, M. J. W. (2009). What are the learning affordances of 3-D virtual environments? *British Journal of Educational Technology, 41*(1), 10–32. doi:10.1111/j.1467-8535.2009.01038.x

Garrison, D. R. (2009). Communities of inquiry in online learning. In P. L. Rogers (Ed.), *Encyclopedia of distance learning* (2nd ed., pp. 352–355). IGI Global. doi:10.4018/978-1-60566-198-8.ch052

Gilbert, R. L., Murphy, N. A., & Avalos, M. C. (2011). Communication patterns and satisfaction levels in three-dimensional versus real-life intimate relationships. *Cyberpsychology, Behavior, and Social Networking, 14*(10), 585–589. doi:10.1089/cyber.2010.0468 PMID:21381970

Girvan, C., & Savage, T. (2013). Guidelines for conducting text based interviews in virtual worlds. In Understanding learning in virtual worlds (pp. 21-40). Springer. doi:10.1007/978-1-4471-5370-2_2

Girvan, C., & Savage, T. (2019). Virtual worlds: A new environment for constructionist learning. *Computers in Human Behavior, 99*, 396–414. doi:10.1016/j.chb.2019.03.017

Gunawardena, C., & Zittle, F. (1997). Social presence as a predictor of satisfaction within a computer mediated conferencing environment. *American Journal of Distance Education, 11*(3), 8–26. doi:10.1080/08923649709526970

Gunawardena, C. N. (1995). Social presence theory and implications for interaction and collaborative learning in computer conferences. *International Journal of Educational Telecommunications, 1*(2/3), 147–166.

Hostetter, C., & Busch, M. (2013). Community matters: Social presence and learning outcomes. *The Journal of Scholarship of Teaching and Learning, 13*(1), 77–86.

Jiang, W. (2017). Interdependence of roles, role rotation, and sense of community in an online course. *Distance Education, 38*(1), 84–105. doi:10.1080/01587919.2017.1299564

Konstantinidis, A. (2017). Using SmallWorlds to enhance social presence, group cohesion, and group identity in an online postgraduate course. In G. Panconesi & M. Guida (Eds.), *Handbook of Research on Collaborative Teaching Practice in Virtual Learning Environments* (pp. 92–110). IGI Global. doi:10.4018/978-1-5225-2426-7.ch005

Lambert, J. L., & Fisher, J. L. (2013). Community of inquiry framework: Establishing community in an online course. *Journal of Interactive Online Learning, 12*(1), 1–16.

Liou, H. C. (2012). The roles of Second Life in a college computer-assisted language learning (CALL) course in Taiwan, ROC. *Computer Assisted Language Learning, 25*(4), 365–382. doi:10.1080/09588221.2011.597766

Lowenthal, P. R., & Dunlap, J. C. (2018). Investigating students' perceptions of instructional strategies to establish social presence. *Distance Education, 39*(3), 281–298. doi:10.1080/01587919.2018.1476844

McVey, M. H. (2008). Observations of expert communicators in immersive virtual worlds: Implications for synchronous discussion. *ALT-J. Research in Learning Technology, 16*(3), 173–180. doi:10.3402/rlt.v16i3.10896

Mount, N. J., Chambers, C., Weaver, D., & Priestnall, G. (2009). Learner immersion engagement in the 3D virtual world: Principles emerging from the DELVE project. *Innovation in Teaching and Learning in Information and Computer Sciences*, *8*(3), 40–55. doi:10.11120/ital.2009.08030040

Murgado-Armenteros, E. M., Torres-Ruiz, F. J., & Vega-Zamora, M. (2012). Differences between on-line and face to face focus groups, viewed through two approaches. *Journal of Theoretical and Applied Electronic Commerce Research*, *7*(2), 73–86. doi:10.4067/S0718-18762012000200008

Nussli, N., & Oh, K. (2017). Field research in Second Life: Strategies for discussion group facilitation and benefits of participation. In G. Panconesi & M. Guida (Eds.), *Handbook of Research on Collaborative Teaching Practice in Virtual Learning Environments* (pp. 348–373). IGI Global. doi:10.4018/978-1-5225-2426-7.ch018

Nussli, N., Oh, K., Cuadro, N., & Kaye, M. (2019). An investigation into the effect of communication modality on learner satisfaction and mental effort expended during a lecture and discussion event in Second life - a 3D virtual world. In K. Yang (Ed.), *Cases on Immersive Virtual Reality Techniques* (pp. 89–123). IGI Global. doi:10.4018/978-1-5225-5912-2.ch005

Peterson, M. (2006). Learner interaction management in an avatar and chat-based virtual world. *Computer Assisted Language Learning*, *19*(1), 79–103. doi:10.1080/09588220600804087

Prude, M. A. (2013). A classroom of bunnies, blimps, and werewolves. *ASIANetwork Exchange*, *20*(2), 1–12.

Schmeil, A., Hasler, B., Peachy, A., de Freitas, S., & Nehmzow, C. (2013). Do virtual worlds support engaging social conferencing? In Understanding learning in virtual worlds (pp. 165-179). Springer. doi:10.1007/978-1-4471-5370-2_9

Siriaraya, P., & Ang, C. S. (2012). Age differences in the perception of social presence in the use of 3D virtual world for social interaction. *Interacting with Computers*, *24*(4), 280–291. doi:10.1016/j.intcom.2012.03.003

Tu, C. H. (2001). How Chinese perceive social presence: An examination of interaction in online learning environment. *Educational Media International*, *38*(1), 45–60. doi:10.1080/09523980010021235

Wang, C. X., Anstadt, S., Goldman, J., & Lefaiver, M. L. M. (2014). Facilitating group discussions in Second Life. *MERLOT Journal of Online Learning and Teaching*, *10*(1), 139–152.

Wang, F., & Burton, J. K. (2013). Second Life in education: A review of publications from its launch to 2011. *British Journal of Educational Technology*, *44*(3), 357–371. doi:10.1111/j.1467-8535.2012.01334.x

Wei, C.-W., Chen, N.-S., & Kinshuk, S. (2012). A model for social presence in online classrooms. *Educational Technology Research and Development*, *60*(3), 529–545. doi:10.100711423-012-9234-9

Wigert, B., de Vreede, G., Boughzala, I., & Bououd, I. (2012). The role of the facilitator in virtual world collaboration. *Journal of Virtual Worlds Research*, *5*(2), 1–18. doi:10.4101/jvwr.v5i2.6225

Wigham, C. R., & Chanier, T. (2013). A study of verbal and nonverbal communication in Second Life – the ARCHI21 experience. *ReCALL*, *25*(1), 63–84. doi:10.1017/S0958344012000250

Wigham, C. R., & Chanier, T. (2015). Interactions between text chat and audio modalities for L2 communication and feedback in the synthetic world Second Life. *Computer Assisted Language Learning*, *28*(3), 260–283. doi:10.1080/09588221.2013.851702

Wilkes, S. F. (2016). Communication modality, learning, and Second Life. In S. Gregory, M. J. W. Lee, B. Dalgarno, & B. Tynan (Eds.), *Learning in virtual worlds: Research and applications* (pp. 43–65). Athabasca University Press.

ADDITIONAL READING

Champion, K., & Gunnlaugson, O. (2018). Fostering generative conversation in higher education course discussion boards. *Innovations in Education and Teaching International*, *55*(6), 704–712.

Conrad, M. (2011). Leaving the lindens: Teaching in virtual worlds of other providers. In *Proceedings of Researching Learning in Immersive Virtual Environments (ReLIVE): 28*. Open University.

Conrad, M., Hassan, A., Koshy, L., Kanamgotov, A., & Christopoulos, A. (2017). Strategies and challenges to facilitate situated learning in virtual worlds post-second life. *Computers in Entertainment*, *15*(1). *Article*, *3*, 1–9.

Gallego, M. D., Bueno, S., & Noyes, J. (2015). Second Life adoption in education: A motivational model based on uses and gratifications theory. *Computers & Education*, *100*, 81–93. doi:10.1016/j.compedu.2016.05.001

Girvan, C. (2018). What is a virtual world? Definition and classification. *Educational Technology Research and Development*, *66*(5), 1087–1100. doi:10.100711423-018-9577-y

Mantziou, O., Papachristos, N., & Mikropoulos, M. (2018). Learning activities as enactments of learning affordances in MUVEs: A review-based classification. *Education and Information Technologies*, *23*(4), 1737–1765. doi:10.100710639-018-9690-x

Martin, F., Ritzhaupt, A., Kumar, S., & Budhrani, K. (2019). Award-winning faculty online teaching practices: Course design, assessment and evaluation, and facilitation. *The Internet and Higher Education*, *42*, 34–43. doi:10.1016/j.iheduc.2019.04.001

Merchant, Z., Goetz, E. T., Cifuentes, L., Keeney-Kennicutt, W., & Davis, T. J. (2014). Effectiveness of virtual reality-based instruction on students' learning outcomes in K-12 and higher education: A meta-analysis. *Computers & Education*, *70*, 29–40. doi:10.1016/j.compedu.2013.07.033

Panconesi, G., & Guida, M. (2017). *Handbook of Research on Collaborative Teaching Practice in Virtual Learning Environments*. IGI Global. doi:10.4018/978-1-5225-2426-7

Qian, Y. (Ed.). (2018). *Integrating multi-user virtual environments in modern classrooms*. IGI Global. doi:10.4018/978-1-5225-3719-9

Richards, D., & Taylor, M. (2015). A comparison of learning gains when using a 2D simulation tool versus a 3D virtual world: An experiment to find the right representation involving the marginal value theorem. *Computers & Education*, *86*, 157–171. doi:10.1016/j.compedu.2015.03.009

Salter, S., Douglas, T., & Kember, D. (2017). Comparing face-to-face and asynchronous online communication as mechanisms for critical reflective dialogue. *Educational Action Research*, *25*(5), 790–805. doi:10.1080/09650792.2016.1245626

Tax'en, G., & Naeve, A. (2002). A system for exploring open issues in VR-based education. *Computers & Graphics*, *26*(4), 593–598. doi:10.1016/S0097-8493(02)00112-7

Winograd, D. (2000). *The effects of trained moderation in online asynchronous distance learning*. Paper presented at the Association for Educational Communication and Technology, Denver, CO.

KEY TERMS AND DEFINITIONS

Active Worlds: An online virtual world that allows synchronous communication via text chat and voice, manipulation of three-dimensional objects, and real-time navigation. Users are visually represented by avatars.

Asynchronous: Any type of communication and online interaction that does not happen in real time. A discussion board where students can post their contributions any time is an example of asynchronous communication, whereas the opposite (i.e., synchronous) would be a live lecture, for example, via a video conference or in a virtual world setting where avatars meet and interact in real time.

Communication Modality: A variety of input channels for communication purposes (i.e., text chat, voice chat, video chat).

Second Life®: An online virtual world where users' avatars communicate and interact with each other in real time using text chat, video, and voice. Three-dimensional objects can be manipulated, designed, and built, individually or collaboratively in a team.

Social Cues: Any signs, gestures, features, communication modalities or tools that help to humanize communication, including smiles, waving, laughs, touch, gestures of politeness, acts of sharing, signs of empathy, humor, showing interest, sharing personal opinion, etc.

Social Presence: Commonly referred to as the feeling of being "there" when immersed in a virtual environment.

Synchronous: "Live" communication, for example in a video conference or a group discussion in a virtual world (opposite of asynchronous) where contributors engage with each other in real time.

UDL: Universal design for learning is a theoretical framework designed to acknowledge learner diversity and to support all learners in achieving school success. The principles of UDL encompass multiple means of engagement, representation, action, and expression.

Virtual Discussions in 3D: Group discussions set in a virtual world, for example, for educational purposes.

Virtual World: Shared and simulated online spaces inhabited and designed by their users who are represented as avatars and who engage in communication and interaction with other avatars.

Zoom: A web-based videoconference system with break-out rooms, audio- and video-recordings functions, and digital whiteboard. Popular with educators for synchronous online teaching at all grade levels.

Chapter 6
Developing an Immersive Virtual Classroom: TeachLivE – A Case Study

Kathleen M. Ingraham
University of Central Florida, USA

Annette Romualdo
University of Central Florida, USA

Angelica Fulchini Scruggs
University of Central Florida, USA

Eric Imperiale
University of Central Florida, USA

Lisa Dieker
https://orcid.org/0000-0002-0789-580X
University of Central Florida, USA

Charles E. Hughes
https://orcid.org/0000-0002-2528-3380
University of Central Florida, USA

ABSTRACT

As virtual reality (VR) technologies continue to improve and become more accessible, educators are increasingly incorporating VR learning experiences in teacher education contexts. This chapter is a case study of TeachLivE™, a virtual classroom platform designed for practicing teaching in a safe virtual space. This chapter describes the system, development, and challenges faced when incorporating immersive VR technologies. Recommendations are provided for future research, development, use, and facilitation of immersive VR learning experiences.

DOI: 10.4018/978-1-7998-4960-5.ch006

INTRODUCTION

As virtual reality (VR) technologies continue to advance, opportunities emerge for simulation training to take advantage of new affordances to improve the effectiveness and efficiency of virtual learning experiences. This chapter will examine the development cycle and challenges of incorporating newer immersive VR technologies into existing VR platforms using the TeachLivE™ simulation platform as a case example. The objective of this chapter is to describe how new immersive VR technologies have been introduced to the platform and how these technologies have affected development, system use, and teacher learning. The authors also describe some of the challenges encountered in using an immersive VR system as well as recommendations for future research, use, and development.

BACKGROUND

The immersive VR classroom can provide a dynamic medium to promote meaningful learning. Since the early 1990s, VR has been promoted as a vehicle to facilitate learning across subject domains (Helsel, 1992; Psotka, 1995). The blank canvas nature of the virtual classroom enables developers and users to adapt the classroom, with "active participation, high interactivity and individualization" (Mikropoulous & Natsis, 2011, p. 770) as integral components of the dynamic space.

One such use of the virtual environment has been to prepare preservice teachers for the 21st century, accountability-driven classroom. As background, teacher preparation programs (TPP) ready novice educators for placement; well-prepared beginning educators enter the classroom with a strong background in evidence-based instructional practices and classroom management techniques (Brownell et al., 2010; Every Student Succeeds Act, 2015; Scheeler et al., 2016).

However, high rates of teacher turnover and burnout indicate novice teachers often are under-prepared for the challenge (Carver-Thomas & Darling-Hammond, 2019). First-year teachers may struggle to implement best-practice in both instructional methods and behavior management (Ingersoll, 2001; Cochran-Smith, et al., 2012; Hong, 2010; Lankford et al., 2002). To mitigate this gap, researchers at the University of Central Florida (UCF) implemented an innovative means to prepare beginning teachers (Dieker et al., 2008). Within a VR simulator (TeachLivE™), participants are immersed into a classroom of virtual students. The abstract spaces of the physical room fade (Mikropoulous & Natsis, 2011), and beginning educators use the classroom and its avatar residents to rehearse and hone research-based strategies of teaching practice (Dieker et al., 2007; Dieker et al., 2008; Dieker et al., 2014; Dieker et al., 2017).

This section discusses the evolution of VR, components and characteristics of current VR systems, and VR use in education. VR is described as an interactive virtual environment simulating real-life experiences accomplished in one of two ways: non-immersive and immersive. Non-immersive VR is displayed through traditional media or technologies, such as computer, keyboard, mouse, and/or screen. Users in the non-immersive environment are not required to wear any special equipment (Freina & Ott, 2015; Suh & Prophet, 2018).

Whereas, an immersive VR experience requires the user to wear specialized equipment to experience the simulation. As researchers began to promote VR for the education space, Psotka (1995) promoted the fully-immersive experience for its unique characteristics, including participants' feelings of control and immediacy with its use. Once immersed, the virtual world becomes real-life as participants experience "the feeling of 'being there' or presence" (p. 405). A fading of the external environment promotes feelings of control over one's surroundings (Mikropoulous & Natsis, 2011). User's perception of presence is central to immersion through head and eye movements within a head-mounted display within the VR environment (Hayes et al., 2013; Jung et al., 2018; Winn, 1993).

The Evolution of Virtual Reality

Attempts to immerse audiences have taken on many forms throughout history, each rising in complexity along with emerging technology. In the nineteenth century, panoramic paintings attempted to immerse the viewer by dominating their field of vision with the massive width of their canvasses. Later, stereoscopes like the ViewMaster represented early prototypes for head-mounted displays intended to command the audience's sense of sight (Whiteman, 2009). In the 1950s, a cinematographer named Morton Heilig developed what he called the Sensorama. It was a stationary booth for one person that featured stereo speakers, a stereographic 3D display, fans, odor generators, and a vibrating chair (Heilig, 1962). Though the Sensorama was still unable to adapt to the viewer's movement, Heilig made a revolutionary attempt to create a completely immersive sensory experience granting him the unofficial title of the "Father of Virtual Reality". By the 1960s, head-mounted displays became more capable of representing a viewer's natural vision by correlating the visual input to their head movements via a motion tracking system (Sutherland, 1968). At this time in history, the equipment and the computations necessary to simulate a three-dimensional, virtual world were cumbersome, uncomfortable, and slow: all hindrances to immersion.

While Mr. Heilig's invention may have later dubbed him "Father of Virtual Reality," not until the late 1980s did the term "Virtual Reality" enter the popular lexicon to describe this research field. Jaron Lanier, the founder of the Visual Programming Lab (VPL), popularized the term "Virtual Reality" as his company went on to develop innovations in VR gear. His company was the first to sell VR goggles, which they called the "EyePhone Head Mounted Display" (Pantelidis, 1993). Not only were these goggles lighter than previous iterations of head tracking visual displays, but they also included headphone speakers that could emit 3D directed audio. Lanier's company also developed the "Dataglove," a wearable glove that introduced *haptics* to the VR experience by simulating the user's sense of touch (Pantelidis, 1993). With these devices, three out of five reality-defining senses could be engaged within a wholly artificial environment. By the 1990s, VR devices were appearing in public arcades, represented in mainstream movies, and as consumer-level devices such as Nintendo's Virtual Boy (Zachara & Zagal, 2009). After a lull in development and public interest, VR reemerged in the 21st century, bolstered by advancements in high-density displays, smaller and more powerful 3D computing devices, a drastic reduction in cost, and an enthusiastic and innovative video game industry. Today, products like the Oculus Rift S, PSVR, and the HTC Vive are common, more affordable, and provide a viable platform for expanding immersion in all forms of entertainment, communication, and education. With these newer platforms in mind, the authors provide a description of some of the major components and characteristics of these systems.

Components and Characteristics of Current VR Systems

Headsets

Most interactions with an immersive VR environment involve the use of a VR headset. Virtual reality equipment manufacturers are constantly innovating in order to compete in a quickly evolving marketplace, balancing technological advancements with affordability. As a result, the headsets currently available vary greatly in performance, price, and quality of the user experience. There are three common forms: Mobile, Tethered, or Standalone.

Mobile

With mobile setups, a peripheral device, such as a smartphone or mobile game system, makes the VR calculations. They usually include only one motion controller and are restricted to three degrees of freedom (DOF) for both the headset and motion controller. They have insufficient active sensors to track 3D positioning in space and have a lower threshold for VR computations, but they are also cheap, lightweight, and unencumbered with heavy cables. One such example of a mobile setup is the Samsung Gear VR (Powered by Oculus, requires a smartphone for operation, preferably Samsung devices) (Samsung, 2019). Google Daydream View is similar but more versatile regarding smartphone compatibility (Daydream, 2019). Other examples embody a do-it-yourself perspective and are folded out of cardboard, thus making them the cheapest possible option (Olson et al., 2011). Google Cardboard and Nintendo Labo VR Kit fit this description, the former requiring a smartphone for use (Google Cardboard, 2019) with the latter requiring a Nintendo Switch (Nintendo Labo, 2019).

Tethered

These headsets are physically connected via cables to a dedicated PC or (in the case of PSVR) a PlayStation. The cables can make them awkward to operate but having the processing power offloaded to a separate device not strapped to the head makes for a VR experience that can be complex and responsive. The dedicated displays are superior to smartphone enabled displays in image fidelity and external sensors or outward-facing cameras allow for 6DOF motion tracking. Some common examples include the Oculus Rift S, which was purchased by Facebook in 2014, making it a well-funded producer of consumer-level VR (Oculus, 2019). Another example that is popular with gamers, is the PlayStation VR; the proliferation of PlayStation game systems already in use and affordable pricing make the barrier for entry extremely low (Playstation VR, 2019).

Standalone

Standalone systems require no peripheral devices such as a smartphone, game system, or even a computer, making them truly standalone. Most are considered entry level VR for newcomers and are limited to 3DOF, such as the Oculus Go (Oculus Go, 2019). New advancements have brought forth a new breed of standalone setups, like the Oculus Quest and the HTC Vive Focus Plus. These new devices outperform their standalone peers by being capable of 6DOF without the need for external sensors or connection cables (Oculus Quest, 2019; VIVE Focus Plus, 2019).

VR Treadmills and Gloves

360-degree Treadmills

Incorporating VR treadmills and gloves to the VR system allows for motion in a confined space. With tethered or even wireless headsets, physical limits to the virtual space can be imposed within the limits of the sensor space or the length of the connecting cord. Using a 360-degree treadmill, a participant can essentially run in place while registering as free movement within the virtual space. Various models include foot-tracking sneakers to determine movement direction and speed and/or waist height sensors to determine crouch or jump height. One example is the Virtuix Omni Treadmill (Virtuix Omni, 2019).

VR Gloves

The market has seen an upsurge in several types of VR gloves designed for specific uses. Some gloves simply track finger movement for the purposes of handling 3D manipulatables or driving robotic machinery. Other gloves track finger movement for recording finger animation in conjunction with motion capture or performance capture software. Haptic VR gloves apply vibrations, motions, or other forces to simulate the sensation of touch. Some examples include the Manus VR family of Manus Prime VR, Performance/Motion Capture, or Haptic gloves (HaptX, 2019; Manus VR, 2019).

As we consider these components of VR systems, defining these experiences in higher education provides a context for use in this space. Far from being a homogeneous technology, VR experiences can be structured in many ways.

Structures of VR Systems

Window on World

This system maintains a distance between the user and the virtual world by existing through a window of access such as a television, desktop monitor, laptop computer, tablet, or other mobile devices. This type of system is commonly used as an interactive portal for simulation training scenarios.

Telepresence

With less of an emphasis on virtual constructs, this system's focus is on presence at a distance. Using VR equipment or more conventional audio/visual interfaces, the user remotely operates sensors and/or equipment such as drones, bomb disposal robots, or deep-water exploration vehicles.

Immersive System

This system is the one most often associated with VR. In this system, the user wears a VR headset that translates the virtual 3D perspective according to the user's head movement and usually includes one or two hand-held motion controllers for interacting with the environment. With this system, a user's sense of sight and sound are completely informed by the VR headset, resulting in a greater detachment from the outside world and resulting in an enhanced sense of immersion.

Mixed Reality (MR) and Augmented Reality (AR)

With MR/AR, the virtual is intertwined with the user's existing reality. Computer generated inputs are brought into the user's view of the real world via peripheral glasses, or through the viewport of a hand-held camera such as a smartphone. Devices like the Magic Leap One incorporate sensors that detect real world objects to intersect with the virtual objects in space and occludes the virtual objects accordingly (Magic Leap 1, 2019). Another type of application resembles a heads-up display such as a fighter pilot's helmet visor, where the computer-generated content is displayed over the user's field of vision.

With these technologies becoming increasingly available and accessible, the question becomes how are educators using these technologies?

VR Use in Education

Helsel, in 1992, began discussing VR with educators, in an effort to include the school community in planning for VR's future use in education settings. She felt educators were "responding powerfully to the notion of virtual reality curriculum" (p. 38), and claimed educators expressed an "almost visceral" understanding of the potential for VR in the classroom. Helsel argued VR would facilitate a revolutionary change in instructional practice and student learning; textbooks would be relic, and text-based learning would transition to symbol and imagery-based curriculum. Moreover, she predicted the visual-processing center of the brain would surpass text decoding as the means to information processing.

Helsel concluded her manuscript by urging educators not to leave VR to the computer science field, and to instead involve themselves in the VR development process. Yet, two decades later, VR remains a largely unused means to increase student engagement and learning, within the K-12 education system. To Helsel's point regarding computer science, Freina and Ott (2015) found over 60% of immersive VR education literature, within a two-year time frame (2013-2014), centered around the university-level computer science domain. Further, Freina and Ott found educational VR largely unused for commonplace learning, and instead primarily utilized for scenarios not easily accessed - such as dangerous situations, historical events, physically inaccessible environments, and ethically problematic events (i.e. surgery, fire-fighting, and time travel).

Recently, Kaminska and colleagues (2019) provide an overview of applications of VR in education. Within this overview, they propose three types of VR use in educational environments: (1) VR to present knowledge within a subject domain - often presented on a static display, (2) VR presented through Kinect (Zhang et al., 2018) or MYO Gesture-type platform (Pilatásig et al., 2018); used to impart skill-based knowledge, such as work-safety training, and (3) immersive VR environment, with wearable devices, as a means to overcome challenging tasks, such as medically-based scenarios. According to their survey of literature, the majority of educational VR software centers around health-related or STEM fields; educational domains included are engineering, medical, space technology, mathematics, and general education (the authors used virtual field trips as an example of general education). Within the review, the authors promote VR as a powerful tool to support learning, including in support of diverse learning needs. Much like Helsel (1992), Kaminska and colleagues (2019) conclude by encouraging educators to "embrace" and "prepare for" the immersive VR revolution, particularly when educating digital natives: Generation Z.

Also, of note when considering the current state of VR in education, Suh and Prophet (2018) conducted a systematic review of immersive VR technology research. Like Kaminska and colleagues (2019), Suh and Prophet (2018) report immersive VR is primarily used across science, engineering, and medical domains - with most studies conducted within higher education levels. Their summary of the research concludes: immersive VR enhances motivation and conceptual blending in the education setting.

TEACHLIVE™

A recent and expanding use of VR in the educational domain of teacher education occurred with the creation of a simulation system at UCF. This section provides background on the TeachLivE™ virtual simulation system along with past and current uses of TeachLivE™ in a non-immersive VR environment. The authors provide an overview of future expansion of TeachLivE™, including insight into an immersive version of the simulation, built in the HTC Vive HMD.

As overview, educators in TeachLivE™ practice teaching a diverse group of digital student avatars in a virtual classroom environment. This environment can be accessed through an immersive head-mounted display (HMD), on a large screen or projector, or on any personal computing device equipped with a microphone and camera.

Stepping into the TeachLivE™ virtual classroom, a facilitator assists teachers in putting on and adjusting the HMD or in setting up materials in front of a projector or large screen. In cases where teachers are connecting remotely on a personal computing device or smartphone, facilitators assist teachers in connecting to a device view of the virtual classroom. Teachers can look around the classroom and speak to a group of five to six students either within the HMD or on the screen. The students are controlled remotely by an interactor who provides vocal responses and controls the physical movement of the students. Having a human actively controlling the virtual students allows the students to respond to any lesson or choice the teacher makes during the rehearsal session. Using a webcam, the interactor can hear and see the teacher and react to verbal and non-verbal teaching choices.

To further improve practice, an expert coach can pause the simulation at any point to give feedback to the teacher. The teacher can choose to either replay a moment without the virtual students remembering their previous actions, or they can continue with their lesson. In this way teachers can practice skills that range from identifying and addressing content misconceptions, to practicing classroom management strategies, to differentiating instruction for individual student needs. Coaches also can pre-plan specific content or behavioral challenges for teachers to practice.

Historically, the majority of TeachLivE™ simulations have been provided through a virtual environment in which teachers interact with the virtual classroom on a screen - such as a projector, a laptop computer, desktop computer, smartphone, or large screen display. This VR experience facilitates meeting the "needs of teachers in high-end university laboratories, at regional centers, at their schools and in their homes" (Dieker et al., 2007, p.7). Within this platform, participants and researchers are not required to have special equipment, beyond what is typical within these settings (computer and internet access). Within the simulation, users, coaches, and researchers can collect simple multi-modal data, as well as record and catalog performance. For teachers and other professionals who seek to change behavior within the simulation, the user-friendly, transportable experience facilitates ease of documentation, after action review, and (ultimately) improves development within the profession.

With purposeful design, developers created an experience that affords an open canvas of scenarios. The platform of TeachLivE™ has been host to a myriad of scenarios, ranging across age, experience, and background; including coaching and feedback, professional development, instructional development, and practicing real-life scenarios. Specific examples of usage include:

- Provide in-action coaching and self-reflection for pre-service special education teacher practices
- Address bullying behaviors
- Simulate lock-down scenarios (active assailant drills)

- Increase parent advocacy of parents of children with disabilities; particularly in IEP process
- Increase student exposure to virtual environments, and thereby spark interest in STEM fields
- Practice teaching inquiry-based science
- Increase praise and response rate
- Utilize assessment data to drive instruction
- Illustrate evidence-based English Learner (EL) instruction
- Increase novice teacher problem-solving skills
- Manage classroom dynamics and behaviors
- Practice parent-teacher conference scenarios
- Navigate first day of school management tasks
- Demonstrate evidence-based literacy practices

A benefit of the non-immersive environment is the transportable ease-of-use, and the ability to rehearse real-life scenarios. Ease of use is critical in reaching in-service teachers who may have limited time and willingness to engage with activities difficult to access or use. Thus, a simulation experience designed to help address some root causes of teacher attrition should avoid adding to teacher stress. Within the education field, teacher attrition (teachers leaving the profession) is an urgent crisis, which requires immediate response (Barnes et al., 2007; Ryan et al., 2017). Development of the TeachLivE™ simulation platform was in direct response to waning teacher preparation enrollment and rising teacher attrition. TeachLivE™ was launched to provide an environment in which preservice teachers could safely and effectively develop evidence-based practices of the profession, before stepping into the K-12 classroom. The original and continued vision of TeachLivE™ researchers is to facilitate virtual rehearsal, involving high stakes situations, without risking the loss of valuable resources, such as money, time, and people (Dieker et al., 2013). The team continues to develop the simulated experience with an array of scenarios where mistakes are welcome and discrete skills are coached in real-time.

An additional benefit of the TeachLivE™ VR environment is its capacity to provide access to scenarios uncommon or difficult to practice in a real classroom. Within simulation, traditional obstacles to quality teacher preparation may be overcome. One such obstacle is limited preservice educator classroom experience within diverse classroom environments. The brick-and-mortar nature of TPP may limit experiences to school systems immediately surrounding the providing university. For the novice educator, juggling the myriad of classroom needs while trying to facilitate student learning can be overwhelming. The TeachLivE™ environment can be delivered remotely to rural or distant areas so preservice teachers can practice situations that uncommon in their geographic location. Within TeachLivE™, teacher educators can uncouple pieces of classroom challenges into achievable exercises. Novice teachers can individually rehearse each challenge, before attempting to meet the needs of an entire classroom. This adaptive nature of simulation enables university teacher preparation programs to expand preservice teachers' experiences, allowing for scenario rehearsal, and ultimate educator excellence in practice - even before placement into the brick-and-mortar classroom.

Another obstacle to quality teacher preparation is finding effective in-service educators who can model and mentor evidence-based teaching (Hobson et al., 2009; Jones, 2009). Adding an inexperienced student-teacher to an already busy classroom is a big ask. Complicating the mentoring process in a live classroom, supervisory teachers cannot pause student learning to coach each poor interaction or inadequate presentation of content. As a result, novice teachers may move into the profession while struggling to manage their classrooms, leading to burnout and career abandonment. By coupling the simulation with live coaching, preservice teachers are mentored through the basics of classroom management and pedagogical practice. This coaching feature allows teacher educators to mentor preservice teachers in instructional practice. Simulations can be guided, rehearsed, paused, and reflected upon - all within a supervised, safe learning environment. The novice educator is afforded the opportunity for apprenticeship, even before stepping foot into an internship (real-life classroom). For example, the teacher educator or coach can prepare a simulation involving a student with a disability who may need additional instructional interventions. Through the simulation, a novice teacher can navigate implementing evidence-based practices of intervention to meet the diverse needs of the avatar student. Concurrent with the simulation, the instructional coach can facilitate participant learning through ongoing and reflective feedback on practice.

This coaching process is validated within simulation, as demonstrated through After Action Review (AAR); the preservice teachers can experience valuable returns on improving teaching practice [Hanoun & Nahavandi, 2018, provide a review of the After-Action Review process]. As mentioned, within the simulated environment, teacher educators have used TeachLivE™ to prepare preservice teachers to improve instructional and pedagogical practice. The VR setting has been shown to improve practice; the efficiency of behavior modification within the simulator is supported: Empirical evidence indicates five minutes in a simulator can provide the emotional equivalent of a 30-minute in-person interaction, in terms of emotional taxation on a participant (Alexander et al., 2005; Dieker et al., 2008). Also, four 10-minute simulator sessions on a specific effective teaching practice can change at least one critical teaching behavior (Dieker et al., 2014). In sum, the use of TeachLivE simulation allows experiential learning to take place via realistic, specific scenarios that give learners an opportunity to practice alternative skills and learn from mistakes in a safe environment (Chini et al., 2014).

TEACHLIVE™: IMMERSIVE VR

As improving professional identity and craft becomes increasingly relevant for educators throughout their careers, the adaptive data-gathering components (such as capacity to record eye tracking, facial expressions, and body positioning) within simulation prove critical to improving evidence-based practices in the classroom. Researchers now have the capacity to gather both automated and manual data of participant performance within the simulator; these data may be analyzed to pinpoint pedagogical and instructional areas of need. This capacity may be greater realized within the immersive simulated environment, as full immersion can provide preservice teachers an even greater feeling of presence in the scenario.

The immersive virtual environment provides an experience in which the user can find "specific sense of self-location within it, can move her or his head and eyes to explore it, feels that the space surrounds her or him, and can interact with the objects in it" (Psotka,1995, p. 406). Kaminska et al. (2019) promote a definition of VR found in technology literature:

"interaction + immersion + imagination" (p. 2). Although not widely used in education environments, research has demonstrated the immersive VR experience "can enhance education in at least three ways: by enabling multiple perspectives, situated learning, and transfer" (Dede, 2009, p. 66). Suh and Prophet (2018) agree: Within the field of education, "researchers found that the use of immersive technologies enhanced learning processes, student engagement, and outcomes" (p. 85).

The TeachLivE™ fully immersive experience is designed to implement three critical components of a strong simulated environment: (a) personalized learning, (b) suspension of disbelief, and (c) cyclical procedures (Dieker et al., 2013). Within seconds of entering the simulator, participants experience a "suspension of disbelief," defined as "forgetting…the environment is not natural, but constructed and contrived, to enhance engagement, presence, and belief of the experience" (Dede, 2009; Hayes et al., 2013, p. 144). In this simulated virtual environment, educators can focus on achieving specific, desired outcomes to improve confidence and ultimate success in the field.

To achieve the high level of engagement needed to fully immerse the user (Dede, 2009), the TeachLivE™ simulation blends virtual components with live performance (i.e. Human in the Loop) throughout the simulation. For the TeachLivE™ participant, this blending is fundamental to the dynamic and responsive nature of the experience. In addition to providing human characteristics to the avatars, the combination of the Human in the Loop (HIL), semi-automated, and automated behaviors create a real-life experience which facilitates meaningful dialogue. As the interactor and coach respond to the learning needs of each participant, behavior is modified, and efficient achievement of learning goals is realized; the coaching capacity will be discussed in depth, in later sections.

In the kindergarten classroom, preservice teachers can don the head-mounted display, and step into circle time with five child avatars. Navigating the realistic, evolving nature of an active group of five-year old students can be realized without stepping outside of the university campus. Novice educators can facilitate a simulated story-time or numeracy lesson, often with an instructional mentor or coach facilitating the interaction. Features unique to the fully immersive environment include: automated eye gaze, gestures, and body positioning data (all of which have potential to impact classroom management). Stereo sound within the fully immersive environment also enhances the user experience. "Unlike research in actual classrooms, where controlled data collection is difficult to ascertain, this virtual environment enables consistency in preparation, immediate feedback, and ongoing data collection, as well as refinement of the environment to ensure the maximum impact on teacher performance and student learning" (Dieker et al., 2008, p. 5). These data can be analyzed and reflected upon, by both coach and participant.

Educators use the kindergarten, immersive virtual environment in develop their pedagogical practice in a safe environment. Educators have the opportunity to practice their teaching while research is conducted using student reflections, surveys, interviews, or other forms of data collection. A specific example of use within the immersive classroom is behavior management strategy rehearsal within kindergarten circle-time. Educators may prioritize an explicit teaching practice, such as using *four positive praises to every one criticism*. The educator uses the 4:1 positive praise technique to decrease off-task behavior displayed by the student while providing encouragement and building trust. This behavior management technique can be as simple as a verbal compliment to the student which educators can practice in the virtual environment before working with real students in a classroom. The facilitator or coach can manually tally participant success of the technique. Within the immersive experience, automatic data on eye gaze and physical proximity can be gathered, analyzed, and reflected upon - as means to measure mastery of evidence-based teaching practice.

Researchers can also use the virtual environment to examine pre-service teachers' feelings of self-efficacy, in both instructional practice and behavior management. When four pre-service teachers were asked about their experiences in the immersive kindergarten classroom, three of them shared the following:

- "As a classroom teacher for five years, I stepped into the classroom expecting awkwardness and a distinct awareness of this being a virtual reality. At first, I was taken back by the environment, but within minutes of interacting, everything faded, and it felt like being back in the classroom again. Students were engaging and I was able to teach like I would in my classroom" (User 1).

- "I think that the VR headset really encourages you to be present and that is what is necessary in this classroom setting. You are applying the skills that were learned about being in the classroom and then you are actually sitting with the students and engaging and seeing how you can put skills into practice" (User 3).
- "Circle time is also critical in kindergarten; this is how most kindergarten teachers start their day with students. For preservice teachers (or anyone needed to practice this skill), the Vive would give them a great sense of how this moment will occur in the classroom including, sitting on the floor crisscross, in a circle with students. The Vive allowed me to feel as though I was included in circle time with a group of Kindergarten students in the classroom" (User 4).

Development

A live virtual simulation like TeachLivE™ requires many stages of development including development of the virtual setting and development of the student avatars. In both stages, the unique affordances and challenges of moving toward an immersive VR structure had to be considered.

Virtual Environment

Prior to the construction of the TeachLivE™ kindergarten classroom environment, the production team received input from educators in written and photographic form. Some of the input came from teachers who were already familiar with TeachLivE™'s other incarnations and methods of operation, while others were not. Requests began with open possibilities before being whittled down to what would make a reasonable mix of function, realism, and affordability. The production team studied several variations of kindergarten classes and began finding common elements among them to merge. A series of concept drawings were submitted for review until a few approved finalists informed the resulting design. With a general form in mind of the shape and function the classroom would take; the production team artist began designing an idealized version of a kindergarten classroom. Many of the reference images submitted by teachers portrayed windowless, crowded, disheveled rooms, which may have represented a more realistic depiction of today's kindergarten classrooms. However, these were prohibitively expensive to construct in 3D as well as being resource-heavy for some of the older computers the software is intended to run on. With the critical elements in mind, such as floor circle time or semi-circle table time, the artist sought to create a roomy, well-lit, modern-looking environment while incorporating the common elements noted during the study of photo submissions.

Since many of the educator's computers using the TeachLivE™ software may be older generation machines with comparatively limited processing power and memory, an effort was made to construct the classroom using as few resources as possible. This meant low polygon construction, frugal texture dimensions, and minimal dynamic lighting. To conserve resources, items not expected to be in the line of sight of a camera are usually either not constructed, or not made with detail. However, as seen in figure 1, in a free roaming 3D virtual environment, anywhere could potentially be scrutinized by the camera, so every detail is considered. The immersed VR user gets a real sense of the real-world scale and presence of the kindergarten avatars when exploring the environment, leading many to get down on the floor to interact with them, which is not usually seen in cases where the user is connecting via a "window on world" setup. The TeachLivE™ production team artist, after seeing the environment virtually, remarked how much more real the classroom looked to him compared to through his desktop workstation; suggesting that even to digital creators who see the same classroom for weeks during its creation, immersive VR can result in fundamentally more engaging experiences.

Figure 1. Kindergarten classroom virtual environments
Source: E. Imperiale, (2019)

Avatars

To begin development of our kindergarten avatars, researchers started by listening to the elementary teachers who worked with our existing classroom of middle school avatars. They noted how teachers described the middle school avatars as different from the kids that they were teaching. Next, researchers conducted interviews with teachers asking them to describe their teaching experiences, their students, elements of teaching that they found the most challenging, and areas that they wish they had had more practice with before stepping into a classroom. From these conversations, and field observations of real kindergarten classrooms researchers realized that the kindergarten avatars would need to be significantly more dynamic and wigglier than the existing virtual students.

Thus, a team of five master elementary teachers worked with interactors to build behavior palettes and academic profiles for our virtual kindergarten classroom. This team videotaped behavioral references that were then shared with an animator who used a combination of motion capture and hand animation to translate these references into controllable animation sequences that can be used in live rehearsal.

One challenge that emerged in developing the characteristics of these kindergartners was how to include the range of possible behaviors for students with Autism. In order to create an authentic virtual student profile, researchers invited an adult individual with Autism and his family to partner with the team in creating a virtual avatar that would authentically represent his kindergarten self. Real home videos and academic documents were used to create the academic profiles and behavior palettes. Additionally, researchers went through an iterative feedback process where his mother directed performance choices until she felt that they authentically represented her son's behavior in a kindergarten classroom. Thus, while most of the virtual avatars are amalgamated behavior and academic profiles from many sources, Martin, a virtual avatar with Autism, is directly modeled after one individual with Autism.

Additionally, revisions and improvements in the performance profiles and behavior palettes are ongoing. The current available avatars are pictured in figure 2. Researchers actively collect feedback from teachers and expert coaches who use the system in order to improve the authenticity of the virtual students.

Figure 2. Kindergarten avatars
Source: E. Imperiale, (2019)

CHALLENGES

As with any new technology, comes challenges that need to be addressed. These challenges include using the technology, designing and implementing effective scenarios in the virtual space, and challenges encountered by facilitators. In order to describe some of the challenges of using an immersive virtual environment, challenges experienced in the current TeachLivE™ kindergarten classroom are being used as a test case.

Use of Technology

First, most kindergarten classroom teachers want to incorporate objects into the lesson such as manipulatives for math, demonstration materials for science, or books for read-aloud activities. In an HMD that is fully immersive and not mixed with a camera feed of the real physical environment, teachers cannot see real-world objects that they hold in their hands. This makes activities such as writing on a smart board, reading a book out loud, or demonstrating a concept with objects very difficult. In order to use any of these objects in the virtual environment, they would need to be modeled and added in a way in which teachers could use the objects with handheld controllers or haptic gloves. It is an open research question whether the adjustments needed to use objects in the virtual environment may help or hinder teaching practice. Thus, while further development to model and control common classroom objects, like math manipulative, is ongoing, further research is needed to determine if practice with virtual objects influences real world classroom practice. Exploring a more mixed-reality approach integrating elements of a virtual environment with a live camera feed of real-world objects teachers can see and manipulate more naturally may prove to be a better approach. The limitations for object manipulation also may explain why many teachers choose to practice with the virtual kindergarten classroom on a projected screen rather than in an immersive virtual environment even when the more immersive virtual environment is available.

In addition to physical interaction with objects, teaching in an immersive virtual environment seems to affect physical movement during the session. Some teachers seem hesitant when first entering the simulation, perhaps fearing collision with a real-world object they cannot see. Some participants also noted the immersive virtual environment encourages them to get down on the floor to interact with the virtual avatars as they would kids in a real classroom: "The best part of interacting with the kindergarten classroom is the fact that it feels so real. I start talking to the avatars as if they are real students in my classroom and immediately sit on the ground to join them during circle time" (User 2, Nov. 20). Additional research is needed to explore how physical movement during teaching differs between an immersive virtual environment, a projected virtual environment, and a real classroom.

So far, we have primarily described challenges for teachers using the system, however, there are additional challenges for the interactors operating the avatar in an immersive virtual environment. In a projected simulation environment, the interactor can see a teacher's face and body through a webcam video feed so that the interactor can respond to a teacher's facial expressions, body postures, and other non-verbal communication. But when the teacher is wearing an HMD their facial expression is obscured. Additionally, it can be difficult to determine where teachers are looking. Although HMDs are advancing and some offer eye tracking features, these data points have yet to be integrated into a view for the interactor. Preliminary experimentation with giving interactors a screen to show the participant's view through the HMD resulted in significantly negative feedback from the interactors. The constant motion of the view through the HMD made it difficult for the interactors to monitor system puppetry and thus interactors requested a stable view of the virtual students that does not respond to teachers' changes in viewing the environment. Thus, additional development is needed to communicate teachers' gaze data to interactors, so they can respond more accurately to teachers' actions in the virtual system.

Faculty Scenario Design and Implementation

As we have discussed some of the opportunities and challenges regarding the technology components of an immersive virtual environment, it is also worth noting some of the advantages and challenges of using a human-in-the-loop simulation design within the virtual environment. Having an interactor control and perform the avatars in real time allows for great flexibility and responsiveness to teachers. This flexibility of the system allows teachers to teach any lesson in any manner that they choose without needing to reprogram the software. However, this same flexibility can sometimes tempt faculty using the simulation to underplan simulated activities. Teachers need clear, measurable objectives as well as feedback on those objectives for teaching skills to improve in a simulated environment. Past research has shown when performance feedback is not included, teachers do not improve on targeted teaching skills (Straub et al., 2014). Similarly, if objectives are not communicated clearly between teachers, facilitators, and interactors, opportunities to practice targeted skills may be missed.

Facilitation of an Immersive VR Experience

With greater technological advances in VR, unique challenges follow. These challenges can include participant individual differences in reception to the immersive experience, including adverse reactions to the experience. Regarding individual differences, the facilitator may need to navigate gender differences (women are at greater risk of adverse reaction to the simulation), age-related response or reception to the environment, and individual feelings of presence (Suh & Prophet, 2018). Further complicating the immersive VR experience is the (often) bulky, wearable technology; physical discomfort from the headset may inhibit the user from achieving a field of presence. Notably, regarding a coaching model, the wearable headset limits interaction to the immediate virtual environment. This physical, visual, and audio barrier limits the way coaches can provide feedback - modeling behavior can only occur if the coach usurps the simulation; whereas, in non-immersive VR, the coach can saddle alongside the participant to model evidence-based practices.

Facilitators also need to be aware of potential, well-known adverse reactions to immersive VR, which can include physical reactions to the simulation, which are related to balance and eye movement; "although using modern technology in education environment is clearly beneficial, it is not without risks and dangers" (Kaminska et al., 2019, p. 13). User adverse-response to immersive technology may take the form of motion sickness, cognitive overload related to visual input, and distracted attention with limited suspension of disbelief (Suh & Prophet, 2018). When facilitating an immersive experience, researchers should ensure participants are given proper attention, if adverse reactions to the environment materialize.

Relatedly, Freina and Ott (2015) discuss the limited recommendations for use of immersive VR among children, which may be related to "health and safety" warnings associated with immersive technology. These limitations include the Oculus Rift, which limits its recommendations-for-use to participants over age 13. The authors cite ongoing eye development in young children as a limiting factor; use of the headset may impact balance and coordination needed within the immersive setting.

RECOMMENDATIONS TO ADDRESS CHALLENGES

Continuing development, research, and refinement of implementation procedures are needed to address the challenges of using VR in educational contexts, including how participants can naturally interact with objects in an immersive virtual environment. As technology develops new tools, methods of interaction should evolve that can be adapted to virtual classroom contexts. Following are recommendations that address the aforementioned challenges.

Use of Technology

One of the challenges of using an immersive VR headset is an inability to see the outside world. If a user becomes preoccupied with navigating the obscured real world in lieu of interacting with the virtual avatars and objects of the simulation, the goal of immersion is hindered, negating the simulation's benefit. To combat this, the dedicated simulation space should be completely cleared of obstacles except where such obstacles are aligned with objects in the virtual space, boundaries for movement within the virtual space should be obvious, and all required manipulatives would need to be built for use with the handset controller or haptic gloves. However, this solution may not be practical for all cases. An alternate solution could be to utilize mixed/augmented reality glasses to bring the student avatars into an existing real world classroom. Advanced MR glasses like Microsoft's HoloLens 2 could potentially scan the real world environment, project the student avatars in a predetermined configuration in the room, and even project over real world objects with virtual objects, such as making a pencil look and function like a magic wand (Microsoft HoloLens, 2019). The glasses would allow the user to feel comfortable seeing themselves in a natural environment while engaging with the virtual avatars and manipulatives.

Another issue discussed above affects the abilities of an interactor to read the facial expressions of a teacher or determine where their attention is focused. Eye tracking improvements and the implementation of emotion-detecting AI could potentially address these problems but additional features would need to be developed for the TeachLivE™ system, such as a virtual representation of a teacher's facial expressions within the interactor's viewport and a dynamic marker representing the teacher's focal point. A balance is required between the useful features of the software and the cognitive load an interactor must manage while retaining focus on their performance. Similarly, teachers' engagement with the simulation should be intuitive enough for them to remain focused on their lessons rather than fighting the equipment and/or simulation. Improvements to environment scanning, FOV enhancements, eye tracking, and object replacement are new, ongoing, and discussed further in the Future Trends section.

Faculty Design and Implementation

While technology advancements and further development may address some challenges, human-in-the-loop structures are likely to persist, at least until artificial intelligence algorithms improve (Ablanedo et al., 2018). Thus, guidelines for communicating with interactors in the system may be helpful. Provided are four basic recommendations for working with interactors to design high quality virtual simulation sessions:

1. Share lesson materials with the interactor in advance of the session.
2. Make sure that session objectives are clear, specific, observable, and possible in the simulated environment.
3. Discuss a framework for decision making.
4. Give feedback to the interactor on their performance.

First, though it may seem obvious, interactors need lesson materials well in advance of the session, so they can plan responses from different students' perspectives, create differentiated work samples, and seed research-based academic misconceptions if applicable. Even though interactors often are hired for their expertise in improvisational performance and may be very accomplished as improvising authentic student responses, all interactors provide better responses with preparation. Preparing these materials in advance also increases consistency across teachers teaching the same lesson and helps avoid interactor mistakes or misconceptions that are unintentional.

Second, session objectives must be clear not only to teachers participating as the learner, but also to the interactor, so they can plan specific opportunities to practice the targeted skill. For example, if a targeted skill is to practice positive specific praise to students, interactors will plan a session where students respond especially well to praise, and classroom disruptions decrease in response to praise. An interactor would likely also seed several instances of undesirable classroom behaviors the teacher could correct or would pause during the session, offering the teacher an opportunity to praise compliance with classroom expectations. In order to respond positively or negatively to teacher actions, the interactor would need to understand when they are observing effective praise and when praise efforts are missing or inadequate. Finally, if a specific component or skill would be difficult to achieve in the virtual environment the interactor needs to address this issue. For instance, if teachers want to include a token reward system as a part of their praise strategy, faculty would need to determine how that would work in a virtual environment. Handing physical objects to the avatars is not possible, so an alternative solution such as marking points on a board, or verbally telling students to record a point may be alternatives that could be implemented virtually.

Third, a framework for decision making is necessary for the interactor. Every session requires the interactor to make hundreds of decisions including: how to respond to teacher statements or actions, what interactions to instigate, how and when to escalate or deescalate disruptive behavior, how deeply to question content material, which misconceptions to present from student perspectives, and which interpersonal challenges to include. Some decisions will be guided by the session objectives or characteristics of students themselves, but some decisions need to be based on the teacher. Teacher experience level is one factor. The challenge level of the simulation should differ from beginning pre-service teachers who are practicing basic skills to master in-service teachers who are polishing new activities before presenting them to their class. Faculty must also decide if the level of challenge needs to be consistent across participants for purposes of research or evaluation or if the level of challenge should respond to the skill level of individual teachers in the system. This principle of changing the level of challenge based on the individual's actions is called dynamic difficulty scaling (DDS) in game design theory (Arzate Cruz & Ramirez Uresti, 2017). If decision making frameworks are not explicit prior to the session, then interactors will be employing internal decision-making frameworks that may or may not align with faculty goals for the session.

Finally, just as teachers need feedback on their performance in order to improve on targeted skills (Straub et al., 2014), interactors also need feedback from faculty members to improve their performance of the virtual students. Data should be collected not only on teacher actions, but on interactor performance choices so that the interactor can receive targeted feedback regarding the authenticity of their performance, the appropriateness of student responses, and the adherence to session goals and decision-making frameworks. Depending on the complexity of the session, it may be too difficult for one faculty member to attend to both teacher and interactor actions during a session. Video recording and review of sessions can be a very helpful tool to address this issue. Providing video recordings of sessions to teams of interactors also offers an opportunity for interactors to peer review performance techniques.

Facilitation of an Immersive Experience

Utilization of VR in education is in its nascent stages, leaving the field wide-open for facilitators to expand learning opportunities for participants. There are a number of challenges to overcome before the use of VR is ubiquitous in the K-12 setting, including prohibitive cost of materials, age restrictions on recommended use, and adverse reactions to the immersive environment. Yet, research indicates use of VR within education yields positive outcomes for participants, including increased motivation, engagement, and interest in the content (Suh & Prophet, 2018). It is our belief the primary goal of the facilitator is to maximize these positive outcomes to increase student learning and growth within the immersive VR setting.

To enhance immersive VR learning experiences, we offer the following recommendations for facilitators:

1. Develop validated standards for immersive VR learning experiences
2. Maximize data collection opportunities within the enclosed environment
3. Simulate experiences which closely mirror real-life scenarios
4. Decrease adverse effects on users, resulting from immersive technology

As immersive VR technology becomes increasingly ubiquitous within the education setting, development of validated standards should follow. Researchers and facilitators should weigh benefits and risks of sensory and perceptual stimulus levels, with particular care given to users under age 18. Stimulus input should be balanced with learning gains, differentiated according to user stages-of-development, content, and setting. For example, standards-of-use within immersive military education settings may be different from those within a K-12 setting.

This leads to a second recommendation: Maximize data collection opportunities within the enclosed environment, to enhance student learning. Collection of data is essential when developing standards-of-use, particularly when measuring user response to sensory input. The enclosed nature of the immersive experience allows facilitators to quickly and dynamically respond to individual student learning needs; and allows for control of extraneous variables. "Unlike research in actual classrooms, where controlled data collection is difficult to ascertain, this virtual environment enables consistency in preparation, immediate feedback, and ongoing data collection, as well as refinement of the environment to ensure the maximum impact on teacher performance and student learning" (Dieker et al., 2008, p. 5). For instance, researchers in teacher preparation may wish to measure preservice teacher eye-gaze or body proximity within the classroom – this can be easily achieved within an enclosed immersive VR setting.

Aligned, Hanoun and Nahavandi (2018) recommend a number of next steps for facilitators within the VR setting. One recommendation is to ensure collected data is diverse in nature; the VR setting affords measurement of multiple perspectives of the performance or task. Perhaps this translates to including multiple means to track biophysical interaction with the simulated environment. Measures could include movement tracking, voice intonation, verbal response, and interaction with the setting. These data can be measured and compared between participants to determine a standard of performance or as measures of learning.

A third recommendation is to simulate experiences closely mirroring real-life scenarios. Again within teacher preparation, a simulated kindergarten classroom may include circle time or table groupings, while a high school immersive experience may include a science lab. By developing skills, within a simulated kindergarten classroom, preservice teachers are able to immediately apply developed skills directly in the real-life classroom; these skills can include behavior management skills, content delivery, positive praise, and small group or center activities.

As educators and coaches continue to explore student growth within the immersive VR setting, the fourth recommendation is to consider the safety and comfort of participants. To achieve the high level of presence needed to achieve a suspension of disbelief, the user must achieve a level of comfort to ensure psychological ownership of the immersive setting (Suh & Prophet, 2018). Practicing in a safe learning environment allows users to make mistakes, without risk to themselves or others. Users should be encouraged to pause the simulation if they are overwhelmed or uncomfortable. Further, as some immersive technologies are not recommended for users under age 13, facilitators must weigh risks when including VR technology in K-12 settings.

FUTURE TRENDS

With VR development advancing so fast, many of the ideas sounding like science fiction actually come from the present or even the recent past. VR social networking platforms, teleconferencing, and all manner of educational, theatrical, and medical applications have been around for years. Mainstream adoption has been slow to manifest in part due to the prohibitively expensive cost of access for most people, and a level of real-time visual fidelity that has only recently been made more available. Technological advances such as seamless integrated eye tracking, which makes dynamic foveated rendering possible, exist today. Foveated rendering is the technique of reducing the rendering workload by reducing the image quality of objects viewed outside the zone of the eye's fovea (which constitutes the peripheral vision) (Parrish, 2016). More than just being resource efficient, this is also more akin to the natural way humans focus on visual stimuli. Precise eye tracking is also useful for the recording of eye movement for insightful analytics of a user's experience. Microsoft's HoloLens 2 MR glasses use eye tracking to identify users and can customize lens widths to provide a more comfortable, personalized experience. They have also implemented laser technology to create a microelectromechanical systems (MEMS) display. With it, the HoloLens 2 can position waveguides in front of a user's eyes, directed by mirrors. Subsequently enlarging images can be accomplished by shifting the angles of the mirrors, effectively doubling the active FOV (Microsoft HoloLens, 2019). The previously mentioned real-time environment scanning capabilities of devices like the Magic Leap One AR device will continue to improve so that virtual characters will not only convincingly exist in the real world, as seen in Pokemon Go, but real-world objects could be made to appear as virtual objects. For example, your countertop could become a touchscreen.

Emotion-detecting AI software now exists, which coupled with VR devices, could convey the subtler aspects of communication such as eye movement and micro-expressions (Affectiva, 2019). Other advanced developments include the previously mentioned standalone VR 6DOF devices like Oculus Quest and the HTC Vive Focus Plus. These devices connect via Wi-Fi connectivity today, with 5G connectivity waiting tomorrow. 5G networks could potentially reduce latency between connected users to imperceptible levels, making telecommunications feel more natural. These things are here now, are not prolific yet, but are likely to become more common in the future as the cost for these technologies decrease. Once these technologies become affordable to incorporate in classrooms and in professional development contexts for teachers, new and innovative use strategies are likely to emerge.

VR Use in Education

From VR's inception, researchers have predicted VR technology would revolutionize learning within the K-12 education setting (Helsel, 1992; Psotka, 1995). Thirty years post, Kaminska and colleagues (2019) contend this next decade will provide the moment for which VR researchers have been waiting; they argue, "the digital world is as important and immersive as the real one" for Generation Z (Kaminska et al., 2019, p. 13). As Generation Z ages, the challenge remains with the educator to present content in digital format - which includes the use of VR in the classroom (Kaminska et al., 2019). The authors submit numerous advantages associated with VR in education settings. They posit, VR is superior in visual presentation, transportable and inclusive in nature, information-rich in framework, promotes increased engagement of learners, and allows for ease of self-directed learning.

Educators can continue to expand use of immersive VR in ways proven effective within teacher preparation. Ideas for future use within the K-12 system include using the virtual environment to:

- Reduce bullying by altering perceptions of biased participants; reach rural education settings with expert delivery of content (i.e. delivery of Advanced Placement courses);
- Rehearse classroom discussion to reduce student anxiety; reduce negative behaviors using avatars as peer supports;
- Use automated systems of feedback to track participation; incorporate haptic gloves and other additional VR technologies to fully immerse the participant into the environment;
- Include greater use of biofeedback analysis to manage stressful classroom situations, and increase use of a bug-in-ear technology to provide coaching feedback to the participant.

With increasing interest and access to VR, the education community is provided an opportunity to diversify student opportunities for learning. Gutierrez and colleagues (2017) cite an expected $120 billion in VR industry profits in 2020 - the authors anticipate investment will focus on content and wearable creation. They forecast the education community will see residual benefits of increasing accessibility and affordability, as wearable technology (HDM) evolves. The authors further contend, as increases are seen in "power and capabilities of newer mobile devices, increased investment to the development of virtual technologies, and access to user-generated virtual contents through social networks" (p.482) are realized, it will be increasingly possible for VR technology to be present across the education spectrum. As wearables become ubiquitous, students and educators will have a blank canvas with which to shape learner experiences; that is, as access to technology increases, creative response will increase, in turn (Gutierrez et al., 2017). The next decade will reveal the full extent of realized learning benefits; Generation Z, a generation of true digital natives, will advance immersive possibilities beyond the lab-nature of today's VR experience.

Human Performance and Increased Use of Interactors

As we consider future trends in the technology and the use of virtual environments in educational settings, use of human performance, interactors, is likely to become a trend. Although advancing developments in artificial intelligence (AI) may eventually replace human interactors in virtual simulation systems, a gap currently exists as to what those AI algorithms can understand about complex human behavior such as teaching. Digital puppetry is likely to remain a technique used to fill that gap until AI systems catch up (Ablanedo et al., 2018). Thus, it is worth considering the implication of potential future wide-scale use of interactors in virtual simulation.

Performance through technology presents unique opportunities and challenges. Through technology, an actor is freed from the casting confines of their physical appearance. An interactor could potentially play virtual characters different from themselves in age, gender, or cultural background. One interactor can play multiple characters, such as multiple students in a classroom, which provides significant cost savings compared to hiring multiple actors in a live training scenario. In one sense, this freedom has the potential to create more equitable casting opportunities for actors ideally based on skill rather than appearance. However, with this freedom comes increased risk of non-transparent, biased performance that may reinforce negative cultural or gender stereotypes (Reed & Phillips, 2013).

This risk is of concern for educational training applications which are especially vulnerable to negative training reinforcing student deficit biases (Matias et al., 2016). At its worst, poor interactor performance could become a form of digital blackface that reproduces negative racial or gender stereotypes while presenting them as authentic student behavior (Reed & Phillips, 2013). Biased performance of student avatars could influence negative teacher biases and expectations for their real classrooms causing potential harm to real students. Research suggests that virtual representations such as video game avatars may already influence perceptions of race and gender in negative ways (Behm-Morawitz & Ta, 2014; Burgess et al., 2011). Vigilance and sensitivity to performance of gender and culture of virtual avatars is essential to avoid unconscious racism or gender bias in performance.

This risk increases as one imagines future applications scaling into larger widespread use. Computer systems used to control virtual avatars are small and affordable enough that interactors can work from home, remote from potential clients. With a small-scale operation like TeachLivE™ where there are generally eight to twelve interactors on staff, some of these risks can be mitigated by having a diverse team that monitors each other's performance with extra sensitivity to performances outside of an individual's personal background. Expert outside feedback on performance authenticity also is a regular part of performance rehearsal. But, maintaining rigorous performance monitoring becomes more difficult as teams expand and spread geographically.

Additionally, as the availability of customizable scenario design increases, and higher education faculty and interactors use systems without institutional oversight, a risk exists of a normalization of white cultural views could be propagated unconsciously in the simulation system through the feedback cycles meant to monitor performance authenticity (Matias et al., 2016; Nishi et al., 2015). Thus, additional research and exploration of scalable performance monitoring systems is essential for ethical use of human-in-the-loop simulation systems.

CONCLUSION

As discussed throughout the chapter, VR technologies represent an evolution in immersive storytelling and provide innovative approaches to teaching and learning. VR use in education is an open, largely underutilized means to increase teacher effectiveness and student learning. The simulated experience, TeachLivE™, is in direct response to a need for more effective teacher preparation. Providing simulated experiences with avatar students whose movements and voices directly interact, through the use of interactors, is a promising use of technology to increase teacher preparation prior to having one's own classroom of students. Given the use of technologies which is expected to become more widespread in the future, more empirical studies are needed to theorize VR use on experiences and performance. We hope this chapter assists and supports educators in understanding the current state of VR, immersive and non-immersive technology, and develop research agendas for future investigation.

ACKNOWLEDGMENT

The authors would like to thank all the Center for Research in Simulation Education Technology (CREST) partners who have worked with us and informed our practice over the years.

We would also like to thank the CREST team members whose contribution make this research possible including Michael Hynes, Donna Martin, and the CREST interactor team.

REFERENCES

Ablanedo, J., Fairchild, E., Griffith, T., & Rodeheffer, C. (2018). Is this person real? Avatar stylization and its influence on human perception in a counseling training environment. Virtual, Augmented and Mixed Reality: Interaction, Navigation, Visualization, Embodiment, and Simulation, 10909, 279–289. doi:10.1007/978-3-319-91581-4_20

Affectiva | Home. (n.d.). Retrieved December 18, 2019, from https://www.affectiva.com/

Alexander, A. L., Brunyé, T., Sidman, J., & Weil, S. A. (2005). From gaming to training: A review of studies on fidelity, immersion, presence, and buy-in and their effects on transfer in pc-based simulations and games. *DARWARS Training Impact Group*, *5*, 1–14.

Arzate Cruz, C., & Ramirez Uresti, J. A. (2017). Player-centered game AI from a flow perspective: Towards a better understanding of past trends and future directions. *Entertainment Computing*, *20*, 11–24. doi:10.1016/j.entcom.2017.02.003

Barnes, G., Crowe, B., & Schaefer, E. (2007). *The cost of teacher turnover in five school districts: A pilot study*. National Commission on Teaching and America's Future.

Behm-Morawitz, E., & Ta, D. (2014). Cultivating virtual stereotypes?: The impact of video game play on racial/ethnic stereotypes. *The Howard Journal of Communications*, *25*(1), 1–15. doi:10.1080/10646175.2013.835600

Brownell, M. T., Sindelar, P. T., Kiely, M. T., & Danielson, L. C. (2010). Special education teacher quality and preparation: Exposing foundations, constructing a new model. *Exceptional Children*, *76*(3), 357–377. doi:10.1177/001440291007600307

Burgess, M. C. R., Dill, K. E., Stermer, S. P., Burgess, S. R., & Brown, B. P. (2011). Playing with prejudice: The prevalence and consequences of racial stereotypes in video games. *Media Psychology*, *14*(3), 289–311. doi:10.1080/15213269.2011.596467

Carver-Thomas, D., & Darling-Hammond, L. (2019). The trouble with teacher turnover: How teacher attrition affects students and schools. *Education Policy Analysis Archives*, *27*(36), 1–32. doi:10.14507/epaa.27.3699

Chini, J., Straub, C. L., & Thomas, K. H. (2014). Learning from avatars: Learning assistants practice physics pedagogy in a classroom simulator. *Physical Review Physics Education Research, 12*(1), 010117-1- 010117-15.

Cochran-Smith, M., McQuillan, P., Mitchell, K., Terrell, D. G., Barnatt, J., D'Souza, L., Jong, C., Shakman, K., Lam, K., & Gleeson, A. M. (2012). A longitudinal study of teaching practice and early career decisions: A cautionary tale. *American Educational Research Journal*, *49*(5), 844–880. doi:10.3102/0002831211431006

Daydream – Daydream View. (n.d.). Retrieved December 18, 2019, from https://arvr.google.com/daydream/smartphonevr/

Dede, C. (2009). Immersive interfaces for engagement and learning. *Science*, *323*(5910), 66–69. doi:10.1126cience.1167311 PMID:19119219

Dieker, L., Hughes, C., Hynes, M., & Straub, C. (2017). Using simulated virtual environments to improve teacher performance. *School-University Partnerships*, *10*(3), 62–81.

Dieker, L., Hynes, M., Hughes, C., & Smith, E. (2008). Implications of mixed reality and simulation technologies on special education and teacher preparation. *Focus on Exceptional Children*, *40*(6), 1–19. doi:10.17161/foec.v40i6.6877

Dieker, L., Hynes, M., Stapleton, C., & Hughes, C. (2007). Virtual classrooms: STAR simulator. *New Learning Technology SALT*, *4*, 1–22.

Dieker, L., & Rodriguez, J., Lignugaris/Kraft, B., Hynes, M., & Hughes, C. E. (2013). The potential of simulated environments in teacher education: Current and future possibilities. *Teacher Education and Special Education: The Journal of the Teacher Education Division of the Council for Exceptional Children*, *37*(1), 21–33. doi:10.1177/0888406413512683

Dieker, L., Straub, C., Hughes, C., Hynes, M., & Hardin, S. (2014). Learning from virtual students. *Educational Leadership*, *71*(8), 54–58.

Every Student Succeeds Act., Pub. L. No. 114–95, 1177 (2015).

Freina, L., & Ott, M. (2015). A Literature review on immersive virtual reality in education: State of the art and perspectives. *ELearning & Software for Education*, *1*, 133–141. doi:10.12753/2066-026X-15-020

Google Cardboard. (n.d.). Retrieved December 18, 2019, from https://arvr.google.com/cardboard/

Gutierrez, J., Mora, C., Anorbe-Diaz, B., & Gonzalez-Marrero, A. (2017). Virtual technologies trends in education. *Eurasia Journal of Mathematics, Science and Technology Education*, *13*(2), 469–486.

Hanoun, S., & Nahavandi, S. (2018). Current and future methodologies of after action review in simulation-based training. *2018 Annual IEEE International Systems Conference (SysCon), Systems Conference (SysCon), 2018 Annual IEEE International*, 1–6. 10.1109/SYSCON.2018.8369516

Hapt, X. (n.d.). *Haptic gloves for VR training, simulation, and design*. Retrieved December 24, 2019, from https://haptx.com

Hayes, A., Hardin, S., & Hughes, C. (2013). Perceived presence's role on learning outcomes in a mixed reality classroom of simulated students. *Virtual, Augmented & Mixed Reality. Systems & Applications*, *8022*, 142–151. . doi:10.1007/978-3-642-39420-1-16

Heilig, M. L. (1962). *U.S. Patent No. 3,050,870*. Washington, DC: U.S. Patent and Trademark Office.

Helsel, S. (1992). Virtual reality and education. *Educational Technology*, *32*(5), 38–42.

Hobson, A. J., Ashby, P., Malderez, A., & Tomlinson, P. D. (2009). Mentoring beginning teachers: What we know and what we don't. *Teaching and Teacher Education*, *25*(1), 207–216. doi:10.1016/j.tate.2008.09.001

Hong, J. Y. (2010). Pre-service and beginning teachers' professional identity and its relation to dropping out of the profession. *Teaching and Teacher Education, 26*(8), 1530–1543. doi:10.1016/j.tate.2010.06.003

Ingersoll, R. M. (2001). Teacher turnover and teacher shortages: An organizational analysis. *American Educational Research Journal, 38*(3), 499–534. doi:10.3102/00028312038003499

Jones, M. L. (2009). A study of novice special educators' views of evidence-based practices. *Teacher Education and Special Education, 32*(2), 101–120. doi:10.1177/0888406409333777

Jung, S., Wisniewski, P., & Hughes, C. (2018). In Limbo: The Effect of Gradual Visual Transition Between Real and Virtual on Virtual Body Ownership Illusion and Presence. *2018 IEEE Conference on Virtual Reality and 3D User Interfaces (VR), Virtual Reality and 3D User Interfaces (VR), 2018 IEEE Conference*, 267–272. 10.1109/VR.2018.8447562

Kamińska, D., Sapiński, T., Wiak, S., Tikk, T., Haamer, R., Avots, E., Helmi, A., Ozcinar, C., & Anbarjafari, G. (2019). Virtual Reality and Its Applications in Education: Survey. *MDPI: Information, 10*(318), 318. Advance online publication. doi:10.3390/info10100318

Lankford, H., Loeb, S., & Wyckoff, J. (2002). Teacher sorting and the plight of urban schools: A descriptive analysis. *Educational Evaluation and Policy Analysis, 24*(1), 37–62. doi:10.3102/01623737024001037

Magic Leap 1. (n.d.). Retrieved from https://www.magicleap.com/magic-leap-1

Manus, V. R. (n.d.). *World's leading VR Gloves for training*. Retrieved December 18, 2019, from https://manus-vr.com/

Matias, C. E., Montoya, R., & Nishi, N. W. M. (2016). Blocking CRT: How the emotionality of Whiteness blocks CRT in urban teacher education. *Educational Studies, 52*(1), 1–19. doi:10.1080/00131946.2015.1120205

Microsoft HoloLens. (n.d.). *Mixed reality technology for business*. Retrieved December 18, 2019, from https://www.microsoft.com/en-us/hololens/

Mikropoulos, T. A., & Natsis, A. (2011). Educational virtual environments: A ten-year review of empirical research (1999–2009). *Computers & Education, 56*(3), 769–780. doi:10.1016/j.compedu.2010.10.020

Nintendo Labo™ for the NINTENDO Switch™ home gaming system - official site. (n.d.). Retrieved December 18, 2019, from https://labo.nintendo.com/

Nishi, N. W., Matias, C. E., & Montoya, R. (2015). Exposing the white avatar: Projections, justifications, and the ever-evolving American racism. *Social Identities, 21*(5), 459–473. doi:10.1080/13504630.2015.1093470

Oculus, Go. Standalone VR Headset. (n.d.). Retrieved December 18, 2019, from https://www.oculus.com/go/

Oculus | VR Headsets & Equipment. (n.d.). Retrieved December 18, 2019, from https://www.oculus.com/

Oculus Quest. All-in-One VR Headset. (n.d.). Retrieved December 18, 2019, from https://www.oculus.com/quest/

Olson, J. L., Krum, D. M., Suma, E. A., & Bolas, M. (2011). A Design for a Smartphone-Based Head Mounted Display. *Proceedings of the 2011 IEEE Virtual Reality*, 233-234. 10.1109/VR.2011.5759484

Pantelidis, V. (1993). Virtual reality in the classroom. *Educational Technology, 33*(4), 23–27.

Parrish, K. (2016). Nvidia plans to prove that new method improves image quality in virtual reality. *Digital Trends.* Retrieved December 18, 2019, from https://www.digitaltrends.com/virtual-reality/nvidia-research-foveated-rendering-vr-smi/

Pilatásig, M., Tobar, E., Paredes, L., Silva, F. M., Acurio, A., & Pruna, E. … Sánchez, Z. (2018). Virtual system for teaching-learning of initial education using a haptic device. In L. T. De Paolis & P. Bourdot (Eds.), Augmented Reality, Virtual Reality, and Computer Graphics (pp. 118–132). Cham: Springer International Publishing.

PlayStation®VR - over 500 games and Experiences. feel them all. (n.d.). Retrieved December 18, 2019, from https://www.playstation.com/en-us/explore/playstation-vr/

Psotka, J. (1995). Immersive training systems: Virtual reality and education and training. *Instructional Science, 23*(5–6), 405–431. doi:10.1007/BF00896880

Reed, A., & Phillips, A. (2013). Additive race: Colorblind discourses of realism in performance capture technologies. *Digital Creativity, 24*(2), 130–144. doi:10.1080/14626268.2013.808965

Ryan, S. V., Nathaniel, P., Pendergast, L. L., Saeki, E., Segool, N., & Schwing, S. (2017). Leaving the teaching profession: The role of teacher stress and educational accountability policies on turnover intent. *Teaching and Teacher Education, 66*(1), 1–11. doi:10.1016/j.tate.2017.03.016

Samsung Gear VR with Controller. (n.d.). Retrieved December 18, 2019, from https://www.samsung.com/global/galaxy/gear-vr/

Scheeler, M. C., Budin, S., & Markelz, A. (2016). The role of teacher preparation in promoting evidence-based practice in schools. *Learning Disabilities (Weston, Mass.), 14*(2), 171–187.

Straub, C., Dieker, L., Hynes, M., & Hughes, C. (2014). *Year 1 findings using virtual rehearsal in TLE TeachLivE™ mixed reality classroom simulator to determine the effects on the performance of mathematics teachers.* Retrieved from http://teachlive.org/wp-content/uploads/2014/10/2014_GR_Technical_Report_10_20_FINAL.pdf

Suh, A., & Prophet, J. (2018). The state of immersive technology research: A literature analysis. *Computers in Human Behavior, 86*, 77–90. doi:10.1016/j.chb.2018.04.019

Sutherland, I. E. (1968). A head-mounted three-dimensional display. *Proceedings of AFIPS, 68*, 757–764.

Virtuix Omni™. (n.d.). Retrieved December 18, 2019, from https://www.virtuix.com/product/virtuix-omni/

VIVE™ | VIVE Virtual Reality System. (n.d.). Retrieved from https://www.vive.com/us/product/vive-virtual-reality-system/

VIVE Cosmos - a new way of Pc VR: VIVE™. (n.d.). Retrieved December 18, 2019, from https://www.vive.com/us/product/vive-cosmos/features/

VIVE Focus Plus. (n.d.). Retrieved December 18, 2019, from https://enterprise.vive.com/us/product/focus-plus/

Whiteman, D. (2009). View-Master, an icon of souvenirs since 1939, enters nonscenic era. *The New York Times*. Retrieved from https://www.nytimes.com/2009/03/04/business/worldbusiness/04iht-view.4.20593331.html

Winn, W. (1993). *A conceptual basis for educational applications of virtual reality* (Report No. TR-93-9). Human Interface Technology Laboratory, Washington Technology Center.

Zachara, M., & Zagal, J. P. (2009). Challenges for success in stereo gaming: A virtual boy case study. *ACM International Conference Proceeding Series*, 99–106. 10.1145/1690388.1690406

Zhang, M., Zhang, Z., Chang, Y., Aziz, E. S., Esche, S., & Chassapis, C. (2018). Recent developments in game-based virtual reality educational laboratories using the microsoft kinect. *International Journal of Emerging Technologies in Learning*, *13*(1), 138–159. doi:10.3991/ijet.v13i01.7773

KEY TERMS AND DEFINITIONS

Artificial Intelligence (AI): The theory and development of computer systems able to perform tasks that normally require human intelligence, such as visual perception, speech recognition, decision-making, and translation between languages.

Augmented Reality: Technology that enables users to engage with virtual information superimposed on the physical world. This mediated immersion places digital resources throughout the real world, augmenting users' experiences, and interactions.

Dynamic Difficulty Scaling (DDS): Adjusting the level of challenge in a game or simulation based on the skill level of the player or learner.

FOV (Field of View): The open observable area a person can see through their eyes or via an optical device.

Foveated Rendering: The technique of reducing the rendering workload by reducing the image quality of objects viewed outside the zone of the eye's fovea (which makes up the peripheral vision).

HMD: Head-mounted display. This is a display device worn on the head that regulates the user's vision to one (monocular) or two (binocular) digital displays, allowing only computer-generated imagery (CGI) or video input to be seen rather than the physical world.

Human in the Loop: A type of simulation where a human operator plays a role in controlling the events of the simulated scenario.

Immersive Virtual Reality (VR): Users are required to wear a head-mounted display and are completely encompassed by the virtual environment. In an immersive VR environment, user responses can be observed and recorded in a controlled situation.

Interactor: A human operator who controls virtual avatars in a virtual environment using digital puppetry and voice performance.

Kinect: A Microsoft motion-sensing device equipped with cameras, projectors, microphones and sensors in order to function as a natural user interface peripheral. Some capabilities include real-time gesture recognition, speech recognition and body skeletal detection for up to four people at a time.

Mixed Reality: The space where the physical and virtual worlds co-exist. Within the reality virtuality framework, a generic MR environment is a space in which real and virtual objects are presented together within a single display.

MYO Gesture-Type Platform: A platform that utilizes input from a MYO gesture control armband. A MYO gesture control armband is a wireless device worn around a user's forearm that detects muscle activity in the forearm to provide touch-free control of technology via hand gestures and motion. The term MYO is derived from the Greek "mŷs", meaning mouse or muscle.

Non-Immersive Virtual Reality (VR): The VR content is displayed via a computer screen. Traditional media, such as keyboards and mice, are used for the interaction. Non-immersive VR does not require users to wear any equipment.

Sensorama: One of the earliest prototypes of immersive, multimodal technology. Introduced in 1962 by inventor Morton Heilig, it is considered one of the first virtual reality (VR) systems.

Chapter 7
Creating a Virtual Reality Lab:
Using a Student-Centered Approach

Benjamin Zibers
Park University, USA

Judi Simmons Estes
Park University, USA

ABSTRACT

Use of virtual reality (VR) has increased in higher education in recent years and is projected to continue to increase. At the same time, there is a growing emphasis for institutions of higher education to re-envision learning spaces and teaching strategies that are student-centered rather than faculty centered. Use of VR, by faculty, requires a new pedagogy of teaching as well as a willingness to explore the use of an unknown technology in delivering curriculum. Having access to a technology lab that uses VR can be a welcomed support for faculty. VR can be expensive and creating a VR lab may not seem doable in settings other than large, well-funded universities. This chapter describes a technology lab that was established at a small Midwest liberal arts university, funded by a student technology fee and created by a student-led technology committee.

INTRODUCTION

Nineteen years ago, Prensky (2001) posited that learners are 'digital natives' who have grown accustomed to the integration of technology in all aspects of life: for entertainment, communication, consumerism, and education. This observation also applies to students entering higher education today. As one of the latest technologies to be integrated into the higher education teaching-learning process, virtual reality (VR) offers the capacity to enhance instructional processes and impact student learning.

The definition of VR has evolved over time in response to the rapid growth in the depth and breadth of its development. As early as 2005, Dickey stated that three-dimensional immersive virtual worlds are one of the most exciting emerging technologies being successfully implemented to promote learning in higher education. Yet, there often are too few opportunities for students to initiate use of VR to

DOI: 10.4018/978-1-7998-4960-5.ch007

explore their field of study. More often than not, when VR is used, it is faculty led. Teaching pedagogy is slowly shifting from a faculty-centered teaching-learning process to one that is more student-centered. "Teaching practices in higher education are evolving, as student-centered approaches to instruction play a growing role in course design" (Alexander et al., 2019, p. 19). As teaching practices are evolving, VR hardware and software are concurrently evolving; staying current with VR technology is a challenge which requires on-going faculty development opportunities and joint ventures between faculty and students. Institutional support and commitment are crucial to sustainability of staying current with technology in higher education. Providing a state-of-the-art learning experience for students will not only benefit the colleges and universities in their competitive environment, but also aid in preparing students for their entry into the workforce (Miller, 2014).

The goals of this chapter are to provide: 1) background information related to VR and applications in higher education; 2) a discussion of a student-centered approach to teaching in higher education, and 3) a detailed description of a Technology Exploration Lab (hereafter, referred to as The Lab) created at a small, private, liberal arts institution and 4) implications for future practice.

BACKGROUND

"There is no reason why the objects displayed by a computer have to follow the ordinary rules of physical reality with which we are familiar" (Sutherland, 1965, para. 13). And so it began. Some fifty-five years later we find technology integrated into our personal, professional, and social lives in ways that were unimaginable in 1965. The advent of VR has certainly ushered in a new technology medium. While Helig (1962), a cinematographer, has been identified as the "father of virtual reality," VR did not become known as a research field until the late 1980's. Sherman and Craig (2003) defined VR as "a medium composed of interactive computer simulation that senses the participant's position and actions and replaces or augments the feedback to one or more senses, giving the feeling of being mentally immersed or present in the simulation (a virtual world)" (p. 13). Kapp and O'Driscoll (2010) defined a virtual world as an "immersed 3D virtual environment in which a learner acts through an avatar to engage with the other avatars for the explicit purpose of learning" (p. 55). LaValle (2019, p. 2) defined VR as "Inducing targeted behavior in an organism by using artificial sensory stimulation, while the organism has little or no awareness of the interference."

The environment created through VR is referred to as a virtual world (VW) or virtual world environment (VWE). Simply, a VWE is an artificial physical environment created using digital technology viewed two-dimensionally (2D); a complex three-dimensional (3D) environment contains digital objects and human avatars in real-time. Virtual world learning environments (VWLE's) can accommodate a wider range of learning styles and goals, encourage collaborative and resource-based learning and allow greater sharing and re-use of resources (Britain, 1999). These VR environments are used to support multiple learning styles and encourage collaborative exchange, social learning, which evolved when innovators of VR noticed that users were responsive to the collaborative community.

As creators of the VR experience focus on the VWLE and collaborative experiences, users are focused on the type of VR experience provided; having guidelines for user experience becomes a topic of discussion. For example, according to Babich (2019), VR apps should have the following properties:

1. **Immersive.** Designers should strive to create the feeling that users are in an experience. For example, if you develop a history app, make history come alive for students.
2. **Easy to use.** Eliminate the need to have special skills to use a VR app.
3. **Meaningful.** Meaning is really important for students. You can't create a good VR learning experience without a good story. That's why it so important to advance the art of storytelling. Stories quite simply provide the best vehicle for delivering messages that are not only heard and understood, but that also inspire and elicit action.
4. **Adaptable**. VR experiences should allow students to explore at their own pace. The app should provide complete control over the level of difficulty. Designers should establish how students learn and then use this knowledge to design VR products that allow effective learning.
5. **Measurable.** Each educational tool should provide measured impact. Teachers should be able to track the metrics of education so they can measure the resulting knowledge of a subject. When designing experiences for VR education, it's essential to choose appropriate metrics and make it clear what criteria will be used to measure success and failure.

In sum, since the inception of VR, as the capabilities and applications of VR functions have expanded, definitions and instructional practices for VR uses have evolved. Today, visual, auditory, haptic, and other perceptual stimuli are incorporated within VR software and hardware applications of technology in a sequence of programmed events to which a person is expected to react. Collaboration enhances VR development and best practices, both of which are important as VR is applied in higher education.

Applications of Virtual Reality in Higher Education

As designs of VWs have evolved, applications in higher education have also evolved across disciplines. In a survey of literature, Kamińska, et al. (2019) found that a majority of the software used in education pertains to health related or STEM fields, including: engineering, medical, mathematics, and general education. As an example, Taipei Medical University established the world's largest VR anatomy classroom in direct partnership with HTC. The VR anatomy class is furnished with 10 sets of VIVE Pro and 3D Organon VR anatomy software. This enables individual study as well as cooperative use of the same VR environment and allows students to visualize lectures on anatomical structures in-depth to better understand how bodies function. This use of VR also overcomes previous limitations such as unobservable structures or awkward angles (Rogers, 2019). One might expect that as features of VWs become more clearly identified, use of VWs in higher education will increase.

However, despite the persistence of interest, and with the development of many teaching facilities in VWs, teaching in these environments has not become mainstream, and the numbers of educators using such environments for teaching is in fact decreasing. This is evidenced by the number of underutilized and disused builds that are seen in VWs (Gregory et al., 2015). Designs of VWs are quite diverse, ranging from the replication of real classrooms to imaginary worlds (Prasolova-Førland, 2008). As early as 2005, Dickey posited that 3-D VWs typically share three features: 1) the illusion of 3-D space, 2) avatars that serve as visual representations of users and 3) an interactive chat tool for users to communicate with one another. Five years later, Hew and Cheung (2010) added a fourth feature; 4) the ability for a user to 'act' on the VW; this added feature provides the user with more opportunity for active engagement within the VWE. For example, Bojonova (2011) posited that through avatars, users can navigate, explore, create, and communicate in a virtual space as if it were an extension of the real world, but without the physical limitations and risk of the real world.

Within teacher preparation programs, the flexible and low impact affordance of a multi-user virtual environment (MUVE) can allow teacher candidates to concentrate on certain discrete aspects of being a teacher, such as classroom management, conducting parent-teacher conferences, and application of instructional strategies without the need to attend to the myriad of other activities and responsibilities teachers take on during a normal teaching session or workday (Yilmaz et al., 2013). For example, TeachLivE™ is a virtual simulation system that provides teacher candidates an opportunity to practice teaching a diverse group of digital student avatars in a virtual classroom environment that is accessed through an immersive head-mount display, on any screen equipped with a microphone and camera (Dicker et al., 2013).

Using VR can be expensive and this can explain why innovative uses of VR technologies is reportedly lagging in education, the potential and promise for innovative uses of such technologies is evident in fields other than education. There are institutions of higher education that create the types of twenty–first century experiences needed for students, through building relationships with technology companies that provide support using their assets. For example, Full Sail University and Doghead Simulation partnered together to implement a Social VR application to explore the challenge of online courses and lack of connection (see http://bit.ly/2TOqWG4). These types of exploratory partnerships that leverage the VR experience, to help support a current educational model, can be useful in exploring the benefits of VR. One partnership with a paucity of literature is the partnership between faculty and students exploring technology together, using a student-centered approach.

A STUDENT-CENTERED APPROACH IN HIGHER EDUCATION

The concept of student-centered teaching is not new and is sometimes called active learning, collaborative learning, inquiry-based learning, cooperative learning, and/or problem-based learning. In 1972, Holloway and Davis spoke to the topic of a learner-centered approach to education. In 1983, Rogers defined student-centered learning as an approach to learning in which learners choose not only what to study but

also how and why that topic might be of interest. Barr and Tagg (1995) wrote a seminal article based on a paradigm shift in higher education where the focus is moving from faculty teaching to a focus on student outcomes and student learning. This shift changes everything, and yet, twenty-five years later everything has not changed. In most higher education classrooms, faculty continue to teach as the sage on the stage rather than the guide on the side (see King, 1993).

Characteristics of a Student-Centered VR Environment

A student-centered VR learning environment is a pedagogical approach that allows learners to explore, discover and discuss ideas resulting in the acquisition of meaningful content and knowledge construction involving relevant real world problems and tasks that students find relatable. The value of learning in meaningful contexts cannot be over stated. McCombs and Whistler (1997) suggested that in a student-centered teaching environment, learners find the learning process more meaningful when topics are relevant to their lives, needs, and interests, and when they are actively engaged in creating, understanding, and connecting to knowledge. Student-centered learning is about moving power from the instructor to the learner, treating the learner as a co-creator in the teaching and learning process (Barr & Tagg, 1995). Weimer (2002) pointed out, the responsibility for learning naturally shifts to the student in a learner-centered setting. Wilson and Peterson (2006) postulated that the most critical shift in education in the twenty years prior have move away from a conception of "learner as sponge" toward an image of "learner as active constructor of meaning." Jonassen and Land (2012) posit that a student-centered learning environment reflects various assumptions, including a) centrality of the learner in deriving meaning; b) students' participation in authentic tasks and sociocultural procedure; c) importance of prior and everyday experience in meaning construction; d) access to multiple perspectives, resources and representations. The very nature of VR and the ways in which it promotes on-going student interest and cognitive processing, make it an optimal outlet to engage learners today.

The VR experience has the potential to motivate and encourage participation as students become immersed in the setting and become motivated and sustain an initial perseverance (Yahaya et al., 2004). Once students have persevered with what can be an unfamiliar and uncomfortable in the initial VR experience, they are able to develop the forms of familiarity and the skill sets required so that the authentic setting no longer provides a distraction from the cognitive engagement that higher order learning requires. VR technology is useful in situations where real life environments can be explored in a safe environment without risking real patient health, such as nursing. As early as 1992, Bricken and Byrne found that simulation of real world experiences showed to be equally as effective as actual real life experiences.

Student Engagement in Learning

Historically, faculty have taught with a focus on the content of a textbook as the main tool for teaching and learning; the effectiveness of such a delivery can be argued. However, effectiveness likely depends on the individual faculty member and how much student interest was engaged. VR can be used to enhance student learning and engagement. VR education can transform the way educational content is delivered and thereby how students learn. As has been established, VR creates opportunities for users to not only see a new world but also to interact with it. Being engaged in the learning process motivates students. As Babich (2019) posited, while using VR, learners are motivated to take responsibility for their own learning, for their own discoveries. In short, students have an opportunity to learn by doing rather than passively reading a textbook.

Students are looking for ways that academic programs can connect outside the classroom. For example, Alexander Astin (1984) developed a Theory of Involvement which posits that students learn more with increased involvement in both the academic and social aspects of the collegiate experience. In regard to VR gaming and other programs using avatars can result in social activity among the users. VR can also provide opportunity for three types of interaction: 1) interaction with content, 2) interaction with peers, and 3) interaction with instructor, each of which contribute to greater student engagement in each of those areas of interaction for learning.

As previously discussed, Babich (2019) identified five key properties of a good VR learning experience: immersive, easy-to-use, meaningful, adaptable, and measureable. It is easy to see how the first four properties create user engagement. Showing measureable results is also an effective tool for engaging and motivating students, particularly when they are involved in the assessment process. "The integration of VR technology not only enhances learning, but it also provides participants with real life experience that they can relate to" (Yahaya, 2006, p. 2).

Student Academic Benefits

One of the most attractive features of VWs, and their use in learning environments, is the ability to extend beyond mere text and lecture to promote active learning, the application of knowledge and skills, and the ability to put learning into practice. Hence, VWs serve as optimal learning environments to promote the application of both content knowledge and procedural knowledge in a safe space (Noteborn et al., 2013). It is important to educate students to be able to produce, interpret and question information rather than individuals who only consume information (Akdemir & Özçelikm, 2019).

Furthermore, VR promotes 'knowledge creating cultures' (Scardamalia & Bereiter, 2006), which allow learners to not only collaborate virtually, but to create and produce new knowledge and experiences together. Regardless of specific hardware, software, or uses for VR, Smart, Cascio, and Paffendof (2007) posited that while VWs may appear in different forms, they possess a number of recurrent features including the following:

- Persistence of an in-world environment
- Shared space allowing multiple users to participate simultaneously
- Virtual embodiment in the form of an avatar (a 3D representation of the self)
- Interactions that occur between users and objects in a 3D environment
- Immediacy of action such that interactions occur in real time
- Similarities to the real world (topography, movement, physics); a sense of being in the environment

Collectively, these features influence and have been influenced by practices that evolved in using VR.

Faculty positively influence student cognitive growth, development, and persistence in college; faculty model intellectual work, promote mastery of knowledge and skills, and help students make connections between their studies and post-graduate plans (NSSE, 2014). The annual National Student Survey of Engagement (NSSE) assesses the extent to which undergraduate students are engaged in effective educational practices and experiences supporting personal development. To achieve the kinds of technology uses required for 21st century teaching and learning, teachers need to understand how to use technology to facilitate meaningful learning (Lai, 2008), such as learning that enables students to construct deep and connected knowledge. Yet, there can be a hesitancy to embrace new technologies and to integrate such technologies into instruction. For these reasons, on-going faculty professional development is imperative.

Student Centered Learning: Need for Faculty Development

Applying VR in higher education requires faculty to develop needed technological knowledge and skills as well as transform the teaching and learning process by using technology, including VR in curriculum delivery.

Faculty Development: Technological Knowledge and Skills

Rogers (2003) theorized that individual adoption rates of technological innovations can be visually represented with a bell-shaped curve with representing five categories of users: (a) innovators (2.5%), (b) early adopters (13.5%), (c) early majority (34%), (d) late majority (34%), and (e) laggards (2.5%). Professional development and training opportunities can support educators in adopting new technologies.

VR has the potential to transform the way educational content is delivered by faculty and received by students. However, the learning curve is steep for building knowledge, skills, and application for integration of VR with instruction (Dalgarno et al., 2013). Managing the changing practice of teaching requires that institutions intentionally design faculty support that is not bound by location or time (Alexander, et al., 2019). "Teacher education leaders must attend to leadership practices that set direction, develop people, and redesign their programs of teacher education in order to develop technology, pedagogy, and technology knowledge and skills in preservice teachers" (Dexter et al., 2012, p. 1). Additionally, faculty involvement across disciplines is necessary. "A new technology—especially one that requires significant research and training—needs to be able to work across the curriculum and in sufficient numbers to merit institutional investment" (Alexander et al., 2019, p. 19).

According to Umbach and Wawrzynski (2005), "faculty behaviors and attitudes affect students profoundly, which suggests that faculty members may play the single-most important role in student learning" (p. 176). In order to use technology effectively in the classroom, teachers need relevant knowledge and skills. These knowledge and skills have been discussed in a variety of ways including (1) technological pedagogical content knowledge as well as relevant knowledge of information and communication (AACTE, 2008) and (2) pedagogical technology integration of content knowledge (Brantley-Dias et al., 2007).

Faculty Development: Pedagogy and Curriculum Delivery

The idea of constructivism as student-centered, active learning, is steeped in the theories of Dewey (1859-1952), Piaget (1896-1980), and Vygotsky (1896-1934); collectively these theorists are responsible for the emergence of the pedagogy of constructivism. Constructivism promotes social interaction among students, engagement, and processes that stimulate critical thinking, inquiry, and problem-based learning. Faculty play an integral role in promoting and sustaining critical discourse and constructive social dynamics, managing both learning (e.g., promoting higher level thinking) and social connections between students (Estes, 2015).

It is one thing for faculty to gain depth and breadth of knowledge and skills in using available technology. Believing in a pedagogy of student-centered active learning is quite another. Pedagogical approaches and the way faculty orchestrate classroom learning matters (McKenzie, 2003). Rather than technology creating educational improvement, educational improvement results from technology integration with effective instruction and assessment collectively supporting high-quality student learning (Goldman et al., 2006). King-Sears and Emenova (2007) posit three premises for integrating technology into instruction: 1) technology must be part of students' instructional program, 2) integration ensures that the technology itself does not become the point of instruction, and 3) keeping abreast of the newest advances in technology is a responsibility shared among faculty.

Technology use has accelerated the need for strategically planned faculty support and a reevaluation of the role of teaching and instruction. The increase in offerings of courses online has required professional development supporting the use of digital tools, resulting in collaborations with instructional designers and accelerating the application of new teaching practices. Without this type of support, faculty are challenged to design student-centered environment experiences.

Lipka (2019) identified the top two solutions to student success, each of which involved faculty: 1) reward faculty for experimentation and innovation around teaching and learning, which include taking a research-based approach to their own teaching, 2) promote more research and evidence on how to bring student-success initiatives to scale. Creating a student-led technology lab is a way for smaller or less well-funded institutions of higher education to provide research opportunities for faculty through experimenting and innovating around teaching and learning. Such a lab is can also provide a venue where faculty, students, and staff are learning with one another. A technology lab with a focus on providing opportunities to explore virtual reality does not have to be a high-end lab. In the next section, creation of such a lab will be described. But first, there will be a general discussion of VR labs.

CREATING A STUDENT-LED TECHNOLOGY LAB

Some believe that VR will one day drive the job market and that students need to experience educational content delivery that is transformed through the use of VR to help prepare them for that market. In reviewing the literature, there is a wide range of approaches to establishing a lab, driven by the size of a college or university, the content and associated funding. From an educational perspective, increasing student learning outcomes is a primary goal for most institutions and instructors.

In 2004, Jensen, et al., developed a tool kit for a VR lab to facilitate collaborative experiment for problem-based learning and, using media tools and complex computer simulations, gained data for meteorology. The tool kit shares ways to improve the design of a virtual lab. Toth (2009) showed a significant qualitative effect when combining a learning experience with a virtual DNA lab; students reported preferring working with a virtual environment before the hands-on lab experience. Makransky et al (2014) posited that a gamified lab simulation significantly increased both learning outcomes and motivation levels when combined with traditional teaching. Makransky et al., (2016) conducted a study of the effects of VR use on the knowledge, intrinsic motivation and self-efficacy of a two hour training session with a class of 300 medical students. The students self-reported that the simulation-based learning environment helped the medical students transfer new understanding of disease mechanisms gained in the VR lab setting into everyday clinical practice.

There are commercial companies who provide pre-developed VR modules. For example, Labster provides a catalog of virtual science labs for high schools and colleges. A study was conducted in the Labster commercial simulation environment where students were exposed to real-life situations (with problems that needed to be solved through experimenting with lab equipment and answering quiz questions) (Labster, 2019) and the scores from the quizzes were integrated into a learning system as a tracking tool for the VR experience. Labster demonstrates that virtual laboratories in education can refer to simulation environments that add an environmental and human touch to interface with real laboratory equipment.

There are also well-funded initiatives with a primary that have a purpose focused on introducing students to VR-based learning through the support of science skill acquisition. VR First is an industry-supported global program designed to provide state-of-the-art facilities to creators and educators interested in exploring the power and potential of virtual reality development. As of 2017, VR First network included 581 universities and science parks in 23 countries and VR First committed to create a total of 50 VR First educational labs at universities by the end of 2017. (see https://venturebeat.com/2017/04/13/vr-first-is-creating-50-labs-for-virtual-reality-education-at-universities/).

VR labs don't have to be initiated only in large, well-funded universities. It can be a challenge to set up a technology lab that includes VR experiences, even when the goal is more modest than those previously described. In this section, establishing a student-led technology lab at a small liberal arts university will be described. The background for how a technology lab was envisioned and funded will be presented, the planning and implementation will be described, and obstacles to success and opportunities for improvement will be identified.

Context

In 2015, the lead author of this chapter was in a staff position to advise and guide members of a student government association which was given a fairly unique charge. They were to help distribute and incubate new ideas for student technology use, funded by the addition of a student technology fee. This fee was to be charged to students at a rate of ten dollars per credit hour and was created to improve student technology experiences across the university. The student government was required to vote on this fee and agreed to its implementation pending the establishment of a committee that allowed for student guidance in its distribution.

The committee that was formed to assist with distribution was called the Technology Fee Committee (heretofore referred to as Tech Committee) and was comprised of students, faculty, and staff members who would serve as a sub-committee of the student government association. From its inception, there was no set number of individuals serving on the Tech Committee. A constant was that students served as committee co-chairs, treasurer, and secretary and students were the majority of the committee members. Faculty and staff served in an advisory role; while the composition of the committee changed over the first four years, initially the committee was composed of seven students from the Student Government, including officers, a representative from the Information Technology department, two invited faculty, and the Director for Student Engagement. Each year there were some changes in the committee as deemed appropriate; for example, as new Student Government representatives were elected, as the Information Technology department became more involved, and as Faculty Senate requested two members join, etc. The Tech Committee met weekly throughout each academic year, with sub-committees meeting during the week to complete tasks.

As this was a new initiative, one of the first things that the Tech Committee decided to implement was the request for a physical space to house and explore emerging technologies. The vision was to create an inclusive and accessible "maker space" that contained technology and materials geared toward exploration and creation. Early on, this space was viewed as a Tech Lab. The vision was to encourage students, faculty, and staff to connect with and explore technology in a meaningful way. The space also needed to serve all the stakeholders at the institution. The Tech Lab would ultimately consist of VR experiences and experiences centered on three-dimensional design, 3D printing, and high-end digital gaming. Extensive planning was foundational to success of the Tech Lab. Note that the Tech Lab was not the only student activity funded through the Tech Fee. Although not a focus of this chapter, it is worth mentioning that dollars were spent to provide gaming opportunities in common areas and an e-Sports Team was later developed as an academic competitive sports team, inclusive of student scholarships.

Planning

The Tech Committee was driven by a passion for creating something new and the implicit promises that this future of VR offered; these promises included an implicit expectation to change the teaching-learning process through immersion, simulation, and personal digital interaction. Through a comprehensive review of the literature and research, the decision was made to incorporate existing infrastructure to leverage types of engagement with VR for students, faculty, and staff. The Tech Committee brainstormed on the desired outcomes, understanding that these outcomes would grow and evolve as needed. Over time, the Tech Committee created a plan for the Tech Lab which included: identifying a purpose statement, identifying ideal experiences which align with the purpose, establishing guiding principles and creating an implementation proposal.

The Tech Committee developed a purpose statement connecting the aspirations of the group with the mission and vision of the institution. It was important for the group to have a strong, well-articulated purpose statement given the broad definition of technology, to ensure the Tech Lab's opportunities could keep pace with the group's ability to facilitate experiences well. After much consideration, the committee settled on the following purpose statement:

The Tech Lab will be supported by the University's Student Government and Audio-Visual Services and will provide access to a variety of new technology for instruction and learning. The Lab will include VR systems that will have experiences displayed outside the lab area for audiences passing by the space. Audio for these VR units will be supported in a lab only with in-ceiling speakers. During VR downtime, the external display will be switched to digital signage.

After the Tech Committee decided on the purpose statement, the next step was to identify the types of experiences the group could create to align with the purpose statement. When the Tech Committee was thinking about these opportunities, they started with statements and then began to ask supporting questions. The group gathered background from existing student experiences, existing consumer technology-centered publications, and information described in trade shows where VR was the highlight to refine the guiding principles of the experience. Following is the original list of ideas for VR experiences within the lab:

- Travel and explore historical sites
- Experience culturally significant locations
- Engage in oceanography and library sciences
- Study new journalism / journalistic experiences
- Create and engage with interactive storytelling
- Offer simulations
- Offer laboratory simulations
- Offer opportunities for city building
- Explore career development and virtual interviews
- Engage in creative art projects

After some revision, the group agreed to the following four guiding principles for VR experiences: *Enhancement, Experience, Exposure, and Empowerment.* These four principles were refined through the process of presenting updates to the institution's leadership team and continued to drive the VR experience choices by the Tech Committee. To help provide clarity for the principles, an explanation of each principle and an overview of the guiding questions centered on each principle are provided below.

1. The Principle of Enhancement. One of the functions of providing VR opportunities was to enhance and, in essence transform, the teaching and learning process. This was chosen to describe VR op-

portunities that centered on reality enhancement for students and on the teaching/learning process in particular. Questions that were generated included the following:

a. Within the Technology Lab, could students create personal and group experiences that weren't plausible or cost-effective before?
b. Can students from various disciplines on campus, use the lab to experience their discipline in a transformed way?
c. Can VR take existing experiences and positively enhance them?
d. Can VR be extended to a virtual online classroom or virtually connect or collaborate in a meeting?

2. The Principle of Experience. Creating VR opportunities that provided an enjoyable and worthwhile experience and which resulted in customer satisfaction, was deemed important. Given that students entered their first VR experience with a variety of feelings, it was also important to tailor the experience to each person so that they would be motivated to come back. Related questions include:
    a. Can we create spaces and places that foster experimentation and where cost does not need to be a factor?
    b. Can we paint and create new artwork in 3 dimensions?
    c. Are there experiences that foster learning that would be otherwise impossible?
    d. Can a VR experience impact behavior?
    e. Is it a safe place to simulate real-world experiences from classroom management to chemistry labs, to medical applications?
3. The Principle of Exposure. The VR opportunities which center on exposure are focused on the possibility of enhanced learning experiences that allow the user to interact and explore recreated content at different times, places, and spaces. Related questions included:
    a. Would it be possible to visit factual recreations of planets or historical events?
    b. Can users visit places where it is too dangerous or too costly to visit in reality?
    c. Could users be exposed to VR to provide an element of change in that person?
    d. Would it be possible to take a trip to the Great Pyramids of Giza and explore Google Maps data?
4. The Principle of Empowerment. These were VR opportunities that center on empowerment; providing access to cutting edge technology for students, faculty and staff, while creating a focused exposure to new trends and new ideas. Related questions include:
    a. Would VR be helpful as a tool for job training?
    b. Could it have a place in training and safety?
    c. Is it possible to provide training opportunities that would be otherwise costly?
    d. Would it be possible to simulate experiences that have been difficult previously?
    e. Can virtual reality provide an opportunity for folks to experience learning moments or simulations that would be dangerous to the learner or others in a safe and preparation focused way?

With these principles in mind, the last aspect of the Tech Committee was to create an implementation proposal for the University to approve. The Tech Committee partnered with existing university offices to create a proposal which allowed for the use of existing University space, was accessible, and could meet the needs of showcasing the virtual experiences for individual and group learning. The Tech Committee created a proposal which included requirements for facilities space, new technology, and access control.

Establishing the Tech Lab

After a few months of weekly meetings, refining the purpose, space requirements, and value of the Tech Lab, university leadership identified and approved a 14x14 feet room that could serve as a Tech Lab to explore emerging technology. This was an existing room located along a high-traffic hallway, with four windows for outside viewing. The Tech Committee felt it was important to provide access to the Tech Lab to the widest range of potential users. Locating the Tech Lab in a highly-trafficked, centralized location was deemed critical. There was a commitment from the Tech Committee and the university to invest in infrastructure as well as emergent technology. Additionally, there was a commitment to include a keycard door access point, a mounted TV monitor outside with a speaker system, and the necessary audio-visual display in the interior of the room to allow for the VR experience to be shared with others inside the room. This design would highlight the lab during campus tours, enhance social use of VR by streaming what was happening in the "virtual world" to the monitors outside the room and helped market the experience to those unaware or unfamiliar with the Tech Lab.

In terms of the Head Mounted Display (HMD) technology, the Tech Committee chose to purchase the HTC Vive headset; this unit has wall-mounted tracking sensors, two hand controllers, a full headset and earbuds. The HTC Vive hardware had a preferred pairing with a windows software system called "Steam" which provided a software interface for the virtual reality experiences. At the time, Steam was the more well-rounded ecosystem where developers could easily create and distribute their VR applications for users to purchase. The HTC system was fairly user intuitive and allowed exploration of applications purchased on a mobile device. The other need was a VR capable computer to connect the hardware to software. The aforementioned components connected to the standard data, visual, and audio ports on the computer.

The Tech Committee worked through logistics and obstacles of installing the system and connected it to the existing University audio and visual infrastructure. The Tech Committee members became experts in the hardware, software, and structure of the systems and served as guides for students and faculty who wanted to be among the first users of the Tech Lab and a VR experience. The University also provided assistance for the Tech Lab with staff from the information technology department.

In the initial days of the Tech Lab implementation, the following software programs (and developer noted in parentheses) were chosen to meet the formerly discussed guiding principles of the Lab:

Enhancement

- Google Earth (Google)
- Chernobyl VR Project Game (The Farm 51 Group SA)
- Virtual Desktop (Virtual Desktop, Inc.)
- Sketchup Viewer (Tremble)

Experience

- Tilt Brush (Google)
- Human Anatomy VR on Gear VR (Oculus)
- Guided Meditation VR (Cubicle Ninjas)

Exposure

- The Blu (Wevr, Inc.)
- Everest VR (Sólfar Studios)
- The Crystal Reef (Virtual Human Interaction Lab)
- Spacetours VR (Vibrant Visuals - Christian Klötzel)

Empowerment

- Job Simulator: the 2050 Archives (Owlchemy Labs)
- Disassembly VR (Khor Chin Heong)
- Handpass VR (Constructive Media)

The software was downloaded to the Tech Lab computing device and all programs and components were integrated. After a few test runs, the Tech Committee opened the Tech Lab for interested students and faculty.

The VR First Experiences

The Tech Lab had no formal opening but rather a series of open houses in which the University community was invited to explore. These open houses were advertised via social media, digital billboards located throughout the campus, presentations at Faculty Senate, and word of mouth. The first few open house sessions for students involved the cumbersome process of connecting students with the headset, making sure they were comfortable, running them through a tutorial, and then executing an experience or two based on the student's interest. Students orally reported that the experience was a joy and delight to explore the technology-based innovation; in short it was a unique experience.

The Student Experience

There really is nothing quite like putting on a VR headset for the first time. For many students, they likened it to a leap of faith. Others described it as the first step from the safety of solid land to the unpredictability of a boat tossed on the water. The experience itself can be jarring. For those who have not experienced a VR yet, imagine putting goggles over your eyes to start. Your view turns from full color to pitch black. In the dark, you then are asked to find and grab controllers. You grab them. You are asked if you are ready and then, all of a sudden, the world in front of your eyes is created. You can see two virtual hands and virtual space in front of you; the world is now yours to explore.

A student's first experience generally started with a low-risk activity, a program called "Tilt Brush." In this creative program the student is an artist, complete with a brush in one hand and an upgraded painting palette in the other. After some basics on controls and perspective (the biggest concern was avoiding obstacles such as other people and walls), the user was asked to pick any color and write their name in the air; most students were able to easily complete this task. Then, the user would be asked to follow the guide's voice; usually a few feet away from their painting. The user would approach the guide and then be asked to turn around to see what they had just painted from a different perspective. The goal was for the user to see their painting in three dimensions. The experience with "Tilt Brush" is just one example of how VR can completely change perspective.

Students who were apprehensive started in a stationary VR experience, a roller coaster. The user would be asked to grab a hand set in the middle of the room and move to a sitting position. The student would then start the VR experience and watch in amazement while going through the ups and downs, twists and turns, of a simulated roller coaster experience. The motion would be simulated via the headset without any additional need for movement or vibrations in the Tech Lab.

Members of the Tech committee reported that it was amazing to join students travelling to places they wanted to visit through the use of Google Earth VR, an interactive experience similar to what it might feel like to have the ability to fly. One starts the experience suspended above the Grand Canyon; in the air, looking down. One then learns how to "fly" through virtual space with the ability to zoom in and out as well as travel across the land toward a horizon. Perhaps what was most surprising was the number of students who wanted to show and share their home; going home was usually the first place a student wanted to travel. The University has students from over 60 countries, and it was fascinating to see the global perspective provided by students as they visited their homes. It was those moments that we know VR, at its best, was about students connecting.

The Faculty Experience

While students became interested in the Tech Lab immediately, it took almost a full semester before the first faculty member brought in a class of their students, unaware of how to embrace technology capabilities for their course. Working with faculty to integrate the use of VR with curriculum and instruction was important. The Tech Committee believed that VR use could transform instruction for every department and field of study with on-going positive impact. Over time, the Tech Lab developed different programs for different subject areas. For example, students in Management or Human Resources courses would be encouraged to engage with an experience such as "Job Simulator - the 2050 Archives" (Owlchemy Labs). This VR activity allows the user to experience common day jobs (such as chef or office worker) through a simulated recreation. While the experience is a cartoony representation, it is helpful in exploring and explaining VR's possibilities. After each student completed their time with VR, there were conversations with the professor and a class debriefing to understand the impact of their experiences.

Similarly, faculty who brought students from the College of Liberal Arts and Sciences began with an exploration of possibilities of VR creatively using "Tilt Brush" or another experience called "Beat Saber" (a rhythmic, virtual movement experience that helps orient the student to the motion controls and perspective shift in VR). It was an ideal partnership as many of the Tech Committee members were familiar with the programs; what evolved was a creative partnering.

Considerations for Sustainability

During the first academic year of implementation the primary users of the lab were students. By year two of the Tech Lab implementation, the lab had additional faculty, staff, and students, who hadn't participated year one, wanting to explore. While the Tech Committee experienced elements of success in the first year of implementation, the Tech Committee wanted to ensure sustained growth for the Tech Lab and address lessons learned. For example, in the original proposal, the Tech Committee had proposed having the Tech Lab open twenty-four hours a day, seven days a week, for anyone who wanted to use the resources. It was proposed that access would be granted through an existing University key card system. However, after initial experiences with students and faculty, the Tech Committee reevaluated this proposal and it was modified. It was very important to the Tech Committee to ensure that the experience with VR was a pleasant and safe experience. The Tech Committee wanted to ensure that users understood the VR options available to them, were safe throughout their experience, the system ran successfully, and users were able to ask questions. One of the ways that the committee ensured these objectives was to provide restricted access to the Tech Lab that required a member of the Tech Committee to be present to assist and be a guide each individual or faculty's class of students.

The Technology Ambassador Program

Requiring a member of the Tech Committee to be present in the Tech Lab during any user time was a significant commitment and didn't seem feasible, even though it was desired. Thus, the Tech Committee decided to ask for support from the Student Government Association. Specifically, the Tech Committee asked for assistance with objectives related to funding, vetting new opportunities, and staffing. The Student Government Association showed interest in forging a partnership with the Tech Committee. This partnership allowed for numerous conversations for the purpose of brainstorming a new staffing model for the Tech Lab. The new staffing model involved the creation of a "Technology Ambassador Program" composed of students. The Ambassador Program aimed to help equip and train students on VR experiences and develop leadership skills. The leadership role would involve guiding and leading individual and groups of students through VR experiences. The idea was for the Technology Ambassadors to take primary responsibility for operating the Tech Lab and helping to ensure the Tech Lab was serviced and available to the University's community of constituents.

The Technology Ambassador Program was created not only to help distribute information about VR to university students, faculty and staff but also for the purpose of increasing student feedback and student participation. To help implement the Technology Ambassador Program, the Tech Committee instituted a referral program which distributed responsibility for Ambassadors to every member of the Tech Committee. The idea was that each member of the Tech Committee was responsible for becoming a Technology Ambassador as well as recruiting potential Ambassadors.

In order to become a Technology Ambassador, students submitted a digital application which was reviewed by the Tech Committee. After the application was reviewed, the members of the Tech Committee met with the applicant to complete a short interview and, if approved, the applicant was given access to training materials and later, the ability to enter the Tech Lab anytime. This process allowed the Tech Committee to focus on the Ambassador applicants that truly enjoyed the VR experience and felt comfortable after their first brush in deep space, virtual mountains, or jump-scare haunted houses. Unsurprisingly, many of the residential students were the first to become Ambassadors and they were often the first group to help become natural promoters to other students, staff, and faculty members.

Obstacles

Upon powering the system and engaging in the first few experiences, the Tech Committee identified a few obstacles that needed to be addressed: sharing the experience with those outside of the virtual reality for teaching and learning, marketing, and engagement; accessibility for non-technical participants, and VR curriculum content integration. Each of these had their own set of unique challenges and the committee was able to work through these obstacles for targeted solutions.

The first obstacle the Tech Committee identified was **sharing the experience** with those outside of the virtual reality for teaching and learning, marketing, and engagement. VR is inherently a solitary activity. It is the user who is putting on the headset, experiencing the digital world, and interacting with the physical world. The learning and experiencing is taking place in an immersive way which is not easy to share. How can we extend this technology and experience to others around the individual for marketing or simply classroom engagement? The Tech Committee synthesized the idea to help share the experience by mirroring the computer's display both inside and outside the lab. By positioning a capable television with audio outside and inside the lab, there was the ability to share a large portion of the VR experience with observers. They could now see what the user was "doing" and the actions that were taking place. The added bonus was that the Technology Ambassadors could now effectively guide the VR user and explain what was happening on the screen for any observers. It was this act of sharing that was one of the primary drivers in helping socialize information about the lab with other students and interested faculty. It was also this distribution of sharing that allowed for us to showcase the space during University tours.

The next obstacle to overcome pertained to **accessibility**. How could a lab be designed that would be easy to access for individuals with a non-technical background? The HTC system was fairly user intuitive but needed some additional instructions to assist with getting users integrated with the system. To tackle this obstacle, the committee worked with the existing staff members in Information Technology to create a partnership where the equipment could be serviced by technical personnel while the committee would create walkthroughs to the new technology as the primary users. These walkthroughs would then be printed and stored on site for easy reference as well as in an online course shell specifically created for the lab. In addition, the committee utilized the student ambassadors to assist with decreasing the technical need for anyone using the lab. It was a "guided" service that allowed for many of the users to focus on the experience and less on the technical elements "how" the system was implemented. Unfortunately, the software and hardware was not nearly as smooth as was hoped. The technology was not fully optimized for the types of programs used and it required frequent calls to the information technology department to assist with troubleshooting the multiples pieces that were involved in running a single experience.

The third obstacle was VR curriculum **content integration**. The Tech Committee identified that one of the challenges faced was simply the limited amount of VR content that existed in the world and as a result of the limited nature, ensuring a way to share and scale that content. The Tech Committee chose to overcome this obstacle by carefully selecting software and creating a selection process for VR experiences. The ecosystem they chose was called "Steam" and it was originally focused as a personal computer video game distribution platform. It was mentioned above as an element of implementation.

Steam was able to partner early and understand the value in VR, it quickly developed into a VR experience platform. Steam applications could be used in tandem with proprietary programs. The first Steam VR device released was the HTC Vive, a VR HMD similar to Oculus Rift. As a platform, SteamVR, not only supports its own HMDs. but also others such as Rift. Steam applications could be used in tandem with proprietary programs. Users with a Steam account could buy the software once and then have the ability to have it synced with their account - even across multiple PC's. Steam VR games were also transferable – similar to an "app store" concept. This was a great fit as the Tech Committee was unsure if the VR lab model that we were creating here might be able to be distributed to other network distribution locations. The Tech Committee created a single Steam user which would function as the sole "owner" of the material for the Tech Lab. The Tech Committee then shared access to Steam VR platform with the Tech Committee leadership and created a process for software selection among the remaining members. This process served a as "clearing house" for taking requests and trying out new experiences as they were released. The secondary benefit of involving students in the selection process was that they were more likely to participate in the experiences and use the labs themselves. Many students were not only eager to build a library of experiences but viewing completing them all as a personal challenge and a challenge they would talk about frequently inside and outside the classroom. With each obstacle the Tech Committee was able to overcome, the more robust an experience that was able to created.

Reflections

Throughout the creation of the Tech Lab, the Tech Committee was able to leverage student and faculty interest to create a space which helped students experience, enhance and become empowered regarding their knowledge of VR. There are three takeaways from the experience of establishing a Tech Lab that might be helpful for those looking to replicate the experience or learn from the startup process. First, develop a razor-focus on being student-centered; second, develop a sustainable funding model: third, integrate faculty involvement, and lastly, intentionally take time to continue to research VR uses in education to enhance and transform the teaching and learning experiences.

Student-focused, Student-driven

First, there is a need to develop a razor-focus on being student-centered. One thing that enhanced our success was to involve students at every-step of the process of creating a Tech Lab. The institution created pathways to involve students through funding mechanisms used, the structure of the Tech Committee primarily involving students, and the planning and implementation process. This involvement of students provided a sense of ownership and a sense of purpose which laid the foundation for the Tech Lab's success. Students embraced the idea of starting something new and innovative and asked, "What is possible?" Students were able to help share their experiences with their peers, their faculty, and their community. It would have been easier to have the University's Information Technology Team create a lab with what they thought was needed for "today's student." It would have been easier to create a committee of solely staff and faculty to create the Tech Lab. It would have been much easier to create the space that the University "thought" students needed without doing the hard work of involving students in the process. If the project were to start over, the recommendation would be to involve students in the process even more.

Financial Sustainability

Second, there is a need to develop a sustainable funding model. Technology in general, and VR technology specifically, can be expensive and difficult to scale. One of the things that caught the Tech Committee by surprise was that the exponential growth of opportunities and costs associated with the Tech Lab. While the Tech Committee had substantial capital for the initial investment ($50,000), after the first year of the Tech Lab's opening, the Tech Committee realized the need for sustained funding. The funding needs that were not originally taken into account were the expansion of the VR experiences, replacement of the VR hardware, sanitization materials for the hardware, and replacement of accidentally damaged hardware. While the Tech Committee had the authority and oversight to use the Technology Fee funding for this purpose, there could be alternative funding models worth exploring in further development of the Tech Lab. These alternative funding models might include the opportunity to charge participants on a rate basis, similar to a per-minute or per-hour cost. Another would be to expand the availability of the lab to community members outside the University. To date, the Tech Lab is not open for public use or consumption, but it would not be difficult to create a framework where there was a monetary exchange for use of the Tech Lab's facilities. Creating or leveraging a renewable funding source will be necessary for long-term success. The reality is that sustainability of a program is difficult when a program has not become part of the institutional fabric. For example, when the lead author of this chapter transferred to another campus with the university system, the position was not refilled. Without a leader, sustainability of the program is in question. A social work faculty who used the Tech Lab for her classes saw the value of VR in enhancing and transforming instruction. At this time that individual has applied for a grant to support the operations of the Tech Lab.

Faculty Involvement and Training

Third, there is a need to integrate faculty involvement. As previously discussed, it was nearly a full semester before the first faculty member set foot inside of the Tech Lab. One of the Tech Committee's biggest regrets in this project was to not work more diligently to intentionally integrate faculty members into the Tech Lab's operational framework. While there were experiences that the Tech Committee knew could be useful in the classroom, a crucial step of connecting and inviting each faculty member to participate was missed. If the Tech Lab were to be recreated, one suggestion would be to involve interested faculty as much as possible to showcase the potential of the technology. This could look like a formal faculty sponsor for the program or construct open houses and showcase the potential for classroom involvement even in a single college, program, or class. As early adopters of the new technology, we could have provided demonstration and possible learning opportunities for more students. For example, one of these learning opportunities might be to showcase VR's value as an alternative to traditional classroom expectations and expenses. If one was to examine traditional sources of expenditures, which might include field trips, lab supplies, museum trips, and risks associated with travel, there could be an opportunity to help curb or redistribute spending. Field trips could be digital experiences which students could take an even more active role in exploring historically relevant places, modern spaces, or opportunities that might be cost or safety prohibited. Another example of learning opportunity might also include working with museums and historical/cultural institutions to help digitize and distribute interactive elements of culture.

Ongoing Research & Development

Lastly, it is critical to intentionally take time to continue to research VR uses in education to enhance and transform the teaching and learning experiences. Establishing the Tech Lab was time consuming and the Tech Committee did not focus on continuing to research emergent uses of VR in higher education. For example, in reviewing literature for preparation for this chapter a document was located that may be useful for those considering setting up a VR Tech Lab. Springboard VR (2019) has developed a "A 30-day guide for implementing virtual reality seamlessly in educational institutions." This guide covers the following topics: setting up hardware & software; holding an open house; hosting a follow up event; integrating content into curriculum; and making your case to decision-makers.

Having this information could have been useful as a check point for our process. It was interesting to note in reflection that these are the very steps that were followed in implementation of this case study. A final point is that, in retrospect, there could have been more of a focus on record-keeping and data collection while creating and implementing the Tech Lab experience. For example, user feedback was primarily gained from taking anecdotal records and student oral report after completing a VR experience. Such record keeping and data collection would be valuable in telling the story of the creation of the Tech Lab and to evaluate implementation, both of which could support replication.

IMPLICATIONS FOR FUTURE PRACTICE

1. It is imperative that institutions of higher education recognize the value that VR hardware and software offer to broaden and deepen the student learning experience.
2. Institutional infrastructure is needed to assure that resources are provided and sustainable systems are established, including funding.
3. Future research in VR should focus on how VR technology can be effectively integrated with other educational activities.
4. On-going faculty exposure to VR and professional development must be provided.
5. Smaller institutions who are establishing Tech Labs for the purpose of providing VR opportunities for students need to publish their case studies.

CONCLUSION

Students come to institutions of higher education with a variety of experiences, skills, and interests in technology, and more specifically VR. While use of VR in higher education is increasing, faculty may struggle to provide adequate student opportunities to explore emergent technologies. Opportunities that are provided are often faculty-initiated to complete an assignment and tend to neglect student exploration and application. This practice grows out of a faculty-centered approach to teaching and learning. In this chapter we emphasized the importance of a student-centered approach. Creating a VR lab can be costly and found primarily at high-end universities. In this chapter a description of the creation of a student-led technology lab, at a small Midwest liberal arts institution, has been discussed. Such a technology lab provides an environment for, not only individual student exploration but also for faculty to bring their classes to use VR for topic-focused exploration. Institutional support is needed to initiate any university-wide initiative and this is certainly the case for establishing a VR lab, regardless of size or scope. Support not only includes a designated budget but must also opportunities for faculty professional technology development.

REFERENCES

AACTE Committee on Innovation and Technology. (2008). *Handbook of technological pedagogical content knowledge (TPCK) for educators*. Routledge.

Akdemir, E., & Özçelik, C. (2019). The investigation of the attitudes of teachers towards using student centered teaching methods and techniques. *Universal Journal of Educational Research, 7*(4), 1147-1153. Retrieved from http://www.hrpub.org

Alexander, B., Ashford-Rowe, K., Barajas-Murphy, N., Dobbin, G., Knott, J., McCormack, M., & Pomerantz, J. (2019). *EDUCAUSE Horizon Report: 2019 Higher Education Edition*. EDUCAUSE.

Babich, N. (2019). *How VR in education will change how we learn and teach*. Retrieved from: https://xd.adobe.com/ideas/principles/emerging-technology/virtual-reality-will-change-learn-teach/

Barr, R., & Tagg, J. (1995, November/December). From teaching to learning: A new paradigm for undergraduate education. *Change*, 13–25.

Bojanova, I. (2011). Physical presence through virtual worlds. *IT Professional, 13*(4), 4–5. doi:10.1109/MITP.2011.66

Bricken, M., & Byrne, C. (1992). *Summer students in virtual reality: A pilot study on educational applications of VR technology*. University of Washington, Human Interface Technology Laboratory.

Britain, S. (1999). A framework for pedagogical evaluation of virtual world learning environments. JISC Technology Applications Programme, Report 41: Joint Information Systems Committee of the Higher Educational Funding Council.

Dalgarno, B., Gregory, S., Carlson, L., Lee, M. J. W., & Tynan, B. (2013). *A systematic review and environmental analysis of the use of 3D immersive virtual worlds in Australian and New Zealand higher education institutions* (Final Report). Armidale, Australia: DEHub: Innovation in Distance Education, University of New England. Retrieved from http://www.dehub.edu.au/downloads/VWSSP_Report_V2_TD_200613_dehub.pd

Dexter, S., Herring, M. & Thomas, T. (2012). Editorial: Technology Leadership for the Teacher Education Initiative. *Contemporary Issues in Technology and Teacher Education, 12*(3), 255-263.

Dickey, M. D. (2005). Brave new (interactive) worlds: A review of the design affordances and constraints of two 3D virtual worlds as interactive learning environments. *Interactive Learning Environments, 13*(1–2), 121–137. doi:10.1080/10494820500173714

Dieker, L., & Rodriguez, J., Lignugaris/Kraft, B., Hynes, M., & Hughes, C. E. (2013). The potential of simulated environments in teacher education: Current and future possibilities. *Teacher Education and Special Education: The Journal of the Teacher Education Division of the Council for Exceptional Children, 37*(1), 21–33. doi:10.1177/0888406413512683

Estes, J. S. (2015). A call for teacher preparation programs to model integration of technology pedagogy and use throughout coursework. In S. Keengwe (Ed.), *Handbook of research on educational technology integration and active learning*. IGI Global. doi:10.4018/978-1-4666-8363-1.ch004

Goldman, S. R., Lawless, K., Pellegrino, J. W., & Plants, R. (2005). Technology for teaching and learning with understanding. In J. M. Cooper (Ed.), *Classroom Teaching Skills* (8th ed., pp. 185–234). Houghton Mifflin.

Gregory, S., Scutter, S., Jacka, L., McDonald, M., Farley, H., & Newman, C. (2015). Barriers and Enablers to the Use of Virtual Worlds in Higher Education: An Exploration of Educator Perceptions, Attitudes and Experiences. *Journal of Educational Technology & Society*, *18*(1), 3–12.

Helig, M. L. (1962). *U. S. Patent No. 3,050, 870*. Washington, DC: U.S. Patent and Trademark Office.

Hew, K. F., & Cheung, W. S. (2010). Use of three-dimensional (3-D) immersive virtual worlds in K-12 and higher education settings: A review of the research. *British Journal of Educational Technology*, *4*(1), 33–55. doi:10.1111/j.1467-8535.2008.00900.x

Holoway, L. D., & Davis, D. J. (1972). The learner centered approach to instruction. *American Vocational Journal*, *47*(1), 32–34.

Hullinger, J. (2015). *Six innovative uses for virtual reality. The Idea Factory.* Retrieved from http://theweek.com/articles/562851/6

Jensen, N., Seipel, S., von Voigt, G., Raasch, S., Olbrich, S., & Nejdl, W. (2004). Development of a Virtual Laboratory System for Science Education and the Study of Collaborative Action. In L. Cantoni & C. McLoughlin (Eds.), *Proceedings of ED-MEDIA 2004--World Conference on Educational Multimedia, Hypermedia & Telecommunications* (pp. 2148-2153). Lugano, Switzerland: Association for the Advancement of Computing in Education (AACE). Retrieved March 28, 2020 from https://www.learntechlib.org/primary/p/12775/

Jonassen, D., & Land, S. (Eds.). (2012). *Theoretical foundations of learning environments*. Routledge.

Kamińska, D., Sapiński, T., Wiak, S., Tikk, T., Haamer, R., Avots, E., Helmi, A., Ozcinar, C., & Anbarjafari, G. (2019). Virtual Reality and Its Applications in Education: Survey. *MDPI: Information*, *10*(318). Advance online publication. doi:10.3390/info10100318

Kapp, K., & O'Driscoll, T. (2010). *Learning in 3D: Adding a new dimension to enterprise learning and collaboration*. Pfeiffer.

King, A. (1993). *From sage on the stage to guide on the side, College Teaching, 41(1)* . Retrieved from http://www.jstor.org/stable/27558571

King-Sears, M., & Evmenova, A. S. (2007). Premises, principles, and processes for integrating technology into instruction. *Teaching Exceptional Children*, *40*(1), 6–14. doi:10.1177/004005990704000101

Lai, K. W. (2008). ICT supporting the learning process: The premise, reality, and promise. In J. Voogt & G. Knezek (Eds.), *International Handbook of Information Technology in Primary and Secondary Education* (pp. 215–230). Springer. doi:10.1007/978-0-387-73315-9_13

LaValle, S. M. (2019). *Virtual Reality.* Retrieved from http://vr.cs.uiuc.edu/

Linden Lab. (2013). *Infographic: 10 years of Second Life.* Retrieved from http://www.lindenlab.com/releases/infographic

Lipka. (2019). The truth about student success: Myths, realities, and 30 practices that are working. *Chronicle of Higher Education.*

Makransky, G., Bonde, M. T., Wulff, J. S. G., Wandall, J., Hood, M., Creed, P. A., & Nørremølle, A. (2016). Simulation based virtual learning environment in medical genetics counseling: An example of bridging the gap between theory and practice in medical education. *BMC Medical Education, 16*(1), 98. doi:10.118612909-016-0620-6 PMID:27012245

McCombs, B., & Whistler, J. (1997). *The learner centered classroom and school: Strategies for increasing student motivation and achievement.* Jossey-Bass Publishers.

McKenzie, J. (2003). Pedagogy does matter. *The Educational Technology Journal, 13*(1), 1–6.

Miller, R. (2014). The application of virtual reality in higher education distance learning. *Journal of Applied Learning Technology, 4*(4), 15–18.

National Survey of Student Engagement (NSSE). (2014). *Center for Postsecondary Research.* Indiana University School of Education. Retrieved http://nsse.iub.edu/NSSE_2014_Results/pdf/NSSE_2014_Annual_Results.pdf#page=8

Noteborn, G., Dailey-Hebert, A., Bohle-Carbonell, K., & Gijselears, W. (2013). Essential knowledge for academic performance: Educating in the virtual world to promote active learning. *Teaching and Teacher Education, 37*(January), 217–234. http://authors.elsevier.com/sd/article/S0742051X1300156X

Prasolova-Førland, E. (2008). Analyzing place metaphors in 3D educational collaborative virtual environments. *Computers in Human Behavior, 24*(2), 185–204. doi:10.1016/j.chb.2007.01.009

Prensky, M. (2001). Digital natives, digital immigrants part 1. *On the Horizon, 9*(5), 1–6. doi:10.1108/10748120110424816

Pulse Simulation Technology. (2008). Retrieved from https://www.youtube.com/watch?v=Q11aWO6dg2Q

Rogers, E. M. (2003). *Diffusion of innovations* (5th ed.). The Free Press.

Rogers, S. (2019). *Virtual Reality: The learning aid of the 21st Century.* Retrieved from https://www.forbes.com/sites/solrogers/2019/03/15/virtual-reality-the-learning-aid-of-the-21st-century/#65899a28139b

Sherman, W. R., & Craig, A. B. (2003). *Understanding virtual reality. Interface, application and design.* Morgan-Kaufmann Publishers. doi:10.1162/105474603322391668

Smart, J., Cascio, J., & Paffendof, J. (2007). *Metaverse roadmap: pathways to the 3D web.* Retrieved from http://www.metaverseroadmap.org/overview

Springboard, V. R. (2019). *A 30-day guide for implementing virtual reality seamlessly in educational institutions.* Retrieved from https://www.springboardvr.com/

Sutherland, I. (1965). The ultimate display. *Proceedings of International Federation of Information Processing, 2*, 506-509. Retrieved from http://worrydream.com/refs/Stutherland%20-%20The%Ultimate%20Display.pdf

Toth, E. E. (2009). "Virtual inquiry" in the science classroom: What is the role of technological pedagogical content knowledge? *International Journal of Communication Technology in Education*, *5*(4), 78–87. doi:10.4018/jicte.2009041008

Umbach, P. D., & Wawrzynsli, M. R. (2005). Faculty do matter: The role of college faculty in student learning and engagement. *Research in Higher Education*, *46*(2), 153–185. doi:10.100711162-004-1598-1

Weimer, M. (2002). *Learner-centered teaching: Five key changes to practice*. Jossey-Bass.

Wilson, S. M., & Peterson, P. L. (2006). *Theories of learning and teaching: What do they mean for educators?* National Education Association. Retrieved from http://www.nea.org/assets/docs/mf_ltreport.pdf

Yahaya, R. A. (2006). Assessing the Effectiveness of Virtual Reality Technology as part of an Authentic Learning Environment. *Proceedings of the Sixth International Conference on Advanced Learning Technologies (ICALT'06)*. Retrieved from https://eprints.qut.edu.au/9327/1/9327.pdf

Yahaya, R. A., Euler, T., & Godat, M. (2004). Enhancement of Learning in Decision Making and Negotiation within Virtual Reality Environment. In E. McWilliam, S. Danby, & J. Knight (Eds.), *Performing Educational Research: Theories*. Methods and Practices.

Yilmaz, R., Topu, F., Goktas, Y., & Coban, M. (2013). Social presence and motivation in a three dimensional virtual world: An explanatory study. *Australian Journal of Educational Technology, 29*(6).

ADDITIONAL READING

Astin, A. (1984). Student involvement: A development theory for higher education. *Journal of College Student Development*, *49*, 518–529.

Bailenson, J. (2019). *Experience on demand: What virtual reality is, how it works, and what it can do*. Apple Books.

Biocca, F., Harms, C., & Burgoon, J. K. (2003). Toward a more robust theory and measure of social presence: Review and suggested criteria. *Presence (Cambridge, Mass.)*, *12*(5), 456–480. doi:10.1162/105474603322761270

Blaschke & Hase. S. (2015). Heutagogy, technology and lifelong learning for professional part-time learners. In A.Dailey-Hebert & K. Dennis (Eds.), Transformative perspectives & processes in higher education. Springer: London. doi. doi:10.1007/978-3-319-09247-8_5

Brantley-Dias, L., Kinuthia, W., Shoffner, M. B., DeCastro, C., & Rigole, N. (2007). Developing pedagogical technology integration content knowledge in preservice teachers: A case study approach. *Journal of Research on Computing in Teacher Education*, *23*, 143–149.

Chang, L. (2015, June 29). Go shopping from the comfort of your own home with your virtual reality headset. *Digital Trends*. Retrieved from https://www.digitaltrends.com/

First, V. R. (2017). *VR First is creating 50 labs for virtual reality education at universities*. Retrieved from https://venturebeat.com/2017/04/13/vr-first-is-creating-50-labs-for-virtual-reality-education-at-universities/

National Survey of Student Engagement. (2019). *Engagement insights: Survey findings on the quality of undergraduate education-Annual Results 2019*. Indiana University Center for Postsecondary Research.

Ong, S. K., & Nee, A. Y. C. (2013). *Virtual and augmented reality applications in manufacturing*. Springer Science & Business Media.

Rheingold, H. (1991). *Virtual reality: The revolutionary technology of computer generated artificial worlds*. Simon & Schuster Publishing.

Rogers, C. (1983). As a teacher, can I be myself? In *Freedom to learn for the 80s*. Charles E. Merrill Publishing Company.

Saposnik, G., & Levin, M. (2011). Virtual reality in stroke rehabilitation a meta-analysis and implications for clinicians. *Stroke*, *42*(5), 1380–1386. doi:10.1161/STROKEAHA.110.605451 PMID:21474804

Schroeder, R. (2008). Defining Virtual Worlds and Virtual Environments. *Journal of Virtual Worlds Research*, *1*(1). Advance online publication. http://journals.tdl.org/jvwr/article/view/294. doi:10.4101/jvwr.v1i1.294

The New Media Consortium. (2007). *The Horizon Report*. New Media Consortium.

Verloop, N., Driel, J. V., & Meijer, P. (2001). Teacher knowledge and the knowledge base of teaching. *International Journal of Educational Research*, *35*(5), 441–461. doi:10.1016/S0883-0355(02)00003-4

Virtual Reality. (n.d.). Retrieved from http://www.merriamwebster.com/dictionary/virtualreality

KEY TERMS AND DEFINITIONS

Authentic Learning Environment: A teaching environment that uses an instructional approach that allows students to explore, discuss, and meaningfully construct concepts and relationships in contexts that involve real-world problems and projects that are relevant to the learner.

HTC: In partnership with the gaming company, Valve, is a Taiwanese-based maker of the Vive headset (and its variations).

Oculus: Oculus is owned by Facebook and has been credited with "brining back VR" in 2012 after a successful Kickstarter campaign.

Pedagogical Content Knowledge: A combination of content and teaching knowledge.

Pedagogy: The method and practice of teaching aligned with a certain set of beliefs about how students best learn.

Student Engagement: Student engagement involves active participation, critical thinking, synthesis, and application of content to real-life experiences. Highly engaged students tend to feel a connection to the process of learning, to their peers, and to the institutions of higher education in which they are enrolled.

Student Services: Student Services is a department of a institutions of higher education that provides supports for student success and enhance student growth and development.

Student-Centered Learning: Student-centered learning is a pedagogy of teaching and learning that views the teacher as a co-facilitator with students in an active and engaging learning process. Student-centered learning is also discussed as a constructivist approach to teaching and learning, active learning and/or problem-solving.

Technology Integration: Technology integration refers to a process of choosing and using specific technology tools to enhance the teaching and learning process.

Technology Lab: The Tech Lab discussed in this chapter was an interactive environment for creating and conducting simulated experiments, a type of playground for experimentation. The majority of focus, chosen by students, involved VR.

Chapter 8
Engaging Students in a Computer Diversity Course Through Virtual Worlds

Yvonne Pigatt
https://orcid.org/0000-0001-5103-5770
Community College of Baltimore County, USA

James Braman
https://orcid.org/0000-0001-6080-3903
Community College of Baltimore County, USA

ABSTRACT

Virtual world technology allows for an immersive 3D experience with rich content and interactive potential for students. Through this richness and interactivity, educators have abundant creative power to design and facilitate meaningful learning experiences and collaboration opportunities. In this chapter, the authors discuss one such initiative using Second Life as an educational space for a community college course activity to enhance student engagement. A brief literature review of the educational use of virtual worlds will be presented, which underpin our pedagogical methodology for the project framework. Focusing on a specific community college course titled "Diversity in a Technological Society," the course goals and project requirements will be discussed. The chapter concludes with a detailed description of the proposed methodology for the next phase, recommendations, and future work.

INTRODUCTION

Student engagement is one key component in the process of learning and often coincides with attaining learning outcomes (Carini et al., 2006). There are many techniques to engage students and to spark additional interest in course topics. Some methods are aimed at classroom activities, while others are more aligned as homework or outside activities for practice and discovery. Student engagement can be achieved through the gamification of activities (Domíngues et al., 2013), flipped classrooms (Roehl

DOI: 10.4018/978-1-7998-4960-5.ch008

et al., 2013), augmented reality (Dunleavy et al., 2009), virtual reality (Putman & Id-Deen, 2019) and mobile applications (Arnone et al., 2011), which are just a few methods using technology to engage students through active learning. Selecting the technology that best supports student learning depends on the instructional content and core learning outcomes. Certain course topics demand extra focus on specific skill sets and skill levels, while others are designed to sharpen skills in a more general sense. Technology in these courses can greatly enhance an educator's ability to reach students and provide them with unique learning opportunities.

Within the community college environment, teaching a general education course can be challenging due to the diverse set of student skill levels, varied technology literacy, and course workload balance. This is compounded by differences in age and enrollment statuses compared to students enrolled in more traditional four-year institutions (Cohen & Brawer, 2003). Adding to this complexity are the many challenges faced when dealing with underprepared (Gabriel & Flake, 2008) or at-risk learners (Zheng et al., 2014). Reaching all students and keeping them engaged in the content and context of the class becomes increasingly complex and dynamic. Therefore, instructors need to be resourceful and open to change as new challenges arise. This also applies to the need to be resourceful and knowledgeable with and about technology.

With the many available technologies and web 2.0 sites available today, educators have a wide array of tools to use in the classroom. Social media for instance now permeates many facets of everyday life and social interaction. Society has grown accustomed to everyday reliance on many forms of digital information (Pew, 2009; Lenhart et al., 2010). However, some technologies do not work or fit well in some contexts, nor are they always appropriate for education. Using technology in the classroom poses its own set of problems and challenges. Instructors may not have knowledge about a particular technology, or even have the resources available. Computing resources, space and internet connectivity all pose potential problems. In some cases, students may be apprehensive of learning with a new technology or may have limited use of a particular resource outside of a school setting. While some schools may have open labs or computing resources available through the library, these can be a challenge to maintain or monitor since they are often outside of the instructor's domain of control.

Despite these challenges for this project, the virtual world of Second Life® (SL) was selected as the virtual world technology of choice. SL is a 3-dimensional (3D) virtual world created by Linden Lab that can be accessed through the Internet via a downloadable client application. Users are represented in this world through an *avatar*, where one can interact with other users, content, and explore their surroundings. This online world has seen a large influx of users over the last several years, with an estimated number of "residents" reaching over 57 million accounts worldwide (Linden Lab, 2018). It also estimated that there have been over 482,000 years of time spent in-world collectively. This immense amount of time has contributed to SL's richness in content and unique user experiences. There are many categories of virtual worlds other than SL, each can be classified by their technology, graphics, goals or specific design. Some worlds are designed to be very open-ended and creative, while other worlds are designed to be more game-like or specific for a particular age group. SL should not be generalized as a game in the traditional sense, but instead as an open collaborative space that lends itself to much potential.

Students are accustomed to working with interactive media for learning and using educational games. While SL itself is not a game, it does have several game-like qualities that work well in teaching certain types of content or topics. As students are often attracted by games and other forms of interactive media, SL is an intriguing medium to use. Some studies have shown that many users of games also enjoyed being immersed in a simulated environment (Yee, 2006). Following Csikszentmihalyi's research on flow (1990) and applying this into areas of virtual environments to create an engaging and immersive space for learning is a useful goal. Using this approach for assignments can create engaging educational material for students. Additionally, virtual environments can provide students with a sense of presence, which some researchers have noted as a key benefit of using the technology (Holmberg & Huvila, 2008; Salmon, 2009).

Many other 3D virtual environments are available, such as IMVU, Twinity, Active Worlds and Minecraft (just to name a few). While these other technologies are competitors, SL still has a strong user base and strong attraction for new users looking to create and share content, with some attributing its popularity to the large amount of varying in-world activities (Wagner, 2008). There have also been a growing number of available 3D environments that are intended for more targeted users and age groups (Kzero, 2014). Minecraft, in particular, has seen an increase in use for the gamification of material for younger students (Gallagher, 2014) or for project-based learning (Callaghan, 2016).

Virtual worlds and other 3D spaces have been used for an array of educational purposes over the last several years (Kapp & O'Driscoll, 2010; Vincenti & Braman, 2011; Dudley & Braman, 2015); including use in general education curriculum in some schools as a vehicle for research and social exploration (Braman et al., 2013). As virtual worlds continue to grow in popularity, so too will the possibilities of their use. Virtual worlds have also been used in wider areas, such as in theater, art, geography, science and English courses, and many more (Vincenti & Braman, 2011; Vincenti & Braman, 2010; Braman & Yancy, 2017). Second Life® has been used in more specific domains, such as computer science and in computer ethics (Wang et al., 2009). The perception of use of Second Life in computing courses has generally been positive (Braman et al., 2011; Braman & Yancy, 2017).

SL was best suited for the pilot study discussed in this chapter due to the authors' experience, the diversity of in-world users, the capabilities of the platform, and the potential for dynamic interactivity through built-in scripting language. In addition, it is possible to link Second Life to external programs and applications to extend its capabilities. Finally, one of the authors has extensive experience conducting workshops and training on Second Life® which helped to facilitate the project. The purpose of using SL in the diversity course discussed in this chapter was twofold: 1) To increase student engagement in the context of the course by increasing participation, student enthusiasm and assignment quality and 2) To teach a new emerging technology. This chapter will begin with background discussion of virtual worlds and creating and using a virtual educational space. Secondly, a pilot study completed at a community college will be described, including the difficulties experienced inside and outside the classroom. A third section will discuss the pilot study and recommendations. Lastly, future research directions and conclusions will be provided.

BACKGROUND

Virtual worlds can be defined as "an electronic environment that visually mimics complex physical spaces, where people can interact with each other and with virtual objects, and where people are represented by animated characters" (Bainbridge, 2007, p. 472). The realism of virtual worlds and the "animated characters" or Avatars, have increased over the years as hardware and video capabilities have improved. The origins of virtual worlds are rooted in online text-based "worlds", referred to as Multi-User Dungeons or Multi-Users Dimension (MUDs) (Bartle, 2003). As technologies have improved, so too have their capabilities, features and representations, which have evolved into the many environments and games seen today. There are other terms that can be used to refer to virtual worlds such as Multi-User Virtual Environments (MUVEs) which can encompass many online worlds, and more specifically, in the context of education, Virtual Learning Environments (VLEs). Typically, VLEs are web-based, are less open-ended compared to MUVEs, and are more focused on learning, communication and include assessment tools (Britain & Liber, 2004). VLEs can be used in a broader sense to include virtual worlds that are focused on education. Common tools are supported in most virtual environments which include capabilities for communication, voice interaction, building tools, polygon mesh, and other 3D support. Adding to realism of virtual worlds is the increase in support for platforms such as the Oculus Rift, making for a very immersive experience. The Oculus Rift is a virtual reality head mounted display device that can be used to create realistic immersive experiences for the wearer. With the increase in realism, the potential for new ways of interaction may become more commonplace. There has also been work to enhance the social interaction between users through emotive avatars that capture real expressions, as in the virtual world High Fidelity (High Fidelity, 2015). Through the use technologies like Google Cardboard (Google VR, 2019), virtual reality can be brought into the classroom where Oculus Rift would not be possible due to costs or other constraints.

While the use of simulations, video and other computerized tools in education are not new, the use of virtual 3D worlds is still experimental. 3D worlds have potential as an educational tool due to the creative nature and capabilities. 3D worlds do present some design challenges in term of creating an educational resource or "space" for the students to work. Unlike the traditional classroom, the virtual classroom has fewer restrictions on time, space and movement. In the next section we examine the creation and use of virtual educational space.

Creating and Using a Virtual Educational Environment

What does it mean to have an education space in a virtual world? What does it look like? In a virtual world, educators are not bound by many of the same physical limitations inherent in the traditional physical classroom. Educators are also not bound by the same limitations of websites or Content Management Systems (CMS) such as Blackboard or Moodle. As John Lester pointed out during his Keynote Talk at the e-LEOT 2014 conference, there is a tendency among educators "to use new tools like old tools" (Lester, 2014). While educators have the power of virtual worlds, which can be used to create new imaginary environments the tendency is to recreate a 3D replica of a traditional classroom. A replica of a classroom in virtual worlds certainly does not guarantee that learning will take place. A virtual world activity for a class needs deliberate planning, testing and integration with specific content to be successful. Unlike some virtual environments where everything is pre-created by the creating company, Second Life relies on the content creation of its residents (users). Content creation in Second Life is more difficult compared to virtual worlds with environments created by software developers, such as World of Warcraft (McArthur et al., 2010). Since many educators may lack the time needed to successfully build all the components needed for their online virtual environment, other options are possible such - as purchasing premade content from other users (via in-world stores or the Second Life Marketplace) or even hiring someone to create the space for a fee. Before designing a space, it is recommended that one spends time in-a virtual world in order to get a sense of the possibilities, and what other educators have designed. Educational spaces can consist of open areas of land which can contain replicas and models of particular systems. These spaces may include interactive kiosks, or somewhat more traditional areas that include meeting spaces like offices with desks. More often, these spaces are more open, creative and unique.

Students benefit from learning new technological platforms such as Second Life®. 3D platforms and games are increasingly commonplace, thus having knowledge of how to operate one can be useful in learning to operate another. Having an avatar can be useful in the operation of various multiuser applications. As noted by Bélisle and Bodur (2010), with the increasing use of consumers today having avatars, it is important to understand how avatars are being used to improve marketing. Many researchers agree that Second Life® can provide an engaging learning environment for students compared to current education platforms, including an "around the clock" accessible meeting place (Bradshaw, 2009; The Schome Community, 2007; Wang & Braman, 2009). Engaging students is also enhanced when instructors maintain additional office hours in-world or include additional training material in a 3D format. This has been observed broadly when teaching in an all online format while engaging and interacting with students using video conferencing tools such as Zoom (Pigatt & Braman, 2018). A search on video sites, such as www.youtube.com, yield many choices of videos showcasing educational designs. Students may be more willing to interact with an interactive training kiosk in Second Life in addition to lecture notes from class or the required text, rather than just reading the textbook alone. As discussed by Antonacci et al. (2008), there are three major educational benefits from using virtual worlds:

1. Virtual worlds give users the ability to carry out tasks that could be difficult for them in the "real world" due to constraints, including cost, scheduling or location;
2. Virtual worlds' persistence allows for continuing and growing social interactions, which can serve as a basis for collaborative education;
3. Virtual worlds can adapt and grow to meet user needs.

These three benefits, particularly for some topics, provide the dynamic flexibility needed to complete projects that would be difficult to complete in the normal time frame of a class.

Duncan et al. (2012) reviewed virtual world educational literature and summarized several advantages of using virtual worlds in an educational setting.

1. The use of SL provides an intuitive modern approach for distance teaching in terms of the use of avatars.
2. Collaboration is greatly facilitated when conducting educational activities in-world.
3. Experimental and constructive learning can be achieved in SL.
4. Higher order thinking, such as analyzing, evaluating and creating can be achieved in virtual worlds as well as lower order thinking, such as remembering, understanding and applying (Falloon, 2010).
5. As geographical boundaries are broken down in SL, there is a large diverse background among participants.

As noted previously, the flexibility of the environment to be changed and adapted to the dynamics of student needs or to the content of a particular course is quite useful. This is dependent however on the instructor and available resources in the classroom. Successful lesson plans using a virtual world needs to be carefully planned, often more so than a traditional lecture. These characteristics are indeed important for integration of a virtual environment into any classroom. As engagement through visual and interactive components can promote active learning, attention needs to be placed carefully on this element. Once students are acclimated to the software, teachers can serve as a guide of the lesson plan to facilitate collaboration between students, assist with challenges and problem solving, and keep the class on task. Instructors can also lead classes on virtual fields trips and create immersive content to enhance and reinforce class topics.

USING SECOND LIFE®: A PILOT PROJECT – CASE 1

A computing course titled "Diversity in a Technological Society" was selected for the Second Life® Pilot Project. The official course catalogue description reads:

Explores the influences of technology on human diversity. Students are introduced to basic human relationship factors, international cultures, technologies, people with disabilities, human and data communications, artificial intelligence, computer security, and various individuals who have influenced technology.

This course is a popular general education course offered by the Computer Science / Information Technology Department and is offered each semester including winter and summer semesters. This course was selected due to the nature and flexibility of the course, and due to the instructor's schedule to carry out the pilot project. In this course the instructor discusses a variety of diversity-related topics, as seen in the real-world. For example, personal and social barriers to success, teamwork, and leadership. The use of computer technology topics helps the learner realize and appreciate the value of technology and how it supports and improves the quality of life, and the role it plays in the success of people working together around the world. For example, topics discussed are global social media, the global digital divide, collaboration software and emerging technologies. An essential outcome for the course is to raise the diversity consciousness of the learner and to teach students to work with people of all ages, races, ethnicities, religions, cultures, and other isms by using technology as the means for communication and collaboration. The instructor in the course has taken a constructivist approach to teach this course. Constructivism focuses on learning how to think and understand. Constructivism gives students ownership of what they learn since learning is based on students' questions and explorations. Constructivism promotes social and communication skills by creating a classroom environment that emphasizes collaboration and the exchange of ideas (Laureate Education, 2014).

In the course for a final semester project, students were assigned a topic from their normal class textbook which served as a basis for a group project. In semesters prior to the Pilot Study, students were to work in a small group of three or four people to construct a detailed written report on a given course related topic. Once the report was complete, students were to present the topic to the class using Microsoft PowerPoint (or similar presentation tool). The report topics included: Artificial Intelligence, virtual reality, military applications of technology, electronic health records, medical information systems, etc., and several other emerging technology trends. Based on assigned topics, through their own research, and from the information in the textbook chapter, students were required to write a summarizing report and presentation (both were graded). This assignment was typical for the course, and was a normal activity assigned at the end of each semester. Students are normally required to attend the presentations of other groups, take notes and ask questions. However, for the pilot study, the "traditional" assignment for the course was altered for use in Second Life.

Introducing Second Life® to Students

In class, students were assigned groups and group topics for the report they would be completing as a course assignment, the same procedure as used pre-pilot study. Groups consisted of three to four students. Students were also asked to create a SL account. Next, the class was introduced to SL in two ways: 1) A homework assignment was administered where students had to watch a documentary on SL and virtual worlds, titled Life 2.0. As part of this homework assignment students were asked to create an avatar; and 2). Students were introduced to SL by means of an in-class lecture and a training session including the in-world navigation controls. Based on our experience, when students spend some time learning about virtual worlds and navigation elements before an actual SL graded project, students are better acclimated to the requirements of the assignment and there is less stress related to learning new software.

The initial in-class practice assignment using SL reviewed the main features and controls, such as chatting, basic avatar control, flying and teleportation. In the exercise, all of these features were included, and students were asked to explore various aspects of the "grid" while paying extra attention to the layout and design of buildings, stores and general places they visited. Students were asked to make notes of their observations. Students were also introduced to aspects of the economy and how to purchase items if needed. In the last 15 - 20 minutes of class, a brief building tutorial was conducted to give students a very basic understanding on how to build and shape objects. This overview was a beneficial method of showing to the class how much time other users put into creating virtual items and buildings.

After students completed these initial practice assignments, the changed aspect of the group project (compared to past semesters) was revealed. Students were instructed that the presentation for the given topic would not be conducted in the "traditional sense" but instead would be presented to the class through Second Life® using their new skills. In addition, each group was asked to upload their final presentations slides into SL, and also to create an interactive kiosk area as an alternative presentation medium for their given topic. For example, if the group's topic was on artificial intelligence, they were asked to create an inviting space to capture their audience's attention, provide a seating area, presentation area and also include decorative items and/or posters or pictures to emphasize their topic. This required some creativity from the students and an understanding of the topic. The group kiosk areas also needed to include several interactive components which could be accessed by the class. The interactive components could include objects that linked to external websites and dispensed other objects or virtual notecards with additional information. An instructor led discussion on the topics, through the Second Life based learning kiosks, served as a content source for the class while immersed in-world. In order to complete the assignment, students needed prior experience in SL to control and manipulate their avatars, understand the interface, and communicate effectively with other students (as avatars). To facilitate this experience, students were exposed to several deliberate exercises within Second Life to learn the controls. Students needed basic building knowledge and, in some cases, basic scripting knowledge in order to create the interactive kiosks. Thus, an outline was developed for the approach that would be used to teach students how to use SL for completion of a report presentation assignment.

Assignment (Version 1)

Outline for Integrating Second Life® into an Assignment

1. Introduce students to Second Life® through homework assignments:
    a. Search for basic information online about SL and similar virtual worlds
    b. Create a free basic SL account by going to http://www.secondlife.com
    c. Watch a video on SL and virtual worlds titled: Life 2.0: https://www.imdb.com/title/tt1518809/
2. Class 1 (Lecture / Discussion):
    a. Lecture topic on virtual worlds, SL (in general) and the SL culture. Emphasis on how SL can be used for education, collaboration, business and for entertainment.
    b. Class discussion questions related to virtual worlds
    c. Textbook assignment: "Real Self vs. Virtual Self"
3. Class 2 (Applied Learning):
    a. Using SL / Create an avatar
    b. Learn navigation controls / Flying / Teleporting
    c. Learn Communication / Search /Editing Appearance / Inventory System
    d. In-world Exploration Assignment
    e. Getting started with groups and coordination of Projects
4. Class 3 (Applied Learning):
    a. Assign groups to in-world spaces
    b. Groups work on designs and upload presentation files in-world
    c. Group Assignment:
        i. Read textbook chapter, complete presentation with interactive kiosk area in SL that discusses an emerging technology topic and group research
5. Class 4 (Applied Learning):
    a. Class exploration and group topic presentations in SL and real life
    b. Class feedback and conclusions

Students were given in-class time to work on their project and to collaborate with their groups to complete the project. Extra time outside of class was also needed, as most groups needed extra study time on the topics and also time to complete the presentation files. In Second Life®, an area was purchased in the main grid by the instructors, specifically in the Goodnight region. This area was 16,384 square meters and was sufficient for several class sections to work. The virtual space was divided into multiple sections and separated by fences. The space was also sufficient in size to have enough space in between each group area for additional separation. Each group was assigned a specific area to build and to contain their design. It is important to let students know that there is a specific number of virtual objects (or "prims", short for primitive objects) that are housed in an area to avoid an excessive number of unneeded objects in their design. It is also important to remind students not to build in other student areas or disrupt other groups. When students are using the in-world chat feature, other conversations can be "heard" by other groups if they are too close.

By the last in-class building session, student groups had managed to complete most of the assignment. Some groups struggled to build kiosk areas that were related to their topic and some had problems getting their presentation slides uploaded without help. On the last day of the project, each of the groups

Figure 1. Beginning of group kiosk building within fenced in areas

presented the research completed on their assigned topic. The presentations took place in-world and in real life simultaneously. In real life, the presenting group stood in front of the class at the instructor station. One group member was logged into SL at the instructor station with Second Life projected on the overhead screen. The other members of the group were also at the front of the room to discuss their section of the presentation. These students were logged in at their desk computers, but physically located at the front of the classroom. The remainder of the class was able to watch and listen to the presentation though Second Life® (by being logged into SL as their avatar) and in Real Life at the same time. Being in-world and in the real-life class had the advantage of allowing students multiple ways to interact with the content and at the same time provide a real life overlay of the presentation in which they were more accustomed. The class did experience a few technical difficulties during two presentations, which included the platform crashing for one group, and another group had their presentation slides inadvertently reset. Having the real-life aspect of the presentation, allowed the group to continue presenting during the challenges. At the conclusion of each presentation, students asked questions to the presenting group via SL through the chat window where each presenting group responded through SL and in person to the class. Several of the presenting groups also posed their own created quiz questions to the class virtually, creating a multi-layered discussion. Figure 2 illustrates a group of students, represented by avatars, in a virtual presentation area.

At the conclusion of the project, the instructors had open discussions with the class to elicit feedback on their experiences with Second Life® and the alternate form of presenting. The instructors also wanted to gain key insights into what parts of the project were useful, difficult or lacking in order to make improvements for the future. As mentioned previously, this was a preliminary pilot study in the early testing phase where more in-depth analysis will occur in the future. Feedback was elicited through class discussion and was not explicitly recorded. Student feedback after the project was generally positive on this mixed reality mode of presenting. Many expressed surprise in presenting in this format, as it was something very new that they had never experienced before. During the presentations there were very minimal technical problems or complications and by this time in the project, students were much more

Figure 2. Students in-world listening to a group presentation

comfortable being able to navigate and control the avatars for the presentation without help. There were some challenges encouraged in and out of the classroom, beyond those of a technical nature.

USING SECOND LIFE®: A PILOT PROJECT – CASE 2

Following the pilot study as outlined above in Case 1, the same course and general design of the project was repeated in the Fall 2019 semester. Like the previous final project, students worked in groups of 3 to 4 students to research and write a report on a specific topic and to present their findings to the class. This time however, the topics were not emerging technologies but instead were related to virtual worlds. As the course relates to diversity and the impacts of technology, we adjusted the topics and approach compared to Case 1. The topics included conducting research on: subcultures in virtual worlds, virtual relationships, 3D technologies, future of virtual worlds, security and privacy in virtual worlds, impacts of virtual world and gaming addiction, identity in virtual worlds, discrimination in virtual worlds, etc. As there was only a brief mention of virtual worlds in the course textbook, the instructor recommended some additional readings to align with course activity objectivities. In alignment with the constructivist approach to teaching, this assignment required additional creative thinking and deeper research and analysis than what was required compared to Case 1 due to the nature of the research topics. Students were asked to use scholarly sources for their research but were allowed to intertwine a few recent news articles if it would enhance their report and presentation. As the topics were not as simple as reporting on an issue directly, they had to piece together evidence to support their overall group topic to build a case. For instance, the group that was focusing on discrimination in virtual words was quite surprised and intrigued by what they discovered in the literature about how avatars were treated differently based on appearance. In addition to their research, the group decided to carry out their own in-world experiment by exploring populated places in SL and observing how they were treated. Specifically, they were surprised at some of the rude comments directed at them for looking like a "noob" or new user to the world and how little effort they had put into their appearance. They expressed feelings of overall rejection and were unsettled about some additional harsh comments that some residents made about their appearance and lack of knowledge about in-world norms. Students learned firsthand about micro-aggressions, discrimination and social barriers to success. Of particular interest was the lesson on discrimination faced by students who felt that they had never been judged by their differences. For the research on virtual world topics, students were not limited to only SL, but many concentrated on that world due to their familiarity from class and the literature.

Changes to the Assignment

Although we followed the overall structure outlined for Case 1, there were some adjustments made to the overall class activity Due to limited class time during the semester and the desire to adjust the research topics. As before, students were asked to create free SL accounts at home for a homework assignment. Groups and topics were assigned in class for the project. Students were introduced in a similar way through an in-class lecture and discussion about virtual world technology, their impact and usage. During the second pilot study, we only had one in-world training session as an introduction to SL which covered basic needed skills of how to control one's avatar. A primary change to the assignment was the removal of the presentation requirement from within SL. While this was desired, we removed this requirement due to limited time and had students present in a traditional format within class. This also removed the additional time needed for students to build a space in the world and the need for additional training sessions on building. However, due to the more complex nature of the topics, more time was needed for researching and assisting in the writing process of the report which included significant time outside of class and homework time.

Assignment (Version 2)

Outline for Integrating Second Life® Into an Assignment

1. Introduce students to Second Life through homework assignments:
    a. Search for basic information online about SL and similar virtual worlds
    b. Create a free basic SL account by going to http://www.secondlife.com
    c. Assigned to Watch a video on SL and virtual worlds titled: Life 2.0: https://www.imdb.com/title/tt1518809/
2. Class 1 (Lecture / Discussion):
    a. Lecture topic on virtual worlds, SL (in general) and the SL culture. Emphasis on how SL can be used for education, collaboration, business and for entertainment.
    b. Class discussion questions related to virtual worlds
    c. Brief in-class research assignment on examples of how virtual words are being used.
    d. Find and briefly summarize a scholarly article on virtual worlds (with suggestions to the class such as looking at the Journal of Virtual Worlds Research).
3. Class 2 (Applied Learning):
    a. Create an avatar in SL
    b. Learn navigation controls / Flying / Teleporting
    c. Learn Communication / Search /Editing Appearance / Inventory System
    d. In-world Exploration Assignment
    e. Getting started with groups and coordination of Projects

4. Class 4 (Presentations):
   a. During the following week all groups presented to the class
   b. Class feedback and conclusions

CHALLENGES IN AND OUT OF THE CLASSROOM

This section highlights some issues that were encountered during both Pilot Projects, both inside the classroom and for at home assignments.

Inside the Classroom

The real-life classroom was a typical computer lab setting with twenty-four computers. The computers were positioned around the perimeter of the room, so that the instructor could easily assist students that were having problems and keep students on task. This also helped with the collaboration component of the project, as other students could easily maneuver around the class to help other group members. The computers used for the first pilot study were 3.2 Ghz with i5 processors with 4GB of RAM, all running the Windows 7 operating system. During the second study, the same classroom was used but the computers were running Windows 10 with 3.2 Ghz with i5 processors with 4GB of RAM. The instructors were pleasantly surprised with the low number of technical difficulties encountered in the classroom. There were issues during the second pilot with student computers that resulted from the campus wireless network signal being weak in the classroom. Several students that wanted to use their own laptop, had to use a computer in the classroom instead.

To make installation and access less problematic, the instructors were able to obtain a large set of 2 gigabyte USB flash drives. These flash drives were generously donated by the college to assist in the first pilot project. A copy of SL was installed on each flash drive. The intention was to have flash drives readily available with a SL install so that students could use it in class, on another computer on campus, or off-campus. Providing a flash drive, with SL installed was a support system so students could keep working without needing to worry about installing additional software. There were a few issues with defective flash drives, and in those cases the students temporarily installed SL on the lab computer as needed. At the end of the activity, the flash drives were collected back from students who expressed that they would not need the drive or would not use SL in the future. During the second pilot, we purchased a new set of flash drives and preloaded SL for the students. Software security in the labs had changed, and no software could be added to the system, so this was the only option to run the program in class. Again, these were collected back after the class period.

Additionally, the class did not encounter many problems with the video cards or graphics capabilities during class. Most installations of the SL software defaulted to the highest video settings (which later needed to be adjusted in some instances). During the first project pilot about 10-15% of the computers experienced periodic crashes, causing SL to need restarting. Lowering the graphic settings one to two levels below maximum seemed to limit the number of crashes. Crashing often occurred when users were moving between regions or teleporting, or when students were located within graphically rich areas. Being close to large bodies of water in SL also seemed to cause problem with some of the graphics cards. The instructors made sure to notify students of these issues as they became known. This was not the case during the second pilot, as only one computer needed to be restarted.

Outside the Classroom

A first challenge outside for the classroom pertained to documentary Life 2.0 by Jason Spingarn-Koff that students were asked to watch. While the instructors considered this to be a useful documentary that revealed several motivations of why some people use or are attracted to SL, student feedback, was mixed. The class had a discussion about the video, along with several related instructor led questions about how students felt about the video. It is important to note that this discussion was held prior to the students experience within the virtual world of SL. One perception that was communicated during the discussion was that many students had the impression that users of SL were addicted to the environment, led unfulfilled lives and that SL was not a useful space for "normal" people. Other students had opinions that were different and observed that indeed SL has very useful purposes in many contexts and could be an interesting collaborative and social space. Overall, students' first impressions of SL were more negative than positive. In the future an alternative video that provides more focus on SL content or several shorter introductory videos on virtual worlds will be used.

A second challenge that occurred was related to those students that did not complete the avatar creation assignment prior to class. Students that failed to complete this homework assignment had difficulties creating their accounts while on campus. After a few students created their account, additional students were blocked from registering because the Internet Protocol (IP) address for the campus location that was temporarily blocked from creating additional accounts. As of the time of this writing, this is still a problem, and additional accounts cannot be created on campus. The remaining students were able to complete the registration process by using their internet connection on their phone (using their own data plan and different IP address). In future semesters, the need to complete the registration process prior to the class will be stressed in order to alleviate this challenge in the future.

DISCUSSION AND RECOMMENDATIONS

Overall, the Pilot Project using SL in a "Diversity in a Technological Society" course was successful. We gained key insights for increasing student engagement from the project, and additionally identified improvements. The original instructor for the course noted improvement in enthusiasm and detail in submitted projects compared to non-SL usage. Anecdotal evidence from the experience suggests that using a virtual world can have a positive impact on student perception of the project and it can increase enthusiasm for some assignments. Some students did report seeing a positive benefit pertaining to gaining knowledge about virtual worlds for future use. After participating in the assignment, most students that previously had a negative view of SL, had changed their viewpoints. This initial negative opinion may be due to the novelty of the software, but additional research is needed in order to understand preconceived negative perceptions. Understanding these perceptions would be helpful as they could be addressed in the beginning of the assignment.

In future incarnations of this project there are several elements that the instructors wish to change and improve. To assist in streamlining the assignment in the future, the instructors plan on creating additional videos on virtual worlds, in addition to video tutorials on how to create objects, upload the presentation files and purchase items in-world. The assignment instructions themselves will also be enhanced to include more detail. Video recorded training sessions will provide additional context for the students of the importance of knowing about virtual world software. It is our wish that other educators can gain insight on how similar projects for their classes may be adapted and used for other diverse content. By placing several of the training videos online, other educators could make use of the information in their classes.

Adjusting the topics from emerging technologies to virtual world related topics infused with the course topics were beneficial and were well received by the class as interesting and important. It also reinforced research and writing skills. The topics also seemed to capture the attention of the class during the presentations as the topics were very new to the students and related to current events and class topics. Groups presenting also had to ask the class two discussion questions related to the topic which sparked some very interesting and lively debates and discussions. As we continue to make improvements to the assignment, the new adjusted research topics may be used as a replacement to the emerging technology topics for this activity.

RECOMMENDATIONS

Following is a list of recommendations for integrating the virtual world of SL into a college course using an approach similar to the Pilot Projects discussed in this chapter. With each recommendation is a discussion of how the authors plan to implement the changes in future courses.

1. **Include at least two smaller training sessions for students to increase awareness of virtual worlds.**

Overall, the initial lectures and discussion sessions about SL, combined with several training sessions on the use of SL were helpful for students based on their general comments in class and observations during the project. These training sessions (which included controls, communication, building etc.) were instrumental for student success in using SL to complete the assignment. As students became conformable with the SL technology and understood its application in a wider scope, communication and collaboration expectations were established. Students were able to communicate effectively with their group in-world to complete assigned tasks. Anecdotal evidence, gathered through the author's observations, suggests that training (even at a basic level) greatly improves overall outcomes when using SL for an educational purpose. There are several orientation areas (e.g., Orientation Island) premade and maintained within SL that can be used by students when instructors do not have a readily available class module for orientation.

2. **Require students to complete virtual world activities outside of the classroom.**

It is beneficial for both the students and instructors to conduct some preliminary research about virtual worlds outside of the classroom. This allows students to pursue topics related to virtual worlds that may be interesting to them. It would be useful to provide a set of guiding questions, depending on the context of a particular course and how virtual worlds could be useful in that domain. For example, in a business course, an instructor could assign specific readings on the value of virtual goods, or articles on virtual world marketing. In the case of this project students were asked to watch a video related to SL. There are many other such videos available that are more general that may be appropriate. Based on student feedback, an alternate video (yet to be determined) will be selected for future semesters. An additional benefit of having students do a portion of the investigation outside of class time is that more time can be focused on the technology and on the collaboration component. A flipped classroom approach for the individual group project topics is useful.

3. **Evaluate the available resources and technology.**

Having backup plans for technical problems will allow for a much smoother class activity. It is important to test the equipment available in the labs especially that of the video card and internet speed. Since SL relies on both components, problems with the video card or internet speeds can easily derail an activity, and frustrate students. Furthermore, be sure to check for any scheduled updates for SL, as it may pose some complications if there are any glitches. One major problem that many may face is the lack of ability to install the SL client application on lab computers. Without administrator rights, installation can be difficult or impossible. Also needed updates to the platform that occur periodically can cause problems if instructors lack administrator rights to perform the updates. In this pilot we used flash drives with pre-installed copies of SL which cut down many problems in the classroom. Even though we did have the ability to install software as needed, computers are reset each day which would have required the reinstallation of the program. Be aware however, that the downside of the flash drive approach is the amount of time needed to install the software on each drive. This should be completed well in advance to the actual class activity.

4. **Provide students with sufficient use of context for the use of Second Life.**

It is important that students understand the importance of virtual worlds and that it is a technology that is increasingly being used in education, business settings and for social interactions. Having an understanding of the technology and its impacts can be advantageous. To help students become more fluent and comfortable with the technology in a general sense (not just with SL), then sufficient knowledge of virtual worlds is helpful. If students can use a virtual world throughout the semester, and not just for one project, then additional skills may develop. Students can learn more advanced features and skills that can be used in outer areas. If a course does not lend itself to using a virtual world platform all semester, then be sure to provide students with enough context information about how the technology can be used and examples of its current use. For example, show the class how businesses are using the technology to reinforce that it's not just a "game" but a serious place to conduct work. One could also show the class how it could be used in the medical field by describing its usage in medical education for simulation and information display (Meskó, 2008). There are numerous examples of how educators and researchers are using the platforms in many areas.

5. **Aim to reduce costs of conducting an in-class project.**

The cost of conducting and implementing SL into a course, especially if there are many students or a large land requirement, can be rather expensive. One needs to purchase an area of land, and then in addition to that expense, a monthly land rental fee is assessed. For example, a smaller 2,048 square meter parcel costs $15.00 USD or a 32,768 square meter parcel costs $125.00 USD as a repeating monthly fee. A full link to the Mainland Pricing and fees can be found at: https://secondlife.com/land/pricing.php. It is important to access the particular needs for implementation prior to purchasing space to avoid incurring unneeded costs. There are alternative worlds available, some of which are free that can be hosted locally and customized, such as OpenSim. As an added benefit of using a locally hosted world to that institution, security and control of the space can be better maintained.

An additional cost that was incurred as part of this Pilot Project was the purchase cost for each group's PowerPoint presentation boards. In order for the students to present their slides on the topic, they needed a presentation object to do so (discussed more in the next section). For the duration of the Pilot Project each group was given a limited amount of virtual currency (Linden dollars) so that they could purchase a presentation viewer to display their presentation slides. Any additional money that remained could be used by the group to purchase additional decorative items for their space if needed. The students were encouraged to use as many freely available items and content as possible. Students did quickly discover how to obtain and search for free items in the SL marketplace: https://marketplace.secondlife.com. Students did learn valuable knowledge on how to make real purchases and how to work with alternate virtual currencies for the project, as well as how to buy from the web, items for their avatar and how to un-package items. There is a large amount of content available in the marketplace and within Second Life for the needs of most projects.

In the second pilot (Case 2) the removal of the requirement of building a static presentation space helped to reduce the cost of in-world building. As a class we briefly experimented with building in a free open zone, but we did not need to keep these objects or need a dedicated area. Instead we only visited popular free areas which reduced the cost significantly. We also did not need to purchase the presentation boards as we did previously.

6. **Use a created display board instead of a purchased display board for the activity.**

Part of the Pilot Project required that students upload their final version of their presentation files to SL as image files (either in .jpg or .png format) to be integrated into an in-world presenter object. These presenter objects act as an interactive display board, where a presenter can show a slide and then advance to the next one while speaking. It is similar to using the instructor station in a classroom to go through a set of PowerPoint slides.. Initially, to save time and to allow students a chance to actually purchase goods in SL, the instructors requested that students visit the SL Marketplace to purchase a specific item for the assignment. In order for this to work, each group needed approximately $500L (500 Linden dollars) which was supplied by the instructors. This amount of virtual currency is approximate equivalent to $1.89 USD, but the exchange rate of the virtual current changes daily and is controlled by Linden Lab (Bray & Konsynski, 2008). While this is not a substantial amount of money, it could become problematic if there are a large number of groups across many sections. In the future it is planned to create a specific presentation object for the activity that can be copied and modified by each group for no cost. If time allows, students could be given instructions to create this presentation object on their own (given adequate time and directions). This would be a more advanced exercise. As previously noted in the second pilot this requirement was removed and we had presentations in the classroom and not in Second Life which removed the need of a purchased display board and removed the time needed to setup the presentations. Groups were instructed to use presentation software such as Prezi, Google Slides or Microsoft PowerPoint.

7. **Train instructors to be fluent with Second Life® and acclimated to the platform.**

It is also strongly recommended that educators stay current in topics related to virtual worlds so that they can provide relevance to students about why they are using the technology and how it can be useful in their future as a technology tool. Providing relevance to using virtual worlds in class can strengthen the relationship of its importance as a learning activity. This can often be accomplished by adding additional readings or discussions that highlight high profile uses of the platform in the business world, educational institutions, government, and in medicine.

Additionally, due to the technical nature of the software and the many changing features, it is helpful for students to have an instructor that is able to help if, and when problems occur during use. Students can face an array of challenges and raise many questions during the activity. As some students are hesitant about using the software or quickly overwhelmed by it, having a background in the features often helps to calm student fears if something happens. It is also helpful as an educator to be familiar with many of the advanced features and how to use many of the building tools as one can then create much more inviting and engaging learning spaces. This advanced ability could lend itself to being able to link the learning space to outside resources such as websites or to create very engaging self-directed learning tools for outside class time learning.

8. **Decide on a design for the virtual world space.**

As the nature of the virtual learning space is very fluid, the environment can take on many forms. The authors recommend analyzing the needs of a particular project to help determine the form of the virtual space early. The size of the area, the amount of avatars for the class that need to be supported, the need for a sandbox area, and the need for certain tools are all main elements to consider. Visiting public educational areas in SL, to get a sense of what is possible and to see what tools are available in-world (such as display areas, simulations, posters, lecture areas, or video screens, etc.), is recommended. It can be a daunting task to figure out how one's educational space should appear, balancing both functionally and having an interesting and inviting landscape. Often virtual learning environments are designed very differently depending on the subject matter of a course and discipline. Virtual environments can range from being a recreation of a scene from a science fiction novel or a play, which could be used by an English course, or an area that is visually simpler such as a lecture style amphitheater for class presentations. Alternatively, the environment could be a replica of a full scale campus. Simulations through Second Life have great potential (Teoh, 2012).

FUTURE RESEARCH DIRECTIONS

In this section, future goals for the Pilot Project are discussed, specifically addressing improvements needed. A first goal is to integrate SL further into the curriculum and also compare retention and learning outcomes in courses integrating SL and those that do not. Although specific measurable feedback from students or grade outcomes from the assignment were not measured at this time, the instructors observed that this Pilot Project, was extremely beneficial in increasing student confidence for using SL in the future and enthusiasm for the assignment. A more detailed and integrated approach using SL earlier in the course, and in multiple assignments would be advantageous. However, further experimentation on selecting specific assignments and best practices are needed.

A second goal is to seek feedback from students using Second Life for class activities. Student feedback is essential for making improvements in the assignment and for understanding strategies that were helpful. Hepplestone et al. (2011) discusses the importance of student feedback regarding technology used within courses and particularly use that encourages engagement. While the teaching methods and features may be quite different with technology providing a 3D environment compared to more traditional technology, student involvement and feedback is equally essential. Instructors using any virtual world or classroom assignment based on SL should continually seek student comments. These environments change often, and content and directions will need to be updated and checked regularly. Using additional student feedback will be useful in implementing changes noted earlier in the chapter.

A third goal, is to use varied quantitative and qualitative methods for collecting detailed feedback from students through discussions, assignments and also through surveys using a more detailed research methodology. Using a more solid project framework that measures student skills and knowledge as well as perceptions about engagement and perceptions would be greatly beneficial. The authors plan to adopt a similar set of survey questions following Wang and Braman (2009) and Braman et al. (2011) with additional questions aimed at engagement and student perception of virtual worlds. A fourth goal is to create and maintain a more permanent space within Second Life that could be used for additional projects, virtual office hours and display of student and faculty projects. Having a fixed space to serve as a location online where students can meet virtually could help improve the project's visibility and encourage more collaboration. As the cost of maintaining a permanent space can be difficult, we intend to explore OpenSimulator as a solution. A space here can be maintained with more control and no cost due to the open source and multi-platform nature (OpenSimulator, 2019).

While these future directions pertaining to the Pilot Projects provides ideas for those who are interested in the next steps for the authors, there is a need to make specific directions for use of SL in higher education courses in general. To date, use of SL in higher education has been limited compared to other technology adoption. For those readers who have not yet implemented a virtual world tool, following are future directions suggested as an extension of this chapter.

1. Identify colleagues that are interested in identifying tools to engage students in active learning and begin the processing of exploring SL (or other virtual worlds), such as those described in this chapter, for the purpose of increasing instructor knowledge, skills, and self-efficacy with virtual world technology.
2. Meet regularly to share what has been learned individually; use journal articles and book chapters that describe the use of SL in college courses; develop a reference list. The list at the end of this chapter could be an initial resource.
3. Stay current in educational trends related to virtual worlds and aim to tailor 3D content to be relevant to the course using the technology.
4. Seek continuous student and faculty feedback from those involved in using virtual worlds in a course to enhance content and interaction. Including students in the process is helpful in increasing engagement and for making improvements.

CONCLUSION

In this chapter, the authors have discussed a Pilot Project using Second Life® in a diversity course to help foster interest and increase student engagement. The original pilot study as well as a secondary version was presented. As discussed in this chapter, there have been many changes in this technology over the years including how it can be used in an educational context. By using tools such as SL to increase student engagement, educators can improve their courses and teach materials in new ways. In this chapter we have provided key background on virtual worlds including how they can be used in higher education. Following, a discussion on a pilot project using SL in a diversity course at a community college where the goal was to increase student engagement and teach a new technology tool. This discussion included the project outline and key activities and student feedback. A discussion about difficulties, both in and out of the classroom was presented as well as a set of recommendations for educators interested in incorporating SL into their own classes. A set of future research goals were also presented as the authors move forward into more detailed research questions and collection of student feedback.

It is a sincere hope that more educators decide to use virtual worlds or similar platforms for educational purposes. SL can be an effective tool to excite and engage students in new ways and extend the capabilities of the traditional classroom setting. With the growing set of features and affordances of virtual worlds, they can become even more commonplace where educators are encouraged to experiment more. While much research is still needed to determine best practices, the literature suggests many positive aspects and potential learning outcomes using virtual worlds as a teaching resource for student engagement, critical thinking, verbal and written communication skill improvement

REFERENCES

Antonacci, D., DiBartolo, S., Edwards, N., Fritch, K., McMullen, B., & Murch-Shafer, R. (2008). *The power of virtual worlds in education: A second primer and resource for exploring the potential of virtual worlds to impact teaching and learning. ANGEL Learning ISLE Steering Committee*. Retrieved December 15, 2014, from http://www.angellearning.com/products/secondlife/downloads/The%20Power%20of%20Virtual%20Worlds%20in%20Education_0708.pdf

Arnone, M., Small, R., Chauncey, S., & McKenna, H. (2011). Curiosity, interest and engagement in technology-pervasive learning environments: A new research agenda. *Educational Technology Research and Development, 59*(2), 181–198. doi:10.100711423-011-9190-9

Bainbridge, W. (2007). The scientific research potential of virtual worlds. *Science, 317*(5837), 472–476. doi:10.1126cience.1146930 PMID:17656715

Bartle, R. (2003). *Designing virtual worlds*. New Riders Publishing.

Bélisle, J., & Bodur, H. (2010). Avatars as information: Perception of consumers based on their avatars in virtual worlds. *Psychology and Marketing, 27*(8), 741–765. doi:10.1002/mar.20354

Bradshaw, D. (2009). *New practices in flexible learning: virtual worlds – real learning! Pedagogical Reflections*. Retrieved Jan. 30, 2009, from http://virtualworlds.flexiblelearning.net.au/reports/VWRL_pedagog_reflect.pdf

Braman, J., Dudley, A., Colt, K., Vincenti, V., & Wang, Y. (2011). Gaining insight into the application of second life in a computer course: Student's perspectives. *Proceedings of the 14th HCI International Conference on Online Communities and Social Computing*. 10.1007/978-3-642-21796-8_3

Braman, J., Meiselwitz, G., & Vincenti, G. (2013). Virtual worlds in the general education curriculum. *Proceedings of the Society for Information Technology & Teacher Education International Conference, 2013*(1), 2692-2697.

Braman, J., & Yancy, B. (2017). Infusing Writing and Research in Technology Courses through Multi-User Virtual Environments. *Proceedings of the 11th International Multi-Conference on Society, Cybernetics and Informatics (IMSCI 2017).*

Bray, D. A., & Konsynski, B. (2008). Virtual worlds, virtual economies, virtual institutions. *Proceedings of Virtual Worlds and New Realities Conference*.

Britain, S., & Liber, O. (2004). A framework for pedagogical evaluation of virtual learning environments. *JISC Technology Applications Program*, (41). Retrieved from https://hal.archives-ouvertes.fr/hal-00696234/document

Callaghan, N. (2016). Investigating the role of Minecraft in educational learning environments. *Educational Media International, 53*(4), 244–260. doi:10.1080/09523987.2016.1254877

Carini, R., Kuh, G., & Klein, S. (2006). Student engagement and student learning: Testing the linkages. *Research in Higher Education, 47*(1), 1–32. doi:10.100711162-005-8150-9

Cohen, A., & Brawer, F. (2003). *The American community college* (4th ed.). Jossey-Bass Publishing.

Csikszentmihalyi, M. (1990). *Flow: The psychology of optimal experience*. Harper Perennial Modern Classics.

De Freitas, S. (2008). *Serious virtual worlds: A scoping study.* Joint Information Systems Committee. Retrieved February 28th, 2020 from https://www.jisc.ac.uk/media/documents/publications/seriousvirtualworldsv1.pdf

Domínguez, A., Saenz-de-Navarrete, J., de-Marcos, L., Fernández-Sanz, L., Pagés, C., & Martínez-Herráiz, J. (2013). Gamifying learning experiences: Practical Implications and Outcomes. *Computer Education, 63*, 380–392. doi:10.1016/j.compedu.2012.12.020

Dudley, A., & Braman, J. (2015). Using virtual worlds in ethical case studies: Evaluating computer students' perceptions. Proceedings from the 19th World Multi-conference on Systemics, Cybernetics and Informatics.

Duncan, I., Miller, A., & Jiang, S. (2012). A taxonomy of virtual world usage in education. *British Journal of Educational Technology, 43*(6). DOI: 10:1111/j.1467-8535.2011.01263.x

Dunleavy, M., Dede, C., & Mitchell, R. (2009). Affordances and limitations of immersive participatory augmented reality simulations for teaching and learning. *Journal of Science Education., 18*, 7–22.

Falloon, G. (2010). Using avatars and virtual and virtual environments in learning: What do they have to offer? *British Journal of Educational Technology, 41*(1), 108–122. doi:10.1111/j.1467-8535.2009.00991.x

Gabriel, K., & Flake, S. (2008). *Teaching unprepared students: strategies for promoting success and retention in higher education*. Stylus Publishing.

Gallagher, C. (2014). *Minecraft in the classroom: Ideas, inspiration, and student projects for teachers*. Peachpit Press.

Google, V. R. (2019). *Google Cardboard*. Retrieved https://arvr.google.com/cardboard/

Hepplestone, S., Holden, G., Irwin, B., Parkin, H., & Thorpe, L. (2011). Using technology to encourage student engagement with feedback: A literature review. *Research in Learning Technology*, *19*(2), 117–127. doi:10.3402/rlt.v19i2.10347

High Fidelity. (2015). *High Fidelity Inc*. Retrieved May 1, 2015 from: https://highfidelity.com/

Holmberg, K., & Huvila, I. (2008). Learning together apart: Distance education in a virtual world. *First Monday*, *13*(10). Advance online publication. doi:10.5210/fm.v13i10.2178

Kapp, K., & O'Driscoll, T. (2010). *Learning in 3D: adding a new dimension to enterprise learning and collaboration*. Pfeiffer.

KZero. (2014). *KZero Reports – Universe Charts*. Retrieved May1, 2015 from http:// kzero.co.uk/

Laureate Education (Producer). (2014). Anatomy of eLearning: Conceptual framework [interactive media]. Baltimore, MD: Author.

Lenhart, A., Purcell, K., Smith, A., & Zickuhr, K. (2010). *Social media & mobile internet use among teens and young adults*. Pew Research Center. Retrieved November 20 2014 http://67.192.40.213/~/media/Files/Reports/2010/PIP_Social_Media_and_Young_Adults_Report_Final_with_toplines.pdf

Lester, J. (2014). *Augmented mind- The evolution of learning tools from language to immersive reality*. Keynote speech presented at the 1st International Conference on e-Learning e-Education and Online Training, Bethesda, MD.

Linden Lab. (2015). *Mainland Pricing and Fees*. Retrieved July 10, 2015 from https://secondlife.com/land/pricing.php

Linden Lab. (2018). *Infographic - 15 Years of Second Life*. Retrieved December 10, 2019 from https://community.secondlife.com/blogs/entry/2349-celebrating-15-years-second-life-infographic-town-hall-video/

McArthur, V., Teather, R., & Stuerzlinger, W. (2010). Comparing 3D content creation interfaces in two virtual worlds: World of Warcraft and second life. *Journal of Gaming & Virtual Worlds.*, *2*(3), 239–258. doi:10.1386/jgvw.2.3.239_1

Meskó, B. (2008, August 17). Unique medical simulation in second life! *Science Roll Blog*. https://scienceroll.com/2008/08/17/unique-medical-simulation-in-second-life/

OpenSimulator. (2019). *What is Open Simulator?* Retrieved from http://opensimulator.org/wiki/Main_Page

Pew Internet. (2009). *Internet, broadband, and cell phone statistics*. Retrieved September 18, 2011 http://www.distributedworkplace.com/DW/Research/Internet%20broadband%20and%20cell%20phone%20statistics%20-%20Pew%20Internet%20Report%20Jan%202010.pdf

Pigatt, V., & Braman, J. (2018). *Promoting success and engagement in online programming courses.* Poster presented at the League of Innovations Conference, National Harbor, MD.

Putman, S., & Id-Deen, L. (2019). "I Can See It!" Math understanding through virtual reality. *Educational Leadership, 76*(5), 36.

Roehl, A., Reddy, S., & Shannon, G. (2013). The flipped classroom: An opportunity to engage millennial students through active learning strategies. *Journal of Family and Consumer Sciences, 105*(2), 44–49. doi:10.14307/JFCS105.2.12

Salmon, G. (2009). The future for (second) life and learning. *British Journal of Educational Technology, 40*(3), 526–538. doi:10.1111/j.1467-8535.2009.00967.x

Teoh, J. (2012). Pre-service teachers in second life: Potential of simulations. *Journal of Educational Technology Systems, 40*(4), 415–441. doi:10.2190/ET.40.4.g

The Schome Community. (2007). *The schome-NAGTY teen second life pilot final report: a summary of key findings and lessons learnt.* http://kn.open.ac.uk/public/getfile.cfm?documentfileid-11344

Vincenti, G., & Braman, J. (2010). *Teaching through multi-user virtual environments: Applying dynamic elements to the modern classroom.* Information Science Reference.

Vincenti, G., & Braman, J. (2011). *Multi-User virtual environments for the classroom: Practical approaches to teaching in virtual worlds.* IGI Global. doi:10.4018/978-1-60960-545-2

Wagner, M. (2008). Second life's popularity rests on breadth of activities. *Information Week.* https://www.informationweek.com/news/personal_tech/virtualworlds/showArticle.jhtml?articleID=210602197

Wang, Y., & Braman, J. (2009). Extending the classroom through second life. *Journal of Information Systems, 20*(2). 235-247.

Wang, Y., Dudley, A., Braman, J., & Vincenti, G. (2009). Simulating ethical dilemmas: Teaching ethics through immersive virtual environments. *Proceedings of the 12th IASTED International Conference on Computers and Advanced Technology in Education.*

Yee, N. (2006). The demographics, motivations, and derived experiences of users of massively multi-user online graphical environments. *Presence (Cambridge, Mass.), 15*(3), 309–329. doi:10.1162/pres.15.3.309

Zheng, B., Warschauer, M., Hwang, J. K., & Collins, P. (2014). Laptop use, interactive science software, and science learning among at-Risk students. *Journal of Science Education and Technology, 1*(5), 591–603. doi:10.100710956-014-9489-5

ADDITIONAL READING

Aldrich, C. (2009). *Learning online with games, simulations, and virtual worlds: strategies for online instruction.* John Wiley & Sons.

Balkin, J., & Noveck, S. (2006). *The state of play: law, games, and virtual worlds*. New York University Press.

Bartle, R. A. (2004). *Designing virtual worlds*. New Riders.

Boellstorff, T., Nardi, B., Pearce, C., & Taylor, T. L. (2012). *Ethnography and virtual worlds: A handbook of method*. Princeton University Press. doi:10.2307/j.cttq9s20

Castronova, E. (2007). *Exodus to the virtual world: how online fun is changing reality*. Palgrave Macmillan.

Corneliussen, H., & Rettberg, W. (2008). Digital culture, play, and identity: a world of warcraft reader. The MIT Press. Cambridge, Massachusetts. London, England.

Duncan, I., Miller, A., & Jiang, S. (2012). A taxonomy of virtual world usage in education. *British Journal of Educational Technology*, *43*(6), 949–964. doi:10.1111/j.1467-8535.2011.01263.x

Gregory, S., Lee, M. J., Dalgarno, B., & Tynan, B. (Eds.). (2016). *Learning in virtual worlds: Research and applications*. Athabasca University Press. doi:10.15215/aupress/9781771991339.01

Hai-Jew, S. (2010). Virtual immersive and 3D learning spaces: Emerging technologies and trends. *IGI Publishing*, *ISBN-10*, 1616928255.

Heaton, J. (2007). *Scripting recipes for second life*. Heaton Research Inc.

Hinrichs, R., & Wankel, C. (2012). *Engaging the avatar: new frontiers in immersive education*. Information Age Publishing.

Hodge, E., Collins, S., & Giordana, T. (2011). *The virtual worlds handbook: how to use second life and other 3D virtual environments*. Jones and Bartlett Publishers.

Jerald, J. (2015). *The VR book: Human-centered design for virtual reality*. Morgan & Claypool. doi:10.1145/2792790

Kapp, K., & O'Driscoll, T. (2010). *Learning in 3D: adding a new dimension to enterprise learning and collaboration*. Pfeiffer.

Lakkaraju, K., Sukthankar, G., & Wigand, R. T. (Eds.). (2018). *Social Interactions in Virtual Worlds: An Interdisciplinary Perspective*. Cambridge University Press. doi:10.1017/9781316422823

Martinelli, R. J., Waddell, J. M., & Rahschulte, T. J. (2017). *Projects without boundaries: Successfully leading teams and managing projects in a virtual world*. John Wiley & Sons.

Nelson, B., & Erlandson, B. (2012). *Design for learning in virtual worlds: Interdisciplinary Approaches to Educational Technology*. Routledge. doi:10.4324/9780203836378

Turkle, S. (1995). *Life on the screen: identity in the age of the internet*. Simon & Schuster Paperbacks.

Vincenti, G., & Braman, J. (2010). *Teaching through multi-user virtual environments: applying dynamic elements to the modern classroom*. Information Science Reference.

Vincenti, G., & Braman, J. (2011). *Multi-user virtual environments for the classroom: practical approaches to teaching in virtual worlds*. IGI Global., doi:10.4018/978-1-60960-545-2

Wankel, C., & Kingsley, J. (2009). *Higher education in virtual worlds: teaching and learning in second life. International Perspectives on Education and Society*. Emerald Group Publishing.

Wankel, C., & Malleck, S. (2009). *Emerging ethical issues of life in virtual worlds*. Information Age Publishing.

KEY TERMS AND DEFINITIONS

Active Worlds: Is an online 3D world and social space initially released in 1995. Similar to other online worlds, user can create and view 3D content, chat and explore. The main website is https://www.activeworlds.com/.

Avatar: A 3D representation of a user within a virtual world. Avatars can take many shapes and forms such as a humanoid representation, animal, shape, or other figure which allows the use to interact within the world and with other users.

Educational Game: A game in which the main goal is a specific learning outcome. Educational games are often used to increase student engagement.

Educational Space: A web-based, 3D or virtual representation of a classroom or learning area. In relation to virtual worlds, an educational space is often related to the 3D area used for learning which can be represented in a myriad of ways.

IMVU: Founded in 2004, IMVU is an online 3D virtual world and social networking platform. In 2014 there were an estimated four million active users. The main website is https://secure.imvu.com/.

Minecraft: Is a 3D "blocks" based world that can be used as a game, a creative space or in a multi-player mode with other users. The program can be run on multiple device types offline, or setup to run on a server for other users to connect.

Multi-User Virtual Environment: Also known as a MUVE. This term can be used to describe a virtual world that can be used for a collaborative purpose where users can interact in real-time.

OpenSimulator: An open source 3D virtual world available on many platforms which is similar to the Second Life virtual world.

Second Life®: A popular internet-based 3D world created by Linden Labs.

Script: A set of instructions or a small program designed to carry out a specific function or task. In Second Life the Linden Scripting Language is used (LSL) to make objects interactive.

Social Networking Site (SNS): A website that is aimed at social interaction that often includes a public profile, ability to post user generated content and also to connect to other users.

Student Engagement: Increasing student interest, focus and, or motivation for a particular learning activity.

Twinity: Is an online 3D virtual world and social platform originally released in 2008 and considered by some to be a mirror world. The main website is http://www.twinity.com.

Virtual Reality: A term that can refer to a virtual representation of a scene or reality simulation in 3D. Virtual Reality can be viewed on a traditional display or using immersive VR goggles.

Virtual World: A virtual world often refers to an internet-based 3D or 2 ½ D environment where users can interact within the world or with other users through an avatar. Often virtual worlds are persistent environments where a large number of users can participate.

Chapter 9
Board Games, Zombies, and Minecraft:
Gamification in Higher Education

Susan Keim
Park University, USA

Zac Jarrard
Park University, USA

ABSTRACT

Games have been played throughout human history and in all cultures, exposing almost everyone to gameplay in some form. Higher education is exploring ways faculty can leverage games to enhance course development and the student learning experience. The primary pedagogical use of games is gamification, in which gaming is used to transform learning activities. This chapter will 1) provide an overview of gamification theory and practice in higher education, 2) share ideas for faculty to consider when using gamification as a teaching tool, and 3) explore how the game Minecraft was used through educational and practical applications to teach a local government course.

INTRODUCTION

People have played games throughout history. In ancient times, humans gathered bones to create a version of dominoes (Kelley, 1999). Kings and queens from the medieval time period played a form of chess (Averbakh, 2012). Modern games occur on different platforms from traditional boards to digital worlds, are easily accessible, and have a broad range of genres. Digital platforms, where players fight zombies and other enemies, create virtual economies, and interact socially, are rapidly increasing in popularity. This chapter examines the linkages between gamification and higher education through the lenses of engagement, motivation, faculty and student perspectives, and educational and practical applications.

DOI: 10.4018/978-1-7998-4960-5.ch009

BACKGROUND

In any gaming environment, McGonigal (2011) suggests four basic game elements are present. The first element is a goal players are working to achieve. The second is establishing game rules and ways a player can go about achieving goals. The third is a feedback system showing players the progress they are making towards achieving goals. Fourth, players voluntarily participate and agree on the goals, rules, and feedback system within the game. These four principles form the foundation for gamification theory which applies to digital and non-digital games.

In a literature review of game-based learning and e-learning, Doney (2019) found seven common themes that occur in practice.

- Challenge: "the level of difficulty and ability to stretch" players (p. 3). The challenge of a game is intrigue and what captures the player's interest. This can vary from player to player;
- Competition: the competition is between players or game elements. Players participate in games for simple rewards such as bragging rights among friends or more complex rewards and prizes. Games can even have groups of players vying to win or players competing against game elements like traps, zombies, and monsters;
- Control: the amount of control players have to manipulate the game environment. Some games are narrow and limit player actions. Other games give players more choices and freedom to customize the game;
- Feedback: the feedback enables players to reflect on actions taken within a game and to learn from their mistakes. Feedback comes to players through game prompts such as a point system. This helps players measure game progress and identify areas of improvement;
- Context: the environment of a game and realistic situations using visuals and media. The context of a game could vary depending on player activities and goals. Digital and non-digital games have different contexts based on how they are designed;
- Rules: the rules help players know how to play the game and what achievements they are seeking. Rules set the boundaries for acceptable behavior and consistency. They establish desired outcomes and steps for players to win the game; and
- Reflection: the power of reflection is a positive influence to encourage learning. Players review their game performance—what went well, what did not go well, and how to improve in the next game. The goal of reflection is continuous improvement.

Student Engagement

When Doney's (2019) principles are imported into an educational context, games can be viewed as a tool in classroom engagement. Since today's students are considered digital natives, their learning styles naturally incorporate openness to using digital games for motivation and engagement in learning (Kiryakova et al., 2013). These students have experienced a variety of gamification learning tools in K-12 and their free time. In fact, 97% of K-12 youth play some type of digital or video games (McGonigal, 2011). Many students filling college classrooms today have spent their whole lives playing video games and can see where games align with coursework (Lorenzo, 2016). They have built vast online worlds and enjoy high engagement through game mechanics such as boss fights or competitive multiplayer systems. This gamification trend is important to stay relevant and keep students engaged today and in the future (McGonigal, 2011).

Games encourage engagement in two primary ways. First, they facilitate both internal and external motivation in learning. Traditionally, students are predominantly internally or externally motivated. Internal or intrinsic motivation refers to a fascination or passion from within which drives students to learn a new activity or pursue a new goal. External or extrinsic motivation refers to the external environment surrounding students and involves their recognition, achieving a goal or reward, and competition in learning (Schinnerer, 2018). Motivation in college students facilitates persistence and grit which determines how far students will go to learn a difficult task. Multidimensional learning at the college level increases complexity by stretching students to be simultaneously intrinsically and extrinsically motivated in the classroom (Lei, 2010).

Galbis-Córdova et al. (2017) conducted a qualitative study with on-campus students exploring the use of digital games for competency-based learning. The study found that students recognized online educational digital games as a tool to make learning relevant competencies more engaging and exciting. This information is important for faculty to consider when using gamification in online and traditional classrooms. Many students today have grown up playing digital games, and often they relate more to interactive digital games compared to class lectures or traditional discussion.

In higher education, classes without high engagement activities may be vulnerable to attrition and student fatigue which results in low academic performance. To combat these problems, faculty and students could collaborate to gamify parts of a course. Students will enjoy working with faculty who are open to leveraging new tools such as gamification to deliver an engaging and fun course. This focus on student-faculty collaboration increases student ownership and improves student-faculty relationships.

Finding ways to use gamification increases student motivation and engagement in any type of real or virtual classroom (Huang & Soman, 2013). Beyond higher education, gamification is emerging in the private sector to promote employee performance and customer engagement (Caponetto et al., 2013). As the Chief Information Officer of a Fortune 500 company explained in a presentation at Park University, using gamification improved their employee engagement and reporting policy saving $2.1 million in one year (Graff, 2017). Future employment opportunities for students are enhanced when they have worked on projects in a virtual environment which reflect the way employers use gamification in the workplace. Thanks, in part, to some of their college courses, students experiencing gamification are well suited to navigate through their future workplace experience and civic participation.

Citizen Engagement

Employing ideas similar to student engagement, the role of citizens in government is important, especially at the local level. A standard definition of citizen engagement is “a fundamental right of all citizens to have a say in the decisions that affect their lives” (Lukensmeyer & Torres, 2006, p. 9). In a continuum, citizen participation ranges from one-way communication of local governments to residents all the way to citizens engaged directly with local government officials in the process of shared governance (Leighninger, 2006). A broad definition of citizen engagement is active engagement of citizens within their communities.

Traditionally, citizen engagement is face-to-face interaction between citizens and community leaders (Leighninger, 2006). This occurs through town hall meetings, community forums or voting. One key limitation is that governments hold these activities in person. However, civic participation may suffer for a variety of reasons. Often, city meetings are held during work hours. With no childcare provided for evening meetings, parents are not able to attend. Schedule conflicts, lack of awareness, or lack of interest are also reasons for nonparticipation. The traditional methods for citizen engagement are not enough to meet the demands of the modern world and suggest the need for digital citizen engagement.

In the past, it was assumed that elected officials were the instigators of civic participation. However, research suggests citizens, rather than elected officials, choose to make the difference (Mathews, 1999). When citizens work together in deliberative two-way processes, they build both trust and a communal expectation of what they can achieve as a body: "People become a public when they acknowledge their interconnectedness and the consequences of their ties with others" (p. 203). One such way for citizens to engage in this sort of community building is through digital games; a new tool used to increase civic participation between citizens and community leaders. There is an opportunity for communities to motivate citizens and promote the common good.

Motivation

Gamification provides internal and external motivation since students using games in the classroom receive a deep internal sense of self fulfillment and external rewards for achievement (Lei, 2010). In addition to facilitating motivation, games help faculty engage students throughout the semester to reduce student fatigue. Fatigue occurs when students feel frustrated, overwhelmed, or stressed which decreases student performance (Transcription Wing, 2020). Students juggle coursework on top of other community, family, and work obligations. Game use in courses presents an opportunity to engage students and insert fun into the learning process.

Fotaris et al. (2016) leveraged games to motivate students with Kahoot! and Who Wants To Be A Millionaire? These games were used within the class structure to ask course-based questions. Kahoot! measured individual understanding of class lectures as compared to peers. After each timed question, results were displayed and the overall winner received a candy reward. In the same class, students were organized into teams to play Who Wants to be a Millionaire? Teams were given opportunities to earn points by collaborating together to answer progressively difficult questions. The winning team was rewarded with the title of "Pythonista of the Year" and chocolate bars. Through these examples, students found playing these games stimulated learning, encouraged peer communication, and improved understanding of class concepts.

These educational benefits are harnessed when course activities are gamified. Burke (2014) defines gamification as "the use of game mechanics and experience design to digitally engage and motivate people" (p. 6). Digital games include commercial video games and online educational games. To create a digital gamification experience, multiple factors are necessary including game mechanics, excellent user experience, and a strong engagement mechanism (Burke, 2014). Gamification digitally engages people through technology including computers, smart phones, or other electronic devices.

Gamification is unique because technology makes it possible to scale digital games across an entire organization at a low cost. Organizations are able to leverage "digital engagement to extend motivation beyond the limits of the physical world" (Burke, 2014, p. 32). Digital games can be asynchronous and always available to players. These games are playable anywhere and anytime, create a sense of connection between people, and provide cost savings, as they are easier to scale than non-digital games and less expensive than face-to-face models (Burke, 2014).

This technology makes it easier than ever to monitor, track, and reward individual and team progress. Digital game performance is constantly available to players who can see their scores on the leaderboard. Game information is located in one place and easily accessible to all players. Game goals for individuals and teams can be reviewed on a regular basis. These goals may encourage players to develop new behaviors, learn new skills, or promote new ideas.

Gamification can produce engagement that aligns with organizational and individual goals in the classroom. In classic organization theory, Etzioni (1964) describes an organizational goal as "a desired state of affairs which the organization attempts to realize" (p. 6). Organizational goals are objectives set by an employer to provide direction to employees. In a university setting, while faculty and student roles may differ, their overall goals include student success, teaching, research, and service.

A personal or "private goal consists of a future state that the individual desires" (Gross, 1969, p. 278). Personal goals are objectives individuals work towards achieving to improve their personal growth, overall happiness, or sense of fulfillment. Personal goals for faculty may include life-long learning, innovative teaching opportunities, and tenure. Personal goals for students in higher education might include mastering course material, passing courses, and graduating from college. While the faculty and student goals are different, they are not mutually exclusive. This intersection of goals makes gamification a desirable method for engagement and goal realization. Gamification offers universities help with their teaching goals, faculty with lifelong learning, and students with achieving their personal learning goals.

GAMIFICATION INSTRUCTIONAL DESIGN

In higher education, customizing gamification to fit a course than rather making the course fit into gamification, is a great starting point. Gamification is meant to complement instead of become the entire course. The primary component of a course is the subject matter which goes hand in hand with course learning outcomes. Adding gamification to boost course delivery options is secondary.

Balanced design is a basic learning framework to consider when faculty add games to a course. It divides learning into three interconnected models of content, evidence, and task (Groff, 2018). The content model refers to the knowledge, skills, or abilities being targeted within a specific activity. Evidence examines ways faculty know students have mastered content. The task model considers what activities will engage students and shows evidence to demonstrate content mastery throughout the class. This framework creates a three-pronged approach with a meaningful gamification experience for students and faculty.

A more complex blueprint for gamification instructional design, laid out by Huang and Soman (2013), is similar to the structure of a course. Initially, a course is developed based on the target audience and minimization of pain points which block student learning. Before the course is developed, learning objectives are defined. As the course is created, the student experience is considered. Course tools such as texts, videos, online sources, and other resources are identified for class use. Gamification resources are tools to be used in the course design.

Nicholson (2013) developed a recipe for meaningful gamification in the classroom. Play facilitates students' freedom to fail fast---explore, experiment, and try new ideas. The game environment gives students the opportunity to make mistakes in a short period of time, evaluate their failure, and try again, a process known as failing fast (IBM, 2020). This process enables quick correction and progress for students rather than a more traditional method of drafting an assignment, waiting several days or weeks for faculty feedback, and then not discussing the assignment again. When failing fast, students may even celebrate failure and use it as a chance to engage in reflective learning!

Students are motivated to play through gamification. Exposition creates real world stories for students to co-create with classmates and faculty. Students are more responsive when they have input into the activities developed. Students have the ability to make meaningful choices within the game which adds to their motivation and engagement. Information provides students with the contextual knowledge of the "why" and "how" of the gamification experience to include real-world context and transferable skills in their activities. Engagement encourages students to explore and learn from classmates in a real world setting. Reflection finds students' other interests and experiences deepening engagement and learning. Through this adaptive learning, students push the boundaries of what is possible (Heifetz et al., 2009).

In Table 1, the concepts from Huang and Soman (2013) and Nicholson (2013) are compared. Using gamification in education, they mirror traditional course development and implementation. Course learning objectives, content, readings, and pain points are determined *before* considering gamification. Effective course gamification is integrated into the course to enhance conventional course work of lectures, discussions, essays, and texts (Jenkins et al., 2003). To be clear, the objective is to gamify the learning process rather than the outcomes or learning objectives (Hall, 2014).

Table 1. Course development using gamification

Huang and Soman (2013) Gamification instructional design	Nicholson (2013) Recipe for meaningful gamification in classroom
Understand student needs when developing course.	Play—facilitate freedom to explore and fail fast.
Minimize student pain points.	Exposition—create stories to integrate with real-world settings.
Define course learning objectives.	Choice—develop systems with power given to participants.
Create student experience.	Information—use gamification to learn real-world context.
Link resources to course work.	Engagement—encourage participants to learn from others.
Apply game mechanics.	Reflection—assist participants to deepen engagement and learning.

According to Bloom's Taxonomy, applying this framework promotes high-level learning for students. When adding game designs to help students demonstrate skill mastery, faculty can look to Bloom's Taxonomy for defining the level of skills they want students to learn from a class (Shabatura, 2018). In this way, games gradually expose students to more complex tasks and keep them engaged through celebrating failure and incremental improvement (Petrovic-Dzerdz, 2019). Just like developing a traditional course, Bloom's Taxonomy is helpful in determining learning outcomes for courses using gamification. This helps pull students up to higher cognitive levels and push students to learn skills outside of their comfort zone. Faculty may customize or use games which align with course learning outcomes since they have greater flexibility integrating games into pieces of the curriculum.

By working with students, faculty can help them achieve the highest level of learning in Bloom's Taxonomy. In the create level of Bloom's Taxonomy, students apply course content by assembling complex elements together or developing new ideas. Games give students a unique place where they can investigate class concepts in a safe environment and create new virtual worlds. The use of games also works well with adult learners who come to the classroom highly motivated, independent, and curious (Colman, 2019). All types of students get a sense of achievement, confidence, and ownership when they build virtual worlds and share it with their peers.

FACULTY CONSIDERATIONS

As faculty move to implement gamification in their courses, they will need to consider user experience, the expectations for student success, faculty perspectives, and assessment of gamified course content. User experience refers to the gamification environment in conjunction with the student journey through a game and is the first point for faculty to consider (Burke, 2014). Student success includes access to the appropriate resources for playing the game in the classroom. Reference material for students to use helps them quickly learn the game and apply it to coursework. Along with providing written and video reference material, when faculty take time to explain game rules and expectations, students learn the class boundaries and begin to practice digital citizenship and teamwork. Developing a brief tutorial and example will go a long way in helping students understand how to play the game.

Early on in a gamified course, students might be confused when they hear the term gamification or see games being played in a classroom. Faculty can help students understand how and why gamification is used through "pointing out the benefits of using online educational video games and the suitability of using online educational video games to develop students' competencies to avoid students' prejudices about the use of video games in education" (Galbis-Córdova et al., 2017, p. 141). As digital natives, students are used to playing games and may have difficulty adjusting to an educational perspective of gaming. With faculty assistance, students can reflect on their experiences and relate them to course work. This helps students see the bridge between games, coursework, and new skills.

Faculty perspective is the second point to examine. For faculty unfamiliar with digital games, gamification presents a change in the teaching pedagogy which identifies strongly held teaching values and philosophies and explores ways these philosophies can be incorporated into a gamified system (Hung et al., 2017). While traditional teaching modes have a strong pull, faculty can use gamification as a way to reimagine their teaching approach in parts of their courses. In considering gamification and online classes, faculty "…can break out of traditional, linear teaching models and offer complex pathways, self-guided learning, and personalized instruction with gamification as the guiding mechanism for students" (Hung et al., 2017, p.15). Despite these differences, breaking from traditional academic pedagogy still requires clear classroom structure and student expectations.

Faculty are on the frontlines delivering the curriculum to students, engaging with the community, and conducting research to advance their academic discipline. Introducing gamification to the classroom can also "vary from personal costs (e.g. time devoted to preparing new teaching materials) to institutional costs (e.g. new equipment like digital blackboards or computers)" (Sánchez-Mena & Martí-Parreño, 2017, p. 434). Personal costs include learning gamification skills, reconfiguring courses, and working with administrative departments. Institutional costs include game licensing, funding, and administrative time. The main drivers for using gamification in online courses include maintaining the students' attention and using games to promote interactive learning.

When faculty consider gamifying course content, it is important to remember gamification expertise may be found outside the academic discipline. Creating a gamification support team from Information Technology (IT), Instructional Design, Academic Support, Student Life, and other departments will help facilitate a positive experience. Look to students for gamification ideas, expertise, and enthusiasm. They can be the gamification facilitators and problem solvers. When faculty develop a trusting relationship with students, they can co-create a dynamic gamification experience within a course.

A third area to reflect upon is clarifying expectations when using gamification in the classroom. Games are intended to enhance teaching and learning so students are more engaged with course material. Students can use games to apply course content to solve real world problems. Games are an avenue for faculty to provide students with exciting hands-on learning. Because students have greater ownership in game-based activities, they are more likely to learn additional skills beyond the course objectives which can be applicable towards future employment. Even with increased student engagement, boundaries established within the course syllabus encourage scholarly and civil behavior. Expectations for time spent within games should be clear at the outset of the course and closely monitored.

Assessment is the fourth consideration facing faculty who use games in the classroom. Gamified portions of a class can be assessed in several ways. From the course design, consider what student outcomes are being measured in a particular class. Review game mechanics and examine how well games measure student learning objectives. Since games are fun, students may put more time and effort into the competition of a game or moving to a higher level. This is a win-win. Students win by learning additional skills as they play a game and applying theory to practice in imaginative ways. The faculty win by having engaged students pushing them for continuous learning opportunities. In today's complex world, learning a broad range of skills is a key to achieving career and personal success (Ware, 2018). Faculty may find ways to create student learning outcomes which are broad enough to recognize the additional skills, including soft skills students learn when using games in the classroom.

Given the pervasiveness of digital gameplay by youth, faculty and administrators can count on future students and workers being engaged by thoughtful gamification within their courses and workplaces. Inside higher education, there is a unique opportunity for faculty to shape the minds of students and plant seeds which will someday grow into happy and fulfilling professional pursuits (Addision, 2018). This is a way to leverage games to meet students where they are with effective engagement via gamification.

A ROADMAP TO INTEGRATE GAMIFICATION

This research began in 2017 with a graduate student gamer and a professor casually discussing similarities between virtual world communities and real world communities. These conversations developed into the process of co-creating a virtual local government course and bringing gamification into our university. Based on the experience of that gamification adventure, we have come to believe in the pedagogical power of games and it has spurred our interest in its theory and application. The following information provides a brief overview of gamification theory, benefits to teaching and learning, and a course development checklist that instructors can utilize when considering or seeking to integrate such work into their practice.

Step 1. Consider the Role of Gamification and Evaluate Course Delivery Options

Gamification has a broad range of applications within higher education. Although gamification is not limited to digital games, we shall focus on digital games for its cost-savings and scalability make it most

Table 2. Gamification and course development checklist

Step 1	Consider the role of gamification and evaluate course delivery options.
Step 2	Test gaming tools for user fit and create the course gamification experience.
Step 3	Pilot the course gamification experience and assess the student experience.
Step 4	Connect gamification to broader real world experiences and global community.

appealing for higher education. Similar to the strategies for gamification and technology, awareness of all user needs is the first step to get started in gamification. Since faculty may serve a multi-generational student body, games with broad appeal to traditional and nontraditional students are good choices. Introducing a game heavily reliant on technology might be an obstacle for some nontraditional students, but appropriate reference material and peer interaction can make it easier for them to learn a new digital game. Intuitive games are easy for students to grasp in a short period of time.

Step 1. Questions to consider:

- What are your learning objectives for the course?
- How might gamification improve the learning experience?
- Which gaming tools are either free of charge or low cost for student use?
- What are the benefits or learning gains anticipated by integrating a gaming option?
- What course activities are well suited for gamification?

In the authors' experience, using games is not the answer to all classroom engagement challenges and faculty should not feel compelled to gamify an entire course. Broad faculty concerns may be issues like: Does this trivialize my course content? How much gamification is needed to be effective? What classroom activities are best for gamification? The authors found using digital games enhances rather than marginalizes course content. The students became more involved in the subject matter and were motivated to dig deeper into their coursework. Almost any course activity could have a gamification component to interject variety into course delivery. For example, lectures or quizzes using Kahoot! instantly gamify course activities. There is no single way to gamify elements of a course and collaborating with students for gamification ideas may provide the best outcomes.

Step 2. Test Gaming Tools for User Fit and Create the Course Gamification Experience

When evaluating methods to gamify course activities, three fundamental things need to be evaluated: (1) platforms or way in which gamified content will be delivered; (2) student perspective on gamified content; (3) and faculty concerns. Platforms are the systems which support digital games. They can be self-contained and simple depending on the game being used. A few examples include gaming consoles, computers, or mobile devices. The student experience is a key to success with gamification in the classroom. They will know what gaming platforms to use, system requirements, and gameplay for successful gamified class activities. Faculty can alleviate some concern by developing the course gamification experience through rigorous testing of gaming platforms, communicating with students in advance about system requirements, and providing reference documentation on gameplay.

Step 2. Questions to consider:

- What gaming platforms are available for use?
- Who will help test the gaming platforms?
- What are the system requirements for accessing the gaming platform?
- What additional technical or administrative resources are required?
- How will faculty and students be able to access the gaming platform?
- What other resources are required for a positive faculty gamification experience?

Finding the right mix of platform and student engagement is a bit of trial and error. There may be some tweaking involved through the first semester of a gamified course. This is no different than introducing any other type of innovation within a course—a new textbook, a new video, or a new assignment. Faculty consideration might include questions like: How will I know a gaming platform will work for my course? Will students enjoy the gamification platform? Will students still enroll in the class? The authors found incorporating existing platforms are easier to navigate as compared to developing a customized platform. Kahoot!, Who Wants To Be A Millionaire?, and Minecraft are examples of games on existing platforms. This will make it as easy as possible for faculty to manage the course while students play the game and maximize the learning value.

Step 3. Pilot the Course Gamification Experience and Assess Student Experience

Here are the hot tips on faculty expertise and piloting a course! Faculty expertise in the subject matter is critical to the success of a course. *Faculty expertise in computers, computer science, gamification or video games is not necessary for gaming to be effectively implemented in a course.* This is where co-creating with students makes the difference by encouraging their engagement. Let the students begin engaging throughout the course pilot. After all, they are digital natives and will lead the way through gaming while offering many creative possibilities.

Step 3. Questions to consider:

- What does success look like for the course?
- In what ways can faculty encourage students to co-create the gaming experience?
- What gaming expertise do students need to have to be identified as potential technical gaming experts for the course?
- Where do gaming activities fit within course assessment?
- What steps are needed to gather and evaluate student learning and feedback?
- What parts of the course need to be tweaked for future success?

Piloting a course is a unique opportunity for faculty to test new teaching and learning methods. Consider it a form of ethnographic research. After defining core course learning outcomes, the next step is identifying digital games to enhance them. Evaluate those games through student input and small scale testing with a class or student club. Faculty may have questions like: How do I run a pilot course? How do I determine what is not enough and what is too much student management of gamification in my course? How do I create a role for student management in my course? In the authors' experience, assistance from students, student-workers, graduate assistants or additional resources makes the transition to gamification easier. When working with students, faculty can introduce games into classroom activities, review feedback, and determine initial effectiveness in the classroom. An added bonus, for students assisting faculty, is gaining valuable work experience and leadership skills. For final assessment, analyze data to measure the outcome of adding gamification to enhance student learning.

Step 4. Connect Gamification to Broader Real World Experiences and Global Community

Innovation in teaching and learning through gamification opens many new doors. Faculty and students working together initiate larger discussions via course gamification activities to help solve real world problems. Sharing this experience with other faculty and administrators begins the process of validating the significance gamification brings to the classroom. Community organizations across the world are becoming curious about linkages between educational gamification experiences and solving real world problems. By bringing faculty, students, and the global community together, the possibilities appear unlimited.

Step 4. Questions to consider:

- What opportunities are available to share the course gamification experience with others?
- How is the course gamification experience relevant and transferrable to real world experience?
- In what ways can faculty network with practitioners on projects to enhance student learning and career development?
- What research, presentation, and publishing opportunities are connected to the course?
- What university or community service components are compatible with the course gamification experience—student club, kids' activities, or other opportunities?

As content experts, faculty leverage students' expertise in games to enhance teaching and learning. Students get to enjoy the learning process and appreciate using games to make classroom activities interactive and fun! Faculty may be wondering: How do I sustain course gamification? What support networks are available? Are faculty at other universities really successful with gamification? The authors have found using larger institutional bodies such as department meetings, teaching and learning programs, and faculty senate meetings begin a larger discussion on best fits for gamification within the overall curriculum. This experience may be shared with the larger academic community and plant seeds which might change the world. There are also research opportunities which could lead to new publications while helping faculty stay current in their field.

MINECRAFT: IT'S MORE THAN A VIDEO GAME

Released in 2009, Minecraft is a digital game developed by Mojang which was later acquired by Microsoft (Nebel et al., 2016). This is a low-cost digital game mimicking Legos. Players build vast virtual worlds in a variety of different types of gameplay. One option is survival mode where the game imitates real life. The focus of this game type is to gather resources for survival while fighting monsters and zombies.

Another option is creative mode where players are immortal and have all the game resources at their disposal. This game type is appealing to players who want to unleash their creativity and build vast worlds.

Several game mechanics make Minecraft unique. Game objects appear as building blocks and are easy to understand. The game replicates daytime and nighttime. Animals are similar to real life such as horses, cows, and sheep. At the same time, Minecraft has monsters which spawn during the night or in dark spaces. Players often have to fight zombies and use lights to create safe spaces. The terrain varies depending on the map settings so players can choose custom terrains ranging from plains to mountains to islands.

There is a seemingly endless amount of activities players can pursue in Minecraft (Callaghan, 2016). A few of the most common activities include building a house, creating a farm to establish a food supply, and exploring the map. Player groups will normally build a city together so they can share resources. Some players will go out during the night to fight zombies and monsters while gathering experience points. Advanced players may want to explore different areas and fight more difficult monsters while also gathering important materials for potions or other rare items.

Minecraft is easy to access and play. It resembles building blocks similar to Legos or puzzle pieces children play with across the world. Players can access the game through a smartphone, console, or personal computer. Game dynamics stay the same regardless of what device is being used to play Minecraft. The controls are intuitive and players learn how to play through tutorials, exploration, and trial and error. Players can also adjust settings to control the game environment such as no harming other players, respawning with materials a player had before dying, or immortality.

A fascinating component of Minecraft is the multi-generational community behind it. Young children can play the game and learn how to make basic structures. Elementary and middle school students are able to create more sophisticated designs and start working in groups. High school and college students can form larger groups while also appreciating the educational value of the game. Adults are able to play the game to rediscover their imagination while taking time to connect with their peers, children, or grandchildren. Minecraft community events such as Minefaire or Minecon are the real-life activities which bring together thousands of people who enjoy playing the game.

Minecraft is intentionally designed as a kid-friendly game. While there is some cartoon violence with fighting monsters, Minecraft does not have the blood, gore, or guts present in other violent video games. The relaxing music within the game, creative mode and open world environment encourage players to build new worlds. There is a game culture to encourage creativity and innovation through manipulating building blocks and other in-game resources. This safe and Rated PG or E environment is an important reason why Minecraft is a natural choice for faculty to use in the classroom.

MINECRAFT EDUCATIONAL APPLICATIONS

Minecraft gives students an opportunity to own their learning and collaborate on creative educational projects. In November 2016, Microsoft released Minecraft: Education Edition for primary and secondary education schools (Wong, 2016). This version is intended for educational use in a course. Features include a classroom mode to monitor students, student ability to take pictures with an in-game camera to share their work, and a ratio of thirty students to one game. The Minecraft: Education Edition website has open source lesson plans created by faculty from across the world for a broad range of classroom activities.

Minecraft is a dynamic game faculty can leverage in a variety of disciplines to maximize students' involvement in classroom activities and teach in diverse academic disciplines. Adapted by K-12, Minecraft: Education Edition is inspiring young students in a broad range of classes. Examples include art, business, education, public administration, science, and social studies. The blocks inside the game "can be arranged in a way that could reproduce almost every static object or shape, thus providing stimuli for a very different set of educational or research projects" (Nebel et al., 2016, p. 359). Faculty can explore the Minecraft: Education Edition website to develop lessons with an educational focus and learn about Minecraft as a valuable educational tool. The Minecraft: Education Edition website makes it easy to find free training and mentors who are available to provide support.

As an open world game, faculty can add Minecraft to their teaching tool kit. Callaghan (2016) conducted a K-12 study with a classroom and student club using Minecraft to gather student feedback about the game. The majority of students playing Minecraft in the classroom found the game "allowed them to attain twenty-first century learning skills of collaborating with their peers, problem-solving, critical thinking and being creative" (Callaghan, 2016, p. 251). Students were willing to share their game expertise and the most skilled students led their groups. All students were found to be applying Bloom's Taxonomy higher-order create and evaluate learning skills while noting Minecraft helped them achieve their desired learning outcomes. Instead of fighting each other, players worked together for their overall survival using soft skills of teambuilding, leadership, and communication skills.

The primary and secondary schools leveraging Minecraft in the classroom recognize this benefit to students. Karsenti et al. (2017) conducted a study of 118 elementary school students from the Montréal metropolitan area who used Minecraft to master classroom activities. They built a wide range of structures in Minecraft including a replica of Titanic, soccer stadium, and spaceship. The pursuit of these activities in Minecraft increased students' self-efficacy, ability to work in teams, and communication skills (p. 26). For example, Steve Isaacs, a middle school teacher in New Jersey, is using Minecraft for teaching students about game design. Students built mini-games and storyboards which taught them computational thinking skills and gave them an opportunity to publish the games they created (Microsoft Education Team, 2018). Guill Strougo, a high school teacher in Georgia, is using Minecraft for teaching advanced placement students about economic concepts (Agostinelli, 2019). Students applied what they learned in class through building their own corporations and engaging in free trade.

The authors also had their own experience with primary and secondary students through two Minecraft camps Park University hosted during the 2019-2020 academic year. Students between the ages of 6-15 participated and worked in teams on several projects. Using Minecraft: Education Edition, they built cities, sailed pirate ships, and traveled on the Oregon Trail. Participants learned about citizenship and history while developing a broad range of skills including communication, empathy, and leadership. They presented their creations to parents at the end of each day. A few unintended benefits observed included young girls taking leadership roles and students exceeding expectations through transformative teamwork.

Another experience the authors had was attending Minefaire Chicago. Minefaire is a series of two-day unofficial Minecraft community events held across the United States. These events bring together a diverse group of faculty, parents, and young students to learn while having fun playing Minecraft. Chief Executive Officer of Creative Minds, Stephen Reid, shared in his Inspiration Stage presentation, the variety of ways he uses Minecraft in the classroom to teach students throughout the world. His examples ranged from DNA and biology in France, World War I and history in the United Kingdom, and contemporary issues of political science in Egypt (Reid, 2019). This presentation demonstrated Minecraft as a universal design teaching tool and its vast educational applications.

Beginning in Spring, 2018, the Hauptmann School of Public Affairs at Park University piloted an online, eight-week, graduate course in Virtual Local Government using Minecraft as the learning platform. Within the pilot course, dual modalities of face to face and distance learning were successfully tested. Students accessed open education resources in public administration and applied theories learned in class to practice by building a city in Minecraft. A few of the key concepts covered included city planning, governance, citizen engagement, and economic development. Faculty assessed student learning through online discussion posts and a final paper.

At the end of the semester, students reflected on their experience and shared what they learned about local government. Student feedback was overwhelmingly positive with praise given to playing Minecraft, using open source articles and resources, and taking a unique class which challenged them to work as a team. Students collectively said that they learned a lifetime of knowledge about their respective cities and towns in an eight-week class. The course was a success and is now part of the Public Administration core curriculum.

GAMIFICATION LESSONS—ONE SIZE DOES NOT FIT ALL!

Lesson 1: Faculty are Content Experts and Students are Digital Gaming Experts

Faculty are the experts in their academic disciplines. They have pursued graduate degrees, doctoral programs, post-doctoral programs, and often have significant industry experience. This qualifies them to be faculty and teach a specific set of classes. Many faculty are publishing articles which advance their academic discipline, presenting at conferences across the world, giving back through student organizations or other community engagement, and teaching classes.

Students are the experts in games. They have grown up playing games and often play them for several years. This qualifies them to play video games and teach others how to play. Many students are also leading video game groups, running large projects within games, learning how to play new games to stay current, and taking classes! Because they are not academic experts, the challenge for students is connecting their digital game experience to the classroom or making the switch from just playing for fun to playing while thinking for academic purposes.

Lesson 2: Faculty and Students are Co-Creators of the Course Gamification Experience

The role of the modern student is transforming ways faculty approach teaching. Internet resources give students access to vast amounts of information which is easily accessible on their smartphones. By partnering with students, faculty encourage students to drive innovation in their courses and higher education while maintaining expertise in the interpretation of the subject. Introducing games into courses creates ripples of positive influence on higher education.

Students are in an excellent position to assist faculty by facilitating gamification in the classroom. They spend a great deal of time playing digital games, and as digital natives, are often able to troubleshoot a situation because of their game knowledge. Student workers, as gamification experts, can take pressure off faculty and allow them to stay focused on course content. When using gamification, there is a fascinating opportunity for students and faculty to co-create classes. When partnering with faculty, students can reflect upon their experience with games and engage in open discussions about gamification in the classroom. This could help students relate academic concepts to what they learned or applied in a game. Students making the linkage between games and theory can further faculty awareness and integration of games within the curriculum.

Students have an opportunity to share their game experience with faculty and the student body. By collaborating with faculty, students will help identify and adopt games which enhance engagement and learning. Games can improve the curriculum and make learning fun. Students may start a broader discussion among faculty and other higher education institutions about other ways to use games and perhaps there is also an option for students to co-author publications and co-present at conferences. This valuable experience helps students prepare for successful careers and make positive contributions to the world.

Lesson 3: Games Complement Rather than Distract

Games are not intended to be a distraction or stand in the way of learning. They are specific tools used to motivate students to learn and apply academic concepts while having fun. Faculty considering the addition of games in the classroom can set boundaries, run a pilot course, and use student feedback to gauge success. Another idea is to collaborate with other faculty or explore academic literature to see if there are cases for certain games within specific courses.

Lesson 4: Digital Gamification has Costs

Despite being more scalable and affordable than in-person games, there are potential cost barriers of time and money associated with developing or scaling some digital games. Common cost barriers include game licensing fees, server costs, IT technical support, and development costs. There are workarounds to reduce or eliminate costs such as partnering with IT, looking for educational versions of digital games, using commercial games and taking advantage of educational discounts. Versions of some digital games are free or have a free trial period. Kahoot! is free and Minecraft: Education Edition has a free trial. Developing a course has set up and learning curve time costs which will decrease with experience. Initial time costs include learning how to play the digital game, evaluating and testing digital game options, finding internal champions, identifying student experts, and sustaining a team to deliver a gamified course.

Lesson 5: Resistance to Gamification is Expected

There are plenty of reasons for skepticism when considering gamification in the classroom. College students taking courses online are spread throughout different time zones in the country or world where communication is asynchronous. Online course learning platforms vary in ability to accommodate gamification. Most professors have expertise in their respective disciplines rather than games. Some may see gamification as less than serious and eschew playing games in class.

There is bound to be pushback to playing games in class since some perceive gamification as frivolous. Anticipate some resistance to gamification when introducing games in the classroom. Higher educational institutions may not be willing to spend the time or resources pursuing games in the curriculum. To raise awareness, faculty can start by having open conversations about the benefits of gamification and classes which lend themselves to enhancement through games. Likeminded colleagues, networks and students are champions for using gamification in the classroom. If faculty are even the least bit curious about using gamification in the classroom, the authors' recommendation is to give it a try.

Lesson 6: Zombie Attacks Are Part of Gamification

When testing gamification in a course, prepare for zombie attacks. These are the unintended consequences which appear when introducing gamification in the classroom. Digital games require technology to operate effectively, so getting the IT department involved early is important. The authors have learned that zombies can appear when IT is not engaged in the process. Knowing the system requirements prior to the start of the course are key for student success. Academic department buy-in might be difficult if gamification is misunderstood. This is addressed by introducing digital games incrementally into a course. Overall, faculty may alleviate zombie attacks through regular communication with information technology, students, and academic departments.

Lesson 7: Digital Gamification in Higher Education is Worth It!

Gamification is worth the fight! Higher education is operating in a digital era where students are engaged in virtual worlds without the accompanying digital, pedagogical engagement. Faculty have a chance to seize the opportunity to meet these students where they are while advancing teaching and learning. Students can share their expertise and gain valuable experience to make them more employable. Fun, play, and games within courses make the college experience exciting, motivate students, and provide deep dives into topics on top of learning real life skills without realizing it! Together, faculty and students can use games in the classroom to help solve real world problems.

Lesson 8: Gamification Builds Community and Workplace Skills

Workplace skills such as communication, cooperation, empathy, leadership, and teambuilding learned by digital natives through playing video games, can be purposefully engaged in the classroom and readily employed in the workplace. Gamification provides transferable skills from the classroom to the workplace, another benefit for the digital natives. Faculty can be the bridge between digital games and communities by encouraging students to apply strategies and skills learned from games to real-life situations.

MINECRAFT PRACTICAL APPLICATIONS

Just as student engagement is important in the classroom, citizen engagement is important in communities. Higher educational institutions and cities serve diverse multi-generational populations. Technology makes it possible to connect people and share ideas in classes and communities. Activities such as clubs, games, professional organizations, and festivals are common events which bring people together for a shared purpose. Minecraft builds the bridge of motivation and engagement with students in the traditional or virtual classroom and with citizens in local government. Students enhance the curriculum and citizens enhance communities. When paired together in a classroom, they create a vibrant learning environment.

In Minecraft, players create cities and naturally work together as a community to protect themselves from monsters and zombies. Minecraft cities develop guidelines and rules similar to city ordinances or laws. Governance is necessary for Minecraft cities which replicates delivery of government services needed for everyday life to function well. The link between the real world of city administration and the virtual world of Minecraft cities is clear. Minecraft, in its existing platform, lends itself to virtual development of real-world cities. Activities Minecraft players go through within the game simulate rules and regulations established by local governments.

MINECRAFT PRACTICAL APPLICATIONS TO LOCAL GOVERNMENT

The terms local government and citizen engagement are typically found in Public Administration theory and practice. Gamification creates a new type of community or citizen engagement for consideration—games, technology, and the common good. Through games, citizen engagement is not limited to attending long and sometimes boring city council meetings. Games bring motivation, fun, and creativity together to solve societal problems for the common good. When local governments engage youth with gamification, they are learning to make positive contributions to their community for a life time.

Local governments come in all different shapes and sizes ranging from boroughs, townships, towns, counties, to cities. They are governed by a municipal charter which outlines structure of the city, its powers, and functions. In most cities, citizens elect the mayor and council who then appoint a city manager to oversee the city's functions. Local government is closest to the people and touches everyday life by providing essential city services such as safety, transportation, sanitation, and health.

Minecraft is a tool used around the world as a platform to connect young citizens with their communities. As a predominant international organization, the United Nations and UN-Habitat, used Minecraft to partner with cities and promote their mission of "socially and environmentally sustainable towns and cities while advocating adequate shelter for all" (Westerberg & Rana, 2016). UN-Habitat focuses on enhancing public spaces through partnerships with local authorities and community organizations. Public spaces including parks, sidewalks, markets, and playgrounds can improve the quality of life for communities.

By 2012, UN-Habitat created Block by Block through an innovative partnership with Mojang, the developer of Minecraft (Westerberg & Rana, 2016). This introduced residents to real world citizen engagement through a virtual world where they reimagined their communities. Since then, Block by Block has deployed Minecraft as a community development tool into communities to broaden participation and citizen engagement in cities around the world. UN-Habitat and Block by Block have successfully used Minecraft to engage marginalized citizens and bring them together to co-create public space designs. Diverse neighbors come together with the help of neighborhood youth to visualize and design new public spaces through Minecraft. Local governments build those spaces to the communities' specifications. Block by Block benefits cities in their visualization, collaboration, voice, self-confidence, and community ownership by showing young citizens how they make a difference in their world.

MINECRAFT PRACTICAL APPLICATIONS: CITIES OF ANAHEIM AND MUMBAI

Coves Park Playground, Anaheim, California

In 2016, Block by Block partnered with the City of Anaheim to reinvigorate a derelict area on the banks of the Santa Ana River. Together with city officials and design professionals, neighbors of all ages, especially neighborhood children, learned to play Minecraft, read plans, design a park, and build the park in Minecraft. In the end, the neighbors chose from the park designs presented by the children. The park was built by the City of Anaheim Parks Department and the children were honored at the park dedication (Wright, 2018).

The City of Anaheim noted the unintended consequences using Minecraft in the park building experience (Wright, 2018). Previous attempts at traditional community outreach with open houses and craft sessions had limited success. Minecraft built the bridge to citizen engagement and brought more people to participate in the planning process. Minecraft is not only a tool for community engagement; it is a way to broaden horizons, especially for the children. These young citizens became proficient in computer use, video games, communication, and cooperation. Working with landscape architects and city officials in the process gave the children opportunities to explore completely new career paths in urban planning, landscape architecture and public service.

M-Ward, City of Mumbai, India

After several failed attempts at citizen engagement in the poorest and most neglected part of Mumbai, the Mumbai Environmental Social Network turned to Block by Block for help engaging residents to work together with government agencies to improve the only spot of public space in M-Ward for almost 200,000 residents (Carr, 2017). Basic services of clean water, proper drainage and electricity were a struggle, and, in some areas, there was no access to a toilet. Despite attempts to engage citizens, there was little interest, perhaps because simply getting basic necessities was such an overwhelming task. Then, Minecraft was introduced as a planning and engagement tool.

The most marginalized and illiterate residents of the city in M-Ward—women, children, and the elderly were asked to imagine change in their community through designing dream gardens and playgrounds. Initially the women were not involved, however, their children were drawn into the process through Minecraft and began bringing their mothers, fathers, and neighbors to the meetings. Together they designed Minecraft models of their ideal public space. Their ideal designs of public areas included green space with trees, walkways, playgrounds for kids, benches for adults, and other dynamic outside gym structures.

In the end, five groups presented their practical and maintainable models to key stakeholders, government officials, local leaders, civic organizations, and community members (Carr, 2017). The groups collaborated to make the best choices for the community. Today, the open area is completed and 90% of the community's designs were incorporated into the public space. In a testament to citizen engagement, the public space is in constant use and the community has kept it clean and maintained. Minecraft engaged children who brought their community together to co-create their unique public space. In this way, the Minecraft digital tool captivated these communities and engaged residents in a shared governance process solving community problems with their local government. As a gamification platform, Minecraft is a universal catalyst for inspiring communities and students.

CONCLUSION

This chapter examines gamification as a teaching tool to motivate and engage both students and citizens. Gameplay has evolved over time from primitive games to digital games. Advances in technology have made scaling digital games possible to connect students in classrooms and citizens in cities to vast virtual worlds. Gamification utilizes game mechanics to drive engagement and skill development. Using gamification captivates individuals while motivating them to achieve higher levels of cognitive thinking.

Digital natives, who had fun growing up playing digital games, now fill college classrooms. For faculty considering gamification in the classroom to reach these students, a check list and lessons learned provide a roadmap. Important points include knowing student needs and expectations of having fun while learning, co-creating the gamification experience with students, addressing time and cost barriers, and preparing for institutional resistance. The benefits to students and the community outweigh any challenges and zombie attacks.

As a transformative digital game, Minecraft has become a popular choice to motivate and engage students and citizens. With its vast international user base, Minecraft lends itself to diverse educational, practical, and global applications. Students have the opportunity to use their gamification experiences to explore the virtual world, apply academic concepts, address adaptive challenges, and develop workforce skills. Examples in Anaheim and Mumbai highlight young citizens pioneering Minecraft as a citizen engagement and teaching tool as they bring neighbors together and collectively build their future one block at a time.

While the common thread between student and citizen engagement seems tenuous, playing Minecraft unites them in co-creation of their worlds. Not only is Minecraft appropriate for the classroom, it has an international application. UN-Habitat and Block by Block provide hands on ways of inspiring young people around the world to build stronger local communities. Within the virtual world of Minecraft, students and residents have found opportunities to benefit the common good.

REFERENCES

Addision, R. (2018). How higher education is preparing students for the jobs of the future. *Guild Digital Limited*. https://guild.co/blog/how-higher-education-is-preparing-students-for-the-jobs-of-the-future/

Agostinelli, M. (2019). *Simulating Trade and Industry with Minecraft: Education Edition*. Northwest Council for Computer Education. http://blog.ncce.org/2019/05/30/simulating-trade-and-industry-with-minecraft-education-edition/

Averbakh, I. (2012). *A History of Chess : From Chaturanga to the Present Day*. Russell Enterprises, Inc.

Burke, B. (2014). *Gamify: How gamification motivates people to do extraordinary things*. Gartner, Inc.

Callaghan, N. (2016). Investigating the role of Minecraft in educational learning environments. *Educational Media International*, *53*(4), 244–260. doi:10.1080/09523987.2016.1254877

Caponetto, I., Earp, J., & Ott, M. (2014). Gamification and education: a literature review. In *Eighth European Conference on Games Based Learning* (pp.50-57). https://books.google.com/books?id=IedEBQAAQBAJ&pg=PA50&lpg=PA50&dq=itd+cnr+genova+italy+caponetto&source=bl&ots=bF0j6T6qYY&sig=ACfU3U3fzuqibaUDmOIdMFWZzVDlWkNP_Q&hl=en&ppis=_c&sa=X&ved=2ahUKEwjU9aqLmM3oAhWbl3IEHaq2C5kQ6AEwAHoECAsQKA#v=onepage&q=itd%20cnr%20genova%20italy%20caponetto&f=false

Carr, C. (2017). *Using Minecraft to engage the public and plan better public spaces.* Rivard Report. https://therivardreport.com/using-minecraft-to engage-the-public-and-plan-better-public-spaces/

Colman, H. (2019). *6 adult learning theories and how to put them into practice.* iSpring Solutions, Inc. https://www.ispringsolutions.com/blog/adult-learning-theories

Doney, I. (2019). Research into effective gamification features to inform e-learning design. *Research in Learning Technology*, *27*(0), 1–17. doi:10.25304/rlt.v27.2093

Etzioni, A. (1964). *Modern Organizations*. Prentice- Hall.

Fotaris, P., Mastoras, T., Leinfellner, R., & Rosunally, Y. (2016). Climbing up the Leaderboard: An Empirical Study of Applying Gamification Techniques to a Computer Programming Class. *Electronic Journal of E-Learning*, *14*(2), 94–110.

Galbis-Córdova, A., Martí-Parreño, J., & Currás-Pérez, R. (2017). Higher Education Students' Attitude Towards the Use of Gamification for Competencies Development. *Journal of E-Learning & Knowledge Society*, *13*(1), 129–146.

Graff, B. (2017, September). *Business and Investment Student Club Meeting*. Lecture conducted from Park University, Parkville, MO.

Groff, J. S. (2018). The potentials of game-based environments for integrated, immersive learning data. *European Journal of Education*, *53*(2), 188–201. doi:10.1111/ejed.12270

Gross, E. (1969). The definition of organizational goals. *The British Journal of Sociology*, *20*(3), 277–294. doi:10.2307/588953

Hall, M. (2014). *What is gamification and why use it in teaching?* https://ii.library.jhu.edu/2014/05/13/what-is-gamification-and-why-use-it-in-teaching/

Heifetz, R., Linsky, M., & Grashow, A. (2009). *The Practice of Adaptive Leadership: Tools and Tactics for Changing Your Organization and the World*. Harvard Business Press.

Huang, W., & Soman, D. (2013). *A practitioner's guide to gamification of education.* University of Toronto. https://inside.rotman.utoronto.ca/behaviouraleconomicsinaction/files/2013/09/GuideGamificationEducationDec2013.pdf

Hwang, G.-J., Sung, H.-Y., Hung, C.-M., Yang, L.-H., & Huang, I. (2013). A knowledge engineering approach to developing educational computer games for improving students' differentiating knowledge. *British Journal of Educational Technology*, *44*(2), 183–196. doi:10.1111/j.1467-8535.2012.01285.x

IBM. (2020). *Fail fast and learn fast.* https://www.ibm.com/garage/method/practices/culture/failing-fast

Jenkins, H., Klopfer, E., Squire, K., & Tan, P. (2003). Entering the education arcade. *ACM Computers in Entertainment, 1*(1), 1-11. https://dl.acm.org/doi/10.1145/950566.950591

Karsenti, T., Bugmann, J., & Gros, P. P. (2017). *Transforming Education with Minecraft? Results of an exploratory study conducted with 118 elementary-school students.* Montréal: CRIFPE. https://education.minecraft.net/wp-content/uploads/Minecraft_Research_Report_Karsenti-Bugmann_2017.pdf

Kelley, J. (1999). *The Great Book of Domino Games*. Sterling Publishing Co., Inc.

Kiryakova, G., Angelova, N., & Yordanova, L. (2013). *Gamification in education.* https://www.sun.ac.za/english/learning-teaching/ctl/Documents/Gamification%20in%20education.pdf

Lei, S. (2010). *Intrinsic and extrinsic motivation: evaluating benefits and drawbacks from college instructors' perspectives*. https://go.gale.com/ps/i.do?v=2.1&it=r&sw=w&id=GALE%7CA231807635&prodId=HRCA&sid=googleScholarFullText&userGroupName=park19302

Leighninger, M. (2006). *The Next Form of Democracy*. Vanderbilt University Press.

Lukensmeyer, C., & Torres, L. (2006). Today's Leadership Challenge—Engaging Citizens. *Public Management*, *35*(3), 26–31.

Mathews, D. (1999). *Politics for People*. University of Illinois Press.

McGonigal, J. (2011). *Reality is broken: Why games make us better and how they can change the world* (2nd ed.). Penguin Books Ltd.

Microsoft Education Team. (2018). *How a New Jersey middle school uses Minecraft: Education Edition to teach game design.* https://educationblog.microsoft.com/en-us/2018/02/minecraft-education-edition-teach-game-design-middle-school/

Nebel, S., Schneider, S., & Rey, G. D. (2016). Mining learning and crafting scientific experiments: A literature review on the use of Minecraft in education and research. *Journal of Educational Technology & Society*, *19*(2), 355.

Nicholson, S. (2013). *A RECIPE for Meaningful Gamification.* To be published. In L. Wood & T. Reiners (Eds.), *Gamification in Education and Business*. Springer. Available online at http://scottnicholson.com/pubs/recipepreprint.pdf

Petrovic-Dzerdz, M. (2019). Gamifying Online Tests to Promote Retrieval-Based Learning. *International Review of Research in Open and Distance Learning*, *20*(2), 24–42. doi:10.19173/irrodl.v20i2.3812

Reid, S. (2019, September). *Game Changer: Teaching with Minecraft.* Lecture conducted from Minefaire Chicago, Chicago, IL.

Sánchez-Mena, A., & Martí-Parreño, J. (2017). Drivers and Barriers to Adopting Gamification: Teachers' Perspectives. *Electronic Journal of E-Learning*, *15*(5), 434–443.

Schinnerer, J. (2018). *The power of positive internal motivation.* Psych Central. https://psychcentral.com/lib/the-power-of-positive-internal-motivation/

Shabatura, J. (2018). *Using bloom's taxonomy to write effective learning objectives.* Technological Innovation & Pedagogical Support. https://tips.uark.edu/using-blooms-taxonomy/

Transcription Wing. (2020). *How to avoid student burnout or academic fatigue.* https://www.transcriptionwing.com/how-to-avoid-student-burnout-or-academic-fatigue/

Ware, M. (2018). *The importance of teaching soft skills in today's classrooms.* LearnWell. https://learnwelleducation.com/the-importance-of-teaching-soft-skills-in-todays-classrooms/

Westerberg, P., & Rana, S. (2016). *Using Minecraft for community participation.* United Nations Habitat. https://unhabitat.org/manual-using-minecraft-for-community-participation

Wong, W. (2016). *Getting started with Minecraft: Education Edition.* EdTech. https://edtechmagazine.com/k12/article/2016/11/getting-started-minecraft-education-edition

Wright, A. (2018). *Building real-world community with Minecraft.* The Dirt. https://dirt.asla.org/2018/10/23/building-real-world-community-with-minecraft/

KEY TERMS AND DEFINITIONS

Anaheim: City of Anaheim, California.

Block by Block: A collaboration between Mojang, Microsoft, and UN-Habitat.

Chess: Two-player checkerboard strategy game.

Citizen Engagement and Civic Participation: Active engagement of citizens within their communities.

Dominoes: Tile-based board game with rectangular pieces.

Games: Activity or sport with fixed rules involving skill, knowledge, or chance.

Kahoot!: An interactive online quiz tool using mobile devices to make classes more interactive.

Minecon: An annual event where Minecraft players where Minecraft players come together from across the world.

Minecraft: A 'sandbox' computer game resembling a complex digital Lego. Allows players to build structures out of textured cubes in a three-dimensional generated video game world.

Minefaire: Local Minecraft community events intended for 7-14 year olds. These events bring together faculty, kids, and Minecraft content developers.

Mumbai: City of Mumbai, India.

Mumbai Environmental Social Network: A think-tank within Mumbai which advocates for advancing urban issues.

Student Engagement: Students actively engaged in the learning process.

Student Motivation: Students' desire to participate in the learning process.

UN-Habitat: A United Nations agency whose mission is to promote the development of socially and environmentally sustainable human settlements and adequate shelter for all.

Video Games: Also computer games or digital games—interactive games played on different electronic display platforms.

Who Wants To Be A Millionaire?: A game where participants answer questions and compete to win $1,000,000.

Chapter 10
AI and AR:
A Copacetic Approach in the New Educational Environment

Anita M. Cassard
H. W. Taft University, USA

Brian W. Sloboda
https://orcid.org/0000-0003-0007-1725
University of Phoenix, USA

ABSTRACT

This chapter presents some of the possibilities and approaches that are used in the application of AI (artificial intelligence) and AR (augmented reality) in the new learning environments. AI will add another dimension to distance learning or eLearning that in some cases already includes AR (augmented reality) virtual learning environments. Because of this advent in available technology and the impact it will have on learning, assessment of newly structured parameters and their impact on student outcomes is crucial when measuring student learning. For some of us there might be a concern about the domination of AI as seen in the movie The Terminator, but we can take ease in the notion that it is not only AI versus humans. A new version of human augmented intelligence (HI) is being developed as we speak.

INTRODUCTION

Rensselaer Polytechnic Institute (RPI) introduced Virtual Reality (VR) that uses a 360-degree virtual environment to teach Chinese to its students. Partnering with IBM Research, two RPI faculty members initiated the project to replicate the benefits of language immersion in social interactions and role-playing games, maximizing language retention. During the pilot program in 2017, researchers noted a significant qualitative improvement in engagement, and these improvements helped students master Chinese (Hao, 2019). Beyond language learning, immersive virtual experience has the ability to link students to hyper-realistic events in history. As Artificial Intelligence (AI) simulations improve in quality, based on the responses by user inputs from a variety of sensors such as microphones and cameras, *learning by doing*

DOI: 10.4018/978-1-7998-4960-5.ch010

will become an educational norm through personalized AI output and VR immersion. With professional skill sets, language eloquence, and engineering competency, learning will be available to all students, and their learning will be tailored to their educational objectives (Diamandis, 2019; Hao, 2019).

As the Internet grew exponentially from 40 million users in 1996 to more than 300 million users by 2000, it has now reached a staggering number of 4,536,258,808 users (internetworldstats). Internet usage is soaring exponentially, and the use of eLearning parallels this rise as well. eSchool News cited that the use of AI in education will grow by 47.5% through 2021 as the world becomes more interconnected (Ascione, 2017).

Briefly, Augmented Reality (AR) enhances the learning experiences of students by using 3D synthetic objects for them to interact. That is, AR enables students to use 3D synthetic objects to augment the visual perception of some target. Augmented Reality has exceeded over 2,000 AR apps on a staggering number of more than 1.4 billion active iOS devices. Whether we choose to embrace it or not, the fact is that this technology is now penetrating our lives. The International Data Corporation (IDC) forecasts that over the next four years, AR headset production will rise 141% each year, reaching 32 million units by 2023 (Diamandis, 2019). Also, the AR market had record growth in 2018, and the Augmented Reality market is expected to earn $61.39 billion by 2023 according to research firm Markets and Markets (Diamandis, 2019). Moreover, AR is continuing to be one of the technological trends to watch for in the next decade. AR is here to stay and take over all industries, which includes use in education and training.

We can imagine the impact this technology may have in our education settings and some of the seemingly obvious benefits. Assistance for students with disabilities is one of those areas. We have approximately 3.5 million visually impaired individuals living in the United States alone (Varma et al., 2016). Developments in AI integrated smart glasses show that associated limitations could soon be reduced in severity. New ideas such as NavCog, AIServe, and MyEye, along with Microsoft's development of a Seeing AI app, which translates surroundings into audio descriptions for the blind through the lens of a smartphone's camera, will change our society. As technology evolves, AI will become more sophisticated, and advances in AI will have an impact on the US economy. Frey and Osborne (2017) examined automation via AI and identified the effects of automation of jobs. From their analysis, 47% of current US jobs are at high-risk of being replaced by machines. As indicated by Autor and Dorn (2013), the impact of automation harms middle-income jobs because these jobs are reflective of the tasks that are susceptible to automation.

More importantly, learning via AR often includes real-time feedback and provides verbal as well as nonverbal cues to foster students' sense of learning by being present, immediacy, and immersion (Kotranza et al., 2009). We must keep in mind that using AR does not replace actual learning, but it supplements students' learning. The main advantage for using AR systems in education could help students develop skills and knowledge more effectively (El Sayed et al., 2011). Because the AR tools present lessons in a 3D format, students can manipulate a variety of learning objects and handle the information in an interactive way that improves their learning. AR has an advantage to personalize the learning for each student and appeals to a multitude of learning styles that helps students improve their learning experiences. In addition to improved student outcomes, earlier research has concluded that AR has promising effects to enable AR to be blended with content to improve learning outcomes. Students who participate in kinesthetically-enhanced learning activities in AR have shown higher levels of student engagement (Anastopoulou et al., 2011; Dunleavy et al., 2009). From these studies, students provided their perceptions and attitudes towards this enhanced learning via the use of surveys. From these responses, embodied interaction via AR may improve student motivation in learning and improved outcomes.

One of the more refined uses of AR involves translation. Whether decoding a list of program options or accessing subtitles while conversing across a language barrier, instantaneous translation is improving exponentially with the rise of AI-powered AR glasses. Google Translate can already convert simple text and street signs in real time through one's smartphone. Companies like Mojo Vision are exploring AR contact lenses, offering us heads-up display capabilities without the requirement of glasses.

The outline of this chapter is as follows. Section II briefly defines Artificial Intelligence. Section III reviews the applications of AI and AR. Section IV describes the New Paradigm - A Mixed Reality and the adoption of artificial intelligence and augmented reality. In Section V, we delve more deeply into the effects of AI and AR in education. Section VI presents the opposing viewpoints of AI and AR in education. Finally, in Section VIII, we provide some closing thoughts and conclusions.

CURRENT STATE OF ARTIFICAL INTELLIGENCE

The technology and the mastery behind artificial intelligence attempts to replicate human qualities with the goal to create 'intelligent entities' that have the potential to think, reason, predict, and manipulate their surroundings as could be performed by human beings (Russell & Norvig, 1995). A later definition by Shubhendu and Vijay (2013) refined this definition that AR consists of software systems that "make decision[s] which normally require [a] human level of expertise," and "these systems help people anticipate problems or deal with issues as they come up." To further define what constitutes Artificial Intelligence, Shubhendu and Vijay (2013) along with West and Allen (2018) identified that AI systems possess the following characteristics: intentionality, intelligence, and adaptability. We shall delve more into these characteristics of Artificial Intelligence systems.

Intentionality. Algorithms using artificial intelligence are designed to make decisions, often using real-time data which are not passive machines. That is, these algorithms would use sensors, digital data, or remote inputs. Once the AI system receives the data, these algorithms combine information from a variety of different sources, analyze the material, and act upon the results derived from the data. In recent years, tremendous improvements have been made in storage systems, system speeds to enable processing of the data, and various analytic methods that could provide greater insights into the data to assist decision-makers in improving their decisions.

Intelligence. Artificial Intelligence does not operate on its own, but it is used in conjunction with machine learning and data analytics. The main motif for machine learning and data analytics is used in prediction but not so much in causality relationships. The interest in the examination of causal relationships is increasing in the economics and social science literature to identify causality (Athey & Imbens, 2019). In brief, machine learning clearly examines the data, and the algorithm looks for underlying trends in the data. Once the algorithm identifies the relevancy in the data, the decision-makers can use this information to analyze specific issues. The main requirement is that the data are suitable, so the machine learning algorithms can identify these useful patterns. The data can consist of digital information, satellite imagery, visual information, text, or unstructured data (Mullainathan & Spiess, 2017).

Adaptability. Artificial Intelligence (AI) systems have the ability to learn and adapt as they make decisions. In education, students will use an application to learn the concepts of probability. As the student learns each rule of probability, the student will practice this concept via problems. The algorithm will assess the students' responses and provide the necessary feedback not only to the students but to the teacher. The advanced algorithms embedded into the software and the use of dashboards, as well as visual displays to present information in real time, allow the students to assess their progress and mastery of the probability concepts. Once the student masters the concepts of probability, the student will advance to the next topic in the learning module.

These three characteristics of Artificial Intelligence will have an abundance of applications in education. The combination of the algorithms of machine learning in conjunction to Artificial Intelligence will prove valuable to students. That is, given the replication of these human qualities we can harness via Artificial Intelligence, it could be beneficial in the classroom to promote learning. The use of AI could help students learn the material while simultaneously helping the instructor to perform normal responsibilities in the classroom, and the teachers can focus more on assisting students with their learning (Adams Becker et al., 2016).

APPLICATIONS

Popular games in recent years such as Pokémon Go represent good examples for the use of Augmented Reality. Because of the popularity of these games, educators have sought to use the applications of AR as a means to improve learning by students. The use of the AR technology uses three-dimensional (3D) concepts in various disciplines (e.g., teaching of geography to understand the various topographic elements of the continents or the 3D geometric tools for used in mathematics and geometry). The 3D visualization requires that the students can visualize objects or processes. Then, after understanding this 3D visualization, the students can improve their comprehension of the material. Augmented Reality experiences can take a variety of forms. Some examples would include Smartphone-based AR applications that would enable students to travel through their environments while looking at their augmented world through a mobile device (Xu et al., 2012), but the mobile device limits the students' ability to physically interact in an augmented space. In addition, there are webcam-based AR applications that make use of a computer camera to capture a physical space and display this on a screen. In turn, the students can use movements to manipulate the required content to improve their learning. In fact, some AR webcam applications would be similar to Kinect and Wii platforms that enable full body movements to respond the stimuli given in the scenario.

Reality Virtual Hackathon hosted by Magic Leap at MIT in January 2019 revealed that two of the top three winners had disabilities. CleARsite provided environment reconstruction and the Soundfield Audio overlay to enable a visually impaired individual to be able to interact with the world. At the same time, HeAR used a Magic Leap 1 headset to translate voice or translate the sign language into readable text in speech bubbles that the individual could see. Given these advances in such applications, Magic Leap is dedicated to the development of these applications, which improves the quality of life for the individuals.

The convergence of today's AI revolution with AR advancements enables us to develop customized learning environments for each student. When adding sensors for tracking of neural and physiological data, students will soon be empowered to better mediate a growth mindset and even work towards achieving a flow state. Research has shown that this blend of AI and AR can vastly improve the learning outcomes for students. The merging of AR with biometric sensors and AI will provide a new platform, and it will present an amazingly different educational system (Diamandis & Cotler, 2020). Offering a delocalized, individually customizable, responsive, and accelerated learning environment, this new system presents a transformation without qualitative changes to the existing system's constituent elements. Seeing the world while sitting in a classroom that encompasses the planet and showing the Earth how it appeared

100 years ago might soon become the norm. Augmented Reality will provide this dynamic and immersive digital world of our choice. In fact, the AI-enabled AR headset can deliver physics lessons, historical scenes, or be used in linguistics. Virtual educators appear on demand, providing answers to nearly any question one could possibly think of. Some operating systems such as Magic Leap One's Lumin allow several wearers to participate/share in a digital experience. For example, students can use Magic Leap's CAD application to collaborate on 3D designs (Diamandis & Cotler, 2020).

From a job-training standpoint, AR will allow low cost training in almost any environment. Based on data from (internetworldstat) in 2017, there are 14.56 million college students in the United States enrolled in public colleges, while 5.1 million students are enrolled in private colleges. The latter estimates are expected to increase to 14.98 million and 5.33 million by 2028, respectively.

AI is defined as machine intelligence which is demonstrated by some non-living entity compared to natural intelligence as shown by human beings. In fact, many technologists, researchers, and economists have described these developments in AI as the third era of computing which may spring us into the Fourth Industrial Revolution as attributed to the advancements in machine intelligence and the availability of Big Data (Cukier & Mayer-Schoenberger, 2013; Schwab, 2016). The Fourth Industrial Revolution would be marked by the convergence of physical, digital, and biological technologies that not only change how or what people do, but it also changes the role of human beings in contrast to the preceding three Industrial Revolutions that were notably marked by the advent of steam, electricity, and internet communication technologies, respectively. In fact, the advent of these advances in technology have been predicted to lead to an expansion in technologic advancements and economic growth. At the same time, it will be marked with some caution as some of these advances may lead to greater economic inequality and disruption of existing labor markets (Schwab, 2016). More specifically, the latter leads to the exponential increase in the sharing economy (or the gig economy). In this new economic arrangement, we are essentially providing a range of services to strangers in exchange for money, but employment would be less stable in earnings, benefits, etc. because workers would no longer be treated as employees but as contractors (Sundararajan, 2016). What roles will AI and AR play, and what influence might these technologies exert? What impacts would AI and AR have on future educational delivery?

In conclusion, AI and AR provide a great learning environment for students because it promotes self-directed learning that cannot be matched in a traditional classroom. Despite the robustness of the AI and AR in learning, such learning consists of complex interactions between students, behaviors, and the learning tool. Consequently, there must be an assessment of the students' perceptions of these learning tools in AI and AR because it will help the course developers and IT designers to understand when and how students perceive their learning in these self-regulated environments via AI and AR. This section will further explore the impact of AI and AR on educational delivery and the role of teachers to facilitate this learning.

Impact of AI and AR on Educational Delivery: Role of Teachers and the AI-AR Classroom

There has been much discussion in recent years concerning the impacts of AI and AR on education (Allen, 2018; Nadrljanski et al., 2018). As part of education in the United States, the role of "teacher" may be archaic, and the role of "teacher" may have a different role in educational delivery and experience by students. That is, the teaching and learning requirements would be substantially revamped, and the dynamics of educational delivery will change under an AI-based system of education. Given this new role of "teacher," it will likely raise questions about the role of the 'for-teaching' degrees and related certificates. In addition, what will be the new adaption of the science of pedagogy to these changes? The advent of technology in education will alter the scope and delivery of education because the future of education will mix AI and AR, and new technologies and paradigms for new design have yet to emerge (Rizzotto, 2017).

What is the impact of this new learning on classrooms? Will the classrooms of today or the physical spaces continue into the future or become virtual? The answer is yes to both questions, and the student in tomorrow's AI based educational experience would no doubt be exposed to these advanced technologies. The thought of the development of the virtual classroom would be great, but we do not know the size of the potential in the development of the virtual classroom. Once the virtual classroom has been introduced, how do we measure the learning outcomes of students in the AI-AR educational process? Students will most likely become more involved in their learning and the measurement of learning could be measured as students' progress through their daily lessons (Hasse et al., 2019). The AI-AR system could, in fact, measure student learning after each section of the lesson and provide the necessary remediation for concepts not mastered. In a perfect world, we will know at the end of each student's day if the student is meeting academic requirements and corrected their deficiencies as they arise so the student can stay on track. Despite the positive benefits of such learning, one could argue there are moral questions to consider with a system such as this one. Consequently, educators and policymakers must be cognizant of this type of learning and fully understand how these technologies can be used to ensure that the benefits of such approaches in educational delivery provides benefits (Allen, 2018; Hasse et al., 2019).

Hasse et al. (2019) acknowledges the advantages for the use of AI-AR in the classroom to enhance educational outcomes for students (e.g., intelligent tutoring systems, AI-based curriculum plans, and intelligent virtual reality). In fact, the adoption of AI-AR could offer personalized learning that can improve outcomes of learning for students. The latter could be referred to as "curriculum playlists," and intelligent tutoring systems because they offer personalized learning experiences for students by providing feedback for students based on their performance and remediation to help the students master the content. This approach would provide daily, individualized learning activities and the use of one-on-one tutoring that nearly mimics face-to-face tutoring. Given the increase in the use of AI-AR, costs of educational delivery would decrease, and access would be improved for students using AI-AR technologies to help them learn from anywhere. The latter could personalize learning and provide greater educational opportunities for students. Further advances may also include the development of additional tools for education by accessing these AI-AR tools via mobile devices beyond the classroom, feedback on tasks, suggested educational resources, and activities that promote 21st century skills in leadership and creativity.

As indicated by Rizzotto (2017) and Allen (2018), the educational system is static, applies general learning to all students, and does not put as much effort on the individual self-development as it should, despite the advent of technological advances in education. More importantly, students often do not know what they are learning and why they are learning these topics. Rizzotto (2017) also posits that there are three important ingredients for effective learning experiences: personalized learning, experiential learning, and mastery-based learning. These learning experiences would improve educational delivery and the students' educational experiences. Table 1 shows these three important ingredients for effective learning.

Unfortunately, the three ingredients to learning (as summarized in Table 1) are not fully utilized at educational institutions for the following three reasons:

Table 1. Three ingredients for effective learning

Learning Type	Description
Personalized Learning	Diverse variety of programs, learning experiences, instructional approaches, and strategies that address the distinct learning. preferences, interests, aspirations, weaknesses, or cultural backgrounds of individual students. More individualized. Personalized learning improves outcomes and promotes greater academic progress among students.
Experimental Learning	The process of learning through experience or "learning through reflection on doing". Experience-based learning also encourages experimentation, embraces curiosity and (perhaps most importantly) turns mistakes into a natural part of the learning process rather than grounds for punishment of students.
Mastery-based Learning	When dealing with cumulative subjects (e.g., mathematics, sciences) where past knowledge is essential to understanding what is next, a student should *only* move forward with the subject once they have mastered all the concepts preceding it. This is a deeply personal and individualized approach, and students do not advance to the next course until the current course is mastered.

Source: Rizzotto (2017)

1. Developing new ways to teach subjects like math, biology, and history experientially is a major design challenge, particularly when there are budgetary constraints. After all, we have been taught using books and a blackboard (whiteboard) for as long as anyone can remember, so how would we go about engaging all senses, making learning active and social, keeping the costs low, and achieving all learning goals? This becomes a challenge.
2. The reason that we do not do these things is because the implementation of the types of learning as shown in Table 1 would require many monetary and financial resources to effectively implement. Given the fiscal restraints of today, this could be difficult to do effectively.
3. Full personalized learning also requires a flexible and non-linear educational curriculum to be fully realized because this is the only way educators can embrace students' differences and create individualized learning for each student. However, today's approach to education is the antithesis of today's rigid solutions.

The increasing range of data capturing devices (e.g., biological data, voice recognition, and eye tracking) will enable AI to provide ways to assess learning for easy and more difficult material. For example, a practice-based learning that incorporates elements of problem-solving or collaboration might be assessed using a combination of data sources to include voice recognition (to identify who is doing and saying what) and eye tracking (to explore which student is focusing on which learning element of the learning task at any given point in the student's learning). The main advantage of the AI tools will enable the collection of data about which teaching and learning tools work best. Such data can be used to track students' progress. The ability to be able to track this progress will examine what modules of learning works best and what refinements need to be made in the AI tool. In addition, the AI systems can maintain the data from these systems that can be used to assess different skills and capabilities because the future jobs in the 21st century will cover a myriad of skills that are important (Luckin et al., 2016).

In brief, as stated in the previous discussion, the role of the teacher will undoubtedly change as the AI becomes more advanced and is used more in education. More specifically, the use of AI can replace some of the tasks performed by teachers (e.g., grading assignments and record keeping). Hence, the use of AI would enable teachers to spend less time on routine, time-consuming tasks and devote more of their time to students while providing greater assistance in the students' education.

A NEW PARADIGM? A MIXED REALITY

The focus of this chapter looks at the adoption of artificial intelligence and augmented reality. What about the possibility of a Mixed Reality (MR)? The standard approach to look at the MR is the continuum posited by Kishino and Milgram (1994), and it illustrates the mixed reality continuum. This continuum would cross from real to virtual, which defines four classes of display with two poles (reality and virtual reality). Then, there are two intermediate classes (augmented reality and augmented virtuality). Kishino and Milgram (1994) indicate that the computer generates these realities and can be placed on a continuum according to how much of the user's world. Moving from left to right, this would result in an increase in the virtual imagery, and the connection with reality would then weaken. In fact, AR technology could be used to transition users smoothly along this continuum as shown by the MagicBook work (Billinghurst et al., 2001).

In other words, MR would integrate the tangible, physical world being mixed with virtual and digitized elements. This continuum can result in the development of new paradigms, tools, techniques, and instrumentation that would enable the visualization at different and multiple scales, and this could result in the design and implementation of MR pedagogy across various disciplines (Magana, 2014). The 2017 NMC Higher Education Horizon Report (Adams Becker et al., 2017) specifically highlights these technologies as key educational technologies leading to innovative and new technology-led pedagogy that could initiate improved learning that would improve the learning outcomes for students.

Why the use of AR and VR in education? Learning tools that use AR is the game and some applications to architecture because the AR-based game allows players to interact directly with their environment. In turn, this makes the distinction clearer. AR is not only using two-dimensional (2D), but it also uses three-dimensional (3D) visualization. This combination of 2D and 3D makes the object looks more real with a dimensionless aspect. The advent of computer applications has enabled the development of the AR technology to be used to simulate the real world and enhance learning. The tools of AR have enabled a rapid development as a direct consequence of the IT that enables the development of AR tools for learning. Humans have a desire to interact with a virtual environment in various ways because of the availability of the AR technology. Much interaction using AR is currently being developed via the interaction of sound and visualization. Until a virtual environment can perform the brain waves, the tools of AR can simulate these interactions to make these interactions more prevalent (Ariyana & Wuryandari, 2012).

Dalgarno and Lee (2010) outline a set of unique characteristics for 3D virtual learning environments that are focused on the right-hand side of the scale shown in Figure 1. These include greater opportunities for experiential learning, increased engagement, and improved contextualization of learning. Cheng and Tsai (2013) also provide insights into the use of AR learning by indicating that student's spatial ability, practical skills, and conceptual understanding would be afforded using this technology. On the other hand, more work must be done on the outcomes of the learning experiences and how students' characteristics affect outcomes from this learning.

To experience a mixed reality, an MR headset is used because these headsets offer a holographic experience using specialized glasses. Some common products used for the MR experience include the Microsoft's HoloLens, Acer Windows Mixed Reality, Lenovo Explorer, and Samsung Odyssey. It's the gesture/gaze/voice recognition technology through a pair of motion controllers or through the MR headset that enables the delivery of the MR experience. On the other hand, more processing power is required to enable a MR experience than it does for the VR and AR experiences.

EXAMPLES OF USE OF AI IN EDUCATION

The use of AI and AR in the education requires the ability to process large amounts of data that provides value to the user. More importantly, the collection of massive data enables course designers and IT developers to use this collection of data to customize the data to be used in the development of various education programs to help students learn. Using Big Data also provides insights about the services processes to understand the student's performance during a lesson that can be assessed in real time to enable personalization and customization of the educational lessons (Kitchin, 2014; Mosco, 2015). Put differently, Big Data practices take place by providing new opportunities to maximize the potential of data collection that can be used in online learning that includes AR and VR. Moreover, Big Data would encourage innovative teaching that enables students to focus on the material that requires additional work with a greater optimization of student learning that benefits both the students and educators. Using Big Data can be quite useful to analyze students' learning in detail with the major goal for the use of the data to assess skills that match the learning objectives (Ariyana & Wuryandari 2012). The subsequent subsections will some specific examples for the use of AI in education: smart content, intelligence tutoring systems, and virtual facilitators as well as learning environments.

Smart Content

To help students review the material, smart content is a technology that attempts to condense textbooks into useful information for preparation for upcoming examinations. Content Technologies, Inc., an artificial intelligence development company specializing in automation of business processes and intelligent instruction design, has created a suite of smart content services for use in secondary education and higher. For example, they created Cram101, and it uses AI to help breakdown textbook content into digestible "smart" study guides that provide summaries, true false and multiple-choice tests, and flashcards. JustTheFacts101 is another company that also uses AI to prepare review materials. JusttheFacts1010 highlights and creates text and chapter-specific summaries, and these are archived digitally and available from Amazon. Other companies are creating smart digital content platforms, complete with content delivery, practice exercises, and real-time feedback and assessment. An example would be Netex Learning that allows teachers to design digital curriculum and content across a myriad of devices that enables the integration of videos and other tools as well as an online assessment by the students.

Given the advantages for the students, smart content software provides teachers and tutors with a detailed analysis on what their students got right and wrong. Then, the software, in conjunction with the input from the teachers and tutors, can provide individualized tutoring to each student or even re-teach entire concepts if necessary. There is some concern that this type of software will replace the role of teachers and tutors. In fact, there is no concern because the teachers and tutors see this tool as a means to help students improve their comprehension of the material. One commonality between each of these educational tools, however, is that they are used to provide value to teachers and tutors rather than replacing them. "The way I think about it, there are seven billion people on this earth, and about half of them don't have access to good education," Professor Goel said in a conversation with Quartz. "If we can take artificial intelligence and provide those people with minimal question answering, who knows what a difference it could make in someone's life?"

Intelligence Tutoring Systems (ITS)

The field of Intelligent Tutoring Systems (ITS) has been investigated since the early 1970s for how to leverage AI techniques to create educational technologies that are personalized to the needs of individual students with the goal to provide students the necessary one-on-one instruction (du Boulay, 2016). More specifically, ITS can improve the students' motivation to learn by providing an accurate assessment of the students' learning during an educational exercise. The goal of ITS is to model, predict, and monitor relevant student behaviors and abilities in a variety of learning activities that provide more personalized help and feedback for students (Woolf, 2009). The ITS system must be able to able to capture and process information from the teaching process: (1) the target instructional domain (domain model), (2) the relevant pedagogical knowledge (pedagogical model), and (3) the students. The latter components define the conceptual development of the instructional modelling and interaction of ITS since the 1970s (du Boulay, 2016). More importantly, ITS has evolved rapidly in recent years with the advent of machine learning (ML). Techniques from ML are instrumental in addressing the challenges in the enhancement of ITS because ML can analyze the data that might be challenging to obtain from human reviews. Moreover, ML can analyze the students' cognitive states in a much higher dimension than the analysis by teachers. In traditional tutoring, the tutor adapts to the tutoring session by engaging the student. Stated differently, it is not just showing the student the correct way of doing an exercise, but it is about being believable and spontaneous during the session. In a typical tutoring session, answering questions is the dominant activity. Alexander et al. (2008) showed that question-answering activities occurred 92% of the time during a typical tutoring session. On the other hand, tutors were engaged 71% of the time (e.g., asking questions, asking for additional information, and delivering immediate feedback). Thus, it becomes important for the ITS systems to also develop the necessary spontaneity to mimic actual tutoring sessions to improve student learning.

Other companies are creating digital content platforms that contain content delivery, practice exercises, and real-time feedback. Netex Learning allows educators to design the curriculum and content across devices, integrating digital media such as video and audio, as well as self or online instructor assessments. Nextex also provides a personalized learning cloud platform which is designed for learning in the workplace. Employers can design customizable learning systems with the appropriate apps; gamification and simulations; virtual courses; self-assessments; video conferencing; and other tools for their learning. These learning platforms in the workplace are designed to allow employees to master additional skills and receive continuous feedback. When used strategically, this type of training has the potential to help improve performance and increase the productivity of the employees. Intelligent Tutoring Systems (ITS) have progressed significantly since their inception. Chaudhri et al. (2013) noted that the use of ITS does not possess the negative stigma of tutors. That is, there is evidence to suggest that ITS performs quite well and perhaps better than individual tutors for many students. Major publishing companies for education have been involved in the development of ITS. For example, Pearson collaborates with University College London Knowledge Lab. These types of collaborations enable ITS to be more transparent which allows educators to understand how a system arrived at a next-step decision. This structure makes ITS a robust tool that can be used in teaching.

IBM's fellow Chieko Asakawa promoted the idea of a robot shaped prototype suitcase using artificial intelligence guiding visually impaired people. A collaborative effort between IBM, Mitsubishi, Alps Alpine, Omron, and Shimizu is working on this project, which could possibly yield applications used by students in various situations such as science classes, field trips, and sports (asahi.com).

Virtual Facilitators and Learning Environments

There has been some research and development to create virtual human guides and facilitators for use in educational and therapeutic environments. That is, the creation of human-like objects that can think, act, react, and interact in a natural way, and they respond to both verbal and nonverbal communication as encountered by human teachers with their students. As an example, Captivating Virtual Instruction for Training (CVIT) aims to integrate live classroom methods with best-fit virtual technologies (e.g., virtual facilitators, augmented reality, intelligent tutor, and other digital tools). The use of the CVIT would be applicable to those students who are in remote areas and need educational assistance (Timms, 2016).

In brief, these tools, especially AI, have the ability to analyze large amounts of data in real-time. That is, students' performance in a particular topic across subjects over the course of an academic year can be assessed. This type of student feedback will provide new content or create new learning parameters instantaneously. Thus, this feedback will help students, and their need for feedback, and focus on topics that give students difficulties. The latter approach makes it sound as if teachers were no longer going to be needed. Not quite. This feedback for students will help teachers better understand student performance and develop more personalized learning plans for students to master the material. Additionally, we may want to look at the concepts of Declarative knowledge (also known as Metalinguistic knowledge) and procedural knowledge, which is obtained through inferences from already existing knowledge. Will AI enhance both? Some of the latest innovation occurring today does not always involve breakthrough technologies but rather the creation of fundamentally new models. The question arises if AI will become our ecosystem (including networks such as local education, medical, employment, and other communication systems, which influence our microsystems), and if so, what might be the level of control we (humans) exercise over the system? Will this new virtual reality be similar to pulling apart a Matryoshka doll and finding another? Higher learning institutions must take a good look at the future technology intensive teaching platforms. The idea of demonetizing and democratizing education is growing, and to some degree, it already exists. Universities are implementing programs that require less time, are cheaper, and are geared toward the future needs of society. In addition, specializing for example in areas of Analytics and Logistics will enable students to procure jobs without a traditional, lengthy and expensive path involving completion of a formal degree but rather earn a certificate in their field of expertise.

OPPOSING VIEWPOINT

Gary Marcus (2020), a trained neuroscientist and NYU professor, thinks that deep learning and the relationship to AI has been overemphasized and cites both "technical and ethical concerns." According to Marcus and technically speaking, deep learning may be mirroring the perceptual tasks of the human brain but hardly understands conversations or causal relationships, which could lead to precarious situations. One of his examples states the following:

AlphaGo can play very well on a 19x19 board but actually has to be retrained to play on a rectangular board. Or you take your average deep-learning system, and it can recognize an elephant as long as the elephant is well lit and you can see the texture of the elephant. But if you put the elephant in silhouette, it might well not be able to recognize it anymore.

During traditional teacher-led approach to learning, students move in lock step. On the other hand, mastery systems encourage the idea that learning can be personalized, and students work on the skills they need help with the most. Given these transformations in learning, our brains would seamlessly connect to the Cloud by 2035 as predicted by Ray Kurzweil (Diamandis & Kotler, 2020). Considering his 86% prediction accuracy rate, this prediction seemed somewhat ambitious. But Neuralink's, a company owned by Elon Musk, recent announcement adds significant credence to Kurzweil's prediction and timeline. Neuralink announced pioneering progress on its Brain-Computer Interface (BCI) technology, striving towards a 2 gigabit-per-second wireless connection between a patient's brain and the cloud in the next few years (Diamandis & Kotler, 2020).

Recently, Technology Company Sage conducted surveys pertaining to AI and individuals' understanding of it. In total, 43% of respondents in the United States and 47% of respondents in the United Kingdom indicated that they had no idea what AI is capable of in business and/or education.

Bakhshi et al. (2020) discuss the lack of gender diversity in AI and the increased possibility that the technology will discriminate against women. They maintain that an all-male research team tends to neglect various points of view and is less prone to address the social implications of their work than teams with at least one woman. Emphasizing gender bias reflected in AI, Bakhshi et al (2020) urge schools, governments, and organizations to eliminate any barriers faced by women, specifically in AI as well as in science, technology, engineering, and mathematics (STEM).

The authors point to a review published by the AI Now Institute, which shows that less than 20% of the researchers applying to AI conferences are women, and a small number of undergraduates studying AI at Stanford and the University of California at Berkeley are female (Myers West et al., 2019).

Bakhshi's et al., (2020) analysis confirms the idea that there is a gender diversity crisis in AI research. There also appears to be a significant difference between countries and research fields. The authors found a robust presence of women in AI research in the Netherlands, Norway, and Denmark with a lower representation in Japan and Singapore. Additional findings showed that women working in physics, education, biology, and social aspects of computing were more likely to publish work on AI compared to those working in computer science or mathematics. What adds another nugget to the study is the authors' exploration of semantic differences between research papers that included female contributions versus male only. To do this, a machine learning technique referred to as word embedding (https://arxiv.org/pdf/1402.3722.pdf) was used to show papers with at least one female author versus papers with males only. Their study was conducted in the United Kingdom, and it would be interesting to see a similar study in the United States.

It is critical for leaders in the field of education to develop a firm understanding of the differences between AI, ML (Machine Learning), and DL (Deep Learning). The increasing levels of insights that can be gained from a shared understanding of AI is evident when understanding exactly how these ever-growing, disruptive technologies can be harnessed.

CONCLUDING THOUGHTS

There is a belief that we are genetically disposed to comment, arbitrate, work on reaching consensus, and engage in dialogue about what we need and want. If all of this fails, we attack and pounce like the predators we are.

What if, and unbeknownst to us, we exhibit a psychological reaction that is based on a theological and mythical oriented gene that triggers reactions and opinions solely based on ancestral experience? Embedded in our genetic make-up and placed there for reasons unidentified to us? Advanced AI would not be able to replicate this phenomenon. As Mr. Spock would say, "it is illogical," and based on this illogical assumption, we maintain a thread of non-replicable humanity… (StarTrek)

REFERENCES

Adams Becker, S., Cummins, M., Davis, A., Freeman, A., Hall Giesinger, C., & Ananthanarayanan, V. (2017). *NMC Horizon Report: 2017 Higher Education Edition*. New Media Consortium.

Adams Becker, S., Freeman, A., Giesinger Hall, C., Cummins, M., & Yuhnke, B. (2016). *NMC/CoSN Horizon Report: 2016 K-* (12th ed.). The New Media Consortium.

Alexander, S., Sarrafzadeh, A., & Hill, S. (2008). Foundation of an affective tutoring system: Learning how human tutors adapt to student emotion. *International Journal of Intelligent Systems Technologies and Applications*, *4*(3), 355. doi:10.1504/IJISTA.2008.017278

Allen, J. R. (2018). Why we need to rethink education in the artificial intelligence age? Brown *Journal of Philosophy, Politics, and Economics*. https://www.brownjppe.com/john-allen-feature

Anastopoulou, S., Sharples, M., & Baber, C. (2011). An evaluation of multimodal interactions with technology while learning science concepts. *British Journal of Educational Technology*, *42*(2), 266–290. doi:10.1111/j.1467-8535.2009.01017.x

Ariyana, Y., & Wuryandari, A. I. (2012). Virtual interaction on augmented reality for education with nonparametric belief propagation algorithm. *Procedia: Social and Behavioral Sciences*, *67*, 590–599. doi:10.1016/j.sbspro.2012.11.364

Ascione, L. (2017). *Brace yourself: AI is set to explode in education in the next four years*. https://www.eschoolnews.com/2017/05/22/brace-ai-set-explode-next-4-years/

Athey, S., & Imbens, G. W. (2019). Machine learning methods that economists should know about. *Annual Review of Economics*, *11*(1), 685–725. doi:10.1146/annurev-economics-080217-053433

Autor, D., & Dorn, D. (2013). The growth of low-skill service jobs and the polarization of the US labor market. *The American Economic Review*, *103*(5), 1553–1597. doi:10.1257/aer.103.5.1553

Bakhshi, H., Hargreaves, I., & Mateos-Garcia, J. (2013). *A manifesto for the creative economy*. Retrieved from http://orca.cf.ac.uk/49323/

Billinghurst, M., Kato, H., & Poupyrev, I. (2001). The magicbook-moving seamlessly between reality and virtuality. *IEEE Computer Graphics and Applications*, *21*(3), 6–8.

Chaudhri, V. K., Gunning, D., Lane, H. C., & Roschelle, J. (2013). Intelligent learning technologies Part 2: Applications of artificial intelligence to contemporary and emerging educational challenges. *AI Magazine*, *34*(4), 10–12. doi:10.1609/aimag.v34i4.2518

Cheng, K. H., & Tsai, C. C. (2013). Affordances of augmented reality in science learning: Suggestions for future research. *Journal of Science Education and Technology*, *22*(4), 449–462. doi:10.100710956-012-9405-9

Cukier, K., & Mayer-Schoenberger, V. (2013). The rise of big data: How it's changing the way we think about the world. *Foreign Affairs*, *92*(3), 28–40.

Dalgarno, B., & Lee, M. J. W. (2010). What are the learning affordances of 3-D virtual environments? *British Journal of Educational Technology*, *40*(6), 10–32. doi:10.1111/j.1467-8535.2009.01038.x

Diamandis, P. (2019). *How augmented reality will overall our most crucial industries*. https://singularityhub.com/2019/09/27/how-augmented-reality-will-overhaul-our-most-crucial-industries/

Diamandis, P., & Kotler, S. (2020). *The future is faster than you think*. Simon & Schuster.

du Boulay, B. (2016). Artificial intelligence as an effective classroom assistant. *IEEE Intelligent Systems*, *31*(6), 76–81. doi:10.1109/MIS.2016.93

Dunleavy, M., Dede, C., & Mitchell, R. (2009). Affordances and limitations of immersive participatory augmented reality simulations for teaching and learning. *Journal of Science Education and Technology*, *18*(1), 7e22.

El Sayed, N. A. M., Zayed, H. H., & Sharawy, M. I. (2011). ARSC: Augmented reality student card – an augmented reality solution for the education field. *Computers & Education*, *56*(4), 1045–1061. doi:10.1016/j.compedu.2010.10.019

Frey, C. B., & Osborne, M. A. (2017). The future of employment: How susceptible are jobs to computerisation? *Technological Forecasting and Social Change*, *114*, 254–280. doi:10.1016/j.techfore.2016.08.019

Hao, K. (2019). *A new immersive classroom uses AI and VR to teach Mandarin Chinese*. https://www.technologyreview.com/s/613963/ai-vr-education-immersive-classroom-chinese-ibm/?utm_campaign=Abundance%20Insider&utm_source=hs_email&utm_medium=email&_hsenc=p2ANqtz-_k8VqBgYDI-vXEJhLfjX4CuZd1lhBsXV34IrJVT7QDBM_yM3i-eNrGAImmyMGwZfXWjbiO

Hasse, A., Cortesi, S., Lombana-Bermudez, A., & Gasser, U. (2019). *Youth and artificial intelligence: Where we stand*. Youth and Media, Berkman Klein Center for Internet & Society. https://cyber.harvard.edu/publication/2019/youth-andartificial-intelligence/where-we-stand

Internet World Stats. Retrieved March 18, 2020, from https://www.internetworldstats.com/stats.htm

Kishino, F., & Milgram, P. (1994). A Taxonomy of Mixed Reality Visual Displays. *IEICE Transactions on Information and Systems*, *E77-D*(12), •••.

Kitchin, R. (2014). Big Data, new epistemologies and paradigm shifts. *Big Data & Society*, *1*(April–June), 1–12. doi:10.1177/2053951714528481

Kotranza, A., Lind, D. S., Pugh, C. M., & Lok, B. (2009). *Real-time in-situ visual feedback of task performance in mixed environments for learning joint psychomotorcognitive tasks* (pp. 125–134). Paper presented at the 8th IEEE International Symposium on Mixed and Augmented Reality (ISMAR), Orlando, FL.

Luckin, R., Holmes, W., Griffiths, M., & Forcier, L. B. (2016). *Intelligence unleashed: An argument for AI in education*. http://oro.open.ac.uk/50104/1/Luckin%20et%20al.%20-%202016%20%20Intelligence%20 Unleashed.%20An%20argument%20for%20AI%20in%20Educ.pdf

Magana, A. J. (2014). Learning strategies and multimedia techniques for scaffolding size and scale cognition. *Computers & Education*, *72*, 367–377. doi:10.1016/j.compedu.2013.11.012

Marcus, G. (2020). The next decade in AI: four steps towards robust artificial intelligence. *arXiv preprint arXiv:2002.06177.*

Mosco, V. (2015). *To the cloud: Big data in a turbulent world*. Routledge. doi:10.4324/9781315631554

Mullainathan, S., & Spiess, J. (2017). Machine learning: An applied econometric approach. *The Journal of Economic Perspectives*, *31*(2), 87–106. doi:10.1257/jep.31.2.87

Myers West, S., Whittaker, M., & Crawford, K. (2019). *Discriminating systems (report)*. AI Now.

Rizzotto, L. (2017). *The future of education: How A.I. and immersive tech will reshape learning forever*. https://perma.cc/2PYJ-GGPG

Russell, S. J., & Norvig, P. (1995). *Artificial intelligence: A modern approach*. Prentice Hall.

Schwab, K. (2016). *The fourth industrial revolution: What it means, how to respond* [Blog post]. https://www.weforum.org/agenda/2016/01/the-fourth-industrial-revolution-what-it-means-and-how-to-respond/

Shukla Shubhendu, S., & Vijay, J. (2013). Applicability of artificial intelligence in different fields of life. *International Journal of Scientific and Engineering Research*, *1*(1), 28–35.

Sundararajan, A. (2016). *The sharing economy: The end of employment and the rise of crowd-based capitalism*. MIT Press.

Timms, M. J. (2016). Letting artificial intelligence in education out of the box: Educational robots and smart classrooms. *International Journal of Artificial Intelligence in Education*, *26*(2), 701–712. doi:10.100740593-016-0095-y

Varma, R., Vajaranant, T. S., Burkemper, B., Wu, S., Torres, M., Hsu, C., Choudhury, F., & McKean-Cowdin, R. (2016). Visual impairment and blindness in adults in the United States: Demographic and geographic variations from 2015 to 2050. *JAMA Ophthalmology*, *134*(7), 802–809. doi:10.1001/jamaophthalmol.2016.1284 PMID:27197072

West, D. M., & Allen, J. (2018). *How artificial intelligence is transforming the world*. https://www.brookings.edu/research/how-artificial-intelligence-is-transforming-the-world/

Woolf, B. (2009). *Building Intelligent Interactive Tutors*. Morgan Kaufmann., doi:10.1016/B978-0-12-373594-2

Xu, Y., Mendenhall, S., Ha, V., Tillery, P., & Cohen, J. (2012). *Herding nerds on your table: NerdHerder, a mobile augmented reality game. Proceedings of the 2012 ACM annual conference extended abstracts on human factors in computing systems extended abstracts*, 1351–1356. 10.1145/2212776.2212453

KEY TERMS AND DEFINITIONS

Artificial Intelligence: Artificial intelligence is the use of computer systems able to perform tasks that typically mimics human actions, such as the visual perception, speech recognition, decision-making, and translation between languages.

Augmented Reality: This is an interactive experience of the real world where the objects from the real world are enhanced by computer-generated perceptual information. These computer-generated information sometimes combine the different senses, e.g., visual, auditory, haptic, somatosensory, and olfactory.

Big Data: The use of extremely large data sets that may be analyzed computationally to reveal patterns, trends, and associations, that can be used to describe human interactions which can be used to assess learning, evaluate marketing behavior, determine the effects of a policy and other forms of assessment.

Captivating Virtual Instruction for Training: Captivating virtual instruction for training aims to shape the future learning through the delivery of course material that is not only informative and educational but provides after learning for the students. In some cases, this type of instruction blends virtual realities and actual classroom instruction.

Causality: This concept shows a relationship between two events where one event is affected by the other. Statistically, if one variable, increases or decreases as a result of other variable, then there is causation exists.

Intelligence Tutoring Systems: It is a computer system provides immediate and customized instruction or feedback to students without the intervention from a teacher.

Mixed Reality: It is the merging of real and virtual worlds to produce new environments and visualizations. At the same time, the physical and digital objects co-exist and also interact in real time.

Virtual Reality: It is the use of computer technology to create a simulated environment. This simulation uses as many senses as possible, such as vision, hearing, touch, and smell. The computer and its algorithms transform this information into the artificial world.

Chapter 11
Virtual Reality in Social Work Education:
Models, Meaning, and Purpose for Enhanced Learning

Debra L. Olson-Morrison
Park University, USA

ABSTRACT

The use of virtual reality (VR) as a learning tool occupies a whole new and exciting domain for social work education. Engaging in virtual worlds expands the potential for students to connect with the learning experience on multiple levels, pedagogically aligns with stimulating affective processes to enhance cognitive engagement, and aligns with the domains of knowledge acquisition in competency-based social work education. In this chapter the author outlines the affordances necessary for student engagement in a virtual learning experience (VLE). The author explores applications for virtual reality in social work education and outlines several distinct opportunities for virtually-enhanced classroom learning. Practical guidelines to assist instructors in facilitating a VR learning experience are proposed, and the chapter concludes with commentary on the future of VR in social work education.

INTRODUCTION

Social work education reflects the essence of what it means to instruct students in an applied profession. Social work curriculum is constructed on and rotates around *nine behaviorally-based competencies*: *(1) Demonstrate ethical and professional behavior; (2) Engage diversity and difference in practice; (3) Advance human rights in social, economic and environmental justice; (4) Engage in practice-informed research and research-informed practice; (5) Engage in Policy Practice; (6) Engage in practice with individuals, families, groups, communities and organizations; (7) Assess individuals, families, groups, communities and organizations; (8) Intervene with individuals, families, groups, communities and organizations; and (9) Evaluate practice with individuals, families, groups, communities and organizations*

DOI: 10.4018/978-1-7998-4960-5.ch011

(CSWE, 2015). Competence in social work means the student demonstrates the ability to integrate and apply social work knowledge, values, and skills to practice situations in a purposeful, intentional, and professional manner to promote human and community well-being. Students are expected to use critical thought and judgement to determine best action and interventions in multiple settings, on multiples levels, with individuals, families, groups, organizations and communities. Assessment of social work competencies encompasses the five domains of knowledge, skills, values, and cognitive and affective processes. In sum, social work programming aims to teach students how to behave as professional social workers through demonstrating competencies on multiple levels across multiple domains.

As a human services profession, social work programs are charged with providing students opportunities to develop specific social work competencies through classroom learning and field education. Field education bares equal importance to classroom learning. Students transfer skills learned in the classroom to real world settings in a structured environment that promotes professional socialization (Miller, 2010). In their field placement, students are charged with developing the professional behaviors that demonstrate acquisition of the competencies and use critical thought and judgement to determine best action and intervention.

The charge to educate students in the field presents challenges. First, not all students are exposed to situations where they work with all levels of practice inclusive of individual, family, group, organization and community practice. Secondly, some students feel unprepared for field work because classroom practice activities simply do not provide adequate real-world experience. Lastly, although students are expected to develop empathy skills as they relate to interpersonal relationships, many experiences in the classroom fall short in eliciting the necessary conditions to learn about and process empathy as a therapeutic tool.

The use of simulation in social work education has proven successful in helping students bridge the gap between classroom learning and demonstration of learned skills in the field (Bogo et al., 2014). Simulation provides students with a safe way to practice skills prior to using them in high stakes, real-world situations. Simulation also gives students the opportunity to process behaviors post-simulation and can be an effective arena for reflecting on knowledge, values, and cognitive and affective processes that precipitated and accompanied the skills demonstrated in the simulated experience. However, facilitating simulation activities can be labor intensive, time-consuming and costly. Further, simulations, while mimicking real world practice scenarios, may lack authenticity and are limited by the quality and quantity of resources available to the instructor.

With the advent of fully online social work education, the field is no stranger to integration of virtual technology to enhance learning. According to Merriam-Webster's dictionary, virtual reality is defined as an artificial environment which is experienced through sensory stimuli (such as sights and sounds) provided by a computer and in which one's actions partially determine what happens in the environment (Merriam-Webster, n.d.). Virtual reality may simply be thought of as computer-generated experiences that can simulate physical presence in real or imagined environments (Curcio et al., 2016; Kerrebrock et al., 2017). The virtual platform called Second Life® (SL) has been used to simulate learning around interpersonal engagement, and direct practice skills development (Huttar & BrintzenhofeSzoc, 2020; Martin, 2017; Wilson et al., 2013). Yet, SL programming has failed to gain traction in the field due to cost and difficulty of use, and reviews on the benefits of integrating SL into curriculum remain mixed (Anstadt et al., 2013; Martin, 2017). Social work programs are slowly beginning to explore other augmented reality and virtual reality learning experiences to engage students in education content despite its strong presence in other allied health professions (Alakar et al., 2016; Huttar & BrintzenhofeSzoc,

2020; Pelargos et al., 2017), including clinical psychology (Atzori et al., 2018; Chesham et al., 2018), social work is in the early phases of discovering the possibilities of using virtual reality to enhance educational outcomes. Even with advances in technology and improved accessibility of virtual reality, the integration of this type of technology in social work face-to-face classrooms has yet to be fully realized.

Like simulation, VR in the social work classroom has potential to enhance learning related to the social work competencies through development of techniques, empathy, and skills in the safety of a classroom environment (Blakeman, 2018). While the VR experience has potential to enhance learning, literature suggests the use has been hindered by the cost and capability of program applications (Birt et al., 2017). As the power of using VR to engage students in the learning process becomes more accessible, social work educators will have more options to use VR as an important part of curriculum development for learning social work competencies (Huttar & BrintzenhofeSzoc, 2019). A handful of higher education institutions have opened VR labs and created or purchased specialized applications (Getz, 2018). While such pursuits will likely be more commonplace over the next decade, many schools yet lack funding and infrastructure to develop this type of technology (Internet2, 2018). Yet, innovative ways to introduce virtually enhanced learning, such as with cardboard or portable head mounted displays, or VR headsets, and free smartphone applications, make VR accessible to most social work programs.

The focus of this chapter is to present a comprehensive framework for application of VR for virtually enhanced learning in the higher education social work classroom. First, the author introduces the theoretical model of affordances (Shin, 2017, 2018) to assist with engaging students in virtual learning. Secondly, the author presents a detailed discussion on the application of VR to social work education and includes methods on how to incorporate social work competencies in designing a virtual learning experience. The author provides guidelines to assist instructors in facilitating the VR experience in the classroom, and the chapter concludes with a commentary on the future of VR in social work education. The aim of this chapter is to introduce social work educators to VR and provide practical information so they begin to become knowledgeable and feel comfortable with using this medium to accomplish social work educational goals. It is also important to note that content and guidelines center on the less costly use of free virtual reality smartphone applications used with inexpensive portable headsets.

AFFORDANCES NECESSARY FOR STUDENT ENGAGEMENT

The theoretical concept of affordances provides a useful framework for considering important factors that contribute to the effectiveness of VR in student learning. Affordances are defined as the characteristics of the learning environment that provide, or *afford*, the opportunity for action and engagement (Gibson, 1986). Affordance refers to how the quality of the virtual environment facilitates a connection that provides ample enough opportunity to meet the desired outcome for those involved in the virtual learning environment (VLE). According to Shin (2017), understanding how affordances relate to learning outcomes in VR may facilitate a more successful interaction between the user and the experience. Steffen et al. (2019) explain that viewing the VLE through the lens of affordances is useful for three primary reasons: (1) they help create a link between technology and user goals, thus providing the reasons driving use of VR to enhance learning, (2) they are generalizable and applicable across settings and therefore provides a common language to compare and contrast experiences across virtual platforms, and (3) they provide a means to compare virtual reality to physical reality, assisting in our understanding of why physical reality would need to be enhanced in order to meet learning goals.

The research of Shin (2017, 2018) on elements needed to maximize learning opportunities in the virtual reality environment points to five main affordances*: presence, immersion, usability, empathy and embodiment.* These affordances interrelate with one another, and influence, and are influenced by, the user. The complex relationship between affordances, the user, and five elements of student engagement are worth exploring in order to assist instructors in facilitating a meaningful VR experience in the classroom.

Presence

Presence implies that students feel more connected to the material and each other when they can fully experience the interactive nature and togetherness of the VLE. Presence is also defined as a sense of being in the virtual world or a feeling of being in a world that exists outside the self (Riva et al., 2007; Shin, 2017). The quality of the VLE mediates presence, with better quality applications correlating with increased sense of presence (Shin, 2017).

Immersion

Immersion refers to the degree to which students feel they are present in the simulation as influenced by the realism of environment. Immersion strongly relates to both presence and embodiment and may help with feelings of embodiment. When interviewing users on the conceptual framework for this affordance, Shin (2017) found his users used words like "absorption," "concentration," and "engrossment" to describe immersion (p. 1830).

Usability

Arguably one of the most important factors in the success of VR learning, usability refers to tolerance and comfort of the equipment (Shin, 2017). This basic affordance predicates all others in that if the user does not understand how to operate the equipment, or if the equipment causes discomfort and undesirable physical symptoms, engagement is less likely to occur. In Shin's research (2017) users reported usability pertained to physical comfort versus the degree to which the equipment was able to used, pointing to the magnitude to which students were wary of engagement when they experienced nausea, dizziness, headaches, or other motion-related symptoms.

Empathy

The importance of the empathy affordance cannot be understated and underscores the pedagogical significance of connecting affective and cognitive processes in learning acquisition. Empathy, or the ability to understand and share the feelings of another, elicits student engagement with the virtual learning environment. As students immerse themselves in the learning environment, they experience the thoughts and feelings of another and may take them on as their own. Empathetic experience leads to embodied cognition, creating a sensation of personally having experiences of those simulated in the VR simulation. Shin (2018) contends that an embodied experience can lead to empathetic development, but also changes how the user identifies with themselves as an empathetic person. Thus, developing empathy through the VLE may significantly alter how a user perceives others, profoundly influencing thoughts, feelings and behaviors towards "the other."

Embodiment

Embodiment is strongly connected to empathy and is defined as the extent students feel they are actually in the simulation, usually through the experience of being an avatar. In Shin's (2017) study students reported perceiving the avatar's experience as their own, thus becoming immersed both affectively and cognitively in the VLE. Embodied cognition begins the learning process, and is necessary for user's to fully engage in the VLE. Therefore, the embodiment affordance is another essential component to determining the learnability in the VR experience.

Shin's research (2017, 2018) demonstrates a strong positive relationship between the affordances and success of student engagement with VR. However, while each affordance embodies distinct characteristics, they are highly interrelated, built upon one another, and influential to each other. For example, immersion results from presence and usability, and usability influences empathy and embodiment. Empathy requires embodiment, but embodiment may not occur without an affective connection to the VR content. Ultimately, Shin (2017) found empathy and usability the best predictors of student engagement.

Adding to the complexity around understanding factors related to student engagement, research supports individual user factors strongly influence degree of engagement. Weibel et al. (2010) report user's tendency to be immersed in a virtual environment relied on factors of willingness to try, openness to explore, innovativeness, and extroversion. User characteristics interact with the affordances to determine the holistic success of the virtual experience (refer to Figure 1).

Figure 1. Interaction with affordances and user

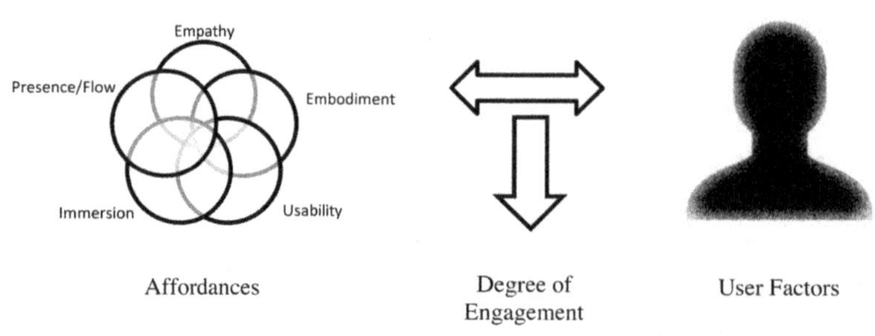

The affordances influence each other and influence and are influenced by the user to predict total degree of engagement

Recognizing the role of affordances and user characteristics may facilitate successful implementation of VR to accomplish social work learning goals. While minimal research exists on applying affordances to social work education, a study by Blakeman (2018) used this framework to understand how undergraduate and graduate social work students engaged in a safety training simulation using VR with google maps. He found that while students enjoyed the experience and viewed it as favorable in terms of a novel learning experience, when no interaction was planned with the VLE embodiment occurred but not empathy. His research supports the tenet that the application of a theoretical framework strengthens outcomes in VLEs (Stefen et al., 2019).

VIRTUAL REALITY'S APPLICATION FOR THE SOCIAL WORK EDUCATION

Virtual Reality can serve diverse purposes in social work education. The instructor's choice of how to use VR to enhance learning predominantly depends on the learning goals and objectives for the content being taught. Further, the targeted social work competency should frame the learning objective. While VR may serve educational purposes, it is important for the instructor to be clear on the overarching structure for the lesson so integration of VR is both logical and consistent with learning objectives. The instructor who plans the lesson with intentionality and purpose, with consideration of affordances as related to the meaning students make of the VR experience, can anticipate successful implementation. Conversely, an instructor who uses VR with little thought to preparation and planning will likely join their students in feelings of confusion and/or disappointment about its purpose. For example, when the author incorporated VR to simply expose student to the medium, she found students "liked" the VR experience and thought it was "cool," but the use of VR did not necessarily enhance learning outcomes.

When considering the Social Work competencies, VR capabilities, and VR learning affordances, four main applications emerge: *context exposure experience, practical skills development, engaging empathy, and advanced clinical practice skill development*. These applications do not represent an exhaustive list of uses, nor are each meant to be exclusive of one another. Instructors may find when using VR, the learning expands beyond a single goal; the educational purposes for a single lesson often converge with multiple implicit and explicit learning goals. However, in identifying one or two explicit goals for the VLE, the instructor creates a purposeful environment where the student users can mentally prepare for the experience. Further, students can stay focused on the desired learning goals rather than be distracted by the novelty of the VLE.

Context Exposure Experience

In the virtual reality story "Francis - Mental Health in Ghana" the user is transported to a small African village, where the sights and sounds of the natural world envelop the senses. Francis begins to tell his story about living with mental illness and receiving care from the village healers. As the narrative unfolds the user is brought into the healing tent, and viscerally senses Francis's fear, isolation, and despair. The story ends with Francis recalling his release from the tent to receive standard psychiatric care. In the closing scene, the user sees Francis happily interacting with his tribal family.

Virtual reality has the potential to elevate understanding while eliciting critical thought around an educational topic. When students enter the virtual world, they gain a deeper appreciation for the stories of diverse cultures, contexts and experiences pertaining to topics relevant to social work education. The applications engage students in a powerful way through visual and aural exposure to the environment and conditions of the narrator. Social work educators may use the stories and scenarios to process national and global policies related to the story, assess the strengths and challenges of the narrator living in their environment, and brainstorm how social workers might intervene on a micro, mezzo and macro level. Further, many VR smartphone applications expose the stories and conditions where social workers have opportunities to assess and intervene (CSWE competencies 6, 7; CSWE, 2015). Unlike simply watching a video, students may find the realism of virtually entering the world completing absorbing, resulting in cognitive and affective connection to the story. Feeling as though one were looking through the eyes of the narrator, reacting to story on the level of the senses, embodies the learning and strengthens students' capacity to grasp the learning objectives. As one student commented after experiencing the story of Francis, "This taught me more than I could have learned from writing 100 papers."

The aforementioned story of Francis illustrates a case study approach to using VR to enhance learning goals (Shin, 2018). This approach targets all affordances, but a social work educator ultimately will rely on empathy and cognitive embodiment affordances to engage students in the Context Exposure Experience. The VLE targets the social work domains of knowledge, values, and cognitive and affective processes. Context exposure uniquely addresses the social work competencies centering on professional identity, diversity and difference in practice, policy practice, and advancing human rights and social justice (CSWE competencies 1-3, 5) (CSWE, 2015).

Following the story of Francis, in the debriefing the instructor can facilitate critical thought discussion on the following:

- Cultural sensitivity
- The role of families and communities in caretaking
- Access to care, and types of care
- Mental illness
- Global issues on mental health care

Delving deeper into the social work values and professional identity, the instructor may also use the story to explore students' implicit feelings and reactions around topics such as:

- Personal beliefs and biases around mental health care in different cultures
- Values around the role of global social work
- Perceptions on the role of family and community in facilitating care
- The role of self-determination in a tribal community

The case study approach represents one common way to facilitate a context exposure experience. If the goal of the educator is simply to see or understand a topic on a cognitive level, the empathy affordance may prove less important to the learning goals. Some examples of VR programs for context exposure experience are listed in Table 1. The author suggests the instructor decides ahead of time which CSWE competencies may be targeted with accompanying domains and minimum affordances necessary for learning. Once the instructor begins to explore VR for context exposure experience, the possibilities are only limited by the instructor's imagination.

Practical Skills Development

In the application titled "VR Social Training Demo," the user becomes a social worker on a child protective services home visit tasked with identifying safety hazards in an around the home. The visit begins on the sidewalk in front of the home. After identifying outside hazards, the user proceeds with the visit by approaching the door and knocking. A scowling-faced woman answers the door, and the user must navigate optional responses listed on their visual screen to identify the most appropriate way to request entry into the home. The worker gains entry and is then tasked with identifying safety hazards inside the home, such as needles, open beer bottles, and exposed wires. The mother stands close by and the child is seen hiding behind a door. The simulation ends when hazards are identified and explanations of each one are provided by the program to the user.

Facilitation of learning to enhance acquisition of applied practical skills, particularly in health care, illustrates one common use of VR across different disciplines (see Westwood, 2011). Like simulation, VR allows students to practice skills in a safe, low-stakes environment. In social work, VR applications for skills development are less common. Beyond literature on programs such as Second Life® that target interpersonal skill development (Anstadt et al., 2013) applications to develop practical skills in social work prove scarce. This may be because practical simulations require contracting with an outside entity to develop the virtual learning experience, which are costly and resource intensive.

In the application "VR Social Training Demo" described above, the company Immersive 365 created software to assist social workers in practicing the skills needed to perform well on a child welfare field visit. This stressful scenario begins to seem real as the child looks on fearfully behind the door and the mother stands in front of the user tapping her toe against the floor with an air of frustration and urgency. Beyond the benefit of learning practical skills, this VLE allows students to learn how to manage strong emotional reactions associated with anxiety, fear or anger while they focus on developing skills needed to protect a child from environmental safety hazards.

Social work competencies 6 and 7 apply to this Practical Skills Development activity, targeting the domains of knowledge, skills, cognitive and affective processes. The explicit learning goals for this application may be:

- Students will demonstrate skills needed to perform a safety hazards check on a home visit:
    - Students will identify all safety hazards in the VLE.
    - Students will choose the best responses to characters in the simulation.

In debriefing, the instructor may facilitate critical thought and discussion on topics such as:

- What was it like to do a home visit with the mother in the room?
- What feelings came up for you, and how did you manage those feelings?
- Did you identify with the worker in the VR experience?
    - What elements of being a social worker were included in this identification?
- Which social work values pertain to this type of work?
- What advice would you give a new child welfare worker?
- As you begin to explore your professional identify in social work, do you think you would want to child protective home visits? Why or why not.

Many existing practical skills applications, particularly those targeting interpersonal skills development, require students' onsite presence in a VR lab, limiting accessibility for online or remote students. However, as the market demands more options for practical skill development in social work, for both face to face and online classrooms, it is anticipated that developers will create more authentic VR applications like the example given for simulation in a safe, low-stakes virtual setting.

Engaging Empathy

In "Angst: The Panic Attack" the VR simulation begins with a heavy sound of breathing as the visual environment transitions from blackness to a high school science classroom. The user, who has embodied a student, looks at the board while her teacher and peers enter the room. The student/user is thinking to herself outload. The anxiety increases as the class begins. Soon the teacher distributes an exam, and the student's internal dialogue becomes quick and pressured as she spirals into a panic attack. The user hears frantic words and fast shallow breathing as the screen turns to black. From a distance faint words of reassurance slowly enter the aural field. The teacher attempts to calm the user, and eventually the student/user can press pause on the panic just long enough to open to the suggestions. The user begins to feel some relief and the simulation ends with the student thinking "okay I can do this. I got this."

Virtual reality programs designed to stimulate empathy have grown in popularity. Empathy can be used as a powerful learning tool to enhance understanding of what it is like to live the life of another person, and to experience being vulnerable, disenfranchised, or marginalized. The VR application of living through someone else's eyes to stimulate empathy and prosocial behavior is called virtual reality perspective taking (VRPT), has become one focus of recent research in VR learning applications -Stanford University's Virtual Human Interaction Lab is at the forefront of developing applications for VRPT (Asher et al., 2018; Cogburn et al., 2018; van Loon et al., 2018). The application titled *1000 Cut Journey* simulates life as a person of color and *Becoming Homeless: A Human Experience* allows the user to understand the path to homelessness. While these applications have yet to be developed for use with smartphones, several applications for portable headsets and smartphones do exist that simulate experiences of living with a variety of circumstances. Some of these applications are listed in Table 1.

Several factors should be considered when using VR to stimulate empathy. Shin (2018) studied factors related to emphatic attunement in the virtual reality environment and found that the impact of the immersive experience on empathy and embodied cognition largely relied on individual factors. Further, the intention of the user and how they made sense of the VR environment predicted how the user responded to the simulation. Shin's research suggests that when attempting to engage students in an empathetic experience, the quality of the interface does not predict student immersion, but the authenticity of the story does.

In using VR to develop empathy in social work students, it is unknown whether the student's prior knowledge of the VR application is beneficial or harmful to full immersion in order to develop empathy. When the author led students in a VR experience simulating what it was like to live with schizophrenia, students who were unaware of the signs and symptoms of schizophrenia reported an increased fear response after hearing voices in the virtual world than students who knew the diagnosis of the avatar. In this particular instance, during the debriefing students who did not understand the signs and symptoms of schizophrenia felt more empathy than students who knew the symptoms associated with the mental illness.

A step beyond empathy, therapeutic empathy refers to the multilayered intersubjective approach to relating to others thoughts, feelings and behaviors (Bizzari et al., 2019) and is comprised of three distinct elements: understanding what a disease means to a patient, communicating that understanding, and acting on that shared understanding in a helpful way (Howick et al., 2018). While developing empathy should be a major focus of any social work program, learning how to use empathy to enhance therapeutic interactions represents an important advanced clinical skill set. Because the student is immersed in the experience, VR potentially expedites learning therapeutic empathy, and therefore should be considered as a learning medium for direct practice social work classes.

When the facilitator's goal centers on empathetic development, questions for students should aim to at least address CSWE competencies 1, 2, and 3 under the knowledge and values domain. As the student embodies the other in the virtual world, the questions center on what students think and feel when taking on the perspective of the other, thus develop greater understanding of what other endures. For example, the facilitator could pose questions on "Angst: The Panic Attack" such as:

- What did the experience feel like?
- What was going through your head as you were experiencing the panic attack?
- What is it like to experience a panic attack in front of peers?
- Did the experience scare you? Why or why not?

When the facilitator aims to teach therapeutic empathy, the questions in the debrief should elicit a higher level of critical thought and judgement so the students begin to understand how empathy can facilitate a therapeutic interaction and contribute to therapeutic outcomes. Engaging therapeutic empathy addresses CSWE competencies 6 and 8, in the domains of knowledge, values, skills, cognitive and affective processes. Based on Howick et al. (2018) documented components of therapeutic empathy, the facilitator may ask students to break into groups to discuss and demonstrate skills:

- Communicate your understanding of what it is like to experience a panic attack.
- Communicate what it is like to live with a panic disorder.
- If you had a panic attack, what could I do that would be helpful?
- What did the teacher do that was helpful? In your answer, address tone of voice, presence, and suggestions.
- What was it like to use suggestions to help calm yourself down?
- At the end of the simulation, how did you feel after calming down?
- What was the teachers' role versus the avatar's role in handling this situation? Critically analyze teacher's use of self and avatar's use of skills in reaching the desired outcome.

Depending on the facilitator's goal for the VR experience, the amount of preparation prior to the VR seems dependent on the lessons to be learned. It should be noted that when students are not prepared in advance for the VR experience, the instructor must set clear guidelines for students to be able to remove the headset if they become flooded or overwhelmed. Students with a history of anxiety, homelessness, or other mental illnesses may be triggered by the immersive experience, and the instructor should proceed with caution. The author discusses preparing for affective reactions later in this chapter.

Using VR for engaging empathy and developing therapeutic empathy represents a powerful and effective learning tool. With knowledge of the affordances, the social work classroom transforms into a laboratory where students try on different personas. In doing so, deeper understanding of clients' experiences shapes students' ability to engage the head *and* the heart, while challenging personal biases and judgmental assumptions that may arise when working with vulnerable populations. Table 1 lists a variety of applications instructors can use for engaging empathy and developing therapeutic empathy.

Advanced Clinical Practice Skill Development

Virtual reality in therapy has existed over two decades (Rizzo et al., 2019; Schafer et al., 2019). Early VR experiences for clinical purposes consisted of simulations that mimicked exposure therapy concepts in a virtual environment. For example, clients seeking therapy for phobias could be exposed to heights, flying, spiders, or public speaking in the virtual realm (Rizzo et al., 2019). With improvements in technology, over the last decade the field has witnessed an expansion of VR technology in many aspects of mental health therapy. Extensive research demonstrates positive outcomes when using VR in therapy for a wide range of mental health concerns, such as phobias, panic, post-traumatic stress disorder, anxiety and addictions (see Maples-Keller et al., 2017). As social work practitioners and large organizations began incorporating VR more frequently into therapy, the equipment and programs decreased in cost and increased in accessibility. Because VR therapy is gaining popularity in mental health care settings, at the very least social work students would benefit from exposure to VR technology. Introducing students to VR lessens fears about incorporating technology in practice, thus tackling this significant mental hurdle to using novel interventions. It is also important for students to understand that VR is not a stand-alone treatment but used as an adjunct to traditional therapy where the social worker is still needed to support and guide the client through the intervention.

Several companies provide excellent VR therapy platforms that are relatively inexpensive. These cloud-based programs require only headsets and computers to facilitate the therapy experience and are ideal to train social work students how to use VR to enhance therapeutic outcomes. However, many social work programs are not ready to invest in such programs and desire to simply expose students to use of VR in a therapeutic setting. Fortunately, many smartphone applications for headsets exist to facilitate such exposure. VR in therapy can promote mindfulness and relaxation; expose clients to fear-based stimuli in order to desensitize them to phobias or traumas (called Virtual Reality Exposure Therapy or VRET); and assist clients in managing addictions. Each application is briefly discussed below to guide the social work instructor to facilitate learning on using VR in therapy.

Mindfulness Applications

In "Tranquil Reality" the user choses their favored environment for a deep relaxation experience. Tropical oceans, soothing mountain lakes, or serene winter sceneries envelop the user in a world apart from their own. Soft music plays and a gentle voice guides the user in relaxation exercises such as deep breathing, softening muscles, and staying present. The mind hardly affords the opportunity to wander to other thoughts while beholding the beauty of the surroundings in virtual environment.

Virtual reality's journey into the area of mindfulness proves exciting for mental health practitioners. Those in the field know the challenges of teaching mindfulness to clients. Moreover, motivating the client to practice skills at home presents even greater barriers. In its most basic practice, mindfulness requires the participants to become aware in the here and now, observe the breath, and empty the mind. While traditional mindfulness training requires the participant to manage the mind's activity independently or with aural guidance only, incorporating VR helps deepen the relaxation response by transporting the client to a world of calm and serenity using all the senses. Clients easily engage in a virtual environment of soft-sand beaches, serene ocean floors, and verdant forests. The addition of sound envelops the participant into a full experience of being there. Some mindfulness applications are accompanied by voices guiding a meditation practice, while others allow the participant to just enjoy the surroundings. VR headsets with smartphone applications can be used anywhere, including outside the therapy office.

Free or inexpensive mindfulness applications are readily available on smartphones and come with relatively few side effects outside those associated with motion-related physical discomfort. Minimal training is necessary for students to begin using mindfulness applications with clients. Thus, training students to use VR to enhance mindfulness in therapy is the perfect place for instructors to start VR therapy exposure in the classroom. As the instructor designs learning goals to address intervening with VR (CSWE competency 8), several options exist for advanced clinical practice skills. Group or peer to peer interaction simulates a therapy encounter with a client where students can practice using VR as an intervention by:

- teaching peers about mindfulness programs for VR
- showing peers how to use the technology (including downloading smartphone applications) and equipment (positioning the headset correctly)
- monitoring others for adverse side-effects related to motion sickness
- debriefing with peers on the experience to assess effectiveness of intervention

For metacognitive debriefing, the instructor may facilitate group processing by asking the following questions:

- As the therapist, how comfortable did you feel using VR as an intervention? Please explain whether comfort had to do with confidence in using technology, confidence in facilitating the intervention, confidence in client's body language during the VR experience and/or confidence in assessing client's experience.
- What did you do that worked/did not work?
- What were the greatest challenges? Successes?
- As you monitored the client using the equipment, what did you notice in their body posture/nonverbal communication and how did you interpret this?
- What are your thoughts related to the client's reported experience on using VR?
- What would you do differently next time?

Many of the practical skill development debriefing questions outlined earlier in this section can also be used in advanced clinical practice skills development debriefing. Table 1 lists free applications to use in class to facilitate mindfulness training.

Although minimal research exists investigating virtual reality and mindfulness, preliminary studies suggest using VR in conjunction with mindfulness interventions elicits stronger relaxation responses, increase states of mindfulness, decreased sadness and anxiety, and increased attention span. (Minkesh & Taizo, 2019; Navarro-Haro et al., 2017). Other studies demonstrate the potential for VR as a tool for pain and anxiety management (Chan et al., 2018; Haisley et al., 2020).

Virtual Reality Exposure Therapy

In "Spider Phobia Cardboard" the user experiences gradual exposure to spiders. Before beginning, the user agrees to the statement "I want to do my best to conquer my fear of spiders." The instructions provide gentle reassurance to the user that fear is temporary and the spider in the scenes in not real. The user then notices they are sitting at a desk, and if the user looks down, they will see their hands resting gently in front of them on the top of the desk. In the first scene, the spider crawls around in a jar on the desk. If the user looks away from the jar, they are guided to turn their eyes back to the jar. Once the user completes this simulation level, they rate their experience of discomfort on a scale from one to ten. The application consists of 15 levels. By level 15, the spider is crawling around the desk and may crawl on the user's hands.

While virtual reality exposure therapy (VRET) has existed since the early 1990's, due to recent improvements in technology, affordability, and logistic accessibility for clinicians, VRET has gained popularity in direct practice application (Rizzo et al., 2019). Otherwise called immersion therapy, VRET gradually exposes users to the feared object or situation. Unlike real world simulations, many aspects of the VR simulation are controlled by the user and the therapist. VRET has long been purported as a safer and possibly more effective way to use exposure therapy in practice (Maples-Keller et al., 2017). The breadth of research on the effectiveness of VRET warrants at least minimal in-class exposure for student learning (Huttar & BrintzenhofeSzoc, 2019). In some areas of practice, particularly working with veterans, using VRET in practice requires advanced specialized training. However, students can get a feel for exposure therapy by the introduction of free applications on headsets, such as the spider application described above. In the controlled simulated environment students experience undergoing VRET to reduce phobic response and build knowledge and empathy around the client's experience of undergoing VRET. In the simulation of practicing how to use VRET, students may guide peers in relaxation exercises, assess discomfort using Likert-type scales, and assist others in containing and mastering fears. In addition to the practice exercises detailed in the previous section, the social work instructor may ask the students to work with each other as clients in simulating VRET to:

- Help clients understand what triggers anxiety, and neurobiological responses associated with anxiety and panic. Teach clients to become aware of body responses associated with anxiety, such as stomach pain or tightening chest.
- Teach clients about deep breathing and relaxation exercises prior to undergoing VRET so the client can employ those skills when they begin to feel anxious.
- Monitor non-verbal behavior for signs of distress and intervene as necessary by either guiding client to take deep breaths or discontinue.
- Ask clients to rate level of discomfort and teach clients how to manage self at each level of discomfort.
- Highlight client strengths used in the VRET and discuss mastery of feared stimuli. Process with client their reaction to VRET.
- Practice grounding exercises after VRET.

For meta-cognitive debriefing, the instructor may consider asking students the debriefing questions in the previous section, along with advanced processing questions on feelings of competence and safety using VRET:

- Were you nervous about the client's fear and anxiety? Why?
- How did you manage your own affect?

- Did your affect interfere with the VRET and the client's experience? How do you know?
- How did you know if the client was in distress during the VRET? When did you know you needed to intervene? How did you intervene? If you intervened, was it successful?
- What are your thoughts about exposure therapy to help clients master fears?
- What place does mindfulness and relaxation training hold when conducting VRET?
- What training would you consider adequate in order to help you feel confident in using VRET?

VRET for direct practice transfer skills addresses CSWE competencies 6-9 with individuals on the domain levels of knowledge, skills, and cognitive and affective processes.

In more refined VRET programs that can be purchased for social work education, the social work clinician has the option to accompany the participant into the virtual world and provide advice and support for managing anxiety and panic. In such applications, the therapist imports visual and auditory relaxation cues into the virtual world to encourage the client to relax, breathe deeply and soften muscles. More sophisticated applications integrate biofeedback into the simulation. Students benefit from practicing all these advanced clinical practice skills. Since VRET only recently became accessible for many practice organizations, no standardized training protocols exist other than those used in large organizations, such as the Veterans Administration Hospital.

Virtual Reality and Managing Addictions

Several professional applications simulate an environment where the participant is exposed to an addictive substance, such as drugs, alcohol, cigarettes, and even internet gaming (Zhang & Ho, 2017). The purpose of engaging in such applications is to expose users to environmental cues that elicit cravings (North et al., 2014). The user learns coping strategies to manage cravings in the virtual environment, with the hope that the skills will generalize into real-world situations. In more refined applications, a therapist can accompany the participant into the virtual world to provide advice and support in managing addiction triggers. While research supports that VR successfully elicits cue-reactivity (Pericot-Valverde et al., 2016), minimal research exists supporting the effectiveness of such interventions. However, this may be due to the fact that this type of intervention is still emerging.

Virtual Reality Cognitive Behavior Therapy (VR-CBT) combines traditional CBT/relapse prevention training with exposure and skill practice in VR-based environments (e.g., bar, party, smoking lounge in an airport) (Bordnick et al., 2011). Like VRET, students may appreciate being exposed to VR interventions for managing addictions and may even benefit from skill development on how to accompany the participant in the virtual world to support management of cravings. However, VR-CBT for addictions requires advanced training and students must be made aware that exposure VR-CBT does not equate to competence in facilitating this intervention. Therefore, students should not attempt to intervene with clients using VR-CBT without specialized training on addictions therapies. Like VRET, the standardization of VR-CBT protocols has yet to be developed.

Free smartphone applications available to the public for VR-CBT are significantly limited. However, social work programs at larger institutions have created programs for research and some train students on using VR to manage addictions (Getz, 2018)

Table 1. Examples of VR headset smartphone applications

Application Title with Program Title	Social Work Application	Type	CSWE Competencies
VR 360 ° Movies: Francis - Mental Health in Ghana	Content Exposure Experience	Follow Francis as he receives mental health treatment	2, 3, 5
Within: Clouds over Sidra	Content Exposure Experience	Follow a child around a refugee camp	2, 3, 5
Within: Waves of Grace	Content Exposure Experience	Follow.and Ebola survivor who uses her immunity to help orphaned children in Africa	2, 3, 5
Within: My Mother's Wing	Content Exposure Experience	Mother coping with the loss of her two children from shelling attack in their school (Gaza)	2, 3, 5
VR Social Training Demo	Practical Skills Training	Simulate being a child welfare worker	6, 7
VR Movies 3D: Mental VR-Autism Experience	Empathetic Engagement	Simulate someone with Autism	2
Mental Health VR	Empathetic Engagement	Simulate someone with schizophrenia	2
Application Title with Program Title	Social Work Application	Type	CSWE Competency
Within: Notes on Blindness	Empathetic Engagement	Experience of being blind	2
Tranquil Reality	Advanced Clinical Skills Development	Mindfulness	7, 8
Relax	Advanced Clinical Skills Development	Mindfulness	7, 8
Serene VR	Advanced Clinical Skills Development	Mindfulness	7, 8
Within: BreathethePeace World	Advanced Clinical Skills Development	Mindfulness	6, 8
Spiderphobia Cardboard	Advanced Clinical Skills Development	VRET: Arachnophobia	6, 8
VR Movies 360 3D: Fear of Heights – Virtual	Advanced Clinical Skills Development	VRET: Heights	6, 8

BASIC GUIDELINES FOR FACILITATING THE VIRTUAL REALITY CLASSROOM EXPERIENCE

A VLE enables the student to fully immerse themselves in the VR experience. Therefore, the instructor must adequately prepare for facilitating the VLE in order to maximize learning outcomes. Three distinct stages emerge for facilitating the classroom VR experience: preparation, implementation, and debriefing. In this section the author provides detailed and practical considerations for each stage.

Preparation

Preparation is arguably the most important part of the entire VLE. A well-prepared instructor shows confidence in using the equipment, can allay student concerns, and can navigate challenges that may arise. The amount of instructor preparation positively correlates with student and instructor satisfaction with the VR learning experience, and predicts educational outcomes. Therefore, this section outlines steps for preparing in four distinct areas: the technology, the lesson, the students and the instructor.

Prepare the Technology: Understand and Ready the Equipment

Many easy to use headsets for smartphones can be purchased off the internet. While cardboard headsets may be the cheapest option, they also provide the least opportunity for full immersion. Cardboard headsets cost between 5 and 15 dollars, and several other types of portable headsets can be purchased for less than 100 dollars. Higher-end headsets offer sound with Bluetooth, providing a more authentic and engaging experience for the student. These headsets usually cost less than 75 dollars, and many average between 30 and 40 dollars.

Bluetooth headsets require charging prior to use, which can be time consuming for instructors. If the headsets do not operate using Bluetooth but have sound capability, an adaptive device, or dongle, must be purchased in order for some students to connect their phones to the audio feature on the headset. Strong Wi-Fi reception is essential to download and play the smartphone applications. Please refer to Image 2 for a picture of a portable VR headset for smartphones.

Technical challenges may arise that will prohibit the students from engaging in the learning aspect of the VR experience. Following the usability affordance, the student will not engage, therefore not learn, if they are challenged to get the equipment to work properly. Instructors should anticipate a trial and error period using the technology and give the class ample time to learn the equipment in the first VR class. The author experienced several unanticipated challenges when first using VR. In one instance, when all students simultaneously tried pairing their phones with their Bluetooth headsets, they ended up syncing with each other's headsets. The author became flustered and frozen wondering what to do, but the students jumped to solving the problem themselves by choosing music to play off their individual phones and then playing "hide and seek" to find the headset with their music. The author enjoyed watching the students creatively work together to solve the problem, but from that point on asked students to turn on their headsets one at a time to identify the correct pairing prompt from *their* headset to *their* phone.

The instructor should anticipate and prepare for hiccups when downloading applications for smartphones. Some students have difficulty downloading the VR application programs to their smartphone due to the age of their phones or even the brand. Further, it is important to note that some applications are not available on some application marketplaces. The author recommends asking the students to download the applications ahead of time and alert the instructor of any problems before the VR class. Some students do not own smartphones, or despite best attempts still cannot download the applications. In these times students can share headsets and/or phones, and some VR application videos can be found on the web and can be played movie-style to the whole class. However, this medium proves far less effective than VR experience. While not all problems can be anticipated beforehand, it would behoove the instructor to always have a "plan B" for students who simply find the technology overwhelming or inaccessible.

In sum, instructors using smartphones applications with headsets should know how to download the applications, hook up to Bluetooth, properly place the phone in the headset, comfortably place the headset on the head, adjust the optical view and volume, and use the eyes to activate aspects of the application on the smartphone screen. If the instructor intends to use the campus VR lab, specialized training may be required. The instructor should explore options to employ an assistant to help operate the equipment in a VR lab. Even with the help of an assistant or technology expert, the instructor should gain familiarity with the VR lab equipment to a minimum degree so they can assist students.

Figure 2. A portable bluetooth VR headset for use with smartphone

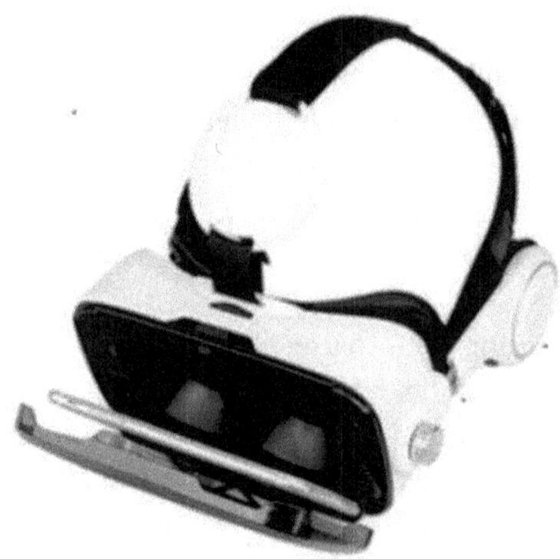

Prepare the Lesson: Articulate Educational Goals and Objectives

Sometimes the instructor simply wants to introduce students to VR. Exposing students to the technology and equipment can be fun, but certainly does not maximize the potential for enhanced learning. In this chapter, the author discussed addressing social work competencies through development of practical skills, context content exposure, engaging empathy, and development of advanced clinical practice skills. Prior to teaching a lesson using VR, the instructor should operationalize how VR will be used to enhance the learning goals. Further, the instructor should identify the social work competencies and domains targeted. It is recommended that the instructor pose questions for thought at the beginning of the class, such as those provided as examples in previous sections. As debriefing has been thought to be one of the most powerful aspects of simulated learning (Bogo, et al., 2014; Coomes, 2019), the instructor should write debriefing questions and prompts prior to the lesson. More on debriefing is discussed later in this section.

Prepare the Students: Articulate Precautions and Expectations

While it is not the aim to scare the students prior to a VR simulation, they should receive general precautionary material prior to the VR class. The first set of precautions relate to entering the virtual world through use of a headset. Some students experience health-related side effects such as nausea, disorientation, loss of balance, and other feelings related to motion sickness while wearing the VR headsets

(Lawson, 2015). In the author's experience, most students who in their past suffered from motion sickness were willing to try the headset. While some removed the headset early, most students could tolerate a stationary VR experience. The author noticed increased discomfort for those students who struggled to adjust the focus properly and see a clear (versus blurry) picture. Sometimes students need reminders to make sure the headset is tight enough against their heads lest the picture remains out of focus despite attempts to adjust. Further, the quality and type of application may also predict the level of undesirable motion-related symptoms. Motion-simulated VR applications, such as riding a roller coaster or climbing mountains, may prove more challenging for students as opposed to stationary experiences where the user simply observes their surroundings. While many VR headsets are designed for use with eye glasses, the students should be informed ahead of time that the shape and size of their glasses may alter the comfort of the headset. Finally, some students avoid wearing the headsets because they fear damage to their facial cosmetics or hairstyles. Instructors should plan for all possible adverse side-effects and warn students of them prior to using VR.

The second precaution relates to the emotional impact of the VR experience. VLE's can produce physiological and emotional change in the participant because the brain views the situation as real (Riva et al., 2007). Since stimulating empathy is both an affordance and a learning goal, emotional engagement should be encouraged. However, some students may find the affective engagement triggers anxiety or other unanticipated/overwhelming feeling states. While unanticipated emotional responses prove difficult to prepare for, the instructor can assist students in self-regulation activities prior to the VR lessons. Practicing deep breathing and other grounding skills teaches students to manage emotional states that may be triggered in the VR world. Further, students should be given permission to pause the VR video as needed and use self-talk to remind themselves they are in a simulated learning environment (the experience is not real). In the author's experience, showing students how to manage strong feelings and sensations prior to the engaging empathy VR applications proves beneficial on many levels. Part of skills development for direct social work practice involves teaching students to cope with strong affective states. Social workers in the field regularly encounter emotional situations that may unexpectedly provoke anxiety, fear and sadness. Affording the opportunity for students to learn self-regulation skills in real time offers a powerful learning experience they can generalize to the field. Finally, the instructor may also lead the class in mindfulness activities before and after the VR experience as a lesson in self-care.

Beyond anticipating challenges with equipment use and emotional responses, the instructor should consider diversity factors related to virtual learning activities. As mentioned previously, most headsets are designed for use with glasses, but the instructor must remember this consideration when choosing headsets. Further, the instructor should ask themselves "can all the students in class easily access the learning opportunity?" or "will any student be excluded from the activity based on differing physical, cognitive or emotional abilities?" The instructor should account for challenges and diversity factors by following the guidelines for student preparation, and always offer alternative means of learning the material aside from VR.

Prepare the Instructor: Become Personally Immersed in the Virtual Learning Experience

Lastly, it almost goes without stating that the instructor should undergo all VR learning experiences themselves prior to implementation with students. In doing so, they can accurately assess the quality of the experience, reflect on cognitive and emotional reactions, and process personal direct and indirect learning as a result of the experience. Instructors can try out many applications that may be relevant to the learning goals, and then reflectively journal on the challenges and benefits of each VR application. The instructor should also reflect on affordances (usability, presence, immersion, empathy and cognitive embodiment) evoked by the application.

Please refer to Appendix 1 for a preparation checklist for facilitating VR learning in the social work classroom.

Implementation

Extensive preparation pays off in the implementation and debriefing stages. Planning in advance for pitfalls with technology and student reactions enables the instructor to address problems that arise efficiently without much disruption to the class experience. Therefore, in the implementation phase the instructor uses preparation work to facilitate full engagement in the VLE. Despite best efforts, sometimes the technology fails. Flexibility, creativity and ingenuity prove beneficial at these times and instructors should always prepare a back-up plan should insurmountable obstacles occur. It is worth noting that many smartphone applications have the option to view the video without a headset as an augmented reality experience, or the video may be accessed online and viewed as two-dimensional video.

Debriefing

Debriefing is loosely defined as the process by which students can reflect on an experiential or simulated learning experience in order to consolidate learning (Bogo et al., 2014). In the debriefing process students integrate theoretical and practical knowledge into the lessons learned in the simulated experience to develop new insights and strengthen existing ideas and perceptions. Debriefing is thought to be the most important part of the simulated learning experience (Fey & Jenkins, 2015; Palaganas, 2016). According to Coomes (2019), debriefing should incorporate the following attributes: (1) engagement; (2) emotional awareness; (3) reflection; (4) critical analysis; (5) integration; and (6) facilitation. The last attribute, facilitation, refers to the role of the instructor as facilitator of the entire debriefing process that incorporates attributes 1-5.

The debriefing process identified for simulation-based learning experiences transfers nicely to VLE's. The attributes cited by Coomes (2019) provide a framework for formulating questions to assess the competency-based social work learning goals and the domains of knowledge acquisition. In the debrief, the conversation may grow organically as students gain new insights in the group processing environment. Yet, debriefing works best when the instructor prepares carefully considered and purposeful questions and discussion prompts in advance. Ideas for questions were posed earlier in the chapter under specific learning opportunities for VR. Many social work instructors have experience in group work which may benefit the facilitation and management of discussion and associated reactions in the debriefing following the VLE.

Lastly, attention needs to be paid to supporting students who were triggered during the VLE or debriefing process. Depending on the intensity of emotional engagement in the VLE, instructors should offer individual time outside of class for students needing extra support following debriefing. The instructor may give students information about accessing outside resources, such as the campus counseling center, if more structured or professional help is needed.

THE FUTURE OF VR IN SOCIAL WORK

Virtual Reality has the potential to change the landscape of social work education. Recently more and more universities are using VR labs to power the educational experience (Getz, 2018). As the quality and affordability of VR applications improve, it is anticipated programs will endeavor to use virtual reality more readily, finding creative and innovative ways to enhance competency development in social work education (Huttar & BrintzenhofeSzoc, 2019). Social work instructors are encouraged to keep an open mind when using new technology and set aside fears around use of equipment or concerns that using VR may replace the traditional classroom experience. Technology is meant to strengthen the learning experience, providing novel ways for students to grasp concepts and skills in order to generalize the classroom learning into their practice environment.

Currently the creation of specialized applications and videos for use with VR equipment remains costly. Some programs exist that allow users to create their own VR video, but without professional assistance these programs are difficult to work with. In the near future, it is anticipated users will be able to make VR content more easily using their smartphones, increasing the potential for social work programs to inexpensively design VR content for specific purposes. Applications akin to SL, where students use VLE's to improve inter and intrapersonal skills are likely to be developed for broad use outside specialized VR labs. Lastly, VR programs are gaining traction with improving authenticity to strengthen immersive experiences.

CONCLUSION

Despite advancements with using VR in social work clinical practice (Smokowski & Hartung, 2003), arguably social work education should continue to find ways to incorporate VR to accomplish learning goals, particularly in the areas of teaching students how to use VR in the field (Huttar & BrintzenhofeSzoc, 2019). Further, as the popularity of online education increases, social work programs will need to find alternative ways to educate students with more interactive mediums. By its very nature social work is an applied profession reliant on practical and interpersonal skill attainment as reflected in the social work practice competencies (CSWE, 2015). Online education in social work programs encounter unique challenges with practice competency development more easily attained through simulation and face to face experiential classroom opportunities (Levin et al., 2018). While field education provides the setting for developing practical and interpersonal skills, virtual-based learning experiences afford students similar opportunities to practice skills in the classroom setting.

It is the intent of this chapter to demystify the process of using VR in social work education. The author outlined the affordances necessary for student engagement in the VLE, provided applications for VR in the social work classroom, outlined practical guidelines for facilitating the VR experience, and briefly explored future trends for VR in social work education. By providing helpful guidelines for creating social work specific competency-based educational goals, using the equipment, and structuring the VR class, the author hopes to allay fears and motivate instructors to push the boundaries when engaging students in the learning process. When innovation is modeled in the classroom, students become inspired to create new uses for technology to enhance social well-being across the spectrum of practice. VLE's hold the potential to catapult social work education into the next era by creating new and exciting ways to increase professional competency that address and help resolve society's most pressing concerns.

REFERENCES

Alaker, M., Wunn, G. R., & Arulampalam, T. (2016). Virtual reality training in laparoscopic surgery: A systematic review. *International Journal of Surgery*, *29*, 85–94. doi:10.1016/j.ijsu.2016.03.034 PMID:26992652

Anstadt, S. P., Bradley, S., Burnette, A., & Medley, L. L. (2013). Virtual worlds: Relationship between real life and experience in second life. *International Review of Research in Open and Distance Learning*, *14*(4), 160–190. doi:10.19173/irrodl.v14i4.1454

Asher, T., Ogle, E., Bailenson, J. N., & Herrera, F. (2018). *Becoming homeless: A human experience*. ACM SIGGRAPH Virtual, Augmented, and Mixed Reality. doi:10.1145/3226552.3226576

Atzori, B., Messeri, A., Vagnoli, L., Grotto, R. L., & Hoffman, H. G. (2019). Virtual reality as distraction technique for pain management in children and adolescents. Encyclopedia of information science and technology, 5955-5965. doi:10.4018/978-1-5225-2255-3.ch518

Birt, J., Hovorka, D., & Nelson, J. (2016). *Interdisciplinary translation of comparative visualization*. Working Paper. https://arxiv.org/ftp/arxiv/papers/1606/1606.03551.pdf

Bizzari, V., Dambha-Miller, H., Laughaey, W. F., & Carvalho, C. (2019). Defining therapeutic empathy: The philosopher's view. *Journal of the Royal Society of Medicine*, *112*(3), 91–95. doi:10.1177/0141076819831869 PMID:30868927

Blakeman, P. (2018). Virtual Reality: What it offers, and how it can be used easily (and inexpensively) by health & social care tutors. *Journal of Practice Teaching & Learning*, *16*(1), 81–93.

Bogo, M., Rawlings, M., Katz, E., Logie, C., & Council on Social Work Education (CSWE). (2014). *Using simulation in assessment and teaching: OSCE adapted for social work*. Council on Social Work Education.

Bordnick, P. S., Carter, B. L., & Traylor, A. C. (2011). What virtual reality research in addictions can tell us about the future of obesity assessment and treatment. *Journal of Diabetes Science and Technology*, *5*(2), 265–271. doi:10.1177/193229681100500210 PMID:21527092

Chan, E., Foster, S., Sambell, R., & Leong, P. (2018). Clinical efficacy of virtual reality for acute procedural pain management: A systematic review and meta-analysis. *PLoS One*, *13*(7), 1–13. doi:10.1371/journal.pone.0200987 PMID:30052655

Chesham, R. K., Malouff, J. M., & Schutte, N. S. (2018). Meta-Analysis of the efficacy of virtual reality exposure therapy for social anxiety. *Behaviour Change*, *35*(3), 152–166. doi:10.1017/bec.2018.15

Cogburn, C. D., Bailenson, J. N., Ogle, E., Asher, T., & Nichols, T. (2018). *1000 cut journey. ACM SIGGRAPH 2018 Virtual*. Augmented, and Mixed Reality. doi:10.1145/3226552.3226575

Coomes, G. (2019). Debriefing in simulation-based learning experiences: A Concept analysis. *The Midwest Quarterly*, *60*(3), 298–310.

Council on Social Work Education. (2015). 2015 *Educational policy and accreditation standards*. Author. https://www.cswe.org/getattachment/Accreditation/Accreditation-Process/2015- EPAS/2015EPAS_Web_FINAL.pdf.aspx

Curcio, I. D. D., Dipace, A., & Norlund, A. (2016). Virtual realities and education. *Research on Education and Media, 8*(2). 1-9. https://doi:10.1515/rem-2016-0019

Fey, M. K., & Jenkins, L. S. (2015). Debriefing practices in nursing education programs: Results from a national study. *Nursing Education Perspectives, 36*(6), 361–366. doi:10.5480/14-1520 PMID:26753294

Getz, L. (2018). Social services innovations: A whole new world — Virtual reality in social work. *Social Work Today, 18*(2), 6. https://www.socialworktoday.com/archive/MA18p6.shtml

Gibson, J. J. (1986). *The ecological approach to visual perception*. Houghton Mifflin.

Haisley, K. R., Straw, O. J., Müller, D. T., Antiporda, M. A., Zihni, A. M., Reavis, K. M., Bradley, D. D., & Dunst, C. M. (2020). Feasibility of implementing a virtual reality program as an adjuvant tool for peri-operative pain control; Results of a randomized controlled trial in minimally invasive foregut surgery. *Complementary Therapies in Medicine, 49*. doi:10.1016/j.ctim.2020.102356

Howick, J., Bizzari, V., & Dhamba-Miller, H. (2018). Therapeutic empathy: What it is and what it isn't. *Journal of the Royal Society of Medicine, 111*(7), 233–236. https://doi:10.1177/0141076818781403

Huttar, C. M., & BrintzenhofeSzoc, K. (2020). Virtual Reality and computer simulation in social work education: A systematic review. *Journal of Social Work Education, 56*(1), 131–141. doi:10.1080/10437797.2019.1648221

Internet2. (2018). *2018 VR/AR in research and education survey.* https://meetings.internet2.edu/media/medialibrary/2019/03/08/20190306-Fineman- MetaverseWG.pdf

Kerrebrock, H., Brengman, M., & Willems, K. (2017). Escaping the crowd: An experimental study on the impact of Virtual Reality experience in a shopping mall. *Computers in Human Behavior, 77,* 437-461. https://doi:10.1016/j.chb.2017.07.019

Lawson, B. D. (2015). Motion sickness symptomology and origins. In K. S. Hale & K. M. Stanney (Eds.), *Handbook of virtual environments: Design, implementation, and applications* (2nd ed., pp. 531–599). Taylor & Francis Group.

Levin, S., Fulginiti, A., & Moore, B. (2018). The perceived effectiveness of online social work education: Insights from a national survey of social work educators. *Social Work Education, 37*(6), 775–789. doi:10.1080/02615479.2018.1482864

Maples-Keller, J. L., Bunnell, B. E., Kim, S. J., & Rothbaum, B. O. (2017). The Use of virtual reality technology in the treatment of anxiety and other psychiatric disorders. *Harvard Review of Psychiatry, 25*(3), 103–113. https://doi:10.1097/HRP.0000000000000138

Martin, J. (2017). Virtual worlds in social work education. *Australian Social Work, 70*(2), 197–208. doi:10.1080/0312407X.2016.1238953

Merriam-Webster. (n.d.). Citation. In *Merriam-Webster.com dictionary*. Retrieved March 10, 2020 from https://www.merriam-webster.com/dictionary/virtualreality

Miller, S. E. (2010). A conceptual framework for the professional socialization of social workers. *Journal of Human Behavior in the Social Environment*, *20*(7), 924–938. doi:10.1080/10911351003751934

Minkesh, A., & Taizo, M. (2019). *Short virtual reality mindfulness meditation training for sustained attention*. Working paper. http://arxiv.org/abs/1907.04487

Navarro-Haro, M. V., López-del-Hoyo, Y., Campos, D., Linehan, M. M., Hoffman, H. G., García-Palacios, A., Modrego-Alarcón, M., Borao, L., & García-Campayo, J. (2017). Meditation experts try Virtual Reality mindfulness: A pilot study evaluation of the feasibility and acceptability of Virtual Reality to facilitate mindfulness practice in people attending a mindfulness conference. *PLoS One*, *12*(11), e0187777. Advance online publication. doi:10.1371/journal.pone.0187777 PMID:29166665

North, L., Robinson, C., Haffegee, A., Sharkey, P. M., & Hwang, F. (2014). Using virtual environments for trigger identification in addiction treatment. *International Journal on Disability and Human Development: IJDHD*, *13*(3), 369–375. doi:10.1515/ijdhd-2014-0330

Palaganas, J. C., Fey, M., & Simon, R. (2016). Structured debriefing in simulation-based education. *AACN Advanced Critical Care*, *27*(1), 78–85. doi:10.4037/aacnacc2016328 PMID:26909457

Pelargos, P. E., Nagasawa, D. T., Lagman, C., Tenn, S., Demos, J. V., Lee, S. J., Bui, T. T., Barnette, N. E., Bhatt, N. S., Ung, N., Bari, A., Martin, N. A., & Yang, I. (2017). Utilizing virtual and augmented reality for educational and clinical enhancements in neurosurgery. *Journal of Clinical Neuroscience*, *35*, 1–4. doi:10.1016/j.jocn.2016.09.002 PMID:28137372

Pericot-Valverde, I., Germeroth, L. J., & Tiffany, S. T. (2016). The use of virtual reality in the production of cue-specific craving for cigarettes: A meta-analysis. *Nicotine & Tobacco Research, 18*(5), 538–546. https://doi:10.1093/ntr/ntv216

Riva, G., Mantovani, F., Capideville, S. C., Preziosa, A., Morganti, F., Villani, D., Gaggioli, A., & Botella, C. A. (2007). Affective interactions using virtual reality: The link between presence and emotions. *Cyberpsychology & Behavior, 10*(1), 45-56. https://doi:10.1089/cpb.2006.9993

Rizzo, A., Koening, T., & Talbot, T. B. (2019). Clinical results using virtual reality. *Journal of Technology in Human Services, 37,* 51-74. https://doi:10.1080/15228835.2019.1604292

Schafer, E. D., O'Reilly, A. E.-S., & Pass, A. D. (2019). *Virtual reality as an alternative therapy*. Salem Press Encyclopedia of Health.

Shin, D. (2017). The role of affordance in the experience of virtual reality learning: Technological and affective affordances in virtual reality. *Telematics and Informatics, 34,* 1826-1836. https//:doi:10.1016/j.tele.2017.05.013

Shin, D. (2018). Empathy and embodied experience in virtual environment: To what extent can virtual reality simulate empathy and embodied experience. *Computers in Human Behavior*, *78*, 64–73. doi:10.1016/j.chb.2017.09.012

Smokowski, P. R., & Hartung, K. (2003). Computer simulation and virtual reality: The practice of school social work. *Journal of Technology in Human Services*, *21*(1–2), 5–30. doi:10.1300/J017v21n01_02

Steffen, J. H., Gaskin, J. E., Meservy, T. O., Jenkins, J. L., & Wolman, I. (2019). Framework of Affordances for Virtual Reality and Augmented Reality. *Journal of Management Information Systems, 36*(3), 683–729. https//:doi:10.1080/07421222.2019.1628877

van Loon A, Bailenson, J., Zaki, J., Bostick, J., & Willer, R. (2018) Virtual reality perspective-taking increases cognitive empathy for specific others. *PLoS ONE 13*(8). Article e0202442. https//:doi:10.1371/journal.pone.0202442

Westwood, J. D. (2011). *Medicine Meets Virtual Reality: Nextmed*. IOS Press.

Wilson, A., Brown, S., Wood, Z., & Farkas, K. (2013). Teaching direct practice skills using web-based simulations: Home visiting in the virtual world. *Journal of Teaching in Social Work*, *33*(4-5), 421–437. doi:10.1080/08841233.2013.833578

Zhang, M. W. B., & Ho, R. C. M. (2017). Smartphone applications for immersive virtual reality therapy for internet addiction and internet gaming disorder. *Technology and Health Care*, *25*(2), 367–372. doi:10.3233/THC-161282 PMID:27911347

KEY TERMS AND DEFINITIONS

Affordances: The characteristics of the learning environment that provide, or *afford*, the opportunity for action and engagement.

Cognitive Embodiment: The concept describing the totality of engagement through incorporating cognition, affect, and physical sensation.

Competencies: The knowledge, skills, and behaviors necessary for effective practice in the social work field.

Debriefing: The process by which students can reflect on an experiential or simulated learning experiences in order to consolidate learning.

Therapeutic Empathy: The multilayered intersubjective approach to the other that facilitates relationship building and resonance.

Virtual Learning Experience: Any experience that uses virtual reality.

Virtual Reality Perspective Taking: The virtual experience of living through someone else's eyes to stimulate empathy and prosocial behavior.

APPENDIX

Instructor Preparation Checklist: Facilitating VR Classroom Experience With Portable Headsets and Smartphones in the Social Work Classroom

Table 2.

Technical Preparation	
Strong Wi-Fi Reception	
Bluetooth Headsets Charged	
Applications can be downloaded for free	
Lesson Preparation	
Learning goals and objectives identified (based on SW competencies)	
Student Instructions prepared	
Debriefing questions prepared	
Necessary affordances identified	
Student Preparation	
Students are aware of sensory precautions	
Students are aware of cosmetic precautions and eyeglasses restrictions	
Students have access to learning goals, and possibly debriefing questions	
Students instructed how to download applications before class	
Instructor Preparation	
Instructor can easily use equipment	
Instructor has undergone VLE and reflected on experience	
Instructor has anticipated challenges	

Chapter 12
Using Virtual Reality in College Student Mental Health Treatment

Nidhi Sinha
https://orcid.org/0000-0003-0357-4344
Indian Institute of Technology, Hyderabad, India

ABSTRACT

When students leave home to attend college, they encounter many adjustments and new experiences. Some students have difficulty coping with the challenges they experience and over time may develop mild to severe mental health issues. Mental health illness among college students is associated with long-term adverse academic outcomes, including dropout. With an exponential rise in mental health issues among university students, there is a dire need to reach out to newer technologies to help students effectively cope with academic and social challenges. Given the increased accessibility and practicality of virtual reality (VR) use in mental health, it becomes paramount to extend the utility of VR to university counselling settings including the preliminary assessment, diagnosis, and treatment strategies to guide students to effectively address any mental health challenges. There are potential implications and challenges associated with the use of VR within universities' counselling settings as well.

INTRODUCTION

With the advent of technological advancement in the counselling and psychotherapy, Virtual Reality (VR) has emerged as a promising tool, which has demonstrated its utility in assessing, diagnosing and treating mental health conditions, as precisely indicated by the last two decades of research in this area (Emmelkamp et al., 2002; Krijn et al., 2004; Krijn et at., 2007). The subsequent paragraphs, therefore, aim to provide a richer understanding of the rising mental health issues among university students, followed by a brief glimpse into the existing applications of VR for mental health treatment in clinical settings. Moreover, with an overview of an existing subset of literature in the field of VR with a particular emphasis of its application in mental health, this chapter also aspires to illuminate its readers

DOI: 10.4018/978-1-7998-4960-5.ch012

and campus counselling services to identify opportunities, strengths, and future directions to integrate virtual reality in university settings.

BACKGROUND

Mental Health Among University Students

Even though university years are touted as a decisive developmental period where most of the personal and professional development of an individual occurs (Evans et al., 2009), it also marks a time which is highly represented by the onset and prevalence of mental illnesses (Ibrahim et al., 2013). As research studies highlight, 12-46 percent of university students are estimated to experience mental health issues in learning, relationships, family and employment at a point of their academic life (Auerbach et al., 2016; Blanco et al., 2008; Eisenberg et al., 2013). According to the World Health Organization (WHO), mental disorders account for at least half of the illness burden of young adults in high-income countries. This illness burden among young students is broadly associated with long-term adverse academic outcomes, including dropout (Hysenbegasi et al., 2005; Ishii et al., 2018).

Despite the availability of treatments for mental disorders, there is a severe treatment gap in university students afflicted with mental illness, with only one in five students receiving care and treatment (Auerbach et al., 2016). The analysis of data on mental health problems of university students by Auerbach and colleagues (2016) also found that individuals suffering from psychological issues were least likely to attend university and were also unable to receive necessary treatment for their illnesses when attending university. Multiple cases of untreated mental disorders have documented poor clinical outcomes in later life. Depression, eating disorders, phobia and social anxiety are some of the prominent mental disorders that affect students (Ricky & O'Donnell Siobhan, 2017). Likewise, in their cross-cultural study of 23 nations, Steptoe et al. (2007) investigated the prevalence of depressive symptoms in 17,348 university going students between the ages of 17 and 30. The findings of this study concluded in context with mental health hazards among this college-going population. It was found that the extent of severe depressive symptoms was most common in students from East Asia (e.g., Japan and Korea) with 38 percent of students self-reporting experiencing such symptoms, followed by students from western countries with 31 percent.

In a similar vein, excessive academic burden and failure to achieve goals in both academic and personal domains has been also found to be contributory in suicidal tendencies among students; suicide among college students has tripled since the 1950s (Burrell, 2020). An undergraduate mental health survey of a premier Indian engineering institute found that approximately 84 percent engineering students felt that mental health was a real challenge on the campus, with 72 percent having experienced depression or anxiety and 24 percent having suicidal ideations at one point of their academic lives. One of the reasons for the increasing prevalence of mental illness within campuses could be because of many students are unable to cope up with this invariable amount of pressure they encounter (Deb, 2019). Considering that most of the universities are residential in nature, establishing and defining a proper support system within the university campus deems essential for better and faster accessibility to mental health services (McLaughlin, 1999).

In summary, mental health issues among university students leave landmark negative footprints on their academic performance and social functioning (Richardson et al., 2012). Failing to provide early intervention could result in a vicious circle of propensity towards adverse life events in the future. For instance, a longitudinal study by Weissman et al. (1999) found that persisting depression and anxiety symptoms influenced adolescents' job turnover rate as well as their likelihood of getting married. This indicates strongly that mental health issues emerging during university life may manifest in students' later life, if not treated effectively on time.

Treatment Efficacy of VR in Mental Health Treatment

The history of healthcare applications of VR can be traced back to the early 1990s when the uses of VR was primarily confined to the diagnostic purposes, visualization of the complex medical data, and surgical procedures (Chinnock, 1994). The application of VR later shifted from physical illnesses to mental health treatment (Hodges et al., 1995). In their research on acrophobic patients, Hodges and colleagues (1995) created a virtual environment to provide patients with fear-inducing experiences of heights. Viewing a virtual environment using a VR headset encouraged a sense of safety and real-like experience among participants. The findings of this study and other similar studies strongly suggested that VR exposure therapy was as effective as traditional *in vivo* exposure therapy (Emmelkamp et al., 2002; Krijn et al., 2007). Since the first reported study of VR use in mental health, twenty-five years ago, additional research studies have continued to broaden applications of VR treatment in mental health conditions (Eichenberg & Wolters, 2012; Krijn et al., 2007). For example, phobias, post-traumatic stress disorders (PTSD), anxiety-related issues or disorders, and more recently mood and psychotic disorders have been studied. (Gerardi et al., 2010).

The shift of VR application from physical illness to mental disorders brought a variety of acceptance and reservations comments. While there are several studies that predict VR as a next-generation treatment tool, there is no dearth of other research that contradicts its suggested effectiveness (Meyerbröker & Emmelkamp, 2010). Despite these contradictions and disputes, VR has garnered undivided attention as a cost-effective and promising technology for enhancing the diagnosis and treatment of various psychological disorders. Virtual Reality Exposure (VRE) has particularly emerged as effective treatment tool for anxiety disorders (Krijn et al., 2007; Rothbaum et al., 2000, 2002; Wiederhold et al., 2002). post-traumatic stress disorder and phobia as in vivo Exposure or IVE (Gerardi et al., 2010). However, the quality of evidence supporting VR as a next-generation therapeutic tool is slightly disputable (Meyerbröker & Emmelkamp, 2010). The primary characteristics of the work in the field of VR and healthcare highlights the significance of full immersion through VR in patient's overall therapeutic experience. Most of the work to improve the effectiveness of psychotherapy centres around the technology advancements to allow patients to have a better and realistic treatment experience. To illustrate, VRE therapy in patients with fear of heights involves placing individuals in a virtual atrium via virtual reality headsets. This allows patients to interact and manipulate their virtual environment freely and in their level of comfort without outside noise.

An insight into the existing research on VR and mental health informs that two types of therapies are predominantly used in the treatment of mental disorders, which include VR- enhanced Cognitive Behaviour Therapy (CBT) and VRE. These two VR-based treatments have been found effective when compared with the patients receiving traditional CBT in person, IE (Imaginal Exposure), and IVE (in vivo exposure). This line of research, therefore, highly recommends virtual reality as a suitable treatment for various mental health problems and encompasses different behavioral health domains, such as anxiety, eating disorders, psychosis, addiction, mood disorders, and trauma (Clus et al., 2018; Fodor et al., 2018)

There are numerous occasions when VR has been integrated with the treatment of associated pain and anxiety in physical illness. For instance, medical procedures evoke a certain level of anxiety and stress, especially among pediatric patients undergoing surgery. VR therapy, therefore, could ensure that the patients undergo stress-relief training and anxiety management through virtual reality headsets that simulates a relaxing environment (for a systematic review of VR in paediatrics (Eijlers et al., 2019). A review of the present literature presents a solidified case, which indicates the effectiveness of VR as a potential supplement of behavior therapy, especially with individuals suffering from a plethora of anxiety disorders (Eichenberg & Wolters, 2012).

In a nutshell, psychological treatment based on VR technology offers substantial success in treating mental health issues among individuals, experiencing symptoms of psychological distress, anxiety, etc. Provided the effectiveness, accessibility, and portability that VR offers, utilizing this treatment technology for college students with mental health problems, is a strategy worthy of use in university counselling settings.

FROM CLINICAL SETTINGS TO UNIVERSITY CAMPUS

Various studies suggest that most of the mental illnesses occurs between the ages of 18-25 (Kessler et al., 2007), the ages that many students pursue higher education. Many universities have enhanced their mental health counselling services with full-time resident assistants as well as suicide and depression awareness programs (Campbell & Dahir, 1997). Nonetheless, providing students with better mental health services and helping them respond to the inevitable flow of challenges in academic and social life presents reasons for universities to modify existing counselling services (Herr, 2001). One modification being used at some universities is including VR opportunities in diagnosis and treatment.

Use of VR in University Mental Health Services

There are some universities presently researching mental health issues to assess, understand, and treat mental health problems using immersive VR technology. For example, the University of Oxford, Department of Psychiatry, and Clinical Psychology uses immersive VR technology to gain insights into mental health problems (Freeman et al, 2017). One of their VR studies led to the treatment of phobia of heights using a virtual atrium. This treatment was found to be as effective as face-to-face therapy. Such studies indicate that VR can also be used as an alternative to other traditional psychotherapies in universities because such VR assisted therapy will only require users to be placed in a virtual environment using portable headsets. While the University of Oxford is presently working in developing new VR technologies for addressing mental health issues, Colorado University Boulder's Counselling and Psychiatric Services (CAPS) is also involved in a visionary pilot study to help treat students with mental health conditions using VR. This program, which is now accessible for its students, aims to help students understand, address and treat their psychological issues, such as the fear of public speaking, fear of insects, fear of heights, or more common mental health issues, such as anxiety or depression.

In a similar vein, senior secondary schools in Singapore have started an awareness programme called *Do You M.I.N.D?,* which allows students to have a chance to understand what it is like to have depression using VR headsets. The two-minute virtual environment enables students to take on the persona of a virtual girl suffering from depression and listen to her inner thoughts and feelings. Such programmes on mental health themes encourage students to become more vigilant about the signs and symptoms of mental health issues. (Choo, 2018).

Even when the students feel that they are in the borderline or risk of developing any mental health condition, VR can serve as a tool to reduce symptoms and may further allow students to have a sense of psychological empowerment; the VR experience can be a psychologically empowering experience, where the students are assured that nothing that happens in the virtual environment "really" happened (Botella et al., 1998). With such assurance, VR can become a powerful intermediate pathway that bridges the students with their internal thoughts and feelings. In a time where students are specifically engrossed in their smartphones, VR therapy would expose them to artificially created environments where they can improve their social skills. Case in point, students suffering from social anxiety could be placed in virtual equivalents of the cafeteria or bus. The students can then work their way up on the levels of difficulty, such as being in a café that has few people to a crowded café. Such a virtual environment would allow students to improve their social skills without worrying too much about what others think of their lack of social skills. To conclude, mental health issues are inseparable from students' environment, and these aforementioned examples demonstrate that technological advancements in mental health settings within universities is emerging.

An Interdisciplinary Approach to the Use of VR

An introduction of VR in student mental health counselling requires serious attempts to enhance VR technologies through more collaborative efforts. Students and faculty domains with programming skills collaborate with their university counseling services and mental health clinicians to design more real-life virtual environment than what are used presently. For instance, since an extensive programming expertise is required in order to create a suitable virtual environment, university counselling services can serve as a bridging gap between technology and clinical care settings by collaborating between various departments, such as computer science and cognitive science, among others. An interdisciplinary approach, therefore, might help render technological, reliability and credibility related deficits in the present VR applications in mental health settings (Cipresso et al., 2018).

Use of VR in Student Counselling Services

The introduction of VR in university student counselling services isn't as challenging as it might seem initially. The use of VR in university counselling settings offers two key advantages. First, with VR technology, it would be easier to integrate all different methods (cognitive, behavior, experimental, and exposure) mainly used in the treatment of common mental health disorders, such as depression or anxiety, within a single virtual experience (Riva, 2005). Secondly, VR can be used to induce the students in a controlled sensory experience (Krijn et al., 2004), which may help unconsciously reorganize their mental schemas relevant to a distressing life event (academic or interpersonal). When individuals experience a world through a VR system, they are independent of rearranging and manipulating their sensory experience based on the visual or auditory cues (Scarfe& Glennerster, 2015). While the inputs and expertise of counselors are indisputable, such virtual experience techniques induced by VR might thus lessen the burden of over-dependence on the skill sets of the university counselors.

To illustrate, one of the initial premises of any counselling session is maintaining confidentiality (APA, 2002). If a university counselor attempts to take a student with social anxiety into a crowded cafeteria for exposure therapy, it might risk and breach the counselor- patient confidentiality. Provided that mental illnesses are still considered a taboo globally (Corrigan & Bink, 2005), students may also avoid such treatment because of the risks associated with getting caught on campus with a counsellor. Similarly, students with extreme phobia usually avoid triggering situations (Wakefield, Horwitz, & Schmitz, 2005) and making students experience exposure to a crowded space might not be a feasible option in the first place. With VR, however, this is not the case. The virtual environment is indeed less threatening than in-vivo exposure, and it also allows students to freely experience a realistic scenario behind the four walls of the counselor's office or a lab setting.

What distinguishes VR therapy from traditional psychotherapy is the existence of two basic components: presence and immersion (Rothbaum et al., 2000). Immersion in VR refers to a state of consciousness in which the users' feel as if being physically present in a non-physical world. This immersion is mainly achieved via the usage of realistic visual and auditory inputs, and sometimes also by using tactile stimulation. A sensation of presence, on the other hand, results as the feeling of being physically immersed in a virtual environment, wherein users perceive the environment as being real and in control of themselves in that virtual world in the context of spatial presence, involvement, and realness.

Since the university student counselling office is often perceived as a dull place by most students, the use of VR, therefore, might increase the therapy motivation among students. For example, in one study, young German participants majorly responded with a "maybe and a 'yes" when asked if they are willing to make use of VR treatment if they are suffering from phobia (Eichenberg & Brahler, as cited in Eichenberg & Wolters, 2012). The integration of the applications of VR with the college aged population will, therefore, not only lead to increased awareness among students about mental health, but it will also increase the use of university counselling services, which, unfortunately, are not appropriately utilized by students on numerous occasions (Russell, Thomson, & Rosenthal, 2008). Moreover, the fact that VR applications simulate real-life experiences and induce physiological symptoms, such as sweating and nausea, highlight their potential in replacing traditional psychotherapeutic interventions in university settings as well.

In university settings, VR technology in fact can also be used in assessing whether or not the students present typical symptoms of some sort of mental health issue. For instance, instead of students attempting to describe their fear of social situations, a mental health clinician can more accurately label the extent of social phobia or anxiety using a virtual situation. Likewise, such VR situations can also unearth deep-level information, which may be grounded so overwhelmingly in the student's unconscious that a student may not even remember the event. Therefore, the ability of VR in administering robust and realistic situational examinations might contribute to enhancing the accuracy of the students' subjective clinical assessment (Krueger & Schkade, 2008). Alternately, VR technology can also shed substantial light into the understanding of the aetiology of mental health disorders and individual differences in mental health (Freeman et al., 2017), such as identifying student environmental characteristics contributing to the risk of adverse psychological conditions.

STRATEGIES FOR VR USE IN STUDENT COUNSELLING SESSIONS

While the logistics issues that majorly cloud university counselling services could not be largely ignored, some of the psychotherapeutic practices using VR technology that have been successfully utilized in clinical settings can also be redesigned and integrated in the improvement of students' mental health.

This section, therefore, aims to provide insights into the possible benefits of VR for the treatment of a plethora of mental health disorders, conditions, syndromes, and issues, which are widely utilized in the hospital care and clinical settings. First and foremost, every university student counselling services needs to have a thorough plan for building mental health awareness that reaches every student. Once a mental health awareness program is in place, there are at least five ways through which VR can be applied in university counselling services: 1) assisted empty chair therapy, 2) assisted exposure therapy, 3) emotion perception therapy, 4) communication skills training, and 5) stress reduction therapy.

Building Mental Health Awareness

Despite the fact that mental disorders, such as depression, make up for one of the leading causes of disability among young adults around globe (Friedrich, 2017) and suicide rates are at its highest point among students in 20 years (Miron et al., 2019), students are often unaware of indicators of a need for mental health counselling. For instance, a student could be depressed without knowing the clinical signs of depression or how depression is actually impacting their social and academic life. This suggests that students who are suicidal feel alone with no way out of the misery they are feeling and may not know that seeking mental health treatment can relieve symptoms. To enhance such awareness, universities often use modern multimedia courseware (such as pictures or videos). While these two-dimensional approaches are one way to promote mental health awareness, this treatment strategy can sometimes fail to serve the purpose it intends to. Adding VR technology, however, might aid in making students grasp the graving concept of mental illness, more realistically, psychologically, and emotionally. Case in point, when teaching about ill-effects of depressive symptoms, VR technology can indeed allow students to experience critical moments of living with depression more intuitively and profoundly, which cannot be otherwise experienced in real life or through traditional courseware (Choo, 2018).

Assisted Empty Chair Therapy

Most of the student encounters various interpersonal disputes in their academic life, including conflict of interest with their professors, research supervisors, and faculty advisors, or with their significant others (Hunt & Eisenberg, 2010). In order to help people with such interpersonal issues, traditional empty chair techniques have been prominently used in many therapeutic procedures (Samoilov & Goldfried, 2000). Herein therapists and clients interact using an empty chair to provide proper ventilation of negative emotions of the client. In such a therapeutic interaction, if the psychotherapist's skills and imaginative cues are not sufficient and rich enough to captivate the client's imagination, it would be difficult for the client to dive deeper into their subconscious and project his/her own character in the treatment.

The VR-assisted empty chair therapy, however, sort of nullifies that issue, for it allows individuals to virtualize and make a significant connection easily. Even if the clients' imaginations are not strong enough, the technology will compensate for the induction of the therapeutic effect by providing a realistic social context. The efficacy of VR empty chair treatment, moreover, has an edge when used in university settings. For instance, students who feel hesitant to approach counselling services because they feel that a counselor who himself/ herself is a part of the university system and he/she might be judgmental and opinionated since they are themselves closely linked with university administration would feel more secured interacting with a virtual system, as it doesn't come up with its own sets of presumptions and biases.

Assisted Exposure Therapy

Exposure therapy is usually employed to treat patients with symptoms of anxiety or phobia (Parsons & Rizzo, 2008). This therapy exposes the patients' fear and anxiety through frequent face-to-face interactions with things they feel more anxious about. Anxiety and phobia are some of the major psychological issues that the majority of students seem to experience (Purdon et al., 2001). Many students experience anxiety due to their academic life, including exam anxiety, landing a job or internships, etc., or anxiety related to the social situation, such as meeting new people or facing a panel of interviewers, etc. (Tillfors & Furmark, 2007). As mentioned earlier, traditional exposure therapies carry their own set of flaws, as individuals, especially young adults, with anxiety or phobia, are reluctant to interact face-to-face with the triggering stimuli.

In addition, students in higher education are appropriately concerned about their social standing and have a need for affiliation and social status (Gavin & Furman, 1989). They may assume that the treatment of their anxiety and phobia in a social setting (such as their university) may consequently damage their social repute in terms of how their peers view them. VR can be, therefore, employed either as a primary technique or supporting tool in order to facilitate a therapeutic environment wherein the students feels safe and stable, which in turn encourages better and productive treatment progress. Exposure therapy, when clubbed with VR technology, allows students to freely explore and interact with an artificially created anxiety environment, where they can actually manipulate the degree of trauma. Moreover, sensor induced virtual environment also helps improve them improve their emotion regulation and social interactions inability.

Likewise, as various research studies document that the majority of suicidal incidences happen around the time of exams and tests, such therapy in the university settings will indeed allow students to reach during exam months, when test anxiety and exam phobia are at their peak onset. VR induced relaxation therapy, for instance, can also be provided to students, which will be discussed in detail in the later section.

Emotion Perception Training

Students' life is inundated with challenges in different domains, including academic, social, and interpersonal (Li et al., 2010; Ryder et al., 2013). Trading from high school life to a university/college life multiplies these challenges at an exponential rate. Most of the students with a comfortable high school life find it extremely challenging to meet their present university demands, which makes them highly prone to a nervous breakdown in case any roadblock emerges (Geller & Greenberg, 2009). This nervous breakdown often results in the lack of one's emotional sensitivity. Research suggests that negative emotions arise due to the lack of ones' inability to regulate their emotions and that impaired emotion regulation plays a major role in the development of adolescents' psychopathology (Wante et al., 2018).

Since emotional health is a pre-requisite to a healthy individual life, teaching students how to cope effectively with their existing academic and social demands would be like taking a step closer to enhancing their emotion and perceptual abilities. With the help of advanced VR technology, a real-life environment can be re-created, which can be simulated on the students to help perfect their emotional intelligence. The emotional experience recreated with the help of VR technology will also facilitate students to carefully scrutinize their current environment in a virtual manner and manipulate that environment differently and learn from the manipulations they have made, which they can later incorporate in their real life.

In addition, VR technology may also serve influential in emotion perception training in university settings through creating a personalized virtual character, where students can perform objective emotion perception training by observing the facial expressions, behavioural actions, and mood orientations of their virtual character.

Communication Skills Training

The periphery of universities and colleges is not merely limited to students' academics, but they also extend beyond lectures or studies to extra-curricular activities, such as participating in other class activities, clubs, cultural events, etc., which may serve as life stressors (Clark, 2005). Most anxiety and phobias of students stem from their inabilities to engage in social interactions. Since these extra-curricular require one to engage interpersonally with other students, faculty, and staff, students' mental health is largely compromised because some students feel that they are not competent enough to handle the crowd. Furthermore, one of the reasons for frequent job rejections during university placements could also be explained by students' poor communication skills (Morgan, 2019). Even though universities usually conduct workshops for communication training, they are primarily not successful because students do not feel comfortable and rather feel anxious practicing in front of another unknown crowd.

University counselling services, therefore, can apply VR technology to facilitate a safe and protected environment where students can be trained on their communication skills in a virtually created environment. For instance, constructing a virtual interview set up or social environment would allow students to practice their communication skills and have a virtual dialogue training for themselves. VR is competent to store a lot of data, including facial expressions and head movement. In fact, sometimes along with physiological monitoring, it can also help us understand our emotional valence and arousal toward a particular emotion-arousing event. Therefore, these dialogue drills using VR would not only help students detect the shortcomings in their communication skills, but it would equally allow them to improve their confidence and self-esteem- two of the major instrumental factors in improved resilience and overall mental health.

Stress Reduction Training

Stress is one of the leading variables that contribute to the overall mental health problems of students (Keller et al., 2012). As mentioned earlier, stress among students could mainly arise due to academic pressure, interpersonal issues, family pressure, economic dependency, etc. Most of the campus counselling services either provide talk therapy or recommend students to nearby psychological clinics or psychotherapy centres (Schmidt, 2003), which provide services, such as relaxation therapy. Relaxation therapy is conducted in various formats, such as Progressive Muscle Relaxation (PMR), abdominal breathing training or music relaxation therapy, etc.

Taking cues from such psychotherapeutic settings, universities can also employ VR assisted stress-relief training in the place of traditional stress management techniques for students. With the assistance of VR technology, even the most abstract environment, which the students are expected to create, can be submerged into a specific virtual environment. Moreover, these abstract yet traditional environments, when incorporated with VR technology can be converted into more students' centric three-dimensional environment for inducing relaxation. Using sound, feelings of temperature, or vibration as students navigate through the virtual environment, for instance. Such stress relief training would lead to better productivity and improved mental health among students, who are constantly preoccupied with one or the other academic deadlines and challenges.

STRENGTHS AND LIMITATIONS

Researchers in the field of VR assisted mental health studies contend that the underlying issue with the VR technology is not associated with the lack of innovative ideas to deal with these disorders (Freeman et al., 2017). Instead, VR encourages a more user-friendly experience and, technically speaking, is indeed capable of replacing the traditional psychotherapeutic treatment for a number of reasons, such as: a) the recent availability of low-cost VR technologies, such as Oculus Rift, Sony VR, etc.; b) the multisensory experience of VR allowing users to profoundly interact with their emotions even without the existence of that real-life situation, and; c) the portability of VR technologies to almost anywhere effortlessly.

Yet as exciting as this VR technology and the promise it offers are, there are certain daunting measurements and theoretical challenges, which advocates of VR still need to satisfy, some of which also appear in clinical studies. The role of VR in mental health diagnosis and treatment has been majorly informed by the medical studies on patients with mental health conditions, such as phobia, depression, trauma, etc., among many. Some major criticisms, however, emerge from this complex and rich literature. Following are four limitations that were encountered by the author in using VR in student mental health counselling services.

The first criticism stems from the lack of sufficient literature to contend for VR treatment effectiveness over traditional practices. While a whole body of research that compares VR treatment effectiveness with the conventional psychotherapy methods, there are only a few subsets of research that conclude with a significant difference. The proven effectiveness of these two treatment methods is hence controversial and requires more research inputs to further validate its experience.

The second and, in fact, the one of other major disadvantages of VR treatment in mental health student counselling is that it does not work for everyone. Individuals who have poor concentration, for instance, usually have difficulties focusing on a single event and experience distractibility issues, and thus they may find immersion in a virtual environment somewhat burdensome. Similarly, while the head-mounted VR devices provide flexibility in movements, the PC-based VR system, unfortunately, suffers from a severe lack of the flexibilities necessary to individualize the therapy according to patients (Riva, 2005). In addition, simulator sickness and nausea may happen in virtual scenarios which are poorly realized (Kennedy & Lilienthal, 1995). Simulator sickness, therefore, may be problematic for therapy effectiveness in such individuals.

A third criticism of VR finds its roots in the lack of standardization, both in the context of VR devices and the virtual environment used for treatment purposes. This lack of standardization somehow questions the efficacy of VR psychotherapy to begin with. Even though psychotherapeutic approaches are more individually tailored, there is still a consensus on how and what carries the treatment forward, unlike the VR treatment, which is still in its infancy stage.

Finally, the fourth limitation of the use of VR in college student mental health treatments involves the associated costs of VR assisted counselling services. VR headsets and allied technological tools are immersive, effective, and confidential. With VR technology becoming less costly, portable, and widely available online, mental health treatment within university seems like a near reality that could revolutionize present days' university counselling services by length and width. Even though the costs of VR headsets have sunk dramatically, the cost associated with setting up a VR lab along with the supportive hardware could still be expensive than traditional counselling offices for some colleges with low funding (Glanz et al., 2003). Provided the lack of budget spent over the counselling services in universities or overall expenses allocated by the government on the education system, setting up a VR counselling service certainly emerges as a challenging task, if not impossible.

FUTURE RESEARCH SUGGESTIONS

Given that the use of VR in mental health settings is still in its infancy stage and applications to student counselling in higher education are also emerging, there is a need for research to examine the effectiveness of VR in these settings. Following are suggestions based on this author's review of the literature and experiences within a university that uses VR in the counselling setting:

1. The use of VR seems like a viable option in mental health treatment. Research regarding the use of VR in mental health therapy, in general, is needed to establish the credibility and validity of VR as a therapeutic tool.
2. Investigations into the broader application of VR in mental health diagnosis, assessment, and treatment are needed; currently there is a paucity of research demonstrating that VR therapy is an effective replacement to commonly used clinical and psychotherapeutic options.
3. Individuals who are using VR in student mental health therapy are needed to publish papers describing their work; case studies are thus required specifically. Such publications can be a vehicle for professional connections.
4. University leadership needs to fiscally and organizationally support student counselling services and demonstrate a commitment to student mental health.

CONCLUSION

Facing the challenges of being in an academic setting can result in a student accumulating a range of mental health problems among students. Thus, an intention of on-going improvement in the student counselling system within university settings is critically important. When mental health issues among students are addressed effectively, the result can be, not only students that have the coping mechanisms to deal with stress during their college years but throughout life.

The introduction of VR into the health care treatments, and subsequently into university student counselling offers another strategy for engaging students in recognizing and addressing mental health issues. Given the immersive characteristics and easier accessibility of the VR technology, as well as the shift toward mental health reforms within the university settings, the prospects of VR technology in addressing students' mental health problems also seem promising. The increasing cost-effectiveness and mobility that VR allows, has encouraged universities to also consider VR as one of the counselling tools to serve students dealing with mental health challenges. For example, VR technology can provide students with social anxiety a platform to initiate and practice in a virtual social environment before they apply new skills in the real social world.

Likewise, an introduction of VR induced psychotherapeutic techniques in university can also help promote student's initiative for mental health education awareness and can consequently reduce psychological health burdens owing to the competitive academic and social environment. Such introduction of VR within the university settings indeed requires an on-going collaboration and persistent efforts among different knowledge domains (such as computer science, cognitive science, clinical psychology, and design) to develop more user-friendly virtual environments to treat mental health disorders. Considering the technological aspects that VR provide, clinical applications of VR in improving the mental health treatment, especially among students within the university settings has promising potential.

REFERENCES

American Psychological Association. (2002). Ethical principles of psychologists and code of conduct. *The American Psychologist*, *57*(12), 1060–1073. doi:10.1037/0003-066X.57.12.1060 PMID:12613157

Auerbach, R. P., Alonso, J., Axinn, W. G., Cuijpers, P., Ebert, D. D., Green, J. G., ... Nock, M. K. (2016). Mental disorders among college students in the World Health Organization world mental health surveys. *Psychological Medicine*, *46*(14), 2955–2970. doi:10.1017/S0033291716001665 PMID:27484622

Blanco, C., Okuda, M., Wright, C., Hasin, D. S., Grant, B. F., Liu, S. M., & Olfson, M. (2008). Mental health of college students and their non-college-attending peers. *Archives of General Psychiatry*, *65*(12), 1429–1437. doi:10.1001/archpsyc.65.12.1429 PMID:19047530

Botella, C., Perpiña, C., & Baños, R. M. (1998). Virtual reality: A new clinical setting lab. *Studies in Health Technology and Informatics*, *58*, 73–81. PMID:10350931

Burrell, J. (2020, March 16). *The grim numbers behind adolescent suicides and attempts* [Web log post]. https://www.verywellmind.com/college-and-teen-suicide-statistics-3570768

Campbell, C. A., & Dahir, C. A. (1997). *Sharing the vision: The ASCA national standards for school counseling programs*. American School Counselor Association.

Chinnock, C. (1994). Virtual reality in surgery and medicine. *Hospital Technology Series*, *13*(18), 1–48. PMID:10172193

Choo, F. (2018, October 31). *Learning about depression via VR tools*. https://www.straitstimes.com/singapore/health/learning-about-depression-via-vr-tools

Cipresso, P., Giglioli, I. A. C., Raya, M. A., & Riva, G. (2018). The past, present, and future of virtual and augmented reality research: A network and cluster analysis of the literature. *Frontiers in Psychology*, *9*, 2086. doi:10.3389/fpsyg.2018.02086 PMID:30459681

Clark, M. R. (2005). Negotiating the freshman year: Challenges and strategies among first-year college students. *Journal of College Student Development*, *46*(3), 296–316. doi:10.1353/csd.2005.0022

Clus, D., Larsen, M. E., Lemey, C., & Berrouiguet, S. (2018). The use of virtual reality in patients with eating disorders: Systematic review. *Journal of Medical Internet Research*, *20*(4), e157. doi:10.2196/jmir.7898 PMID:29703715

Corrigan, P., & Bink, A. B. (2005). *On the stigma of mental illness*. American Psychological Association.

Deb, S. (2019, July 26). Opinion I What do you do about this 'IIT dream' madness of parents? [Web log post]. https://www.livemint.com/opinion/columns/opinion-what-do-you-do-about-this-iit-dream-madness-of-parents-1564136143781.html

Eichenberg, C., & Brähler, E. (2013). Internet as a guide for mental health problems. *Psychotherapist, 58*(1), 63–72. doi:10.100700278-012-0893-0

Eichenberg, C., & Wolters, C. (2012). Virtual Realities in the treatment of mental disorders: A Review of the current state of research. *Virtual Reality in Psychological. Medical and Pedagogical Applications, 2*, 35–64.

Eijlers, R., Utens, E. M., Staals, L. M., de Nijs, P. F., Berghmans, J. M., Wijnen, R. M., Hillegers, M. H. J., Dierckx, B., & Legerstee, J. S. (2019). Meta-Analysis: Systematic Review and Meta-analysis of Virtual Reality in Pediatrics: Effects on Pain and Anxiety. *Anesthesia and Analgesia, 129*(5), 1344–1353. doi:10.1213/ANE.0000000000004165 PMID:31136330

Eisenberg, D., Hunt, J., & Speer, N. (2013). Mental health in American colleges and universities: Variation across student subgroups and across campuses. *The Journal of Nervous and Mental Disease, 201*(1), 60–67. doi:10.1097/NMD.0b013e31827ab077 PMID:23274298

Emmelkamp, P. M., Krijn, M., Hulsbosch, A. M., De Vries, S., Schuemie, M. J., & van der Mast, C. A. (2002). Virtual reality treatment versus exposure in vivo: A comparative evaluation in acrophobia. *Behaviour Research and Therapy, 40*(5), 509–516. doi:10.1016/S0005-7967(01)00023-7 PMID:12038644

Evans, N. J., Forney, D. S., Guido, F. M., Patton, L. D., & Renn, K. A. (2009). *Student development in college: Theory, research, and practice*. John Wiley & Sons.

Fodor, L. A., Coteț, C. D., Cuijpers, P., Szamoskozi, Ș., David, D., & Cristea, I. A. (2018). The effectiveness of virtual reality based interventions for symptoms of anxiety and depression: A meta-analysis. *Scientific Reports, 8*(1), 1–13. doi:10.103841598-018-28113-6 PMID:29985400

Freeman, D., Reeve, S., Robinson, A., Ehlers, A., Clark, D., Spanlang, B., & Slater, M. (2017). Virtual reality in the assessment, understanding, and treatment of mental health disorders. *Psychological Medicine, 47*(14), 2393–2400. doi:10.1017/S003329171700040X PMID:28325167

Friedrich, M. J. (2017). Depression is the leading cause of disability around the world. *Journal of the American Medical Association, 317*(15), 1517–1517. doi:10.1001/jama.2017.3826 PMID:28418490

Gavin, L. A., & Furman, W. (1989). Age differences in adolescents' perceptions of their peer groups. *Developmental Psychology, 25*(5), 827–834. doi:10.1037/0012-1649.25.5.827

Geller, L. L., & Greenberg, M. (2009). Managing the transition process from high school to college and beyond: Challenges for individuals, families, and society. *Social Work in Mental Health, 8*(1), 92–116. doi:10.1080/15332980902932466

Gerardi, M., Cukor, J., Difede, J., Rizzo, A., & Rothbaum, B. O. (2010). Virtual reality exposure therapy for post-traumatic stress disorder and other anxiety disorders. *Current Psychiatry Reports, 12*(4), 298–305. doi:10.100711920-010-0128-4 PMID:20535592

Glanz, K., Rizzo, A. S., & Graap, K. (2003). Virtual reality for psychotherapy: Current reality and future possibilities. *Psychotherapy (Chicago, Ill.), 40*(1-2), 55–67. doi:10.1037/0033-3204.40.1-2.55

Herr, E. L. (2001). The impact of national policies, economics, and school reform on comprehensive guidance programs. *Professional School Counseling, 4*, 236–245.

Hodges, L. F., Kooper, R., Meyer, T. C., Rothbaum, B. O., Opdyke, D., De Graaff, J. J., Williford, J. S., & North, M. M. (1995). Virtual environments for treating the fear of heights. *Computer, 28*(7), 27–34. doi:10.1109/2.391038

Hunt, J., & Eisenberg, D. (2010). Mental health problems and help-seeking behavior among college students. *The Journal of Adolescent Health, 46*(1), 3–10. doi:10.1016/j.jadohealth.2009.08.008 PMID:20123251

Hysenbegasi, A., Hass, S. L., & Rowland, C. R. (2005). The impact of depression on the academic productivity of university students. *The Journal of Mental Health Policy and Economics, 8*(3), 145–151. PMID:16278502

Ibrahim, A. K., Kelly, S. J., Adams, C. E., & Glazebrook, C. (2013). A systematic review of studies of depression prevalence in university students. *Journal of Psychiatric Research, 47*(3), 391–400. doi:10.1016/j.jpsychires.2012.11.015 PMID:23260171

Ishii, T., Tachikawa, H., Shiratori, Y., Hori, T., Aiba, M., Kuga, K., & Arai, T. (2018). What kinds of factors affect the academic outcomes of university students with mental disorders? A retrospective study based on medical records. *Asian Journal of Psychiatry, 32*, 67–72. doi:10.1016/j.ajp.2017.11.017 PMID:29216609

Keller, A., Litzelman, K., Wisk, L. E., Maddox, T., Cheng, E. R., Creswell, P. D., & Witt, W. P. (2012). Does the perception that stress affects health matter? The association with health and mortality. *Health Psychology, 31*(5), 677–684. doi:10.1037/a0026743 PMID:22201278

Kennedy, R. S., & Lilienthal, M. G. (1995). Implications of balance disturbances following exposure to virtual reality systems. *Proceedings of the Virtual Reality Annual International Symposium '95*, 35-39. 10.1109/VRAIS.1995.512477

Kessler, R. C., Amminger, G. P., Aguilar-Gaxiola, S., Alonso, J., Lee, S., & Ustun, T. B. (2007). Age of onset of mental disorders: A review of recent literature. *Current Opinion in Psychiatry, 20*(4), 359. doi:10.1097/YCO.0b013e32816ebc8c PMID:17551351

Krijn, M., Emmelkamp, P. M., Biemond, R., de Ligny, C. D. W., Schuemie, M. J., & van der Mast, C. A. (2004). Treatment of acrophobia in virtual reality: The role of immersion and presence. *Behaviour Research and Therapy, 42*(2), 229–239. doi:10.1016/S0005-7967(03)00139-6 PMID:14975783

Krijn, M., Emmelkamp, P. M., Olafsson, R. P., Schuemie, M. J., & Van Der Mast, C. A. (2007). Do self-statements enhance the effectiveness of virtual reality exposure therapy? A comparative evaluation in acrophobia. *Cyberpsychology & Behavior, 10*(3), 362–370. doi:10.1089/cpb.2006.9943 PMID:17594260

Krueger, A. B., & Schkade, D. A. (2008). The reliability of subjective well-being measures. *Journal of Public Economics, 92*(8-9), 1833–1845. doi:10.1016/j.jpubeco.2007.12.015 PMID:19649136

Li, G., Chen, W., & Duanmu, J. (2010). Determinants of international students' academic performance: A comparison between Chinese and other international students. *Journal of Studies in International Education*, *14*(4), 389–405. doi:10.1177/1028315309331490

McLaughlin, C. (1999). Counselling in schools: Looking back and looking forward. *British Journal of Guidance & Counselling*, *27*(1), 13–22. doi:10.1080/03069889908259712

Meyerbröker, K., & Emmelkamp, P. M. (2010). Virtual reality exposure therapy in anxiety disorders: A systematic review of process-and-outcome studies. *Depression and Anxiety*, *27*(10), 933–944. doi:10.1002/da.20734 PMID:20734361

Miron, O., Yu, K. H., Wilf-Miron, R., & Kohane, I. S. (2019). Suicide rates among adolescents and young adults in the United States, 2000-2017. *Journal of the American Medical Association*, *321*(23), 2362–2364. doi:10.1001/jama.2019.5054 PMID:31211337

Morgan, H. (2019, April 13). *41 Reasons Why You Didn't Get the Job* [Web log post]. https://careersherpa.net/41-reasons-why-you-didnt-get-the-job

Parsons, T. D., & Rizzo, A. A. (2008). Affective outcomes of virtual reality exposure therapy for anxiety and specific phobias: A meta-analysis. *Journal of Behavior Therapy and Experimental Psychiatry*, *39*(3), 250–261. doi:10.1016/j.jbtep.2007.07.007 PMID:17720136

Purdon, C., Antony, M., Monteiro, S., & Swinson, R. P. (2001). Social anxiety in college students. *Journal of Anxiety Disorders*, *15*(3), 203–215. doi:10.1016/S0887-6185(01)00059-7 PMID:11442139

Richardson, M., Abraham, C., & Bond, R. (2012). Psychological correlates of university students' academic performance: A systematic review and meta-analysis. *Psychological Bulletin*, *138*(2), 353–387. doi:10.1037/a0026838 PMID:22352812

Ricky, C., & O'Donnell Siobhan, M. N. (2017). Factors associated with delayed diagnosis of mood and/or anxiety disorders. *Health Promotion and Chronic Disease Prevention in Canada: Research. Policy & Practice*, *37*(5), 137.

Riva, G. (2005). Virtual reality in psychotherapy. *Cyberpsychology & Behavior*, *8*(3), 220–230. doi:10.1089/cpb.2005.8.220 PMID:15971972

Rothbaum, B. O., Hodges, L., Anderson, P. L., Price, L., & Smith, S. (2002). Twelve-month follow-up of virtual reality and standard exposure therapies for the fear of flying. *Journal of Consulting and Clinical Psychology*, *70*(2), 428–432. doi:10.1037/0022-006X.70.2.428 PMID:11952201

Rothbaum, B. O., Hodges, L., Smith, S., Lee, J. H., & Price, L. (2000). A controlled study of virtual reality exposure therapy for the fear of flying. *Journal of Consulting and Clinical Psychology*, *68*(6), 1020–1026. doi:10.1037/0022-006X.68.6.1020 PMID:11142535

Russell, J., Thomson, G., & Rosenthal, D. (2008). International student use of university health and counselling services. *Higher Education*, *56*(1), 59–75. doi:10.100710734-007-9089-x

Ryder, A. G., Alden, L. E., Paulhus, D. L., & Dere, J. (2013). Does acculturation predict interpersonal adjustment? It depends on who you talk to. *International Journal of Intercultural Relations*, *37*(4), 502–506. doi:10.1016/j.ijintrel.2013.02.002

Samoilov, A., & Goldfried, M. R. (2000). Role of emotion in cognitive-behavior therapy. *Clinical Psychology: Science and Practice*, *7*(4), 373–385. doi:10.1093/clipsy.7.4.373

Scarfe, P., & Glennerster, A. (2015). Using high-fidelity virtual reality to study perception in freely moving observers. *Journal of Vision (Charlottesville, Va.)*, *15*(9), 3–3. doi:10.1167/15.9.3 PMID:26161632

Schmidt, J. J. (2003). *Counseling in schools: Essential services and comprehensive programs*. Allyn & Bacon.

Steptoe, A., Tsuda, A., & Tanaka, Y. (2007). Depressive symptoms, socio-economic background, sense of control, and cultural factors in university students from 23 countries. *International Journal of Behavioral Medicine*, *14*(2), 97–107. doi:10.1007/BF03004175 PMID:17926438

Tillfors, M., & Furmark, T. (2007). Social phobia in Swedish university students: Prevalence, subgroups and avoidant behavior. *Social Psychiatry and Psychiatric Epidemiology*, *42*(1), 79–86. doi:10.100700127-006-0143-2 PMID:17160591

Wakefield, J. C., Horwitz, A. V., & Schmitz, M. F. (2005). Are we overpathologizing the socially anxious? Social phobia from a harmful dysfunction perspective. *Canadian Journal of Psychiatry*, *50*(6), 317–319. doi:10.1177/070674370505000604 PMID:15999945

Wante, L., Van Beveren, M. L., Theuwis, L., & Braet, C. (2018). The effects of emotion regulation strategies on positive and negative affect in early adolescents. *Cognition and Emotion*, *32*(5), 988–1002. doi:10.1080/02699931.2017.1374242 PMID:28880723

Weissman, M. M., Wolk, S., Wickramaratne, P., Goldstein, R. B., Adams, P., Greenwald, S., Ryan, N. D., Dahl, R. E., & Steinberg, D. (1999). Children with prepubertal-onset major depressive disorder and anxiety grown up. *Archives of General Psychiatry*, *56*(9), 794–801. doi:10.1001/archpsyc.56.9.794 PMID:12884885

Wiederhold, B. K., Jang, D. P., Gevirtz, R. G., Kim, S. I., Kim, I. Y., & Wiederhold, M. D. (2002). The treatment of fear of flying: A controlled study of imaginal and virtual reality graded exposure therapy. *IEEE Transactions on Information Technology in Biomedicine*, *6*(3), 218–223. doi:10.1109/TITB.2002.802378 PMID:12381038

KEY TERMS AND DEFINITIONS

Emotion Perception: One's ability to recognize and identify subjective experience of emotions in others by interpreting their biological and physiological changes.

Emotion Regulation: One's ability to respond to one's ongoing demands of emotional experience, when needed or demanded.

Mental Health: A person's optimal level of psychological and emotional well-being.

Phobia: A type of anxiety disorder that underlies excessive and long-lasting fear of objects and situations.

Progressive Muscle Relaxation: A relaxation technique, which involves simple tensing or tightening of muscles followed by a relaxation phase, lasting usually for 10-20 mins.

Psychotherapeutic Techniques: Psychological, cognitive, or behavioral techniques used by psychiatrists, psychologists, licensed counsellors to treat individuals with mental health challenges using therapist-client collaboration.

Social Anxiety: A mental health condition leading individuals to fear social situations (e.g., leaving one's home or interacting with others in public).

Stress: A feeling of emotional and physiological tension owing to an external challenges or demands.

Student Counselling: Includes use of various psychological and behavioral tools and suggestive measures to help students cope with their mental health issues.

University Counselling Services: The psychological services offered to the students and staffs within a college or university settings.

Compilation of References

3D . Organon V. R. Anatomy. (2016). [Windows application software]. Retrieved December 19, 2019 from https://store.steampowered.com/app/548010/3D_Organon_VR_Anatomy/

3. Glasses. (n.d.). Retrieved December 19, 2019 from https://www.3glasses.com/en

AACTE Committee on Innovation and Technology. (2008). *Handbook of technological pedagogical content knowledge (TPCK) for educators*. Routledge.

Ablanedo, J., Fairchild, E., Griffith, T., & Rodeheffer, C. (2018). Is this person real? Avatar stylization and its influence on human perception in a counseling training environment. Virtual, Augmented and Mixed Reality: Interaction, Navigation, Visualization, Embodiment, and Simulation, 10909, 279–289. doi:10.1007/978-3-319-91581-4_20

Adams Becker, S., Cummins, M., Davis, A., Freeman, A., Hall Giesinger, C., & Ananthanarayanan, V. (2017). *NMC Horizon Report: 2017 Higher Education Edition*. New Media Consortium.

Adams Becker, S., Freeman, A., Giesinger Hall, C., Cummins, M., & Yuhnke, B. (2016). *NMC/CoSN Horizon Report: 2016 K-* (12th ed.). The New Media Consortium.

Adams, E. W. (2004). Postmodernism and the three types of immersion. *Gamasutra*. Retrieved from http://designers-notebook.com/Columns/063_Postmodernism/063_postmodernism.htm

Addision, R. (2018). How higher education is preparing students for the jobs of the future. *Guild Digital Limited*. https://guild.co/blog/how-higher-education-is-preparing-students-for-the-jobs-of-the-future/

Affectiva | Home. (n.d.). Retrieved December 18, 2019, from https://www.affectiva.com/

Agostinelli, M. (2019). *Simulating Trade and Industry with Minecraft: Education Edition*. Northwest Council for Computer Education. http://blog.ncce.org/2019/05/30/simulating-trade-and-industry-with-minecraft-education-edition/

Ahn, S. J., Bostick, J., Ogle, E., & Bailenson, J. N. (2015). *Embodying nature's experiences: Taking the perspective of nature with immersive virtual environments to promote connectedness with nature*. Paper to be presented at the Annual Association for Education in Journalism and Mass Communication (AEJMC) Conference, San Francisco, CA. Retrieved May 2020 from https://vhil.stanford.edu/pubs/

Akdemir, E., & Özçelik, C. (2019). The investigation of the attitudes of teachers towards using student centered teaching methods and techniques. *Universal Journal of Educational Research, 7*(4), 1147-1153. Retrieved from http://www.hrpub.org

Alaker, M., Wunn, G. R., & Arulampalam, T. (2016). Virtual reality training in laparoscopic surgery: A systematic review. *International Journal of Surgery, 29*, 85–94. doi:10.1016/j.ijsu.2016.03.034 PMID:26992652

Alexander, B., Ashford-Rowe, K., Barajas-Murphy, N., Dobbin, G., Knott, J. McCormack, M., Pomerantz, J., Seilhamer, R., & Weber, N. (2019). Educause Horizon Report: 2019 Higher Education Edition. Louisville, CO: Educause.

Alexander, A. L., Brunyé, T., Sidman, J., & Weil, S. A. (2005). From gaming to training: A review of studies on fidelity, immersion, presence, and buy-in and their effects on transfer in pc-based simulations and games. *DARWARS Training Impact Group*, *5*, 1–14.

Alexander, B., Ashford-Rowe, K., Barajas-Murphy, N., Dobbin, G., Knott, J., McCormack, M., & Pomerantz, J. (2019). *EDUCAUSE Horizon Report: 2019 Higher Education Edition*. EDUCAUSE.

Alexander, S., Sarrafzadeh, A., & Hill, S. (2008). Foundation of an affective tutoring system: Learning how human tutors adapt to student emotion. *International Journal of Intelligent Systems Technologies and Applications*, *4*(3), 355. doi:10.1504/IJISTA.2008.017278

Alexander, T., Westhoven, M., & Conradi, J. (2017). Virtual environments for competency-oriented education and training. In J. I. Kantola, T. Barath, S. Nazir, & T. Andre (Eds.), *Advances in Human Factors, Business Management, Training and Education* (pp. 23–29). Springer. doi:10.1007/978-3-319-42070-7_3

Al-Hatem, A. I., Masood, M., & Al-Samarraie, H. (2018). Fostering student nurses' self-regulated learning with the Second Life environment: An empirical study. *Journal of Information Technology Education*, *17*, 285–307. doi:10.28945/4110

Ali, N., Ullah, S., Alam, A., & Rafique, J. (2014). 3D interactive virtual chemistry laboratory for simulation of high school experiments. *Conference: International Conference on Computer Graphics, Animation and Gaming Technologies (EURASIA Turkey 2014)*, 1-6.

Allen, J. R. (2018). Why we need to rethink education in the artificial intelligence age? Brown *Journal of Philosophy, Politics, and Economics*. https://www.brownjppe.com/john-allen-feature

American Psychological Association. (2002). Ethical principles of psychologists and code of conduct. *The American Psychologist*, *57*(12), 1060–1073. doi:10.1037/0003-066X.57.12.1060 PMID:12613157

Ammanuel, S., Brown, I., Uribe, J., & Rehani, B. (2019). Creating 3D models from radiologic images for virtual reality medical education modules. *Journal of Medical Systems*, *43*(6), 166. doi:10.100710916-019-1308-3 PMID:31053902

Anastopoulou, S., Sharples, M., & Baber, C. (2011). An evaluation of multimodal interactions with technology while learning science concepts. *British Journal of Educational Technology*, *42*(2), 266–290. doi:10.1111/j.1467-8535.2009.01017.x

Anatomy 4D. (2017). [Mobile application software]. Retrieved May 20, 2020 from https://www.google.com/search?source=univ&tbm=isch&q=Anatomy+4D+(2017).&sa=X&ved=2ahUKEwjTq4Ca4MPpAhVRb60KHcYNDj0QsAR6BAgGEAE&biw=1370&bih=604

Andersen, S. M., & Thorpe, J. S. (2009). An IF–THEN theory of personality: Significant others and the relational self. *Journal of Research in Personality*, *43*(2), 163–170. doi:10.1016/j.jrp.2008.12.040

Andreas, K., & Tsiatsos, T. (2008, March). Selecting a networked virtual environment platform and the design of a collaborative e-learning environment. In *22nd International Conference on Advanced Information Networking and Applications-Workshops (aina workshops 2008)* (pp. 44-49). IEEE.

Angle of View. (n.d.). In *Wikipedia*. Retrieved December 15, 2019, from https://en.wikipedia.org/wiki/Angle_of_view#Measuring_a_camera's_field_of_view

Anstadt, S. P., Bradley, S., Burnette, A., & Medley, L. L. (2013). Virtual worlds: Relationship between real life and experience in second life. *International Review of Research in Open and Distance Learning*, *14*(4), 160–190. doi:10.19173/irrodl.v14i4.1454

Anthes, C., García-Hernandez, R. J., Wiedemann, M., & Kranzlmüller, D. (2016, March). *State of the art of virtual reality technology*. Paper presented at the 2016 IEEE Aerospace Conference, Yellowstone, MT. 10.1109/AERO.2016.7500674

Antonacci, D., DiBartolo, S., Edwards, N., Fritch, K., McMullen, B., & Murch-Shafer, R. (2008). *The power of virtual worlds in education: A second primer and resource for exploring the potential of virtual worlds to impact teaching and learning. ANGEL Learning ISLE Steering Committee.* Retrieved December 15, 2014, from http://www.angellearning.com/products/secondlife/downloads/The%20Power%20of%20Virtual%20Worlds%20in%20Education_0708.pdf

Arango-López, J., Valdivieso, C. C. C., Collazos, C. A., Vela, F. L. G., & Moreira, F. (2019). CREANDO: Tool for creating pervasive games to increase the learning motivation in higher education students. *Telematics and Informatics*, *38*, 62–73. doi:10.1016/j.tele.2018.08.005

Ariyana, Y., & Wuryandari, A. I. (2012). Virtual interaction on augmented reality for education with nonparametric belief propagation algorithm. *Procedia: Social and Behavioral Sciences*, *67*, 590–599. doi:10.1016/j.sbspro.2012.11.364

Arnone, M., Small, R., Chauncey, S., & McKenna, H. (2011). Curiosity, interest and engagement in technology-pervasive learning environments: A new research agenda. *Educational Technology Research and Development*, *59*(2), 181–198. doi:10.100711423-011-9190-9

Arzate Cruz, C., & Ramirez Uresti, J. A. (2017). Player-centered game AI from a flow perspective: Towards a better understanding of past trends and future directions. *Entertainment Computing*, *20*, 11–24. doi:10.1016/j.entcom.2017.02.003

Ascione, L. (2017). *Brace yourself: AI is set to explode in education in the next four years.* https://www.eschoolnews.com/2017/05/22/brace-ai-set-explode-next-4-years/

Asher, T., Ogle, E., Bailenson, J. N., & Herrera, F. (2018). *Becoming homeless: A human experience.* ACM SIGGRAPH Virtual, Augmented, and Mixed Reality. doi:10.1145/3226552.3226576

Astheimer, P., Dai, F., Göbel, M., Kruse, R., Müller, S., & Zachmann, G. (1994). Realism in virtual reality. In *Artificial life and virtual reality* (pp. 189–209). John Wiley.

Athey, S., & Imbens, G. W. (2019). Machine learning methods that economists should know about. *Annual Review of Economics*, *11*(1), 685–725. doi:10.1146/annurev-economics-080217-053433

Atzori, B., Messeri, A., Vagnoli, L., Grotto, R. L., & Hoffman, H. G. (2019). Virtual reality as distraction technique for pain management in children and adolescents. Encyclopedia of information science and technology, 5955-5965. doi:10.4018/978-1-5225-2255-3.ch518

Auerbach, R. P., Alonso, J., Axinn, W. G., Cuijpers, P., Ebert, D. D., Green, J. G., ... Nock, M. K. (2016). Mental disorders among college students in the World Health Organization world mental health surveys. *Psychological Medicine*, *46*(14), 2955–2970. doi:10.1017/S0033291716001665 PMID:27484622

Auliya, R. N., & Munasiah, M. (2019, October). Mathematics learning instrument using augmented reality for learning 3D geometry. *Journal of Physics: Conference Series*, *1318*(1), 012069. doi:10.1088/1742-6596/1318/1/012069

Autor, D., & Dorn, D. (2013). The growth of low-skill service jobs and the polarization of the US labor market. *The American Economic Review*, *103*(5), 1553–1597. doi:10.1257/aer.103.5.1553

Averbakh, I. (2012). *A History of Chess : From Chaturanga to the Present Day.* Russell Enterprises, Inc.

Aydoğan, H., Aras, F., & Karakas, E. (2010, June). An assessment on distance education in a 3D virtual environment: How to produce electricity in a hydroelectric power plant. In *2010 2nd International Conference on Education Technology and Computer* (Vol. 1, pp. V1-346). IEEE.

Aydogan, H., & Aras, F. (2019). Design, simulation and virtual implementation of a novel fundamental programmable logic controllers laboratory in a 3D virtual world. *International Journal of Electrical Engineering Education*. Advance online publication. doi:10.1177/0020720919856249

Azuma, R. (1997). A Survey of Augmented Reality. *Presence (Cambridge, Mass.)*, *6*(4), 355–385. doi:10.1162/pres.1997.6.4.355

B.F.A. in Immersive Reality. (n.d.). Retrieved May 20, 2020, from https://www.scad.edu/academics/programs/immersive-reality/degrees/bfa

Babich, N. (2019). *How VR in education will change how we learn and teach.* Retrieved from: https://xd.adobe.com/ideas/principles/emerging-technology/virtual-reality-will-change-learn-teach/

Bainbridge, W. (2007). The scientific research potential of virtual worlds. *Science*, *317*(5837), 472–476. doi:10.1126cience.1146930 PMID:17656715

Bajura, M., Fuchs, H., & Ohbuchi, R. (1992). Merging virtual objects with the real world: Seeing ultrasound imagery within the patient. *Computer Graphics*, *26*(2), 203–210. doi:10.1145/142920.134061

Baker, S. C., Wentz, R. K., & Woods, M. M. (2009). Using virtual worlds in education: Second Life® as an educational tool. *Teaching of Psychology*, *36*(1), 59–64. doi:10.1080/00986280802529079

Bakhshi, H., Hargreaves, I., & Mateos-Garcia, J. (2013). *A manifesto for the creative economy.* Retrieved from http://orca.cf.ac.uk/49323/

Bal, A., Crittenden, V., Halvorson, W., Pitt, L., & Parent, M. (2015, January). Second best in Second Life: Teaching marketing cases in a virtual world environment. In *Proceedings of the 2010 Academy of Marketing Science (AMS) Annual Conference* (pp. 211-211). Springer International Publishing. 10.1007/978-3-319-11797-3_119

Balcikanli, C. (2012). Language learning in Second Life: American and Turkish Students' Experiences. *Turkish Online Journal of Distance Education*, *13*(2), 131–146.

Barnes, G., Crowe, B., & Schaefer, E. (2007). *The cost of teacher turnover in five school districts: A pilot study.* National Commission on Teaching and America's Future.

Barrett, M. (2012*). Using virtual reality modelling to enhance electrical safety and design in the built environment* (Unpublished doctoral dissertation). Technological University Dublin, Republic of Ireland. doi:10.21427/D7W31P

Barr, R., & Tagg, J. (1995, November/December). From teaching to learning: A new paradigm for undergraduate education. *Change*, 13–25.

Barry, D. M., Kanematsu, H., Fukumura, Y., Kobayashi, T., Ogawa, N., & Nagai, H. (2013). US Students Carry out Nuclear Safety Project in a Virtual Environment. *Procedia Computer Science*, *22*, 1354–1360. doi:10.1016/j.procs.2013.09.224

Bartle, R. (2003). *Designing virtual worlds*. New Riders Publishing.

Ba, S., Ke, D., Stallaert, J., & Zhang, Z. (2010). Why give away something for nothing? Investigating virtual goods pricing and permission strategies. *ACM Transactions on Management Information Systems*, *1*(1), 1–22. doi:10.1145/1877725.1877729

Bauer, M., Bruegge, B., Klinker, G., MacWilliams, A., Reicher, T., Riss, S., & Wagner, M. (2001, October). Design of a component-based augmented reality framework. In *Proceedings IEEE and ACM International Symposium on Augmented Reality* (pp. 45-54). IEEE. 10.1109/ISAR.2001.970514

Behm-Morawitz, E., & Ta, D. (2014). Cultivating virtual stereotypes?: The impact of video game play on racial/ethnic stereotypes. *The Howard Journal of Communications*, *25*(1), 1–15. doi:10.1080/10646175.2013.835600

Bélisle, J., & Bodur, H. (2010). Avatars as information: Perception of consumers based on their avatars in virtual worlds. *Psychology and Marketing*, *27*(8), 741–765. doi:10.1002/mar.20354

Benford, S., Greenhalgh, C., Reynard, G., Brown, C., & Koleva, B. (1998). Understanding and constructing shared spaces with mixed-reality boundaries. *ACM Transactions on Computer-Human Interaction*, *5*(3), 185–223. doi:10.1145/292834.292836

Bers, M., & Chau, C. (2010). The virtual campus of the future: Stimulating and simulating civic actions in a virtual world. *Journal of Computing in Higher Education*, *22*(1), 1–23. doi:10.100712528-009-9026-3

Bhattarai, A., Alsadoon, A., Prasad, P. W. C., Pham, L., Haddad, S., Hsu, J., & Deva, A. (2019). A novel multiple communication paths for surgical telepresence videos delivery of the maxilla area in oral and maxillofacial surgery. *International Journal of Computer Assisted Radiology and Surgery*, *14*(5), 873–883. doi:10.100711548-018-01904-y PMID:30649669

Billinghurst, M. (2002). *Augmented Reality in Education*. Retrieved from http://solomonalexis.com/downloads/ar_edu.pdf

Billinghurst, M., Kato, H., & Poupyrev, I. (2001). The MagicBook: A transitional AR interface. *Computers & Graphics*, *25*(5), 745–753. doi:10.1016/S0097-8493(01)00117-0

Billinghurst, M., Kato, H., & Poupyrev, I. (2001). The magicbook-moving seamlessly between reality and virtuality. *IEEE Computer Graphics and Applications*, *21*(3), 6–8.

Biocca, F., Harms, C., & Burgoon, J. K. (2003). Toward a more robust theory and measure of social presence: Review and suggested criteria. *Presence (Cambridge, Mass.)*, *12*(5), 456–480. doi:10.1162/105474603322761270

Birt, J., Hovorka, D., & Nelson, J. (2016). *Interdisciplinary translation of comparative visualization.* Working Paper. https://arxiv.org/ftp/arxiv/papers/1606/1606.03551.pdf

Birt, J., Stromberga, Z., Cowling, M., & Moro, C. (2018). Mobile mixed reality for experiential learning and simulation in medical and health sciences education. *Information*, *9*(2), 31. doi:10.3390/info9020031

Bizzari, V., Dambha-Miller, H., Laughaey, W. F., & Carvalho, C. (2019). Defining therapeutic empathy: The philosopher's view. *Journal of the Royal Society of Medicine*, *112*(3), 91–95. doi:10.1177/0141076819831869 PMID:30868927

Björk, S., & Holopainen, J. (2004). *Patterns in Game Design*. Charles River Media.

Blakeman, P. (2018). Virtual Reality: What it offers, and how it can be used easily (and inexpensively) by health & social care tutors. *Journal of Practice Teaching & Learning*, *16*(1), 81–93.

Blanco, C., Okuda, M., Wright, C., Hasin, D. S., Grant, B. F., Liu, S. M., & Olfson, M. (2008). Mental health of college students and their non-college-attending peers. *Archives of General Psychiatry*, *65*(12), 1429–1437. doi:10.1001/archpsyc.65.12.1429 PMID:19047530

Blascovich, J., & Bailenson, J. (2005). Immersive virtual environments and education simulations. In S. Cohen, K. E. Portney, D. Rehberger, & C. Thorsen (Eds.), *Virtual decisions: Digital simulations for teaching reasoning in social science and humanities immersive virtual environments* (pp. 229–253). Lawrence Erlbaum Associates.

Blascovich, J., & Bailenson, J. (2011). *Infinite reality: Avatars, eternl life, new worlds, and the dawn of the virtual evolution*. William Morrow & Company.

Bogo, M., Rawlings, M., Katz, E., Logie, C., & Council on Social Work Education (CSWE). (2014). *Using simulation in assessment and teaching: OSCE adapted for social work*. Council on Social Work Education.

Bojanova, I. (2011). Physical presence through virtual worlds. *IT Professional*, *13*(4), 4–5. doi:10.1109/MITP.2011.66

Bordnick, P. S., Carter, B. L., & Traylor, A. C. (2011). What virtual reality research in addictions can tell us about the future of obesity assessment and treatment. *Journal of Diabetes Science and Technology*, *5*(2), 265–271. doi:10.1177/193229681100500210 PMID:21527092

Botella, C., Perpiña, C., & Baños, R. M. (1998). Virtual reality: A new clinical setting lab. *Studies in Health Technology and Informatics*, *58*, 73–81. PMID:10350931

Boulos, M. N. K., Hetherington, L., & Wheeler, S. (2007). Second Life: An overview of the potential of 3-D virtual worlds in medical and health education. *Health Information and Libraries Journal*, *24*(4), 233–245. doi:10.1111/j.1471-1842.2007.00733.x PMID:18005298

Bowman, D. A., & Hodges, L. F. (1999). Formalizing the design, evaluation, and application of interaction techniques for immersive virtual environments. *Journal of Visual Languages and Computing*, *10*(1), 37–53. doi:10.1006/jvlc.1998.0111

Bowman, D. A., Koller, D., & Hodges, L. F. (1998). A methodology for the evaluation of travel techniques for immersive virtual environments. *Virtual Reality (Waltham Cross)*, *3*(2), 120–131. doi:10.1007/BF01417673

BoyV. (2020, April 1). Retrieved 2020, from https://en.wikipedia.org/wiki/Virtual_Boy

Bradshaw, D. (2009). *New practices in flexible learning: virtual worlds – real learning! Pedagogical Reflections.* Retrieved Jan. 30, 2009, from http://virtualworlds.flexiblelearning.net.au/reports/VWRL_pedagog_reflect.pdf

Braman, J., Meiselwitz, G., & Vincenti, G. (2013). Virtual worlds in the general education curriculum. *Proceedings of the Society for Information Technology & Teacher Education International Conference, 2013*(1), 2692-2697.

Braman, J., Dudley, A., Colt, K., Vincenti, V., & Wang, Y. (2011). Gaining insight into the application of second life in a computer course: Student's perspectives. *Proceedings of the 14th HCI International Conference on Online Communities and Social Computing.* 10.1007/978-3-642-21796-8_3

Braman, J., & Yancy, B. (2017). Infusing Writing and Research in Technology Courses through Multi-User Virtual Environments. *Proceedings of the 11th International Multi-Conference on Society, Cybernetics and Informatics (IMSCI 2017).*

Brand, C., & Repenning, A. (2017). Helping teacher and students learn to use 3D in agent cubes online. 2017 IEE Blocks and beyond workshop (B & B), 103-104.

Bray, D. A., & Konsynski, B. (2008). Virtual worlds, virtual economies, virtual institutions. *Proceedings of Virtual Worlds and New Realities Conference.*

Bricken, M., & Byrne, C. (1992). *Summer students in virtual reality: A pilot study on educational applications of VR technology.* University of Washington, Human Interface Technology Laboratory.

Brightman, J. (2017). Global esports revenue to hit $2.3 billion in 2022. *Gamesindustry.biz.* Retreived from: https://www.gamesindustry.biz/articles/2017-12-11-global-esports-revenue-to-hit-usd2-3-billion-in-2020-superdata

Britain, S. (1999). A framework for pedagogical evaluation of virtual world learning environments. JISC Technology Applications Programme, Report 41: Joint Information Systems Committee of the Higher Educational Funding Council, Manchester, UK.

Britain, S. (1999). A framework for pedagogical evaluation of virtual world learning environments. JISC Technology Applications Programme, Report 41: Joint Information Systems Committee of the Higher Educational Funding Council.

Britain, S., & Liber, O. (2004). A framework for pedagogical evaluation of virtual learning environments. *JISC Technology Applications Program*, (41). Retrieved from https://hal.archives-ouvertes.fr/hal-00696234/document

Bronack, S., Sanders, R., Cheney, A., Riedl, R., Tashner, J., & Matzen, N. (2008). Presence Pedagogy: Teaching and Learning in a 3D Virtual Immersive World. *International Journal on Teaching and Learning in Higher Education*, *20*(1), 59–69.

Brooks, F. P. (1999). What's real about virtual reality? *IEEE Computer Graphics and Applications, 19*(6), 16–27. doi:10.1109/38.799723

Brownell, M. T., Sindelar, P. T., Kiely, M. T., & Danielson, L. C. (2010). Special education teacher quality and preparation: Exposing foundations, constructing a new model. *Exceptional Children, 76*(3), 357–377. doi:10.1177/001440291007600307

Brown, R., Rasmussen, R., Baldwin, I., & Wyeth, P. (2012). Design and implementation of a virtual world training simulation of ICU first hour handover processes. *Australian Critical Care, 25*(3), 178–187. doi:10.1016/j.aucc.2012.02.005 PMID:22436543

Buesing, M., & Cook, M. (2013). Augmented reality comes to physics. *The Physics Teacher, 51*(4), 226–228. doi:10.1119/1.4795365

Burdea, G. C., & Coiffet, P. (2003). *Virtual reality technology* (2nd ed.). Wiley-IEEE Press. doi:10.1162/105474603322955950

Burgess, M. C. R., Dill, K. E., Stermer, S. P., Burgess, S. R., & Brown, B. P. (2011). Playing with prejudice: The prevalence and consequences of racial stereotypes in video games. *Media Psychology, 14*(3), 289–311. doi:10.1080/15213269.2011.596467

Burke, B. (2014). *Gamify: How gamification motivates people to do extraordinary things*. Gartner, Inc.

Burrell, J. (2020, March 16). *The grim numbers behind adolescent suicides and attempts* [Web log post]. https://www.verywellmind.com/college-and-teen-suicide-statistics-3570768

Byrne, C. M. (1996). *Water on tap: The use of virtual reality as an educational tool* (Doctoral dissertation). University of Washington.

Callaghan, M. J., McCusker, K., Losada, J. L., Harkin, J. G., & Wilson, S. (2009, August). *Integrating virtual worlds & virtual learning environments for online education. In 2009 International IEEE Consumer Electronics Society's Games Innovations Conference*. IEEE.

Callaghan, N. (2016). Investigating the role of Minecraft in educational learning environments. *Educational Media International, 53*(4), 244–260. doi:10.1080/09523987.2016.1254877

Calongne, C., & Hiles, J. (2007). Blended Realities: A Virtual Tour of Education in Second Life. *Proceedings of TCC Worldwide Online Conference 2007*, 70-90. Retrieved from http://etec.hawaii.edu/proceedings/2007/calongne.pdf

Campbell, C. A., & Dahir, C. A. (1997). *Sharing the vision: The ASCA national standards for school counseling programs*. American School Counselor Association.

Caponetto, I., Earp, J., & Ott, M. (2014). Gamification and education: a literature review. In *Eighth European Conference on Games Based Learning* (pp.50-57). https://books.google.com/books?id=IedEBQAAQBAJ&pg=PA50&lpg=PA50&dq=itd+cnr+genova+italy+caponetto&source=bl&ots=bF0j6T6qYY&sig=ACfU3U3fzuqibaUDmOIdMFWZzVDlWkNP_Q&hl=en&ppis=_c&sa=X&ved=2ahUKEwjU9aqLmM3oAhWbl3IEHaq2C5kQ6AEwAHoECAsQKA#v=onepage&q=itd%20cnr%20genova%20italy%20caponetto&f=false

Carini, R., Kuh, G., & Klein, S. (2006). Student engagement and student learning: Testing the linkages. *Research in Higher Education, 47*(1), 1–32. doi:10.100711162-005-8150-9

Carr, C. (2017). *Using Minecraft to engage the public and plan better public spaces*. Rivard Report. https://therivardreport.com/using-minecraft-to engage-the-public-and-plan-better-public-spaces/

Carver-Thomas, D., & Darling-Hammond, L. (2019). The trouble with teacher turnover: How teacher attrition affects students and schools. *Education Policy Analysis Archives, 27*(36), 1–32. doi:10.14507/epaa.27.3699

Case Study: How VR Assists in Writing Skills Training. (2019). Retrieved May 20, 2020, from https://en-vr.101.com/news/06182019/053429513.shtml

Caudell, T. P., & Mizell, D. W. (1992, January). Augmented reality: An application of heads-up display technology to manual manufacturing processes. In *Proceedings of the twenty-fifth Hawaii international conference on system sciences* (Vol. 2, pp. 659-669). IEEE. 10.1109/HICSS.1992.183317

Chan, E., Foster, S., Sambell, R., & Leong, P. (2018). Clinical efficacy of virtual reality for acute procedural pain management: A systematic review and meta-analysis. *PLoS One*, *13*(7), 1–13. doi:10.1371/journal.pone.0200987 PMID:30052655

Chang, L. (2015). Go shopping from the comfort of your own home with your virtual reality headset. *Digital Trends.* Retrieved July 1, 2015 from http://www.digitaltrends.com/cool/retail/

Chang, C.-M., Hsu, C.-H., Hsu, C.-F., & Chen, K.-T. (2016). Performance measurements of virtual reality systems: Quantifying the timing and positioning accuracy. In *Proceedings of the 24th ACM International Conference on Multimedia* (pp. 655-659). ACM. 10.1145/2964284.2967303

Chart, S. (2019). [Mobile application software]. Retrieved May 20, 2020 from https://play.google.com/store/apps/details?id=com.escapistgames.starchart&hl=en_US

Chaudhri, V. K., Gunning, D., Lane, H. C., & Roschelle, J. (2013). Intelligent learning technologies Part 2: Applications of artificial intelligence to contemporary and emerging educational challenges. *AI Magazine*, *34*(4), 10–12. doi:10.1609/aimag.v34i4.2518

Chen, C. P., & Wang, C. H. (2015, December). The effects of learning style on mobile augmented-reality-facilitated English vocabulary learning. In *2015 2nd International Conference on Information Science and Security (ICISS)* (pp. 1-4). IEEE. 10.1109/ICISSEC.2015.7371036

Cheng, K. H., & Tsai, C. C. (2013). Affordances of augmented reality in science learning: Suggestions for future research. *Journal of Science Education and Technology*, *22*(4), 449–462. doi:10.100710956-012-9405-9

Cheng, Y., & Wang, S.-H. (2011). Applying a 3D virtual learning environment to facilitate student's application ability–The case of marketing. *Computers in Human Behavior*, *27*(1), 576–584. doi:10.1016/j.chb.2010.10.008

Chen, X., Siau, K., & Nah, F. F.-H. (2009). 3-D virtual worlds: Education and learning. *Proceedings of the Eighth Annual Workshop on HCI Research in MIS (SIGHCI 2009).*

Chen, X., Siau, K., & Nah, F. F.-H. (2010). 3-D Virtual World Education: An Empirical Comparison With Face-To-Face Classroom. *Thirty First International Conference on Information Systems (ICIS)*, 260.

Chesham, R. K., Malouff, J. M., & Schutte, N. S. (2018). Meta-Analysis of the efficacy of virtual reality exposure therapy for social anxiety. *Behaviour Change*, *35*(3), 152–166. doi:10.1017/bec.2018.15

Chiang, T. H. C., Yang, S. J., & Hwang, G. J. (2014). An augmented reality-based mobile learning system to improve students' learning achievements and motivations in natural science inquiry activities. *Journal of Educational Technology & Society*, *17*(4), 352–365.

Childs, M. (2007). Real Learning in Virtual Worlds. *Warwick International Journal, 30*(2).

Childs, M. (2010). *Learners' experience of presence in Virtual Worlds* (Doctoral dissertation). Institute of Education. Retrieved from https://files.warwick.ac.uk/mchilds1/files/childs+thesis+final.pdf

Chini, J., Straub, C. L., & Thomas, K. H. (2014). Learning from avatars: Learning assistants practice physics pedagogy in a classroom simulator. *Physical Review Physics Education Research, 12*(1), 010117-1- 010117-15.

Chinnock, C. (1994). Virtual reality in surgery and medicine. *Hospital Technology Series, 13*(18), 1–48. PMID:10172193

Choo, F. (2018, October 31). *Learning about depression via VR tools.* https://www.straitstimes.com/singapore/health/learning-about-depression-via-vr-tools

Chouhan, R., & Sharma, G. K. (2015). Virtual Reality: In gaming. *International Journal of Multidisciplinary Consortium, 2*(2), 36.

Cinganotto, L. (2019). Gamification and virtual worlds for language learning. *Form@ re-Open Journal per la formazione in rete, 19*(1), 133-148.

Cipresso, P., Giglioli, I. A. C., Raya, M. A., & Riva, G. (2018). The past, present, and future of virtual and augmented reality research: A network and cluster analysis of the literature. *Frontiers in Psychology, 9*, 2086. doi:10.3389/fpsyg.2018.02086 PMID:30459681

Civelek, T., Ucar, E., Ustunel, H., & Aydın, M. K. (2014). Effects of a Haptic Augmented Simulation on K-12 Students' Achievement and their Attitudes towards Physics. *Eurasia Journal of Mathematics. Science and Technology Education, 10*(6), 565–574. doi:10.12973/eurasia.2014.1122a

Claman, F. L. (2015). The impact of multiuser virtual environments on student engagement. *Nurse Education in Practice, 15*(1), 13–16. doi:10.1016/j.nepr.2014.11.006 PMID:25532889

Clark, M. R. (2005). Negotiating the freshman year: Challenges and strategies among first-year college students. *Journal of College Student Development, 46*(3), 296–316. doi:10.1353/csd.2005.0022

Clark, S., & Maher, M. L. (2001). The role of place in designing a learner centred virtual learning environment. In *Computer Aided Architectural Design Futures 2001* (pp. 187–200). Springer. doi:10.1007/978-94-010-0868-6_15

Clus, D., Larsen, M. E., Lemey, C., & Berrouiguet, S. (2018). The use of virtual reality in patients with eating disorders: Systematic review. *Journal of Medical Internet Research, 20*(4), e157. doi:10.2196/jmir.7898 PMID:29703715

Cochran-Smith, M., McQuillan, P., Mitchell, K., Terrell, D. G., Barnatt, J., D'Souza, L., Jong, C., Shakman, K., Lam, K., & Gleeson, A. M. (2012). A longitudinal study of teaching practice and early career decisions: A cautionary tale. *American Educational Research Journal, 49*(5), 844–880. doi:10.3102/0002831211431006

Cogburn, C. D., Bailenson, J. N., Ogle, E., Asher, T., & Nichols, T. (2018). *1000 cut journey. ACM SIGGRAPH 2018 Virtual.* Augmented, and Mixed Reality. doi:10.1145/3226552.3226575

Cohen, A., & Brawer, F. (2003). *The American community college* (4th ed.). Jossey-Bass Publishing.

Colman, H. (2019). *6 adult learning theories and how to put them into practice.* iSpring Solutions, Inc. https://www.ispringsolutions.com/blog/adult-learning-theories

Coomes, G. (2019). Debriefing in simulation-based learning experiences: A Concept analysis. *The Midwest Quarterly, 60*(3), 298–310.

Corrigan, P., & Bink, A. B. (2005). *On the stigma of mental illness.* American Psychological Association.

Costello, S. (2020). Everything you need to know about virtual reality on i-phone. *Lifewire.* Retrieved May 3, 2020 from https://www.lifewire.com/virtual-reality-on-iphone-4125903

Council on Social Work Education. (2015). 2015 *Educational policy and accreditation standards.* Author. https://www.cswe.org/getattachment/Accreditation/Accreditation-Process/2015- EPAS/2015EPAS_Web_FINAL.pdf.aspx

Crăciun, D., & Bunoiu, M. (2016, July). Augmented reality in Romanian science education Pros and cons. In *The International Scientific Conference eLearning and Software for Education* (*Vol. 3*, pp. 193-199). "Carol I" National Defence University.

Crăciun, D., & Bunoiu, M. (2017, December). Boosting physics education through mobile augmented reality. In. AIP Conference Proceedings: Vol. 1916. *No. 1* (p. 050003). AIP Publishing. doi:10.1063/1.5017456

Croatti, A., & Ricci, A. (2018, June). A model and platform for building agent-based pervasive mixed reality systems. In *International Conference on Practical Applications of Agents and Multi-Agent Systems* (pp. 127-139). Springer. 10.1007/978-3-319-94580-4_10

Csikszentmihalyi, M. (1990). *Flow: The psychology of optimal experience*. Harper Perennial Modern Classics.

CubeS. A. S. (n.d.). Retrieved 2020, from https://benayoun.com/z_a/sascube/index.en.html

Cukier, K., & Mayer-Schoenberger, V. (2013). The rise of big data: How it's changing the way we think about the world. *Foreign Affairs*, *92*(3), 28–40.

Cummings, J. J., & Bailenson, J. N. (2015). How immersive is enough? A meta-analysis of the effect of immersive technology on user presence. *Media Psychology*, 1–38.

Curcio, I. D. D., Dipace, A., & Norlund, A. (2016). Virtual realities and education. *Research on Education and Media, 8*(2). 1-9. https://doi:10.1515/rem-2016-0019

Dafoulas, G., Saleeb, N., & Loomes, M. (2012, June). The impact of 3D virtual environments on communication patterns. In *2012 International Conference on Information Technology Based Higher Education and Training (ITHET)* (pp. 1-5). IEEE. 10.1109/ITHET.2012.6246065

Dailey-Hebert, A., Donnelli-Sallee, E., & DiPadova-Stocks, L. (2008). Service-eLearning as integrated pedagogy: An introduction. In A. Dailey-Hebert, E. Donnelli-Sallee, & L. DiPadova-Stocks (Eds.), *Service-eLearning: Educating for citizenship* (pp. 1–5). Information Age Publishing.

Dalgarno, B., Gregory, S., Carlson, L., Lee, M. J. W., & Tynan, B. (2013). *A systematic review and environmental analysis of the use of 3D immersive virtual worlds in Australian and New Zealand higher education institutions* (Final Report). Armidale, Australia: DEHub: Innovation in Distance Education, University of New England. Retrieved from http://www.dehub.edu.au/downloads/VWSSP_Report_V2_TD_200613_dehub.pd

Dalgarno, B., & Lee, M. J. W. (2009). What are the learning affordances of 3-D virtual environments? *British Journal of Educational Technology*, *41*(1), 10–32. doi:10.1111/j.1467-8535.2009.01038.x

Damer, B. (1997). *Avatars! Exploring and building virtual worlds on the Internet*. Retrieved from http://www.digital-space.com/avatars/book/chtu/chtu1.htm

Davis, I. I. J., Goel, M., Hylands, C., Kienhuis, B., Lee, E. A., Liu, J., Liu, X., Muliadi, L., Neuendorffer, S., Reekie, J., Smyth, N., Tsay, J., & Xiong, Y. (1999). *Overview of the Ptolemy project* (Vol. 99). ERL Technical Report UCB/ERL No. M99/37, Dept. EECS, University of California, Berkeley, CA.

Dawley, L. (2009). Social network knowledge construction: Emerging virtual world pedagogy. *On The Horizon, 17*(2), 109-121. doi:10.1108/10748120910965494

Daydream – Daydream View. (n.d.). Retrieved December 18, 2019, from https://arvr.google.com/daydream/smartphonevr/

De Freitas, S. (2008). *Serious virtual worlds: A scoping study.* Joint Information Systems Committee. Retrieved February 28th, 2020 from https://www.jisc.ac.uk/media/documents/publications/seriousvirtualworldsv1.pdf

De Freitas, S. (2008). *Serious virtual worlds: A scoping study.* Retrieved from http://citeseerx.ist.psu.edu/viewdoc/download?doi=10.1.1.176.1630&rep=rep1&type=pdf

De Lucia, A., Francese, R., Passero, I., & Tortora, G. (2009). Development and evaluation of a virtual campus on Second Life: The case of SecondDMI. *Computers & Education*, *52*(1), 220–233. doi:10.1016/j.compedu.2008.08.001

Deb, S. (2019, July 26). Opinion | What do you do about this 'IIT dream' madness of parents? [Web log post]. https://www.livemint.com/opinion/columns/opinion-what-do-you-do-about-this-iit-dream-madness-of-parents-1564136143781.html

Dede, C. (2009). Immersive interfaces for engagement and learning. *Science*, *323*(5910), 66–69. doi:10.1126cience.1167311 PMID:19119219

Desktop, V. (2019). [Windows application software]. Retrieved December 7th, 2019 from https://www.vrdesktop.net/

Detlefsen, J. (2014). *The Cosmic Perspective: Teaching Middle-School Children Astronomy Using Ego-Centric Virtual Reality* (Unpublished master's thesis). Alborg University, Alborg, Denmark. Retrieved June 2, 2020 from https://projekter.aau.dk/projekter/files/198097322/Portfolio_JanDetlefsen.pdf

Dexter, S., Herring, M. & Thomas, T. (2012). Editorial: Technology Leadership for the Teacher Education Initiative. *Contemporary Issues in Technology and Teacher Education, 12*(3), 255-263.

Di Blas, N., & Poggi, C. (2007). European virtual classrooms: Building effective "virtual" educational experiences. *Virtual Reality (Waltham Cross)*, *11*(2-3), 129–143. doi:10.100710055-006-0060-4

Diamandis, P. (2019). *How augmented reality will overall our most crucial industries*. https://singularityhub.com/2019/09/27/how-augmented-reality-will-overhaul-our-most-crucial-industries/

Diamandis, P., & Kotler, S. (2020). *The future is faster than you think.* Simon & Schuster.

Dickey, M. D. (2003). Teaching in 3D: Pedagogical Affordances and Constraints of 3D Virtual Worlds for Synchronous Distance Education. *Distance Education*, *24*(1), 105–121. doi:10.1080/01587910303047

Dickey, M. D. (2005a). Brave new (interactive) worlds: A review of the design affordances and constraints of two 3D virtual worlds as interactive learning environments. *Interactive Learning Environments*, *13*(1-2), 121–137. doi:10.1080/10494820500173714

Dickey, M. D. (2005b). Three-dimensional virtual worlds and distance learning: Two case studies of Active Worlds as a medium for distance learning. *British Journal of Educational Technology*, *36*(3), 439–451. doi:10.1111/j.1467-8535.2005.00477.x

Dieker, L. A., Lignugaris-Kraft, B., Hynes, M., & Hughes, C. E. (2016). Mixed reality environments in teacher education: Development and future applications. *Online in Real Time: Using WEB 2.0 for Distance Education in Rural Special Education*, 122-131.

Dieker, L., Hughes, C., Hynes, M., & Straub, C. (2017). Using simulated virtual environments to improve teacher performance. *School-University Partnerships*, *10*(3), 62–81.

Dieker, L., Hynes, M., Hughes, C., & Smith, E. (2008). Implications of mixed reality and simulation technologies on special education and teacher preparation. *Focus on Exceptional Children*, *40*(6), 1. doi:10.17161/foec.v40i6.6877

Dieker, L., Hynes, M., Stapleton, C., & Hughes, C. (2007). Virtual classrooms: STAR simulator. *New Learning Technology SALT*, *4*, 1–22.

Dieker, L., & Rodriguez, J., Lignugaris/Kraft, B., Hynes, M., & Hughes, C. E. (2013). The potential of simulated environments in teacher education: Current and future possibilities. *Teacher Education and Special Education: The Journal of the Teacher Education Division of the Council for Exceptional Children*, *37*(1), 21–33. doi:10.1177/0888406413512683

Dieker, L., Straub, C., Hughes, C., Hynes, M., & Hardin, S. (2014). Learning from virtual students. *Educational Leadership*, *71*(8), 54–58.

Domínguez, A., Saenz-de-Navarrete, J., de-Marcos, L., Fernández-Sanz, L., Pagés, C., & Martínez-Herráiz, J. (2013). Gamifying learning experiences: Practical Implications and Outcomes. *Computer Education*, *63*, 380–392. doi:10.1016/j.compedu.2012.12.020

Doney, I. (2019). Research into effective gamification features to inform e-learning design. *Research in Learning Technology*, *27*(0), 1–17. doi:10.25304/rlt.v27.2093

Dong, P., Ma, B., & Wang, F. (2010, May). Development and evaluation of an experiential learning service in 3D virtual world. In *2010 International Conference on Service Sciences* (pp. 374-378). IEEE. 10.1109/ICSS.2010.37

dos Santos, F. R., Guetl, C., Bailey, P. H., & Harward, V. J. (2010, April). Dynamic virtual environment for multiple physics experiments in higher education. In *IEEE EDUCON 2010 Conference* (pp. 731-736). IEEE. 10.1109/EDUCON.2010.5492507

Dreher, C., Reiners, T., Dreher, N., & Dreher, H. (2009, June). 3D virtual worlds as collaborative communities enriching human endeavours: Innovative applications in e-Learning. In *2009 3rd IEEE International Conference on Digital Ecosystems and Technologies* (pp. 151-156). IEEE.

DU Amache Research Project. (n.d.). Retrieved May 20, 2020, from http://portfolio.du.edu/amache

du Boulay, B. (2016). Artificial intelligence as an effective classroom assistant. *IEEE Intelligent Systems*, *31*(6), 76–81. doi:10.1109/MIS.2016.93

Dudley, A., & Braman, J. (2015). Using virtual worlds in ethical case studies: Evaluating computer students' perceptions. Proceedings from the 19th World Multi-conference on Systemics, Cybernetics and Informatics.

Duncan, I., Miller, A., & Jiang, S. (2012). A taxonomy of virtual world usage in education. *British Journal of Educational Technology, 43*(6). DOI: 10:1111/j.1467-8535.2011.01263.x

Duncan, I., Miller, A., & Jiang, S. (2012). A taxonomy of virtual worlds usage in education. *British Journal of Educational Technology*, *43*(6), 949–964. doi:10.1111/j.1467-8535.2011.01263.x

Dunleavy, M., Dede, C., & Mitchell, R. (2009). Affordances and limitations of immersive participatory augmented reality simulations for teaching and learning. *Journal of Science Education and Technology, 18*(1), 7e22.

Dunleavy, M., Dede, C., & Mitchell, R. (2009). Affordances and Limitations of Immersive Participatory Augmented Reality Simulations for Teaching and Learning. *Journal of Science Education and Technology*, *18*(1), 7–22. doi:10.100710956-008-9119-1

Dunleavy, M., Dede, C., & Mitchell, R. (2009). Affordances and limitations of immersive participatory augmented reality simulations for teaching and learning. *Journal of Science Education.*, *18*, 7–22.

Dunne, J. R., & McDonald, C. L. (2010). Pulse!!: A model for research and development of virtual-reality learning in military medical education and training. *Military Medicine*, *175*(7S), 25–27. doi:10.7205/MILMED-D-10-00158 PMID:23634475

Earth, V. R. (2017). [Mobile application software]. Retrieved May 20, 2020 from https://play.google.com/store/apps/details?id=uk.hls.earth&hl=en

Edirisingha, P., Nie, M., Pluciennik, M., & Young, R. (2009). Socialisation for learning at a distance in a 3-D multi-user virtual environment. *British Journal of Educational Technology*, *40*(3), 458–479. doi:10.1111/j.1467-8535.2009.00962.x

Eichenberg, C., & Brähler, E. (2013). Internet as a guide for mental health problems. *Psychotherapist*, *58*(1), 63–72. doi:10.100700278-012-0893-0

Eichenberg, C., & Wolters, C. (2012). Virtual Realities in the treatment of mental disorders: A Review of the current state of research. *Virtual Reality in Psychological. Medical and Pedagogical Applications*, *2*, 35–64.

Eijlers, R., Utens, E. M., Staals, L. M., de Nijs, P. F., Berghmans, J. M., Wijnen, R. M., Hillegers, M. H. J., Dierckx, B., & Legerstee, J. S. (2019). Meta-Analysis: Systematic Review and Meta-analysis of Virtual Reality in Pediatrics: Effects on Pain and Anxiety. *Anesthesia and Analgesia*, *129*(5), 1344–1353. doi:10.1213/ANE.0000000000004165 PMID:31136330

Eisenberg, D., Hunt, J., & Speer, N. (2013). Mental health in American colleges and universities: Variation across student subgroups and across campuses. *The Journal of Nervous and Mental Disease*, *201*(1), 60–67. doi:10.1097/NMD.0b013e31827ab077 PMID:23274298

El Sayed, N. A. M., Zayed, H. H., & Sharawy, M. I. (2011). ARSC: Augmented reality student card – an augmented reality solution for the education field. *Computers & Education*, *56*(4), 1045–1061. doi:10.1016/j.compedu.2010.10.019

Ellison, K., & Matthews, C. (2010). Virtual history: A socially networked pedagogy of Enlightenment. *Educational Research*, *52*(3), 297–307. doi:10.1080/00131881.2010.504065

Emmelkamp, P. M., Krijn, M., Hulsbosch, A. M., De Vries, S., Schuemie, M. J., & van der Mast, C. A. (2002). Virtual reality treatment versus exposure in vivo: A comparative evaluation in acrophobia. *Behaviour Research and Therapy*, *40*(5), 509–516. doi:10.1016/S0005-7967(01)00023-7 PMID:12038644

Encyclopædia Britannica. (2019). Virtual Reality (VR). *Encyclopædia Britannica Online*. Retrieved from: https://www.britannica.com/technology/virtual-reality#ref884313

Englund, C., Olofsson, A. D., & Price, L. (2017). Teaching with technology in higher education: Understanding conceptual change and development in practice. *Higher Education Research & Development*, *36*(1), 73–87. doi:10.1080/07294360.2016.1171300

Eschenbrenner, B., Nah, F. F.-H., & Siau, K. (2008). 3-D virtual worlds in education: Applications, benefits, issues, and opportunities. *Journal of Database Management*, *19*(4), 91–110. doi:10.4018/jdm.2008100106

eSports. (2019). Collegiate varsity esports programs. *Game Designing*. Retrieved from https://www.gamedesigning.org/schools/varsity-esports/

Estes, J. S. (2015). A call for teacher preparation programs to model integration of technology pedagogy and use throughout coursework. In S. Keengwe (Ed.), *Handbook of research on educational technology integration and active learning*. IGI Global. doi:10.4018/978-1-4666-8363-1.ch004

Etzioni, A. (1964). *Modern Organizations*. Prentice- Hall.

Evans, N. J., Forney, D. S., Guido, F. M., Patton, L. D., & Renn, K. A. (2009). *Student development in college: Theory, research, and practice*. John Wiley & Sons.

Eve, E. J., Koo, S., Alshihri, A. A., Cormier, J., Kozhenikov, M., Donoff, R. B., & Karimbux, N. (2014). Performance of dental students versus prosthodontics residents on a 3D immersive haptic simulator. *Journal of Dental Education, 78*(4), 630–637. PMID:24706694

Every Student Succeeds Act., Pub. L. No. 114–95, 1177 (2015).

Falloon, G. (2010). Using avatars and virtual environments in learning: What do they have to offer? *British Journal of Educational Technology, 41*(1), 108–122. doi:10.1111/j.1467-8535.2009.00991.x

Fan, S., Ng, T. T., Koenig, B. L., Herberg, J. S., Jiang, M., Shen, Z., & Zhao, Q. (2017). Image visual realism: From human perception to machine computation. *IEEE Transactions on Pattern Analysis and Machine Intelligence, 40*(9), 2180–2193. doi:10.1109/TPAMI.2017.2747150 PMID:28866484

Feiner, S. (2002, April). Augmented Reality: A New Way of Seeing. *Scientific American, 286*(4), 36–41. doi:10.1038c ientificamerican0402-48 PMID:11905108

Feiner, S., Macintyre, B., & Seligmann, D. (1993). Knowledge-based augmented reality. *Communications of the ACM, 36*(7), 53–62. doi:10.1145/159544.159587

Fernández-Avilés, D., Dotor, D., Contreras, D., & Salazar, J. C. (2016, February). Virtual labs: A new tool in the education: Experience of Technical University of Madrid. In *2016 13th International Conference on Remote Engineering and Virtual Instrumentation (REV)* (pp. 271-272). IEEE.

Fey, M. K., & Jenkins, L. S. (2015). Debriefing practices in nursing education programs: Results from a national study. *Nursing Education Perspectives, 36*(6), 361–366. doi:10.5480/14-1520 PMID:26753294

Fırat, M. (2010). Learning in 3D virtual worlds and current situation in Turkey. *Procedia: Social and Behavioral Sciences, 9*, 249–254. doi:10.1016/j.sbspro.2010.12.145

Fodor, L. A., Coteț, C. D., Cuijpers, P., Szamoskozi, Ș., David, D., & Cristea, I. A. (2018). The effectiveness of virtual reality based interventions for symptoms of anxiety and depression: A meta-analysis. *Scientific Reports, 8*(1), 1–13. doi:10.103841598-018-28113-6 PMID:29985400

Fonseca, D., Villagrasa, S., Navarro, I., Redondo, E., Valls, F., & Sánchez, A. (2017, April). Urban gamification in architecture education. In *World Conference on Information Systems and Technologies* (pp. 335-341). Springer.

Fotaris, P., Mastoras, T., Leinfellner, R., & Rosunally, Y. (2016). Climbing up the Leaderboard: An Empirical Study of Applying Gamification Techniques to a Computer Programming Class. *Electronic Journal of E-Learning, 14*(2), 94–110.

Frederiksen, J. G., Sørensen, S. M. D., Konge, L., Svendsen, M. B. S., Nobel-Jørgensen, M., Bjerrum, F., & Andersen, S. A. W. (2020). Cognitive load and performance in immersive virtual reality versus conventional virtual reality simulation training of laparoscopic surgery: A randomized trial. *Surgical Endoscopy, 34*(3), 1244–1252. doi:10.100700464-019-06887-8 PMID:31172325

Freeman, D., Reeve, S., Robinson, A., Ehlers, A., Clark, D., Spanlang, B., & Slater, M. (2017). Virtual reality in the assessment, understanding, and treatment of mental health disorders. *Psychological Medicine, 47*(14), 2393–2400. doi:10.1017/S003329171700040X PMID:28325167

Freina, L., & Ott, M. (2015, April). A literature review on immersive virtual reality in education: state of the art and perspectives. In *The International Scientific Conference eLearning and Software for Education* (*Vol. 1*, p. 133). "Carol I" National Defence University.

Freina, L., & Ott, M. (2015). A Literature review on immersive virtual reality in education: State of the art and perspectives. *ELearning & Software for Education, 1*, 133–141. doi:10.12753/2066-026X-15-020

Frey, C. B., & Osborne, M. A. (2017). The future of employment: How susceptible are jobs to computerisation? *Technological Forecasting and Social Change, 114*, 254–280. doi:10.1016/j.techfore.2016.08.019

Friedrich, M. J. (2017). Depression is the leading cause of disability around the world. *Journal of the American Medical Association, 317*(15), 1517–1517. doi:10.1001/jama.2017.3826 PMID:28418490

Furness, T. (n.d.). *Thomas Furness: American Electrical Engineer.* Retrieved May 20, 2020 from https://www.britannica.com/biography/Thomas-Furness

Gabbard, J. L. (1997*). A taxonomy of usability characteristics in virtual environments* (Unpublished doctoral dissertation). Virginia Tech.

Gabriel, K., & Flake, S. (2008). *Teaching unprepared students: strategies for promoting success and retention in higher education.* Stylus Publishing.

Gadh, R. (1998). *Virtual reality—a new technology for the mechanical engineer.* John Wiley & Sons, Inc.

Galbis-Córdova, A., Martí-Parreño, J., & Currás-Pérez, R. (2017). Higher Education Students' Attitude Towards the Use of Gamification for Competencies Development. *Journal of E-Learning & Knowledge Society, 13*(1), 129–146.

Gallagher, A. G., Ritter, E. M., Champion, H., Higgins, G., Fried, M. P., Moses, G., Smith, C. D., & Satava, R. M. (2005). Virtual reality simulation for the operating room: Proficiency-based training as a paradigm shift in surgical skills training. *Annals of Surgery, 241*(2), 364–372. doi:10.1097/01.sla.0000151982.85062.80 PMID:15650649

Gallagher, C. (2014). *Minecraft in the classroom: Ideas, inspiration, and student projects for teachers.* Peachpit Press.

Gallego, M. D., Bueno, S., & Noyes, J. (2016). Second Life adoption in education: A motivational model based on Uses and Gratifications theory. *Computers & Education, 100*, 81–93. doi:10.1016/j.compedu.2016.05.001

Gamage, V., Tretiakov, A., & Crump, B. (2011). Teacher perceptions of learning affordances of multi-user virtual environments. *Computers & Education, 57*(4), 2406–2413. doi:10.1016/j.compedu.2011.06.015

Gao, F., Noh, J. J., & Koehler, M. J. (2009). Comparing role-playing activities in Second Life and face-to-face environments. *Journal of Interactive Learning Research, 20*(4), 423–443.

Garb, Y. (Winter 1987). Virtual Reality, *Whole Earth Review,* (57).

Garcia-Zubia, J., Irurzun, J., Angulo, I., Hernandez, U., Castro, M., Sancristobal, E., Orduna, P., & Ruiz-de Garibay, J. (2010, April). SecondLab: A remote laboratory under Second Life. In *IEEE EDUCON 2010 Conference* (pp. 351-356). IEEE.

Garrison, D. R. (2009). Communities of inquiry in online learning. In P. L. Rogers (Ed.), *Encyclopedia of distance learning* (2nd ed., pp. 352–355). IGI Global. doi:10.4018/978-1-60566-198-8.ch052

Gavin, L. A., & Furman, W. (1989). Age differences in adolescents' perceptions of their peer groups. *Developmental Psychology, 25*(5), 827–834. doi:10.1037/0012-1649.25.5.827

Gazave, C. M., & Hatcher, A. R. (2017). Evaluating the use of Second Life™ for virtual team-based learning in an online undergraduate anatomy course. *Medical Science Educator, 27*(2), 217–227. doi:10.100740670-017-0374-8

Geller, L. L., & Greenberg, M. (2009). Managing the transition process from high school to college and beyond: Challenges for individuals, families, and society. *Social Work in Mental Health, 8*(1), 92–116. doi:10.1080/15332980902932466

Gerardi, M., Cukor, J., Difede, J., Rizzo, A., & Rothbaum, B. O. (2010). Virtual reality exposure therapy for post-traumatic stress disorder and other anxiety disorders. *Current Psychiatry Reports, 12*(4), 298–305. doi:10.100711920-010-0128-4 PMID:20535592

Getz, L. (2018). Social services innovations: A whole new world — Virtual reality in social work. *Social Work Today, 18*(2), 6. https://www.socialworktoday.com/archive/MA18p6.shtml

Ghanbarzadeh, R., Ghapanchi, A. H., & Blumenstein, M. (2015, May). Characteristics of research on the application of three-dimensional immersive virtual worlds in health. In *International Conference on Health Information Science* (pp. 213-224). Springer. 10.1007/978-3-319-19156-0_22

Ghanbarzadeh, R., Ghapanchi, A. H., Blumenstein, M., & Talaei-Khoei, A. (2014). A Decade of Research on the Use of Three-Dimensional Virtual Worlds in Health Care: A Systematic Literature Review. *Journal of Medical Internet Research, 16*(2), e47. doi:10.2196/jmir.3097 PMID:24550130

Ghezzi, T. L., & Corleta, O. C. (2016). 30 years of robotic surgery. *World Journal of Surgery, 40*(10), 2550–2557. doi:10.100700268-016-3543-9 PMID:27177648

Gibson, J. J. (1986). *The ecological approach to visual perception*. Houghton Mifflin.

Gilbert, R. L., Murphy, N. A., & Avalos, M. C. (2011). Communication patterns and satisfaction levels in three-dimensional versus real-life intimate relationships. *Cyberpsychology, Behavior, and Social Networking, 14*(10), 585–589. doi:10.1089/cyber.2010.0468 PMID:21381970

Girvan, C., & Savage, T. (2013). Guidelines for conducting text based interviews in virtual worlds. In Understanding learning in virtual worlds (pp. 21-40). Springer. doi:10.1007/978-1-4471-5370-2_2

Girvan, C. (2018). What is a virtual world? Definition and classification. *Educational Technology Research and Development, 66*(5), 1087–1100. doi:10.100711423-018-9577-y

Girvan, C., & Savage, T. (2019). Virtual worlds: A new environment for constructionist learning. *Computers in Human Behavior, 99*, 396–414. doi:10.1016/j.chb.2019.03.017

Glanz, K., Rizzo, A. S., & Graap, K. (2003). Virtual reality for psychotherapy: Current reality and future possibilities. *Psychotherapy (Chicago, Ill.), 40*(1-2), 55–67. doi:10.1037/0033-3204.40.1-2.55

Goldman, S. R., Lawless, K., Pellegrino, J. W., & Plants, R. (2005). Technology for teaching and learning with understanding. In J. M. Cooper (Ed.), *Classroom Teaching Skills* (8th ed., pp. 185–234). Houghton Mifflin.

Google Cardboard. (n.d.). Retrieved December 18, 2019, from https://arvr.google.com/cardboard/

Google, V. R. (2019). *Google Cardboard*. Retrieved https://arvr.google.com/cardboard/

Graff, B. (2017, September). *Business and Investment Student Club Meeting*. Lecture conducted from Park University, Parkville, MO.

Green, J., Wyllie, A., & Jackson, D. (2014). Virtual worlds: A new frontier for nurse education? *Collegian (Royal College of Nursing, Australia), 21*(2), 135–141. doi:10.1016/j.colegn.2013.11.004 PMID:25109212

Gregory, S., O'Connell, J., Butler, D., McDonald, M., Kerr, T., Schutt, S., . . . Gregory, B. (2019). *New applications, new global audiences: Educators repurposing and reusing 3D virtual and immersive learning resources*. Retrieved from https://ro.uow.edu.au/cgi/viewcontent.cgi?article=4204&context=eispapers1

Gregory, S., Scutter, S., Jacka, L., McDonald, M., Farley, H., & Newman, C. (2015). Barriers and enablers to the use of virtual worlds in higher education: An exploration of educator perceptions, attitudes and experiences. *Journal of Educational Technology & Society, 18*(1), 3–12.

Gregory, S., Scutter, S., Jacka, L., McDonald, M., Farley, H., & Newman, C. (2015). Barriers and Enablers to the Use of Virtual Worlds in Higher Education: An Exploration of Educator Perceptions, Attitudes and Experiences. *Journal of Educational Technology & Society, 18*(1), 3–12.

Gregory, S., & Wood, D. (2018). Conclusion. In S. Gregory & D. Wood (Eds.), *Authentic Virtual World Education.* Springer. doi:10.1007/978-981-10-6382-4_12

Grenfell, J. (2013). Immersive interfaces for art education teaching and learning in virtual and real world learning environments. *Procedia: Social and Behavioral Sciences, 93*, 1198–1211. doi:10.1016/j.sbspro.2013.10.016

Grimes, G., & Bartolacci, M. (2012). Second Life: a virtual world platform for profiling online behavior for network and information security education? An initial investigation. In M. Bartolacci & S. Powell (Eds.), *Research, practice, and educational advancements in telecommunications and networking* (pp. 285–289). Information Science Reference., doi:10.4018/978-1-4666-0050-8.ch017

Grivokostopoulou, F., Perikos, I., & Hatzilygeroudis, I. (2016, December). An innovative educational environment based on virtual reality and gamification for learning search algorithms. In *2016 IEEE Eighth International Conference on Technology for Education (T4E)* (pp. 110-115). IEEE. 10.1109/T4E.2016.029

Groff, J. S. (2018). The potentials of game-based environments for integrated, immersive learning data. *European Journal of Education, 53*(2), 188–201. doi:10.1111/ejed.12270

Gross, E. (1969). The definition of organizational goals. *The British Journal of Sociology, 20*(3), 277–294. doi:10.2307/588953

Guérin, E., Tosan, E., & Baskurt, A. (2002). *Modeling and approximation of fractal surfaces with projected IFS attractors. In Emergent Nature: Patterns, Growth and Scaling in the Science*. World Scientific.

Gunawardena, C. N. (1995). Social presence theory and implications for interaction and collaborative learning in computer conferences. *International Journal of Educational Telecommunications, 1*(2/3), 147–166.

Gunawardena, C., & Zittle, F. (1997). Social presence as a predictor of satisfaction within a computer mediated conferencing environment. *American Journal of Distance Education, 11*(3), 8–26. doi:10.1080/08923649709526970

Gupta, A., Scott, K., & Dukewich, M. (2018). Innovative technology using virtual reality in the treatment of pain: Does it reduce pain via distraction, or is there more to it? *Pain Medicine, 19*(1), 151–159. doi:10.1093/pm/pnx109 PMID:29025113

Haisley, K. R., Straw, O. J., Müller, D. T., Antiporda, M. A., Zihni, A. M., Reavis, K. M., Bradley, D. D., & Dunst, C. M. (2020). Feasibility of implementing a virtual reality program as an adjuvant tool for peri-operative pain control; Results of a randomized controlled trial in minimally invasive foregut surgery. *Complementary Therapies in Medicine, 49*. doi:10.1016/j.ctim.2020.102356

Hall, M. (2014). *What is gamification and why use it in teaching?* https://ii.library.jhu.edu/2014/05/13/what-is-gamification-and-why-use-it-in-teaching/

Hamacher, A., Kim, S. J., Cho, S. T., Pardeshi, S., Lee, S. H., Eun, S. J., & Whangbo, T. K. (2016). Application of virtual, augmented, and mixed reality to urology. *International Neurourology Journal, 20*(3), 172–181. doi:10.5213/inj.1632714.357 PMID:27706017

Hamada, E. K., Mohamed, E. A., Mohamed, S., & Youssef, M. (2016). An augmented reality approach to integrate practical activities in e-learning systems. *International Journal of Advanced Computer Science & Applications, 1*(7), 107–117.

Hanoun, S., & Nahavandi, S. (2018). Current and future methodologies of after action review in simulation-based training. *2018 Annual IEEE International Systems Conference (SysCon), Systems Conference (SysCon), 2018 Annual IEEE International*, 1–6. 10.1109/SYSCON.2018.8369516

Hao, K. (2019). *A new immersive classroom uses AI and VR to teach Mandarin Chinese*. https://www.technologyreview.com/s/613963/ai-vr-education-immersive-classroom-chinese-ibm/?utm_campaign=Abundance%20Insider&utm_source=hs_email&utm_medium=email&_hsenc=p2ANqtz-_k8VqBgYDI-vXEJhLfjX4CuZd1lhBsXV34IrJVT7QD-BM_yM3i-eNrGAImmyMGwZfXWjbiO

Hapt, X. (n.d.). *Haptic gloves for VR training, simulation, and design*. Retrieved December 24, 2019, from https://haptx.com

Harrington, C. M., Kavanagh, D. O., Quinlan, J. F., Ryan, D., Dicker, P., O'Keeffe, D., Traynor, O., & Tierney, S. (2018). Development and evaluation of a trauma decision-making simulator in Oculus virtual reality. *American Journal of Surgery*, *215*(1), 42–47. doi:10.1016/j.amjsurg.2017.02.011 PMID:28262203

Harris, S. R., & Gerich, E. (1996). Retiring the NSFNET backbone service: Chronicling the end of an era. *ConneXiona, 10*(4). Retrieved June 2, 2020 from https://www.merit.edu/wp-content/uploads/2019/06/Retiring-the-NSFNET-Backbone-Service_-Chronicling-the-End-of-an-Era-1.pdf

Harris, A. L., & Rea, A. (2019). Web 2.0 and virtual world technologies: A growing impact on IS education. *Journal of Information Systems Education*, *20*(2), 3.

Harrison, G. A., Smith, D. A., Black, J. M., & Ghaneie, E. (2019). *U.S. Patent No. 10,215,989*. Washington, DC: U.S. Patent and Trademark Office.

Hasse, A., Cortesi, S., Lombana-Bermudez, A., & Gasser, U. (2019). *Youth and artificial intelligence: Where we stand*. Youth and Media, Berkman Klein Center for Internet & Society. https://cyber.harvard.edu/publication/2019/youth-andartificial-intelligence/where-we-stand

Hayes, A., Hardin, S., & Hughes, C. (2013). Perceived presence's role on learning outcomes in a mixed reality classroom of simulated students. *Virtual, Augmented & Mixed Reality. Systems & Applications*, *8022*, 142–151. . doi:10.1007/978-3-642-39420-1-16

Heifetz, R., Linsky, M., & Grashow, A. (2009). *The Practice of Adaptive Leadership: Tools and Tactics for Changing Your Organization and the World*. Harvard Business Press.

Heili, J., & Michel, H. (2011, October). Do students Trained using serious games become better sales representatives? An experiment to study the performance of academic serious games. In *European Conference on Games-Based Learning* (p. 230). Redding, UK: Academic Conferences International Limited. Retrieved June 2, 2020 from http://ja.games.free.fr/ludoscience/EVirtuoses/AppelAComEVirtuo2012/Articles/01_ImpactSG.pdf

Heilig, M. L. (1962). *U.S. Patent No. 3,050,870*. Washington, DC: U.S. Patent and Trademark Office.

Helig, M. L. (1962). *U. S. Patent No. 3,050, 870*. Washington, DC: U.S. Patent and Trademark Office.

Helsel, S. (1992). Virtual reality and education. *Educational Technology*, *32*(5), 38–42.

Hemp, P. (2006). Avatar-based marketing. *Harvard Business Review*, *84*(6), 48–57.

Hepplestone, S., Holden, G., Irwin, B., Parkin, H., & Thorpe, L. (2011). Using technology to encourage student engagement with feedback: A literature review. *Research in Learning Technology*, *19*(2), 117–127. doi:10.3402/rlt.v19i2.10347

Herr, E. L. (2001). The impact of national policies, economics, and school reform on comprehensive guidance programs. *Professional School Counseling*, *4*, 236–245.

Hew, K. F., & Cheung, W. S. (2010). Use of three-dimensional (3-D) immersive virtual worlds in K-12 and higher education settings: A review of the research. *British Journal of Educational Technology*, *4*(1), 33–55. doi:10.1111/j.1467-8535.2008.00900.x

Hew, K. F., & Cheung, W. S. (2013). Use of Web 2.0 technologies in K-12 and higher education: The search for evidence-based practice. *Educational Research Review*, *9*, 47–64. doi:10.1016/j.edurev.2012.08.001

High Fidelity. (2015). *High Fidelity Inc*. Retrieved May 1, 2015 from: https://highfidelity.com/

History of Sega. (n.d.). Retrieved May 20, 2020 from https://segaretro.org/History_of_Sega

History, N. (n.d.). Retrieved May 20, 2020 from https://www.nintendo.co.uk/Corporate/Nintendo-History/Nintendo-History-625945.html

Hobson, A. J., Ashby, P., Malderez, A., & Tomlinson, P. D. (2009). Mentoring beginning teachers: What we know and what we don't. *Teaching and Teacher Education*, *25*(1), 207–216. doi:10.1016/j.tate.2008.09.001

Hodges, L. F., Kooper, R., Meyer, T. C., Rothbaum, B. O., Opdyke, D., De Graaff, J. J., Williford, J. S., & North, M. M. (1995). Virtual environments for treating the fear of heights. *Computer*, *28*(7), 27–34. doi:10.1109/2.391038

Hodgson, P., Lee, V. W. Y., Chan, J. C. S., Fong, A., Tang, C. S. Y., Chang, L., & Wong, C. (2019). Immersive virtual reality (VR) in higher education: development and implementation. In M. C. Dieck & T. Jung (Eds.), *Augmented reality and virtual reality: The power of AR and VR in business* (pp. 161–173). Springer. doi:10.1007/978-3-030-06246-0_12

Hoffmann, M., Meisen, T., & Jeschke, S. (2016). Shifting virtual reality education to the next level–Experiencing remote laboratories through mixed reality. In *Engineering Education 4.0* (pp. 235–249). Springer. doi:10.1007/978-3-319-46916-4_19

Höllerer, T. H., & Feiner, S. K. (2004). Mobile Augmented Reality. In H. A. Karimi & A. Hammad (Eds.), *Telegeoinformatics: Location-Based Computing and Services* (pp. 392–421). CRC Press.

Holley, D., & Hobbs, M. (2020). Augmented Reality For Education. In Encyclopedia of Educational Innovation. Delhi, India: Springer Nature.

Holley, D., & Hobbs, M. (2020). Augmented Reality For Education. In: Peters, M.A and Heraud, R., eds. Encyclopedia of Educational Innovation. Delhi, India: Springer Nature.

Holloway, S., Black, P., Hoffman, K., & Pierce, D. (2009). Some considerations of the import of the 2008 EPAS for curriculum design. *Council on Social Work Education*. Retrieved May 4, 2020 from https://www.bu.edu/ssw/files/pdf/2008EPASCurriculumDesign1.pdf

Holmberg, K., & Huvila, I. (2008). Learning together apart: Distance education in a virtual world. *First Monday*, *13*(10). Advance online publication. doi:10.5210/fm.v13i10.2178

Holoway, L. D., & Davis, D. J. (1972). The learner centered approach to instruction. *American Vocational Journal*, *47*(1), 32–34.

Hong, J. Y. (2010). Pre-service and beginning teachers' professional identity and its relation to dropping out of the profession. *Teaching and Teacher Education*, *26*(8), 1530–1543. doi:10.1016/j.tate.2010.06.003

Hostetter, C., & Busch, M. (2013). Community matters: Social presence and learning outcomes. *The Journal of Scholarship of Teaching and Learning*, *13*(1), 77–86.

Howard, M. (2019). Virtual reality interventions for personal development: A meta-analysis of hardware and software. *Human-Computer Interaction*, *34*(3), 205–239. doi:10.1080/07370024.2018.1469408

Howick, J., Bizzari, V., & Dhamba-Miller, H. (2018). Therapeutic empathy: What it is and what it isn't. *Journal of the Royal Society of Medicine, 111*(7), 233–236. https://doi:10.1177/0141076818781403

Hsu, L. (2012). Web 3D simulation-based application in tourism education: A case study with Second Life. *Journal of Hospitality, Leisure, Sport and Tourism Education, 11*(2), 113–124. doi:10.1016/j.jhlste.2012.02.013

Huang, W., & Soman, D. (2013). *A practitioner's guide to gamification of education.* University of Toronto. https://inside.rotman.utoronto.ca/behaviouraleconomicsinaction/files/2013/09/GuideGamificationEducationDec2013.pdf

Huang, Y.-C., Backman, S. J., Chang, L.-L., Backman, K. F., & McGuire, F. A. (2013). Experiencing student learning and tourism training in a 3D virtual world: An exploratory study. *Journal of Hospitality, Leisure, Sport and Tourism Education, 13*, 190–201. doi:10.1016/j.jhlste.2013.09.007

Hughes, C. E., Stapleton, C. B., Hughes, D. E., & Smith, E. M. (2005). Mixed reality in education, entertainment, and training. *IEEE Computer Graph, 25*(6), 24–30. doi:10.1109/MCG.2005.139 PMID:16315474

Hullinger, J. (2015). *Six innovative uses for virtual reality. The Idea Factory.* Retrieved from http://theweek.com/articles/562851/6

Hullinger, J. (2015). *Six innovative uses for virtual reality. The Idea Factory.* Retrieved July 1, 2015 from http://theweek.com/articles/562851/6

Hunt, J., & Eisenberg, D. (2010). Mental health problems and help-seeking behavior among college students. *The Journal of Adolescent Health, 46*(1), 3–10. doi:10.1016/j.jadohealth.2009.08.008 PMID:20123251

Husson University to Demonstrate New Augmented Reality App for Theatrical Set Designers. (2019). Retrieved December 19, 2020, from https://www.husson.edu/news/2019/04/husson-university-to-demonstrate-new-augmented-reality-app-for-theatrical-set-designers

Huttar, C. M., & BrintzenhofeSzoc, K. (2020). Virtual Reality and computer simulation in social work education: A systematic review. *Journal of Social Work Education, 56*(1), 131–141. doi:10.1080/10437797.2019.1648221

Hwang, G.-J., Sung, H.-Y., Hung, C.-M., Yang, L.-H., & Huang, I. (2013). A knowledge engineering approach to developing educational computer games for improving students' differentiating knowledge. *British Journal of Educational Technology, 44*(2), 183–196. doi:10.1111/j.1467-8535.2012.01285.x

Hysenbegasi, A., Hass, S. L., & Rowland, C. R. (2005). The impact of depression on the academic productivity of university students. *The Journal of Mental Health Policy and Economics, 8*(3), 145–151. PMID:16278502

Ibáñez, M. B., & Delgado-Kloos, C. (2018). Augmented reality for STEM learning: A systematic review. *Computers & Education, 123*, 109–123. doi:10.1016/j.compedu.2018.05.002

IBM. (2020). *Fail fast and learn fast.* https://www.ibm.com/garage/method/practices/culture/failing-fast

Ibrahim, A. K., Kelly, S. J., Adams, C. E., & Glazebrook, C. (2013). A systematic review of studies of depression prevalence in university students. *Journal of Psychiatric Research, 47*(3), 391–400. doi:10.1016/j.jpsychires.2012.11.015 PMID:23260171

Image resolution. (n.d.). In *Wikipedia.* Retrieved May 20, 2020, from https://en.wikipedia.org/wiki/Image_resolution

Ingersoll, R. M. (2001). Teacher turnover and teacher shortages: An organizational analysis. *American Educational Research Journal, 38*(3), 499–534. doi:10.3102/00028312038003499

Inman, C., Wright, V. H., & Hartman, J. A. (2010). Use of Second Life in K-12 and higher education: A review of research. *Journal of Interactive Online Learning, 9*(1), 44–63.

International Society for Technology in Education. (2012). *Digital age coaching*. Retrieved July 7, 2015 from http://www.iste.org/standards/nets-for-coaches

Internet World Stats. Retrieved March 18, 2020, from https://www.internetworldstats.com/stats.htm

Internet2. (2018). *2018 VR/AR in research and education survey*. https://meetings.internet2.edu/media/medialibrary/2019/03/08/20190306-Fineman- MetaverseWG.pdf

Internet2. (n.d.). Retrieved 2020, from https://www.internet2.edu/

Irwin, P., Coutts, R., & Graham, I. (2019, September). Looking Good Sister! The Use of a Virtual World to Develop Nursing Skills. In *Australasian Simulation Congress* (pp. 33-45). Springer. 10.1007/978-981-32-9582-7_3

Ishii, T., Tachikawa, H., Shiratori, Y., Hori, T., Aiba, M., Kuga, K., & Arai, T. (2018). What kinds of factors affect the academic outcomes of university students with mental disorders? A retrospective study based on medical records. *Asian Journal of Psychiatry*, *32*, 67–72. doi:10.1016/j.ajp.2017.11.017 PMID:29216609

Jacka, L., & Booth, K. (2019). Students as designers of virtual world learning environments. In Pre-Service and In-Service Teacher Education: Concepts, Methodologies, Tools, and Applications (pp. 1697-1712). IGI Global. doi:10.4018/978-1-5225-7305-0.ch079

Jee, H. K., Lim, S., Youn, J., & Lee, J. (2014). An augmented reality-based authoring tool for E-learning applications. *Multimedia Tools and Applications*, *68*(2), 225–235. doi:10.100711042-011-0880-4

Jenkins, H., Klopfer, E., Squire, K., & Tan, P. (2003). Entering the education arcade. *ACM Computers in Entertainment, 1*(1), 1-11. https://dl.acm.org/doi/10.1145/950566.950591

Jensen, N., Seipel, S., von Voigt, G., Raasch, S., Olbrich, S., & Nejdl, W. (2004). Development of a Virtual Laboratory System for Science Education and the Study of Collaborative Action. In L. Cantoni & C. McLoughlin (Eds.), *Proceedings of ED-MEDIA 2004--World Conference on Educational Multimedia, Hypermedia & Telecommunications* (pp. 2148-2153). Lugano, Switzerland: Association for the Advancement of Computing in Education (AACE). Retrieved March 28, 2020 from https://www.learntechlib.org/primary/p/12775/

Jestice, R. J., & Kahai, S. (2010). *The effectiveness of virtual worlds for education: an empirical study*. Paper presented at the Sixteenth Americas Conference on Information Systems (AMCIS), Lima, Peru.

Jiang, W. (2017). Interdependence of roles, role rotation, and sense of community in an online course. *Distance Education*, *38*(1), 84–105. doi:10.1080/01587919.2017.1299564

Johnson, E. (2016). *What are the differences among virtual, augmented and mixed reality?* Retrieved from https://www.vox.com/2015/7/27/11615046/whats-the-difference-between-virtual-augmented-and-mixed-reality

Johnston, A. P., Rae, J., Ariotti, N., Bailey, B., Lilja, A., Webb, R., ... McGhee, J. (2018). Journey to the centre of the cell: Virtual reality immersion into scientific data. *Traffic (Copenhagen, Denmark)*, *19*(2), 105–110. doi:10.1111/tra.12538 PMID:29159991

Jonassen, D., & Land, S. (Eds.). (2012). *Theoretical foundations of learning environments*. Routledge.

Jones, M. L. (2009). A study of novice special educators' views of evidence-based practices. *Teacher Education and Special Education*, *32*(2), 101–120. doi:10.1177/0888406409333777

Jose, J., Unnikrishnan, R., Marshall, D., & Bhavani, R. R. (2016, December). Haptics enhanced multi-tool virtual interfaces for training carpentry skills. In *2016 International Conference on Robotics and Automation for Humanitarian Applications (RAHA)* (pp. 1-6). IEEE. 10.1109/RAHA.2016.7931900

Jung, S., Wisniewski, P., & Hughes, C. (2018). In Limbo: The Effect of Gradual Visual Transition Between Real and Virtual on Virtual Body Ownership Illusion and Presence. *2018 IEEE Conference on Virtual Reality and 3D User Interfaces (VR), Virtual Reality and 3D User Interfaces (VR), 2018 IEEE Conference*, 267–272. 10.1109/VR.2018.8447562

Kamińska, D., Sapiński, T., Wiak, S., Tikk, T., Haamer, R., Avots, E., Helmi, A., Ozcinar, C., & Anbarjafari, G. (2019). Virtual Reality and Its Applications in Education: Survey. *MDPI: Information*, *10*(318), 318. Advance online publication. doi:10.3390/info10100318

Kapp, K., & O'Driscoll, T. (2010). *Learning in 3D*. Pfeiffer.

Kapp, K., & O'Driscoll, T. (2010). *Learning in 3D: adding a new dimension to enterprise learning and collaboration*. Pfeiffer.

Kapp, K., & O'Driscoll, T. (2010). *Learning in 3D: Adding a new dimension to enterprise learning and collaboration*. Pfeiffer.

Kapp, S., Thees, M., Strzys, M. P., Beil, F., Kuhn, J., Amiraslanov, O., Javaheri, H., Lukowicz, P., Lauer, F., Rheinländer, C., & Wehn, N. (2019). Augmenting Kirchhoff's laws: Using augmented reality and smartglasses to enhance conceptual electrical experiments for high school students. *The Physics Teacher*, *57*(1), 52–53. doi:10.1119/1.5084931

Karsenti, T., Bugmann, J., & Gros, P. P. (2017). *Transforming Education with Minecraft? Results of an exploratory study conducted with 118 elementary-school students*. Montréal: CRIFPE. https://education.minecraft.net/wp-content/uploads/Minecraft_Research_Report_Karsenti-Bugmann_2017.pdf

Kastoudi, D. (2011). *Using a Quest in a 3D Virtual Environment for Student Interaction and Vocabulary Acquisition in Foreign Language Learning. In European Association for Computer-Assisted Language Learning*. EUROCALL.

Kaufmann, H., & Schmalstieg D. (2003). Mathematics and geometry education with collaborative augmented reality. *Computers and Graphics*, *27*(3), 7. doi:10.1016/S0097- 8493(03)00028-1358

Kawulich, B. B., & D'Alba, A. (2019). Teaching qualitative research methods with Second Life, a 3-dimensional online virtual environment. *Virtual Reality (Waltham Cross)*, *23*(4), 375–384. doi:10.100710055-018-0353-4

Keengwe, J., & Onchwari, G. (2011). Fostering meaningful student learning through constructivist pedagogy and technology integration. In L. A. Tomei (Ed.), *Learning tools and teaching approaches through ICT advancements* (pp. 239–249). IGI Global.

Keller, A., Litzelman, K., Wisk, L. E., Maddox, T., Cheng, E. R., Creswell, P. D., & Witt, W. P. (2012). Does the perception that stress affects health matter? The association with health and mortality. *Health Psychology*, *31*(5), 677–684. doi:10.1037/a0026743 PMID:22201278

Kelley, J. (1999). *The Great Book of Domino Games*. Sterling Publishing Co., Inc.

Kennedy, R. S., & Lilienthal, M. G. (1995). Implications of balance disturbances following exposure to virtual reality systems. *Proceedings of the Virtual Reality Annual International Symposium '95*, 35-39. 10.1109/VRAIS.1995.512477

Kerrebrock, H., Brengman, M., & Willems, K. (2017). Escaping the crowd: An experimental study on the impact of Virtual Reality experience in a shopping mall. *Computers in Human Behavior, 77*, 437-461. https://doi:10.1016/j.chb.2017.07.019

Kessler, R. C., Amminger, G. P., Aguilar-Gaxiola, S., Alonso, J., Lee, S., & Ustun, T. B. (2007). Age of onset of mental disorders: A review of recent literature. *Current Opinion in Psychiatry*, *20*(4), 359. doi:10.1097/YCO.0b013e32816ebc8c PMID:17551351

Kim, S. J., Bae, Y. M., & Choi, Y. J. (2018). Design and Implementation of Real-time Augmented Reality Building Information System Combined with 3D Map. *Journal of The Korea Computer Graphics Society*, *24*(4), 39–54. doi:10.15701/kcgs.2018.24.4.39

Kim, S. S., Dohler, M., & Dasgupta, P. (2018). The Internet of Skills: Use of fifth-generation telecommunications, haptics and artificial intelligence in robotic surgery. *BJU International*, *122*(3), 356–358. doi:10.1111/bju.14388 PMID:29750403

King, A. (1993). *From sage on the stage to guide on the side, College Teaching, 41(1)* . Retrieved from http://www.jstor.org/stable/27558571

King-Sears, M., & Evmenova, A. S. (2007). Premises, principles, and processes for integrating technology into instruction. *Teaching Exceptional Children*, *40*(1), 6–14. doi:10.1177/004005990704000101

Kiryakova, G., Angelova, N., & Yordanova, L. (2013). *Gamification in education.* https://www.sun.ac.za/english/learning-teaching/ctl/Documents/Gamification%20in%20education.pdf

Kishino, F., & Milgram, P. (1994). A Taxonomy of Mixed Reality Visual Displays. *IEICE Transactions on Information and Systems*, *E77-D*(12), •••.

Kitchin, R. (2014). Big Data, new epistemologies and paradigm shifts. *Big Data & Society*, *1*(April–June), 1–12. doi:10.1177/2053951714528481

Kleven, N. F. (2014). *Virtual University hospital as an arena for medical training and health education.* Institutt for datateknikk og informasjonsvitenskap. Retrieved May 20, 2020 from https://ntnuopen.ntnu.no/ntnu-xmlui/handle/11250/253752

Kolb Antarctica Experience. (2018). Kolb (1.0.077) [Windows application software]. Retrieved May 20, 2020 from https://store.steampowered.com/app/831450/Kolb_Antarctica_Experience/

Kononowicz, A. A., Woodham, L., Georg, C., Edelbring, S., Stathakarou, N., Davies, D., Masiello, I., Saxena, N., Tudor Car, L., Car, J., & Zary, N. (2016). Virtual patient simulations for health professional education. *Cochrane Database of Systematic Reviews*, 5. doi:10.1002/14651858.CD012194

Konstantinidis, A. (2017). Using SmallWorlds to enhance social presence, group cohesion, and group identity in an online postgraduate course. In G. Panconesi & M. Guida (Eds.), *Handbook of Research on Collaborative Teaching Practice in Virtual Learning Environments* (pp. 92–110). IGI Global. doi:10.4018/978-1-5225-2426-7.ch005

Kopp, G., & Burkle, M. (2010). Using Second Life for just-in-time training: Building teaching frameworks in virtual worlds. *International Journal of Advanced Corporate Learning*, *3*(3), 19–25. doi:10.3991/ijac.v3i3.1373

Kotranza, A., Lind, D. S., Pugh, C. M., & Lok, B. (2009). *Real-time in-situ visual feedback of task performance in mixed environments for learning joint psychomotorcognitive tasks* (pp. 125–134). Paper presented at the 8th IEEE International Symposium on Mixed and Augmented Reality (ISMAR), Orlando, FL.

Krijn, M., Emmelkamp, P. M., Biemond, R., de Ligny, C. D. W., Schuemie, M. J., & van der Mast, C. A. (2004). Treatment of acrophobia in virtual reality: The role of immersion and presence. *Behaviour Research and Therapy*, *42*(2), 229–239. doi:10.1016/S0005-7967(03)00139-6 PMID:14975783

Krijn, M., Emmelkamp, P. M., Olafsson, R. P., Schuemie, M. J., & Van Der Mast, C. A. (2007). Do self-statements enhance the effectiveness of virtual reality exposure therapy? A comparative evaluation in acrophobia. *Cyberpsychology & Behavior*, *10*(3), 362–370. doi:10.1089/cpb.2006.9943 PMID:17594260

Krueger, A. B., & Schkade, D. A. (2008). The reliability of subjective well-being measures. *Journal of Public Economics*, *92*(8-9), 1833–1845. doi:10.1016/j.jpubeco.2007.12.015 PMID:19649136

Krueger, M. W. (1991). *Artificial reality* (2nd ed.). Addison-Wesley.

KZero. (2013). *Kzero Worldswide*. Retrieved May 15, 2013 from http://www.kzero.co.uk/blog/category/education-and-academia

KZero. (2014). *KZero Reports – Universe Charts*. Retrieved May1, 2015 from http:// kzero.co.uk/

Lai, K.-W. (2008). ICT supporting the learning process: The premise, reality, and promise. In J. Voogt & G. Knezek (Eds.), *International Handbook of Information Technology in Primary and Secondary Education* (pp. 215–230). Springer. doi:10.1007/978-0-387-73315-9_13

Lambert, J. L., & Fisher, J. L. (2013). Community of inquiry framework: Establishing community in an online course. *Journal of Interactive Online Learning*, *12*(1), 1–16.

Lanier, J. (1989). Interview with Jaron Lanier. *Whole Earth Review*, *64*, 108–119.

Lankford, H., Loeb, S., & Wyckoff, J. (2002). Teacher sorting and the plight of urban schools: A descriptive analysis. *Educational Evaluation and Policy Analysis*, *24*(1), 37–62. doi:10.3102/01623737024001037

Lan, Y. J., Lyu, B. N., & Chin, C. K. (2019). Does 3D immersive experience enhance Mandarin writing by CSL students? *Language Learning & Technology*, *23*(2), 125–144.

Latifi, K., & Latifi, R. (2018). Telemedicine and Telepresence for Surgery and Trauma. *Surgical Critical Care and Emergency Surgery: Clinical Questions and Answers*, 477-481.

Lau, K. W., & Lee, P. Y. (2015). The use of virtual reality for creating unusual environmental stimulation to motivate students to explore creative ideas. *Interactive Learning Environments, 23*, 3-18. doi:10. 1080/10494820.2012.745426

Laughlin, B. D., Murrish, R. E., & Vandenbrande, J. H. (2018). *U.S. Patent No. 10,026,227*. Washington, DC: U.S. Patent and Trademark Office.

Laureate Education (Producer). (2014). Anatomy of eLearning: Conceptual framework [interactive media]. Baltimore, MD: Author.

LaValle, S. M. (2019). *Virtual Reality*. Retrieved from http://vr.cs.uiuc.edu/

Lawson, B. D. (2015). Motion sickness symptomology and origins. In K. S. Hale & K. M. Stanney (Eds.), *Handbook of virtual environments: Design, implementation, and applications* (2nd ed., pp. 531–599). Taylor & Francis Group.

Lee, E. A., & Wong, K. W. (2014). Learning with desktop virtual reality:low spatial ability learners are more positively affected. *Computers & Education*, *79*, 49–58. doi:10.1016/j.compedu.2014.07.010

Lei, S. (2010). *Intrinsic and extrinsic motivation: evaluating benefits and drawbacks from college instructors' perspectives*. https://go.gale.com/ps/i.do?v=2.1&it=r&sw=w&id=GALE%7CA231807635&prodId=HRCA&sid=googleScholarFullText&userGroupName=park19302

Leighninger, M. (2006). *The Next Form of Democracy*. Vanderbilt University Press.

Lenhart, A., Purcell, K., Smith, A., & Zickuhr, K. (2010). *Social media & mobile internet use among teens and young adults*. Pew Research Center. Retrieved November 20 2014 http://67.192.40.213/~/media/Files/Reports/2010/PIP_Social_Media_and_Young_Adults_Report_Final_with_toplines.pdf

Lépinard, P., & Vandangeon-Derumez, I. (2019). Apprendre le management autrement: la ludopédagogie au service du développement des soft skills des étudiant·e·s. *XXVIIIe Conférence Internationale de Management Stratégique*.

Le, Q. T., & Park, C. S. (2012, August). Construction safety education model based on second life. In *Proceedings of IEEE International Conference on Teaching, Assessment, and Learning for Engineering (TALE) 2012* (pp. H2C-1). IEEE. 10.1109/TALE.2012.6360336

Lester, J. (2014). *Augmented mind- The evolution of learning tools from language to immersive reality*. Keynote speech presented at the 1st International Conference on e-Learning e-Education and Online Training, Bethesda, MD.

Levien, R. E. (1972). *The Emerging Technology: Instructional Uses of the Computer in Higher Education*. McGraw-Hill Book Company.

Levin, S., Fulginiti, A., & Moore, B. (2018). The perceived effectiveness of online social work education: Insights from a national survey of social work educators. *Social Work Education, 37*(6), 775–789. doi:10.1080/02615479.2018.1482864

Lewis, L. A., Koston, Z., Quartley, M., & Adsit, J. (2011). Virtual communities of practice: Bridging research and practice using Web 2.0. *Journal of Educational Technology Systems, 39*(2), 155–161. doi:10.2190/ET.39.2.e

Li, G., Chen, W., & Duanmu, J. (2010). Determinants of international students' academic performance: A comparison between Chinese and other international students. *Journal of Studies in International Education, 14*(4), 389–405. doi:10.1177/1028315309331490

Lim, D. H., Han, S. J., Oh, J., & Jang, C. S. (2019). Application of Virtual and Augmented Reality for Training and Mentoring of Higher Education Instructors. In *Handbook of Research on Virtual Training and Mentoring of Online Instructors* (pp. 325–344). IGI Global. doi:10.4018/978-1-5225-6322-8.ch015

Linden Lab. (2013). *Infographic: 10 years of Second Life*. Retrieved from http://www.lindenlab.com/releases/infographic

Linden Lab. (2013). *Infographic: 10 years of second life*. Retrieved July 1, 2015 from http://www.lindenlab.com/releases/infographic

Linden Lab. (2015). *Mainland Pricing and Fees*. Retrieved July 10, 2015 from https://secondlife.com/land/pricing.php

Linden Lab. (2018). *Infographic - 15 Years of Second Life*. Retrieved December 10, 2019 from https://community.secondlife.com/blogs/entry/2349-celebrating-15-years-second-life-infographic-town-hall-video/

Linden Research. (2011). *Second Life education: The virtual learning advantage*. Retrieved from http://lecs-static-secondlife-com.s3.amazonaws.com/work/SL-Edu-Brochure-010411.pdf

Linganisa, A., Ako-Nai, A., & Ajayi, N. (2018, December). The Potential of Second Life as a Platform for Learning: Student's Perspective. In *2018 International Conference on Intelligent and Innovative Computing Applications (ICONIC)* (pp. 1-5). IEEE. 10.1109/ICONIC.2018.8601201

Liou, H. C. (2012). The roles of Second Life in a college computer-assisted language learning (CALL) course in Taiwan, ROC. *Computer Assisted Language Learning, 25*(4), 365–382. doi:10.1080/09588221.2011.597766

Lipka. (2019). The truth about student success: Myths, realities, and 30 practices that are working. *Chronicle of Higher Education.*

Liu, Y. (2014, July). Virtual neurosurgical education for image-guided deep brain stimulation neurosurgery. In *Audio, Language and Image Processing (ICALIP), 2014 International Conference on* (pp. 623-626). IEEE. 10.1109/ICALIP.2014.7009869

Liu, W., Cheok, A. D., Mei-Ling, C. L., & Theng, Y. L. (2007, September). Mixed reality classroom: learning from entertainment. In *Proceedings of the 2nd international conference on Digital interactive media in entertainment and arts* (pp. 65-72). ACM.

Lorenzo-Alvarez, R., Ruiz-Gomez, M. J., & Sendra-Portero, F. (2019). Medical students' and family physicians' attitudes and perceptions toward radiology learning in the Second Life virtual world. *AJR. American Journal of Roentgenology, 212*(6), 1295–1302. doi:10.2214/AJR.18.20381 PMID:30860900

Lorenzo, C.-M., Ángel Sicilia, M., & Sánchez, S. (2012). Studying the effectiveness of multi-user immersive environments for collaborative evaluation tasks. *Computers & Education, 59*(4), 1361–1376. doi:10.1016/j.compedu.2012.06.002

Loureiro, A., & Bettencourt, T. (2011). The Extended Classroom: Meeting students' needs using a virtual environment. *Procedia: Social and Behavioral Sciences, 15*, 2667–2672. doi:10.1016/j.sbspro.2011.04.167

Lowenthal, P. R., & Dunlap, J. C. (2018). Investigating students' perceptions of instructional strategies to establish social presence. *Distance Education, 39*(3), 281–298. doi:10.1080/01587919.2018.1476844

Luckin, R., Holmes, W., Griffiths, M., & Forcier, L. B. (2016). *Intelligence unleashed: An argument for AI in education.* http://oro.open.ac.uk/50104/1/Luckin%20et%20al.%20-%202016%20%20Intelligence%20Unleashed.%20An%20argument%20for%20AI%20in%20Educ.pdf

Lukensmeyer, C., & Torres, L. (2006). Today's Leadership Challenge—Engaging Citizens. *Public Management, 35*(3), 26–31.

Maas, M. J., & Hughes, J. M. (2020). Virtual, augmented and mixed reality in K–12 education: A review of the literature. *Technology, Pedagogy and Education, 29*(2), 231–249. doi:10.1080/1475939X.2020.1737210

Magana, A. J. (2014). Learning strategies and multimedia techniques for scaffolding size and scale cognition. *Computers & Education, 72*, 367–377. doi:10.1016/j.compedu.2013.11.012

Magic Leap 1. (n.d.). Retrieved from https://www.magicleap.com/magic-leap-1

Makransky, G., Bonde, M. T., Wulff, J. S. G., Wandall, J., Hood, M., Creed, P. A., & Nørremølle, A. (2016). Simulation based virtual learning environment in medical genetics counseling: An example of bridging the gap between theory and practice in medical education. *BMC Medical Education, 16*(1), 98. doi:10.118612909-016-0620-6 PMID:27012245

Malaquias, R., DeOliveira Malzquias, F., Borges, D., Junior., & Zambra, P. (2018). The use of a serious game and academic performance of undergraduate accounting students: an empirical analysis. *Turkish Online Journal of Distance Education, 19*(2), 117-127. Retrieved May 25, 2020 from http://static.dergipark.org.tr/article-download/7b29/972a/43f3/5ad4fcaca63ef.pdf?

Ma, M., Jain, L. C., & Anderson, P. (2014). *Virtual, augmented reality and serious games for healthcare 1* (Vol. 1). Springer. doi:10.1007/978-3-642-54816-1

Manus, V. R. (n.d.). *World's leading VR Gloves for training*. Retrieved December 18, 2019, from https://manus-vr.com/

Maples-Keller, J. L., Bunnell, B. E., Kim, S. J., & Rothbaum, B. O. (2017). The Use of virtual reality technology in the treatment of anxiety and other psychiatric disorders. *Harvard Review of Psychiatry, 25*(3), 103–113. https://doi:10.1097/HRP.0000000000000138

Marcelino, R., Silva, J. B., Gruber, V., & Bilessimo, M. S. (2012, July). 3D virtual worlds using open source platform and integrated remote experimentation. In *2012 9th International Conference on Remote Engineering and Virtual Instrumentation (REV)* (pp. 1-2). IEEE.

Marcus, G. (2020). The next decade in AI: four steps towards robust artificial intelligence. *arXiv preprint arXiv:2002.06177.*

Marino, P. (2004). *The art of machinima: 3D game-based filmmaking*. ParaglyphPress.

Martín-Gutiérrez, J., Mora, C. E., Añorbe-Díaz, B., & González-Marrero, A. (2017). Virtual technologies trends in education. *Eurasia Journal of Mathematics, Science and Technology Education, 13*(2), 469–486.

Martin, J. (2017). Virtual worlds in social work education. *Australian Social Work, 70*(2), 197–208. doi:10.1080/0312407X.2016.1238953

Mathews, D. (1999). *Politics for People*. University of Illinois Press.

Mathews, S., Andrews, L., & Luck, E. (2012). Developing a Second Life virtual field trip for university students: An action research approach. *Educational Research, 54*(1), 17–38. doi:10.1080/00131881.2012.658197

Matias, C. E., Montoya, R., & Nishi, N. W. M. (2016). Blocking CRT: How the emotionality of Whiteness blocks CRT in urban teacher education. *Educational Studies, 52*(1), 1–19. doi:10.1080/00131946.2015.1120205

Matsuda, T., Nakayama, H., & Tamada, K. (2015). Using 3D virtual reality technology in cyber ethics education: How can we really evaluate and change students' attitudes? In Human rights and ethics: concepts, methodologies, tools, and applications (pp. 1621-1636). Hershey, PA: Information Science Reference. doi:10.4018/978-1-4666-6433-3.ch089

May, S. (2015, December 12). *STEM Engagement at Johnson.* Retrieved 2020, from https://www.nasa.gov/centers/johnson/stem/home/index.html

Mazuryk, T., & Gervautz, M. (1996). *Virtual reality, history, applications, technology and future, 1-72. Institute of Computer Graphics.* Vienna University of Technology, Austria. Retrieved August 29, 2015 from https://www.cg.tuwien.ac.at/research/publications/1996/mazuryk-1996-VRH/TR-186-2-96-06Paper.pdf

McArthur, V., Teather, R., & Stuerzlinger, W. (2010). Comparing 3D content creation interfaces in two virtual worlds: World of Warcraft and second life. *Journal of Gaming & Virtual Worlds., 2*(3), 239–258. doi:10.1386/jgvw.2.3.239_1

McCombs, B., & Whistler, J. (1997). *The learner centered classroom and school: Strategies for increasing student motivation and achievement.* Jossey-Bass Publishers.

McCormack, M., Brooks, D. C., & Shulman, B. (2020). *The Top 10 Strategic Technologies for 2020.* EDUCAUSE Center for Analysis and Research (ECAR).

McCoy, B. (2016). Digital distractions in the classroom: Student classroom use of digital devices for non-class related purposes. *Journal of Medical Education, 7*(1), 5–32.

McGonigal, J. (2011). *Reality is broken: Why games make us better and how they can change the world* (2nd ed.). Penguin Books Ltd.

McKenzie, J. (2003). Pedagogy does matter. *The Educational Technology Journal, 13*(1), 1–6.

McKeown, L. (2007). Taking action learning online in the 3D virtual worlds of Second Life. *International Review of Research in Open and Distance Learning, 8*(3). Advance online publication. doi:10.19173/irrodl.v8i3.507

McLaughlin, C. (1999). Counselling in schools: Looking back and looking forward. *British Journal of Guidance & Counselling, 27*(1), 13–22. doi:10.1080/03069889908259712

McVey, M. H. (2008). Observations of expert communicators in immersive virtual worlds: Implications for synchronous discussion. *ALT-J. Research in Learning Technology, 16*(3), 173–180. doi:10.3402/rlt.v16i3.10896

Mechdyne Corporation. (2012). *CAVE 2: The hybrid work environment.* Retrieved May 24, 2020 from https://www.mechdyne.com/hardware.aspx?name=CAVE2

Meldrum, D., Glennon, A., Herdman, S., Murray, D., & McConn-Walsh, R. (2012). Virtual reality rehabilitation of balance: Assessment of the usability of the Nintendo Wii® Fit Plus. *Disability and Rehabilitation. Assistive Technology*, *7*(3), 205–210. doi:10.3109/17483107.2011.616922 PMID:22117107

Mendonça, R. F., Carreira, S. M., & Sampaio, P. N. (2011, April). VirtualLabs@ UMa: A customizable 3D learning platform for experimental activities. In *2011 International Conference on Multimedia Computing and Systems* (pp. 1-6). IEEE. 10.1109/ICMCS.2011.5945594

Merchant, Z., Goetz, E. T., Keeney-Kennicutt, W., Kwok, O. M., Cifuentes, L., & Davis, T. J. (2012). The learner characteristics, features of desktop 3D virtual reality environments, and college chemistry instruction: A structural equation modeling analysis. *Computers & Education*, *59*(2), 551–568. doi:10.1016/j.compedu.2012.02.004

Merriam-Webster. (n.d.). Citation. In *Merriam-Webster.com dictionary*. Retrieved March 10, 2020 from https://www.merriam-webster.com/dictionary/virtualreality

Meskó, B. (2008, August 17). Unique medical simulation in second life! *Science Roll Blog*. https://scienceroll.com/2008/08/17/unique-medical-simulation-in-second-life/

Meyerbröker, K., & Emmelkamp, P. M. (2010). Virtual reality exposure therapy in anxiety disorders: A systematic review of process-and-outcome studies. *Depression and Anxiety*, *27*(10), 933–944. doi:10.1002/da.20734 PMID:20734361

Michel, H. (2013, January). From «Haute-Couture» to «Ready-to-Wear»: Typology of Serious Games Implementation Strategies in Higher Education. In *European Conference on Games Based Learning* (p. 386). Academic Conferences International Limited.

Microsoft Education Team. (2018). *How a New Jersey middle school uses Minecraft: Education Edition to teach game design*. https://educationblog.microsoft.com/en-us/2018/02/minecraft-education-edition-teach-game-design-middle-school/

Microsoft HoloLens. (n.d.). *Mixed reality technology for business*. Retrieved December 18, 2019, from https://www.microsoft.com/en-us/hololens/

Mikropoulos, T. A., & Natsis, A. (2011). Educational virtual environments: A ten-year review of empirical research (1999–2009). *Computers & Education*, *56*(3), 769–780. doi:10.1016/j.compedu.2010.10.020

Milgram, P., & Kishino, F. (1994). A taxonomy of mixed reality visual displays. *IEICE Trans. Information and Systems. E (Norwalk, Conn.)*, *77-D*(12), 1321–1329. http://etclab.mie.utoronto.ca/people/paul_dir/IEICE94/ieice.html

Milgram, P., Takemura, H., Utsumi, A., & Kishino, F. (1994). Augmented reality: A class of displays on the reality-virtuality continuum, *SPIE. Telemanipulator and Telepresence Technologies*, *2351*, 282–291. doi:10.1117/12.197321

Millar, R. (1991). Why is science hard to learn? *Journal of Computer Assisted Learning*, *7*(7), 66–74. doi:10.1111/j.1365-2729.1991.tb00229.x

Miller, R. (2014). The application of virtual reality in higher education distance learning. *Journal of Applied Learning Technology*, *4*(4), 15–18.

Miller, S. E. (2010). A conceptual framework for the professional socialization of social workers. *Journal of Human Behavior in the Social Environment*, *20*(7), 924–938. doi:10.1080/10911351003751934

Mine, M. R. (1995). *Virtual environment interaction techniques*. UNC Chapel Hill CS Dept.

Minkesh, A., & Taizo, M. (2019). *Short virtual reality mindfulness meditation training for sustained attention*. Working paper. http://arxiv.org/abs/1907.04487

Miron, O., Yu, K. H., Wilf-Miron, R., & Kohane, I. S. (2019). Suicide rates among adolescents and young adults in the United States, 2000-2017. *Journal of the American Medical Association, 321*(23), 2362–2364. doi:10.1001/jama.2019.5054 PMID:31211337

Mladenovic, S., Kuvac, H., & Štula, M. (2012). Virtual learning environment. In *Virtual learning environments: concepts, methodologies, tools and applications* (pp. 1–16). Information Science Reference., doi:10.4018/978-1-4666-0011-9.ch101

Molka-Danielsen, J., & Chabada, M. (2010, January). Application of the 3D multi user virtual environment of second life to emergency evacuation simulation. In *2010 43rd Hawaii international conference on system sciences* (pp. 1-9). IEEE.

Molnar, A. R. (1975). Viable Goals for New Educational Technology Efforts: Science Education and the New Technological Revolution. *Educational Technology, 15*(9), 16–22.

Morgan, H. (2019, April 13). *41 Reasons Why You Didn't Get the Job* [Web log post]. https://careersherpa.net/41-reasons-why-you-didnt-get-the-job

Moro, C., Stromberga, Z., Raikos, A., & Stirling, A. (2017). The effectiveness of virtual and augmented reality in health sciences and medical anatomy. *Anatomical Sciences Education, 10*(6), 549–559. doi:10.1002/ase.1696 PMID:28419750

Moro, C., Stromberga, Z., & Stirling, A. (2017). Virtualisation devices for student learning: Comparison between desktop-based (Oculus Rift) and mobile-based (Gear VR) virtual reality in medical and health science education. *Australasian Journal of Educational Technology, 33*(6), 1–10. doi:10.14742/ajet.3840

Mosco, V. (2015). *To the cloud: Big data in a turbulent world.* Routledge. doi:10.4324/9781315631554

Mount, B., Latta, S., Poulos, A., McCulloch, D., Bennett, D., Hastings, R., & Scott, J. (2016). *U.S. Patent No. 9,497,501.* Washington, DC: U.S. Patent and Trademark Office.

Mount, N. J., Chambers, C., Weaver, D., & Priestnall, G. (2009). Learner immersion engagement in the 3D virtual world: Principles emerging from the DELVE project. *Innovation in Teaching and Learning in Information and Computer Sciences, 8*(3), 40–55. doi:10.11120/ital.2009.08030040

Mueller, J., Wood, E., Willoughby, T., Ross, C., & Specht, J. (2008). Identifying discriminating variables between teachers who fully integrate computers and teachers with limited integration. *Computers & Education, 51*(4), 1523–1537. doi:10.1016/j.compedu.2008.02.003

Muhanna, M. A. (2015). Virtual reality and the CAVE: Taxonomy, interaction challenges and research directions. *Journal of King Saud University-Computer and Information Sciences, 27*(3), 344–361. doi:10.1016/j.jksuci.2014.03.023

Mullainathan, S., & Spiess, J. (2017). Machine learning: An applied econometric approach. *The Journal of Economic Perspectives, 31*(2), 87–106. doi:10.1257/jep.31.2.87

Müller, D., Chilliischi, A., & Langer, S. (2012, July). Integrating immersive 3D worlds and real lab equipment for teaching mechatronics. In *2012 9th International Conference on Remote Engineering and Virtual Instrumentation (REV)* (pp. 1-6). IEEE.

Murgado-Armenteros, E. M., Torres-Ruiz, F. J., & Vega-Zamora, M. (2012). Differences between online and face to face focus groups, viewed through two approaches. *Journal of Theoretical and Applied Electronic Commerce Research, 7*(2), 73–86. doi:10.4067/S0718-18762012000200008

Mutekwe, E., Ndofirepi, A., Maphosa, C., Wadesango, N., & Machingambi, S. (2013). A swot analysis of the rise and pedagogical implications of the social constructivist epistemology in educational practice. *Anthrpologist, 15*(1), 53–65. doi:10.1080/09720073.2013.11891292

Myers West, S., Whittaker, M., & Crawford, K. (2019). *Discriminating systems (report)*. AI Now.

Nanome (2019). Nanome (1.15) [Windows application software]. Retrieved from https://nanome.ai/

NASA Spacesuit User Interface Technologies for Students (SUITS). (2019). Retrieved 2020, from https://www.nasa.gov/stem-ed-resources/nasa-spacesuit-user-interface-technologies-for-students-suits-design-challenge.html

National Survey of Student Engagement (NSSE). (2014). *Center for Postsecondary Research*. Indiana University School of Education. Retrieved http://nsse.iub.edu/NSSE_2014_Results/pdf/NSSE_2014_Annual_Results.pdf#page=8

Navarro-Haro, M. V., López-del-Hoyo, Y., Campos, D., Linehan, M. M., Hoffman, H. G., García-Palacios, A., Modrego-Alarcón, M., Borao, L., & García-Campayo, J. (2017). Meditation experts try Virtual Reality mindfulness: A pilot study evaluation of the feasibility and acceptability of Virtual Reality to facilitate mindfulness practice in people attending a mindfulness conference. *PLoS One*, *12*(11), e0187777. Advance online publication. doi:10.1371/journal.pone.0187777 PMID:29166665

Nebel, S., Schneider, S., & Rey, G. D. (2016). Mining learning and crafting scientific experiments: A literature review on the use of Minecraft in education and research. *Journal of Educational Technology & Society*, *19*(2), 355.

Neri, S. G., Cardoso, J. R., Cruz, L., Lima, R. M., De Oliveira, R. J., Iversen, M. D., & Carregaro, R. L. (2017). Do virtual reality games improve mobility skills and balance measurements in community-dwelling older adults? Systematic review and meta-analysis. *Clinical Rehabilitation*, *31*(10), 1292–1304. doi:10.1177/0269215517694677 PMID:28933612

Nicholls, J., & Philip, R. (2012). Solo life to Second Life: The design of physical and virtual learning spaces inspired by the drama classroom. *Research in Drama Education*, *17*(4), 583–602. doi:10.1080/13569783.2012.727628

Nicholson, S. (2013). *A RECIPE for Meaningful Gamification*. To be published. In L. Wood & T. Reiners (Eds.), *Gamification in Education and Business*. Springer. Available online at http://scottnicholson.com/pubs/recipepreprint.pdf

Nikolaou, A., & Tsolakidis, C. (2012, September). The role of three dimensional virtual environments in the development of Personal Learning Networks. In *2012 15th International Conference on Interactive Collaborative Learning (ICL)* (pp. 1-7). IEEE. 10.1109/ICL.2012.6402114

Nintendo Labo™ for the NINTENDO Switch™ home gaming system - official site. (n.d.). Retrieved December 18, 2019, from https://labo.nintendo.com/

Nishide, R. (2011). Prospects for digital campus with extensive applications of virtual collaborative space. *Journal of Interactive Learning Research*, *22*(3), 421–443.

Nishide, R., & Ueshima, S. (2004, January). Digital campus project: A" dream university" over the Internet Web. *Proceedings. Second International Conference on Creating, Connecting and Collaborating through Computing*, *2004*, 122–129.

Nishi, N. W., Matias, C. E., & Montoya, R. (2015). Exposing the white avatar: Projections, justifications, and the ever-evolving American racism. *Social Identities*, *21*(5), 459–473. doi:10.1080/13504630.2015.1093470

Niu, Z., Wang, A., Xu, H., Li, L., & Li, Z. (2014). Teaching reform of the Introduction to Metal Cutting Machine Tools course for the Excellent Engineers Training Plan. *World Transactions on Engineering and Technology Education*, *12*(2), 294–297.

North, L., Robinson, C., Haffegee, A., Sharkey, P. M., & Hwang, F. (2014). Using virtual environments for trigger identification in addiction treatment. *International Journal on Disability and Human Development: IJDHD*, *13*(3), 369–375. doi:10.1515/ijdhd-2014-0330

Noteborn, G., Dailey-Hebert, A., Bohle-Carbonell, K., & Gijselears, W. (2013). Essential knowledge for academic performance: Educating in the virtual world to promote active learning. In *Teacher and Teacher Education*. Elsvier. http://authors.elsevier.com/sd/article/S0742051X1300156X

Noteborn, G., Dailey-Hebert, A., Bohle-Carbonell, K., & Gijselears, W. (2013). Essential knowledge for academic performance: Educating in the virtual world to promote active learning. *Teaching and Teacher Education*, *37*(January), 217–234. http://authors.elsevier.com/sd/article/S0742051X1300156X

Nussli, N., & Oh, K. (2017). Field research in Second Life: Strategies for discussion group facilitation and benefits of participation. In G. Panconesi & M. Guida (Eds.), *Handbook of Research on Collaborative Teaching Practice in Virtual Learning Environments* (pp. 348–373). IGI Global. doi:10.4018/978-1-5225-2426-7.ch018

Nussli, N., Oh, K., Cuadro, N., & Kaye, M. (2019). An investigation into the effect of communication modality on learner satisfaction and mental effort expended during a lecture and discussion event in Second life - a 3D virtual world. In K. Yang (Ed.), *Cases on Immersive Virtual Reality Techniques* (pp. 89–123). IGI Global. doi:10.4018/978-1-5225-5912-2.ch005

Oculus | VR Headsets & Equipment. (n.d.). Retrieved December 18, 2019, from https://www.oculus.com/

Oculus Quest. All-in-One VR Headset. (n.d.). Retrieved December 18, 2019, from https://www.oculus.com/quest/

Oculus Rift, S. (n.d.). Retrieved May 20, 2020 from https://www.oculus.com/rift-s/features/

Oculus, Go. Standalone VR Headset. (n.d.). Retrieved December 18, 2019, from https://www.oculus.com/go/

Office of Science and Technology Policy (OSTP). (1992). *Grand Challenges: High Performance Computing and Communications.* Retrieved July 25, 2015 from http://www.hpcc.gov

Office of Social and Economic Data Analysis (OSEDA). (2001). *Final results from the e-MINTS teacher survey*. Author.

Office of Technology Assessment (OTA). (1995). *Teachers and technology: Making the connection*. U.S. Government Printing Office.

Office of Technology Assessment. (1982). Informational technology and its impact on American education. U.S. Congress.

Okutsu, M., DeLaurentis, D., Brophy, S., & Lambert, J. (2013). Teaching an aerospace engineering design course via virtual worlds: A comparative assessment of learning outcomes. *Computers & Education*, *60*(1), 288–298. doi:10.1016/j.compedu.2012.07.012

Oliver, M., & Carr, D. (2009). Learning in virtual worlds: Using communities of practice to explain how people learn from play. *British Journal of Educational Technology*, *40*(3), 14. doi:10.1111/j.1467-8535.2009.00948.x

Olson, J. L., Krum, D. M., Suma, E. A., & Bolas, M. (2011). A Design for a Smartphone-Based Head Mounted Display. *Proceedings of the 2011 IEEE Virtual Reality*, 233-234. 10.1109/VR.2011.5759484

Ong, S. K., & Nee, A. Y. C. (2013). *Virtual and augmented reality applications in manufacturing*. Springer Science & Business Media.

OpenSimulator. (2019). *What is Open Simulator?* Retrieved from http://opensimulator.org/wiki/Main_Page

Orlosky, J., Kiyokawa, K., & Takemura, H. (2017). Virtual and augmented reality on the 5G highway. *Journal of Information Processing*, *25*(0), 133–141. doi:10.2197/ipsjjip.25.133

Ota, D., Loftin, B., Saito, T., Lea, R., & Keller, J. (1995). Virtual reality in surgical education. *Computers in Biology and Medicine*, *25*(2), 127–137. doi:10.1016/0010-4825(94)00009-F PMID:7554831

Palaganas, J. C., Fey, M., & Simon, R. (2016). Structured debriefing in simulation-based education. *AACN Advanced Critical Care*, *27*(1), 78–85. doi:10.4037/aacnacc2016328 PMID:26909457

Pantelidis, V. (1993). Virtual reality in the classroom. *Educational Technology*, *33*(4), 23–27.

Parrish, K. (2016). Nvidia plans to prove that new method improves image quality in virtual reality. *Digital Trends*. Retrieved December 18, 2019, from https://www.digitaltrends.com/virtual-reality/nvidia-research-foveated-rendering-vr-smi/

Parsons, T. D., & Rizzo, A. A. (2008). Affective outcomes of virtual reality exposure therapy for anxiety and specific phobias: A meta-analysis. *Journal of Behavior Therapy and Experimental Psychiatry*, *39*(3), 250–261. doi:10.1016/j.jbtep.2007.07.007 PMID:17720136

PC SDK. (n.d.). In *Oculus Developer Center, Overview*. Retrieved May 20, 2020 from https://developer.oculus.com/rift/

Pelargos, P. E., Nagasawa, D. T., Lagman, C., Tenn, S., Demos, J. V., Lee, S. J., Bui, T. T., Barnette, N. E., Bhatt, N. S., Ung, N., Bari, A., Martin, N. A., & Yang, I. (2017). Utilizing virtual and augmented reality for educational and clinical enhancements in neurosurgery. *Journal of Clinical Neuroscience*, *35*, 1–4. doi:10.1016/j.jocn.2016.09.002 PMID:28137372

Penland, J. L., Laviers, K., Bassham, E., & Nnochiri, V. (2019). Virtual Learning: A Study of Virtual Reality for Distance Education. In Handbook of Research on Blended Learning Pedagogies and Professional Development in Higher Education. IGI Global. doi:10.4018/978-1-5225-5557-5.ch009

Pensieri, C., & La Marca, A. (2019). Virtual worlds and virtual reality. An analysis in the healthcare education. *Form@re*, *19*(1), 256.

Pereira, M. M., Artemiou, E., McGonigle, D., Köster, L., Conan, A., & Sithole, F. (2019). Second Life and Classroom Environments: Comparing Small Group Teaching and Learning in Developing Clinical Reasoning Process Skills. *Medical Science Educator*, *29*(2), 431–437. doi:10.100740670-019-00706-4

Pérez-López, D., & Contero, M. (2013). Delivering educational multimedia contents through an augmented reality application: A case study on its impact on knowledge acquisition and retention. *Turkish Online Journal of Educational Technology-TOJET*, *12*(4), 19–28.

Pericot-Valverde, I., Germeroth, L. J., & Tiffany, S. T. (2016). The use of virtual reality in the production of cue-specific craving for cigarettes: A meta-analysis. *Nicotine & Tobacco Research, 18*(5), 538–546. https://doi:10.1093/ntr/ntv216

Pestalozzi, H. (1803). *ABC der Anschauung, oder Anschauungs-Lehre der Massverhaltnisse*. Gessner.

Peterson, M. (2006). Learner interaction management in an avatar and chat-based virtual world. *Computer Assisted Language Learning*, *19*(1), 79–103. doi:10.1080/09588220600804087

Petrakou, A. (2010). Interacting through avatars: Virtual worlds as a context for online education. *Computers & Education*, *54*(4), 1020–1027. doi:10.1016/j.compedu.2009.10.007

Petrovic-Dzerdz, M. (2019). Gamifying Online Tests to Promote Retrieval-Based Learning. *International Review of Research in Open and Distance Learning*, *20*(2), 24–42. doi:10.19173/irrodl.v20i2.3812

Pew Internet. (2009). *Internet, broadband, and cell phone statistics*. Retrieved September 18, 2011 http://www.distributedworkplace.com/DW/Research/Internet%20broadband%20and%20cell%20phone%20statistics%20-%20Pew%20Internet%20Report%20Jan%202010.pdf

Pierce, D. (2015, March 6). The Future of Virtual Reality is inside your smartphone. *Wired*. Retrieved from http://www.wired.com/2015/03/future-virtual-reality-inside-smartphone/

Pigatt, V., & Braman, J. (2018). *Promoting success and engagement in online programming courses.* Poster presented at the League of Innovations Conference, National Harbor, MD.

Pilatásig, M., Tobar, E., Paredes, L., Silva, F. M., Acurio, A., & Pruna, E. … Sánchez, Z. (2018). Virtual system for teaching-learning of initial education using a haptic device. In L. T. De Paolis & P. Bourdot (Eds.), Augmented Reality, Virtual Reality, and Computer Graphics (pp. 118–132). Cham: Springer International Publishing.

Pimax Vision 8K X. (n.d.). Retrieved May 20, 2020, from https://www.tomshardware.com/news/pimax-vision-8k-x-vr-headset

PlayStation®VR - over 500 games and Experiences. feel them all. (n.d.). Retrieved December 18, 2019, from https://www.playstation.com/en-us/explore/playstation-vr/

Postlethwaite, D., Zboray, D., Gandee, C., Aditjandra, A., Wallace, M., & Lenker, Z. (2017). *U.S. Patent No. 9,836,987.* Washington, DC: U.S. Patent and Trademark Office.

Prasolova-Forland, E. (2004, November). Supporting social awareness among university students in 3D CVEs: Benefits and limitations. In *2004 International Conference on Cyberworlds* (pp. 127-134). IEEE. 10.1109/CW.2004.59

Prasolova-Førland, E. (2008). Analyzing place metaphors in 3D educational collaborative virtual environments. *Computers in Human Behavior, 24*(2), 185–204. doi:10.1016/j.chb.2007.01.009

Prensky, M. (2001). Digital natives, digital immigrants part 1. *On the Horizon, 9*(5), 1–6. doi:10.1108/10748120110424816

Pricer, W. F. (2011). At issue: Immersive Education, an Annotated Webliography. *Community College Enterprise, 17*(1), 41–50.

Prude, M. A. (2013). A classroom of bunnies, blimps, and werewolves. *ASIANetwork Exchange, 20*(2), 1–12.

Psotka, J. (1995). Immersive training systems: Virtual reality and education and training. *Instructional Science, 23*(5–6), 405–431. doi:10.1007/BF00896880

Puentedura, R. (2006). Transformation, technology, and education [Blog post]. Retreived May 3, 2020 from http://hippasus.com/resources/tte/

Pulse Simulation Technology. (2008). Retrieved from https://www.youtube.com/watch?v=Q11aWO6dg2Q

Pulse Simulation Technology. (2008). Retrieved July 1, 2015 from https://www.youtube.com/watch?v=Q11aWO6dg2Q

Purdon, C., Antony, M., Monteiro, S., & Swinson, R. P. (2001). Social anxiety in college students. *Journal of Anxiety Disorders, 15*(3), 203–215. doi:10.1016/S0887-6185(01)00059-7 PMID:11442139

Putman, S., & Id-Deen, L. (2019). "I Can See It!" Math understanding through virtual reality. *Educational Leadership, 76*(5), 36.

Quest, O. (n.d.). In *Oculus*. Retrieved May 20, 2020, from https://www.oculus.com/quest/?locale=en_US

Quint, F., Sebastian, K., & Gorecky, D. (2015). A mixed-reality learning environment. *Procedia Computer Science, 75*, 43–48. doi:10.1016/j.procs.2015.12.199

Realities, M. (2020, March). Retrieved May 20, 2020, from https://lethbridgecollege.ca/mergingrealities

Reed, A., & Phillips, A. (2013). Additive race: Colorblind discourses of realism in performance capture technologies. *Digital Creativity, 24*(2), 130–144. doi:10.1080/14626268.2013.808965

Reid, S. (2019, September). *Game Changer: Teaching with Minecraft*. Lecture conducted from Minefaire Chicago, Chicago, IL.

Repenning, A., Lamprou, A., Petralito, S., & Basawapatna, A. (2019). *Mandatory pre-service teacher Computer Science Education: Exploring a demographic shift in Switzerland*. Paper presented at the Innovation and Technology in computer Science Education, (ITiCSE'19), Aberdeen, UK.

Repenning, A., Webb, D., & Ioannidou, A. (2010). *Scalable game design and the development of a checklist for getting computational thinking into public schools*. Association for Computer Machinery (ACM).

Rheingold, H. (1991). *Virtual reality: The revolutionary technology of computer generated artificial worlds*. Simon & Schuster Publishing.

Richardson, M., Abraham, C., & Bond, R. (2012). Psychological correlates of university students' academic performance: A systematic review and meta-analysis. *Psychological Bulletin*, *138*(2), 353–387. doi:10.1037/a0026838 PMID:22352812

Ricky, C., & O'Donnell Siobhan, M. N. (2017). Factors associated with delayed diagnosis of mood and/or anxiety disorders. *Health Promotion and Chronic Disease Prevention in Canada: Research. Policy & Practice*, *37*(5), 137.

Ritz, L. T., & Buss, A. R. (2016). A framework for aligning instructional design strategies with affordances of CAVE immerisive virtualy reality systesm. *Techn Trends: Linking Research in Practice to Improve Learning*, *60*(6), 549–556. doi:10.100711528-016-0085-9

Riva, G., Mantovani, F., Capideville, S. C., Preziosa, A., Morganti, F., Villani, D., Gaggioli, A., & Botella, C. A. (2007). Affective interactions using virtual reality: The link between presence and emotions. *Cyberpsychology & Behavior, 10*(1), 45-56. https://doi:10.1089/cpb.2006.9993

Riva, G. (2005). Virtual reality in psychotherapy. *Cyberpsychology & Behavior*, *8*(3), 220–230. doi:10.1089/cpb.2005.8.220 PMID:15971972

Riva, G. (2006). *Virtual reality. In Encyclopaedia of Biomedical Engineering*. John Wiley & Sons.

Rizzo, A., Koening, T., & Talbot, T. B. (2019). Clinical results using virtual reality. *Journal of Technology in Human Services, 37,* 51-74. https://doi:10.1080/15228835.2019.1604292

Rizzotto, L. (2017). *The future of education: How A.I. and immersive tech will reshape learning forever*. https://perma.cc/2PYJ-GGPG

Robinson, A. (2016). Oculus Rift Review: Virtual reality is always almost here. *The Verge*. Retrieved May 24, 2020 from https://www.theverge.com/2016/3/28/11284590/oculus-rift-vr-review

Roehl, A., Reddy, S., & Shannon, G. (2013). The flipped classroom: An opportunity to engage millennial students through active learning strategies. *Journal of Family and Consumer Sciences*, *105*(2), 44–49. doi:10.14307/JFCS105.2.12

Rogers, S. (2019). *Virtual Reality: The learning aid of the 21st Century*. Retrieved from https://www.forbes.com/sites/solrogers/2019/03/15/virtual-reality-the-learning-aid-of-the-21st-century/#65899a28139b

Rogers, E. M. (2003). *Diffusion of innovations* (5th ed.). The Free Press.

Rosenblum, L. J., & Cross, R. A. (1997). The challenge of virtual reality. In W. R. Earnshaw, J. Vince, & H. Jones (Eds.), *Visualization & Modeling* (pp. 325–399). Academic Press.

Rothbaum, B. O., Hodges, L., Anderson, P. L., Price, L., & Smith, S. (2002). Twelve-month follow-up of virtual reality and standard exposure therapies for the fear of flying. *Journal of Consulting and Clinical Psychology*, *70*(2), 428–432. doi:10.1037/0022-006X.70.2.428 PMID:11952201

Rothbaum, B. O., Hodges, L., Smith, S., Lee, J. H., & Price, L. (2000). A controlled study of virtual reality exposure therapy for the fear of flying. *Journal of Consulting and Clinical Psychology*, *68*(6), 1020–1026. doi:10.1037/0022-006X.68.6.1020 PMID:11142535

Roussou, M. (2004, June). Examining young learners' activity within interactive virtual environments. In *Proceedings of the 2004 conference on Interaction design and children: building a community* (pp. 167-168). ACM. 10.1145/1017833.1017872

Russell, J., Thomson, G., & Rosenthal, D. (2008). International student use of university health and counselling services. *Higher Education*, *56*(1), 59–75. doi:10.100710734-007-9089-x

Russell, S. J., & Norvig, P. (1995). *Artificial intelligence: A modern approach.* Prentice Hall.

Ryan, S. V., Nathaniel, P., Pendergast, L. L., Saeki, E., Segool, N., & Schwing, S. (2017). Leaving the teaching profession: The role of teacher stress and educational accountability policies on turnover intent. *Teaching and Teacher Education*, *66*(1), 1–11. doi:10.1016/j.tate.2017.03.016

Ryder, A. G., Alden, L. E., Paulhus, D. L., & Dere, J. (2013). Does acculturation predict interpersonal adjustment? It depends on who you talk to. *International Journal of Intercultural Relations*, *37*(4), 502–506. doi:10.1016/j.ijintrel.2013.02.002

Sala, N. (2016). Virtual Reality and Education: Overview Across Different Disciplines. In Emerging Tools and Applications of Virtual Reality in Education (pp. 1-25). IGI Global.

Sala, N. (2009). Fractal Geometry in Artificial Worlds and in Second Life. *Chaos and Complexity Letters*, *4*(1), 23–34.

Sala, N., Metzeltin, S., & Sala, M. (2002). Applications of mathematics in the real world: territory and landscape. *Proceedings International Conference The Humanistic Renaissance in Mathematics Education*, 326-333.

Sala, N., & Sala, M. (2005). Virtual reality in education. In D. Carbonara (Ed.), *Technology literacy applications in learning environments* (pp. 358–367). Idea Group Inc. doi:10.4018/978-1-59140-479-8.ch025

Saleeb, N., & Dafoulas, G. (2010a, June). Architectural propositions for enhancement of learning spaces within 3D virtual learning environments. In *2010 International Conference on Information Society* (pp. 410-415). IEEE. 10.1109/i-Society16502.2010.6018738

Saleeb, N., & Dafoulas, G. (2010b, June). Pedagogical immigration to 3D virtual worlds: A critical review of underlying themes and their concepts. In *2010 International Conference on Information Society* (pp. 401-409). IEEE. 10.1109/i-Society16502.2010.6018737

Salmon, G. (2009). The future for (second) life and learning. *British Journal of Educational Technology*, *40*(3), 13. doi:10.1111/j.1467-8535.2009.00967.x

Salmon, G., Nie, M., & Edirisingha, P. (2010). Developing a five-stage model of learning in Second Life. *Educational Research*, *52*(2), 169–182. doi:10.1080/00131881.2010.482744

Samoilov, A., & Goldfried, M. R. (2000). Role of emotion in cognitive-behavior therapy. *Clinical Psychology: Science and Practice*, *7*(4), 373–385. doi:10.1093/clipsy.7.4.373

Samsung Gear VR with Controller. (n.d.). Retrieved December 18, 2019, from https://www.samsung.com/global/galaxy/gear-vr/

Samsung Gear, V. R. (n.d.). Retrieved May 20, 2020 from https://www.samsung.com/global/galaxy/gear-vr/

Sánchez-Mena, A., & Martí-Parreño, J. (2017). Drivers and Barriers to Adopting Gamification: Teachers' Perspectives. *Electronic Journal of E-Learning*, *15*(5), 434–443.

Saposnik, G., & Levin, M. (2011). Virtual reality in stroke rehabilitation a meta-analysis and implications for clinicians. *Stroke*, *42*(5), 1380–1386. doi:10.1161/STROKEAHA.110.605451 PMID:21474804

Sargent, D. L. (2020). The Evolution of Teacher Education Through Emerging Technologies of Mixed Reality Simulation. In *Next Generation Digital Tools and Applications for Teaching and Learning Enhancement* (pp. 16–30). IGI Global. doi:10.4018/978-1-7998-1770-3.ch002

Scardamalia, M., & Bereiter, C. (2006). Knowledge building: Theory, pedagogy, and technology. In K. Sawyer (Ed.), *Cambridge Handbook of the Learning Sciences* (pp. 97–118). Cambridge University Press.

Scarfe, P., & Glennerster, A. (2015). Using high-fidelity virtual reality to study perception in freely moving observers. *Journal of Vision (Charlottesville, Va.)*, *15*(9), 3–3. doi:10.1167/15.9.3 PMID:26161632

Scarlett, M. (2015). Gaming Geography: Using Minecraft to Teach Essential Geographic Skills. In D. Rutledge & D. Slykhuis (Eds.), *Proceedings of SITE 2015--Society for Information Technology & Teacher Education International Conference* (pp. 838-840). Las Vegas, NV: Association for the Advancement of Computing in Education (AACE). Retrieved November 5, 2019 from https://www.learntechlib.org/primary/p/150098/

Schafer, E. D., O'Reilly, A. E.-S., & Pass, A. D. (2019). *Virtual reality as an alternative therapy*. Salem Press Encyclopedia of Health.

Scheeler, M. C., Budin, S., & Markelz, A. (2016). The role of teacher preparation in promoting evidence-based practice in schools. *Learning Disabilities (Weston, Mass.)*, *14*(2), 171–187.

Schinnerer, J. (2018). *The power of positive internal motivation*. Psych Central. https://psychcentral.com/lib/the-power-of-positive-internal-motivation/

Schmalsteig, D., Fuhrmann, A., Szalavari, Z., & Gervautz, M. (1996). Studierstube – An Environment for Collaboration in Augmented Reality. *CAVE '96 Workshop Proceedings*.

Schmeil, A., Hasler, B., Peachy, A., de Freitas, S., & Nehmzow, C. (2013). Do virtual worlds support engaging social conferencing? In Understanding learning in virtual worlds (pp. 165-179). Springer. doi:10.1007/978-1-4471-5370-2_9

Schmidt, M., Beck, D., Glaser, N., & Schmidt, C. (2017) A Prototype Immersive, Multi-user 3D Virtual Learning Environment for Individuals with Autism to Learn Social and Life Skills: A Virtuoso DBR Update. Communications in Computer and Information Science, 725, 185-188.

Schmidt, J. J. (2003). *Counseling in schools: Essential services and comprehensive programs*. Allyn & Bacon.

Schroeder, R. (2008). Defining VirtualWorlds and Virtual Environments. *Journal of Virtual Worlds Research*, *1*(1). Advance online publication. doi:10.4101/jvwr.v1i1.294

Schwab, K. (2016). *The fourth industrial revolution: What it means, how to respond* [Blog post]. https://www.weforum.org/agenda/2016/01/the-fourth-industrial-revolution-what-it-means-and-how-to-respond/

Shabatura, J. (2018). *Using bloom's taxonomy to write effective learning objectives*. Technological Innovation & Pedagogical Support. https://tips.uark.edu/using-blooms-taxonomy/

Shakya, K., Khanal, S., Alsadoon, A., Prasad, P. W. C., Hsu, J., Deva, A., ... Elchouemic, A. (2019). Remote surgeon hand motion and occlusion removal in mixed reality in breast surgical telepresence: Rural and remote care. *American Journal of Applied Sciences*, *15*(11), 497–509. doi:10.3844/ajassp.2018.497.509

Sharma, S., Agada, R., & Ruffin, J. (2013, April). *Virtual reality classroom as an constructivist approach. In 2013 Proceedings of IEEE Southeastcon*. IEEE.

Shen, L. C., Wu, T. T., & Hsu, W. C. (2019, December). The Application of Augmented Reality to the Education of Chemistry–Take the Course of Nature Science in Junior High School as an Example. In *International Conference on Innovative Technologies and Learning* (pp. 41-48). Springer. 10.1007/978-3-030-35343-8_5

Sherman, W. R., & Craig, A. B. (2003). *Understanding virtual reality. Interface, application and design.* Morgan-Kaufmann Publishers. doi:10.1162/105474603322391668

Sherman, W. R., & Craig, A. B. (2018). *Understanding virtual reality: Interface, application, and design.* Morgan Kaufmann.

Sherman, W. R., & Craig, A. B. (2019). *Understanding virtual reality: interface, application, and design.* Elsevier.

Shin, D. (2017). The role of affordance in the experience of virtual reality learning: Technological and affective affordances in virtual reality. *Telematics and Informatics, 34,* 1826-1836. https//:doi:10.1016/j.tele.2017.05.013

Shin, D. (2018). Empathy and embodied experience in virtual environment: To what extent can virtual reality simulate empathy and embodied experience. *Computers in Human Behavior, 78*, 64–73. doi:10.1016/j.chb.2017.09.012

Shukla Shubhendu, S., & Vijay, J. (2013). Applicability of artificial intelligence in different fields of life. *International Journal of Scientific and Engineering Research, 1*(1), 28–35.

Silva, M., Freitas, D., Neto, E., Lins, C., Teichrieb, V., & Teixeira, J. M. (2014). Glassist: using augmented reality on Google Glass as an aid to classroom management. *2014 XVI Symposium on Virtual and Augmented Reality*, 37-44. 10.1109/SVR.2014.41

Siriaraya, P., & Ang, C. S. (2012). Age differences in the perception of social presence in the use of 3D virtual world for social interaction. *Interacting with Computers, 24*(4), 280–291. doi:10.1016/j.intcom.2012.03.003

Skinner. (1954). *The science of learning and art of teaching.* Cambrige, MA: Harvard Education Review.

Slater, M. (2009). Place illusion and plausibility can lead to realistic behaviour in immersive virtual environments. *Philosophical Transactions of the Royal Society of London. Series B, Biological Sciences, 364*(1535), 3549–3557. doi:10.1098/rstb.2009.0138 PMID:19884149

Smart, J., Cascio, J., & Paffendof, J. (2007). *Metaverse roadmap: pathways to the 3D web.* Retrieved from http://www.metaverseroadmap.org/overview

Smart, J., Cascio, J., & Paffendof, J. (2007). *Metaverse roadmap: pathways to the 3D web.* Retrieved July 5. 2015, from http://www.metaverseroadmap.org/overview

Smokowski, P. R., & Hartung, K. (2003). Computer simulation and virtual reality: The practice of school social work. *Journal of Technology in Human Services, 21*(1–2), 5–30. doi:10.1300/J017v21n01_02

Song, H., Chen, F., Peng, Q., Zhang, J., & Gu, P. (2018). Improvement of user experience using virtual reality in open-architecture product design. *Proceedings of the Institution of Mechanical Engineers. Part B, Journal of Engineering Manufacture, 232*(13), 2264–2275. doi:10.1177/0954405417711736

Springboard, V. R. (2019). *A 30-day guide for implementing virtual reality seamlessly in educational institutions.* Retrieved from https://www.springboardvr.com/

Stefan, L. (2016). Virtual worlds in online Education and Training–an evaluation report. In *Conference proceedings of "eLearning and Software for Education"* (No. 2, pp. 453-459). "Carol I" National Defence University Publishing House.

Steffen, J. H., Gaskin, J. E., Meservy, T. O., Jenkins, J. L., & Wolman, I. (2019). Framework of Affordances for Virtual Reality and Augmented Reality. *Journal of Management Information Systems, 36*(3), 683–729. https//:doi:10.1080/07421222.2019.1628877

Steptoe, A., Tsuda, A., & Tanaka, Y. (2007). Depressive symptoms, socio-economic background, sense of control, and cultural factors in university students from 23 countries. *International Journal of Behavioral Medicine, 14*(2), 97–107. doi:10.1007/BF03004175 PMID:17926438

Stiubiener, I., Barbosa, W., Kamienski, C. A., & Schweitzer, C. M. (2011, October). Using Virtual Worlds in distance learning environments. In 2011 Frontiers in Education Conference (FIE) (pp. F3C-1). IEEE. doi:10.1109/FIE.2011.6142822

Straub, C., Dieker, L., Hynes, M., & Hughes, C. (2014). *Year 1 findings using virtual rehearsal in TLE TeachLivE™ mixed reality classroom simulator to determine the effects on the performance of mathematics teachers.* Retrieved from http://teachlive.org/wp-content/uploads/2014/10/2014_GR_Technical_Report_10_20_FINAL.pdf

Strzys, M. P., Kapp, S., Thees, M., Kuhn, J., Lukowicz, P., Knierim, P., & Schmidt, A. (2017). Augmenting the thermal flux experiment: A mixed reality approach with the HoloLens. *The Physics Teacher, 55*(6), 376–377. doi:10.1119/1.4999739

Sugar, W., & Slagter van Tryon, P. J. (2014). Development of a virtual technology coach to support technology integration for K-12 educators. *TechTrends, 58*(3), 54–62. doi:10.100711528-014-0752-7

Suh, A., & Prophet, J. (2018). The state of immersive technology research: A literature analysis. *Computers in Human Behavior, 86*, 77–90. doi:10.1016/j.chb.2018.04.019

Sundararajan, A. (2016). *The sharing economy: The end of employment and the rise of crowd-based capitalism.* MIT Press.

Sutherland, I. (1965). The ultimate display. *Proceedings of International Federation of Information Processing, 2*, 506-509. Retrieved from http://worrydream.com/refs/Stutherland%20-%20The%Ultimate%20Display.pdf

Sutherland, I. E. (1965). The ultimate display. Multimedia: From Wagner to virtual reality. In *Proceedings of the IFIP Congress.* INFERENCE.

Sutherland, I. E. (1968). A head-mounted three-dimensional display. *Proceedings of AFIPS, 68*, 757–764.

Sutori. (n.d.). Retrieved May 20, 2020 from https://www.sutori.com/item/1961-headsight-developed-by-comeau-and-bryan-the-headsight-projected-screen-f

Sweller, J. (2008). Cognitive load theory and the use of educational technology. *Educational Technology, 48*, 32–35. doi:10.100711423-019-09701-3

Tang, Y. M., Au, K. M., & Leung, Y. (2018). Comprehending products with mixed reality: Geometric relationships and creativity. *International Journal of Engineering Business Management, 10.* Advance online publication. doi:10.1177/1847979018809599

Teoh, J. (2012). Pre-service teachers in second life: Potential of simulations. *Journal of Educational Technology Systems, 40*(4), 415–441. doi:10.2190/ET.40.4.g

Terzidou, T., Tsiatsos, T., Dae, A., Samaras, O., & Chasanidou, A. (2012, July). Utilizing virtual worlds for game based learning: Grafica, a 3D educational game in second life. In *2012 IEEE 12th International Conference on Advanced Learning Technologies* (pp. 624-628). IEEE.

The Associated Press. (2014). *Facebook to buy Oculus virtual reality firm for $2B.* Retrieved July 1, 2015 from http://www.cbc.ca/news/technology/facebook-to-buy-oculus-virtual-reality-firm-for-zb-1,2586318

The New Media Consortium. (2007). *The Horizon Report.* New Media Consortium.

The Schome Community. (2007). *The schome-NAGTY teen second life pilot final report: a summary of key findings and lessons learnt.* http://kn.open.ac.uk/public/getfile.cfm?documentfileid-11344

Thomas, M., Benini, S., Schneider, C., Rainbow, C. A., Can, T., Simsek, T., ... Cinganotto, L. (2018). Digital Game-Based Language Learning in 3D Immersive Environments: The Guinevere Project. *Conference Proceedings: Innovation in Language Learning.*

Thorsteinson, G. (2002). Innovation and practical use of knowledge. *DATA International Research Conference 2002. The Design and Technology Association*, 177–183.

Thorsteinsson, G. (2013). Developing an understanding of the pedagogy of using a virtual reality learning environment (VRLE) to support innovation education. In L. Shavinina (Ed.), The Routledge International handbook of innovation education (pp. 454-470). London: Routledge.

Thorsteinsson, G., & Page, T. (2008). Innovative technology education using a virtual reality learning environment. Pedagogy Studies/Pedigogika: Vilnius Pedagogical University.

Thorsteinsson, G., Page, T., & Niculescu, A. (2010). Using virtual relity for developing design communication. *Studies in Informatics and Control, 19*(1), 93–106. doi:10.24846/v19i1y201010

Tilhou, R., Taylor, V., & Crompton, H. (2020). 3D Virtual Reality in K-12 Education: A Thematic Systematic Review. In *Emerging Technologies and Pedagogies in the Curriculum* (pp. 169–184). Springer. doi:10.1007/978-981-15-0618-5_10

Tillfors, M., & Furmark, T. (2007). Social phobia in Swedish university students: Prevalence, subgroups and avoidant behavior. *Social Psychiatry and Psychiatric Epidemiology, 42*(1), 79–86. doi:10.100700127-006-0143-2 PMID:17160591

Timms, M. J. (2016). Letting artificial intelligence in education out of the box: Educational robots and smart classrooms. *International Journal of Artificial Intelligence in Education, 26*(2), 701–712. doi:10.100740593-016-0095-y

Tindell, D. R., & Bohlander, R. W. (2012). The use and abuse of cell phones and text messaging in the classroom: A survey of college students. *College Teaching, 60*(1), 1–9. doi:10.1080/87567555.2011.604802

Toth, E. E. (2009). "Virtual inquiry" in the science classroom: What is the role of technological pedagogical content knowledge? *International Journal of Communication Technology in Education, 5*(4), 78–87. doi:10.4018/jicte.2009041008

Trahan, M. P., Adams, N. B., & Dupre, S. (2012). Virtual learning environments: Second Life MUVEs to leverage student ownership. In Virtual Learning Environments: Concepts, Methodologies, Tools and Applications (pp. 200-213). Hershey, PA: Information Science Reference. doi:10.4018/978-1-4666-0011-9.ch113

Transcription Wing. (2020). *How to avoid student burnout or academic fatigue.* https://www.transcriptionwing.com/how-to-avoid-student-burnout-or-academic-fatigue/

Translate, G. (2019). [Mobile application software]. Retrieved from https://apps.apple.com/us/app/google-translate/id414706506

Traphagan, T. W., Chiang, Y.-V., Chang, H. M., Wattanawaha, B., Lee, H., Mayrath, M. C., Woo, J., Yoon, H.-J., Jee, M. J., & Resta, P. E. (2010). Cognitive, social and teaching presence in a virtual world and a text chat. *Computers & Education, 55*(3), 923–936. doi:10.1016/j.compedu.2010.04.003

Trelease, R. B. (2016). From chalkboard, slides, and paper to e-learning: How computing technologies have transformed anatomical sciences education. *Anatomical Sciences Education, 9*(6), 583–602. doi:10.1002/ase.1620 PMID:27163170

Tretsiakova-McNally, S., Maranne, E., Verbecke, F., & Molkov, V. (2017). Mixed e-learning and virtual reality pedagogical approach for innovative hydrogen safety training of first responders. *International Journal of Hydrogen Energy*, *42*(11), 7504–7512. doi:10.1016/j.ijhydene.2016.03.175

Tsai, J. P., Kao, Y. C., & Lee, R. S. (2012, July). Investigating the effect of virtual reality application on teaching assistance for machine tools operation education. In *2012 IEEE/ASME International Conference on Advanced Intelligent Mechatronics (AIM)* (pp. 626-631). IEEE. 10.1109/AIM.2012.6265919

Tsaramirsis, G., Buhari, S. M., Al-Shammari, K. O., Ghazi, S., Nazmudeen, M. S., & Tsaramirsis, K. (2016). Towards simulation of the classroom learning experience: Virtual reality approach. *3rd International Conference on Computing for Sustainable Global Development (INDIACom)*, 1343-1346.

Tu, C. H. (2001). How Chinese perceive social presence: An examination of interaction in online learning environment. *Educational Media International*, *38*(1), 45–60. doi:10.1080/09523980010021235

Umbach, P. D., & Wawrzynsli, M. R. (2005). Faculty do matter: The role of college faculty in student learning and engagement. *Research in Higher Education*, *46*(2), 153–185. doi:10.100711162-004-1598-1

Uppot, R. N., Laguna, B., McCarthy, C. J., De Novi, G., Phelps, A., Siegel, E., & Courtier, J. (2019). Implementing virtual and augmented reality tools for radiology education and training, communication, and clinical care. *Radiology*, *291*(3), 570–580. doi:10.1148/radiol.2019182210 PMID:30990383

van Krevelen, D. W. F., & Poelman, R. (2010). A survey of augmented reality technologies, applications and limitations. *The International Journal of Virtual Reality: a Multimedia Publication for Professionals*, *9*(2), 1–20. doi:10.20870/IJVR.2010.9.2.2767

van Loon A, Bailenson, J., Zaki, J., Bostick, J., & Willer, R. (2018) Virtual reality perspective-taking increases cognitive empathy for specific others. *PLoS ONE 13*(8). Article e0202442. https//:doi:10.1371/journal.pone.0202442

Varma, R., Vajaranant, T. S., Burkemper, B., Wu, S., Torres, M., Hsu, C., Choudhury, F., & McKean-Cowdin, R. (2016). Visual impairment and blindness in adults in the United States: Demographic and geographic variations from 2015 to 2050. *JAMA Ophthalmology*, *134*(7), 802–809. doi:10.1001/jamaophthalmol.2016.1284 PMID:27197072

Vera, L. (2019, Apr 10). What does extended reality mean? *Premo*. Retreived from: https://3dcoil.grupopremo.com/blog/what-does-extended-reality-mean/

Vincenti, G., & Braman, J. (2010). *Teaching through multi-user virtual environments: Applying dynamic elements to the modern classroom*. Information Science Reference.

Vincenti, G., & Braman, J. (2011). *Multi-User virtual environments for the classroom: Practical approaches to teaching in virtual worlds*. IGI Global. doi:10.4018/978-1-60960-545-2

Violante, M. G., & Vezzetti, E. (2015). Virtual interactive e-learning application: An evaluation of the student satisfaction. *Computer Applications in Engineering Education*, *23*(1), 72–91. doi:10.1002/cae.21580

Virtual Immersive Teaching and Learning (VITaL). (n.d.). Retrieved May 20, 2020, from https://its.sdsu.edu/vital/

Virtual Reality & Immersive Media Program. (n.d.). Retrieved May 20, 2020 from https://drexel.edu/westphal/academics/undergraduate/virtual-reality/

Virtual Reality (VR) in Higher Ed. (2017, August 3). Retrieved May 20, 2020, from https://blogs.gartner.com/marty-resnick/virtual-reality-vr-in-higher-ed/

Virtual Reality Design. (n.d.). Retrieved May 20, 2020, from https://www.su.edu/applied-technology/virtual-reality-design/

Virtual Reality in the Healthcare Industry. (n.d.). Retrieved 2May 20, 2020, from https://visualise.com/virtual-reality/virtual-reality-healthcare

Virtual Reality. (n.d.a). Retrieved June 24, 2015, from http://www.merriamwebster.com/dictionary/virtualreality

Virtual Reality. (n.d.b). Retrieved June 24, 2015, from https://en.wikipedia.org/wiki/Virtual_reality

Virtual Speech, V. R. (2016). VirtualSpeech (2.28) [Mobile application software]. Retrieved from https://virtualspeech.com/

Virtuality. (n.d.). Retrieved May 20, 2020, from https://virtuality.com/ /

Virtuix Omni™. (n.d.). Retrieved December 18, 2019, from https://www.virtuix.com/product/virtuix-omni/

VIVE Cosmos - a new way of Pc VR: VIVE™. (n.d.). Retrieved December 18, 2019, from https://www.vive.com/us/product/vive-cosmos/features/

VIVE Focus Plus. (n.d.). Retrieved December 18, 2019, from https://enterprise.vive.com/us/product/focus-plus/

VIVE Focus. (n.d.). In *VIVE Enterprise*. Retrieved May 20, 2020, from https://enterprise.vive.com/us/product/vive-focus/

VIVE Pro Eye. (n.d.). In *VIVE Enterprise*. Retrieved May 20, 2020 from https://enterprise.vive.com/us/product/vive-pro-eye-office/

VIVE™ | VIVE Virtual Reality System. (n.d.). Retrieved from https://www.vive.com/us/product/vive-virtual-reality-system/

Wagner, M. (2008). Second life's popularity rests on breadth of activities. *Information Week*. https://www.informationweek.com/news/personal_tech/virtualworlds/showArticle.jhtml?articleID=210602197

Wagner, C., & Ip, R. K. (2019). Action learning with Second Life-A pilot study. *Journal of Information Systems Education*, *20*(2), 13.

Wakefield, J. C., Horwitz, A. V., & Schmitz, M. F. (2005). Are we overpathologizing the socially anxious? Social phobia from a harmful dysfunction perspective. *Canadian Journal of Psychiatry*, *50*(6), 317–319. doi:10.1177/070674370505000604 PMID:15999945

Wang, Y., & Braman, J. (2009). Extending the classroom through second life. *Journal of Information Systems*, *20*(2). 235-247.

Wang, Y., Dudley, A., Braman, J., & Vincenti, G. (2009). Simulating ethical dilemmas: Teaching ethics through immersive virtual environments. *Proceedings of the 12th IASTED International Conference on Computers and Advanced Technology in Education.*

Wang, C. X., Anstadt, S., Goldman, J., & Lefaiver, M. L. M. (2014). Facilitating group discussions in Second Life. *MERLOT Journal of Online Learning and Teaching*, *10*(1), 139–152.

Wang, F., & Burton, J. K. (2013). Second Life in education: A review of publications from its launch to 2011. *British Journal of Educational Technology*, *44*(3), 357–371. doi:10.1111/j.1467-8535.2012.01334.x

Wang, F., & Lockee, B. B. (2010). Virtual Worlds in Distance Education: A Content Analysis Study. *Quarterly Review of Distance Education*, *11*(3), 183–186.

Wang, T., & Zhu, Q. (2009, March). A software engineering education game in a 3-D online virtual environment. In *2009 First International Workshop on Education Technology and Computer Science* (Vol. 2, pp. 708-710). IEEE. 10.1109/ETCS.2009.418

Wang, Y., & Braman, J. (2019). Extending the classroom through Second Life. *Journal of Information Systems Education, 20*(2), 12.

Wante, L., Van Beveren, M. L., Theuwis, L., & Braet, C. (2018). The effects of emotion regulation strategies on positive and negative affect in early adolescents. *Cognition and Emotion, 32*(5), 988–1002. doi:10.1080/02699931.2017.1374242 PMID:28880723

Warburton, S. (2009). Second Life in higher education: Assessing the potential for and the barriers to deploying virtual worlds in learning and teaching. *British Journal of Educational Technology, 40*(3), 414–426. doi:10.1111/j.1467-8535.2009.00952.x

Ware, M. (2018). *The importance of teaching soft skills in today's classrooms.* LearnWell. https://learnwelleducation.com/the-importance-of-teaching-soft-skills-in-todays-classrooms/

Warner, T. (2012). E-coaching systems: Convenient, anytime, anywhere, and nonhuman. *Performance Improvement, 51*(9), 22–28. doi:10.1002/pfi.21305

Wave, S. D. K. (n.d.). In *VIVE Developer Resources*. Retrieved May 20, 2020 from https://developer.vive.com/resources/mobile-vr/

Webb, D., Repenninga, A., & Koh, K. (2012). Toward an emergent theory of broadening participation in computer science education. In *Proceeding of the Association for Computer Machinery (ACM) Special Interest Group on Computer Science Conference (SIGCSE)*. Raleigh, NC: ACM. 10.1145/2157136.2157191

Wei, C.-W., Chen, N.-S., & Kinshuk, S. (2012). A model for social presence in online classrooms. *Educational Technology Research and Development, 60*(3), 529–545. doi:10.100711423-012-9234-9

Weimer, M. (2002). *Learner-centered teaching: Five key changes to practice*. Jossey-Bass.

Weissman, M. M., Wolk, S., Wickramaratne, P., Goldstein, R. B., Adams, P., Greenwald, S., Ryan, N. D., Dahl, R. E., & Steinberg, D. (1999). Children with prepubertal-onset major depressive disorder and anxiety grown up. *Archives of General Psychiatry, 56*(9), 794–801. doi:10.1001/archpsyc.56.9.794 PMID:12884885

Welch, G., & Foxlin, E. (2002). Motion tracking survey. *IEEE Computer Graphics and Applications, 22*(6), 24–38. doi:10.1109/MCG.2002.1046626

West, D. M., & Allen, J. (2018). *How artificial intelligence is transforming the world.* https://www.brookings.edu/research/how-artificial-intelligence-is-transforming-the-world/

Westerberg, P., & Rana, S. (2016). *Using Minecraft for community participation.* United Nations Habitat. https://unhabitat.org/manual-using-minecraft-for-community-participation

Western Carolina University. (2019, April 11). *Nursing students test virtual reality simulation technology at MAHEC.* Retrieved May 20, 2020 from https://news-prod.wcu.edu/2019/04/wcu-school-of-nursing-students-test-virtual-reality-simulation-technology-at-mahec/

Westlake, J. (2019). Exploring the Potential of Using Augmented Reality and Virtual Reality for STEM Education. In *Learning Technology for Education Challenges: 8th International Workshop, LTEC 2019, Proceedings* (36-44). Springer.

Westwood, J. D. (2011). *Medicine Meets Virtual Reality: Nextmed.* IOS Press.

Whiteman, D. (2009). View-Master, an icon of souvenirs since 1939, enters nonscenic era. *The New York Times*. Retrieved from https://www.nytimes.com/2009/03/04/business/worldbusiness/04iht-view.4.20593331.html

Wiederhold, B. K., Jang, D. P., Gevirtz, R. G., Kim, S. I., Kim, I. Y., & Wiederhold, M. D. (2002). The treatment of fear of flying: A controlled study of imaginal and virtual reality graded exposure therapy. *IEEE Transactions on Information Technology in Biomedicine*, *6*(3), 218–223. doi:10.1109/TITB.2002.802378 PMID:12381038

Wigert, B., de Vreede, G., Boughzala, I., & Bououd, I. (2012). The role of the facilitator in virtual world collaboration. *Journal of Virtual Worlds Research*, *5*(2), 1–18. doi:10.4101/jvwr.v5i2.6225

Wigham, C. R., & Chanier, T. (2013). A study of verbal and nonverbal communication in Second Life–the ARCHI21 experience. *ReCALL*, *25*(01), 63–84. doi:10.1017/S0958344012000250

Wigham, C. R., & Chanier, T. (2015). Interactions between text chat and audio modalities for L2 communication and feedback in the synthetic world Second Life. *Computer Assisted Language Learning*, *28*(3), 260–283. doi:10.1080/09588221.2013.851702

Wilkes, S. F. (2016). Communication modality, learning, and Second Life. In S. Gregory, M. J. W. Lee, B. Dalgarno, & B. Tynan (Eds.), *Learning in virtual worlds: Research and applications* (pp. 43–65). Athabasca University Press.

Williams, T., Szafir, D., Chakraborti, T., & Ben Amor, H. (2018, March). Virtual, augmented, and mixed reality for human-robot interaction. In *Companion of the 2018 ACM/IEEE International Conference on Human-Robot Interaction* (pp. 403-404). ACM. 10.1145/3173386.3173561

Williams, T., Szafir, D., Chakraborti, T., & Phillips, E. (2019, March). Virtual, Augmented, and Mixed Reality for Human-Robot Interaction (VAM-HRI). In *2019 14th ACM/IEEE International Conference on Human-Robot Interaction (HRI)* (pp. 671-672). IEEE.

Wilson, A., Brown, S., Wood, Z., & Farkas, K. (2013). Teaching direct practice skills using web-based simulations: Home visiting in the virtual world. *Journal of Teaching in Social Work*, *33*(4-5), 421–437. doi:10.1080/08841233.2013.833578

Wilson, S. M., & Peterson, P. L. (2006). *Theories of learning and teaching: What do they mean for educators?* National Education Association. Retrieved from http://www.nea.org/assets/docs/mf_ltreport.pdf

Winkelmann, K., Keeney-Kennicutt, W., Fowler, D., Lazo Macik, M., Perez Guarda, P., & Ahlborn, C. J. (2019). Learning gains and attitudes of students performing chemistry experiments in an immersive virtual world. *Interactive Learning Environments*, 1–15.

Winn, W. (1993). *A conceptual basis for educational applications of virtual reality* (Report No. TR-93-9). Human Interface Technology Laboratory, Washington Technology Center.

Winn, W. (1993). *A conceptual basis for educational applications of virtual reality (Technical Report TR-93-9)*. Human Interface Technology Laboratory, University of Washington. Retrieved from http://www.hitl.washington.edu/publications/r-93-9/

Wong, W. (2016). *Getting started with Minecraft: Education Edition*. EdTech. https://edtechmagazine.com/k12/article/2016/11/getting-started-minecraft-education-edition

Woods, E., Billinghurst, M., Looser, J., Aldridge, G., Brown, D., Garrie, B., & Nelles, C. (2004). Augmenting the science centre and museum experience. *Proceedings of the 2nd International Conference on Computer Graphics and Interactive Techniques in Australasia and South East Asia (GRAPHITE '04)*, 230–236. 10.1145/988834.988873

Woolf, B. (2009). *Building Intelligent Interactive Tutors*. Morgan Kaufmann., doi:10.1016/B978-0-12-373594-2

Wright, A. (2018). *Building real-world community with Minecraft*. The Dirt. https://dirt.asla.org/2018/10/23/building-real-world-community-with-minecraft/

Wu, F., Liu, Z., Wang, J., & Zhao, Y. (2015, March). Establishment virtual maintenance environment based on VIRTOOLS to effectively enhance the sense of immersion of teaching equipment. In *2015 International Conference on Education Technology, Management and Humanities Science (ETMHS 2015)*. Atlantis Press. 10.2991/etmhs-15.2015.93

Wu, H. K., Lee, S. W. Y., Chang, H. Y., & Liang, J. C. (2013). Current status, opportunities and challenges of augmented reality in education. *Computers & Education*, *62*, 41–49. doi:10.1016/j.compedu.2012.10.024

Wu, P. H., Hwang, G. J., Yang, M. L., & Chen, C. H. (2018). Impacts of integrating the repertory grid into an augmented reality-based learning design on students' learning achievements, cognitive load and degree of satisfaction. *Interactive Learning Environments*, *26*(2), 221–234. doi:10.1080/10494820.2017.1294608

XReality Center. (n.d.). Retrieved May 20, 2020, from https://xrcenter.newschool.edu/

Xu, Y., Mendenhall, S., Ha, V., Tillery, P., & Cohen, J. (2012). *Herding nerds on your table: NerdHerder, a mobile augmented reality game. Proceedings of the 2012 ACM annual conference extended abstracts on human factors in computing systems extended abstracts*, 1351–1356. 10.1145/2212776.2212453

Yahaya, R. A. (2006). Assessing the Effectiveness of Virtual Reality Technology as part of an Authentic Learning Environment. *Proceedings of the Sixth International Conference on Advanced Learning Technologies (ICALT'06)*. Retrieved from https://eprints.qut.edu.au/9327/1/9327.pdf

Yahaya, R. A., Euler, T., & Godat, M. (2004). Enhancement of Learning in Decision Making and Negotiation within Virtual Reality Environment. In E. McWilliam, S. Danby, & J. Knight (Eds.), *Performing Educational Research: Theories*. Methods and Practices.

Yalcinalp, S., Sen, N., Kocer, G., & Koroglu, F. (2012). Higher education student's behaviors as avatars in a web based course in Second Life. *Procedia: Social and Behavioral Sciences*, *46*, 4534–4538. doi:10.1016/j.sbspro.2012.06.291

Ye, E., Liu, C., & Polack-Wahl, J. A. (2007). *Enhancing software engineering education using teaching aids in 3-D online virtual worlds. Frontiers in Education.*

Yee, N. (2006). The demographics, motivations, and derived experiences of users of massively multi-user online graphical environments. *Presence (Cambridge, Mass.)*, *15*(3), 309–329. doi:10.1162/pres.15.3.309

Yilmaz, R., Topu, F., Goktas, Y., & Coban, M. (2013). Social presence and motivation in a three dimensional virtual world: An explanatory study. *Australian Journal of Educational Technology, 29*(6).

Yoshida, S., Kihara, K., Takeshita, H., & Fujii, Y. (2014). Instructive head-mounted display system: Pointing device using a vision-based finger tracking technique applied to surgical education. *Videosurgery, & Techniques Other Miniinvasive, PMC*, *9*(3), 449. doi:10.5114/wiitm.2014.44132 PMID:25337172

Youngblut, C. (1998). *Educational uses of virtual reality technology* (IDA Document D-2128). Retrieved from Institute for Defense Analyses website: https://www.sustainable-design.ie/sustain/VE_Education-D2128.pdf

YouTube VR. (2020). [Mobile application software]. Retrieved December 17, 2019 from https://play.google.com/store/apps/details?id=com.google.android.apps.youtube.vr&hl=en_IN

Zachara, M., & Zagal, J. P. (2009). Challenges for success in stereo gaming: A virtual boy case study. *ACM International Conference Proceeding Series*, 99–106. 10.1145/1690388.1690406

Zhang, B., Robb, N., Eyerman, J., & Goodman, L. (2017). Virtual worlds and gamification to increase integration of international students in higher education: An inclusive design approach. *International Journal of E-Learning & Distance Education/Revue internationale du e-learning et la formation à distance, 32*(2).

Zhang, M. W. B., & Ho, R. C. M. (2017). Smartphone applications for immersive virtual reality therapy for internet addiction and internet gaming disorder. *Technology and Health Care*, *25*(2), 367–372. doi:10.3233/THC-161282 PMID:27911347

Zhang, M., Zhang, Z., Chang, Y., Aziz, E. S., Esche, S., & Chassapis, C. (2018). Recent developments in game-based virtual reality educational laboratories using the microsoft kinect. *International Journal of Emerging Technologies in Learning*, *13*(1), 138–159. doi:10.3991/ijet.v13i01.7773

Zhan, T., Zou, J., Xiong, J., Liu, X., Chen, H., Yang, J., Liu, S., Dong, Y., & Wu, S. T. (2020). Practical Chromatic Aberration Correction in Virtual Reality Displays Enabled by Cost-Effective Ultra-Broadband Liquid Crystal Polymer Lenses. *Advanced Optical Materials*, *8*(2), 1901360. doi:10.1002/adom.201901360

Zhao, W., Sun, K., & Li, X. J. (2011, May). Investigation on Situational Networked Learning Environment in Virtual Campus. In *2011 3rd International Workshop on Intelligent Systems and Applications* (pp. 1-5). IEEE. 10.1109/ISA.2011.5873408

Zhao, H., Sun, B., Wu, H., & Hu, X. (2010, November). Study on building a 3D interactive virtual learning environment based on OpenSim platform. In *2010 International Conference on Audio, Language and Image Processing* (pp. 1407-1411). IEEE. 10.1109/ICALIP.2010.5684986

Zheng, B., Warschauer, M., Hwang, J. K., & Collins, P. (2014). Laptop use, interactive science software, and science learning among at-Risk students. *Journal of Science Education and Technology*, *1*(5), 591–603. doi:10.100710956-014-9489-5

Zhong, Y., & Liu, C. (2012, June). User evaluation of a domain-oriented end-user design environment for building 3D virtual chemistry experiments. In *2012 First International Workshop on User Evaluation for Software Engineering Researchers (USER)* (pp. 5-8). IEEE. 10.1109/USER.2012.6226585

Zhou, N. N., & Deng, Y. L. (2009). Virtual reality: A state-of-the-art survey. *International Journal of Automation and Computing*, *6*(4), 319–325. doi:10.100711633-009-0319-9

Zoller, U. (1990). Students' misunderstandings and misconceptions in college freshman chemistry (general and organic). *Journal of Research in Science Teaching*, *27*(10), 1053–1065. doi:10.1002/tea.3660271011

Zulkanain, N. A., Rahim, E. E. A., & Azizan, F. F. (2016, August). Exploratory study on the relationship of students' perceptions towards the instructors' involvement in Second Life. In *2016 4th International Conference on User Science and Engineering (i-USEr)* (pp. 100-104). IEEE.

Zyda, M. (2005). From visual simulation to virtual reality to games. *Computer*, *38*(9), 25–32. doi:10.1109/MC.2005.297

About the Contributors

Amber Dailey-Hebert has worked, in the United States and abroad, for continuing higher education programs focused on adult learners, distance education and training, and grant-funded projects that serve working professionals. She earned her Ph.D. in Adult Education from Cornell University, and completed her undergraduate & masters studies in Leadership Development and Distance Education at Texas A&M University. As a tenured Full Professor, she has taught traditional, accelerated, and online courses in the Graduate School of Professional Studies at Park University, focusing on critical teaching for social change. Her administrative academic experience includes Department Chair, Program Coordinator, Associate Dean, and Founding & Executive Director of the Center for Excellence in Teaching & Learning (CETL), which provides faculty development for over 1600 full/part time faculty located around the globe.

* * *

James Braman is an Assistant Professor in the Computer Science/Information Technology Department at the Community College of Baltimore County for the School of Technology, Art & Design. He earned a B.S. and M.S. in Computer Science and D.Sc. in Information Technology from Towson University. He is currently pursuing a M.S. in Thanatology from Marian University. From 2009 to 2017 he was a joint editor-in-chief for the European Alliance for Innovation (EAI) endorsed Transactions on E-Learning with Dr. Giovanni Vincenti. Dr. Braman's research interests include thanatechnology, virtual and augmented reality, e-Learning, affective computing, agent-based technologies and information retrieval.

Anita Cassard completed her undergraduate coursework at the Economic Research Institute and Institute of Advanced Studies. She received her MPS from The New School University in New York City, and her PhD from Walden University in Minneapolis, Minnesota (Applied Management and Decision Sciences). Anita collaboratively writes papers published in scientific journals such as Insight – A Journal of Scholarly Teaching, JSBHS- Journal of Social, Behavioral, and Health Sciences, and VDM-Publishing in Germany, published her book, The Sherpa Leadership Model: A Model of Disempowerment, in Europe, Asia, and the United States. She is a member of Sigma Iota Epsilon-Zeta Rho Chapter and Delta Mu Delta, and serves as the Dean of the School of Business at Howard Taft University.

Nicole Cuadro is an Adjunct Professor within the Learning and Instruction department at The University of San Francisco, School of Education. She is currently completing her Doctoral work in the Organization and Leadership department with an emphasis on Digital Accessibility for Online Course

Content. Nicole has over ten years of experience in the Education Technology field, as a technology director for a school, technology teacher, professional development developer and presenter, and in her current role as Distance Learning Administrator for School of Nursing and Health Professions at the University of San Francisco. Her research and instruction focuses include digital accessibility, instructional design, multimedia learning, technology professional development for educators, universal design for learning, and distance education.

Lisa Dieker is a Pegasus Professor and Lockheed Martin Eminent Scholars in the College of Community Innovation and Education at the University of Central Florida (UCF). She serves as the Director of the UCF/Lockheed Martin Mathematics and Science Academy, Program Coordinator for the Ph.D. program in special education, and Co-Director of the UCF Center for Research in Education Simulation Technology (CREST). Her research focuses on harnessing the power of teachers working across disciplines in inclusive settings in teacher education, special education, and simulation.

Angelica Fulchini Scruggs is a technology innovation post-doctoral researcher with the IRIS Center at Vanderbilt University and the Associate Director of CREST Center in the College of Community Innovation and Education at the University of Central Florida. Dr. Fulchini Scruggs is also the Project Director of the United Cerebral Palsy of Central Florida schools Teacher Mentorship Program where she works with first-year teachers in order to retain educators in the classroom. Her research includes using technology to prepare teachers in inclusive classrooms and reducing novice teachers stress using biofeedback.

Reza Ghanbarzadeh is currently a lecturer at the School of Business and Tourism, Southern Cross University, Australia. Reza obtained his PhD in the field of information systems from the School of Information and Communication, Griffith University, Australia. His research mainly focuses on human-computer interaction and the innovative use of technologies in various contexts.

Amir Ghapanchi is currently a senior lecturer at Victoria University, Australia. Amir obtained his PhD from the Australian School of Business, at the University of New South Wales (UNSW), Australia. Amir has published over 80 referred publications including more than 50 journal articles in prestigious journals.

Charles Hughes is Pegasus Professor of Computer Science, Electrical & Computer Engineering, Education, Games & Interactive Media, and Modeling Simulation & Training at the University of Central Florida (UCF). He is co-director of the university's Synthetic Reality Laboratory (SREAL), co-director of the Center for Research in Education Simulation Technology (CREST), and co-lead of the Learning Sciences Faculty Cluster Initiative. He received his BA in Mathematics in 1966 (Northeastern University), and his MS and Ph.D. in Computer Science in 1968 and 1970, respectively (Penn State). He was a National Research Council Postdoctoral Research Associate in 1971-72 and a faculty member at Penn State and the University of Tennessee before coming to UCF in 1980. His research interests are in virtual environments, especially those focused on learning, and the applications of these technologies to interpersonal skills development, teacher preparation, physician training, de-escalation skills, and protective strategies for self and others.

Eric Imperiale is a digital artist and research associate for the Synthetic Reality Lab (SREAL) at the University of Central Florida's Institute for Simulation and Training (IST). His duties include concept art, graphic design, motion capture, 3D modeling, texturing, character rigging and animation. A graduate from the Florida Interactive Entertainment Academy (FIEA), Eric has worked on numerous video games and interactive simulations for military, medical and educational institutions. Previous artistic occupations have involved painting and sculpture as a scenic artist for various Florida theme parks and themed restaurants. He continues to work on personal projects in drawing, painting and sculpture in both digital and traditional formats.

Kathleen Ingraham is the Program Director of the Center for Research in Education Simulation Technologies (CREST) at the University of Central Florida (UCF). Her research explores the intersection of simulation design and improvised interactive performance. She works with faculty at UCF to design and evaluate new interpersonal simulation applications and technologies.

Zac Jarrard is a Project Manager in Information Technology Services and a Professional Tutor for the Academic Success Center. He is pursuing a Master of Information Systems in Business Analytics, while also holding an MPA and MBA from Park University. A few of his duties include delivering operational and strategic projects and assisting students who are struggling with their classes. His research interests include gamification, innovation, and project management. Zac is a gamification, artificial intelligence, and innovation leader at Park University. He is also an Eagle Scout who aspires to make the world a better place for everyone.

Melisa Kaye teaches in the Educational Technology program at the University of San Francisco and in the Occupational Therapy department at San Jose State University. A design team member for the Educational Technology Master's program at the University of San Francisco, her curriculum development work focuses on the meaningful intersections between digital technology and optimal learning. Dr. Kaye's research interests include the use of multimedia strategies to augment complex content learning, the incorporation of technology in healthcare education, sensory processing and integration, trauma-informed care, and children's development of cognitive and perceptual skills. In addition to her teaching work, Dr. Kaye is is the founder and director of a pediatric occupational therapy clinic in the San Francisco Bay Area.

Susan Keim is an Assistant Professor in the Hauptmann School of Public Affairs at Park University. Her areas of expertise are citizen engagement, community development, leadership and followership, local government, public policy, and gamification. In addition, she facilitates community strategic planning, leadership, development and team building for governments, businesses and nonprofits throughout the country. Susan is most proud of her past leadership accomplishments as chair of the All-America City Steering Committee which won the coveted All-America City Award for Kansas City, Kansas/Wyandotte County and founding chair of the Community Foundation of Wyandotte County. She is a Kansas Jayhawk through and through, receiving her BA, MPA, and PhD from the University of Kansas.

Natalie Nussli is a graduate from the Monterey Institute of International Studies (MATESOL) and the University of San Francisco (Ed.D.). She is now a faculty member at the University of Applied Sciences and Arts Northwestern Switzerland at the Institute of Primary Education where she currently trains pre- and in-service primary school teachers in the English Department. Natalie emphasizes the importance of inquiry-based learning, reflective practice, and feedback processes in her teaching. Her research interests revolve around teacher training in three-dimensional virtual worlds, the use of virtual discussion groups to promote reflective practice, and the unique affordances of virtual worlds for special education purposes.

Kevin Oh, Ph.D., is an associate professor at the University of San Francisco in the Learning and Instruction department. After completing his doctorate in special education at the University of Virginia, Kevin accepted a position at the University of San Francisco where he currently trains pre-service and in-service teachers in general education and special education programs. In his current position, Kevin emphasizes the importance of teacher training and the critical role of using data to provide important feedback for in-service teachers. In sum, he prepares teachers to utilize technology appropriately and effectively, and to investigate how technology can be integrated into the curriculum for high-need students with disabilities in urban school settings.

Debra Olson-Morrison, PhD, MSW, LCSW, RPT-S, is an Assistant Professor of Social Work at Park University. Debra earned her PhD in 2009 and her MSW in 2001 from University of Utah, and she has been teaching at Park University since 2015. Debra's research interests vary, and she has publications on field education in social work, Universal Design for Learning, play therapy, and trauma treatment. She is committed to accessibility in secondary education for students with trauma, emotional and psychological disorders, and her most recent work centers on teaching resiliency to new college students. Debra's interest in accessibility in education lead her to discovering the power of VR in social work education.

Yvonne Pigatt is an Assistant Professor in the Computer Science/Information Technology Department at the Community College of Baltimore County for the School of Technology, Art & Design. She teaches a variety of technology courses ranging from Diversity in a Technological Society to Comprehensive Database Design. Prior to teaching, she was a Software Engineer at Verizon Communications. Yvonne has a Bachelor of Science in Management Information Systems from the Columbia Union College and a Master of Science in Management Information Systems from American University. She is currently pursuing a Doctoral degree in Adult Learning and Higher Education from Walden University. Her research interests include student engagement, e-Education, Social Presence in Online Learning, and collaborative technology.

Annette Romualdo is a doctoral candidate and LEAD-IT scholar in the Exceptional Student Education Ph.D. program at the University of Central Florida. With a M.Ed. in Secondary Education (mathematics emphasis) and experience in inclusive settings, Annette's passion is to increase equity and access for students with disabilities in general education K-12 and post-secondary settings.

Nicoletta Sala received the degree in Physics ("Laurea"), applied cybernetics, at the University of Milan (Italy). Ph.D. in Communication Science at Università della Svizzera italiana of Lugano (USI, Lugano, Switzerland). Postgraduates (two years for each) in:"Didactics of the communication and multimedia technologies" and "Journalism and mass media". She is professor in Information Technology and in Electronics and she taught at University of Lugano (Mendrisio, Switzerland). She is founder and co-editor of Chaos and Complexity Letters International Journal of Dynamical System Research (Nova

Science, New York). Her research interests concern various scientific topics from an interdisciplinary point of view and comprise the following areas: Fractal Geometry and Complexity; Mathematics in Arts, Architecture and Industrial Design; New media and IT in the learning environments; Virtual Reality in education. She has authored 20 mathematics and information technology books, and edited 10 others. She has written 300 scientific papers.

Judi Simmons Estes' interest in technology was initially ignited by her son's passion, as early as 1983, when he and his peers were teaching their teachers how to use computers within the classroom. A pioneer in teaching via a community college cable network, partnering with public television to provide training to rural educators, and an early adopter of teaching online, Dr. Estes is committed to finding innovative ways to provide accessible and effective teacher training. Her work emphasizes the need for program-wide and program-deep integration of technology pedagogy and practice that transforms the teaching-learning process, along with institutional support and professional development for student-centered delivery. Academic experience within a Department of Education has included Adjunct faculty, Program Coordinator, Department Chair, Coordinator of an Urban Education graduate program, and Associate Dean.

Nidhi Sinha is a Graduate student in psychology at IIT Hyderabad, India, and is currently working in the field of cognitive psychology. Prior to joining IITH, she worked as a Cognitive Behavior Therapist at NIMHANS, Bangalore. She has published various articles in national and international journals.

Brian Sloboda earned his Bachelor's Degree in Economics from Rowan University in New Jersey and received his Master's and Doctoral Degrees in Economics from Southern Illinois University at Carbondale. His research interests in labor economics, economic growth, finance, and regional economics and entreprenership. He completed the Post Doctoral Bridge (PDB) Program at the Warrington College of Business Administration Hough Graduate School at the University of Florida with a specialization in financial management and corporate finance. Brian has published articles in the Journal of Economics, Journal of Financial Issues, Advances in Econometrics, Crisis Management in Tourism (wrote a chapter on the effects of terrorism on Europe)) Tourism Economics, Journal of Transportation and Statistics, Pennsylvania Economic Review, International Journal of Transport Economics (2), Journal of Educators Online, the Journal of Transportation Research Forum, Public Administration(2), Journal of Business and Economic Studies, and the Virginia Economic Journal. He edited a volume for J Ross Publishers on Transportation Statistics. He is also a committee member for the Federal Forecasters Consortium (FFC) and a board member for the Pennsylvania Economics Association. He is the former president for the Society of Government Economists (SGE) and is now the executive director. He is currently an assistant editor for the Journal of Economics and a senior social science editor for the European Scientific Journal.

Yongzhi Wang received his BS and MS degrees in computer science from Xidian University, China in 2004 and 2007, respectively. He received his PhD in computer science from Florida International University, FL, USA, in 2015. His research interests include software security, network security, and computer education. He has published more than 30 peer-reviewed articles. Some of them are published in top-tiered conferences and journals, including IEEE TIFS, IEEE Transactions on Computers, INFOCOM, etc.

Benjamin Zibers is the Associate Vice President at Park Gilbert, Park University's second traditional campus located in Gilbert, Arizona. As such, he is responsible for leading all aspects of the student lifecycle, enrollment growth and student life. He also leads the development and execution of operations and initiatives with a focus on student enrollment, retention and experiences, strategic academic partnerships and academic delivery. Previously, he served as the Director for Student Engagement at Park University's Flagship Campus in Parkville Missouri.

Index

3DVW 21-22, 25, 28-34, 36-39, 47

A

Active Learning 2, 4, 6-7, 16, 73, 148, 150-151, 164, 166, 169, 171, 174, 187, 191
Active Worlds 13, 31, 42, 59, 112, 117, 172, 193
ADDIE 216
Affordances 4, 7, 13, 17, 31, 43, 60, 64, 113-114, 116, 119, 128, 164, 188-189, 229, 232, 234-238, 241, 250-251, 254-255
AI and eLearning assessment 216
Anaheim 194, 210-212, 215
Artificial Intelligence (AI) 6, 20, 67, 133, 137, 143, 175-176, 216, 218-219, 223-226, 228-231
Asynchronous 117, 197, 208
Augmented Reality (AR) 2-3, 13-17, 20, 48-56, 60-72, 75-76, 82-84, 89, 91-92, 94-95, 122, 133, 136, 142-143, 168, 171, 189, 216-221, 223-224, 226, 228-231, 233, 250, 253-255, 268
Authentic Learning Environment 167-168
Avatar 2, 4, 19-20, 36-37, 39, 47, 56, 58-59, 72, 97, 99-100, 107, 115, 119, 126, 129, 131, 138-139, 141, 146, 150, 171, 174, 176-178, 180, 182, 185, 192-193, 236, 240-241

B

Big Data 220, 224, 229-231
Blackboard 38, 47, 173, 222
Block by Block 194, 210-212, 215

C

Captivating Virtual Instruction for Training 226, 231
Causality 218, 231
Chess 194, 212, 215
Citizen Engagement and Civic Participation 194, 215
Cognitive Embodiment 238, 250, 255
Collaborative Virtual Environments 17, 95, 166
College Teaching 93, 145, 165
Communication Modalities 97-98, 102, 111-113, 117
Communication Modality 96, 102, 115-117
Community College 5, 45, 170-172, 188-189
Competencies 196, 200, 213, 232-234, 237-239, 241, 245, 248, 251, 255
Computer-Mediated Communication 96

D

Debriefing 103, 108, 158, 238-240, 243-244, 246, 248, 250, 252-255
Discussion Facilitation 96, 112
Discussion Group 96, 100, 106, 115
Distance Learning 7, 13, 16, 34, 37-38, 42, 46, 60, 68, 114, 117, 166, 207, 214, 216, 252
Dominoes 194, 215
Dynamic Difficulty Scaling (DDS) 134, 143

E

Education 1-37, 39-48, 52-53, 55-58, 60-72, 74-75, 82-91, 93, 95, 111, 113-120, 122-126, 132, 134-142, 145-152, 161-168, 170-175, 177, 180, 184, 187-194, 196, 198-202, 205-209, 212-215, 217-230, 232-234, 236-237, 245, 251-254, 260, 264, 267-268, 271
Educational Game 46, 193
Educational Space 170, 172-173, 186, 193
Edutainment 54, 72, 85
E-Learning 18-19, 22-23, 34, 37-38, 40, 42, 47, 58-60, 66-67, 71-72, 190, 195, 213-214
eLearning content 216
Embodiment 4, 139, 150, 232, 235-236, 238, 250, 255
Emerging Technologies 1, 70, 143, 145, 153, 175, 179, 183, 192
Emotion Perception 263-265, 273
Emotion Regulation 264, 272-273

Empathy 117, 206, 209, 232-238, 240-241, 244, 248-250, 252-255
Engagement 3, 9, 55, 75, 85, 91, 97-100, 102, 108, 110-113, 115, 117, 123, 126-127, 133-134, 136, 140, 147, 149-151, 153, 159-160, 166-168, 170, 172, 174, 182, 187-191, 193-199, 201-203, 207-212, 215-217, 223, 232-236, 249-251, 255
enhanced learning 126, 155, 216-217, 232, 234, 248
eSports 6-7, 13, 20
Extended Reality (XR) 1-3, 18, 20

F

Faculty Development 145-146, 150-151
FOV (Field of View) 79, 143
Foveated Rendering 136, 143
Fractal Geometry 53, 69, 73

G

Games 3, 10-11, 14, 16, 19-20, 29, 36, 40-41, 57, 60, 76, 81-82, 91-92, 94, 139, 142, 160, 171, 173-174, 191-216, 219
Gamification 60, 64-66, 72-73, 170, 172, 194-204, 207-214, 225

H

Hardware 2, 4, 16, 36-39, 48-51, 56, 73-74, 77, 79-81, 87-89, 91, 95, 146-147, 150, 156, 160, 162-163, 172, 267
Head-Mounted Display (HMD) 20, 75-76, 78, 80, 124
Higher Education 1, 5-7, 11-12, 14-16, 19, 21-36, 39-43, 46-47, 65-67, 69, 72, 74, 83-84, 89-90, 116, 122-123, 138, 145-148, 150, 152, 162-168, 187-190, 193-194, 196, 198, 201-202, 207-209, 212-213, 223, 228, 234, 260, 264, 267, 271
HMD 20, 51, 75-76, 78, 80, 87-88, 124, 130-131, 143, 156, 160
HTC 75, 80-81, 120-121, 124, 136, 147, 156, 160, 168
Human in the Loop 127, 143

I

Immersion 2-4, 20, 36, 48-49, 53, 56, 61-62, 67, 72-73, 75, 78, 80, 115, 120, 122, 126, 132, 139, 143, 153, 216-217, 235-236, 240, 244, 247, 250, 259, 262, 266, 270
Immersive 1-4, 6, 8, 10-14, 20, 22, 33-34, 39, 41, 43-46, 50-51, 53-54, 56, 59-60, 65-66, 70, 74-76, 78, 80, 82-84, 86-90, 92-94, 113-116, 118-120, 122-124, 126-132, 134-138, 140, 142-145, 147-149, 160, 164-165, 170, 172-173, 175, 189-193, 213, 216, 220, 229-230, 239-241, 251, 255, 260, 266-267
Immersive Virtual Reality (VR) 14, 143
Immersive Virtual World 4, 20, 46, 53
IMVU 57, 59, 172, 193
Innovative Technology 1, 14, 18
Inquiry-Based Learning (IBL) 60, 73
Intelligence Tutoring Systems 224-225, 231
Interaction 1, 3-4, 8, 17, 19-20, 22, 30, 37, 43, 48-49, 54, 56, 58, 62-63, 71, 73, 75, 78-80, 82, 87, 89, 91, 98-100, 109, 112-115, 117, 125-127, 131-132, 135, 139, 144, 149, 151, 153, 157, 171, 173, 187, 193, 196, 202, 217, 223, 225, 228, 234, 236, 240-241, 243, 263
Interactive 1-3, 9, 13, 15, 17, 20, 22, 27-28, 35, 43, 45-46, 50, 54, 62, 67-68, 71-73, 75, 89, 94-95, 98, 100, 114, 119, 122, 146-147, 154, 158, 162, 164, 169-171, 173-174, 176-177, 185, 190-191, 193, 196, 200, 204, 215, 217, 231, 235, 251
Interactor 124, 127, 131, 133-134, 137-138, 143

K

Kahoot! 194, 197, 202-203, 208, 215
Kinect 123, 143-144, 219

L

Learning 1-2, 4-23, 25-38, 40-48, 52-73, 75, 83-86, 88, 92-93, 95, 97-98, 100, 106-108, 111-119, 123, 125-127, 134-140, 142-143, 145-152, 154-155, 159-177, 180, 186-210, 212-244, 246-248, 250-252, 254-255, 258, 268
Learning Environment 3, 18, 20, 27, 36, 38, 41-42, 46-47, 57, 60, 69, 75, 84, 92, 95, 115, 126, 135, 148-149, 152, 166-168, 174, 209, 219-220, 234-235, 249, 255
Linden Scripting Language 38, 47, 193

M

Machinima 29, 36, 44, 47
Mental Health 8, 90, 237-238, 242, 257-259, 261-263, 265-270, 273
Mental Health Awareness 263
Minecon 205, 215
Minecraft 7, 17, 172, 189-190, 193, 203-215

Minefaire 205-206, 214-215
Mixed Reality (MR) 2-3, 6, 20, 48, 50-51, 54-55, 62-64, 66-68, 70-71, 73, 83, 95, 122, 139-142, 144, 178, 218, 223, 229, 231, 252
Multi-User Virtual Environment 42, 148, 193
Mumbai 210-212, 215
Mumbai Environmental Social Network 211, 215
MYO Gesture-Type Platform 123, 144

N

Non-Immersive Virtual Reality (VR) 144

O

Oculus 6, 10, 14, 16-18, 75-76, 81-82, 92, 120-121, 132, 136, 141, 156, 160, 168, 173, 266
Open Simulator 30-31, 33, 47, 59, 187, 190, 193

P

Pedagogical Content Knowledge 151, 164, 167-168
Pedagogy 6-7, 9, 11, 13, 15, 17-18, 29, 41-42, 68, 139, 145-146, 151, 164, 166, 168-169, 200, 221, 223
Phobia 243, 258-260, 262, 264, 266, 272-273
Preservice teacher 118, 135
Progressive Muscle Relaxation 265, 273
Psychotherapeutic Techniques 268, 273

R

Robotics 62, 67, 73

S

Script 193
Second Life 4, 6-7, 15, 19, 27-34, 37-38, 40-48, 58-60, 62-63, 65-69, 71, 73, 96-97, 100, 102, 110, 112-117, 165, 170-180, 184-193, 233, 239, 252
Sensorama 75-76, 120, 144
Simulation 2, 8-11, 14, 17-19, 23, 25-26, 29, 34-35, 37, 40-41, 43, 45, 47, 49, 54-55, 57, 59, 63-65, 70, 73, 78, 84, 89-90, 93-94, 117-119, 122, 124, 126-128, 131-135, 137-140, 143, 146, 148-149, 152-153, 166, 184, 190, 193, 231-236, 239-241, 244-245, 248, 251-253, 255
Social Anxiety 252, 258, 261, 267, 271, 273
Social Cues 111, 117
Social Networking Site (SNS) 193
Social Presence 12, 31, 94, 100-101, 114-115, 117, 167
Software 2, 4, 14, 29-30, 37, 46-48, 50, 56, 64-65, 70, 73-77, 79-80, 85-86, 89-95, 122-123, 128, 131, 133, 136, 140, 146-147, 150, 156-157, 160-163, 173-176, 181-182, 184-186, 191, 218, 224, 239
Stress 125, 142, 176, 242, 259-260, 263, 265, 267, 269-270, 273
Student Counselling 261-263, 266-267, 273
Student Counselling Services 261, 263, 267
Student Engagement 85, 97, 112-113, 123, 126, 149, 153, 166, 168, 170, 172, 182, 188-190, 193, 195-196, 201, 203, 209, 215, 217, 232, 234-236, 251
Student Mental Health Treatment 257
Student Motivation 166, 196, 215, 217
Student Services 168
Student-Centered Learning 145, 148-149, 169
Synchronous 22, 35, 64, 96-98, 100, 102, 107, 110, 112, 114, 117

T

Teacher education 16-17, 64, 67, 70, 111, 118, 124, 140-142, 151, 164, 166-167, 189
Teaching 5-7, 9, 11-13, 15, 18-19, 21-23, 25-27, 29-33, 35-38, 40-41, 43-46, 48, 53-56, 59-62, 64, 68-72, 83, 85, 90, 93, 101, 110, 112, 114-119, 124-127, 129-131, 133, 137-142, 145-152, 154-155, 159-169, 171, 174, 179, 187-194, 198, 200-201, 203-204, 206-207, 209, 212-215, 219-220, 222, 224-226, 229, 242-243, 248-249, 251-252, 255, 263-264
TeachLivE 54, 118-119, 124-130, 133, 138, 142, 148
Technology Assignment 170
Technology Integration 1, 5, 7-8, 15, 18, 151, 164, 167, 169
Technology Lab 145, 151-152, 155, 163, 169
Therapeutic Empathy 240-241, 252-253, 255
Three-Dimensional (3D) 1, 3, 8, 10-11, 13-14, 21, 23, 42-43, 47-49, 51, 58, 60, 66, 75, 96-97, 114, 117, 120, 142, 145-146, 153, 165, 215, 219, 223, 265
Three-Dimensional Virtual World (3DVW) 21, 47
Three-Dimensional Virtual Worlds 13, 21, 42-43
Twinity 172, 193
Two-Dimensional (2D) 20, 97, 223

U

UDL 111, 117
UN-Habitat 210, 212, 215
University Counselling Services 261-263, 265-266, 273
Uses and Gratification Theory (UGT) 58, 73

V

Video Games 3, 19-20, 36, 139, 195, 197, 200, 203, 205, 207, 209, 211, 215
Virtal World (VW) 20
Virtual classroom 10, 27, 31-32, 39-40, 118-119, 124, 132, 148, 173, 196, 209, 221
Virtual Discussions in 3D 117
Virtual Learning 1, 20, 22, 28, 37-38, 41-42, 44-47, 69, 71, 75, 92, 114-116, 119, 145, 166, 173, 186, 189, 216, 223, 232, 234-235, 239, 249, 255
Virtual Learning Environment (VLE) 20, 38, 41-42, 46-47, 69, 75, 92, 166, 234-235
Virtual Learning Experience 232, 234, 239, 249, 255
Virtual Lecturing 25-27, 34-35, 40, 47
Virtual Prototyping (VP) 73
Virtual Reality (VR) 1-3, 6, 8-10, 12-20, 42, 44, 46, 48, 54, 56, 60, 62-74, 76-87, 89-95, 113, 115, 118-120, 123, 127, 140-147, 152, 155-156, 159-160, 162, 164-168, 171, 173, 175, 191-193, 216, 221, 223, 226, 231-235, 237, 240, 242-246, 251-255, 257-260, 268-272
Virtual reality performance 118
Virtual Reality Perspective Taking 240, 255
Virtual Reality Simulators 20
Virtual Reality Systems 73, 78, 82, 90, 270
Virtual World(s) 1-4, 9, 12-14, 16-17, 19-23, 27-31, 33, 37-39, 41-62, 64-70, 72-75, 78, 87, 91, 95-101, 107, 110-117, 119-120, 122, 144-146, 156, 164-168, 170-174, 176-177, 179-180, 182-184, 186-193, 199-201, 204, 209-210, 212, 231-232, 235, 237, 240-241, 245, 248, 252-253, 255, 262
VR Assisted Counselling Services 257, 266

W

Wearables 20, 137
Who Wants To Be A Millionaire? 197, 203, 215

Z

Zoom 80, 103, 108, 117, 158, 174

Premier Reference Source
Emerging GIS Applications for Emergency and Disaster Management

Premier Reference Source
Managerial Strategies and Green Solutions for Project Sustainability

Premier Reference Source
Comparative Approaches to Using R and Python for Statistical Data Analysis

Premier Reference Source
Solutions for High-Touch Communications in a High-Tech World

www.ingramcontent.com/pod-product-compliance
Lightning Source LLC
LaVergne TN
LVHW060420300926
849162LV00006B/1478
9781799849605